CODE OF FEDERA REGULATIONS

Title 22
Foreign Relations

Part 300 to End

Revised as of April 1, 2019

Containing a codification of documents
of general applicability and future effect

As of April 1, 2019

Published by the Office of the Federal Register
National Archives and Records Administration
as a Special Edition of the Federal Register

Table of Contents

Page

Finding Aids:

Cite this Code: CFR

To cite the regulations in this volume use title, part and section number. Thus, 22 CFR 301.1 *refers to title 22, part 301, section 1.*

Explanation

The Code of Federal Regulations is a codification of the general and permanent rules published in the Federal Register by the Executive departments and agencies of the Federal Government. The Code is divided into 50 titles which represent broad areas subject to Federal regulation. Each title is divided into chapters which usually bear the name of the issuing agency. Each chapter is further subdivided into parts covering specific regulatory areas.

Each volume of the Code is revised at least once each calendar year and issued on a quarterly basis approximately as follows:

Title 1 through Title 16 .... as of January 1
Title 17 through Title 27 .... as of April 1
Title 28 through Title 41 .... as of July 1
Title 42 through Title 50 .... as of October 1

The appropriate revision date is printed on the cover of each volume.

LEGAL STATUS

The contents of the Federal Register are required to be judicially noticed (44 U.S.C. 1507). The Code of Federal Regulations is prima facie evidence of the text of the original documents (44 U.S.C. 1510).

HOW TO USE THE CODE OF FEDERAL REGULATIONS

The Code of Federal Regulations is kept up to date by the individual issues of the Federal Register. These two publications must be used together to determine the latest version of any given rule.

To determine whether a Code volume has been amended since its revision date (in this case, April 1, 2019), consult the "List of CFR Sections Affected (LSA)," which is issued monthly, and the "Cumulative List of Parts Affected," which appears in the Reader Aids section of the daily Federal Register. These two lists will identify the Federal Register page number of the latest amendment of any given rule.

EFFECTIVE AND EXPIRATION DATES

Each volume of the Code contains amendments published in the Federal Register since the last revision of that volume of the Code. Source citations for the regulations are referred to by volume number and page number of the Federal Register and date of publication. Publication dates and effective dates are usually not the same and care must be exercised by the user in determining the actual effective date. In instances where the effective date is beyond the cut-off date for the Code a note has been inserted to reflect the future effective date. In those instances where a regulation published in the Federal Register states a date certain for expiration, an appropriate note will be inserted following the text.

OMB CONTROL NUMBERS

The Paperwork Reduction Act of 1980 (Pub. L. 96–511) requires Federal agencies to display an OMB control number with their information collection request.

Many agencies have begun publishing numerous OMB control numbers as amendments to existing regulations in the CFR. These OMB numbers are placed as close as possible to the applicable recordkeeping or reporting requirements.

PAST PROVISIONS OF THE CODE

Provisions of the Code that are no longer in force and effect as of the revision date stated on the cover of each volume are not carried. Code users may find the text of provisions in effect on any given date in the past by using the appropriate List of CFR Sections Affected (LSA). For the convenience of the reader, a "List of CFR Sections Affected" is published at the end of each CFR volume. For changes to the Code prior to the LSA listings at the end of the volume, consult previous annual editions of the LSA. For changes to the Code prior to 2001, consult the List of CFR Sections Affected compilations, published for 1949-1963, 1964-1972, 1973-1985, and 1986-2000.

"[RESERVED]" TERMINOLOGY

The term "[Reserved]" is used as a place holder within the Code of Federal Regulations. An agency may add regulatory information at a "[Reserved]" location at any time. Occasionally "[Reserved]" is used editorially to indicate that a portion of the CFR was left vacant and not accidentally dropped due to a printing or computer error.

INCORPORATION BY REFERENCE

What is incorporation by reference? Incorporation by reference was established by statute and allows Federal agencies to meet the requirement to publish regulations in the Federal Register by referring to materials already published elsewhere. For an incorporation to be valid, the Director of the Federal Register must approve it. The legal effect of incorporation by reference is that the material is treated as if it were published in full in the Federal Register (5 U.S.C. 552(a)). This material, like any other properly issued regulation, has the force of law.

What is a proper incorporation by reference? The Director of the Federal Register will approve an incorporation by reference only when the requirements of 1 CFR part 51 are met. Some of the elements on which approval is based are:

(a) The incorporation will substantially reduce the volume of material published in the Federal Register.

(b) The matter incorporated is in fact available to the extent necessary to afford fairness and uniformity in the administrative process.

(c) The incorporating document is drafted and submitted for publication in accordance with 1 CFR part 51.

What if the material incorporated by reference cannot be found? If you have any problem locating or obtaining a copy of material listed as an approved incorporation by reference, please contact the agency that issued the regulation containing that incorporation. If, after contacting the agency, you find the material is not available, please notify the Director of the Federal Register, National Archives and Records Administration, 8601 Adelphi Road, College Park, MD 20740-6001, or call 202-741-6010.

CFR INDEXES AND TABULAR GUIDES

A subject index to the Code of Federal Regulations is contained in a separate volume, revised annually as of January 1, entitled CFR INDEX AND FINDING AIDS. This volume contains the Parallel Table of Authorities and Rules. A list of CFR titles, chapters, subchapters, and parts and an alphabetical list of agencies publishing in the CFR are also included in this volume.

An index to the text of "Title 3—The President" is carried within that volume.

The Federal Register Index is issued monthly in cumulative form. This index is based on a consolidation of the "Contents" entries in the daily Federal Register.

A List of CFR Sections Affected (LSA) is published monthly, keyed to the revision dates of the 50 CFR titles.

REPUBLICATION OF MATERIAL

There are no restrictions on the republication of material appearing in the Code of Federal Regulations.

INQUIRIES

For a legal interpretation or explanation of any regulation in this volume, contact the issuing agency. The issuing agency's name appears at the top of odd-numbered pages.

For inquiries concerning CFR reference assistance, call 202–741–6000 or write to the Director, Office of the Federal Register, National Archives and Records Administration, 8601 Adelphi Road, College Park, MD 20740-6001 or e-mail *fedreg.info@nara.gov.*

SALES

The Government Publishing Office (GPO) processes all sales and distribution of the CFR. For payment by credit card, call toll-free, 866-512-1800, or DC area, 202-512-1800, M-F 8 a.m. to 4 p.m. e.s.t. or fax your order to 202-512-2104, 24 hours a day. For payment by check, write to: US Government Publishing Office – New Orders, P.O. Box 979050, St. Louis, MO 63197-9000.

ELECTRONIC SERVICES

The full text of the Code of Federal Regulations, the LSA (List of CFR Sections Affected), The United States Government Manual, the Federal Register, Public Laws, Public Papers of the Presidents of the United States, Compilation of Presidential Documents and the Privacy Act Compilation are available in electronic format via *www.govinfo.gov.* For more information, contact the GPO Customer Contact Center, U.S. Government Publishing Office. Phone 202-512-1800, or 866-512-1800 (toll-free). E-mail, *ContactCenter@gpo.gov.*

The Office of the Federal Register also offers a free service on the National Archives and Records Administration's (NARA) World Wide Web site for public law numbers, Federal Register finding aids, and related information. Connect to NARA's web site at *www.archives.gov/federal-register.*

The e-CFR is a regularly updated, unofficial editorial compilation of CFR material and Federal Register amendments, produced by the Office of the Federal Register and the Government Publishing Office. It is available at *www.ecfr.gov.*

OLIVER A. POTTS,
Director,
Office of the Federal Register
April 1, 2019.

THIS TITLE

Title 22—Foreign Relations is composed of two volumes. The first volume, parts 1—299 contains Chapter I—Department of State regulations and Chapter II—Agency for International Development regulations. The second volume, part 300 to End is composed of Chapter III—Peace Corps; Chapter IV—International Joint Commission, United States and Canada; Chapter V—Broadcasting Board of Governors; Chapter VII—Overseas Private Investment Corporation; Chapter IX—Foreign Service Grievance Board; Chapter X—Inter-American Foundation; Chapter XI—International Boundary and Water Commission, United States and Mexico, United States Section; Chapter XII—United States International Development Cooperation Agency; Chapter XIII—Millennium Challenge Corporation; Chapter XIV—Foreign Service Labor Relations Board; Federal Labor Relations Authority; General Counsel of the Federal Labor Relations Authority; and the Foreign Service Impasse Disputes Panel; Chapter XV—African Development Foundation; Chapter XVI—Japan-United States Friendship Commission; and Chapter XVII—United States Institute of Peace. The contents of these volumes represent all current regulations codified under this title of the CFR as of April 1, 2019.

For this volume, Susannah C. Hurley was Chief Editor. The Code of Federal Regulations publication program is under the direction of John Hyrum Martinez, assisted by Stephen J. Frattini.

Title 22—Foreign Relations

(This book contains part 300 to end)

CHAPTER III—PEACE CORPS

PART 300 [RESERVED]

PART 301—PUBLIC ACCESS TO CLASSIFIED MATERIAL

AUTHORITY: E.O. 12356, 43 FR 14874 dated April 2, 1982.

SOURCE: 49 FR 13692, Apr. 6, 1984, unless otherwise noted.

§ 301.1 Introduction.

The following regulations implement Executive Order 12356 and provide guidance for members of the public desiring a review for declassification of a document of the Peace Corps.

§ 301.2 Requests for mandatory declassification review.

(a) All information originally classified by the Peace Corps shall be subject to review for declassification.

(b) Requests for review of such information for declassification shall be in writing, addressed to the Peace Corps Director of Security, Peace Corps, Washington, DC 20526, and reasonably describe the information sought with sufficient specificity to enable its location with a reasonable amount of effort. Only requests made by a United States citizen or a permanent resident alien, a Federal agency or a State or local government will be considered.

(c) Requests relating to information, either derivatively classified by the Peace Corps or originally classified by another agency but in the possession of the Peace Corps, shall be forwarded, together with a copy of the record, to the originating agency. The transmittal may contain in Peace Corps recommendation for action.

§ 301.3 Action on requests for declassification review.

(a) The Director of Security shall present each request for declassification to the Peace Corps Classification Review Committee, which shall consist of the Associate Director for International Operations, the Associate Director for Management and the General Counsel, or their designees, together with his or her recommendation for action.

(b) Every effort will be made to complete action on each request within 60 days of receipt thereof.

(c) Information shall be declassified or downgraded as soon as national security considerations permit. If the Classification Review Committee determines that the material for which review is requested no longer requires this protection, it shall be declassified and made available to the requester unless withholding is otherwise authorized by law.

(d) If the Peace Corps Classification Review Committee determines that requested information must remain classified, the requester shall be given prompt notice of the decision and, if possible, a brief explanation of why the information cannot be declassified.

(e) The Peace Corps may refuse to confirm or deny the existence or non-existence of requested information whenever the fact of its existence or non-existence is itself classified under E.O. 12356.

(f) A requester may appeal a refusal to declassify information to the Director of the Peace Corps, or the Director's designee. Appeals shall be in writing, addressed to the Director of the Peace Corps, Washington, DC 20526, and shall briefly state the reasons why the requester believes that the Peace Corps Classification Review Committee decision is in error. Appeals must be submitted within 30 days after receipt of notice of the Classification Review Committee decision. The decision of the Peace Corps Director, or designee, will be based on the entire record, and will be rendered in writing within 60 days after receipt of an appeal. The decision of the Director or Director's designee is the final Peace Corps action on a request.

PART 303—PROCEDURES FOR DISCLOSURE OF INFORMATION UNDER THE FREEDOM OF INFORMATION ACT

AUTHORITY: 5 U.S.C. 552; 22 U.S.C. 2501, et. seq.; E.O. 12137, 44 FR 29023, 3 CFR, 1979 Comp., p. 389; E.O. 12600, 52 FR 23781, 3 CFR, 1987 Comp., p. 235.

SOURCE: 68 FR 66008, Nov. 25, 2003, unless otherwise noted.

§ 303.1 Purpose.

This part sets out the rules and procedures the Peace Corps follows in making records available to the public under the Freedom of Information Act (FOIA).

§ 303.2 Definitions.

As used in this part—

(a) *Commercial use request* means a request from or on behalf of one who seeks information for a use or purpose that furthers the commercial, trade, or profit interests of the requester or the person on whose behalf the request is made. In determining whether a requester has made a commercial use request, the Peace Corps will look to the use to which a requester will put the documents requested. When the Peace Corps has reasonable cause to doubt the requester's stated use of the records sought, or where the use is not clear from the request itself, it will seek additional clarification before assigning the request to a category.

(b) *Duplication* means the process of making a copy of a record requested pursuant to this part. Such copies can take the form of paper copy, microform, audio-visual materials, or machine readable electronic documents, among others.

(c) *Educational institution* means a preschool, a public or private elementary or secondary school, an institution of undergraduate or graduate higher education, or an institution of professional or vocational education which operates a program or programs of scholarly research.

(d) *Expedited processing* means the process set forth in the FOIA that allows requesters to ask for expedited processing of their FOIA request if they can demonstrate a compelling need.

(e) *Fee waiver* means the waiver or reduction of processing fees if a requester can demonstrate that certain statutory standards are satisfied including that the information is in the public interest and is not requested for a commercial interest.

(f) *FOIA Public Liaison* means an agency official who is responsible for assisting in reducing delays, increasing transparency and understanding of the status of requests, and assisting in the resolution of disputes.

(g) *Non-commercial scientific institution* means an institution that is not operated on a "commercial" basis and which is operated solely for the purpose of conducting scientific research, the results of which are not intended to promote any particular product or industry.

(h) *OIG records* means those records as defined generally in this section which originated with or are in the possession and control of the Office of Inspector General (OIG) of the Peace Corps which have been compiled for law enforcement, audit, and investigative functions and/or any other purpose authorized under the IG Act of 1978, as amended.

(i) *Records* means books, papers, maps, photographs, or other documentary materials, regardless of whether the format is physical or electronic, made or received by the Peace Corps in connection with the transaction of Peace Corps' business and preserved by the Peace Corps as evidence of the organization, functions, policies, decisions, procedures, operations, or other activities of the Peace Corps, or because of the informational value of data in them. The term does not include, *inter alia*, books, magazines, or other materials acquired solely for library purpose, or that are otherwise publicly available.

(j) *Representative of the news media* means any person actively gathering news for an entity that is organized and operated to publish or broadcast news to the public. The term "news" means information that is about current events or that would be of current interest to the public. Examples of news media entities include television or radio stations broadcasting to the public at large and publishers of periodicals (but only in those instances when they can qualify as disseminators of "news") who make their products available for purchase or subscription by the general public. These examples are not intended to be all-inclusive. Moreover, as traditional methods of news delivery evolve (*e.g.*, electronic dissemination of newspapers through telecommunications services), such alternative media would be included in this category. In the case of "freelance" journalists, they will be regarded as working for a news organization if they can demonstrate a solid basis for expecting publication through that organization, even though not actually employed by it.

(k) *Requester category* means one of the three categories that agencies place requesters in for the purpose of determining whether a requester will be charged fees for search, review and duplication, including commercial requesters; non-commercial scientific or educational institutions or news media requesters, and all other requesters.

(l) *Review* means the process of examining a document located in response to a request to determine whether any portion of such document is exempt from disclosure. It also includes processing any such document for disclosure. Review does not include time spent resolving general legal or policy issues regarding the application of exemptions.

(m) *Search* means the process of looking for and retrieving records that are responsive to a request for records. It includes page-by-page or line-by-line identification of material within documents and also includes reasonable efforts to locate and retrieve information from records maintained in electronic form or format. Searches may be conducted manually or by automated means and will be conducted in the most efficient and least expensive manner. If the Agency cannot identify the requested records after a 2 hour search, it can determine that the records were not adequately described and ask the requester to provide a more specific request.

(n) *Submitter* means any person or entity providing potentially confidential commercial information to an agency, which information may be subject to a FOIA request. The term submitter includes, but is not limited to, individuals, corporations, state governments, and foreign governments.

[68 FR 66008, Nov. 25, 2003, as amended at 79 FR 19818, Apr. 10, 2014]

§ 303.3 Policy.

The Peace Corps will make its records concerning its operations, activities, and business available to the public consistent with the requirements of the FOIA. As a matter of policy, the Peace Corps makes discretionary disclosures of records or information that may be exempt from disclosure under the FOIA whenever disclosure would not foreseeably harm an interest protected by a FOIA exemption, but this policy does not create any right enforceable in court.

[79 FR 19818, Apr. 10, 2014]

§ 303.4 Records published in the Federal Register.

The Peace Corps publishes its notices and substantive regulations in the FEDERAL REGISTER. It also publishes information on its basic structure and operations necessary to inform the public how to deal effectively with the Peace Corps in the *United States Government Manual*, a special publication of the FEDERAL REGISTER. The Peace Corps will make reasonable efforts to currently update such information, which includes information on Peace Corps' location and functions, and how the public may obtain information or forms, or make submittals or requests. The Peace Corps' published regulations are at 22 CFR Chapter III.

§ 303.5 Public reading room.

(a) The Peace Corps maintains a public reading room at its headquarters at 1111 20th Street NW., Washington DC 20526. This room is supervised and is open to the public during Peace Corps' regular business hours for inspecting and copying records described in paragraph (b) of this section.

(b) Subject to the limitation stated in paragraph (c) of this section, the Peace Corps makes the following records available in the public reading room:

(1) All final public opinions, including concurring and dissenting opinions, and orders issued in the adjudication of cases that involve the Peace Corps;

(2) Statements of policy and interpretations adopted by the Peace Corps that are not published in the FEDERAL REGISTER;

(3) Administrative staff manuals and instructions to the staff that affect the public;

(4) Copies of records, regardless of form or format, released to any person in response to a public request for records which the Peace Corps determines are likely to become subject to subsequent requests for substantially the same records, and a general index of such records;

(5) The index required by § 303.7; and

(6) Other records the Peace Corps has determined are of general interest to members of the public in understanding activities of the Peace Corps or in dealing with the Peace Corps in connection with those activities.

(c) Certain records otherwise required by FOIA to be available in the public reading room may be exempt from mandatory disclosure pursuant to § 552(b) of the FOIA. Such record will not be made available in the public reading room. Other records maintained in the public reading room may be edited by the deletion of identifying details concerning individuals to prevent a clearly unwarranted invasion of personal privacy. In such cases, the record shall have attached to it an explanation of the deletion. The extent of the deletion shall be indicated, unless doing so would harm an interest protected by the exemption under which the deletion is made. It technically feasible, the extent of the deletion shall be indicated at the place in the record where the deletion was made.

(d) *Electronic reading room.* Records required by the FOIA to be maintained and made available in the public reading room created by the Peace Corps on or after November 1, 1996, are made available electronically on the Peace Corps Web site at *http://www.peacecorps.gov.*

[68 FR 66008, Nov. 25, 2003, as amended at 79 FR 19818, Apr. 10, 2014]

§ 303.6 Procedures for use of public reading room.

Any member of the public may inspect or copy records described in § 303.5(b) in the public reading room during regular business hours. Because it will sometimes be impossible to produce records or copies of records on short notice, a person who wishes to inspect or copy records shall arrange a time in advance, by telephone or letter request made to the Peace Corps FOIA Officer. Persons submitting a request by telephone for a record in the public reading room will be notified whether a written request would be advisable to aid in the identification and expeditious processing of the records sought. Written requests should identify the records sought in the manner described in § 303.8(b) and should request a specific date for inspecting the records. The requester will be advised as promptly as possible if, for any reason, it may not be possible to make the records sought available on the date requested.

[79 FR 19818, Apr. 10, 2014]

§ 303.7 Index of records.

The Peace Corps will maintain a current index identifying any matter within the scope of § 303.4 or § 303.5(b)(1) through (5). The index will be maintained and made available for public inspection and copying at the Peace Corps' headquarters in Washington, DC. The cost of a copy of the index will not exceed the standard charge for duplication set out in § 303.13(e). The Peace Corps will also make the index available on its public Web site.

§ 303.8 Requests for records.

(a) Except for records required by the FOIA to be published in the FEDERAL REGISTER or to be made available in the public reading room, the Peace Corps will make its records promptly available, upon request, to any person in accordance with this section, unless it is determined that such records should be withheld and are exempt from mandatory disclosure under the FOIA.

(b) *Requests.* Requests for records under this section shall be made in writing via regular mail, email, facsimile, or online web portal and, as applicable, the envelope and the letter or other form of request should be clearly marked "Freedom of Information Request." All requests shall be addressed to the FOIA Officer. Requests by letter shall use the address given in § 303.5(a). Requests by email must be sent to the FOIA electronic mailbox, *foia@peacecorps.gov.* Regarding requests submitted via online web portal (accessible on the agency Web site, *www.peacecorps.gov*), requesters shall fill in all of the fields as required. Any request not marked and addressed as specified in this paragraph will be so marked by Peace Corps personnel as soon as the request is properly identified. The request will be forwarded immediately to the FOIA Officer. A request improperly addressed will not be deemed to have been received for purposes of the time period set out in paragraph (h) of this section until it has been received by the FOIA Officer. Upon receipt of an improperly addressed request, the FOIA Officer shall notify the requester of the date on which the time period began. Requests by letter shall be stamped "received" on the date received by the FOIA Office. Requests by email shall be "received" on the date the email arrived, if a business day, or on the next business day. Requests by online web portal will be entered automatically in the FOIA tracking system. Requests sent via mail or email will be entered manually in the FOIA tracking system. Requesters may utilize the online web portal for purpose of checking status of requests (open/closed) for requests from all sources.

(c) A request must reasonably describe the records requested so that employees of the Peace Corps who are familiar with the subject area of the request are able, with a reasonable amount of effort, to determine which particular records are within the scope of the request. If it is determined that a request does not reasonably describe the records sought, the requester shall be so informed and provided an opportunity to confer with Peace Corps personnel in order to attempt to reformulate the request in a manner that will meet the needs of the requester and the requirements of this paragraph (c). If the Agency cannot identify the requested records after a 2 hour search, it may determine that the records were not adequately described and ask the requester to provide a more specific request.

(d) To facilitate the location of records by the Peace Corps, a requester should try to provide the following kinds of information, if known;

(1) The specific event or action to which the record refers;

(2) The unit or program of the Peace Corps which may be responsible for or may have produced the record;

(3) The date of the record or the date or period to which it refers or relates;

(4) The type of record, such as an application, a particular form, a contract, or a report;

(5) Personnel of the Peace Corps who may have prepared or have knowledge of the record; or

(6) Citations to newspapers or publications which have referred to the record.

(e) The Peace Corps is not required to create a record or to perform research to satisfy a request.

(f) Any request for a waiver or reduction of fees should be included in the FOIA request, and any such request should indicate the grounds for a waiver or reduction of fees, as set out in § 303.13(f). The Peace Corps shall respond to such request as promptly as possible.

(g) *Format.* The Peace Corps will provide records in the form or format indicated by the requester to the extent such records are readily reproducible in the requested form or format.

(h) *Initial response/delays.* (1) The FOIA Officer, upon request for any records made in accordance with this section, except in the case of a request for OIG records, shall assign a tracking number to each individual request and send an acknowledgement letter or email to each requester. The acknowledgement letter or email will inform the requester of the assigned tracking number. The FOIA Officer will make an initial determination of whether to comply with or deny such request and dispatch such determination to the requester within 20 business days after receipt of such request. Peace Corps will acknowledge all FOIA requests within 20 working days, except for unusual circumstances, in which case the time limit may be extended for up to 10 business days by written notice to the requester setting forth the reasons for such extension and the date on which a determination is expected to be dispatched.

(2) If the FOIA Officer determines that a request or portion thereof is for OIG records, the FOIA Officer shall promptly refer the request or portion thereof to the OIG and send notice of such referral to the requester. In such case, the OIG FOIA Officer shall make an initial determination of whether to comply with or deny such request and dispatch such determination to the requester within 20 business days after receipt of such request, except for unusual circumstances, in which case the time limit may be extended for up to 10 business days by written notice to the requester setting forth the reasons for such extension and the date on which a determination is expected to be dispatched. If for any reason, a request for Agency information goes directly to the OIG rather than through the FOIA Officer, the OIG shall provide notice to the FOIA Officer of its receipt of the request. The FOIA Office and the OIG should normally consult with each other whenever they receive requests for the same or similar records.

(3) *Unusual circumstances.* As used in this part, "unusual circumstances" are limited to the following, but only to the extent reasonably necessary for the proper processing of the particular request:

(i) The need to search for and collect the requested records from components or locations that are separate from the office processing the request;

(ii) The need to search for, collect, and appropriately examine a voluminous amount of separate and distinct records which are demanded in a single request; or

(iii) The need for consultation, which shall be conducted with all practicable speed, with another agency or organization having a substantial interest in the determination of the request or among two or more components of the Peace Corps having a substantial subject matter interest therin.

(i) If a request is particularly broad or complex so that it cannot be completed within the time periods stated in paragraph (h) of this section, the Peace Corps may ask the requester to narrow the request or agree to an additional delay.

(j) When no determination can be dispatched within the applicable time limit, the FOIA Officer or the OIG FOIA Officer shall inform the requester of the reason for the delay, the date on which a determination may be expected to be dispatched, and the requester's right to treat the delay as a denial and to appeal to the Associate Director for the Office of Management or the Inspector General, in accordance with §303.12. If no determination has been dispatched by the end of the 20-day period, or the last extension thereof, the requester may deem the request denied, and exercise a right of appeal in accordance with §303.12. The FOIA Officer or the OIG FOIA Officer may ask the requester to forego an appeal until a determination is made.

(k) After it has been determined that a request will be granted, the responsible official will act with due diligence in providing a prompt response.

(l) *Expedited treatment.* (1) Requests and appeals will be taken out of order and given expedited treatment whenever the requester demonstrates a compelling need. A compelling need means:

(i) Circumstances in which the lack of expedited treatment could reasonably be expected to pose an imminent threat to the life or physical safety of an individual;

(ii) An urgency to inform the public about an actual or alleged Peace Corps or Federal government activity and the request is made by a person primarily engaged in disseminating information;

(iii) The loss of substantial due process rights; or

(iv) A matter of widespread and exceptional media interest in which there exist possible questions about the Peace Corps' or the Federal government's integrity which affect public confidence.

(2) A request for expedited processing may be made at the time of the initial request for records or at any later time. For a prompt determination, a request for expedited processing must be properly addressed and marked and received by the Peace Corps pursuant to paragraph (b) of this section.

(3) A requester who seeks expedited processing must submit a statement demonstrating a compelling need that is certified by the requester to be true and correct to the best of that person's knowledge and belief, explaining in detail the basis for requesting expedited processing.

(4) Within ten business days of its receipt of a request for expedited processing, the FOIA Officer or the OIG FOIA Officer shall decide whether to grant the request and shall notify the requester of the decision. If a request for expedited treatment is granted, the request shall be given priority and shall be processed as soon as practicable. If a request for expedited processing is denied, any appeal of that decision shall be acted on expeditiously by the Peace Corps.

(5) Appeals shall be made to the Associate Director for the Office of Management, who shall respond within 10 business days of receipt of the appeal.

[68 FR 66008, Nov. 25, 2003, as amended at 72 FR 27055, May 14, 2007; 79 FR 19818, Apr. 10, 2014]

§ 303.9 Exemptions for withholding records.

(a) The Peace Corps may withhold a requested record from public disclosure only if the record fits within one or more of the following FOIA exemptions:

(1) Matter specifically authorized under criteria established by an Executive Order to be kept secret in the interest of national defense or foreign policy and is in fact properly classified pursuant to such Executive Order;

(2) Matter which is related solely to the internal personnel rules and practices of the Peace Corps;

(3) Matter which is specifically exempted from disclosure by statute (other than exemptions under FOIA at 5 U.S.C. 552(b)), provided that such statute requires that the matter be withheld from the public in such a manner as to leave no discretion on the issue, or establishes particular criteria for withholding, or refers to particular types of matters to be withheld;

(4) Trade secrets and commercial or financial information obtained from a person and privileged or confidential;

(5) Inter-agency or intra-agency memoranda or letters which would not be available by law to a party other than an agency in litigation with the Peace Corps;

(6) Personnel and medical files and similar files, the disclosure of which would constitute a clearly unwarranted invasion of personal privacy;

(7) Records or information compiled for law enforcement purposes including enforcing the Peace Corps Act or any other law, but only to the extent that the production of such law enforcement records or information:

(i) Could reasonably be expected to interfere with enforcement proceedings;

(ii) Would deprive a person or a recipient of a right to a fair trial or an impartial adjudication;

(iii) Could reasonably be expected to constitute an unwarranted invasion of personal privacy;

(iv) Could reasonably be expected to disclose the identity of a confidential source, including a State, local, or foreign agency or authority or any private institution which furnished information on a confidential basis; and, in the case of a record or information compiled by a criminal law enforcement authority in the course of a criminal investigation, information furnished by a confidential source;

(v) Would disclose techniques and procedures for law enforcement investigations or prosecutions, or would disclose guidelines for law enforcement investigations or prosecutions if such disclosure could reasonably be expected to risk circumvention of the law; or

(vi) Could reasonably be expected to endanger the life or physical safety of any individual.

(8) Contained in or related to examination, operating, or condition reports prepared by, on behalf of, or for the use of an agency responsible for the regulation or supervision of financial institutions; or

(9) Geological and geophysical information and data, including maps, concerning wells.

(b) In the event that one or more of the above exemptions in paragraph (a) of this section apply, any reasonably segregable portion of a record shall be provided to the requester after deletion of the portions that are exempt. The Peace Corps shall indicate, if technically feasible, the precise amount of information deleted and the exemption under which the deletion is made at the place in the record where the deletion is made, and indicate the exemption under which a deletion is made on the released portion of the record, unless including that indication would harm an interest protected by the exemption. At the discretion of the Peace Corps officials authorized to grant or deny a request for records, it may be possible to provide a requester with:

(1) A summary of information in the exempt portion of a record; or

(2) An oral description of the exempt portion of a record.

(c) No requester shall have a right to insist that any or all of the techniques in paragraph (b) of this section should be employed in order to satisfy a request.

(d) Records that may be exempt from disclosure pursuant to paragraph (a) of this section may be made available at the discretion of the Peace Corps.

(e) Proprietary information. (1) It is the policy of the Peace Corps to withhold proprietary information that falls within the protection of paragraph (a)(4) of this section. Proprietary information includes trade secrets, or commercial or financial information obtained from a person, the disclosure of which could reasonably be expected to cause substantial competitive harm.

(2) It is also the policy of the Peace Corps to give submitters of arguably proprietary information an adequate opportunity to provide information to the Peace Corps to establish that the information constitutes protected proprietary information.

(3) A person submitting arguably proprietary information to the Peace Corps will be notified in writing by the Peace Corps if there is a FOIA request for the information, unless:

(i) The Peace Corps has already decided that the information should be withheld;

(ii) The information has been lawfully published or has been officially made available to the public; or

(iii) Disclosure of the information is required by law.

(4) The notice shall afford the submitter at least ten business days in which to object to the disclosure of any requested information. Whenever the Peace Corps provides such notice to the submitter, it shall also notify the requester that notice and an opportunity to comment are being provided to the submitter.

(5) A submitter's request for protection for information under paragraph (a)(4) of this section shall:

(i) Specifically identify the exact material claimed to be confidential proprietary information;

(ii) State whether the information identified has ever been released to a person who is not in a confidential relationship with the submitter;

(iii) State the basis for the submitter's belief that the information is not commonly known or readily ascertainable by outside persons; and

(iv) State how release of the information would cause harm to the submitter's competitive position.

(6) The Peace Corps shall consider the submitter's objections and specific grounds for non-disclosure when deciding whether to disclose the information. If the Peace Corps decides to disclose the information, it shall, to the extent permitted by law, provide the submitter at least ten business days notice of its decision before the information is disclosed and a statement of its reasons for not sustaining the objection to disclosure. Whenever the Peace Corps notifies the submitter of its final decision, it shall also notify the requester.

(7) Whenever a FOIA requester brings suit seeking to compel disclosure of proprietary information, the Peace Corps shall promptly notify the submitter.

[68 FR 66008, Nov. 25, 2003; 69 FR 68695, Dec. 9, 2003; 79 FR 19819, Apr. 10, 2014]

§303.10 Responsibilities and authorities.

(a) *Legal counsel.* The General Counsel (GC) shall furnish legal advice to Peace Corps officials and staff as to their obligations under this part and shall take such other actions as may be necessary or appropriate to assure a consistent and equitable application of the provisions of this part by and within the Peace Corps. The OIG Legal Counsel will coordinate with GC, as appropriate and necessary, when furnishing legal advice to the OIG FOIA Officer and Inspector General.

(b) *Authority to grant or deny requests.* The FOIA Officer is authorized to grant or deny requests for records, except for OIG records, under this part. The OIG FOIA Officer is authorized to grant or deny requests for OIG records under this part. The FOIA Officer and the OIG FOIA Officer shall consult with each other when a request includes both Peace Corps and OIG records in order to ensure consistency and lack of duplication in processing the request.

(c)(1) *Records received from other agencies.* When the Peace Corps receives a request for a record in its possession that it has received from another agency, it shall determine whether the other agency is better qualified to decide whether the record is exempt from disclosure and, if so, whether it should be disclosed as a matter of discretion. If the Peace Corps determines it is better qualified to process the record in response to the request, then it shall do so. If the Peace Corps determines it is not better qualified to process the request, it shall either:

(i) Consult with the other agency before responding to the request; or

(ii) Refer the responsibility for responding to the request for the record to the other agency (but only if the agency is subject to FOIA). Ordinarily, the agency that originated a record will be presumed to be best able to determine whether to disclose it.

(2) *Law enforcement and classified information.* Notwithstanding paragraph (c)(1) of this section:

(i) Whenever the Peace Corps receives a request for a record containing information that relates to an investigation of a possible violation of law that was originated by another agency, the Peace Corps will either consult with the other agency before responding or refer the responsibility for responding to the request to the other agency; and

(ii) Whenever a request is made for a record containing information that has been classified by another agency or may be appropriate for classification under Executive Order 13525 or any other executive order concerning the classification of records, the Peace Corps shall refer the responsibility for responding to the request regarding that information to the agency that classified the information, should consider the information for classification, or has the primary interest in the information, as appropriate.

(3) *Notice of referral.* Whenever the Peace Corps refers all or any part of the responsibility for responding to a request to another agency, it ordinarily shall notify the requester of the referral and inform the requester of the name of the agency to which the request has been referred and the part of the request that has been referred and provide the requester with a point of contact within the receiving agency to whom the requester can speak regarding the referral.

(4) *Effect of consultations and referrals on timing of response.* All consultations and referrals will be handled according to the date the FOIA request was initially received by the Peace Corps.

(5) *Agreements with other agencies.* The Peace Corps may make agreements with other agencies to eliminate the need for consultations or referrals for particular types of records.

[68 FR 66008, Nov. 25, 2003, as amended at 79 FR 19819, Apr. 10, 2014]

§303.11 Denials.

(a) A denial of a written request for a record that complies with the requirements of §303.8 shall be in writing and shall include, as applicable:

(1) A reference to the applicable exemption or exemptions in §303.9(a) upon which the denial is based;

(2) An explanation of how the exemption applies to the requested records;

(3) A statement explaining why it is deemed unreasonable to provide segregable portions of the record after deleting the exempt portions;

(4) An estimate of the volume of requested matter denied unless providing such estimate would harm the interest protected by the exemption under which the denial is made, if other than the FOIA Officer;

(5) The name and title of the person or persons responsible for denying the request, if other than the FOIA Officer; and

(6) An explanation of the right to appeal the denial and the procedures for submitting an appeal, including the address of the official to whom appeals should be submitted.

(b) A partial deletion of a record made available to a requester shall be deemed a denial of a record for purposes of paragraph (a) of this section. All denials shall be treated as final opinions under § 303.5(b).

§ 303.12 Appeals.

(a) Any person whose written request has been denied is entitled to appeal the denial within 30 business days by writing to the Associate Director of the Office of Management or, in the case of a denial of a request for OIG Records, the Inspector General, at the address given in 303.5(a). An appeal need not be in any particular form, but should adequately identify the denial, if possible, by describing the requested record, identifying the official who issued the denial, and providing the date on which the denial was issued. If the appeal is sent via mail, the envelope and the letter should be clearly marked "Freedom of Information Appeal" and the appeal shall be addressed to the Associate Director, Office of Management. Appeals by letter shall use the address given in § 303.5(a). Appeals are accepted via email. Appeals by email must be sent to the FOIA electronic mailbox, *foia@peacecorps.gov*. In appeals submitted via online web portal (accessible on the agency Web site, *www.peacecorps.gov*), requesters shall fill in all of the fields as required. Appeals by online web portal will be entered automatically in the FOIA tracking system. Persons submitting an appeal may utilize the online web portal for purpose of checking status of requests (open/closed) for requests from all sources.

(b) A response to an appeal will advise the requester that the 2007 FOIA amendments created the Office of Government Information Services (OGIS) to offer mediation services to resolve disputes between FOIA requesters and Federal agencies as a non-exclusive alternative to litigation. A requester may contact OGIS in any of the following ways:

Office of Government Information Services, National Archives and Records Administration, 8601 Adelphi Road—OGIS, College Park, MD 20740, *ogis.archives.gov*, Email: *ogis@nara.gov*, Telephone: 202–741–5770, Facsimile: 202–741–5769, Toll-free: 1–877–684–6448.

(c) The decision of the Associate Director for the Office of Management or the Inspector General on an appeal shall be in writing and, in the event the denial is in whole or in part upheld, shall contain an explanation responsive to the arguments advanced by the requester, the matters described in § 303.11(a)(1) through (4), and the provisions for judicial review of such decision under section 552(a)(4) of the FOIA. The decision shall be dispatched to the requester within 20 business days after receipt of the appeal, unless an additional period is justified pursuant to § 303.8(i) and such period taken together with any earlier extension does not exceed 10 business days. The decision by the Associate Director for the Office of Management or the Inspector General shall constitute the final action of the Peace Corps. All such decisions shall be treated as final opinions under § 303.5(b).

[68 FR 66008, Nov. 25, 2003, as amended at 79 FR 19819, Apr. 10, 2014]

§ 303.13 Fees.

(a) For information routinely provided by the Peace Corps to the public in the normal course of doing business, such as informational or recruiting brochures, no fees will be charged.

(b) For each commercial use request, fees will be limited to reasonable standard charges for document search, review, and duplication.

(c) For each request for records sought by a representative of the news media or by an educational or noncommercial scientific institution, fees shall be limited to reasonable standard charges for document duplication after the first 100 pages.

(d) For all other requests, fees shall be limited to reasonable standard charges for search time after the first 2 hours and duplication after the first 100 pages.

(e) The schedule of reasonable standard charges for services regarding the production or disclosure of the Peace Corps records is as follows:

(1) Manual search and review of records: Salary rate of employee[s] performing the search and review plus 16%. Charges for search and review time less than a full hour will be billed by quarter-hour segments;

(2) Computer time: Actual costs as incurred;

(3) Duplication by paper copy: 15 cents per page;

(4) Duplication by other methods: Actual costs as incurred;

(5) Certification of true copies: $1.00 each;

(6) Packing and mailing records: Actual costs as incurred; and

(7) Special delivery or express mail: Actual charges as incurred.

(f) *Fee waivers:* Fees will be waived or reduced below the fees established under paragraph (e) of this section if disclosure of the information is in the public interest because it is likely to contribute significantly to public understanding of the operations or activities of the Peace Corps or Federal government and is not primarily in the commercial interest of the requester.

(1) In order to determine whether the disclosure of the information is in the public interest because it is likely to contribute significantly to public understanding of the operations or activities of the Federal government, the Peace Corps shall consider the following four criteria:

(i) The subject of the request: Whether the subject of the requested records concerns the operations or activities of the Peace Corps or Federal government;

(ii) The informative value of the information to be disclosed: Whether the disclosure is "likely to contribute" to an understanding of Peace Corps or Federal government operations or activities;

(iii) The contribution to an understanding of the subject by the general public likely to result from disclosure: Whether disclosure of the requested information will contribute to "public understanding;" and

(iv) The significance of the contribution to public understanding: Whether the disclosure is likely to contribute "significantly" to public understanding of Peace Corps or Federal government operations or activities.

(2) In order to determine whether disclosure of the information is not primarily in the commercial interest of the requester, the Peace Corps shall consider the following two factors:

(i) The existence and magnitude of a commercial interest: Whether the requester has a commercial interest that would be furthered by the requested disclosure; and if so,

(ii) The primary interest in disclosure: Whether the magnitude of the identified commercial interest of the requester is sufficiently large, in comparison with the public interest in disclosure, that disclosure is "primarily in the commercial interest of the requester."

(3) These fee waiver/reduction provisions will be subject to appeal in the same manner as appeals from denial under §303.12.

(g) No fee will be charged under this section unless the cost of routine collection and processing of the fee payment is likely to exceed the average cost of processing a payment.

(h) Requesters must agree to pay all fees charged for services associated with their requests. The Peace Corps will assume that requesters agree to pay all charges for services associated with their requests up to $25 unless otherwise indicated by the requester.

(i) No requester will be required to make an advance payment of any fee unless:

(1) The requester has previously failed to pay a required fee to another federal agency or to Peace Corps within 30 days of the date of billing, in which case an advance deposit of the full amount of the anticipated fee together with the fee then due plus interest accrued may be required. (The request will not be deemed to have been

received by the Peace Corps until such payment is made.); or

(2) The Peace Corps determines that an estimated fee will exceed $250, in which case the requester shall be notified of the amount of the anticipated fee or such portion thereof as can readily be estimated. Such notification shall be transmitted as soon as possible, but in any event within 5 business days of receipt of the request by the Peace Corps. The notification shall offer the requester the opportunity to confer with appropriate representatives of the Peace Corps for the purpose of reformulating the request so as to meet the needs of the requester at a reduced cost. The request will not be deemed to have been received by the Peace Corps for purposes of the initial 20-day response period until the requester makes a deposit on the fee in an amount determined by the Peace Corps.

(j) Interest may be charged to those requesters who fail to pay the fees charged. Interest will be assessed on the amount billed, starting on the 31st day following the day on which the billing was sent. The rate charged will be as prescribed in 31 U.S.C. 3717.

(k) The Agency is not required to process a request for a requester who has not paid FOIA fees owed to another Federal agency.

(l) If the Peace Corps reasonably believes that a requester or group of requesters is attempting to break a request into a series of requests for the purpose of evading the assessment of fees, the Peace Corps shall aggregate such requests and charge accordingly. Likewise, the Peace Corps will aggregate multiple requests for documents received from the same requester within 45 business days.

(m) The Peace Corps reserves the right to limit the number of copies of any document that will be provided to any one requester or to require that special arrangements for duplication be made in the case of bound volumes or other records representing unusual problems of handling or reproduction.

[68 FR 66008, Nov. 25, 2003, as amended at 72 FR 27056, May 14, 2007; 79 FR 19820, Apr. 10, 2014]

§ 303.14 Procedures for responding to a subpoena.

(a) *Purpose and scope.* (1) This part sets forth the procedures to be followed in proceedings in which the Peace Corps is not a party, whenever a subpoena, order or other demand (collectively referred to as a "demand") of a court or other authority is issued for:

(i) The production or disclosure of any material contained in the files of the Agency;

(ii) The production or disclosure of any information relating to material contained in the files of the Agency;

(iii) The production or disclosure of any information or material acquired by any person while such person was an employee of the Agency as a part of the performance of his official duties or because of his official status, or

(iv) The production of an employee of the Agency for the deposition or an appearance as a witness in a legal action or proceeding.

(2) For purposes of this part, the term "employee of the Agency" includes all officers and employees of the Agency appointed by, or subject to the supervision, jurisdiction or control of, the director of the Agency, including personal services contractors. Also for purposes of this part, records of the Agency do not include records of the Office of Inspector General.

(3) This part is intended to provide instructions regarding the internal operations of the Agency, and is not intended, and does not and may not be relied upon, to create any right or benefit, substantive or procedural, enforceable at law by a party against the Agency.

(4) This part applies to:

(i) State and local court, administrative and legislative proceedings; and

(ii) Federal court and administrative proceedings.

(5) This part does not apply to:

(i) Congressional requests or subpoenas for testimony or documents;

(ii) Employees or former employees making appearances solely in their private capacity in legal or administrative proceedings that do not relate to the Agency (such as cases arising out of traffic accidents or domestic relations). Any question regarding whether the appearance relates solely to the employee's or former employee's private capacity should be referred to the Office of the General Counsel.

(6) Nothing in this part otherwise permits disclosure of information by the Agency except as is provided by statute or other applicable law.

(b) *Procedure in the event of a demand for production or disclosure.* (1) No employee or former employee of the Agency shall, in response to a demand of a court or other authority set forth in § 303.14(a) produce any material, disclose any information or appear in any proceeding, described in § 303.14(a) without the approval of the General Counsel or designee.

(2) Whenever an employee or former employee of the Peace Corps receives a demand for the production of material or the disclosure of information described in § 303.14(a) he shall immediately notify and provide a copy of the demand to the General Counsel or designee. The General Counsel, or designee, shall be furnished by the party causing the demand to be issued or served a written summary of the information sought, its relevance to the proceeding in connection with which it was served and why the information sought is unavailable by any other means or from any other sources.

(3) The General Counsel, or designee, in consultation with appropriate Agency officials, including the Agency's FOIA Officer, or designee, and in light of the considerations listed in § 303.14(d), will determine whether the person on whom the demand was served should respond to the demand.

(4) To the extent he deems it necessary or appropriate, the General Counsel or designee, may also require from the party causing such demand to be issued or served a plan of all reasonably foreseeable demands, including but not limited to names of all employees and former employees from whom discovery will be sought, areas of inquiry, length of time of proceedings requiring oral testimony and identification of documents to be used or whose production is sought.

(c) *Considerations in determining whether production or disclosure should be made pursuant to a demand.* (1) In deciding whether to make disclosures pursuant to a demand, the General Counsel or designee, may consider, among things:

(i) Whether such disclosure is appropriate under the rules of procedure governing the case or matter in which the demand arose; and

(ii) Whether disclosure is appropriate under the relevant substantive law concerning privilege.

(2) Among the demands in response to which disclosure will not be made are those demands with respect to which any of the following factors exist:

(i) Disclosure would violate a statute or a rule of procedure;

(ii) Disclosure would violate the privacy rights of an individual;

(iii) Disclosure would violate a specific regulation;

(iv) Disclosure would reveal classified information, unless appropriately declassified by the originating agency;

(v) Disclosure would reveal trade secrets or proprietary information without the owner's consent;

(vi) Disclosure would otherwise adversely affect the interests of the United States or the Peace Corps; or

(vii) Disclosure would impair an ongoing Inspector General or Department of Justice investigation.

[68 FR 66008, Nov. 25, 2003, as amended at 79 FR 19820, Apr. 10, 2014]

PART 304—CLAIMS AGAINST GOVERNMENT UNDER FEDERAL TORT CLAIMS ACT

GENERAL PROVISIONS

PROCEDURES

AUTHORITY: 28 U.S.C. 2672; 22 U.S.C. 2503(b); E.O. 12137, as amended.

SOURCE: 34 FR 5840, Mar. 28, 1969, unless otherwise noted.

GENERAL PROVISIONS

§ 304.1 Scope; definitions.

(a) This subpart applies to claims asserted under the Federal Tort Claims Act, as amended, accruing on or after January 18, 1967, for money damages against the United States for injury to or loss of property or personal injury or death caused by the negligent or wrongful act or omission of an officer or employee of the Peace Corps, a person serving the Peace Corps under invitational travel orders, or a Peace Corps Volunteer or trainee while acting within the scope of his office or employment.

(b) This subpart is not applicable to claims arising in a foreign country; it is applicable to claims arising in Puerto Rico and the Virgin Islands.

(c) This subpart is issued subject to and consistent with applicable regulations on administrative claims under the Federal Tort Claims Act issued by the Attorney General (28 CFR part 14).

(d) For the purposes of this subpart, the term "General Counsel" means the General Counsel of the Peace Corps or his designee.

[34 FR 5840, Mar. 28, 1969, as amended at 72 FR 4205, Jan. 30, 2007]

PROCEDURES

§ 304.2 Administrative claim; when presented; appropriate Peace Corps Office.

(a) For purposes of this subpart, a claim shall be deemed to have been presented when the Peace Corps receives, at a place designated in paragraph (b) of this section, an executed "Claim for Damages or Injury," Standard Form 95, or other written notification of an incident, accompanied by a claim for money damages in a sum certain for injury to or loss of property, for personal injury, or for death alleged to have occurred by reason of the incident. A claim which should have been presented to the Peace Crops, but which was mistakenly addressed to or filed with another Federal agency, is deemed to have been presented to the Peace Corps as of the date that the claim is received by the Peace Corps. If a claim is mistakenly addressed to or filed with the Peace Corps, the Peace Corps shall forthwith transfer it to the appropriate Federal agency, if ascertainable, or return it to the claimant.

(b) A claimant shall mail or deliver his claim to the General Counsel, Peace Corps, 1111 20th Street, NW., Washington, DC 20526.

[34 FR 5840, Mar. 28, 1969, as amended at 72 FR 4206, Jan. 30, 2007]

§ 304.3 Administrative claim; who may file.

(a) A claim for injury to or loss of property may be presented by the owner of the property, his duly authorized agent, or his legal representative.

(b) A claim for personal injury may be presented by the injured person, his duly authorized agent, or his legal representative.

(c) A claim based on death may be presented by the executor or administrator of the decedent's estate, or by any other person legally entitled to assert such a claim in accordance with applicable State law.

(d) A claim for loss wholly compensated by an insurer with the rights of a subrogee may be presented by the insurer. Claim for loss partially compensated by an insurer with the rights of a subrogee may be presented by the insurer or the insured individually, as their respective interests appear, or jointly. Whenever an insurer presents a claim asserting the rights of a subrogee, he shall present with his claim appropriate evidence that he has the rights of a subrogee.

(e) A claim presented by an agent or legal representative shall be presented in the name of the claimant, be signed by the agent or legal representative, show the title or legal capacity of the person signing, and be accompanied by evidence of his authority to present a claim on behalf of the claimant.

§ 304.4 Administrative claim; evidence and information to be submitted.

(a) *Personal injury.* In support of a claim for personal injury, including pain and suffering, the claimant may be required to submit the following evidence or information:

(1) A written report by his attending physician or dentist setting forth the

nature and extent of the injury, nature and extent of treatment, any degree of temporary or permanent disability, the prognosis, period of hospitalization, and any diminished earning capacity. In addition, the claimant may be required to submit to a physical or mental examination by a physician employed or designated by the Peace Corps or another Federal agency. A copy of the report of the examining physician shall be made available to the claimant upon the claimant's written request provided that he has, upon request, furnished the report referred to in the first sentence of this paragraph and has made or agrees to make available to the Peace Corps any other physician's report previously or thereafter made of the physical or mental condition which is the subject matter of his claim.

(2) Itemized bills for medical, dental, and hospital expenses incurred, or itemized receipts of payment for such expenses.

(3) If the prognosis reveals the necessity for future treatment, a statement of expected expenses for such treatment.

(4) If a claim is made for loss of time from employment, a written statement from his employer showing actual time lost from employment, whether he is a full-or part-time employee, and wages or salary actually lost;

(5) If a claim is made for loss of income and the claimant is self-employed, documentary evidence showing the amount of earnings actually lost.

(6) Any other evidence or information which may have a bearing on either the responsibility of the United States for the personal injury or the damages claimed.

(b) *Death.* In support of a claim based on death, the claimant may be required to submit the following evidence or information:

(1) An authenticated death certificate or other competent evidence showing cause of death, date of death, and age of the decedent.

(2) Decedent's employment or occupation at the time of death, including his monthly or yearly salary or earnings (if any), and the duration of his last employment or occupation.

(3) Full names, addresses, birth dates, kinship, and marital status of decedent's survivors, including identification of those survivors who were dependent for support upon decedent at the time of his death.

(4) Degree of support afforded by decedent to each survivor dependent upon him for support at the time of his death.

(5) Decedent's general physical and mental condition before death.

(6) Itemized bills for medical and burial expenses incurred by reason of the incident causing death, or itemized receipts of payment for such expenses.

(7) If damages for pain and suffering prior to death are claimed, a physician's detailed statement specifying the injuries suffered, duration of pain and suffering, any drugs administered for pain, and decedent's physical condition in the interval between injury and death.

(8) Any other evidence or information which may have a bearing on either the responsibility of the United States for the death or the damages claimed.

(c) *Property damage.* In support of a claim for injury to or loss of property, real or personal, the claimant may be required to submit the following evidence or information.

(1) Proof of ownership.

(2) A detailed statement of the amount claimed with respect to each item of property.

(3) Two or more itemized written estimates of the cost of such repairs and any itemized receipt of payment for necessary repairs.

(4) A statement listing date of purchase, purchase price, and salvage value where repair is not economical.

(5) Any other evidence or information which may have a bearing on either the responsibility of the United States for the injury to or loss of property or the damages claimed.

§304.5 Investigations.

The Peace Corps may investigate, or the General Counsel may request any other Federal agency to investigate, a claim filed under this subpart.

§304.6 Claims investigation.

(a) When a claim has been filed with the Peace Corps, the General Counsel will send a copy of the claim to the head of the office concerned and ask him to designate one employee of that office who shall act as, and who shall be referred to herein as, the Claims Investigating Officer for that particular claim. The Claims Investigating Officer shall, with the advice of the General Counsel, where necessary:

(1) Investigate as completely as is practicable the nature and circumstances of the occurrence causing the loss or damage of the claimant's property.

(2) Ascertain the extent of loss or damage to the claimant's property.

(3) Assemble the necessary forms with required data contained therein.

(4) Prepare a brief statement setting forth the facts relative to the claim (in the case of motor vehicle accidents, facts should be recorded on Standard Form 91–A), a statement whether the claim satisfies the requirements of this subpart, and a recommendation as to the amount to be paid in settlement of the claim.

(5) The head of the office concerned will be responsible for assuring that all necessary forms, statements, and all supporting papers have been procured for the file and will transmit the entire file to the General Counsel.

§ 304.7 Authority to adjust, determine, compromise, and settle claims.

The authority to consider, ascertain, adjust, determine, compromise and settle claims of less than $5,000 under 28 U.S.C. 2672, and this subpart, rests with the Chief Financial Officer, as the designee of the head of the agency. For claims under 28 U.S.C. 2672 and this subpart, subject to § 304.8, the Director of the Peace Corps retains authority to consider, ascertain, adjust, determine, compromise and settle claims of $5,000 or more.

[72 FR 4206, Jan. 30, 2007]

§ 304.8 Limitations on authority.

(a) An award, compromise, or settlement of a claim under section 2672 of title 28, United States Code, and this subpart in excess of $25,000 may be effected only with the prior written approval of the Attorney General or his designee. For the purpose of this paragraph, a principal claim and any derivative or subrogated claim shall be treated as a single claim.

(b) An administrative claim may be adjusted, determined, compromised, or settled only after consultation with the Department of Justice when, in the opinion of the General Counsel:

(1) A new precedent or a new point of law is involved; or

(2) A question of policy is or may be involved; or

(3) The United States is or may be entitled to indemnity or contribution from a third party, and the Peace Corps is unable to adjust the third party claim; or

(4) The compromise of a particular claim, as a practical matter, will or may control the disposition of a related claim in which the amount to be paid may exceed $25,000.

(c) An administrative claim may be adjusted, determined, compromised, or settled only after consultation with the Department of Justice when the Peace Corps is informed or is otherwise aware that the United States or an officer, employee, agent, or cost-type contractor of the United States is involved in litigation based on a claim arising out of the same incident or transaction.

§ 304.9 Referral to the Department of Justice.

When Department of Justice approval or consultation is required under § 304.8, the referral or request shall be transmitted to the Department of Justice by the General Counsel.

[72 FR 4206, Jan. 30, 2007]

§ 304.10 Review of claim.

(a) Upon receipt of the claim file from the head of the office concerned, the General Counsel will ascertain that all supporting papers are contained in the file.

(b) After legal review and recommendation by the General Counsel, the Director of the Peace Corps will make a written determination on the claim, unless the claim is worth less than $5,000, in which case the Chief Financial Officer will make the written determination.

[34 FR 5840, Mar. 28, 1969, as amended at 73 FR 21528, Apr. 22, 2008; 73 FR 49943, Aug. 25, 2008]

§304.11 Final denial of claim.

The General Counsel will send notification of the final denial of an administrative claim to the claimant, his attorney, or legal representative by certified or registered mail. The notification of final denial may include a statement of the reasons for the denial and shall include a statement that, if the claimant is dissatisfied with the Peace Corps action, he may file suit in an appropriate U.S. District Court not later than 6 months after the date of mailing of the notification.

§304.12 Action on approved claim.

(a) Payment of a claim approved under this subpart is contingent on claimant's execution of (1) a "Claim for Damage or Injury," Standard From 95; and (2) a "Voucher for Payment," Standard Form 1145, as appropriate. When a claimant is represented by an attorney, the voucher for payment shall designate the claimant and his attorney as copayees, and the check shall be delivered to the attorney, whose address shall appear on the voucher.

(b) Acceptance by the claimant, his agent, or legal representative of an award, compromise, or settlement made under section 2672 or 2677 of title 28, United States Code, is final and conclusive on the claimant, his agent or legal representative, and any other person on whose behalf or for whose benefit the claim has been presented, and constitutes a complete release of any claim against the United States and against any officer or employee of the Government whose act or omission gave rise to the claim, by reason of the same subject matter.

PART 305—ELIGIBILITY AND STANDARDS FOR PEACE CORPS VOLUNTEER SERVICE

Sec.

AUTHORITY: 22 U.S.C. 2503, 2504 2521; 29 U.S.C. 794; E.O. 12137, 44 FR 29023, 3 CFR, 1979 Comp., p. 389; E.O. 13160, 65 FR 39775, 3 CFR, 2000 Comp., p. 1461.

SOURCE: 82 FR 1188, Jan. 5, 2017, unless otherwise noted.

§305.1 Purpose and general guidelines.

This part states the requirements for eligibility for Peace Corps Volunteer service and the factors considered in the assessment and selection of eligible applicants for Peace Corps Volunteer service.

(a) *Definitions.* For purposes of this part:

(1) *Applicant* means an individual for enrollment as a Volunteer, who has completed and submitted the Peace Corps Volunteer application form.

(2) *Trainee* means an individual for enrollment as a Volunteer during any period of training occurring prior to such enrollment.

(3) *Volunteer* means an individual who has taken the prescribed oath and enrolled for service in the Peace Corps.

(4) *Enrollment* means the act by which an individual becomes a Volunteer upon successful completion of training and taking the prescribed oath of office pursuant to Section 5 of the Peace Corps Act, 22 U.S.C. 2504.

(5) *Dependent* means an individual for whom an applicant or Volunteer has a legal or familial obligation to provide financial support.

(6) *Family member* means any individual related by blood or affinity whose close association with the applicant or Volunteer is the equivalent of a family relationship.

(b) *Selection.* Invitations to serve in the Peace Corps are the result of a highly competitive application process. Many more individuals apply for Peace Corps Volunteer service than can be accepted. Because the Peace Corps cannot accept all eligible and qualified applicants who wish to serve, it evaluates applicants to select the best qualified among eligible applicants. The Peace

Corps determines Applicants' eligibility, and assesses their relative skills, qualifications, and personal attributes, such as motivation, aptitude, fitness for service, emotional maturity, adaptability, productive competence, and ability to serve effectively as a Volunteer in a foreign country and culture.

(c) *Authority.* Under section 5(a) of the Peace Corps Act, 22 U.S.C. 2504(a), the President may enroll in the Peace Corps for service abroad qualified citizens and nationals of the United States. The terms and conditions of the enrollment of Volunteers are exclusively those set forth in the Peace Corps Act and those consistent therewith which the President may prescribe. The President has delegated his authority under section 5(a) of the Peace Corps Act to the Director of the Peace Corps pursuant to Executive Order 12137 (May 16, 1979), as amended.

(d) *Non-discrimination.* The Peace Corps does not discriminate against any person on account of race, color, religion, sex (including but not limited to gender identity and gender expression), national origin, age (40 and over), disability, sexual orientation, gender identity, gender expression, pregnancy, marital status, parental status, political affiliation, union membership, genetic information, or history of participation in the EEO process, any grievance procedure or any authorized complaint procedure. Anyone who feels he or she has been discriminated against should contact the Office of Civil Rights and Diversity, 202.692.2139, *ocrd@peacecorps.gov*, Peace Corps, 1111 20th Street NW., Washington, DC 20526.

(e) *Failure to disclose requested information.* In order for the Peace Corps to be able to make appropriate selection and placement decisions, it is critical that Applicants provide complete and accurate information throughout the application process, including information provided for a mandatory background investigation. The Peace Corps may disqualify an Applicant or separate a Volunteer or Trainee from Peace Corps service at any time if the Peace Corps determines that the Applicant, Volunteer, or Trainee provided materially false, misleading, inaccurate or incomplete information during the Peace Corps application process.

§ 305.2 Eligibility.

In order to be eligible for enrollment as a Volunteer, Applicants must meet mandatory citizenship and age requirements.

(a) *Citizenship.* The Applicant must be a citizen or national of the United States prior to entering on duty as a Trainee.

(b) *Age.* The Applicant must be at least 18 years old at the time of entry on duty as a Trainee.

§ 305.3 Selection standards.

(a) *General.* To qualify for selection for overseas service as a Volunteer, an Applicant must demonstrate that he or she is suitable, possessing the requisite personal and professional attributes required for Peace Corps service generally, and for the particular Volunteer assignment for which he or she is considered. The Peace Corps assesses each Applicant's personal, professional, educational, and legal qualifications in order to select those Applicants most likely to be successful in a Peace Corps assignment, serving under conditions of hardship if necessary to achieve the goals of the Peace Corps. Meeting these qualifications does not in and of itself entitle any individual to serve in the Peace Corps. The Peace Corps endeavors to select the best qualified individuals from among all eligible Applicants.

(b) *Personal attributes.* Applicants must adequately demonstrate the following personal attributes to Peace Corps:

(1) *Motivation.* A sincere desire to carry out the goals of Peace Corps service, and a commitment to serve a full term as a Volunteer.

(2) *Productive competence.* The intelligence and professional experience or educational background to meet the needs of the individual's assignment.

(3) *Emotional maturity and adaptability.* The maturity, flexibility, cultural sensitivity, and self-sufficiency to adapt successfully to life in another culture, and to interact and communicate with other people regardless of cultural, social, and economic differences.

(4) *Skills.* In addition to any educational, professional or other qualifications and prerequisites that an individual must possess in order to be selected for a given assignment, a Trainee must demonstrate competence in the following areas by the end of pre-service training:

(i) *Language.* The ability to communicate effectively in the appropriate language or languages of the country of service with the fluency required to meet the needs of the overseas assignment.

(ii) *Technical competence.* Proficiency in the technical skills needed to carry out the Trainee's assignment as a Volunteer.

(iii) *Knowledge.* Adequate knowledge of the culture and history of the country of assignment to ensure a successful adjustment to, and acceptance by, the host country society, as well as an appropriate understanding of the history and government of the United States which qualifies the individual to represent the United States abroad.

(c) *Failure to meet standards.* Failure to meet initial selection standards, failure to attain any of the selection standards by the completion of training, or failure to maintain these standards during service, may be grounds for de-selection and disqualification from Peace Corps service.

§305.4 Medical status eligibility standard.

(a) *Requirements.* Under the Peace Corps Act (22 U.S.C. 2504(e)), the Peace Corps is responsible for ensuring that Peace Corps Volunteers receive all necessary or appropriate health care during their service. To ensure that the Peace Corps will be capable of doing so, Applicants must be medically qualified for Peace Corps Volunteer service. An Applicant who is otherwise qualified must meet the following requirements:

(1) The Applicant, with or without reasonable accommodation, removal of architectural, communication or transportation barriers, or the provision of auxiliary aids or services, must have the physical and mental capacity required to meet the essential eligibility requirements for a Volunteer. In this context, the essential eligibility requirements for a Volunteer include, without limitation, the capability to:

(i) Live and work independently in an isolated location overseas at the same socio-economic level and in similar conditions as members of the community to which the Applicant is assigned;

(ii) Perform the job to which the Applicant is assigned; and

(iii) Complete a specified tour of service without undue disruption.

(2) The Peace Corps must be capable of providing the Applicant with such health care as the Peace Corps deems to be necessary or appropriate.

(3) The Applicant must not pose a direct threat (as defined in paragraph (c) of this section).

(b) *Individualized assessment.* In determining whether an Applicant is medically qualified, an individualized assessment is required regarding each of the requirements set forth in paragraph (a) of this section.

(c) *Direct threat.* (1) A "direct threat" is a significant risk to the health or safety of others that cannot be eliminated by a reasonable accommodation to policies, practices or procedures, removal of architectural, communication or transportation barriers, or the provision of auxiliary aids or services.

(2) In determining whether an applicant poses a direct threat, the Peace Corps will make an individualized assessment based on reasonable judgment that relies on current medical knowledge or on the best available objective evidence to ascertain:

(i) The nature, duration and severity of the risk;

(ii) The probability that the potential injury will actually occur; and

(iii) Whether reasonable accommodations, removal of architectural, communication or transportation barriers, or the provision of auxiliary aids or services will mitigate the risk.

(d) *Reasonable accommodation.* (1) The term "accommodation" means modifications to the Peace Corps' policies, practices or procedures.

(2) An accommodation is not reasonable if:

(i) It would modify the essential eligibility requirements for a Volunteer;

(ii) It would modify, among other things, the Applicant's Volunteer assignment or the Peace Corps' medical program in a way that would result in a fundamental alteration in the nature of the service, program, or activity; or

(iii) It would impose an undue financial and administrative burden on the operations of the Peace Corps, including its medical program.

(3) In determining whether an accommodation would impose an undue financial and administrative burden on the operations of the Peace Corps, the Peace Corps may take into account, among other things:

(i) The size and composition of the Peace Corps staff at the post of assignment;

(ii) The adequacy of local medical facilities and the availability of other medical facilities;

(iii) The nature and cost of the accommodation compared to the overall number of Volunteers and the overall size of the Peace Corps budget; and

(iv) The capacities of the host country agency and of the host community to which the Applicant would be assigned.

(e) *Medical status eligibility review.* (1) An Applicant who is determined by medical screening staff not to be medically qualified for Peace Corps Volunteer service may request review of that decision by submitting any relevant information to the Office of Medical Services (OMS). The information submitted by the Applicant will be reviewed by a physician, and, unless the physician determines that the Applicant is medically qualified, by a Pre-Service Review Board (PSRB) composed of medical personnel in OMS and advised by the General Counsel. Procedures for such review are subject to approval by the General Counsel.

(2) The PSRB will include as voting members at least one physician as well as other medical professionals in OMS. In any case involving review of issues involving mental health, at least one mental health professional from the Counseling and Outreach Unit will also participate as a voting member.

(3) The decision of the PSRB will be reviewed by the General Counsel for legal sufficiency. Subject to that review, it will constitute the final agency action.

§ 305.5 Legal status eligibility standard.

(a) *General requirements.* The existence of an arrest or conviction record may, but will not automatically, exclude an Applicant from consideration for Peace Corps service. The Peace Corps will consider the nature of the offense, how long ago the offense occurred, whether the Applicant was acquitted of the offense, the terms of any applicable parole or probation, and other relevant facts or indications of rehabilitation.

(b) *Drug and alcohol related offenses.* (1) An Applicant with any drug-related conviction, with a conviction for public intoxication, driving under the influence (DUI), or driving while intoxicated (DWI), with a conviction for reckless driving after having been initially charged with DUI or DWI, or with a similar alcohol-related conviction, is not eligible to have his or her application for Peace Corps service considered until 12 months has passed from the date of the incident.

(2) An Applicant who, at any time on or prior to the day of departure for Peace Corps service, is arrested for any drug offense or for public intoxication, DUI, DWI or any similar alcohol-related offense will have any pending application or invitation for Peace Corps service withdrawn. If the charges are dismissed, an Applicant whose application or invitation for Peace Corps service was terminated may immediately reapply. If the applicant is convicted of the offense, he or she may reapply after 12 months from the date of the incident.

(c) *Review process.* An Applicant who is rejected for a Volunteer position because of an arrest or conviction may request a review of that decision by submitting any relevant information to the Associate Director of the Office of Volunteer Recruitment and Selection (VRS). The Associate Director will review the information submitted and consult with the General Counsel. The decision of the Associate Director will be the final agency decision. The Associate Director may delegate authority to conduct such a review to another senior member of VRS, but not to the supervisor of the office making the original eligibility determination.

(d) *Subsequent application.* An Applicant rejected for service due to failure to meet the legal status eligibility standard may reapply at a later date, but not sooner than 12 months after the final agency decision.

§305.6 Applicants with an intelligence background.

(a) *General.* It has been the longstanding policy of the Peace Corps to exclude from Volunteer service any individuals who have engaged in intelligence activity or related work or who have been employed by or connected with an intelligence agency, either for a specific period of time or permanently (depending on the agency). This policy is founded on the premise that it is crucial to the Peace Corps in carrying out its mission that there be a complete and total separation of Peace Corps from the intelligence activities of the United States Government or any foreign government, both in reality and appearance. Any semblance of a connection between the Peace Corps and the intelligence community would seriously compromise the ability of the Peace Corps to develop and maintain the trust and confidence of the people of the host countries. To ensure that there is not the slightest basis for the appearance of any connection between the Peace Corps and the intelligence community, this policy contains certain temporary and permanent bars to Peace Corps service. Serious doubts about an Applicant's connection with intelligence activities are to be resolved in favor of exclusion.

(b) *Definitions.* For purposes of this section:

(1) *Intelligence activity* includes any activities or specialized training involving or related to the clandestine collection of information, or the analysis or dissemination of such information, intended for use by the United States Government or any foreign government in formulating or implementing political or military policy in regard to other countries. The term "intelligence activity" includes any involvement in covert actions designed to influence events in foreign countries. The fact that the name of an employer or the description of a person's work uses or does not use the term "intelligence" does not, in and of itself, mean that the person has or has not engaged in intelligence activity or related work.

(2) *Intelligence agency* includes:

(i) Any agency, division of an agency, or instrumentality of the United States Government that is a member of the United States Intelligence Community; and

(ii) Any other agency, division of an agency, or instrumentality of the United States Government or any foreign government, a substantial part of whose mission has been determined by the General Counsel to include intelligence activities.

(3) *Employment, employee or employed* refer to the existence of a relationship of employer and employee, whether full-time or part-time, permanent or temporary, whether or not the individual is engaged in intelligence activity for an employer, without regard to the length of time the relationship existed or is proposed to exist, and includes individuals performing duties as volunteers, fellows, interns, consultants, personal services contractors, contractors (non-personal services contractors), and employees of contractors who were assigned to work for an intelligence agency or to engage in intelligence activities. Employees of contractors who were or are not themselves assigned to work for an Intelligence Agency or to engage in intelligence activities are not considered to have been or to be employed by an intelligence agency.

(c) *Employment by an intelligence agency or engagement in intelligence activities.* (1) An Applicant currently or formerly employed by the Central Intelligence Agency (CIA) is permanently ineligible for Peace Corps Volunteer service.

(2) An Applicant who has been employed by an intelligence agency other than the CIA is ineligible for a minimum of 10 years from the last day of employment by such intelligence agency. This bar on an Applicant who is or was employed by an intelligence agency applies whether or not the Applicant was engaged in intelligence activity for the intelligence agency.

(3) An Applicant who has been engaged in intelligence activities is ineligible for service as a Volunteer for a period of 10 years from the last date on which the Applicant engaged in intelligence activities.

(4) An Applicant may be ineligible for service for a period in excess of 10 years if the General Counsel determines that the Applicant's background or work history with regard to intelligence activities warrants such action.

(d) *Relationship to intelligence agency or activity.* (1) An Applicant whose background discloses a relationship to an intelligence agency or intelligence activity may be ineligible to serve as a Peace Corps Volunteer. The term "relationship" means any association with an intelligence agency or with an intelligence activity, if such association could be the basis for an inference or the appearance that an Applicant was engaged in an intelligence activity. The association could include, but not be limited to, one based upon a familial, personal or financial connection to an intelligence agency or with an intelligence activity.

(2) Determinations of the eligibility or periods of ineligibility of such Applicants will be made by the General Counsel on a case by case basis using the criteria set forth below. Examples of the type of relationships among others that could lead to ineligibility are Applicants whose spouses, domestic partners, or parents are or were involved in actual intelligence activities, or members of the immediate family of prominent highly placed officials in an intelligence agency who might be the target of harassment or violence overseas as the result of family connections. Employment by an organization that has been funded by an intelligence agency may also lead to ineligibility.

(3) In determining whether an Applicant's relationship to an intelligence agency or intelligence activity makes the Applicant ineligible for service, or in determining the duration of any ineligibility, the General Counsel will consider the following factors as appropriate:

(i) Nature of the relationship.

(ii) The intelligence agency with which the Applicant has the relationship.

(iii) Duration of the relationship.

(iv) Length of time that has elapsed since the last connection to the intelligence agency.

(v) Where the intelligence activity or work was performed.

(vi) Nature of the connection with intelligence activity or work.

(vii) Whether or not the intelligence activity or work involved contact with foreign nationals.

(viii) Whether the connection was known or unknown to the Applicant at the time it occurred.

(ix) Training received, if any.

(x) Regularity of the contact with foreign nationals, and nature of duties, if any.

(xi) Public knowledge of the activity or connection.

(xii) Any other information which bears on the relationship of the Applicant to an intelligence agency or intelligence activity.

(e) *Determination.* VRS is responsible for the initial screening of Peace Corps Volunteer applications for compliance with the provisions of this policy. In cases where that office is unable to make a decision regarding the eligibility of an Applicant under this policy, the individual's application will be referred to the General Counsel, who will make the determination on eligibility.

(f) *Appeal.* VRS will inform all Applicants promptly and in writing of any decision to disqualify them based on an intelligence background and the reasons for that decision. Applicants have 15 days from the date of receipt of the letter from VRS to appeal the decision to the Director of the Peace Corps. The decision of the Director of the Peace Corps will be the final agency decision.

(g) *Post Peace Corps employment by United States intelligence agencies.* Pursuant to agreements between the Peace Corps and certain intelligence agencies, those intelligence agencies will not employ former Volunteers for a specified period after the end of their Peace Corps service and will not use former Volunteers for certain purposes or in certain positions. Information regarding such agreements may be obtained from the Office of the General Counsel.

§305.7 Special circumstances.

(a) *Couples.* Two Applicants who are married to one another or two unmarried Applicants who are in a same-sex or opposite-sex domestic partnership or other committed relationship are eligible to apply for service as a couple. In the case of an unmarried couple, each member of the couple must provide a sworn statement, in a form acceptable to the Peace Corps, attesting to their domestic partnership status or committed relationship (as the case may be) and their request to be considered for assignment as a couple. In all cases, both members of the couple must apply and qualify for assignment at the same location.

(b) *Serving with dependents and other family members.* In general, dependents and other family members may not accompany a Volunteer during service. However, the Peace Corps may from time to time make exceptions either on a case-by-case basis or for particular categories of Volunteers to the extent permitted by Federal law.

(c) *Military service.* The Peace Corps welcomes applications from veterans, reservists, and active duty military personnel who are interested in Peace Corps service after completion of their military service. After receiving an invitation for Peace Corps service, applicants with reserve obligations are reminded to comply with all requirements to notify their reserve component that they will be unavailable for drills and annual training because of their Peace Corps service. Such applicants are urged to obtain written confirmation from their reserve component that they have complied with these requirements.

§305.8 Background investigation.

Section 22 of the Peace Corps Act requires that each Applicant be investigated to ensure that enrollment of the Applicant as a Volunteer is consistent with the national interest. The Peace Corps therefore obtains an appropriate background investigation for all Applicants who are invited to serve in the Peace Corps. Information revealed by the background investigation may be grounds for disqualification from Peace Corps service. Under the Peace Corps Act, if a background investigation regarding an Applicant develops any data reflecting that the Applicant is of questionable loyalty or is a questionable security risk, the Peace Corps must refer the matter to the Federal Bureau of Investigation for a full field investigation. The results of that full field investigation will be furnished to the Peace Corps for information and appropriate action.

PART 306—VOLUNTEER DISCRIMINATION COMPLAINT PROCEDURE

CROSS REFERENCE: ACTION regulations concerning the volunteer discrimination complaint procedure, appearing in 45 CFR part 1225, are applicable to Peace Corps volunteers. Part 1225 appears at 46 FR 1609, Jan. 6, 1981.

PART 308—IMPLEMENTATION OF THE PRIVACY ACT OF 1974

AUTHORITY: 5 U.S.C. 552a.

SOURCE: 50 FR 1844, Jan. 14, 1985, unless otherwise noted.

§308.1 Purpose.

The purpose of this part is to set forth the basic policies of the Peace Corps governing the maintenance of systems of records containing personal information as defined in the Privacy

Act of 1974 (5 U.S.C. 552a). Records included in this part are those described in the aforesaid Act and maintained by the Peace Corps and/or any component thereof.

§ 308.2 Policy.

It is the policy of the Peace Corps to protect, preserve and defend the right of privacy of any individual as to whom the agency maintains personal information in any records system and to provide appropriate and complete access to such records including adequate opportunity to correct any errors in said records. It is further the policy of the agency to maintain its records in such a fashion that the information contained therein is and remains material and relevant to the purposes for which it is collected in order to maintain its records with fairness to the individuals who are the subject of such records.

§ 308.3 Definitions.

(a) *Record* means any document, collection, or grouping of information about an individual maintained by the agency, including but not limited to information regarding education, financial transactions, medical history, criminal or employment history, or any other personal information which contains the name or personal identification number, symbol, photograph, or other identifying particular assigned to such individual, such as a finger or voiceprint.

(b) *System of Records* means a group of any records under the control of the agency from which information is retrieved by use of the name of an individual or by some identifying number, symbol, or other identifying particular assigned to the individual.

(c) *Routine Use* means, with respect to the disclosure of a record, the use of such record for a purpose which is compatible with the purpose for which it was collected.

(d) The term *agency* means the Peace Corps or any component thereof.

(e) The term *individual* means any citizen of the United States or an alien lawfully admitted to permanent residence.

(f) The term *maintain* includes the maintenance, collection, use or dissemination of any record.

(g) The term *Act* means the Privacy Act of 1974 (5 U.S.C. 552a) as amended from time to time.

§ 308.4 Disclosure of records.

The agency will not disclose any personal information from systems of records it maintains to any individual other than the individual to whom the record pertains, or to another agency, without the express written consent of the individual to whom the record pertains, or his or her agent or attorney, except in the following instances:

(a) To officers or employees of the Peace Corps having a need for such record in the official performance of their duties.

(b) When required under the provisions of the Freedom of Information Act (5 U.S.C. 552).

(c) For routine uses as published in the FEDERAL REGISTER.

(d) To the Bureau of the Census for uses pursuant to title 13.

(e) To an individual or agency having a proper need for such record for statistical research provided that such record is transmitted in a form which is not individually identifiable and that an appropriate written statement is obtained from the person to whom the record is transmitted stating the purpose for the request and a certification under oath that the records will be used only for statistical purposes.

(f) To the National Archives of the United States as a record of historical value under rules and regulations of the Archives or to the Administrator of General Services or his designee to determine if it has such value.

(g) To an agency or instrumentality of any governmental jurisdiction within the control of the United States for civil or criminal law enforcement activities, if the activity is authorized by law, and the head of any such agency or instrumentality has made a written request for such records specifying the particular portion desired and the law enforcement activity for which the record is sought. Such a record may also be disclosed by the agency to the law enforcement agency on its own initiative in situations in which criminal conduct is suspected: *Provided,* That such disclosure has been established as a routine use or in situations in which the misconduct is directly related to the purpose for which the record is maintained.

(h) In emergency situations upon a showing of compelling circumstances affecting the health or safety of any individual provided that after such disclosure, notification of such disclosure must be promptly sent to the last known address of the individual to whom the record pertains.

(i) To either House of Congress or to a subcommittee or committee (joint or of either house) to the extent the subject matter falls within their jurisdiction.

(j) To the Comptroller General, or any of his authorized representatives, in the course of the performance of the duties of the General Accounting Office.

(k) Pursuant to an order by the presiding judge of a court of competent jurisdiction. If any record is disclosed under such compulsory legal process and subsequently made public by the court which issued it, the agency must make a reasonable effort to notify the individual to whom the record pertains of such disclosure.

(l) To consumer reporting agencies as defined in 31 U.S.C. 3701(a)(3) in accordance with 31 U.S.C. 3711, and under contracts for collection services as authorized in 31 U.S.C. 3718.

§308.5 New uses of information.

The agency shall publish in the FEDERAL REGISTER a notice of its intention to establish a new or revised routine use of any system of records maintained by it with an opportunity for public comments on such use. Such notice shall contain the following:

(a) The name of the system of records for which the new or revised routine use is to be established.

(b) The authority for maintaining the system of records.

(c) The categories of records maintained in the system.

(d) The purpose for which the record is to be maintained.

(e) The proposed routine use(s).

(f) The purpose of the routine use(s).

(g) The categories of recipients of such use.

In the event of any request for an addition to the routine uses of the systems which the agency maintains, such request may be sent to the following officer: Director, Office of Administrative Services, Peace Corps, 806 Connecticut Avenue, NW., Washington, DC 20526.

§308.6 Reports regarding changes in systems.

The agency shall provide to Congress and the Office of Management and Budget advance notice of any proposal to establish or alter any system of records as defined herein. This report will be submitted in accord with guidelines provided by the Office of Management and Budget.

§308.7 Use of social security account number in records systems. [Reserved]

§308.8 Rules of conduct.

(a) The head of the agency shall assure that all persons involved in the design, development, operation or maintenance of any systems of records as defined herein are informed of all requirements necessary to protect the privacy of individuals who are the subject of such records. All employees shall be informed of all implications of the Act in this area including the criminal penalties provided under the Act, and the fact the agency may be subject to civil suit for failure to comply with the provisions of the Privacy Act and these regulations.

(b) The head of the agency shall also ensure that all personnel having access to records receive adequate training in the protection of the security of personal records and that adequate and proper storage is provided for all such records with sufficient security to assure the privacy of such records.

§308.9 Records systems—management and control.

(a) The Director, Office of Administrative Services, shall have overall control and supervision of the security of all records keeping systems and shall be responsible for monitoring the security standards set forth in these regulations.

(b) A designated official (System Manager) shall be named who shall have management responsibility for each record system maintained by the agency and who shall be responsible for providing protection and accountability for such records at all times and for insuring that such records are secured in appropriate containers wherever not in use or in the direct control of authorized personnel.

§ 308.10 Security of records systems—manual and automated.

The head of the agency has the responsibility of maintaining adequate technical, physical, and security safeguards to prevent unauthorized disclosure or destruction of manual and automatic record systems. These security safeguards shall apply to all systems in which identifiable personal data are processed or maintained including all reports and outputs from such systems which contain identifiable personal information. Such safeguards must be sufficient to prevent negligent, accidental, or unintentional disclosure, modification or destruction of any personal records or data and must furthermore minimize the extent technicians or knowledgeable persons could improperly obtain access to modify or destroy such records or data and shall further insure against such casual entry by unskilled persons without official reasons for access to such records or data.

(a) *Manual systems.* (1) Records contained in records systems as defined herein may be used, held or stored only where facilities are adequate to prevent unauthorized access by persons within or without the agency.

(2) All records systems when not under the personal control of the employees authorized to use same must be stored in an appropriate metal filing cabinet. Where appropriate, such cabinet shall have a three position dial-type combination lock, and/or be equipped with a steel lock bar secured by a GSA approved changeable combination padlock or in some such other securely locked cabinet as may be approved by GSA for the storage of such records. Certain systems are not of such confidential nature that their disclosure would harm an individual who is the subject of such record. Records in this category shall be maintained in steel cabinets without the necessity of combination locks.

(3) Access to and use of systems of records shall be permitted only to persons whose official duties require such access within the agency, for routine use as defined in § 308.4 and in the Peace Corps' published systems of records notices, or for such other uses as may be provided herein.

(4) Other than for access within the agency to persons needing such records in the performance of their official duties or routine uses as defined herein and in the Peace Corps' systems of records notices or such other uses as provided herein, access to records within systems of records shall be permitted only to the individual to whom the record pertains or upon his or her written request to a designated personal representative.

(5) Access to areas where records systems are stored will be limited to those persons whose official duties require work in such areas and proper accounting of removal of any records from storage areas shall be maintained at all times in the form directed by the Director, Administrative Services.

(6) The agency shall assure that all persons whose official duties require access to and use of records contained in records systems are adequately trained to protect the security and privacy of such records.

(7) The disposal and destruction of records within records systems shall be in accord with rules promulgated by the General Services Administration.

(b) *Automated systems.* (1) Identifiable personal information may be processed, stored or maintained by automatic data systems only where facilities or conditions are adequate to prevent unauthorized access to such systems in any form. Whenever such data contained in punch cards, magnetic tapes or discs are not under the personal control of an authorized person such information must be stored in a metal filing cabinet having a built-in three position combination lock, a metal filing cabinet equipped with a steel lock, a metal filing cabinet equipped with a steel lock bar secured with a General Services Administration (GSA) approved combination padlock, or in adequate containers or in a secured room or in such other facility having greater safeguards than those provided for herein.

(2) Access to and use of identifiable personal data associated with automated data systems shall be limited to those persons whose official duties require such access. Proper control of personal data in any form associated with automated data systems shall be maintained at all times including maintenance of accountability records showing disposition of input and output documents.

(3) All persons whose official duties require access to processing and maintenance of identifiable personal data and automated systems shall be adequately trained in the security and privacy of personal data.

(4) The disposal and disposition of identifiable personal data and automated systems shall be carried on by shredding, burning or in the case of tapes of discs, degaussing, in accord with any regulations now or hereafter proposed by the GSA or other appropriate authority.

§ 308.11 Accounting for disclosure of records.

Each office maintaining a system of records shall keep a written account of routine disclosures (see paragraphs (a) through (e) of this section) for all records within such system in the form prescribed by the Director, Office of Administrative Services. Disclosure made to employees of the agency in the normal course of their official duties or pursuant to the provisions of the Freedom of Information Act need not be accounted for. Such written account shall contain the following:

(a) The date, nature, and purpose of each disclosure of a record to any person or to another agency.

(b) The name and address of the person or agency to whom the disclosure was made.

(c) Sufficient information to permit the construction of a listing of all disclosures at appropriate periodic intervals.

(d) The justification or basis upon which any release was made including any written documentation required when records are released for statistical or law enforcement purposes under the provisions of subsection (b) of the Act.

(e) For the purpose of this part, the system of accounting for disclosure is not a system of records under the definitions hereof and no accounting need be maintained for the disclosure of accounting of disclosures.

§ 308.12 Contents of records systems.

(a) The agency shall maintain in any records contained in any records system hereunder only such information about an individual as is accurate, relevant, and necessary to accomplish the purpose for which the agency acquired the information as authorized by statute or executive order.

(b) In situations in which the information may result in adverse determinations about such individual's rights, benefits and privileges under any Federal program, all information placed in records systems shall, to the greatest extent practicable, be collected from the individual to whom the record pertains.

(c) Each form or other document which an individual is expected to complete in order to provide information for any records system shall have appended thereto, or in the body of the document:

(1) An indication of the authority authorizing the solicitation of the information and whether the provision of the information is mandatory or voluntary.

(2) The purpose or purposes for which the information is intended to be used.

(3) Routine uses which may be made of the information and published pursuant to § 308.7 of this regulation.

(4) The effect on the individual, if any, of not providing all or part of the required or requested information.

(d) Records maintained in any system of records used by the agency to make any determination about any individual shall be maintained with such accuracy, relevancy, timeliness, and completeness as is reasonably necessary to assure fairness to the individual in the making of any determination about such individual: *Provided, however*, That the agency shall not be required to update or keep current retired records.

(e) Before disseminating any record about an individual to any person other than an agency as defined in 5 U.S.C. 552(e) or pursuant to the provsions of the Freedom of Information Act (5 U.S.C. 552), the agency shall make reasonable efforts to assure that such records are accurate, complete, timely and relevant for agency purposes.

(f) Under no circumstances shall the agency maintain any record about an individual with respect to or describing how such individual exercises rights guaranteed by the first amendment of the Constitution of the United States unless expressly authorized by statute or by the individual about whom the record is maintained or unless pertinent to and within the scope of an authorized law enforcement activity.

(g) In the event any record is disclosed as a result of the order of a presiding judge of a court of competent jurisdiction, the agency shall make reasonable efforts to notify the individual whose record was so disclosed after the process becomes a matter of public record.

§ 308.13 Access to records.

(a) The Director, Administrative Services, shall keep a current list of systems of records maintained by the agency and published in accordance with the provisions of these regulations.

(b) Individuals requesting access to any record the agency maintains about him or her in a system of records shall be provided access to such records. Such requests shall be submitted in writing by mail, or in person during regular business hours, to the System Managers identified in the specific system notices. Systems maintained at overseas and dometic field offices may be addressed to the Country Director or Regional Service Center Manager. If assistance is needed, the Director, Office of Administrative Services, will provide agency addresses.

(c) Requests for records from more than one system of records shall be directed to the Director, Office of Administrative Services, Peace Crops, 806 Connecticut Avenue, NW., Washington, DC 20526.

(d) Requests for access to or copies of records should contain, at a minimum, identifying information needed to locate any given record and a brief description of the item or items of information required. If the individual wishes access to specific documents the request should identify or describe as nearly as possible such documents.

(e) A record may be disclosed to a representative of the person to whom a record relates who is authorized in writing to have access to the record by the person to whom it relates.

(f) A request made in person will be promptly complied with if the records sought are in the immediate custody of the Peace Corps. Mailed or personal request for documents in storage which must be complied from more than one location, or which are otherwise not immediately available, will be acknowledge within ten working days, and the records requested will be provided as promptly thereafter as possible.

(g) Medical or psychological records shall be disclosed to an individual unless in the judgment of the agency, access to such records might have an adverse effect upon such individual. When such determination has been made, the agency may require that the information be disclosed only to a physician chosen by the requesting individual. Such physician shall have full authority to disclose all or any portion of such record to the requesting individual in the exercise of his or her professional judgment.

§ 308.14 Specific exemptions.

Records or portions of records in certain record systems specified in paragraphs (a) through (c) of this section shall be exempt from disclosure: *Provided, however,* That no such exemption shall apply to the provisions of § 308.12(a) (maintaining records with accuracy, completeness, etc. as reasonably necessary for agency purposes); § 308.12(b) (collecting information directly from the individual to whom it pertains); § 308.12(c) (informing individuals asked to supply information of the purposes for which it is collected and whether it is mandatory); § 308.12(g) (notifying the subjects of records disclosed under compulsory court process); §308.16(d)(3) (informing prior recipient of corrected or disputed records); §308.16(g) (civil remedies). With the above exceptions the following material shall be exempt from disclosure to the extent indicated:

(a) Material in any system of records considered classified and exempt from disclosure under provisions of section 552(b)(1) of the Freedom of Information Act. Agency systems of records now containing such material are: Legal Files—Staff, Volunteers and Applicants; Security Records Peace Corps Staff/Volunteers and ACTION staff.

(1) Authority: 5 U.S.C. 552a (k)(1)

(2) Reasons: To protect information classified in the interest of national defense or foreign policy.

(b) Investigatory material compiled for the purposes of law enforcement: *Provided, however,* That if any individual is denied any right, privilege, or benefit that he or she would otherwise be entitled to by Federal law, or for which he or she would otherwise be eligible, as a result of the maintenance of such material, such material shall be provided to such individual except to the extent necessary to protect the identity of a source who furnished information to the government under an express promise that his or her identity would be held in confidence, or prior to the effective date of the Privacy Act of 1974, under an implied promise of such confidentiality of the identity of such source. Agency systems of records containing such investigatory material are: Discrimination Complaint Files; Employee Occupational Injury and Illness Reports; Legal Files—Staff, Volunteers and Applicants; Security Records—Peace Corps Staff/Volunteers and ACTION Staff.

(1) Authority: 5 U.S.C. 552a(k)(2)

(2) Reasons: To protect the identity of sources to whom proper promises of confidentiality have been made during investigations. Without these promises, sources will often be unwilling to provide information essential in adjudicating access in a fair and impartial manner.

(c) Investigatory material compiled solely for the purpose of determining suitability, eligibility or qualification for service as an employee or volunteer or for the obtaining of a Federal contract or for access to classified information: *Provided, however,* That such material shall be disclosed to the extent possible without revealing the identity of a source who furnished information to the government under an express promise of the confidentiality of his or her identity or, prior to the effective date of the Privacy Act of 1974, under an implied promise of such confidentiality of identity. Agency systems of records containing such material are: Contractors and Consultant Files; Discrimination Complaint Files; Legal Files—Staff, Volunteers and Applicants; Personal Service Contract Records—Peace Corps Staff/Volunteers and ACTION Staff; Staff Applicant and Personnel Records; Talent Bank; Volunteer Applicant and Service Record Systems.

(1) Authority: 5 U.S.C. 552a(k)(5)

(2) Reasons: To ensure the frankness of information used to determine whether Peace Corps Volunteers applicants and Peace Corps Staff applicants are qualified for service with the agency.

(d) Records in the Office of Inspector General Investigative Files and Records system of records are exempt from certain provisions to the extent provided hereinafter.

(1) To the extent that the system of records pertains to the enforcement of criminal laws, the Office of Inspector General Investigative Files and Records system of records is exempt from all sections of the Privacy Act (5 U.S.C. 552a) except the following sections: (b) relating to conditions of disclosure; (c)(1) and (2) relating to keeping and maintaining a disclosure accounting; (e)(4)(A) through (F) relating to publishing a system notice setting the name, location, categories of individuals and records, routine uses, and policies regarding storage, retrievability, access controls, retention and disposal of the records; (e)(6), (7), (9), (10), and (11) relating to dissemination and maintenance of records and (i) relating to criminal penalties. This system of records is also exempt from the provisions of §308.11 through

§ 308.17 to the extent that the provisions of these sections conflict with this paragraph.

(i) Authority: 5 U.S.C. 552a(j)(2).

(ii) Reasons:

(A) To prevent interference with law enforcement proceedings.

(B) To avoid unwarranted invasion of personal privacy, by disclosure of information about third parties, including other subjects of investigations, investigators, and witnesses.

(C) To protect the identity of Federal employees who furnish a complaint or information to OIG, consistent with section 7(b) of the Inspector General Act of 1978, as amended, 5 U.S.C. App. 3.

(D) To protect the confidentiality of non-Federal employee sources of information.

(E) To assure access to sources of confidential information, including those contained in Federal, State, and local criminal law enforcement information systems.

(F) To prevent disclosure of law enforcement techniques and procedures.

(G) To avoid endangering the life or physical safety of confidential sources.

(2) To the extent that there may exist within this system of records investigative files compiled for law enforcement purposes, other than material within the scope of subsection (j)(2) of the Privacy Act, the OIG Investigative Files and Records system of records is exempt from the following sections of the Privacy Act: (c)(3) relating to access to the disclosure accounting; (d) relating to access to records; (e)(1) relating to the type of information maintained in the records; (e)(4) (G), (H), and (I) relating to publishing the system notice information as to agency procedures for access and amendment, and information as to the categories of sources or records; and (f) relating to developing agency rules for gaining access and making corrections. *Provided, however*, That if any individual is denied any right, privilege, or benefit that they would otherwise be entitled by Federal law, or for which they would otherwise be eligible, as a result of the maintenance of such material, such material shall be provided to such individual except to the extent that the disclosure of such material would reveal the identity of a source who furnished information to the Government under an express promise that the identity of the source would be held in confidence, or, prior to January 1, 1975, under an implied promise that the identity of the source would be held in confidence. This system of records is also exempt from the provisions of § 308.11 through § 308.17 to the extent that the provisions of these sections conflict with this paragraph.

(i) Authority: 5 U.S.C. 552a(k)(2)

(ii) Reasons:

(A) To prevent interference with law enforcement proceedings.

(B) To protect investigatory material compiled for law enforcement purposes.

(C) To avoid unwarranted invasion of personal privacy, by disclosure of information about third parties, including other subjects of investigation, law enforcement personnel, and sources of information.

(D) To fulfill commitments made to protect the confidentiality of sources.

(E) To protect the identity of Federal employees who furnish a complaint or information to the OIG, consistent with Section 7(b) of the Inspector General Act of 1978, as amended, 5 U.S.C. App. 3.

(F) To assure access to sources of confidential information, including those contained in Federal, State, and local criminal law enforcement systems.

(G) [Reserved]

(H) To prevent disclosure of law enforcement techniques and procedures.

(I) To avoid endangering the life or physical safety of confidential sources and law enforcement personnel.

[50 FR 1844, Jan. 14, 1985, as amended at 58 FR 39657, July 26, 1993]

§ 308.15 Identification of requesters.

The agency shall require reasonable identification of all individuals who request access to records to assure that records are not disclosed to persons not entitled to such access.

(a) In the event an individual requests disclosure in person, such individual shall be required to show an identification card such as a driver's license, etc., containing a photo and a sample signature of such individual. Such individual may also be required to sign a statement under oath as to his or her identity acknowledging that he or she is aware of the penalties for improper disclosure under the provisions of the Privacy Act of 1974.

(b) In the event that disclosure is requested by mail, the agency may request such information as may be necessary to reasonably assure that the individual making such request is properly identified. In certain cases, the agency may require that a mail request be notarized with an indication that the notary received an acknowledgment of identity from the individual making such request.

(c) In the event an individual is unable to provide suitable documentation or identification, the agency may require a signed notarized statement asserting the identity of the individual and stipulating that the individual understands that knowingly or willfully seeking or obtaining access to records about another person under false pretenses is punishable by a fine of up to $5,000.

(d) In the event a requester wishes to be accompanied by another person while reviewing his or her records, the agency may require a written statement authorizing discussion of his or her records in the presence of the accompanying representative or other persons.

§ 308.16 Amendment of records and appeals with respect thereto.

(a) In the event an individual desires to request an amendment of his or her record, he or she may do so by submitting such written request to the Director, Administrative Services, Peace Corps, 806 Connecticut Avenue, NW., Washington, DC 20526. The Director, Administrative Services, shall provide assistance in preparing any amendment upon request and a written acknowledgment of receipt of such request within 10 working days after the receipt thereof from the individual who requested the amendment. Such acknowledgment may, if necessary, request any additional information needed to make a determination with respect to such request. If the agency decides to comply with the request within the 10 day period, no written acknowledgment is necessary: *Provided, however,* That a certification of the change shall be provided to such individual within such period.

(b) Promptly after acknowledgment of the receipt of a request for an amendment the agency shall take one of the following actions:

(1) Make any corrections of any portion of the record which the individual believes is not accurate, relevant, timely or complete.

(2) Inform the individual of its refusal to amend the record in accord with the request together with the reason for such refusal and the procedures established for requesting review of such refusal by the head of the agency or his or her designee. Such notice shall include the name and business address of the reviewing official.

(3) Refer the request to the agency that has control of and maintains the record in those instances where the record requested remains the property of the controlling agency and not of the Peace Corps.

(c) In reviewing a request to amend the record the agency shall assess the accuracy, relevance, timeliness and completeness of the record with due and appropriate regard for fairness to the individual about whom the record is maintained. In making such determination, the agency shall consult criteria for determining record quality published in pertinent chapters of the *Federal Personnel Manual* and to the extent possible shall accord therewith.

(d) In the event the agency agrees with the individual's request to amend such record it shall:

(1) Advise the individual in writing,

(2) Correct the record accordingly, and

(3) Advise all previous recipients of a record which was corrected of the correction and its substance.

(e) In the event the agency, after an initial review of the request to amend a record, disagrees with all or a portion of it, the agency shall:

(1) Advise the individual of its refusal and the reasons therefore,

(2) Inform the individual that he or she may request further review in accord with the provisions of these regulations, and

(3) Specify The name and address of the person to whom the request should be directed.

(f) In the event an individual requester disagrees with the initial agency determination, he or she may appeal such determination to the Director of the Peace Corps or his or her designee. Such request for review must be made within 30 days after receipt by the requester of the initial refusal to amend.

(g) If after review the Director or designee refuses to amend the record as requested he or she shall advise the individual requester of such refusal and the reasons for same; of his or her right to file a concise statement in the record of the reasons for disagreeing with the decision of the agency; of the procedures for filing a statement of disagreement and of the fact that such statement so filed will be made available to anyone to whom the record is subsequently disclosed together with a brief statement of the agency summarizing its reasons for refusal, if the agency decides to place such brief statement in the record. The agency shall have the authority to limit the length of any statement to be filed, such limit to depend upon the record involved. The agency shall also inform such individual that prior recipients of the disputed record will be provided a copy of both statements of the dispute to the extent that the accounting of disclosures has been maintained and of the individual's right to seek judicial review of the agency's refusal to amend the record.

(h) If after review the official determines that the record should be amended in accordance with the individual's request, the agency shall proceed as provided above in the event a request is granted upon initial demand.

(i) Final agency determination of an individual's request for a review shall be concluded with 30 working days from the date of receipt of the review request: *Provided, however,* That the Director or designee may determine that fair and equitable review cannot be made within that time. If such circumstances occur, the individual shall be notified in writing of the additional time required and of the approximate date on which determination of the review is expected to be completed.

§ 308.17 Denial of access and appeals with respect thereto.

In the event that the agency finds it necessary to deny any individual access to a record about such individual pursuant to provisions of the Privacy Act or of these regulations, a response to the original request shall be made in writing within ten working days after the date of such initial request. The denial shall specify the reasons for such refusal or denial and advise the individual of the reasons therefore, and of his or her right to an appeal within the agency and/or judicial review under the provisions of the Act.

(a) In the event an individual desires to appeal any denial of access, he or she may do so in writing by addressing such appeal to the attention of the Director, Peace Corps, or designee identified in such denial. Such appeal should be addressed to Director, Peace Corps, c/o Office of Administrative Services, Room P–314, 806 Connecticut Avenue, NW., Washington, DC 20526.

(b) The Director, or designee, shall review a request from a denial of access and shall make a determination with respect to such appeal within 30 days after receipt thereof. Notice of such determination shall be provided to the individual making the request in writing. If such appeal is denied in whole or in part, such notice shall include notification of the right of the person making such request to have judicial review of the denial as provided in the Act.

§ 308.18 Fees.

No fees shall be charged for search time or for any other time expended by the agency to produce a record. Copies of records may be charged for at the rate of 10 cents per page provided that one copy of any record shall be provided free of charge.

PART 309—DEBT COLLECTION

Subpart A—General Provisions

Sec.

Subpart B—Collection Actions

Subpart C—Salary Offset

AUTHORITY: 31 U.S.C. 3701–3719; 5 U.S.C. 5514; 22 U.S.C. 2503(b); 31 U.S.C. 3720A; 31 CFR part 285; 5 CFR 550, subpart K.

SOURCE: 73 FR 18155, Apr. 3, 2008, unless otherwise noted.

Subpart A—General Provisions

§309.1 General purpose.

This part prescribes the procedures to be used by the United States Peace Corps (Peace Corps) in the collection and/or disposal of non-tax debts owed to Peace Corps and to the United States.

§309.2 Scope.

(a) *Applicability of Federal Claims Collection Standards (FCCS).* Peace Corps hereby adopts the provisions of the Federal Claims Collections Standards (31 CFR parts 900–904) and, except as set forth in this part or otherwise provided by law, Peace Corps will conduct administrative actions to collect claims (including offset, compromise, suspension, termination, disclosure and referral) in accordance with the FCCS.

(b) This part is not applicable to:

(1) Peace Corps claims against another Federal agency, any foreign country or any political subdivision thereof, or any public international organization.

(2) Debts arising out of acquisitions contracts subject to the Federal Acquisition Regulation (FAR) shall be determined, collected, compromised, terminated, or settled in accordance with those regulations (see 49 CFR part 32).

(3) Claims where the Peace Corps Director (or designee) determines that the achievement of the purposes of the Peace Corps Act, as amended, 22 U.S.C. 2501 *et seq.*, or any other provision of law administered by the Peace Corps require a different course of action.

§309.3 Definitions.

As used in this part (except where the context clearly indicates, or where the term is otherwise defined elsewhere in this part) the following definitions shall apply:

(a) *Administrative offset* means withholding funds payable by the United States to, or held by the United States for, a person to satisfy a debt owed by the person to the United States.

(b) *Administrative wage garnishment* means the process by which a Federal agency orders a non-Federal employer to withhold amounts from an employee's wages to satisfy a debt the employee owes to the United States.

(c) *Compromise* means that the creditor agency accepts less than the full amount of an outstanding debt in full satisfaction of the entire amount of the debt.

(d) *Debt* or *claim* means an amount of money which has been determined by an appropriate agency official to be owed to the United States from any person. As used in this part, the terms debt and claim are synonymous.

(e) *Debtor* means a person who owes the Federal Government money.

(f) *Delinquent debt* means any debt, which has not been paid by the date specified in an agency's initial written notification or in an applicable agreement, unless other satisfactory payment arrangements have been made.

(g) *Discharge* means the release of a debtor from personal liability for a debt. Further collection action is prohibited.

(h) *Disposable pay* has the same meaning as that term is defined in 5 CFR §550.1103.

(i) Employee means a current employee of the Peace Corps or other Federal agency, including a member of the

Armed Forces or Reserve of the Armed Forces of the United States.

(j) *FCCS* means the Federal Claims Collection Standards jointly published by the Department of the Treasury and the Department of Justice at 31 CFR parts 900–904.

(k) *Person* means an individual, corporation, partnership, association, organization, State or local government, or any other type of entity other than a Federal agency, foreign government, or public international organization.

(l) *Salary offset* means the withholding of amounts from the current pay account of a Federal employee to satisfy a debt owed by that employee to the United States.

(m) *Suspension* means the temporary cessation of an active debt collection pending the occurrence of an anticipated event.

(n) *Termination* means the cessation of all active debt collection action for the foreseeable future.

(o) *Waiver* means the decision to forgo collection of a debt owed to the United States as permitted or required by law.

§ 309.4 Other procedures or actions.

(a) Nothing contained in this regulation is intended to require Peace Corps to duplicate administrative proceedings required by contract or other laws or regulations.

(b) Nothing in this regulation is intended to preclude utilization of informal administrative actions or remedies which may be available.

(c) Nothing contained in this regulation is intended to deter Peace Corps from demanding the return of specific property or from demanding the return of the property or the payment of its value.

(d) The failure of Peace Corps to comply with any provision in this regulation shall not serve as a defense to the debt.

§ 309.5 Interest, penalties, and administrative costs.

(a) Except as otherwise provided by statute, contract or excluded in accordance with FCCS, Peace Corps will assess:

(1) Interest on unpaid debts in accordance with 31 CFR 901.9.

(2) Penalty charges at a rate of 6 percent a year or such other rate as authorized by law on any portion of a claim that is delinquent for more than 90 days.

(3) Administrative charges to cover the costs of processing and handling delinquent debts.

(4) Late payment charges that shall be computed from the date of mailing or hand delivery of the notice of the claim and interest requirements.

(b) When a debt is paid in partial or installment payments, amounts received shall be applied first to outstanding penalty and administrative cost charges, second to accrued interest, and then to outstanding principal.

(c) *Waiver.* Peace Corps will consider waiver of interest, penalties and/or administrative costs in accordance with the FCCS, 31 CFR 901.9(g).

§ 309.6 Collection in installments.

Whenever feasible, and except as required otherwise by law, debts owed to the United States, together with interest, penalties, and administrative costs as required by this regulation, should be collected in one lump sum. This is true whether the debt is being collected under administrative offset, including salary offset, or by another method, including voluntary payment. However, if the debtor is financially unable to pay the indebtedness in one lump sum, payment may be accepted in regular installments. If Peace Corps agrees to accept payment in installments, it may require a legally enforceable written agreement from the debtor that specifies all of the terms of the arrangement and which contains a provision accelerating the debt in the event the debtor defaults. The size and frequency of the payments should bear a reasonable relation to the size of the debt and ability of the debtor to pay. If possible, the installment payments should be sufficient in size and frequency to liquidate the Government's claim within three years.

§ 309.7 Designation.

The Chief Financial Officer is delegated authority and designated to perform all the duties for which the Director is responsible under the forgoing statutes and joint regulations.

Subpart B—Collection Actions

§309.8 Application.

(a) Peace Corps shall aggressively collect claims and debts in accordance with these regulations and applicable law.

(b) Peace Corps will transfer to the Department of the Treasury, Financial Management Service (FMS) any past due, legally enforceable non-tax debt that has been delinquent for 180 days or more so that FMS may take appropriate action to collect the debt or take other appropriate action in accordance with applicable law and regulation.

(c) Peace Corps may transfer any past due, legally enforceable debt that has been delinquent for fewer than 180 days to FMS for collection in accordance with applicable law and regulation. (See 31 CFR part 285.)

§309.9 Notice—written demand for payment.

(a) Upon determination that a debt is owed to Peace Corps or the United States, Peace Corps shall promptly hand deliver or send by first-class mail (to the debtor's most current address in the records of Peace Corps) at least one written notice (e.g. Bill of Collection or demand letter) informing the debtor of the consequences of failing to pay or otherwise resolve a Peace Corps debt, subject to paragraph (c) of this section. Written demand under this subpart may be preceded by other appropriate actions under this part and or the FCCS, including but not limited to actions taken under the procedures applicable to administrative offset, including salary offset.

(b) The written notice shall inform the debtor of:

(1) The nature and amount of the debt, and the facts giving rise to the debt;

(2) The date by which payment should be made to avoid the imposition of interest, penalties, and administrative costs, and the enforced collection actions described in §309.5 of this part;

(3) The applicable standards for imposing interest, penalties and administrative costs to delinquent debts;

(4) Peace Corps' willingness to discuss alternative payment arrangements and how the debtor may enter into a written agreement to repay the debt under terms acceptable to Peace Corps;

(5) The name, address, and telephone number of a contact person or office within Peace Corps;

(6) Peace Corps' intention to enforce collection if the debtor fails to pay or otherwise resolve the debt, by taking one or more of the following actions:

(i) Offset from Federal payments otherwise due to the debtor, including income tax refunds, salary, certain benefit payments, retirement, vendor payments, travel reimbursement and advances, and other Federal payments;

(ii) Referral to private collection agency;

(iii) Report to credit bureaus;

(iv) Administrative wage garnishment;

(v) Referral to Department of Justice for litigation action;

(vi) Referral to Financial Management Service of the Department of the Treasury for collection;

(vii) Other actions as permitted by the FCCS and applicable law.

(7) How the debtor may inspect and copy records related to the debt;

(8) The debtor's opportunity for an internal review of Peace Corps' determination that the debtor owes a debt or the amount of the debt;

(9) The debtor's right, if any, to request waiver of collection of certain debts, as applicable;

(10) Requirement that the debtor advise Peace Corps of any bankruptcy proceeding of the debtor.

(c) Peace Corps may omit from a notice to a debtor one or more of the provisions contained in paragraphs (b) (6) through (10) of this section if Peace Corps determines that any provision is not legally required given the collection remedies to be applied to a particular debt, or which have already been provided by prior notice, applicable agreement, or contract.

§309.10 Review requirements.

(a) For purposes of this section, whenever Peace Corps is required to afford a debtor a review within the agency, Peace Corps shall provide the debtor with an opportunity for an internal review of the existence or the amount of the debt. For offset of current Federal salary under 5 U.S.C. 5514 for certain debts, debtors may also request an outside hearing. (See subpart C of this part)

(b) Any request for a review must be in writing to the contact office by the payment due date stated in the initial notice sent under § 309.9(b) or other applicable provision. The debtor's request shall state the basis for the dispute and include any relevant documentation in support.

(1) Peace Corps will provide for an internal review of the debt by an appropriate agency official. The review may include examination of documents, internal discussions with relevant officials and discussion by letter or orally with the debtor, at Peace Corps' discretion.

(2) An oral hearing is not required when, in Peace Corps' determination, the matter can be decided on the documentary record. Peace Corps will provide a "paper hearing", that is, a determination based upon a review of the written record unless Peace Corps makes a determination that a debt involves issues of credibility or veracity, at which point an oral hearing may be required. Unless otherwise required by law, such oral hearing shall not be a formal evidentiary hearing.

§ 309.11 Collection.

Upon final determination of the existence and amount of a debt, unless other acceptable payment arrangement have been made or procedures under a specific statute apply, Peace Corps shall collect the debt by one or more of the methods described in § 309.9(b) (6) (i-vii) or as otherwise authorized by law and regulation.

(a) *Administrative offset*—(1) Payments otherwise due the debtor from the United States shall be offset from the debt in accordance with 31 CFR 901.3. These may be funds under the control of Peace Corps or other Federal agencies. Collection may be through centralized offset by the Financial Management Service (FMS) of the Department of the Treasury.

(2) Such payments include but are not limited to vendor payments, salary, retirement, lump sum payments due upon Federal employment separation, travel reimbursements, tax refunds, loans or other assistance. Offset of Federal salary payments will be in accordance with 5 U.S.C. 5514.

(3) Before administrative offset is instituted by another Federal agency or the FMS, Peace Corps shall certify in writing to that entity that the debt is past due and legally enforceable and that Peace Corps has complied with all applicable due process and other requirements as described in this part and other Federal law and regulations.

(b) Any other method authorized by law or regulation.

Subpart C—Salary Offset

§ 309.12 Purpose.

This subpart provides Peace Corps' policies and procedures for the collection by salary offset of a Federal employee's pay to satisfy certain past due debts owed the United States Government.

§ 309.13 Scope.

(a) The provisions of this section apply to collection by salary offset under 5 U.S.C. 5514 of debts owed to Peace Corps and debts owed to other Federal agencies by Peace Corps' employees. Peace Corps will make reasonable and lawful efforts to administratively collect amounts owed by employees prior to initiating salary offset action. This section does not apply to debts where collection by salary offset is explicitly provided for or prohibited by another statute (*e.g.* travel advances).

(b) *References.* The following statutes and regulations apply to Peace Corps' recovery of debts due the United States by salary offset:

(1) 5 U.S.C. 5514, as amended, governing the installment collection of debts;

(2) 31 U.S.C. 3716, governing the liquidation of debts by administrative offset;

(3) 5 CFR part 550, subpart K, setting forth the minimum requirements for executive agency regulations on salary offset; and

(4) 31 CFR parts 900 through 904, the Federal Claims Collections Standards.

(c) Nothing in this subpart precludes the compromise, suspension, or termination of collection actions where appropriate under the standards implementing the Federal Claims Collection Standards.

§ 309.14 Coordinating offset with another Federal agency.

(a) When Peace Corps is owed a debt by an employee of another agency, the other agency shall not initiate the requested offset until Peace Corps provides the agency with a written certification that the debtor owes Peace Corps a debt (including the amount and basis of the debt and the due date of payment) and that Peace Corps has complied with these regulations.

(b) When another agency is owed the debt, Peace Corps may use salary offset against one of its employees who is indebted to another agency, if requested to do so by that agency. Such request must be accompanied by a certification that the person owes the debt (including the amount and basis of the debt and the due date of payment) and that the agency has complied with its regulations as required by 5 U.S.C. 5514 and 5 CFR part 550, subpart K.

§ 309.15 Notice requirements before offset.

(a) Deductions under the authority of 5 U.S.C. 5514 shall not be made unless the creditor agency first provides the employee with written notice that he/she owes a debt to the Federal Government at least 30 calendar days before salary offset is to be initiated. When Peace Corps is the creditor agency this notice of intent to offset an employee's salary shall be hand-delivered or sent by certified mail to the most current address that is available. The written notice will state:

(1) That Peace Corps has reviewed the records relating to the claim and has determined that a debt is owed, its origin and nature, and the amount of the debt;

(2) The intention of Peace Corps to collect the debt by means of deduction from the employee's current disposable pay account until the debt and all accumulated interest is paid in full;

(3) The amount, frequency, approximate beginning date, and duration of the intended deductions;

(4) An explanation of the Peace Corps' policy concerning interest, penalties and administrative costs, including a statement that such assessments must be made unless excused in accordance with the FCCS (See § 309.5);

(5) The employee's right to inspect and copy all records of the Peace Corps pertaining to the debt claimed or to receive copies of such records if personal inspection is impractical;

(6) The right to a hearing conducted by a hearing official (an administrative law judge, or alternatively, an individual not under the supervision or control of the Peace Corps) with respect to the existence and amount of the debt claimed, or the repayment schedule, so long as a petition is filed by the employee as prescribed;

(7) If not previously provided, the opportunity (under terms agreeable to the Peace Corps) to establish a schedule for the voluntary repayment of the debt or to enter into a written agreement to establish a schedule for repayment of the debt in lieu of offset. The agreement must be in writing, signed by both the employee and the creditor agency, and documented in the creditor agency's files;

(8) The name, address and telephone number of an officer or employee of the Peace Corps who may be contacted concerning procedures for requesting a hearing;

(9) The method and time period for requesting a hearing;

(10) That the timely filing of a petition for a hearing as prescribed will stay the commencement of collection proceedings;

(11) The name and address of the office to which the petition should be sent;

(12) That the Peace Corps will initiate certification procedures to implement a salary offset, as appropriate, (which may not exceed 15 percent of the employee's disposable pay) not less than 30 calendar days from the date of delivery of the notice of debt, unless the employee files a timely petition for a hearing;

(13) That a final decision on the hearing (if one is requested) will be issued

at the earliest practical date, but not later than 60 calendar days after the filing of the petition requesting the hearing, unless the employee requests and the hearing official grants a delay in the proceedings;

(14) That any knowingly false or frivolous statements, representations or evidence may subject the employee to:

(i) Disciplinary procedures appropriate under the Peace Corps Act or the Foreign Service Act, Peace Corps regulations, or any other applicable statutes or regulations;

(ii) Penalties under the False Claims Act, §§ 3729–3731 of title 31, United States Code, or any other applicable statutory authority; and

(iii) Criminal penalties under 18 U.S.C. sections 286, 287, 1001, and 1002 or any other applicable authority;

(15) Any other rights and remedies available to the employee under statutes or regulations governing the program for which the collection is being made;

(16) That unless there are applicable contractual or statutory provisions to the contrary, amounts paid on or deducted for the debt which are later waived or found not owed to the United States will be promptly refunded to the employee; and

(17) That proceedings with respect to such debt are governed by 5 U.S.C. 5514.

(b) Peace Corps is not required to provide prior notice to an employee when the following adjustments are made by Peace Corps to a Peace Corps employee's pay:

(1) Any adjustment to pay arising out of an employee's election of coverage or a change in coverage under a Federal benefits program requiring periodic deductions from pay if the amount to be recovered was accumulated over four pay periods or less;

(2) A routine adjustment of pay that is made to correct an overpayment of pay attributable to clerical or administrative errors or delays in processing pay documents, if the overpayment occurred within the four pay periods preceding the adjustment, and, at the time of such adjustment, or as soon thereafter as practical, the individual is provided written notice of the nature and the amount of the adjustment and point of contact for contesting the adjustment; or

(3) Any adjustment to collect a debt of $50 or less, if, at the time of such adjustment, or as soon thereafter as practical, the individual is provided written notice of the nature of the amount of the adjustment and a point of contact for contesting the adjustment.

§ 309.16 Review.

(a) *Request for outside hearing.* Except as provided in paragraph (b) of this section, an employee who desires an outside hearing concerning the existence or amount of the debt or the proposed offset schedule must send a request to the office designated in the notice of intent. See § 309.15(a)(8). The request must be received by the designated office not later than 20 calendar days after the date of delivery of the notice as provided in § 309.15(a). The request must be signed by the employee and should identify and explain with reasonable specificity and brevity the facts, evidence and witnesses which the employee believes support his or her position. If the employee objects to the percentage of disposable pay to be deducted from each check, the request should state the objection and the reasons for it. The employee must also specify whether an oral hearing or a review of the documentary evidence is requested. If an oral hearing is desired, the request should explain why the matter cannot be resolved by review of the documentary evidence alone.

(b) *Failure to submit timely.* (1) If the employee files a petition for a review after the expiration of the 20 calendar day period provided for in paragraph (a) of this section, the designated office may accept the request if the employee can show that the delay was the result of circumstances beyond his or her control, or because of a failure to receive the notice of the filing deadline (unless the employee has actual knowledge of the filing deadline).

(2) An employee waives the right to a review, and will have his or her disposable pay offset in accordance with Peace Corps' offset schedule, if the employee fails to file a request for a hearing unless such failure is excused as provided in paragraph (b)(1) of this section.

(3) If the employee fails to appear at an oral hearing of which he or she was notified, unless the hearing official determines failure to appear was due to circumstances beyond the employee's control, his or her appeal will be decided on the basis of the documents then available to the hearing official.

(c) *Representation at the hearing.* The creditor agency may be represented by a representative of its choice. The employee may represent himself or herself or may be represented by an individual of his or her choice and at his or her expense.

(d) *Review of Peace Corps records related to the debt.* (1) An employee who intends to inspect or copy creditor agency records related to the debt in accordance with § 309.15(a)(5), must send a letter to the official designated in the notice of intent to offset stating his or her intention. The letter must be sent within 20 calendar days after receipt of the notice.

(2) In response to a timely request submitted by the debtor, the designated official will notify the employee of the location and time when the employee may inspect and copy records related to the debt.

(3) If personal inspection is impractical, copies of such records shall be sent to the employee.

(e) *Oral Hearing.* (1) If an employee timely files a request for an oral hearing under § 309.16(a), the matter will be conducted by a hearing official not under the supervision or control of Peace Corps.

(2) *Procedure.* (i) After the employee requests a hearing, the hearing official shall notify the employee of the form of the hearing to be provided. If the hearing will be oral, notice shall set forth the date, time and location of the hearing. If the hearing will be paper, the employee shall be notified that he or she should submit arguments in writing to the hearing official by a specified date after which the record shall be closed. This date shall give the employee reasonable time to submit documentation.

(ii) An employee who requests an oral hearing shall be provided an oral hearing if the hearing official determines that the matter cannot be resolved by review of documentary evidence alone (*e.g.* when an issue of credibility or veracity is involved). The hearing is not an adversarial adjudication, and need not take the form of an evidentiary hearing.

(iii) If the hearing official determines that an oral hearing is not necessary, he or she will make a decision based upon a review of the available written record.

(iv) The hearing official must maintain a summary record of any hearing provided by this subpart. Witnesses who provide testimony will do so under oath or affirmation.

(3) *Decision.* The written decision shall include:

(i) A statement of the facts presented to support the origin, nature, and amount of the debt;

(ii) The hearing official's findings, analysis, and conclusions; and

(iii) The terms of any repayment schedules, or the date salary offset will commence, if applicable.

(4) *Failure to appear.* In the absence of good cause shown (*e.g.* excused illness), an employee who fails to appear at a hearing shall be deemed, for the purpose of this subpart, to admit the existence and amount of the debt as described in the notice of intent. The hearing official shall schedule a new hearing upon the request of the creditor agency representative when good cause is shown.

(5) A hearing official's decision is considered to be an official certification regarding the existence and amount of the debt for purposes of executing salary offset under 5 U.S.C. 5514 only. It does not supersede the finding by Peace Corps that a debt is owed and does not affect the Government's ability to recoup the debt through alternative collection methods under other appropriate methods.

§ 309.17 Procedures for salary offset.

Unless otherwise provided by statute or contract, the following procedures apply to salary offset:

(a) *Method.* Salary offset will be made by deduction at one or more officially established pay intervals from the current pay account of the employee without his or her consent.

(b) *Source.* The source of salary offset is current disposable pay.

(c) *Types of collection*—(1) *Lump sum payment.* Ordinarily debts will be collected by salary offset in one lump sum if possible. However, if the amount of the debt exceeds 15 percent of disposable pay for an officially established pay interval, the collection by salary offset must be made in installment deductions.

(2) *Installment deductions.* (i) The size of installment deductions must bear a reasonable relation to the size of the debt and the employee's ability to pay. If possible, the size of the deduction will be that necessary to liquidate the debt in no more than 1 year. However, the amount deducted for any period must not exceed 15 percent of the disposable pay from which the deduction is made, except as provided by other regulations or unless the employee has agreed in writing to greater amount.

(ii) Installment payments of less than $25 per pay period will be accepted only in the most unusual circumstances.

(iii) Installment deductions will be made over a period of not greater than the anticipated period of employment.

§ 309.18 Voluntary repayment agreements as an alternative to salary offset.

(a) In response to a notice of intent, an employee may propose a written agreement to repay the debt as an alternative to salary offset. Any employee who wishes to repay a debt without salary offset shall submit in writing a proposed agreement to repay the debt. The proposal shall admit the existence of the debt and set forth a proposed repayment schedule. Any proposal under this paragraph must be received by the official designated in that notice within 20 calendar days after receipt of the notice of intent.

(b) When the Peace Corps is the creditor agency, in response to a timely proposal by the debtor the agency will notify the employee whether the employee's proposed written agreement for repayment is acceptable. It is within the agency's discretion to accept a repayment agreement instead of proceeding by offset.

(c) If the Peace Corps decides that the proposed repayment agreement is unacceptable, the employee will have 15 calendar days from the date he or she received notice of the decision to file a petition for a review.

(d) If the Peace Corps decides that the proposed repayment agreement is acceptable, the alternative arrangement must be in writing and signed by both the employee and a designated agency official.

§ 309.19 Waiver.

(a) Under certain circumstances, employees may have a statutory right to request a waiver of indebtedness. When an employee makes a request under a statutory right, further collection will be stayed pending an administrative determination on the request.

(b) Waiver of indebtedness is an equitable remedy and as such must be based on an assessment of the facts involved in the individual case under consideration. The burden is on the employee to demonstrate that the applicable waiver standard has been met.

§ 309.20 Compromise.

Peace Corps may attempt to effect compromise in accordance with the standards set forth in the FCCS (31 CFR part 902).

§ 309.21 Suspension of collection.

Suspension of collection action shall be made in accordance with the standards set forth in the FCCS (31 CFR 903.1–903.2).

§ 309.22 Termination of collection.

Termination of collection action shall be made in accordance with the standards set forth in the FCCS (31 CFR 903.1 and 903.3–903.4).

§ 309.23 Discharge.

Once a debt has been closed out for accounting purposes and collection has been terminated, the debt is discharged. Peace Corps will report discharged debt as income to the debtor to the Internal Revenue Service per 26 U.S.C. 6050P and 26 CFR 1.6050P–1.

§ 309.24 Bankruptcy.

Peace Corps generally terminates collection activity on debts that have been discharged in bankruptcy unless otherwise provided for by bankruptcy law. The CFO will seek legal advice by the General Counsel's office if there is the belief that any claims or offset may have survived the discharge of a debtor.

PART 311—NEW RESTRICTIONS ON LOBBYING

Subpart A—General

Subpart B—Activities by Own Employees

Subpart C—Activities by Other Than Own Employees

Subpart D—Penalties and Enforcement

Subpart E—Exemptions

Subpart F—Agency Reports

AUTHORITY: Section 319, Public Law 101–121 (31 U.S.C. 1352); 22 U.S.C. 2503.

CROSS REFERENCE: See also Office of Management and Budget notice published at 54 FR 52306, December 20, 1989.

SOURCE: 55 FR 6737, 6749, Feb. 26, 1990, unless otherwise noted.

Subpart A—General

§311.100 Conditions on use of funds.

(a) No appropriated funds may be expended by the recipient of a Federal contract, grant, loan, or cooperative ageement to pay any person for influencing or attempting to influence an officer or employee of any agency, a Member of Congress, an officer or employee of Congress, or an employee of a Member of Congress in connection with any of the following covered Federal actions: the awarding of any Federal contract, the making of any Federal grant, the making of any Federal loan, the entering into of any cooperative agreement, and the extension, continuation, renewal, amendment, or modification of any Federal contract, grant, loan, or cooperative agreement.

(b) Each person who requests or receives from an agency a Federal contract, grant, loan, or cooperative agreement shall file with that agency a certification, set forth in appendix A, that the person has not made, and will not make, any payment prohibited by paragraph (a) of this section.

(c) Each person who requests or receives from an agency a Federal contract, grant, loan, or a cooperative agreement shall file with that agency a disclosure form, set forth in appendix B, if such person has made or has agreed to make any payment using nonappropriated funds (to include profits from any covered Federal action), which would be prohibited under paragraph (a) of this section if paid for with appropriated funds.

(d) Each person who requests or receives from an agency a commitment providing for the United States to insure or guarantee a loan shall file with that agency a statement, set forth in Appendix A, whether that person has made or has agreed to make any payment to influence or attempt to influence an officer or employee of any agency, a Member of Congress, an officer or employee of Congress, or an employee of a Member of Congress in connection with that loan insurance or guarantee.

(e) Each person who requests or receives from an agency a commitment providing for the United States to insure or guarantee a loan shall file with that agency a disclosure form, set forth in appendix B, if that person has made or has agreed to make any payment to influence or attempt to influence an officer or employee of any agency, a Member of Congress, an officer or employee of Congress, or an employee of a Member of Congress in connection with that loan insurance or guarantee.

§ 311.105 Definitions.

For purposes of this part:

(a) *Agency*, as defined in 5 U.S.C. 552(f), includes Federal executive departments and agencies as well as independent regulatory commissions and Government corporations, as defined in 31 U.S.C. 9101(1).

(b) *Covered Federal action* means any of the following Federal actions:

(1) The awarding of any Federal contract;

(2) The making of any Federal grant;

(3) The making of any Federal loan;

(4) The entering into of any cooperative agreement; and,

(5) The extension, continuation, renewal, amendment, or modification of any Federal contract, grant, loan, or cooperative agreement.

Covered Federal action does not include receiving from an agency a commitment providing for the United States to insure or guarantee a loan. Loan guarantees and loan insurance are addressed independently within this part.

(c) *Federal contract* means an acquisition contract awarded by an agency, including those subject to the Federal Acquisition Regulation (FAR), and any other acquisition contract for real or personal property or services not subject to the FAR.

(d) *Federal cooperative agreement* means a cooperative agreement entered into by an agency.

(e) *Federal grant* means an award of financial assistance in the form of money, or property in lieu of money, by the Federal Government or a direct appropriation made by law to any person. The term does not include technical assistance which provides services instead of money, or other assistance in the form of revenue sharing, loans, loan guarantees, loan insurance, interest subsidies, insurance, or direct United States cash assistance to an individual.

(f) *Federal loan* means a loan made by an agency. The term does not include loan guarantee or loan insurance.

(g) *Indian tribe* and *tribal organization* have the meaning provided in section 4 of the Indian Self-Determination and Education Assistance Act (25 U.S.C. 450B). Alaskan Natives are included under the definitions of Indian tribes in that Act.

(h) *Influencing or attempting to influence* means making, with the intent to influence, any communication to or appearance before an officer or employee or any agency, a Member of Congress, an officer or employee of Congress, or an employee of a Member of Congress in connection with any covered Federal action.

(i) *Loan guarantee* and *loan insurance* means an agency's guarantee or insurance of a loan made by a person.

(j) *Local government* means a unit of government in a State and, if chartered, established, or otherwise recognized by a State for the performance of a governmental duty, including a local public authority, a special district, an intrastate district, a council of governments, a sponsor group representative organization, and any other instrumentality of a local government.

(k) *Officer or employee of an agency* includes the following individuals who are employed by an agency:

(1) An individual who is appointed to a position in the Government under title 5, U.S. Code, including a position under a temporary appointment;

(2) A member of the uniformed services as defined in section 101(3), title 37, U.S. Code;

(3) A special Government employee as defined in section 202, title 18, U.S. Code; and,

(4) An individual who is a member of a Federal advisory committee, as defined by the Federal Advisory Committee Act, title 5, U.S. Code appendix 2.

(l) *Person* means an individual, corporation, company, association, authority, firm, partnership, society, State, and local government, regardless of whether such entity is operated for profit or not for profit. This term excludes an Indian tribe, tribal organization, or any other Indian organization with respect to expenditures specifically permitted by other Federal law.

(m) *Reasonable compensation* means, with respect to a regularly employed officer or employee of any person, compensation that is consistent with the normal compensation for such officer or employee for work that is not furnished to, not funded by, or not furnished in cooperation with the Federal Government.

(n) *Reasonable payment* means, with respect to perfessional and other technical services, a payment in an amount that is consistent with the amount normally paid for such services in the private sector.

(o) *Recipient* includes all contractors, subcontractors at any tier, and subgrantees at any tier of the recipient of funds received in connection with a Federal contract, grant, loan, or cooperative agreement. The term excludes an Indian tribe, tribal organization, or any other Indian organization with respect to expenditures specifically permitted by other Federal law.

(p) *Regularly employed* means, with respect to an officer or employee of a person requesting or receiving a Federal contract, grant, loan, or cooperative agreement or a commitment providing for the United States to insure or guarantee a loan, an officer or employee who is employed by such person for at least 130 working days within one year immediately preceding the date of the submission that initiates agency consideration of such person for receipt of such contract, grant, loan, cooperative agreement, loan insurance commitment, or loan guarantee commitment. An officer or employee who is employed by such person for less than 130 working days within one year immediately preceding the date of the submission that initiates agency consideration of such person shall be considered to be regularly employed as soon as he or she is employed by such person for 130 working days.

(q) *State* means a State of the United States, the District of Columbia, the Commonwealth of Puerto Rico, a territory or possession of the United States, an agency or instrumentality of a State, and a multi-State, regional, or interstate entity having governmental duties and powers.

§311.110 Certification and disclosure.

(a) Each person shall file a certification, and a disclosure form, if required, with each submission that initiates agency consideration of such person for:

(1) Award of a Federal contract, grant, or cooperative agreement exceeding $100,000; or

(2) An award of a Federal loan or a commitment providing for the United States to insure or guarantee a loan exceeding $150,000.

(b) Each person shall file a certification, and a disclosure form, if required, upon receipt by such person of:

(1) A Federal contract, grant, or cooperative agreement exceeding $100,000; or

(2) A Federal loan or a commitment providing for the United States to insure or guarantee a loan exceeding $150,000, unless such person previously filed a certification, and a disclosure form, if required, under paragraph (a) of this section.

(c) Each person shall file a disclosure form at the end of each calendar quarter in which there occurs any event that requires disclosure or that materially affects the accuracy of the information contained in any disclosure form previously filed by such person under paragraphs (a) or (b) of this section. An event that materially affects the accuracy of the information reported includes:

(1) A cumulative increase of $25,000 or more in the amount paid or expected to be paid for influencing or attempting to influence a covered Federal action; or

(2) A change in the person(s) or individual(s) influencing or attempting to influence a covered Federal action; or,

(3) A change in the officer(s), employee(s), or Member(s) contacted to influence or attempt to influence a covered Federal action.

(d) Any person who requests or receives from a person referred to in paragraphs (a) or (b) of this section:

(1) A subcontract exceeding $100,000 at any tier under a Federal contract;

(2) A subgrant, contract, or subcontract exceeding $100,000 at any tier under a Federal grant;

(3) A contract or subcontract exceeding $100,000 at any tier under a Federal loan exceeding $150,000; or,

(4) A contract or subcontract exceeding $100,000 at any tier under a Federal cooperative agreement, shall file a certification, and a disclosure form, if required, to the next tier above.

(e) All disclosure forms, but not certifications, shall be forwarded from tier to tier until received by the person referred to in paragraphs (a) or (b) of this section. That person shall forward all disclosure forms to the agency.

(f) Any certification or disclosure form filed under paragraph (e) of this section shall be treated as a material representation of fact upon which all receiving tiers shall rely. All liability arising from an erroneous representation shall be borne solely by the tier filing that representation and shall not be shared by any tier to which the erroneous representation is forwarded. Submitting an erroneous certification or disclosure constitutes a failure to file the required certification or disclosure, respectively. If a person fails to file a required certification or disclosure, the United States may pursue all available remedies, including those authorized by section 1352, title 31, U.S. Code.

(g) For awards and commitments in process prior to December 23, 1989, but not made before that date, certifications shall be required at award or commitment, covering activities occurring between December 23, 1989, and the date of award or commitment. However, for awards and commitments in process prior to the December 23, 1989 effective date of these provisions, but not made before December 23, 1989, disclosure forms shall not be required at time of award or commitment but shall be filed within 30 days.

(h) No reporting is required for an activity paid for with appropriated funds if that activity is allowable under either subpart B or C.

Subpart B—Activities by Own Employees

§ 311.200 Agency and legislative liaison.

(a) The prohibition on the use of appropriated funds, in § 311.100 (a), does not apply in the case of a payment of reasonable compensation made to an officer or employee of a person requesting or receiving a Federal contract, grant, loan, or cooperative agreement if the payment is for agency and legislative liaison activities not directly related to a covered Federal action.

(b) For purposes of paragraph (a) of this section, providing any information specifically requested by an agency or Congress is allowable at any time.

(c) For purposes of paragraph (a) of this section, the following agency and legislative liaison activities are allowable at any time only where they are not related to a specific solicitation for any covered Federal action:

(1) Discussing with an agency (including individual demonstrations) the qualities and characteristics of the person's products or services, conditions or terms of sale, and service capabilities; and,

(2) Technical discussions and other activities regarding the application or adaptation of the person's products or services for an agency's use.

(d) For purposes of paragraph (a) of this section, the following agencies and legislative liaison activities are allowable only where they are prior to formal solicitation of any covered Federal action:

(1) Providing any information not specifically requested but necessary for an agency to make an informed decision about initiation of a covered Federal action;

(2) Technical discussions regarding the preparation of an unsolicited proposal prior to its official submission; and,

(3) Capability presentations by persons seeking awards from an agency pursuant to the provisions of the Small Business Act, as amended by Public Law 95–507 and other subsequent amendments.

(e) Only those activities expressly authorized by this section are allowable under this section.

§ 311.205 Professional and technical services.

(a) The prohibition on the use of appropriated funds, in § 311.100 (a), does not apply in the case of a payment of reasonable compensation made to an officer or employee of a person requesting or receiving a Federal contract, grant, loan, or cooperative agreement or an extension, continuation, renewal, amendment, or modification of a Federal contract, grant, loan, or cooperative agreement if payment is for professional or technical services rendered directly in the preparation, submission, or negotiation of any bid, proposal, or application for that Federal contract, grant, loan, or cooperative agreement or for meeting requirements imposed by or pursuant to law as a condition for receiving that Federal contract, grant, loan, or cooperative agreement.

(b) For purposes of paragraph (a) of this section, "professional and technical services" shall be limited to advice and analysis directly applying any professional or technical discipline. For example, drafting of a legal document accompanying a bid or proposal by a lawyer is allowable. Similarly, technical advice provided by an engineer on the performance or operational capability of a piece of equipment rendered directly in the negotiation of a contract is allowable. However, communications with the intent to influence made by a professional (such as a licensed lawyer) or a technical person (such as a licensed accountant) are not allowable under this section unless they provide advice and analysis directly applying their professional or technical expertise and unless the advice or analysis is rendered directly and solely in the preparation, submission or negotiation of a covered Federal action. Thus, for example, communications with the intent to influence made by a lawyer that do not provide legal advice or analysis directly and solely related to the legal aspects of his or her client's proposal, but generally advocate one proposal over another are not allowable under this section because the lawyer is not providing professional legal services. Similarly, communications with the intent to influence made by an engineer providing an engineering analysis prior to the preparation or submission of a bid or proposal are not allowable under this section since the engineer is providing technical services but not directly in the preparation, submission or negotiation of a covered Federal action.

(c) Requirements imposed by or pursuant to law as a condition for receiving a covered Federal award include those required by law or regulation, or reasonably expected to be required by law or regulation, and any other requirements in the actual award documents.

(d) Only those services expressly authorized by this section are allowable under this section.

§ 311.210 Reporting.

No reporting is required with respect to payments of reasonable compensation made to regularly employed officers or employees of a person.

Subpart C—Activities by Other Than Own Employees

§ 311.300 Professional and technical services.

(a) The prohibition on the use of appropriated funds, in § 311.100 (a), does not apply in the case of any reasonable payment to a person, other than an officer or employee of a person requesting or receiving a covered Federal action, if the payment is for professional or technical services rendered directly in the preparation, submission, or negotiation of any bid, proposal, or application for that Federal contract, grant, loan, or cooperative agreement or for meeting requirements imposed by or pursuant to law as a condition for receiving that Federal contract, grant, loan, or cooperative agreement.

(b) The reporting requirements in § 311.110 (a) and (b) regarding filing a disclosure form by each person, if required, shall not apply with respect to professional or technical services rendered directly in the preparation, submission, or negotiation of any commitment providing for the United States to insure or guarantee a loan.

(c) For purposes of paragraph (a) of this section, *professional and technical services* shall be limited to advice and analysis directly applying any professional or technical discipline. For example, drafting or a legal document accompanying a bid or proposal by a lawyer is allowable. Similarly, technical advice provided by an engineer on the performance or operational capability of a piece of equipment rendered directly in the negotiation of a contract is allowable. However, communications with the intent to influence made by a professional (such as a licensed lawyer) or a technical person (such as a licensed accountant) are not allowable under this section unless they provide advice and analysis directly applying their professional or technical expertise and unless the advice or analysis is rendered directly and solely in the preparation, submission or negotiation of a covered Federal action. Thus, for example, communications with the intent to influence made by a lawyer that do not provide legal advice or analysis directly and solely related to the legal aspects of his or her client's proposal, but generally advocate one proposal over another are not allowable under this section because the lawyer is not providing professional legal services. Similarly, communications with the intent to influence made by an engineer providing an engineering analysis prior to the preparation or submission of a bid or proposal are not allowable under this section since the engineer is providing technical services but not directly in the preparation, submission or negotiation of a covered Federal action.

(d) Requirements imposed by or pursuant to law as a condition for receiving a covered Federal award include those required by law or regulation, or reasonably expected to be required by law or regulation, and any other requirements in the actual award documents.

(e) Persons other than officers or employees of a person requesting or receiving a covered Federal action include consultants and trade associations.

(f) Only those services expressly authorized by this section are allowable under this section.

Subpart D—Penalties and Enforcement

§ 311.400 Penalties.

(a) Any person who makes an expenditure prohibited herein shall be subject to a civil penalty of not less than $10,000 and not more than $100,000 for each such expenditure.

(b) Any person who fails to file or amend the disclosure form (see appendix B) to be filed or amended if required herein, shall be subject to a civil penalty of not less than $10,000 and not more than $100,000 for each such failure.

(c) A filing or amended filing on or after the date on which an administrative action for the imposition of a civil penalty is commenced does not prevent the imposition of such civil penalty for a failure occurring before that date. An administrative action is commenced with respect to a failure when an investigating official determines in writing to commence an investigation of an allegation of such failure.

(d) In determining whether to impose a civil penalty, and the amount of any such penalty, by reason of a violation by any person, the agency shall consider the nature, circumstances, extent, and gravity of the violation, the effect on the ability of such person to continue in business, any prior violations by such person, the degree of culpability of such person, the ability of the person to pay the penalty, and such other matters as may be appropriate.

(e) First offenders under paragraphs (a) or (b) of this section shall be subject to a civil penalty of $10,000, absent aggravating circumstances. Second and subsequent offenses by persons shall be subject to an appropriate civil penalty between $10,000 and $100,000, as determined by the agency head or his or her designee.

(f) An imposition of a civil penalty under this section does not prevent the United States from seeking any other remedy that may apply to the same conduct that is the basis for the imposition of such civil penalty.

§ 311.405 Penalty procedures.

Agencies shall impose and collect civil penalties pursuant to the provisions of the Program Fraud and Civil Remedies Act, 31 U.S.C. sections 3803 (except subsection (c)), 3804, 3805, 3806, 3807, 3808, and 3812, insofar as these provisions are not inconsistent with the requirements herein.

§ 311.410 Enforcement.

The head of each agency shall take such actions as are necessary to ensure that the provisions herein are vigorously implemented and enforced in that agency.

Subpart E—Exemptions

§311.500 Secretary of Defense.

(a) The Secretary of Defense may exempt, on a case-by-case basis, a covered Federal action from the prohibition whenever the Secretary determines, in writing, that such an exemption is in the national interest. The Secretary shall transmit a copy of each such written exemption to Congress immediately after making such a determination.

(b) The Department of Defense may issue supplemental regulations to implement paragraph (a) of this section.

Subpart F—Agency Reports

§311.600 Semi-annual compilation.

(a) The head of each agency shall collect and compile the disclosure reports (see appendix B) and, on May 31 and November 30 of each year, submit to the Secretary of the Senate and the Clerk of the House of Representatives a report containing a compilation of the information contained in the disclosure reports received during the six-month period ending on March 31 or September 30, respectively, of that year.

(b) The report, including the compilation, shall be available for public inspection 30 days after receipt of the report by the Secretary and the Clerk.

(c) Information that involves intelligence matters shall be reported only to the Select Committee on Intelligence of the Senate, the Permanent Select Committee on Intelligence of the House of Representatives, and the Committees on Appropriations of the Senate and the House of Representatives in accordance with procedures agreed to by such committees. Such information shall not be available for public inspection.

(d) Information that is classified under Executive Order 12356 or any successor order shall be reported only to the Committee on Foreign Relations of the Senate and the Committee on Foreign Affairs of the House of Representatives or the Committees on Armed Services of the Senate and the House of Representatives (whichever such committees have jurisdiction of matters involving such information) and to the Committees on Appropriations of the Senate and the House of Representatives in accordance with procedures agreed to by such committees. Such information shall not be available for public inspection.

(e) The first semi-annual compilation shall be submitted on May 31, 1990, and shall contain a compilation of the disclosure reports received from December 23, 1989 to March 31, 1990.

(f) Major agencies, designated by the Office of Management and Budget (OMB), are required to provide machine-readable compilations to the Secretary of the Senate and the Clerk of the House of Representatives no later than with the compilations due on May 31, 1991. OMB shall provide detailed specifications in a memorandum to these agencies.

(g) Non-major agencies are requested to provide machine-readable compilations to the Secretary of the Senate and the Clerk of the House of Representatives.

(h) Agencies shall keep the originals of all disclosure reports in the official files of the agency.

§311.605 Inspector General report.

(a) The Inspector General, or other official as specified in paragraph (b) of this section, of each agency shall prepare and submit to Congress each year, commencing with submission of the President's Budget in 1991, an evaluation of the compliance of that agency with, and the effectiveness of, the requirements herein. The evaluation may include any recommended changes that may be necessary to strengthen or improve the requirements.

(b) In the case of an agency that does not have an Inspector General, the agency official comparable to an Inspector General shall prepare and submit the annual report, or, if there is no such comparable official, the head of the agency shall prepare and submit the annual report.

(c) The annual report shall be submitted at the same time the agency submits its annual budget justifications to Congress.

(d) The annual report shall include the following: All alleged violations relating to the agency's covered Federal actions during the year covered by the report, the actions taken by the head of the agency in the year covered by the report with respect to those alleged violations and alleged violations in previous years, and the amounts of civil penalties imposed by the agency in the year covered by the report.

Appendix A to Part 311—Certification Regarding Lobbying

Certification for Contracts, Grants, Loans, and Cooperative Agreements

The undersigned certifies, to the best of his or her knowledge and belief, that:

(1) No Federal appropriated funds have been paid or will be paid, by or on behalf of the undersigned, to any person for influencing or attempting to influence an officer or employee of an agency, a Member of Congress, an officer or employee of Congress, or an employee of a Member of Congress in connection with the awarding of any Federal contract, the making of any Federal grant, the making of any Federal loan, the entering into of any cooperative agreement, and the extension, continuation, renewal, amendment, or modification of any Federal contract, grant, loan, or cooperative agreement.

(2) If any funds other than Federal appropriated funds have been paid or will be paid to any person for influencing or attempting to influence an officer or employee of any agency, a Member of Congress, an officer or employee of Congress, or an employee of a Member of Congress in connection with this Federal contract, grant, loan, or cooperative agreement, the undersigned shall complete and submit Standard Form-LLL, "Disclosure Form to Report Lobbying," in accordance with its instructions.

(3) The undersigned shall require that the language of this certification be included in the award documents for all subawards at all tiers (including subcontracts, subgrants, and contracts under grants, loans, and cooperative agreements) and that all subrecipients shall certify and disclose accordingly.

This certification is a material representation of fact upon which reliance was placed when this transaction was made or entered into. Submission of this certification is a prerequisite for making or entering into this transaction imposed by section 1352, title 31, U.S. Code. Any person who fails to file the required certification shall be subject to a civil penalty of not less than $10,000 and not more than $100,000 for each such failure.

Statement for Loan Guarantees and Loan Insurance

The undersigned states, to the best of his or her knowledge and belief, that:

If any funds have been paid or will be paid to any person for influencing or attempting to influence an officer or employee of any agency, a Member of Congress, an officer or employee of Congress, or an employee of a Member of Congress in connection with this commitment providing for the United States to insure or guarantee a loan, the undersigned shall complete and submit Standard Form-LLL, "Disclosure Form to Report Lobbying," in accordance with its instructions.

Submission of this statement is a prerequisite for making or entering into this transaction imposed by section 1352, title 31, U.S. Code. Any person who fails to file the required statement shall be subject to a civil penalty of not less than $10,000 and not more than $100,000 for each such failure.

APPENDIX B TO PART 311—DISCLOSURE FORM TO REPORT LOBBYING

DISCLOSURE OF LOBBYING ACTIVITIES

Approved by OMB 0348-0046

Complete this form to disclose lobbying activities pursuant to 31 U.S.C. 1352
(See reverse for public burden disclosure.)

1. Type of Federal Action:
☐ a. contract
b. grant
c. cooperative agreement
d. loan
e. loan guarantee
f. loan insurance

2. Status of Federal Action:
☐ a. bid/offer/application
b. initial award
c. post-award

3. Report Type:
☐ a. initial filing
b. material change

For Material Change Only:
year ______ quarter ______
date of last report ______

4. Name and Address of Reporting Entity:
☐ Prime ☐ Subawardee
Tier ____, *if known*:

Congressional District, *if known*:

5. If Reporting Entity in No. 4 is Subawardee, Enter Name and Address of Prime:

Congressional District, *if known*:

6. Federal Department/Agency:

7. Federal Program Name/Description:

CFDA Number, *if applicable*: ______

8. Federal Action Number, *if known*:

9. Award Amount, *if known*:
$

10. a. Name and Address of Lobbying Entity *(if individual, last name, first name, MI)*:

b. Individuals Performing Services *(including address if different from No. 10a) (last name, first name, MI)*:

(attach Continuation Sheet(s) SF-LLL-A, if necessary)

11. Amount of Payment *(check all that apply)*:
$ ______ ☐ actual ☐ planned

12. Form of Payment *(check all that apply)*:
☐ a. cash
☐ b. in-kind; specify: nature ______
value ______

13. Type of Payment *(check all that apply)*:
☐ a. retainer
☐ b. one-time fee
☐ c. commission
☐ d. contingent fee
☐ e. deferred
☐ f. other; specify: ______

14. Brief Description of Services Performed or to be Performed and Date(s) of Service, including officer(s), employee(s), or Member(s) contacted, for Payment Indicated in Item 11:

(attach Continuation Sheet(s) SF-LLL-A, if necessary)

15. Continuation Sheet(s) SF-LLL-A attached: ☐ Yes ☐ No

16. Information requested through this form is authorized by title 31 U.S.C. section 1352. This disclosure of lobbying activities is a material representation of fact upon which reliance was placed by the tier above when this transaction was made or entered into. This disclosure is required pursuant to 31 U.S.C. 1352. This information will be reported to the Congress semi-annually and will be available for public inspection. Any person who fails to file the required disclosure shall be subject to a civil penalty of not less than $10,000 and not more than $100,000 for each such failure.

Signature: ______
Print Name: ______
Title: ______
Telephone No.: ______ **Date:** ______

Federal Use Only:

Authorized for Local Reproduction
Standard Form - LLL

INSTRUCTIONS FOR COMPLETION OF SF-LLL, DISCLOSURE OF LOBBYING ACTIVITIES

This disclosure form shall be completed by the reporting entity, whether subawardee or prime Federal recipient, at the initiation or receipt of a covered Federal action, or a material change to a previous filing, pursuant to title 31 U.S.C. section 1352. The filing of a form is required for each payment or agreement to make payment to any lobbying entity for influencing or attempting to influence an officer or employee of any agency, a Member of Congress, an officer or employee of Congress, or an employee of a Member of Congress in connection with a covered Federal action. Use the SF-LLL-A Continuation Sheet for additional information if the space on the form is inadequate. Complete all items that apply for both the initial filing and material change report. Refer to the implementing guidance published by the Office of Management and Budget for additional information.

1. Identify the type of covered Federal action for which lobbying activity is and/or has been secured to influence the outcome of a covered Federal action.
2. Identify the status of the covered Federal action.
3. Identify the appropriate classification of this report. If this is a followup report caused by a material change to the information previously reported, enter the year and quarter in which the change occurred. Enter the date of the last previously submitted report by this reporting entity for this covered Federal action.
4. Enter the full name, address, city, state and zip code of the reporting entity. Include Congressional District, if known. Check the appropriate classification of the reporting entity that designates if it is, or expects to be, a prime or subaward recipient. Identify the tier of the subawardee, e.g., the first subawardee of the prime is the 1st tier. Subawards include but are not limited to subcontracts, subgrants and contract awards under grants.
5. If the organization filing the report in item 4 checks "Subawardee", then enter the full name, address, city, state and zip code of the prime Federal recipient. Include Congressional District, if known.
6. Enter the name of the Federal agency making the award or loan commitment. Include at least one organizational level below agency name, if known. For example, Department of Transportation, United States Coast Guard.
7. Enter the Federal program name or description for the covered Federal action (item 1). If known, enter the full Catalog of Federal Domestic Assistance (CFDA) number for grants, cooperative agreements, loans, and loan commitments.
8. Enter the most appropriate Federal identifying number available for the Federal action identified in item 1 (e.g., Request for Proposal (RFP) number; Invitation for Bid (IFB) number; grant announcement number; the contract, grant, or loan award number; the application/proposal control number assigned by the Federal agency). Include prefixes, e.g., "RFP-DE-90-001."
9. For a covered Federal action where there has been an award or loan commitment by the Federal agency, enter the Federal amount of the award/loan commitment for the prime entity identified in item 4 or 5.
10. (a) Enter the full name, address, city, state and zip code of the lobbying entity engaged by the reporting entity identified in item 4 to influence the covered Federal action.

    (b) Enter the full names of the individual(s) performing services, and include full address if different from 10 (a). Enter Last Name, First Name, and Middle Initial (MI).
11. Enter the amount of compensation paid or reasonably expected to be paid by the reporting entity (item 4) to the lobbying entity (item 10). Indicate whether the payment has been made (actual) or will be made (planned). Check all boxes that apply. If this is a material change report, enter the cumulative amount of payment made or planned to be made.
12. Check the appropriate box(es). Check all boxes that apply. If payment is made through an in-kind contribution, specify the nature and value of the in-kind payment.
13. Check the appropriate box(es). Check all boxes that apply. If other, specify nature.
14. Provide a specific and detailed description of the services that the lobbyist has performed, or will be expected to perform, and the date(s) of any services rendered. Include all preparatory and related activity, not just time spent in actual contact with Federal officials. Identify the Federal official(s) or employee(s) contacted or the officer(s), employee(s), or Member(s) of Congress that were contacted.
15. Check whether or not a SF-LLL-A Continuation Sheet(s) is attached.
16. The certifying official shall sign and date the form, print his/her name, title, and telephone number.

Public reporting burden for this collection of information is estimated to average 30 mintues per response, including time for reviewing instructions, searching existing data sources, gathering and maintaining the data needed, and completing and reviewing the collection of information. Send comments regarding the burden estimate or any other aspect of this collection of information, including suggestions for reducing this burden, to the Office of Management and Budget, Paperwork Reduction Project (0348-0046), Washington, D.C. 20503.

DISCLOSURE OF LOBBYING ACTIVITIES
CONTINUATION SHEET

Approved by OMB
0348-0046

Reporting Entity: ______________________ **Page** ____ **of** ____

Authorized for Local Reproduction
Standard Form - LLL-A

PART 312—GOVERNMENTWIDE REQUIREMENTS FOR DRUG-FREE WORKPLACE (FINANCIAL ASSISTANCE)

AUTHORITY: 22 U.S.C. 2503 (b); 41 U.S.C. 701 *et seq.*

SOURCE: 68 FR 66588, Nov. 26, 2003, unless otherwise noted.

Subpart A—Purpose and Coverage

§ 312.100 What does this part do?

This part carries out the portion of the Drug-Free Workplace Act of 1988 (41 U.S.C. 701 *et seq.*, as amended) that applies to grants. It also applies the provisions of the Act to cooperative agreements and other financial assistance awards, as a matter of Federal Government policy.

§ 312.105 Does this part apply to me?

(a) Portions of this part apply to you if you are either—

(1) A recipient of an assistance award from the Peace Corps; or

(2) A(n) Peace Corps awarding official. (See definitions of award and recipient in §§ 312.605 and 312.660, respectively.)

(b) The following table shows the subparts that apply to you:

If you are . . .	see subparts . . .
(1) A recipient who is not an individual	A, B and E.
(2) A recipient who is an individual	A, C and E.
(3) A(n) Peace Corps awarding official	A, D and E.

§ 312.110 Are any of my Federal assistance awards exempt from this part?

This part does not apply to any award that the Peace Corps Director or designee determines that the application of this part would be inconsistent with the international obligations of the United States or the laws or regulations of a foreign government.

§ 312.115 Does this part affect the Federal contracts that I receive?

It will affect future contract awards indirectly if you are debarred or suspended for a violation of the requirements of this part, as described in § 312.510(c). However, this part does not apply directly to procurement contracts. The portion of the Drug-Free Workplace Act of 1988 that applies to Federal procurement contracts is carried out through the Federal Acquisition Regulation in chapter 1 of Title 48 of the Code of Federal Regulations (the drug-free workplace coverage currently is in 48 CFR part 23, subpart 23.5).

Subpart B—Requirements for Recipients Other Than Individuals

§ 312.200 What must I do to comply with this part?

There are two general requirements if you are a recipient other than an individual.

(a) First, you must make a good faith effort, on a continuing basis, to maintain a drug-free workplace. You must agree to do so as a condition for receiving any award covered by this part. The specific measures that you must take in this regard are described in more detail in subsequent sections of this subpart. Briefly, those measures are to—

(1) Publish a drug-free workplace statement and establish a drug-free awareness program for your employees (see §§ 312.205 through 312.220); and

(2) Take actions concerning employees who are convicted of violating drug statutes in the workplace (see § 312.225).

(b) Second, you must identify all known workplaces under your Federal awards (see § 312.230).

§ 312.205 What must I include in my drug-free workplace statement?

You must publish a statement that—

(a) Tells your employees that the unlawful manufacture, distribution, dispensing, possession, or use of a controlled substance is prohibited in your workplace;

(b) Specifies the actions that you will take against employees for violating that prohibition; and

(c) Lets each employee know that, as a condition of employment under any award, he or she:

(1) Will abide by the terms of the statement; and

(2) Must notify you in writing if he or she is convicted for a violation of a criminal drug statute occurring in the workplace and must do so no more than five calendar days after the conviction.

§ 312.210 To whom must I distribute my drug-free workplace statement?

You must require that a copy of the statement described in § 312.205 be given to each employee who will be engaged in the performance of any Federal award.

§ 312.215 What must I include in my drug-free awareness program?

You must establish an ongoing drug-free awareness program to inform employees about—

(a) The dangers of drug abuse in the workplace;

(b) Your policy of maintaining a drug-free workplace;

(c) Any available drug counseling, rehabilitation, and employee assistance programs; and

(d) The penalties that you may impose upon them for drug abuse violations occurring in the workplace.

§ 312.220 By when must I publish my drug-free workplace statement and establish my drug-free awareness program?

If you are a new recipient that does not already have a policy statement as described in § 312.205 and an ongoing awareness program as described in § 312.215, you must publish the statement and establish the program by the time given in the following table:

If . . .	then you . . .
(a) The performance period of the award is less than 30 days	must have the policy statement and program in place as soon as possible, but before the date on which performance is expected to be completed.
(b) The performance period of the award is 30 days or more ...	must have the policy statement and program in place within 30 days after award.
(c) You believe there are extraordinary circumstances that will require more than 30 days for you to publish the policy statement and establish the awareness program.	may ask the Peace Corps awarding official to give you more time to do so. The amount of additional time, if any, to be given is at the discretion of the awarding official.

§ 312.225 What actions must I take concerning employees who are convicted of drug violations in the workplace?

There are two actions you must take if an employee is convicted of a drug violation in the workplace:

(a) First, you must notify Federal agencies if an employee who is engaged in the performance of an award informs you about a conviction, as required by § 312.205(c)(2), or you otherwise learn of the conviction. Your notification to the Federal agencies must__

(1) Be in writing;

(2) Include the employee's position title;

(3) Include the identification number(s) of each affected award;

(4) Be sent within ten calendar days after you learn of the conviction; and

(5) Be sent to every Federal agency on whose award the convicted employee was working. It must be sent to every awarding official or his or her official designee, unless the Federal agency has specified a central point for the receipt of the notices.

(b) Second, within 30 calendar days of learning about an employee's conviction, you must either__

(1) Take appropriate personnel action against the employee, up to and including termination, consistent with the requirements of the Rehabilitation Act of 1973 (29 U.S.C. 794), as amended; or

(2) Require the employee to participate satisfactorily in a drug abuse assistance or rehabilitation program approved for these purposes by a Federal, State or local health, law enforcement, or other appropriate agency.

§ 312.230 How and when must I identify workplaces?

(a) You must identify all known workplaces under each Peace Corps award. A failure to do so is a violation of your drug-free workplace requirements. You may identify the workplaces__

(1) To the Peace Corps official that is making the award, either at the time of application or upon award; or

(2) In documents that you keep on file in your offices during the performance of the award, in which case you must make the information available for inspection upon request by Peace Corps officials or their designated representatives.

(b) Your workplace identification for an award must include the actual address of buildings (or parts of buildings) or other sites where work under the award takes place. Categorical descriptions may be used (*e.g.*, all vehicles of a mass transit authority or State highway department while in operation, State employees in each local unemployment office, performers in concert halls or radio studios).

(c) If you identified workplaces to the Peace Corps awarding official at the time of application or award, as described in paragraph (a)(1) of this section, and any workplace that you identified changes during the performance of the award, you must inform the Peace Corps awarding official.

Subpart C—Requirements for Recipients Who Are Individuals

§ 312.300 What must I do to comply with this part if I am an individual recipient?

As a condition of receiving a(n) Peace Corps award, if you are an individual recipient, you must agree that—

(a) You will not engage in the unlawful manufacture, distribution, dispensing, possession, or use of a controlled substance in conducting any activity related to the award; and

(b) If you are convicted of a criminal drug offense resulting from a violation occurring during the conduct of any award activity, you will report the conviction:

(1) In writing.

(2) Within 10 calendar days of the conviction.

(3) To the Peace Corps awarding official or other designee for each award that you currently have, unless §312.301 or the award document designates a central point for the receipt of the notices. When notice is made to a central point, it must include the identification number(s) of each affected award.

§312.301 [Reserved]

Subpart D—Responsibilities of Peace Corps Awarding Officials

§312.400 What are my responsibilities as a(n) Peace Corps awarding official?

As a(n) Peace Corps awarding official, you must obtain each recipient's agreement, as a condition of the award, to comply with the requirements in—

(a) Subpart B of this part, if the recipient is not an individual; or

(b) Subpart C of this part, if the recipient is an individual.

Subpart E—Violations of this Part and Consequences

§312.500 How are violations of this part determined for recipients other than individuals?

A recipient other than an individual is in violation of the requirements of this part if the Peace Corps Director or designee determines, in writing, that—

(a) The recipient has violated the requirements of subpart B of this part; or

(b) The number of convictions of the recipient's employees for violating criminal drug statutes in the workplace is large enough to indicate that the recipient has failed to make a good faith effort to provide a drug-free workplace.

§312.505 How are violations of this part determined for recipients who are individuals?

An individual recipient is in violation of the requirements of this part if the Peace Corps Director or designee determines, in writing, that—

(a) The recipient has violated the requirements of subpart C of this part; or

(b) The recipient is convicted of a criminal drug offense resulting from a violation occurring during the conduct of any award activity.

§312.510 What actions will the Federal Government take against a recipient determined to have violated this part?

If a recipient is determined to have violated this part, as described in §312.500 or §312.505, the Peace Corps may take one or more of the following actions—

(a) Suspension of payments under the award;

(b) Suspension or termination of the award; and

(c) Suspension or debarment of the recipient under 22 CFR part 310, for a period not to exceed five years.

§312.515 Are there any exceptions to those actions?

The Peace Corps Director may waive with respect to a particular award, in writing, a suspension of payments under an award, suspension or termination of an award, or suspension or debarment of a recipient if the Peace Corps Director determines that such a waiver would be in the public interest. This exception authority cannot be delegated to any other official.

Subpart F—Definitions

§312.605 Award.

Award means an award of financial assistance by the Peace Corps or other Federal agency directly to a recipient.

(a) The term award includes:

(1) A Federal grant or cooperative agreement, in the form of money or property in lieu of money.

(2) A block grant or a grant in an entitlement program, whether or not the grant is exempted from coverage under the Governmentwide rule [Agency-specific CFR citation] that implements OMB Circular A–102 (for availability, see 5 CFR 1310.3) and specifies uniform administrative requirements.

(b) The term award does not include:

(1) Technical assistance that provides services instead of money.

(2) Loans.

(3) Loan guarantees.

(4) Interest subsidies.

(5) Insurance.

(6) Direct appropriations.

(7) Veterans' benefits to individuals (*i.e.*, any benefit to veterans, their families, or survivors by virtue of the service of a veteran in the Armed Forces of the United States).

(c) Notwithstanding paragraph (a)(2) of this section, this paragraph is not applicable for the Peace Corps.

§312.610 Controlled substance.

Controlled substance means a controlled substance in schedules I through V of the Controlled Substances Act (21 U.S.C. 812), and as further defined by regulation at 21 CFR 1308.11 through 1308.15.

§312.615 Conviction.

Conviction means a finding of guilt (including a plea of nolo contendere) or imposition of sentence, or both, by any judicial body charged with the responsibility to determine violations of the Federal or State criminal drug statutes.

§312.620 Cooperative agreement.

Cooperative agreement means an award of financial assistance that, consistent with 31 U.S.C. 6305, is used to enter into the same kind of relationship as a grant (see definition of grant in §312.650), except that substantial involvement is expected between the Federal agency and the recipient when carrying out the activity contemplated by the award. The term does not include cooperative research and development agreements as defined in 15 U.S.C. 3710a.

§312.625 Criminal drug statute.

Criminal drug statute means a Federal or non-Federal criminal statute involving the manufacture, distribution, dispensing, use, or possession of any controlled substance.

§312.630 Debarment.

Debarment means an action taken by a Federal agency to prohibit a recipient from participating in Federal Government procurement contracts and covered nonprocurement transactions. A recipient so prohibited is debarred, in accordance with the Federal Acquisition Regulation for procurement contracts (48 CFR part 9, subpart 9.4) and the common rule, Government-wide Debarment and Suspension (Nonprocurement), that implements Executive Order 12549 and Executive Order 12689.

§312.635 Drug-free workplace.

Drug-free workplace means a site for the performance of work done in connection with a specific award at which employees of the recipient are prohibited from engaging in the unlawful manufacture, distribution, dispensing, possession, or use of a controlled substance.

§312.640 Employee.

(a) *Employee* means the employee of a recipient directly engaged in the performance of work under the award, including—

(1) All direct charge employees;

(2) All indirect charge employees, unless their impact or involvement in the performance of work under the award is insignificant to the performance of the award; and

(3) Temporary personnel and consultants who are directly engaged in the performance of work under the award and who are on the recipient's payroll.

(b) This definition does not include workers not on the payroll of the recipient (*e.g.*, volunteers, even if used to meet a matching requirement; consultants or independent contractors not on the payroll; or employees of subrecipients or subcontractors in covered workplaces).

§312.645 Federal agency or agency.

Federal agency or agency means any United States executive department, military department, government corporation, government controlled corporation, any other establishment in the executive branch (including the Executive Office of the President), or any independent regulatory agency.

§312.650 Grant.

Grant means an award of financial assistance that, consistent with 31 U.S.C. 6304, is used to enter into a relationship—

(a) The principal purpose of which is to transfer a thing of value to the recipient to carry out a public purpose of support or stimulation authorized by a law of the United States, rather than to acquire property or services for the Federal Government's direct benefit or use; and

(b) In which substantial involvement is not expected between the Federal agency and the recipient when carrying out the activity contemplated by the award.

§312.655 Individual.

Individual means a natural person.

§312.660 Recipient.

Recipient means any individual, corporation, partnership, association, unit of government (except a Federal agency) or legal entity, however organized, that receives an award directly from a Federal agency.

§312.665 State.

State means any of the States of the United States, the District of Columbia, the Commonwealth of Puerto Rico, or any territory or possession of the United States.

§312.670 Suspension.

Suspension means an action taken by a Federal agency that immediately prohibits a recipient from participating in Federal Government procurement contracts and covered nonprocurement transactions for a temporary period, pending completion of an investigation and any judicial or administrative proceedings that may ensue. A recipient so prohibited is suspended, in accordance with the Federal Acquisition Regulation for procurement contracts (48 CFR part 9, subpart 9.4) and the common rule, Governmentwide Debarment and Suspension (Nonprocurement), that implements Executive Order 12549 and Executive Order 12689. Suspension of a recipient is a distinct and separate action from suspension of an award or suspension of payments under an award.

PARTS 313–399 [RESERVED]

CHAPTER IV—INTERNATIONAL JOINT COMMISSION, UNITED STATES AND CANADA

PART 400 [RESERVED]

PART 401—RULES OF PROCEDURE

AUTHORITY: Art. XII, 36 Stat. 2453.

SOURCE: 30 FR 3379, Mar. 13, 1965, unless otherwise noted.

Subpart A—General

§ 401.1 Definitions.

(a) In the construction of the regulations in this part, unless the context otherwise requires, words importing the singular number shall include the plural and words importing the plural number shall include the singular; and,

(b) *Applicant* means the Government or person on whose behalf on application is presented to the Commission in accordance with § 401.12;

(c) *Government* means the Government of Canada or the Government of the United States of America;

(d) *Person* includes Province, State, department or agency of a Province or State, municipality, individual, partnership, corporation and association, but does not include the Government of Canada or the Government of the United States of America;

(e) *Oath* includes affirmation;

(f) *Reference* means the document by which a question or matter of difference is referred to the Commission pursuant to Article IX of the Treaty;

(g) *The Treaty* means the Treaty between the United States of America and His Majesty the King, dated the 11th day of January 1909;

(h) *Canadian section consists of the commissioners appointed by Her Majesty on the recommendation of the Governor in Council of Canada;*

(i) *United States section* consists of the Commissioners appointed by the President of the United States.

§ 401.2 Chairmen.

(a) The commissioners of the United States section of the Commission shall appoint one of their number as chairman, to be known as the Chairman of the United States Section of the International Joint Commission, and he shall act as chairman at all meetings of the Commission held in the United States and in respect to all matters required to be done in the United States by the chairman of the Commission.

(b) The commissioners of the Canadian section of the Commission shall appoint one of their number as chairman, to be known as the Chairman of the Canadian Section of the International Joint Commission, and he shall act as chairman at all meetings of the Commission held in Canada and in respect to all matters required to be done in Canada by the chairman of the Commission.

(c) In case it shall be impracticable for the chairman of either section to act in any matter, the commissioner of such section who is senior in order of appointment shall act in his stead.

§ 401.3 Permanent offices.

The permanent offices of the Commission shall be at Washington, in the

District of Columbia, and at Ottawa, in the Province of Ontario, and, subject to the directions of the respective chairmen acting for their respective sections, the secretaries of the United States and Canadian sections of the Commission shall have full charge and control of said offices, respectively.

§401.4 Duties of secretaries.

(a) The secretaries shall act as joint secretaries at all meetings and hearings of the Commission. The secretary of the section of the Commission of the country in which a meeting or hearing is held shall prepare a record thereof and each secretary shall preserve an authentic copy of the same in the permanent offices of the Commission.

(b) Each secretary shall receive and file all applications, references and other papers properly presented to the Commission in any proceeding instituted before it and shall number in numerical order all such applications and references; the number given to an application or reference shall be the primary file number for all papers relating to such application or reference.

(c) Each secretary shall forward to the other for filing in the office of the other copies of all official letters, documents, records or other papers received by him or filed in his office, pertaining to any proceeding before the Commission, to the end that there shall be on file in each office either the original or a copy of all official letters and other papers, relating to the said proceeding.

(d) Each secretary shall also forward to the other for filing in the office of the other copies of any letters, documents or other papers received by him or filed in his office which are deemed by him to be of interest to the Commission.

§401.5 Meetings.

(a) Subject at all times to special call or direction by the two Governments, meetings of the Commission shall be held at such times and places in the United States and Canada as the Commission or the Chairman may determine and in any event shall be held each year at Washington in April and at Ottawa in October, beginning ordinarily on the first Tuesday of the said months.

(b) If the Commission determines that a meeting shall be open to the public, it shall give such advance notice to this effect as it considers appropriate in the circumstances.

§401.6 Service of documents.

(a) Where the secretary is required by the regulations in this part to give notice to any person, this shall be done by delivering or mailing such notice to the person at the address for service that the said person has furnished to the Commission, or if no such address has been furnished, at the dwelling house or usual place of abode or usual place of business of such person.

(b) Where the secretary is required by the regulations in this part to give notice to a Government, this shall be done by delivering or mailing such notice to the Secretary of State for External Affairs of Canada or to the Secretary of State of the United States of America, as the case may be.

(c) Service of any document pursuant to §401.22 shall be by delivering a copy thereof to the person named therein, or by leaving the same at the dwelling house or usual place of abode or usual place of business of such person. The person serving the notice or request shall furnish an affidavit to the secretary stating the time and place of such service.

§401.7 Conduct of hearings.

Hearings may be conducted, testimony received and arguments thereon heard by the whole Commission or by one or more Commissioners from each section of the Commission, designated for that purpose by the respective sections or the Chairman thereof.

§401.8 Decision by the whole Commission.

The whole Commission shall consider and determine any matter or question which the Treaty or any other treaty or international agreement, either in terms or by implication, requires or makes it the duty of the Commission to determine. For the purposes of this section and §401.7, "the whole Commission" means all of the commissioners appointed pursuant to Article VII of the Treaty whose terms of office have not expired and who are not prevented by serious illness or other circumstances beyond their control from carrying out their functions as commissioners. In no event shall a decision be made without the concurrence of at least four commissioners.

§401.9 Suspension or amendment of rules.

The commission may suspend, repeal, or amend all or any of the rules of procedure at any time, with the concurrence of at least four commissioners. Both Governments shall be informed forthwith of any such action.

§401.10 General rule.

The Commission may, at any time, adopt any procedure which it deems expedient and necessary to carry out the true intent and meaning of the Treaty.

§401.11 Availability of records.

(a) The following items in the official records of the Commission shall be available for public information at the permanent offices of the Commission.

Applications.
References.
Public Notices.
Press Releases.
Statements in Response.
Statements in Reply.
Records of hearings, including exhibits filed.
Brief and formal Statements submitted at hearings or at other times.

(b) Decisions rendered and orders issued by the Commission and formal opinions of any of the Commissioners with relation thereto, shall be available similarly for public information after duplicate originals of the decisions or orders have been transmitted to and filed with the Governments pursuant to Article XI of the Treaty.

(c) Copies of reports submitted to one or both of the Governments pursuant to the Treaty shall be available similarly for public information only with the consent of the Government or Governments to whom the reports are addressed.

(d) Reports, letters, memoranda and other communications addressed to the Commissions, by boards or committees created by or at the request of the Commission, are privileged and shall become available for public information only in accordance with a decision of the Commission to that effect.

(e) Except as provided in the preceding paragraphs of this section, records of deliberations, and documents, letters, memoranda and communications of every nature and kind in the official records of the Commission, whether addressed to or by the Commission, commissioners, secretaries, advisers or any of them, are privileged and shall become available for public information only in accordance with a decision of the Commission to that effect.

(f) A copy of any document, report, record or other paper which under this section is available for public information may be furnished to any person upon payment of any cost involved in its reproduction.

Subpart B—Applications

§401.12 Presentation to Commission.

(a) Where one or the other of the Governments on its own initiative seeks the approval of the commission for the use, obstruction or diversion of waters with respect to which under Articles III or IV of the Treaty the approval of the Commission is required, it shall present to the Commission an application setting forth as fully as may be necessary for the information of the Commission the facts upon which the application is based and the nature of the order of approval desired.

(b) Where a person seeks the approval of the Commission for the use, obstruction or diversion of waters with respect to which under Articles III or IV of the Treaty the approval of the Commission is required, he shall prepare an application to the Commission and forward it to the Government within whose jurisdiction such use, obstruction or diversion is to be made, with the request that the said application be transmitted to the Commission. If such Government transmits the application to the Commission with a request that it take appropriate action thereon, the same shall be filed by the Commission in the same manner as an application presented in accordance with paragraph (a) of this section. Transmittal of the application to the Commission shall not be construed as authorization by the Government of the use, obstruction or diversion proposed by the applicant. All applications by persons shall conform, as to their contents, to the requirements of paragraph (a) of this section.

(c) Where the Commission has issued an Order approving a particular use, obstruction or diversion, in which it has specifically retained jurisdiction over the subject matter of an application and has reserved the right to make further orders relating thereto, any Government or person entitled to request the issuance of such further order may present to the Commission a request, setting forth the facts upon which it is based and the nature of the further order desired. On receipt of the request, the Commission shall proceed in accordance with the terms of the Order in which the Commission specifically retained jurisdiction. In each case the secretaries shall notify both Governments and invite their comments before the request is complied with.

§ 401.13 Copies required.

(a) Subject to paragraph (c) of this section, two duplicate originals and fifty copies of the application and of any supplemental application, statement in response, supplemental statement in response, statement in reply and supplemental statement in reply shall be delivered to either secretary. On receipt of such documents, the secretary shall forthwith send one duplicate original and twenty-five copies to the other secretary.

(b) Subject to paragraph (c) of this section, two copies of such drawings, profiles, plans or survey, maps and specifications as may be necessary to illustrate clearly the matter of the application shall be delivered to either secretary and he shall send one copy forthwith to the other secretary.

(c) Notwithstanding paragraphs (a) and (b) of this section, such additional copies of the documents mentioned therein as may be requested by the Commission shall be provided forthwith.

§ 401.14 Authorization by Government.

(a) Where the use, obstruction or diversion of waters for which the Commission's approval is sought has been authorized by or on behalf of a Government or by or on behalf of a State or Province or other competent authority, two copies of such authorization and of any plans approved incidental thereto shall accompany the application when it is presented to the Commission in accordance with § 401.12.

(b) Where such a use, obstruction or diversion of waters is authorized by or on behalf of a Government or by or on behalf of a State or Province or other competent authority after an application has been presented to the Commission in accordance with § 401.12, the applicant shall deliver forthwith to the Commission two copies of such authorization and of any plans approved incidental thereto.

§ 401.15 Notice of publication.

(a) As soon as practicable after an application is presented or transmitted in accordance with § 401.12, the secretary of the section of the Commission appointed by the other Government shall send a copy of the application to such Government.

(b) Except as otherwise provided pursuant to § 401.19, the secretaries, as soon as practicable after the application is received, shall cause a notice to be published in the Canada Gazette and the FEDERAL REGISTER and once each week for three successive weeks in two newspapers, published one in each country and circulated in or near the localities which, in the opinion of the Commission, are most likely to be affected by the proposed use, obstruction or diversion. Subject to paragraph (c) of this section, the notice shall state that the application has been received, the nature and locality of the proposed use, obstruction or diversion, the time within which any person interested may present a statement in response to the Commission and that the Commission will hold a hearing or hearings at which all persons interested are entitled to be heard with respect thereto.

(c) If the Commission so directs, the notice referred to in paragraph (b) of this section, appropriately modified, may be combined with the notice of hearing referred to in § 401.24 and published accordingly.

§401.16 Statement in response.

(a) Except as otherwise provided pursuant to §410.19, a Government and any interested person, other than the applicant, may present a statement in response to the Commission within thirty days after the filing of an application. A statement in response shall set forth facts and arguments bearing on the subject matter of the application and tending to oppose or support the application, in whole or in part. If it is desired that conditional approval be granted, the statement in response should set forth the particular condition or conditions desired. An address for service of documents should be included in the statement in response.

(b) When a statement in response has been filed, the secretaries shall send a copy forthwith to the applicant and to each Government except the Government which presented the said statement in response. If so directed by the Commission, the secretaries shall inform those who have presented statements in response, of the nature of the total response.

§401.17 Statement in reply.

(a) Except as otherwise provided pursuant to §410.19, the applicant and, if he is a person, the Government which transmitted the application on his behalf, one or both may present a statement or statements in reply to the Commission within thirty days after the time provided for presenting statements in response. A statement in reply shall set forth facts and arguments bearing upon the allegations and arguments contained in the statements in response.

(b) When a statement in reply has been filed, the secretary shall send a copy forthwith to each Government except the Government which presented the said statement in reply, and to all persons who presented statements in response.

§401.18 Supplemental or amended applications and statements.

(a) If it appears to the Commission that either an application, a statement in response or a statement in reply is not sufficiently definite and complete, the Commission may require a more definite and complete application, statement in response or statement in reply, as the case may be, to be presented.

(b) Where substantial justice requires it, the Commission with the concurrence of at least four Commissioners may allow the amendment of any application, statement in response, statement in reply and any document or exhibit which has been presented to the Commission.

§401.19 Reducing or extending time and dispensing with statements.

In any case where the Commission considers that such action would be in the public interest and not prejudicial to the right of interested persons to be heard in accordance with Article XII of the Treaty, the Commission may reduce or extend the time for the presentation of any paper or the doing of any act required by these rules or may dispense with the presentation of statements in response and statements in reply.

§401.20 Interested persons and counsel.

Governments and persons interested in the subject matter of an application, whether in favor of or opposed to is, are entitled to be heard in person or by counsel at any hearing thereof held by the Commission.

§401.21 Consultation.

The Commission may meet or consult with the applicant, the Governments and other persons or their counsel at any time regarding the plan of hearing, the mode of conducting the inquiry, the admitting or proof of certain facts or for any other purpose.

§401.22 Attendance of witnesses and production of documents.

(a) Requests for the attendance and examination of witnesses and for the production and inspection of books, papers and documents may be issued over the signature of the secretary of the section of the Commission of the country in which the witnesses reside or the books, papers or documents may be, when so authorized by the Chairman of that section.

(b) All applications for subpoena or other process to compel the attendance of witnesses or the production of books, papers and documents before the Commission shall be made to the proper courts of either country, as the case may be, upon the order of the Commission.

§ 401.23 Hearings.

(a) The time and place of the hearing or hearings of an application shall be fixed by the Chairmen of the two sections.

(b) The secretaries shall forthwith give written notice of the time and place of the hearing or hearings to the applicant, the Governments and all persons who have presented statements in response to the Commission. Except as otherwise provided by the Commission, the secretaries shall also cause such notice to be published in the Canada Gazette and the FEDERAL REGISTER and once each week for three successive weeks in two newspapers, published one in each country and circulated in or near the localities which, in the opinion of the Commission, are most likely to be affected by the proposed use, obstruction or diversion of water.

(c) All hearings shall be open to the public.

(d) The applicant, the Governments and persons interested are entitled to present oral and documentary evidence and argument that is relevant and material to any issue that is before the Commission in connection with the application.

(e) The presiding chairman may require that evidence to be under oath.

(f) Witnesses may be examined and cross-examined by the Commissioners and by counsel for the applicant, the Governments and the Commission. With the consent of the presiding chairman, cousel for a person other than the applicant may also examine or cross-examine witnesses.

(g) The Commission may require further evidence to be given and may require printed briefs to be submitted at or subsequent to the hearing.

(h) The Commissioners shall be free to determine the probative value of the evidence submitted to it.

(i) A verbatim transcript of the proceedings at the hearing shall be prepared.

(j) The hearing of the application, when once begun, shall proceed at the times and places determined by the Chairmen of the two sections to ensure the greatest practicable continuity and dispatch of proceedings.

§ 401.24 Expenses of proceedings.

(a) The expenses of those participating in any proceeding under this subpart B shall be borne by the participants.

(b) The Commission, after due notice to the participant or participants concerned, may require that any unusual cost or expense to the Commission shall be paid by the person on whose behalf or at whose request such unusual cost or expense has been or will be incurred.

§ 401.25 Government brief regarding navigable waters.

When in the opinion of the Commission it is desirable that a decision should be rendered which affects navigable waters in a manner or to an extent different from that contemplated by the application and plans presented to the Commission, the Commission will, before making a final decision, submit to the Government presenting or transmitting the application a draft of the decision, and such Government may transmit to the Commission a brief or memorandum thereon which will receive due consideration by the Commission before its decision is made final.

Subpart C—References

§ 401.26 Presentation to Commission.

(a) Where a question or matter of difference arising between the two Governments involving the rights, obligations, or interests of either in relation to the other or to the inhabitants of the other along the common frontier between the United States of America and Canada is to be referred to the Commission under Article IX of the Treaty, the method of brining such question or matter to the attention of the Commission and invoking its action ordinarily will be as set forth in this section.

(b) Where both Governments have agreed to refer such a question or matter to the Commission, each Government will present to the Commission, at the permanent office in its country, a reference in similar or identical terms setting forth as fully as may be necessary for the information of the Commission the question or matter which it is to examine into the report upon and any restrictions or exceptions which may be imposed upon the Commission with respect thereto.

(c) Where one of the Governments, on its own initiative, has decided to refer such a question or matter to the Commission, it will present a reference to the Commission at the permanent office in its country. All such references should conform, as to their contents, to the requirements of paragraph (b) of this section.

(d) Such drawings, plans of survey and maps as may be necessary to illustrate clearly the question or matter referred should accompany the reference when it is presented to the Commission.

§ 401.27 Notice and publication.

(a) The secretary to whom a reference is presented shall receive and file the same and shall send a copy forthwith to the other secretary for filing in the office of the latter. If the reference is presented by one Government only, the other secretary shall send a copy forthwith to his Government.

(b) Subject to any restrictions or exceptions which may be imposed upon the Commission by the terms of the reference, and unless otherwise provided by the Commission, the secretaries, as soon as practicable after the reference is received, shall cause a notice to be published in the Canada Gazette, the FEDERAL REGISTER and in two newspapers, published one in each country and circulated in or near the localities which, in the opinion of the Commission, are most likely to be interested in the subject matter of the reference. The notice shall describe the subject matter of reference in general terms invite interested persons to inform the Commission of the nature of their interest and state that the Commission will provide convenient opportunity for interested persons to be heard with respect thereto.

§ 401.28 Advisory boards.

(a) The Commission may appoint a board or boards, composed of qualified persons, to conduct on its behalf investigations and studies that may be necessary or desirable and to report to the Commission regarding any questions or matters involved in the subject matter of the reference.

(b) Such board ordinarily will have an equal number of members from each country.

(c) The Commission ordinarily will make copies of the main or final report of such board or a digest thereof available for examination by the Governments and interested persons prior to holding the final hearing or hearings referred to in § 401.29.

§ 401.29 Hearings.

(a) A hearing or hearings may be held whenever in the opinion of the Commission such action would be helpful to the Commission in complying with the terms of a reference. Subject to any restrictions or exceptions which may be imposed by the terms of the reference, a final hearing or hearings shall be held before the Commission reports to Government in accordance with the terms of the reference.

(b) The time, place and purpose of the hearing or hearings on a reference shall be fixed by the chairmen of the two sections.

(c) The secretaries shall forthwith give written notice of the time, place and purpose of the hearing or hearings to each Government and to persons who have advised the Commission of their interest. Unless otherwise directed by the Commission, the secretaries shall also cause such notice to be published in the Canada Gazette, the FEDERAL REGISTER and once each week for three successive weeks in two newspapers, published one in each country and circulated in or near the localities which, in the opinion of the Commission, are most likely to be interested in the subject matter of the reference.

(d) All hearings shall be open to the public, unless otherwise determined by the Commission.

(e) At a hearing, the Governments and persons interested are entitled to present, in person or by counsel, oral and documentary evidence and argument that is relevant and material to any matter that is within the published purpose of the hearing.

(f) The presiding chairman may require that evidence be under oath.

(g) Witnesses may be examined and cross-examined by the Commissioners and by counsel for the Governments and the Commission. With the consent of presiding chairman, counsel for any interested person may also examine or cross-examine witnesses.

(h) The Commission may require further evidence to be given and may require printed briefs to be submitted at or subsequent to the hearing.

(i) A verbatim transcript of the proceedings at the hearing shall be prepared.

§ 401.30 Proceedings under Article X.

When a question or matter of difference arising between the two Governments involving the rights, obligations or interests of either in relation to the other or to their respective inhabitants has been or is to be referred to the Commission for decision under Article X of the Treaty, the Commission, after consultation with the said Governments, will adopt such rules of procedure as may be appropriate to the question or matter referred or to be referred.

PARTS 402–499 [RESERVED]

CHAPTER V—BROADCASTING BOARD OF GOVERNORS

EDITORIAL NOTE: Nomenclature changes to chapter V appear at 64 FR 54539, Oct. 7, 1999.

PART 500 [RESERVED]

PART 501—APPOINTMENT OF FOREIGN SERVICE OFFICERS

AUTHORITY: Foreign Service Act of 1980 (22 U.S.C. 3901 *et seq.*).

SOURCE: 50 FR 27423, July 3, 1985, unless otherwise noted.

§ 501.1 Policy.

It is the policy of the Broadcasting Board of Governors that Foreign Service Officers occupy positions in which there is a need and reasonable opportunity for interchangeability of personnel between the Board and posts abroad, and which are concerned with (a) the conduct, observation, or analysis of information and cultural activities, or (b) the executive management of, or administrative responsibility for, the overseas operations of the Board's program.

§ 501.2 Eligibility for appointment as Foreign Service Officer.

CROSS-REFERENCE: The regulations governing eligibility for appointment as a Foreign Service Officer are codified in part 11 of this title.

§ 501.3 Noncompetitive interchange between Civil Service and Foreign Service.

(a) An agreement between the Office of Personnel Management and the Board under the provisions of Executive Order 11219 (3 CFR 1964–65 Comp. p. 303) provides for the noncompetitive appointment of present or former Foreign Service employees as career or career conditional Civil Service employees.

(b) Under this agreement former career personnel of the Board's Foreign Service (FSCR, FSRU, FSIO, FSS, FSO, or FP) and such present personnel desiring to transfer, are eligible, under certain conditions, for noncompetitive career or career-conditional appointment in any Federal agency that desires to appoint them. The President has authorized the Office of Personnel Management by executive order to waive the requirements for competitive examination and appointment for such Board career Foreign Service personnel.

(c) A present or former Civil Service employee may be appointed on a competitive basis in any Foreign Service class for which the employee has qualified under the provisions of section 3947 of title 22, United States Code.

§ 501.4 Junior Level Career Candidate Program (Class 6, 5, or 4).

CROSS-REFERENCE: The regulations governing the junior level Career Candidate program are codified in part 11 of this title.

§ 501.5 Mid-level FSO Candidate Program (Class 3, 2, or 1).

(a) *General.* The mid-level FSO Candidate program, under the provisions of section 306 of the Foreign Service Act of 1980, supplements the junior-level Career Candidate program to meet total requirements for Foreign Service Officers at the mid-level in the Foreign Service. Foreign Service limited appointments of FSO Candidates are made to Class 3, 2, or 1 for a period not to exceed five years. Occasionally, appointments may be offered at the Class 4 level. The FSO Commissioning Board will determine whether FSO Candidates have performed at a satisfactory level and demonstrated the required level of growth potential and competence, and will make a recommendation on commissioning as Foreign Service Officers. FSO Candidates who are not recommended for commissioning prior to the expiration of their limited appointment will be separated from the mid-level program.

(b) *Sources of applicants.* (1) The Broadcasting Board of Governors draws a significant number of FSO Candidates from Board employees who apply, and are found qualified by the Board of Examiners for the Foreign Service (BEX).

(2) The Board also draws Candidates from outside applicants who possess skills and abilities in short supply in the Foreign Service and who have capabilities, insights, techniques, experiences, and differences of outlook which would serve to enrich the Foreign Service and enable them to perform effectively in assignments both abroad and in the United States. Minority applicants are recruited for mid-level entry under the COMRAT program. Appointment from sources outside the Board is limited and based on intake levels established in accordance with total Broadcasting Board of Governors FSO workforce and functional requirements. Such appointments are based on successful completion of the examination process, and existing assignment vacancies.

(c) *Eligibility requirement*—(1) *Broadcasting Board of Governors Employees.* On the date of application, employees must have at least three years of Federal Government service in a position of responsibility in the Board. A position of responsibility is defined as service as an Overseas Specialist at Class 4 or above or as a Domestic Specialist at GS–11 or above within the Board. The duties and responsibilities of the position occupied by the applicant must have been similar or closely related to those of a Foreign Service Officer in terms of knowledge, skills, abilities, and overseas experience. Board Domestic and Overseas Specialists must be no more than 58 years of age on the date of redesignation or appointment as an FSO Candidate.

(2) *Applicants Under Special Recruitment Programs.* Minority and women applicants must be no more than 58 years of age, must have approximately nine years of education or experience relevant to work performed in Broadcasting Board of Governors, must be knowledgeable in the social, political and cultural history of the U.S. and be able to analyze and interpret this in relation to U.S. Government policy and American life.

(3) *Outside Applicants.* On the date of appointment, applicants must be no more than 58 years of age, with nine years of relevant work experience and/or education, or proficiency in a language for which the Board has a need, or substantial management expertise. Relevant work experience is defined as public relations work, supervisory or managerial positions in communications media, program director for a museum or university-level teacher of political science, history, English or other relevant disciplines. Appointments from these sources for the limited vacancies available are made on a competitive basis to fill specific Service needs after ensuring that the vacancies cannot be filled by Foreign Service Officers already in the Foreign Service Officer Corps.

(d) *Application Procedures.* (1) Applicants must complete Standard Form 171, Application for Federal Employment; Form DSP–34, Supplement to Application for Federal Employment; a 1,000 word autobiography; a statement affirming willingness and capacity to serve at any post worldwide; and transcripts of all graduate and undergraduate course work and forward them to the Special Recruitment Branch, Office of Personnel (M/PDSE).

(2) The filing of an application for the Foreign Service does not in itself entitle an applicant to examination. The decision to proceed with an oral examination is made by a Qualifications Evaluation Panel after determining the applicant's eligibility for appointment and reviewing the applicant's qualifications including his/her performance, and administrative files (or equivalents), claimed language proficiency and other background or factors which may be related to the work performed by FSOs. An oral examination is given only in those cases where the applicant is found to possess superior qualifications, proven ability, and high potential for success in the Foreign Service.

(e) *Examination process*—(1) *Written Examination.* A written examination will not normally be required of applicants for FSO Candidate appointments. However, if the volume of applications for a given class or classes is such as to make it infeasible to examine applicants orally within a reasonable time, such applicants may be required to take an appropriate written examination prescribed by the Board of Examiners. Those who meet or exceed the passing level set by the Board of Examiners on the written examination will be eligible for selection for the oral examination.

(2) *Oral examination.* (i) Applicants approved by the Qualifications Evaluation Panel for examination will be given an oral examination by a panel of Deputy Examiners approved by the Board of Examiners. The oral examination is designed to enable the Board of Examiners to determine whether applicants are functionally qualified for work in the Foreign Service at the mid-level, whether they would be suitable representatives abroad of the United States, whether they have the potential to advance in the Foreign Service, and whether they have the background and experience to make a contribution to the Foreign Service. The oral examination is individually scheduled throughout the year and is normally given in Washington, D.C. At the discretion of the Board of Examiners, it may be given in other American cities, or at Foreign Service posts, selected by the Board.

(ii) The panel will orally examine each applicant through questioning and discussion. There will also be a writing exercise and an in-basket test. Applicants taking the oral examination will be graded according to the standards established by the Board of Examiners. The application of anyone whose score is at or above the passing level set by the Board will be continued. The application of anyone whose score is below the passing level will be terminated. The applicant may, however, reapply in 12 months by submitting a new application.

(3) *Foreign language requirement.* All applicants who pass the oral examination will be required to take a subsequent test to measure their fluency in foreign languages, or their aptitude for learning them (MLAT) for which a score of 50 points (on a scale of zero to eighty) is necessary to qualify for further processing. No applicant will be recommended for career appointment who has not demonstrated such a proficiency or aptitude. An applicant may be selected, appointed and assigned without first having demonstrated required proficiency in a foreign language, but the appointment will be subject to the condition that the employee may not receive more than one promotion and may not be commissioned as an FSO until proficiency in one foreign language is achieved.

(4) *Medical examination.* Those applicants recommended by the Board of Examiners for an FSO candidacy, and their dependents who will reside with them overseas, are required to pass a physical examination at the Department of State Medical Division.

(5) *Security and suitability considerations.* A background investigation or appropriate security clearance update will be conducted on each applicant, and no application may be continued until a security clearance has been granted.

(6) *Class of appointment.* The Board of Examiners fixes the entry level for appointment as an FSO candidate.

(7) *Certification for appointment.* After completion of all aspects of the examination, the Board of Examiners certifies to the Board successful candidates for appointment as FSO Candidates. Determinations of duly constituted panels of examiners and deputy examiners are final, unless modified by specific action of the Board of Examiners for the Foreign Service.

(8) *FSO Candidate registers.* (i) After approval by the Board of Examiners, and certification as to suitability and security clearance by the Board's Director of Security, successful applicants will have their names placed on a register for the class for which they have been found qualified. Appointments to available openings will be made from the applicants entered on the register for the class of the position to be filled. Inclusion on the register does not guarantee eventual assignment and appointment as an FSO Candidate. Applicants who have qualified but have not been appointed because of lack of openings will be dropped from the register 18 months after the date of placement on it (or the completion of an inside applicant's current overseas tour, whichever is longer). Such applicants may reapply for the program, but will be required to

repeat the entire application process, including BEX testing.

(ii) Any applicant on the register who refuses an assignment offer will be removed from the Register and will not be eligible to reapply for the program for seven years.

(iii) The Board of Examiners may extend the eligibility period when such extension is in its judgment justified in the interest of the Foreign Service.

(f) *Appointment as an FSO Candidate.* (1) An FSO Candidate will be given a four-year Foreign Service limited appointment. Board Career Overseas Specialists will be redesignated as FSO Candidates for a period of four years. The appointment or redesignation may be extended for one year, but must be terminated at the end of the fifth year. The purpose of the FSO Candidacy is to permit on-the-job evaluation of an individual's suitability and capacity for effective service as a Foreign Service Officer.

(2) FSO Candidates will be assigned to Generalist positions overseas, and will compete for promotion with other Generalist officers under the Annual Generalist Selection Boards. FSO Candidates at the Class 1 level may not compete for promotion into the Senior Foreign Service prior to commissioning as an FSO.

(3) The FSO Candidacy may be terminated during the four-year period for unsatisfactory performance (22 U.S.C. 4011) or for such other cause as will promote the efficiency of the Service (22 U.S.C. 4010).

(g) *Commissioning as a Foreign Service Officer.* (1) Upon completion of three years' service (most of which will have been overseas), the FSO Candidate will be eligible for commissioning as a Foreign Service Officer. The FSO Commissioning Board will review all FSO Candidates appointed on or after March 1, 1980 and will recommend on tenure.

(2) The criterion used for deciding whether to recommend commissioning of FSO Candidates is the Candidate's demonstrated potential to perform effectively as a Foreign Service Officer in a normal range of generalist assignments up through the Class 1 level. No quota or numerical limit is placed on the number of affirmative decisions.

(3) If recommended for commissioning, and having satisfied the language proficiency requirements, the name of the FSO Candidate will be forwarded to the President and the Senate and, upon approval, the FSO Candidate will be commissioned as an FSO.

(4) If the FSO Commissioning Board does not recommend commissioning of the FSO Candidate during its review, it may recommend extension of the FSO Candidacy to allow for a future review. Under no circumstances will an FSO Candidacy be extended to a total of more than five years.

(5) Candidates not recommended for commissioning or who have not satisfied the language proficiency requirement will be separated from the Service at the expiration of their appointment. However, FSO Candidates who were appointed from within the Board with career status as a Domestic or Overseas Specialist may exercise reappointment rights to their previous category in lieu of separation.

§ 501.6 Appointment of Overseas Specialists.

(a) *General.* Members of the Board's Foreign Service appointed as Overseas Specialists serve on rotational U.S.-overseas assignments in the following types of positions: General Administration; Publication Writers and Editors; Exhibit Managers; Printing Specialists; English Teaching Specialists; Correspondents; Engineers for the Voice of America; Regional Librarian Consultants; and Secretaries. Appointees serve a trial period of service as Specialist Candidates under Foreign Service limited appointments (or redesignation) for a period not to exceed five years. Appointments are made to F.S. classes 8 through 1. Specialist Candidates are given career appointments as Overseas Specialists based on the recommendations of Specialist Selection Boards. Specialist candidates not recommended for tenuring will be separated from the Foreign Service, or reinstated in the Civil Service.

(b) *Sources of applicants.* Qualified Broadcasting Board of Governors domestic employees comprise a significant recruitment source for Overseas Specialist appointments. Such employees will be given priority consideration over outside applicants when applying for Overseas Specialist positions, when qualifications are otherwise equal.

(c) *Eligibility requirements.* All applicant must be citizens of the United States, and must be at least 21 years of age and no more than 58 years of age at the time of appointment. The 21-year age requirement may be waived by the Director, Office of Personnel (M/P or VOA/P) when she or he determines that the applicant's services are urgently needed. Broadcasting Board of Governors employee applicants must also have at least three years of Federal government experience and occupy a position at the GS–11 level (or equivalent) or above (GS–10 for Electronic Technicians in the Voice of America). All applicants must be available for worldwide assignment to positions in their occupational category.

(d) *Application procedures.* (1) Applications for all specialties except secretarial should include a current SF–171, Application for Federal Employment; a DSP–34, Supplement to Application for Federal Employment; university transcripts; a 1,000 word autobiographical statement which should include mention of the qualifications the applicant would bring to the job and reason for desiring to work for the Board; and a statement affirming willingness and capacity to serve at any post worldwide.

(2) *Special requirements for Foreign Service Secretaries.* Secretarial applicants must submit a current SF–171, Application for Federal Employment, and a 250 word essay on a commonly understood subject to demonstrate grammatical competence. The following specific requirements must be met by applicants: Ability to type accurately at 60 words per minute; four years of secretarial or administrative experience (business school or college training may be substituted for up to two years of required work experience); and attainment of an acceptable score in verbal ability and spelling tests. Applicants will subsequently be given a written examination to measure administrative aptitude.

(e) *Examination process*—(1) *Application review.* All applications are to be sent to the Special Recruitment Staff, Office of Personnel (M/PDSE), or to the Foreign Personnel Advisor (VOA/PF) for Voice of America positions.

(2) *Qualifications Evaluation Panel.* A Qualifications Evaluation Panel will evaluate the applicant's qualifications including his/her performance and administrative files (or equivalent), claimed language proficiency and other background or factors which may be related to the work performed by an Overseas Specialist Officer in the relevant specialty.

(3) *Oral examination.* (i) Applicants who are passed on by the Qualifications Evaluation Panel to the Board of Examiners will be given an oral examination to evaluate the applicant's total qualifications for service as an Overseas Specialist in the desired functional specialty.

(ii) The Board panel examining all candidates except those of the Voice of America will consist of one Broadcasting Board of Governors Overseas Specialist and two BEX Deputy Examiners. For VOA candidates, the panel will consist of the Foreign Personnel Advisor, a BEX Deputy Examiner assigned to the Voice of America, and a Deputy Examiner assigned to the Board of Examiners.

(iii) The panel will examine each applicant through questioning and discussion. Hypothetical problem-solving exercises, a writing exercise and an inbasket test may also be required. The panel will also recommend the F.S. entry level for appointment. If the panel's recommendation is unfavorable, the application process will be discontinued. An unsuccessful applicant may apply again in 12 months.

(4) The same medical and security requirements applicable to FSO Candidates pertain to Specialist Candidates.

(5) *Overseas Specialist Candidate register.* If an applicant is successful in the examination, and medical and security clearances have been successfuly completed, his/her name will be added to the appropriate Overseas Specialist register for a period of 18 months, or completion of an inside candidate's current tour of duty overseas, whichever is longer, at the Foreign Service class determined in the examination process and based on previous experience. Inclusion on the register does not

guarantee eventual assignment and appointment as an Overseas Specialist Candidate.

(f) *Appointment as a Specialist Candidate.* (1) When the Office of Personnel identifies an overseas vacancy which cannot be filled from the existing ranks of Overseas Specialists, applicants on the Overseas Specialist register will be considered for the assignment. An applicant will not be appointed unless an overseas position has been identified and a need for the individual in the Foreign Service has been certified by the Director, Office of Personnel (M/P or VOA/P). Any applicant selected from the register who refuses an assignment offer will be dropped from the register and precluded from reapplying for a period of seven years.

(2) Applicants will be given a Foreign Service limited appointment (or redesignation) for a period of four years at the Foreign Service Class determined in the examination process. The purpose of this untenured appointment is to allow the Board to evaluate and assess the Specialist Candidate's abilities and future potential prior to offering career appointment as an Overseas Specialist. The limited appointment may be extended for one additional year, but must be terminated at the end of the fifth year if the Candidate does not obtain career tenure.

(3) The Candidate will receive the orientation and training necessary to serve overseas and will be assigned overseas in a position in his or her specialty. Broadcasting Board of Governors Civil Service employees selected as Overseas Specialist Candidates will be appointed only if the Board element to which they are currently assigned is willing to affirm in writing that a position at the appropriate level will be made available for the employee should the candidacy end unsuccessfully. Broadcasting Board of Governors Civil Service applicants will be appointed as Overseas Specialist Candidates on or about the date of their departure for post of assignment or upon assumption of an assignment (which has been identified and will follow a period of orientation in Washington). The Board may also assign a Candidate to a U.S.-based position for an initial assignment of up to 24 months when the Candidate will spend the majority of his/her time traveling overseas and will, except for the U.S. basing, be fully functioning as an Overseas Specialist. Specialist Candidates will compete for promotion by the Annual Overseas Specialist Selection Board with other officers in the same specialty and at the same class level. Specialist Candidates at the Class 1 level are ineligible for promotion into the Senior Foreign Service.

(4) The Specialist candidacy may be terminated at any time for unsatisfactory performance (22 U.S.C. 4011) or for such cause as will promote the efficiency of the Service (22 U.S.C. 4010).

(g) *Career appointment as an Overseas Specialist.* In accordance with section 3946 of title 22 United States Code, the decision to offer a Specialist Candidate a career appointment will be based on the recommendation made by the Annual Overseas Specialist Selection Board which reviews all employees in the Candidate's occupational category and class level.

(1) *Eligibility.* Specialist Candidates who have performed at least two years of overseas service will be eligible for review for career status at the time of the Candidate's third Board review. Candidates serving an initial tour in the U.S. but spending the majority of time working overseas will be credited with up to one year's overseas service, but no more than half of the time based in the U.S. If a Specialist Candidate is not recommended for career status during the initial review, the Candidate may be reviewed again when the next Annual Overseas Specialist Selection Board convenes if the initial Board so recommends.

(2) *Selection Board Review.* The Selection Board(s) will review the official performance file of the eligible Specialist Candidates and in accordance with established precepts, will determine whether the Candidates should be recommended for career appointment as Overseas Specialists. Recommendations by the Board will be based on the Candidate's demonstrated aptitude and fitness for a career in the Foreign Service in their occupational specialties. No quota or numerical limit is placed on the number of positive career status

decisions that can be made by Selection Boards. The Specialist candidacy will be terminated if the Candidate fails to be recommended for career status after a second Board review for tenuring. Candidates may be terminated earlier than the expiration of their limited appointment if so recommended by the Board and approved by the Director, Office of Personnel (M/P or VOA/P). Specialist Candidates recommended for career status by the Selection Board will be given Foreign Service career appointments (or redesignation) as Overseas Specialist, to take effect within one month of the Board's recommendation.

§ 501.7 Appointment as Chief of Mission.

(a) *Appointment by President.* Chiefs of mission are appointed by the President, by and with the advice and consent of the Senate. They may be career members of the Foreign Service or they may be appointed from outside the Service.

(b) *Recommendation of Foreign Service career members.* On the basis of recommendations made by the Director of Broadcasting Board of Governors, the Secretary of State from time to time furnishes the President with the names of Foreign Service career members qualified for appointment as chiefs of mission. The names of these officers, together with pertinent information concerning them, are given to the President to assist him in selecting qualified candidates for appointment as chiefs of mission.

(c) *Status of Foreign Service career members appointed as Chiefs of Mission.* Foreign Service career members who are appointed as chiefs of mission retain their career status as Foreign Service career members.

§ 501.8 Reappointment of Foreign Service Officers and Career Overseas Specialists.

The President may, by and with the advice and consent of the Senate, reappoint to the Service a former Foreign Service Officer who is separated from the Service. The Director (Broadcasting Board of Governors) may reappoint to the Service a former career Overseas Specialist.

(a) *Requirements for reappointment.* (1) On the date of application, each applicant must be a citizen of the United States.

(2) No applicant will be considered who has previously been separated from the Foreign Service pursuant to section 608 or 610 of the Foreign Service Act of 1980 (or predecessor section 633, 635, or 637 of the Foreign Service Act of 1946, as amended); or who resigned or retired in lieu of selection out or separation for cause.

NOTE: This requirement will not apply where it has been determined by the Foreign Service Grievance Board under 3 FAM 660 or by the Director, Office of Personnel, that the separation or the resignation or retirement in lieu of selection out or separation for cause was wrongful; where reappointment is determined by the Director, Office of Personnel, as an appropriate means to settle a grievance or complaint of a former Foreign Service career member on a mutually satisfactory basis; or where reappointment is the indicated redress in a proceeding under 3 FAM 130 "Equal Employment Opportunity."

(b) *Application.* Apply by letter addressed to the Director, Office of Personnel. Include the standard application forms, SF–171, Application for Federal Employment; and DSP–34, Supplement to Application for Federal Employment; and a brief resume of work and other experience since resignation from the Foreign Service. Whenever the Director, Office of Personnel, finds that the reappointment of one or more former Foreign Service Career Members may be in the best interest of the Service, all application forms, along with the available personnel files, will be referred as appropriate to the Board of Examiners for the Foreign Service which will conduct an advisory evaluation of the qualifications of each applicant.

(c) *Nature of evaluation.* (1) The Board of Examiners' advisory qualifications evaluation of FSO applicants (i) will be based on a review of all pertinent information relating to the applicant's record of employment in the Foreign Service and to subsequent experience, as well, and (ii) will take into consideration among other factors, the rank of the applicant's contemporaries in the Service in recommending the class in which the applicant will be reappointed under section 308 of the Foreign Service Act of 1980.

(2) In consultation with the Foreign Service Personnel Division (M/PF or VOA/PF) and officials from the pertinent Board elements, the Overseas Specialist applicant's total qualifications and experience will be evaluated based on the application and an interview. On the basis of this review and the recommendations of the appropriate officials, the personnel office will determine whether the application should be continued and, if so, will recommend the appointment class.

(d) *Medical examination and security investigation.* Qualified applicants and their dependents who will accompany them overseas will be given a physical examination. A security investigation will also be conducted. The reappointment action is subject to completion of a satisfactory security investigation and satisfactory medical examination of the applicant and his/her dependents.

(e) *Selection for reappointment.* The Director, Office or Personnel (M/P or VOA/P), taking into consideration (1) the qualifications and experience of each applicant as outlined in the qualifications evaluation performed by the Board of Examiners for the Foreign Service or the personnel office, (2) future placement and growth potential, and (3) the needs of the Service for the applicant's skills determines which applicant, or applicants, are qualified for reappointment and the appointment class that is considered to be appropriate. An Overseas Specialist may not be reappointed until and unless an overseas assignment has been identified. The Director, Office of Personnel (M/P or VOA/P) is responsible for initiating appointment action. Any voluntary applicant who refuses an offer of reappointment will not be considered for reappointment again.

§ 501.9 Interchange of FSOs between Broadcasting Board of Governors and other Foreign Affairs Agencies.

Foreign Service Officers (FSOs) desiring transfer from one agency to another may apply under the following provisions:

(a) *Applications.* Applications for interchange appointments should be sent to the Board of Examiners for the Foreign Service, Department of State, Washington, DC 20520.

(b) *Certification and approval.* (1) When a Foreign Service Officer of another Foreign Affairs Agency wishes to transfer to the Broadcasting Board of Governors, a certification of need is required from the Director, Office of Personnel, Broadcasting Board of Governors, and approval is required by the Director of Personnel for the other agency for the officer's release to Broadcasting Board of Governors.

(2) When a Broadcasting Board of Governors FSO wishes to transfer to another Foreign Affairs Agency, a certification of need is required from the Director of Personnel of the other Agency, and approval is required by the Director, Office of Personnel, Broadcasting Board of Governors, for the officer's release to that Agency.

(3) A review by the Board of Examiners for the Foreign Service will certify the eligibility of candidates for exchange. BEX will notify the Office of Personnel, Broadcasting Board of Governors when a Foreign Service Officer of another Agency has been approved for transfer and Broadcasting Board of Governors will process the necessary employment papers.

(4) A new FSO appointment for officers transferring between another Foreign Affairs Agency and Broadcasting Board of Governors is not required.

PART 502—DOMESTIC REQUESTS FOR BROADCASTING BOARD OF GOVERNORS PROGRAM MATERIALS

Sec.

AUTHORITY: 22 U.S.C. 1461, 1461–1a.

SOURCE: 78 FR 39585, July 2, 2013, unless otherwise noted.

§ 502.1 Authority and scope.

(a) *Authority for this part.* This part is pursuant to Section 1078 of the National Defense Authorization Act for Fiscal Year 2013, Public Law 112–239, as codified in 22 U.S.C. 1461, 1461–1a and the U.S. International Broadcasting Act, 22 U.S.C. 6201 et seq.

(b) *Scope.* This part applies to the public and all divisions of the Federal Government supervised by the Broadcasting Board of Governors under the U.S. International Broadcasting Act of 1994 (collectively "the Agency"). These regulations only cover the procedures for responding to domestic requests for Agency program materials.

(c) *Summary.* (1) The Broadcasting Board of Governors supervises all U.S. non-military international broadcasting activities in accordance with the broadcasting principles and standards in the U.S. International Broadcasting Act of 1994, 22 U.S.C. 6201 et seq., including consistency with the broad foreign policy objectives of the United States.

(2) As stated in the U.S. International Broadcasting Act of 1994, it is the policy of the United States to promote freedom of opinion and expression and to open communication of information and ideas among the people of the world. The Agency has adopted as its mission statement "to inform, engage, and connect people around the world in support of freedom and democracy."

(3) It is the Agency's policy to make its program materials available, upon request, whenever doing so is consistent with all statutory authorities, prohibitions, principles, and standards. However, the Agency reserves the right to deny requests for program materials under circumstances described in Section 502.7 of this regulation.

(4) Pursuant to section 501 of the U.S. Information and Educational Exchange Act, as amended, as codified in 22 U.S.C. 1461, the Agency may, upon request, provide members of the public, organizations, and media with program materials which the Agency disseminated abroad, in accordance with these regulations.

(5) Pursuant to Section 208 of Foreign Relations Authorization Act, Fiscal Years 1986 and 1987, as amended, as codified at 22 U.S.C. 1461–1a, the Agency is prohibited from using appropriated funds to influence public opinion in the United States, however, the statute clarifies that the Agency may:

(i) Provide information about its operations, programs, or program materials to the media, the public, or Congress in accordance with applicable law;

(ii) Make program materials available in the Unites States, when appropriate, and in accordance with other applicable law.

§ 502.2 Definitions.

As used in this part:

(a) *Media entity* means any person or entity, that actively gathers information of potential interest to a segment of the public, turns gathered information into a distinct work, or distributes that work to an audience within the United States, and otherwise serves the purposes described in § 502.4.

(b) *Organization* means any corporation, trust, association, cooperative, or other group organized primarily for scientific, educational, service, charitable, or similar purpose, including but not limited to institutions of higher education, and otherwise serves the purposes described in § 502.4.

(c) *Program materials* means radio broadcasts, television broadcasts, and Internet content that the Agency disseminates to audiences outside of the United States, pursuant to: The U.S. Information and Educational Exchange Act of 1948 (22 U.S.C. 1461 et seq.); The U.S. International Broadcasting Act of 1994 (22 U.S.C. 6201 et seq.); The Radio Broadcasting to Cuba Act (22 U.S.C. 1465 et seq.); or The Television Broadcasting to Cuba Act (22 U.S.C. 1465aa et seq.).

(d) *Requestor* means any private person or entity within the United States that requests program materials from the Agency.

§ 502.3 Availability of program materials on public Web sites.

(a) The Agency makes program materials available to Requestors through the Agency's news and information

Web sites designed for foreign audiences. To access currently-available Agency program materials, please visit *www.voanews.com* and *www.martinoticias.com*. The homepages of these Web sites display a portion of the Agency's most recent news reporting. Additional program materials are available through the Web sites' search functions.

(b) Program materials are available on Agency Web sites, and may be removed from Agency Web sites solely at the Agency's discretion. The Agency will remove program materials from Agency Web sites when a National Archives and Records Administration (NARA) records schedule goes into effect, or when required by licensing agreements with third-party copyright holders. Once these program materials have been removed from Agency Web sites, they are no longer available from the Agency.

(1) When full programs are removed from the Agency's Web sites in accordance with a NARA records schedule, programs designated as permanent will be transferred to NARA. For information on how to request Agency program materials that have been transferred to NARA, see the Agency's records schedules and NARA's regulations at *www.nara.gov*.

(2) Programs designated as temporary under a NARA records schedule will not be retained by the Agency once they are removed from the Agency's Web sites and are no longer needed for the Agency's use.

(c) Segments incorporated into final programs, including music, interviews, reports, and other program elements, will not be transferred to NARA independently of full program recordings, and will not be available after they have been removed from Agency Web sites.

(d) Draft program materials, and any other program materials not selected for dissemination abroad, are not available.

(e) The Agency shall determine the method of making program materials available, as well as the file type, file format, resolution, and storage medium(s) that are available. Program materials are only available in the same form (i.e. radio or television filetype and file format) and language in which the Agency disseminated them abroad.

[78 FR 39585, July 2, 2013, as amended at 78 FR 67026, Nov. 8, 2013]

§ 502.4 Media or organization one-time requests for broadcast quality agency program materials.

Upon request, the Agency may provide a broadcast-quality copy of Agency program materials to media entities, educational organizations, not-for-profit corporations, or other requestors. Requestors will be informed if materials are subject to third party content holders' restrictions. One-time requests for broadcast quality copies of Agency program materials should be directed to:

(a) The Voice of America Office of Public Relations for broadcast-quality copies of Voice of America program materials; and

(b) The TV Marti Division of the Office of Cuba Broadcasting for broadcast-quality copies of TV or Radio Marti program materials.

[78 FR 67026, Nov. 8, 2013]

§ 502.5 Media or organization requests for ongoing subscriptions to broadcast quality agency program materials

(a) Upon request, the Agency may make program materials available on an ongoing basis to Media entities, or other organizations, through a subscription agreement, provided that the Agency determines that entering into a subscription agreement to make program materials available on an ongoing basis would be consistent with the Agency's mission and authorities. Requested, ongoing subscription agreements must be consistent with the Agency's Policy for domestic distribution which incorporates the Broadcasting principles and standards and other requirements, found in 22 U.S.C. 1461, 1461–1a, 1462, 6201, 6202, 6203, 6204, 6205, 6206; Pub. L. 112–239, section 1078(b), 126 Stat. 1632, 1958; agreements with third-parties that hold a copyright in Agency program materials; and Terms of Use on Agency Web sites. Requestors shall secure all necessary licenses from all persons or organizations that hold a copyright in any portion of program materials before making any use of those program materials, except uses of program materials permitted by the Copyright Act of 1976, as amended.

(b) Media entities or other organizations may request ongoing subscriptions by filling out an application form found on the Web site for the Direct System, the Agency's professional distribution system.

[78 FR 67026, Nov. 8, 2013]

§ 502.6 Terms of use for accessing program materials available on agency Web sites.

(a) By accessing Agency Web sites, Requestors agree to all the Terms of Use available on those Web sites.

(b) All Requestors are advised that Agency program materials may contain third-party copyrighted material, unless the Agency specifically informs the Requestor otherwise. Accordingly, and as further explained in the Terms of Use mentioned above, by using Agency Web sites to access program materials:

(1) The Requestor agrees that he or she is solely responsible for his or her use of program materials provided by the Agency and any copyrighted portion(s) of those materials;

(2) The Requestor agrees that he or she shall secure all necessary licenses from all persons or organizations that hold a copyright in any portion of requested program materials before making any use of those program materials, except uses of program materials permitted by the Copyright Act of 1976, as amended.

[78 FR 39585, July 2, 2013, as amended at 78 FR 67026, Nov. 8, 2013]

§ 502.7 Denial of requests.

(a) The Agency reserves the right to deny any request for program materials made pursuant to these regulations for cause, including but not limited to the following circumstances:

(1) For a Requestor's failure to comply with the Terms of Use on Agency Web sites;

(2) For a Requestor's failure to secure necessary rights and licenses to use third-party copyrighted materials when the Requestor uses Agency program materials in any way not explicitly permitted by the Copyright Act of 1976, as amended;

(3) When the Agency's distribution of program materials is restricted by an agreement with a third-party that holds a copyright in a portion of Agency program materials;

(4) If providing the requested materials would be inconsistent with the Agency's statutory authorities, the broadcasting element's charter, or any applicable law or regulation.

(b) For more information on the criteria for accepting or denying requests, please see the Agency's policy for domestic distribution, available at *www.bbg.gov.*

§ 502.8 Fees.

(a) The Agency makes program material available at no cost on *www.voanews.com* and *www.martinoticias.com.*

(b) The Agency may collect a fee for reimbursement of the reasonable costs incurred to fulfill a request for Agency program materials, including ongoing subscriptions for Media entities and one-time requests for broadcast-quality copies of Agency program materials. Fees charged for ongoing subscriptions, if any, will be outlined in an agreement between the Media entity and the Agency.

(c) The Agency reserves the right to establish and change fees in accordance with applicable law and regulation.

PART 503—FREEDOM OF INFORMATION ACT REGULATION

Sec.

AUTHORITY: 5 U.S.C. 552 Reform Act of 1986 as amended by Pub. L. 99–570; sec. 1801–1804; U.S.C. 2658; 5 U.S.C. 301; 13 U.S.C. 8, E.O. 10477, as amended; 47 FR 9320, Apr. 2, 1982, E.O. 12356. 5 U.S.C. 552 (1988 & Supp. III 1991) as amended by Freedom of Information Reform Act of 1986, Pub. L. 99–570, Title I, sections 1801–1804, 100 Stat. 3207, 3207–48–50 (1986)(codified at 5 U.S.C. 552 (1988)); 22 U.S.C. 2658 (1988); 5 U.S.C. 301 (1988); 13 U.S.C. 8 (2988); E.O. 10477, 3 CFR 958 (1949–1953) as amended by E.O. 10822, 3 CFR 355 (1959–1963), E.O. 12292, 3 FR 134 (1982), E.O. 12356, 3 CFR 166 (1983), E.O. 12958 (1995).

SOURCE: 67 FR 8867, Feb. 27, 2002, unless otherwise noted.

§ 503.1 Introduction and definitions.

(a) *Introduction.* The Freedom of Information Act (FOIA) and this part apply to all records of The Broadcasting Board of Governors (BBG). As a general policy BBG follows a balanced approach in administering the FOIA. We recognize the right of public access to information in the Agency's possession, but we also seek to protect the integrity of the Agency's internal processes. This policy calls for the fullest possible disclosure of records consistent with those requirements of administrative necessity and confidentiality which are recognized by the FOIA.

(b) *Definitions:*

Access Appeal Committee or Committee means the Committee delegated by the Agency Head for making final agency determinations regarding appeals from the initial denial of records under the FOIA.

Agency or BBG means the Broadcasting Board of Governors. It includes all parts of the BBG in the U.S. and its worldwide operations.

Commercial use, when referring to a request, means that the request is from, or on behalf of, one who seeks information for a use or purpose that furthers the commercial, trade, or profit interests of the requester or of a person on whose behalf the request is made. Whether a request is for a commercial use depends on the purpose of the request and how the records will be used. The identity of the requester (individual, non-profit corporation, for-profit corporation), or the nature of the records, while in some cases indicative of that purpose or use, is not necessarily determinative. When a request is made by a representative of the news media, the request shall be deemed to be for a non-commercial use.

Department means any executive department, military department, government corporation, government controlled corporation, any independent regulatory agency, or other establishment in the executive branch of the Federal Government. A private organization is not a department even if it is performing work under contract with the Government or is receiving Federal financial assistance. Grantee and contractor records are not subject to the FOIA unless they are in the possession and control of the BBG.

Duplication means the process of making a copy of a record and sending it to the requester, to the extent necessary to respond to the request. Such copies include paper copy, microform, audiovisual materials, and magnetic tapes, cards and discs.

Educational institution means a preschool, elementary or secondary school, institution of undergraduate or graduate higher education, or institution of professional or vocational education.

FOIA means the Freedom of Information Act, section 552 of title 5, United States Code, as amended.

Freedom of Information Officer means the BBG official who has been delegated the authority to release or withhold records and assess, waive, or reduce fees in response to FOIA requests.

Non-commercial scientific institution means an institution that is not operated substantially for the purposes of furthering its own or someone else's business, trade, or profit interests, and that is operated for purposes of conducting scientific research whose results are not intended to promote any particular product or industry.

Records (and any other term used in this section in reference to information) include any information that would be an agency record subject to the requirements of this section when maintained by the Agency in any format, including an electronic format. Records also include any handwritten, typed or printed documents (such as memoranda, books, brochures, studies, writings, drafts, letters, transcripts, and minutes) and documentary material in other forms (such as punchcards, magnetic tapes, cards, or discs; paper tapes; audio or video recordings, maps, photographs, slides, microfilm, and motion pictures). It does not include objects or articles such as exhibits, models, equipment, and duplication machines or audiovisual processing materials. Reports does not include books, magazines, pamphlets, or other reference material in formally organized and officially designated BBG libraries, where such materials are available under the rules of the particular library.

Representative of the news media means a person actively gathering news for an entity organized and operated to publish or broadcast news to the public. *News* means information that is about current events or that would be of current interest to the public. News media entities include television and radio broadcasters, publishers of periodicals (to the extent they publish "news") who make their products available for purchase or subscription by the general public, and entities that may disseminate news through other media (e.g., electronic dissemination of text). Freelance journalists shall be considered representatives of a news media entity if they can show a solid basis for expecting publication through such an entity. A publication contract or a requester's past publication record may show such a basis.

Request means asking in writing for records whether or not the request refers specifically to the FOIA.

Review means examining the records to determine which portions, if any, may be released, and any other processing that is necessary to prepare the records for release. It includes only the first examination and processing of the requested documents for purposes of determining whether a specific exemption applies to a particular record or portion of a record.

Search means looking for records or portions of records responsive to a request. It includes reading and interpreting a request, and also page-by-page and line-by-line examination to identify responsive portions of a document. However, it does not include line-by-line examination where merely duplicating the entire page would be a less expensive and quicker way to comply with the request.

§503.2 Making a request.

(a) *How to request records.* All requests for documents shall be made in writing. Requests should be addressed to The Broadcasting Board of Governors (BBG), FOIA/Privacy Act Officer, Office of the General Counsel, 330 Independence Avenue, SW, Suite 3349, Washington, DC 20237; telephone (202) 260–4404; or fax (202) 260–4394. Write the words "Freedom of Information Act Request" on the envelope and letter.

(b) *Details in your letter.* Your request for documents should provide as many details as possible that will help us find the records you are requesting. If there is insufficient information, we will ask you to provide greater details. Include your telephone number(s) to help us reach you if we have questions. If you are not sure how to write your request or what details to include, you may call the FOIA Office to request a copy of the Agency's booklet "Guide and Index of Records," or access the same information via the Internet on BBG's World Wide Web site (*http://www.ibb.gov*). The more specific the request for documents, the sooner the Agency will be able to respond to your request(s).

(c) *Requests not handled under FOIA.* We will not provide documents requested under the FOIA and this part if the records are currently available in the National Archives, subject to release through the Archives, or commonly sold to the public by it or another agency in accordance with statutory authority (for example, records currently available from the Government Printing Office or the National Technical Information Service). Agency records that are normally freely available to the general public, such as BBG press releases, are not covered by the FOIA. Requests for documents from Federal departments, Chairmen of Congressional committees or subcommittees and court orders are not FOIA requests.

(d) *Referral of requests outside the agency.* If you request records that were created by or provided to us by another Federal department, we may refer your request to or consult with that department. We may also refer requests for classified records to the department that classified them. In cases of referral, the other department is responsible for processing and responding to your request under that department's regulation. When possible, we will notify you when we refer your request to another department.

(e) *Responding to your request*—(1) *Retrieving records*. The Agency is required to furnish copies of records only when they are in our possession and control. If we have stored the records you want in a record retention center, we will retrieve and review them for possible disclosure. However, the Federal Government destroys many old records, so sometimes it is impossible to fill requests. The Agency's record retention policies are set forth in the General Records Schedules of the National Archives and Records Administration and in BBG's Records Disposition Schedule, which establish time periods for keeping records before they may be destroyed.

(2) *Furnishing records*. (i) The Agency is only required to furnish copies of records that we have or can retrieve. We are not compelled to create new records. The Agency will aid requesters by providing records and information in the form requested, including electronic format, if we can readily reproduce them in that form or format.

(ii) We may decide to conserve government resources and at the same time supply the records you need by consolidating information from various records, in paper form or electronically, rather than copying them all. If the effort to produce records in electronic format would significantly interfere with the operations of the Agency, we will consider the effort to be an unreasonable search.

(iii) The Agency is required to furnish only one copy of a record. If we are unable to make a legible copy of a record to be released, we will not attempt to reconstruct it. Rather we will furnish the best copy possible and note its poor quality in our reply or on the copy.

(iv) If we cannot accommodate your request for form or format, we will provide responsive, nonexempt information in a reasonably accessible form.

§ 503.3 Availability of agency records.

(a) *Release of records*. If we have released a record or part of a record to others in the past, we will ordinarily release it to you also. This principle does not apply if the previous release was an unauthorized disclosure. However, we will not release it to you if a statute forbids this disclosure and we will not necessarily release it to you if an exemption applies in your situation and did not apply or applied differently in the previous situation.

(b) *Denial of requests*. All denials are in writing and describe in general terms the material withheld and state the reasons for the denial, including a reference to the specific exemption of the FOIA authorizing the withholding or deletion. The denial also explains your right to appeal the decision and it will identify the official to whom you should send the appeal. Denial letters are signed by the person who made the decision to deny all or part of the request, unless otherwise noted.

(c) *Unproductive searches*. We will make a diligent search for records to satisfy your request. Nevertheless, we may not be able always to find the records you want using the information you provided, or they may not exist. If we advise you that we have been unable to find the records despite a diligent search, you will nevertheless be provided the opportunity to appeal the adequacy of the Agency's search. However, if your request is for records that are obviously not connected with this Agency or your request has been provided to us in error, a "no records" response will not be considered an adverse action and you will not be provided an opportunity to appeal.

(d) *Appeal of denials*. You have the right to appeal a partial or full denial of your FOIA request. To do so, you must put your appeal in writing and address it to the official identified in the denial letter. Your appeal letter must be dated and postmarked within 30 calendar days from the date of the Agency's denial letter. Because we have some discretionary authority in deciding whether to release or withhold records, you may strengthen your appeal by explaining your reasons for wanting the records. However, you are not required to give any explanation.

Your appeal will be reviewed by the Agency's Access Appeal Committee that consists of senior Agency officials. When the Committee responds to your appeal, that constitutes the Agency's final action on the request. If the Access Appeal Committee grants your appeal in part or in full, we will send the records to you promptly or set up an appointment for you to inspect them. If the decision is to deny your appeal in part or in full, the final letter will state the reasons for the decision, name the officials responsible for the decision, and inform you of the FOIA provisions for judicial review.

§503.4 Time limits.

(a) *General.* The FOIA sets certain time limits for us to decide whether to disclose the records you requested, and to decide appeals. If we fail to meet the deadlines, you may proceed as if we had denied your request or your appeal. Since requests may be misaddressed or misrouted, you should call or write to confirm that we have the request and to learn its status if you have not heard from us in a reasonable time.

(b) *Time allowed.* (1) We will decide whether to release records within 20 working days after your request reaches the appropriate area office that maintains the records you are requesting. When we decide to release records, we will actually provide the records at that time, or as soon as possible after that decision, or let you inspect them as soon as possible thereafter.

(2) We will decide an appeal within 20 working days after the appeal reaches the appropriate reviewing official.

(3)(i) The FOIA Officer or appeal official may extend the time limits in unusual circumstances for initial requests or appeals, up to 10 working days. We will notify you in writing of any extensions. "Unusual circumstances" include situations where we: Search for and collect records from field facilities, records centers or locations other than the office processing the records; search for, collect, or examine a great many records in response to a single request; consult with another office or department that has substantial interest in the determination of the request; and/or conduct negotiations with submitters and requesters of information to determine the nature and extent of non-disclosable proprietary materials.

(ii) If an extra ten days still does not provide sufficient time for the Agency to deal with your request, we will inform you that the request cannot be processed within the statutory time limit and provide you with the opportunity to limit the scope of your request and/or arrange with us a negotiated deadline for processing your request.

(iii) If you refuse to reasonably limit the scope of your request or refuse to agree upon a time frame, the Agency will process your case, as it would have, had no modification been sought. We will make a diligent, good faith effort to complete our review within the statutory time frame.

§503.5 Records available for public inspection.

(a) To the extent that they exist, we will make the following records of general interest available for you in paper form or electronically for inspection or copying:

(1) Orders and final opinions, including concurring and dissenting opinions in adjudications. (*See* §503.8(e) of this part for availability of internal memoranda, including attorney opinions and advice.)

(2) Statements of policy and interpretations that we have adopted but which have not been published in the FEDERAL REGISTER.

(3) Administrative staff manuals and instructions to staff that affect the public. (We will not make available, however, manuals or instructions that reveal investigative or audit procedures as described in §503.8(b) and (g) of this part.)

(4) In addition to such records as those described in this paragraph (a), we will make available to any person a copy of all other Agency records, in the format requested, if available, unless we determine that such records should be withheld from disclosure under subsection (b) of the Act and §§503.8 and 503.9 of this part.

(b) Before releasing these records, however, we may delete the names of people, or information that would identify them, if release would invade their personal privacy to a clearly unwarranted degree (*See* § 503.8(f)).

(c) The Agency's FOIA Guide and Index is available electronically via the Internet, or you may request a copy of it by mail.

§ 503.6 Restrictions on some agency records.

Under the U.S. Information and Educational Exchange Act of 1948 (22 U.S.C. 1461, as amended), the BBG is prohibited from disseminating within the United States information about the U.S., its people, and its policies when such materials have been prepared by the Agency for audiences abroad. This includes films, radio scripts and tapes, videotapes, books, and similar materials produced by the Agency. However, this law does provide that upon request, such information shall be made available at BBG, for examination only, by representatives of the press, magazines, radio systems and stations, research students or scholars and available, for examination only, to Members of Congress.

§ 503.7 Fees.

(a) *Fees to be charged—categories of requests.* Paragraphs (a)(1) though (3) and (b) through (e) of this section explain each category of request and the type of fees that we will generally charge. However, for each of these categories, the fees may be limited, waived, or reduced for the reasons given in paragraph (e) of this section. "Request" means asking for records, whether or not you refer specifically to the Freedom of Information Act (FOIA). Requests from Federal agencies and court orders for documents are not included within this definition. "Review" means, when used in connection with processing records for a commercial use request, examining the records to determine what portions, if any, may be withheld, and any other processing that is necessary to prepare the records for release. It includes only the examining and processing that are done the first time we analyze whether a specific exemption applies to a particular record or portion of a record. It does not include the process of researching or resolving general legal, or policy issues regarding exemptions. "Search" means looking for records or portions of records responsive to a request. It includes reading and interpreting a request, and also and line-by-line examination to identify responsive portions of a document.

(1) *Commercial use request.* If your request is for a commercial use, BBG will charge you the costs of search, review and duplication. "Commercial use" means that the request is from or on behalf of one whom seeks information for a use or purpose that furthers the commercial, trade, or profit interests of the requester or of a person on whose behalf the request is made. Whether a request is for a commercial use depends on the purpose of the request and how the records will be used; the identity of the requester (individual, non-profit corporation, for-profit corporation), or the nature of the records, while in some cases may indicate the purpose or use is not necessarily determinative. When a request is made by a representative of the news media, a purpose of use which supports the requester's news dissemination function is deemed to be a non-commercial use.

(2) *Educational and scientific institutions and news media.* If you are an educational institution or a non-commercial scientific institution, operated primarily for scholarly or scientific research, or a representative of the news media, and your request is not for a commercial use, BBG will charge you only for the duplication of documents. Also BBG will not charge you the copying costs for the first 100 pages of duplication. "Educational institution" means a preschool, elementary or secondary school, institution of undergraduate or graduate higher education, or institution of professional or vocational education. "Non-commercial scientific institution" means an institution that is not operated substantially for purposes of furthering its own or someone else's business, trade, or profit interests, and that is operated for purposes of conducting scientific research whose results are not intended to promote any particular product or industry. "Representative of the news media" means a person actively gathering news for an entity organized and operated to publish or broadcast news

to the public. "News" means information that is about current events or that would be of current interest to the public. News media entities include television and radio broadcasters, publishers of periodicals (to the extent they publish "news") who make their products available for purchase or subscription by the general public, and entities that may disseminate news through other media (e.g., electronic dissemination of text). We will treat freelance journalists as representatives of a news media entity if they can show a solid basis for expecting publication through such an entity. A publication contract is such a basis and the requester's past publication record may show such a basis.

(3) *Other requesters.* If your request is not the kind described by paragraph (a)(1) or (a)(2) of this section, then the BBG will charge you only for search and duplication. Also, we will not charge you for the first two hours of search time or for the copying costs of the first 100 pages of duplication.

(b) *Fees to be charged—general provisions.* (1) We may charge search fees even if the records we find are exempt from disclosure, or even if we do not find any records at all.

(2) We will not charge you any fee at all if the costs of routine collection and processing of the fee are likely to equal or exceed the amount of the fee. We have estimated that cost to be $5.00.

(3) If we determine that you are acting alone or with others to break down a single request into a series of requests in order to avoid or reduce the fees charged, we may aggregate all these requests for purposes of calculating the fees charged.

(4) We will charge interest on unpaid bills beginning on the 31st day following the day the bill was sent. The accrual of interest will stop upon receipt of the fee, rather than upon its processing by BBG. Interest will be at the rate prescribed in section 3717 of Title 32 U.S.C.

(c) *Fee schedule—BBG will charge the following fees:* (1) Manual searching for or reviewing of records:

(i) When performed by employees at salary grade GS–1 through GS–8 or FS–9 through FS–5—an hourly rate of $10.00 will be charged;

(ii) When performed by employees at salary grade GS–9 through GS–13 or FS–5 through FS–2—an hourly rate of $20.00 will be charged;

(iii) When performed by employees at salary grade GS–14 or above or FS–2 or above—an hourly rate of $36.00 will be charged.

(iv) When a search involves employees at more than one of these levels, we will charge the appropriate rate for each.

(2) Computer searching and printing. Except in unusual cases, the cost of computer time will not be a factor in calculating the two free hours of search time. In those unusual cases, where the cost of conducting a computerized search significantly detracts from the Agency's ordinary operations, no more than the dollar cost of two hours of manual search time shall be allowed. For searches conducted beyond the first two hours, the Agency shall only charge the direct costs of conducting such searches.

(3) Photocopying standard size pages—$0.15 per page.

(4) Photocopying odd-size documents (such as punchcards or blueprints) or reproducing other records (such as tapes)—the actual cost of operating the machine, plus the actual cost of the materials used, plus charges for the time spent by the operator, at the rates given in paragraph (c)(1) of this section.

(5) Certifying that records are true copies—this service is not required by the FOIA. If we agree to provide it, we will charge $10.00 per certification.

(6) Sending records by express mail, certified mail, or other special methods. This service is not required by the FOIA. If we agree to provide it, we will charge our actual cost.

(7) Performing any other special service that you request and to which we agree—actual cost of operating any machinery, plus actual cost of any materials used, plus charges for the time of our employees, at the rates given in paragraph (c)(1) of this section.

(d) *Procedures for assessing and collecting fees*—(1) *Agreement to pay.* We generally assume that when you request records you are willing to pay the fees we charge for services associated with your request. You may specify a limit on the amount you are willing to spend. We will notify you if it appears that the fees will exceed the limit and ask whether you nevertheless want us to proceed with the search.

(2) *Advance payment.* If you have failed to pay previous bills in a timely manner, or if our initial review of your request indicates that we will charge you fees exceeding $250.00, we will require you to pay your past due fees and/or the estimated fees, or a deposit, before we start searching for the records you want, or before we send them to you. In such cases, the administrative time limits as described in Sec. 503.4(b), will begin only after we come to an agreement with you over payment of fees, or decide that a fee waiver or reduction is appropriate.

(e) *Waiver or reduction of fees.* We will waive or reduce the fees we would otherwise charge if disclosure of the information meets both of the following tests (paragraphs (e)(1) and (e)(2) of this section):

(1) It is in the public interest because it is likely to contribute significantly to public understanding of government operations or activities, regardless of any other public interest it may further. In making this determination, we may consider:

(i) Whether the requester is in a position to contribute to public understanding;

(ii) Whether the requester has such knowledge or expertise as may be necessary to understand the information; and

(iii) Whether the requester's intended use of the information would be likely to disseminate the information among the public.

(2) It is not primarily in the commercial interest of the requester. Commercial interests include interests relating to business, trade, and profit. Not only profit-making corporations have commercial interests; so do nonprofit corporations, individuals, unions, and other associations.

(3) You must make your request for a waiver or reduction at the same time you make your request for records. Only the FOIA Officer may make the decision whether to waive or reduce the fees. If we do not completely grant your request for a waiver or reduction, the denial letter will designate the appeal official.

§ 503.8 Exemptions.

Section 552(b) of the Freedom of Information Act contains nine exemptions to the mandatory disclosure of records. These exemptions and their application by the Agency are described below. In some cases, more than one exemption may apply to the same document. This section does not itself authorize the giving of any pledge of confidentiality by any officer or employee of the Agency.

(a) *Exemption one—National defense and foreign policy.* We are not required to release records that are specifically authorized under criteria established by an Executive Order to be kept secret in the interest of national defense or foreign policy and are in fact properly classified according to such Executive Order. Executive Order No. 12958 (1995) provides for such classification. When the release of certain records may adversely affect U.S. relations with foreign countries, we usually consult with officials with knowledge of those countries and/or with officials of the Department of State. We may also have in our possession records classified by another agency. If we do, we may consult with that agency or may refer your request to that agency for their direct response to you. If possible, we will notify you that we have made such a referral.

(b) *Exemption two—Internal personnel rules and practices.* We are not required to release records that are related solely to the internal personnel rules and practices of an agency. We may withhold routine internal agency procedures such as guard schedules and luncheon periods. We may also withhold internal records the release of which would help some persons circumvent the law or Agency regulations.

(c) *Exemption three—Records exempted by other statutes.* We are not required to release records if another statute specifically allows us to withhold them. Another statute may be used only if it absolutely prohibits disclosure or if it sets forth criteria identifying particular types of material to be withheld (for example, the statute discussed in §503.6).

(d) *Exemption four—Trade secrets and confidential commercial or financial information.* We will withhold trade secrets and commercial or financial information that is obtained from a person and is privileged or confidential.

(1) *Trade secrets:* A trade secret is a secret, commercially valuable plan, formula, process, or device that is used for the making, preparing, compounding, or processing of trade commodities and that can be said to be the end product of either innovation or substantial effort. A direct relationship is necessary between the trade secret and the productive process.

(2) Commercial or financial information, obtained from a person, and is privileged or confidential.

(i) Information is "commercial or financial" if it relates to businesses, commerce, trade, employment, profits, or finances (including personal finances).

(ii) Information is obtained from someone outside the Federal Government or from someone within the Government who has a commercial or financial interest in the information. "Person" includes an individual, partnership, corporation, association, state or foreign government, or other organization. Information is not "obtained from a person" if it is generated by BBG or another Federal agency.

(iii) Information is "privileged" if it would ordinarily be protected from disclosure in civil discovery by a recognized evidentiary privilege, such as the attorney-client privilege, or the work-product privilege. Information may be privileged for this purpose under a privilege belonging to a person outside the Government, unless the providing of the information to the Government rendered the information no longer protectible in civil discovery.

(iv) Information is "confidential" if it meets one of the following tests:

(A) Disclosure may impair the Government's ability to obtain necessary information in the future;

(B) Disclosure would substantially harm the competitive position of the person who submitted the information;

(C) Disclosure would impair other Government interests, such as program effectiveness and compliance; or

(D) Disclosure would impair other private interests, such as an interest in controlling availability of intrinsically valuable records, which are sold in the market by their owner.

(3) *Designation of certain confidential information.* A person who submits records to the Government may designate part or all of the information in such records as exempt from disclosure under Exemption four. The person may make this designation either at the time the records are submitted to the Government or within a reasonable time thereafter. The designation must be in writing. The legend prescribed by a request for proposal or request for quotations according to any agency regulation establishing a substitute for the language is sufficient but not necessary for this purpose. Any such designation will expire ten years after the records were submitted to the Government.

(4) *Predisclosure notification.* The procedures in this paragraph apply to records that were submitted to the Government and where we have substantial reason to believe that information in the records could reasonably be considered exempt under Exemption four. Certain exceptions to these procedures are stated in paragraph (d)(5) of this section.

(i) When we receive a request for such records and we determine that we may be required to disclose them, we will make reasonable efforts to notify the submitter about these facts. The notice will inform the submitter about the procedures and time limits for submission and consideration of objections to disclosure. If we must notify a large number of submitters, we may do this by posting or publishing a notice in a place where the submitters are reasonably likely to become aware of it.

(ii) The submitter has ten (10) working days from receipt of the notice to object to disclosure of any part of the records and to state all bases for its objections.

(iii) We will give consideration to all bases that have been timely stated by the submitter. If we decide to disclose the records and the submitter still does not agree, we will send a written notice to the submitter stating briefly why we did not sustain its objections and we will provide a copy of the records as we intend to release them. The notice will state that we will disclose the records five (5) working days after the submitter receives the notice unless we are ordered by a United States District Court not to release them.

(iv) When a requester files suit under the FOIA to obtain records covered by this paragraph, we will promptly notify the submitter.

(v) Whenever we send a notice to a submitter under paragraph (d)(4)(i) of this section, we will notify you that we are giving the submitter a notice and an opportunity to object.

(5) Exceptions to predisclosure notification. The notice requirements in paragraph (d)(4) of this section do not apply in the following situations:

(i) We decide not to disclose the records;

(ii) The information has previously been published or made generally available;

(iii) We have already notified the submitter of previous requests for the same records and have come to an understanding with that submitter about the records;

(iv) Disclosure is required by a statute other than the FOIA;

(v) Disclosure is required by a regulation, issued after notice and opportunity for public comment that specifies narrow categories of records that are to be disclosed under the FOIA. In this case a submitter may still designate records as described in paragraph (d)(3) of this section and in exceptional cases, at our discretion, may follow the notice procedures in paragraph (d)(4) of this section;

(vi) The designation appears to be obviously frivolous, but in this case we will still give the submitter the written notice required by paragraph (d)(4)(iii) of this section (although this notice need not explain our decision or include a copy of the records); and

(vii) We withhold the information because another statute requires its withholding.

(e) *Exemption five—Internal memoranda.* This exemption covers internal Government communications and notes that fall within a generally recognized evidentiary privilege. Internal Government communications include an agency's communications with an outside consultant or other outside person, with a court, or with Congress, when those communications are for a purpose similar to the purpose of privileged intra-agency communications. Some of the most common applicable privileges are:

(1) *The deliberative process privilege.* This privilege protects predecisional deliberative communications. A communication is protected under this privilege if it was made before a final decision was reached on some question of policy and if it expressed recommendations or opinions on that question. The purpose of this privilege is to prevent injury to the quality of the agency decision making process by encouraging open and frank internal policy discussions, by avoiding premature disclosure of policies not yet adopted, and by avoiding the public confusion that might result from disclosing reasons that were not in fact the ultimate grounds for an agency's decision. This privilege continues to protect pre-decisional documents even after a decision is made. We will release purely factual material in a deliberative document unless that material is otherwise exempt. However, purely factual material in a deliberative document is within this privilege if:

(i) It is inextricably intertwined with the deliberative portions so that it cannot reasonably be segregated; or

(ii) It would reveal the nature of the deliberative portions, or

(iii) Its disclosure would in some other way make possible an intrusion into the decision making process.

(2) *Attorney-client privilege.* This privilege protects confidential communications between a lawyer and an employee or agent of the Government where an attorney-client relationship exists (for example, where the lawyer is acting as attorney for the agency and the employee is communicating on behalf of the agency) and where the employee has communicated information to the attorney in confidence in order to obtain legal advice or assistance,

and/or when the attorney has given advice to the client.

(3) *Attorney work product privilege.* This privilege protects documents prepared by or for an agency, or by or for its representative (usually BBG attorneys) in anticipation of litigation or for trial. It includes documents prepared for purposes of administrative adjudications as well as court litigation. It includes factual material in such documents as well as material revealing opinions and tactics. The privilege continues to protect the documents even after the litigation is closed.

(f) *Exemption six—Clearly unwarranted invasion of personal privacy.* We may withhold personnel, medical, and similar files, and personal information about individuals if disclosure would constitute a clearly unwarranted invasion of personal privacy.

(1) *Balancing test.* In deciding whether to release records that contain personal or private information about someone else to a requester, we weigh the foreseeable harm of invading that individual's privacy against the public benefit that would result from the release of the information. In our evaluation of requests for records, we attempt to guard against the release of information that might involve a violation of personal privacy by a requester being able to "piece together items" or "read between the lines" information that would normally be exempt from mandatory disclosure.

(2) *Information frequently withheld.* We frequently withhold such information as home addresses, home telephone numbers, ages, minority group status, social security numbers, individual's benefits, earning records, leave records, etc.

(g) *Exemption seven—Law enforcement.* We are not required to release information or records that the Government has compiled for law enforcement purposes. The records may apply to actual or potential violations of either criminal or civil laws or regulations. We can withhold these records only to the extent that releasing them would cause harm in at least one of the following situations:

(1) *Enforcement proceedings.* We may withhold information when release could reasonably be expected to interfere with prospective or ongoing law enforcement proceedings, investigations of fraud and mismanagement, employee misconduct, and civil rights violations may fall into this category. In certain cases, we may refuse to confirm or deny the existence of records that relate to violations in order not to disclose that an investigation is in progress or may be conducted.

(2) *Fair trial or impartial adjudication.* We may withhold records when release would deprive a person of a fair trial or an impartial adjudication because of prejudicial publicity.

(3) *Personal privacy.* We are careful not to disclose information that could reasonably be expected to constitute an unwarranted invasion of personal privacy. When a name surfaces in an investigation, that person is likely to be vulnerable to innuendo, rumor, harassment, or retaliation.

(4) *Confidential sources and information.* We may withhold records whose release could reasonably be expected to disclose the identity of a confidential source of information. A confidential source may be an individual; a state, local or foreign Government agency; or any private organization. The exemption applies whether the source provides information under an express promise of confidentiality or under circumstances from which such an assurance could be reasonably inferred. Also, where the record or information in it has been compiled by a criminal law enforcement authority conducting a criminal investigation or by an agency conducting a lawful national security investigation, the exemption also protects all information supplied by a confidential source. Also protected from mandatory disclosure is any information which, if disclosed, could reasonably be expected to jeopardize the system of confidentiality that assures a flow of information from sources to investigatory agencies.

(5) *Techniques and procedures.* We may withhold records reflecting special techniques or procedures of investigation or prosecution not otherwise generally known to the public. In some cases, it is not possible to describe even in general terms those techniques without disclosing the very material to

be withheld. We may also withhold records whose release would disclose guidelines for law enforcement investigations or prosecutions if this disclosure could reasonably be expected to create a risk that someone could circumvent requirements of law or of regulation.

(6) *Life and physical safety.* We may withhold records whose disclosure could reasonably be expected to endanger the life or physical safety of any individual. This protection extends to threats and harassment as well as to physical violence.

(h) *Exemptions eight and nine—Records on financial institutions and records on wells.* (1) Exemption eight permits us to withhold records about regulation or supervision of financial institutions.

(2) Exemption nine permits the withholding of geological and geophysical information and data, including maps concerning wells.

§ 503.9 Electronic records.

(a) *Introduction.* This section applies to all records of the BBG, including all of its worldwide operations. Congress enacted the FOIA to require Federal agencies to make records available to the public through public inspections and at the request of any person for any public or private use. The increase in the Government's use of computers enhances the public's access to Government information. This section addresses and explains how records will be reviewed and released when the records are maintained in electronic format. Documentation not previously subject to the FOIA when maintained in a non-electronic format is not made subject to FOIA by this law.

(b) *Definitions*—(1) *Compelling need.* Obtaining records on an expedited basis because of an imminent threat to the life or physical safety of an individual, or urgently needed by an individual primarily engaged in disseminating information to the public concerning actual or alleged Federal Government activities.

(2) *Discretionary disclosure.* Records or information normally exempt from disclosure will be released whenever it is possible to do so without reasonably foreseeable harm to any interest protected by an FOIA exemption.

(3) *Electronic reading room.* The room provided which makes electronic records available.

(c) *Electronic format of records.* (1) Materials such as agency opinions and policy statements (available for public inspection and copying) will be available electronically by accessing the BBG's Home Page via the Internet at *http://www.ibb.gov.* To set up an appointment to view such records in hard copy or to access the Internet via the BBG's computer, please contact the FOIA/Privacy Act Officer at (202) 260–4404.

(2) We will make available for public inspection and copying, both electronically via the Internet and in hard copy, those records that have been previously released in response to FOIA requests, when we determine the records have been or are likely to be the subject of future requests.

(3) We will provide both electronically through our Internet address and in hard copy a "Guide" on how to make an FOIA request, and an Index of all Agency information systems and records that may be requested under the FOIA.

(4) We may delete identifying details when we publish or make available the index and copies of previously-released records to prevent a clearly unwarranted invasion of personal privacy.

(i) We will indicate the extent of any deletions made from the place the deletion was made, if possible.

(ii) We will not reveal information about deletions if such disclosure would harm an interest protected by an exemption.

(d) *Honoring form or format requests.* We will aid requesters by providing records and information in the form requested, including electronic format, if we can readily reproduce them in that form or format. However, if we cannot accommodate you, we will provide responsive, nonexempt information in a reasonably accessible form.

(1) We will make a reasonable effort to search for records kept in an electronic format. However, if the effort would significantly interfere with the operations of the agency or the agency's use of its computers, we will consider the effort to be unreasonable.

(2) We need not create documents that do not exist, but computer records found in a database rather than in a file cabinet may require the application of codes or some form of programming to retrieve the information. This application of codes or programming of records will not amount to the creation of records.

(3) Except in unusual cases, the cost of computer time will not be a factor in calculating the two free hours of search time available under Sec. 503.7. In those unusual cases, where the cost of conducting a computerized search significantly detracts from the agency's ordinary operations, no more than the dollar cost of two hours of manual search time shall be allowed. For searches conducted beyond the first two hours, the agency shall only charge the direct costs of conducting such searches.

(e) *Technical feasibility of redacting non-releasable material.* We will make every effort to indicate the place on the record where a redaction of non-releasable material is made, and an FOIA citation noting the applicable exemption for the deletion will also be placed at the site. If unable to do so, we will notify you of that fact.

(f) *Ensuring timely response to request.* We will make every attempt to respond to FOIA requests within the prescribed 20 working-day time limit. However, processing some requests may require additional time in order to properly screen material against the inadvertent disclosure of material covered by the exemptions.

(1) *Multitrack first-in first-out processing.* (i) Because the agency expects to be able to process its requests without a backlog of cases, BBG will not institute a multitract system. Those cases that may be handled easily, because they require only a few documents or a simple answer, will be handled immediately by an FOIA specialist.

(ii) If you wish to qualify for faster processing, you may limit the scope of your request so that we may respond more quickly.

(2) *Unusual circumstances.* (i) The agency may extend for a maximum of ten working days the statutory time limit for responding to an FOIA request by giving notice in writing as to the reason for such an extension. The reasons for such an extension may include: the need to search for and collect requested records from multiple offices; the volume of records requested; and, the need for consultation with other components within the agency.

(ii) If an extra ten days still does not provide sufficient time for the Agency to deal with your request, we will inform you that the request cannot be processed within the statutory time limit and provide you with the opportunity to limit the scope of your request and/or arrange with us a negotiated deadline for processing your request.

(iii) If you refuse to reasonably limit the scope of your request or refuse to agree upon a time frame, the agency will process your case, as it would have, had no modification been sought. We will make a diligent, good-faith effort to complete our review within the statutory time frame.

(3) *Grouping of requests.* We will group together requests that clearly involve related material that should be considered as a single request.

(i) If you make multiple or related requests for similar material for the purpose of avoiding costs, we will notify you that we are grouping together your requests, and the reasons why.

(ii) Multiple or related requests may also be grouped, such as those involving requests and schedules but you will be notified in advance if we intend to do so.

(g) *Time periods for agency consideration of requests*—(1) *Expedited access.* We will authorize expedited access to requesters who show a compelling need for access, but the burden is on the requester to prove that expedition is appropriate. We will determine within ten days whether or not to grant a request for expedited access and we will notify the requester of our decision.

(2) *Compelling need for expedited access.* Failure to obtain the records within an expedited deadline must pose an imminent threat to an individual's life or physical safety; or the request must be made by someone primarily engaged in disseminating information, and who has an urgency to inform the

public about actual or alleged Federal Government activity.

(3) *How to request expedited access.* We will be required to make factual and subjective judgments about the circumstances cited by requesters to qualify them for expedited processing. To request expedited access, your request must be in writing and it must explain in detail your basis for seeking expedited access. The categories for compelling need are intended to be narrowly applied:

(i) *A threat to an individual's life or physical safety.* A threat to an individual's life or physical safety should be imminent to qualify for expedited access to the records. You must include the reason why a delay in obtaining the information could reasonably be foreseen to cause significant adverse consequences to a recognized interest.

(ii) *Urgency to inform.* The information requested should pertain to a matter of a current exigency to the American public, where delay in response would compromise a significant recognized interest. The person requesting expedited access under an "urgency to inform," must be primarily engaged in the dissemination of information. This does not include individuals who are engaged only incidentally in the dissemination of information. "Primarily engaged" requires that information dissemination be the main activity of the requester. A requester only incidentally engaged in information dissemination, besides other activities, would not satisfy this requirement. The public's right to know, although a significant and important value, would not by itself be sufficient to satisfy this standard.

(4) *Estimation of matter denied.* The agency will try to estimate the volume of any denied material and provide the estimate to the requester, unless doing so would harm an interest protected by an exemption.

(h) *Computer redaction.* The agency will identify the location of deletions in the released portion of the records, and where technologically possible, will show the deletion at the place on the record where the deletion was made, unless including that indication would harm an interest protected by an exemption.

(i) *Annual report on FOIA activities.* Reports on FOIA activities are submitted each fiscal year to the Department of Justice, and are due by February 1 of every year. The BBG's report will be available both in hard copy and through the Internet. The Department of Justice will also report all Federal agency FOIA activity through electronic means.

(j) *Reference materials and guides.* The agency has available in hard copy, and electronically through the Internet, a guide for requesting records under the FOIA, and an index and description of all major information systems of the agency. The guide is a simple explanation of what the FOIA is intended to do, and how you can use it to access BBG records. The Index explains the types of records that may be requested from the Agency through FOIA requests and why some records cannot, by law, be made available by the BBG.

PART 504—TESTIMONY BY BBG EMPLOYEES, PRODUCTION OF OFFICIAL RECORDS, AND DISCLOSURE OF OFFICIAL INFORMATION IN LEGAL PROCEEDINGS

Subpart A—General Provisions

Subpart B—Demands or Requests for Testimony and Production of Documents

Subpart C—Schedule of Fees

Subpart D—Penalties

504.15 Penalties

AUTHORITY: 22 U.S.C. 6204.

SOURCE: 72 FR 19798, Apr. 20, 2007, unless otherwise noted.

Subpart A—General Provisions

§ 504.1 Scope and purpose.

(a) These regulations in this subpart establish policy, assign responsibilities and prescribe procedures with respect to:

(1) The production or disclosure of official information or records by BBG employees, and

(2) The testimony of current and former BBG employees, relating to official information, official duties, or the BBG's records, in connection with federal or state litigation in which the BBG is not a party.

(b) The BBG intends these provisions to:

(1) Conserve the time of BBG employees for conducting official business;

(2) Minimize the involvement of BBG employees in issues unrelated to BBG's mission;

(3) Maintain the impartiality of BBG employees in disputes between private litigants; and

(4) Protect sensitive, confidential information and the deliberative processes of the BBG.

(c) In providing for these requirements, the BBG does not waive the sovereign immunity of the United States.

(d) This part provides guidance for the internal operations of BBG. It does not create any right or benefit, substantive or procedural, that a party may rely upon in any legal proceeding against the United States.

§ 504.2 Applicability.

This part applies to demands and requests to current and former employees for factual or expert testimony relating to official information or official duties or for production of official records or information, in legal proceedings in which the BBG is not a named party. This part does not apply to:

(a) Demands upon or requests for a BBG employee to testify as to facts or events that are unrelated to his or her official duties or that are unrelated to the functions of the BBG;

(b) Demands upon or requests for a former BBG employee to testify as to matters in which the former employee was not directly or materially involved while at the BBG;

(c) Requests for the release of records under the Freedom of Information Act, 5 U.S.C. 552, or the Privacy Act, 5 U.S.C. 552a; or

(d) Congressional demands and requests for testimony, records or information.

§ 504.3 Definitions.

The following definitions apply to this part:

(a) Demand means an order, subpoena, or other command of a court or other competent authority for the production, disclosure, or release of records or for the appearance and testimony of a BBG employee in a legal proceeding.

(b) General Counsel means the General Counsel of the BBG or a person to whom the General Counsel has delegated authority under this part.

(c) Legal proceeding means any matter before a court of law, administrative board or tribunal, commission, administrative law judge, hearing officer or other body that conducts a legal or administrative proceeding. Legal proceeding includes all phases of litigation.

(d) BBG means the Broadcasting Board of Governors.

(e) BBG employee means:

(1) Any current or former employee of the BBG.

(2) This definition does not include persons who are no longer employed by the BBG and who agree to testify about general matters, matters available to the public, or matters with which they had no specific involvement or responsibility during their employment with the BBG.

(f) Records or official records and information means all information in the custody and control of the BBG, relating to information in the custody and control of the BBG, or acquired by a BBG employee in the performance of his or her official duties or because of his or her official status, while the individual was employed by the BBG.

(g) *Request* means any informal request, by whatever method, for the production of records and information or for testimony which has not been ordered by a court or other competent authority.

(h) *Testimony* means any written or oral statements, including depositions, answers to interrogatories, affidavits, declarations, interviews, and statements made by an individual in connection with a legal proceeding.

Subpart B—Demands or Requests for Testimony and Production of Documents

§ 504.4 General prohibition.

(a) In any United States federal, state, and local proceeding or administrative action, or proceeding or administrative action conducted in a foreign country, in which the BBG is not a party, no BBG employee shall, in response to a demand or request for official records or information, furnish or produce documents or testimony as to any material contained in BBG files, any information relating to or based upon material contained in BBG files, or any information or material acquired as part of the performance of that person's official duties (or because of that person's official status) without the prior written approval of the General Counsel.

(b) Whenever a request or demand for information is made upon a BBG employee, the employee, wherever located, shall immediately prepare a report that specifically describes the testimony or documents sought and immediately notify the General Counsel. The BBG employee shall then await instructions from the General Counsel concerning a response to the request or demand. The failure of any BBG employee to follow the procedures specified in this subpart neither creates nor confers any rights, privileges, or benefits on any person or party.

§ 504.5 Factors the BBG will consider.

The General Counsel, in his or her sole discretion, may grant an employee permission to testify on matters relating to official information, or produce official records and information, in response to a demand or request. Among the relevant factors that the General Counsel may consider in making this decision are whether:

(a) The purposes of this part are met;

(b) Allowing such testimony or production of records would be necessary to prevent a miscarriage of justice;

(c) Allowing such testimony or production of records would assist or hinder the BBG in performing its statutory duties;

(d) Allowing such testimony or production of records would be in the best interest of the BBG or the United States;

(e) The records or testimony can be obtained from other sources;

(f) The demand or request is unduly burdensome or otherwise inappropriate under the applicable rules of discovery or the rules of procedure governing the case or matter in which the demand or request arose;

(g) Disclosure would violate a statute, Executive Order or regulation;

(h) Disclosure would reveal confidential, sensitive, or privileged information, trade secrets or similar, confidential or financial information, otherwise protected information, or information which would otherwise be inappropriate for release;

(i) Disclosure would impede or interfere with an ongoing law enforcement investigation or proceeding, or compromise constitutional rights or national security interests;

(j) Disclosure would result in the BBG appearing to favor one litigant over another;

(k) The request was served before the demand;

(l) A substantial Government interest is implicated;

(m) The demand or request is within the authority of the party making it; and

(n) The demand or request is sufficiently specific to be answered and/or can be limited to information to that which would be consistent with the factors specified herein.

§ 504.6 Filing requirements for litigants seeking documents or testimony.

A litigant must comply with the following requirements when filing a request for official records and information or testimony under this subpart. A request should be filed before a demand.

(a) The request must be in writing and must be submitted to the General Counsel.

(b) The written request must contain the following information:

(1) The caption of the legal proceeding, docket number, and name and address of the court or other authority involved;

(2) A copy of the complaint or equivalent document setting forth the assertions in the case and any other pleading or document necessary to show relevance;

(3) A list of categories of records sought, a detailed description of how the information sought is relevant to the issues in the legal proceeding, and a specific description of the substance of the testimony or records sought;

(4) A statement as to how the need for the information outweighs any need to maintain the confidentiality of the information and outweighs the burden on the BBG to produce the records or provide testimony;

(5) A statement indicating that the information sought is not available from another source, from other persons or entities, or from the testimony of someone other than an BBG employee, such as a retained expert;

(6) If testimony is requested, the intended use of the testimony, and a showing that no document could be provided and used in lieu of testimony;

(7) A description of all prior decisions, orders, or pending motions in the case that bear upon the relevance of the requested records or testimony;

(8) The name, address, and telephone number of counsel to each party in the case; and

(9) An estimate of the amount of time that the requester and other parties will require for each BBG employee for time spent by the employee to prepare for testimony, in travel, and for attendance in the legal proceeding.

(c) The BBG reserves the right to require additional information to complete the request where appropriate.

(d) The request should be submitted at least 30 days before the date that records or testimony is required. Requests submitted in less than 30 days before records or testimony is required must be accompanied by a written explanation stating the reasons for the late request and the reasons for expedited processing.

(e) Failure to cooperate in good faith to enable the General Counsel to make an informed decision may serve as the basis for a determination not to comply with the request.

(f) The request should state that the requester will provide a copy of the BBG employee's statement free of charge and that the requester will permit the BBG to have a representative present during the employee's testimony.

§ 504.7 Service of requests or demands.

Requests or demands for official records or information or testimony under this Subpart must be served on the General Counsel, BBG, 330 Independence Ave., SW., Washington, DC 20237 by mail or fax at (202) 203–4585 and clearly marked "Part 504—Request for Testimony or Official Records in Legal Proceedings."

§ 504.8 Processing requests or demands.

(a) After receiving service of a request or demand for testimony, the General Counsel will review the request and, in accordance with the provisions of this Subpart, determine whether, or under what conditions, to authorize the employee to testify on matters relating to official information and/or produce official records and information.

(b) Absent exigent circumstances, the BBG will issue a determination within 30 days from the date the request is received.

(c) The General Counsel may grant a waiver of any procedure described by this Subpart where a waiver is considered necessary to promote a significant interest of the BBG or the United States, or for other good cause.

(d) Certification (authentication) of copies of records. The BBG may certify that records are true copies in order to facilitate their use as evidence. If a requester seeks certification, the requester must request certified copies from the BBG at least 30 days before the date they will be needed. The request should be sent to the BBG General Counsel.

§ 504.9 Final determinations.

The General Counsel makes the final determination on demands or requests to employees for production of official records and information or testimony in litigation in which the BBG is not a party. All final determinations are within the sole discretion of the General Counsel. The General Counsel will notify the requester and, when appropriate, the court or other competent authority of the final determination, the reasons for the grant or denial of the request, and any conditions that the General Counsel may impose on the release of records or information, or on the testimony of an BBG employee. The General Counsel's decision exhausts administrative remedies for discovery of the information.

§ 504.10 Restrictions that apply to testimony.

(a) The General Counsel may impose conditions or restrictions on the testimony of BBG employees including, for example:

(1) Limiting the areas of testimony;

(2) Requiring the requester and other parties to the legal proceeding to agree that the transcript of the testimony will be kept under seal;

(3) Requiring that the transcript will be used or made available only in the particular legal proceeding for which testimony was requested. The General Counsel may also require a copy of the transcript of testimony at the requester's expense.

(b) The BBG may offer the employee's written declaration in lieu of testimony.

(c) If authorized to testify pursuant to this part, an employee may testify as to facts within his or her personal knowledge, but, unless specifically authorized to do so by the General Counsel, the employee shall not:

(1) Disclose confidential or privileged information; or

(2) For a current BBG employee, testify as an expert or opinion witness with regard to any matter arising out of the employee's official duties or the functions of the BBG unless testimony is being given on behalf of the United States (see also 5 CFR 2635.805).

(d) The scheduling of an employee's testimony, including the amount of time that the employee will be made available for testimony, will be subject to the BBG's approval.

§ 504.11 Restrictions that apply to released records.

(a) The General Counsel may impose conditions or restrictions on the release of official records and information, including the requirement that parties to the proceeding obtain a protective order or execute a confidentiality agreement to limit access and any further disclosure. The terms of the protective order or of a confidentiality agreement must be acceptable to the General Counsel. In cases where protective orders or confidentiality agreements have already been executed, the BBG may condition the release of official records and information on an amendment to the existing protective order or confidentiality agreement.

(b) If the General Counsel so determines, original BBG records may be presented for examination in response to a request, but they may not be presented as evidence or otherwise used in a manner by which they could lose their identity as official BBG records, nor may they be marked or altered. In lieu of the original records, certified copies may be presented for evidentiary purposes.

§ 504.12 Procedure when a decision is not made prior to the time a response is required.

If a response to a demand or request is required before the General Counsel can make the determination referred to in § 504.9, the General Counsel, when necessary, will provide the court or other competent authority with a copy of this part, inform the court or other competent authority that the request is being reviewed, provide an estimate as to when a decision will be made, and seek a stay of the demand or request pending a final determination.

§ 504.13 Procedure in the event of an adverse ruling.

If the court or other competent authority fails to stay a demand or request, the employee upon whom the demand or request is made, unless otherwise advised by the General Counsel, will appear, if necessary, at the stated time and place, produce a copy of this part, state that the employee has been advised by counsel not to provide the requested testimony or produce documents, and respectfully decline to comply with the demand or request, citing *United States ex rel. Touhy* v. *Ragen*, 340 U.S. 462 (1951).

Subpart C—Schedule of Fees

§ 504.14 Fees.

(a) *Generally*. The General Counsel may condition the production of records or appearance for testimony upon advance payment of a reasonable estimate of the costs to the BBG.

(b) *Fees for records*. Fees for producing records will include fees for searching, reviewing, and duplicating records, costs of attorney time spent in reviewing the request, and expenses generated by materials and equipment used to search for, produce, and copy the responsive information. Costs for employee time will be calculated on the basis of the hourly pay of the employee (including all pay, allowances, and benefits). Fees for duplication will be the same as those charged by the BBG in its Freedom of Information Act regulations at 22 CFR Part 503.

(c) *Witness fees*. Fees for attendance by a witness will include fees, expenses, and allowances prescribed by the court's rules. If no such fees are prescribed, witness fees will be determined based upon the rule of the Federal district court closest to the location where the witness will appear and on 28 U.S.C. 1821, as applicable. Such fees will include cost of time spent by the witness to prepare for testimony, in travel and for attendance in the legal proceeding, plus travel costs.

(d) *Payment of fees*. A requester must pay witness fees for current BBG employees and any record certification fees by submitting to the General Counsel a check or money order for the appropriate amount made payable to the Treasury of the United States. In the case of testimony of former BBG employees, the requester must pay applicable fees directly to the former BBG employee in accordance with 28 U.S.C. 1821 or other applicable statutes.

(e) *Waiver or reduction of fees*. The General Counsel, in his or her sole discretion, may, upon a showing of reasonable cause, waive or reduce any fees in connection with the testimony, production, or certification of records.

(f) *De minimis fees*. Fees will not be assessed if the total charge would be $10.00 or less.

Subpart D—Penalties

§ 504.15 Penalties.

(a) An employee who discloses official records or information or gives testimony relating to official information, except as expressly authorized by the BBG, or as ordered by a Federal court after the BBG has had the opportunity to be heard, may face penalties as provided in any applicable enforcement statute.

(b) A current BBG employee who testifies or produces official records and information in violation of this part shall be subject to disciplinary action and, if done for a valuable consideration, may subject that person to criminal prosecution.

PART 505—PRIVACY ACT REGULATION

Sec.

AUTHORITY: Pub. L. 93–579, 88 Stat. 1897; 5 U.S.C. 552a.

SOURCE: 67 FR 8875, Feb. 27, 2002, unless otherwise noted.

§ 505.1 Purpose and scope.

The Broadcasting Board of Governors (BBG) will protect individuals' privacy from misuses of their records, and grant individuals access to records concerning them which are maintained by the Agency's domestic and overseas offices, consistent with the provisions of Public Law 93-579, 88 Stat. 1897; 5 U.S.C. 552a, the Privacy Act of 1974, as amended. The Agency has also established procedures to permit individuals to amend incorrect records, to limit the disclosure of personal information to third parties, and to limit the number of sources of personal information. The Agency has also established internal rules restricting requirements of individuals to provide social security account numbers.

§ 505.2 Definitions.

(a) *Access Appeal Committee (AAC).* The body established by and responsible to the Broadcasting Board for reviewing appeals made by individuals to amend records held by the Agency.

(b) *Agency, BBG, our, we* or *us.* The BBG, its offices, divisions, branches and its worldwide operations.

(c) *Amend.* To make a correction to or expunge any portion of a record about an individual which that individual believes is not accurate, relevant, timely or complete.

(d) *Individual* or *you.* A citizen of the United States or an alien lawfully admitted for permanent residence.

(e) *Maintain.* Collect, use, store, disseminate or any combination of these record keeping functions; exercise of control over and hence responsibility and accountability for systems of records.

(f) *Record.* Any information maintained by the Agency about an individual that can be reproduced, including finger or voice prints and photographs, and which is retrieved by that particular individual's name or personal identifier, such as a social security number.

(g) *Routine use.* With respect to the disclosure of a record, the use of such record for a purpose, which is compatible with the purpose for which it was collected. The common ordinary purposes for which records are used and all of the proper and necessary uses even if any such uses occur infrequently.

(h) *Statistical record.* A record in a system of records maintained for statistical research or reporting purposes only and not used in whole or in part in making any determination about an identifiable individual, except as provided in 12 U.S.C.8.

(i) *System of records.* A group of records under the maintenance and control of the Agency from which information is retrieved by the name or personal identifier of the individual.

(j) *Personnel record.* Any information about an individual that is maintained in a system of records by the Agency that is needed for personnel management or processes such as staffing, employee development, retirement, grievances and appeals.

(k) *Worldwide Operations.* Any of the foreign service establishments of the Agency.

§ 505.3 Procedures for requests.

(a) The agency will consider all written requests received from an individual for records pertaining to herself/ himself as a request made under the Privacy Act of 1974, as amended (5 U.S.C. 552a) whether or not the individual specifically cites the Privacy Act when making the request.

(b) All requests under the Privacy Act should be directed to the FOIA/Privacy Act Office, Office of the General Counsel, Broadcasting Board of Governors, Suite 3349, 330 Independence Avenue, SW, Washington, DC 20237, which will coordinate the search of all systems of records specified in the request. Requests should state name, date of birth, and social security number.

(c) Requests directed to any of the Agency's worldwide establishments which involve routine unclassified, administrative and personnel records available only at those establishments may be released to the individual by the establishment if it determines that such a release is authorized by the Privacy Act. All other requests shall be submitted by the establishment to the

FOIA/Privacy Act Office, Office of the General Counsel, Broadcasting Board of Governors, Suite 3349, 330 Independence Avenue, SW, Washington, DC 20237, and the individual shall be so notified of this section in writing, when possible.

(d) In those instances where an individual requests records pertaining to herself/himself, as well as records pertaining to another individual, group or some other category of the Agency's records, only that portion of the request which pertains to records concerning the individual will be treated as a Privacy Act request. The remaining portions of such a request will be processed as a Freedom of Information Act request and sent to the office noted in paragraph (b) of this section.

§ 505.4 Requirements and identification for making requests.

(a) When you seek access to Agency records, you may present your written request, fax it to (202) 260–4394 or mail it to the FOIA/Privacy Act Office, Office of the General Counsel, Broadcasting Board of Governors, Suite 3349, 330 Independence Avenue, SW, Washington, DC 20237. The FOIA/Privacy Act Office may be visited between the hours of 9 a.m. and 3 p.m., Monday through Friday, except for legal holidays.

(b) When you seek access to Agency records, you will be requested to present identification. You must state your full name, date of birth and social security number. You must also include your present mailing address and zip code, and if possible, a telephone number.

(c) When signing a statement confirming your identity, you should understand that knowingly and willfully seeking or obtaining access to records about another person under false pretenses is punishable by a fine of up to $5,000.

§ 505.5 Disclosure of information.

(a) In order to locate the system of records that you believe may contain information about you, you should first obtain a copy of the Agency's Notice of Systems of Records. By identifying a particular record system and by furnishing all the identifying information requested by that record system, it would enable us to more easily locate those records which pertain to you. At a minimum, any request should include the information specified in Sec. 505.4(b).

(b) In certain circumstances, it may be necessary for us to request additional information from you to ensure that the retrieved record does, in fact, pertain to you.

(c) All requests for information on whether or not the Agency's systems of records contain information about you will be acknowledged within 20 working days of receipt of that request. The requested records will be provided as soon as possible thereafter.

(d) If the Agency determines that the substance of the requested record is exceptionally sensitive, we will require you to furnish a signed, notarized statement that you are in fact the person named in the file before granting access to the records.

(e) Original records will not be furnished subject to and in accordance with fees established in § 505.11.

(f) Denial of access to records:

(1) The requirements of this section do not entitle you access to any information compiled in reasonable anticipation of a civil action or proceeding.

(2) Under the Privacy Act, we are not required to permit access to records if the information is not retrievable by your name or other personal identifier; those requests will be processed as Freedom of Information Act requests.

(3) We may deny you access to a record, or portion thereof, if following a review it is determined that the record or portion falls within a system of records that is exempt from disclosure according to 5 U.S.C. 552a(j) and 552a(k). See §§ 505.13 and 505.14 for a listing of general and specific exemptions.

(4) The decision to deny access to a record or a portion of the record is made by the Agency's Privacy Act Officer. The denial letter will advise you of your right to appeal the denial (See § 505.9 on Access Appeal Committee's review).

§ 505.6 Medical records.

If, in the judgment of the Agency, the release of medical information to you could have an adverse effect, the Agency will arrange an acceptable alternative to granting access of such records directly to you. This normally involves the release of the information to a doctor named by you. However, this special procedure provision does not in any way limit your absolute right to receive a complete copy of your medical record.

§ 505.7 Correction or amendment of record.

(a) You have the right to request that we amend a record pertaining to you which you believe is not accurate, relevant, timely, or complete. At the time we grant access to a record, we will furnish guidelines for you to request amendment to the record.

(b) Requests for amendments to records must be in writing and mailed or delivered to the FOIA/Privacy Act Officer, FOIA/Privacy Act Office, Office of the General Counsel, Broadcasting Board of Governors, Suite 3349, 330 Independence Avenue, SW, Washington, DC 20237, who will coordinate the review of the request to amend the record with the appropriate office(s). Such requests must contain, at a minimum, identifying information needed to locate the record, a brief description of the item or items of information to be amended, and the reason for the requested change. The requester should submit as much documentation, arguments or other data as seems warranted to support the request for amendment.

(c) We will review all requests for amendments to records within 20 working days of receipt of the request and either make the changes or inform you of our refusal to do so and the reasons.

§ 505.8 Agency review of requests for changes.

(a) In reviewing a record in response to a request to amend or correct a file, we will incorporate the criteria of accuracy, relevance, timeliness, and completeness of the record in the review.

(b) If we agree with you to amend your records, we will:

(1) Advise you in writing;

(2) Correct the record accordingly;

(3) And, to the extent that an accounting of disclosure was maintained, advise all previous recipients of the record of the corrections.

(c) If we disagree with all or any portion of your request to amend a record, we will:

(1) Advise you of the reasons for the determination; and

(2) Inform you of your right to further review (see Sec. 505.9).

§ 505.9 Review of adverse agency determination.

(a) When we determine to deny a request to amend a record, or portion of the record, you may request further review by the Agency's Access Appeal Committee. The written request for review should be mailed to the Chairperson, Access Appeal Committee, FOIA/Privacy Act Office, Office of the General Counsel, Broadcasting Board of Governors, Suite 3349, 330 Independence Avenue, SW., Washington, DC 20237. The letter should include any documentation, information or statement, which substantiates your request for review.

(b) The Agency's Access Appeal Committee will review the Agency's initial denial to amend the record and your documentation supporting amendment, within 30 working days. If additional time is required, you will be notified in writing of the reasons for the delay and the approximate date when the review is expected to be completed. Upon completion of the review, the Chairperson will notify you of the results.

(c) If the Committee upholds the Agency's denial to amend the record, the Chairperson will advise you of:

(1) The reasons for our refusal to amend the record;

(2) Your right and the procedure to add to the file a concise statement supporting your disagreement with the decision of the Agency; and

(3) Your right to seek judicial review of the Agency's refusal to amend the file.

(d) When you file a statement disagreeing with our refusal to amend a record, we will clearly annotate the record so that the fact that the record is disputed is apparent to anyone who may subsequently have access to, use of, or reason to disclose the file. If information is disclosed regarding the area of dispute, we will provide a copy of your statement in the disclosure. Any statement, which may be included by the Agency regarding the dispute, will be limited to the reasons given to you for not amending the record. Copies of our statement shall be treated as part of your record, but will not be subject to amendment by you under these regulations.

§ 505.10 Disclosure to third parties.

We will not disclose any information about you to any person or another agency without your prior consent, except as provided for in the following paragraphs:

(a) *Medical records.* May be disclosed to a doctor or other medical practitioner, named by you, as prescribed in Sec. 505.6.

(b) *Accompanying individual.* When you are accompanied by any other person, we will require that you sign a statement granting consent to the disclosure of the contents of your record to that person.

(c) *Designees.* If a person requests another person's file, he or she must present a signed statement from the person of record that authorizes and consents to the release of the file to the designated individual.

(d) *Guardians.* Parents or legal guardians) of dependent minors or of an individual who has been declared by a court to be incompetent due to physical, mental or age incapacity, may act for and on behalf of the individual on whom the Agency maintains records.

(e) *Other disclosures.* A record may be disclosed without a request by or written consent of the individual to whom the record pertains if such disclosure conditions are authorized in accordance, with 5 U.S.C. 552a(b). These conditions are:

(1) *Disclosure within the Agency.* This condition is based upon a "need-to-know" concept, which recognizes that Agency personnel may require access to discharge their duties.

(2) *Disclosure to the public.* No consent by an individual is necessary if the record is required to be released under the Freedom of Information Act (FOIA), 5 U.S.C. 552. The record may be exempt, however, under one of the nine exemptions of the FOIA.

(3) *Disclosure for a routine use.* No consent by an individual is necessary if the condition is necessary for a "routine use" as defined in Sec. 505.2(g). Information may also be released to other government agencies, that have statutory or other lawful authority to maintain such information.

(4) *Disclosure to the Bureau of the Census.* For purposes of planning or carrying out a census or survey or related activity. Title 13 U.S.C. Section 8 limits the uses of these records and also makes them immune from compulsory disclosure.

(5) *Disclosure for statistical research and reporting.* The Agency will provide the statistical information requested only after all names and personal identifiers have been deleted from the records.

(6) *Disclosure to the National Archives.* For the preservation of records of historical value, according to 44 U.S.C. 2103.

(7) *Disclosure for law enforcement purposes.* Upon receipt of a written request by another Federal agency or a state or local government describing the law enforcement purpose for which a record is required, and specifying the particular record. Blanket requests for all records pertaining to an individual are not permitted under the Privacy Act.

(8) *Disclosure under emergency circumstances.* For the safety or health of an individual (e.g., medical records on a patient undergoing emergency treatment).

(9) *Disclosure to the Congress.* For matters within the jurisdiction of any House or Senate committee or subcommittee, and/or joint committee or subcommittee, but only when requested in writing from the Chairman of the committee or subcommittee.

(10) *Disclosure to the General Accounting Office (GAO).* For matters within the jurisdiction of the duties of the GAO's Comptroller General.

(11) *Disclosure according to court order.* According to the order of a court of competent jurisdiction. This does not include a subpoena for records requested by counsel and issued by a clerk of court.

§ 505.11 Fees.

(a) The first copy of any Agency record about you will be provided free of charge. A fee of $0.15 per page will be charged for any additional copies requested by you.

(b) Checks or money orders should be made payable to the United States Treasurer and mailed to the FOIA/Privacy Act Office, Office of the General Counsel, Broadcasting Board of Governors, Suite 3349, 330 Independence Avenue, SW., Washington, DC 20237. The Agency will not accept cash.

§ 505.12 Civil remedies and criminal penalties.

(a) *Grounds for court action.* You will have a remedy in the Federal District Court under the following circumstances:

(1) *Denial of access.* You may challenge our decision to deny you access to records to which you consider yourself entitled.

(2) *Refusal to amend a record.* Under the conditions of 5 U.S.C. 552a(g), you may seek judicial review of the Agency's refusal to amend a record.

(3) *Failure to maintain a record accurately.* You may bring suit against the Agency for any alleged intentional and willful failure to maintain a record accurately, if it can be shown that you were subjected to an adverse action resulting in the denial of aright, benefit, entitlement or employment you could reasonably have been expected to be granted if the record had not been deficient.

(4) *Other failures to comply with the Act.* You may bring an action for any alleged failure by the Agency to comply with the requirements of the Act or failure to comply with any rule published by the Agency to implement the Act provided it can be shown that:

(i) The action was intentional or willful;

(ii) The Agency's action adversely affected you; and

(iii) The adverse action was caused by the Agency's actions.

(b) *Jurisdiction and time limits.* (1) Action may be brought in the district court for the jurisdiction in which you reside or have a place of residence or business, or in which the Agency records are situated, or in the District of Columbia.

(2) The statute of limitations is two years from the date upon which the cause of action arises, except for cases in which the Agency has materially and willfully misrepresented any information requested to be disclosed and when such misrepresentation is material to the liability of the Agency. In such cases the statute of limitations is two years from the date of discovery of the misrepresentation by you.

(3) A suit may not be brought on the basis of injury, which may have occurred as a result of the Agency's disclosure of a record prior to September 27, 1975.

(c) *Criminal penalties*—(1) *Unauthorized disclosure.* It is a criminal violation of the provisions of the Act for any officer or employee of the Agency to knowingly and willfully disclose a record in any manner to any person or agency not entitled to receive it, for failure to meet the conditions of disclosure listed in S U.S.C. 552a(b), or without the written consent or at the request of the individual to whom the record pertains. Any officer or employee of the Agency found guilty of such misconduct shall be fined not more than $5,000.

(2) *Failure to publish a public notice.* It is a criminal violation of the Act to willfully maintain a system of records and not publish the prescribed public notice. Any officer or employee of the Agency found guilty of such misconduct shall be fined not more than $5,000.

(3) *Obtaining records under false pretenses.* The Act makes it a criminal offense to knowingly and willfully request or gain access to a record about an individual under false pretenses. Any person found guilty of such an offense may be fined not more than $5,000.

§ 505.13 General exemptions (Subsection (j)).

(a) General exemptions are available for systems of records which are maintained by the Central Intelligence Agency (Subsection (j)(1)), or maintained by an agency which performs as its principal function any activity pertaining to the enforcement of the criminal laws (Subsection (j)(2)).

(b) The Act does not permit general one exemption of records compiled primarily for a non-criminal purpose, even though there are some quasi-criminal aspects to the investigation and even though the records are in a system of records to which the general exemption applies.

§505.14 Specific exemptions (Subsection (k)).

The specific exemptions focus more on the nature of the records in the system of records than on the agency. The following categories of records may be exempt from disclosure:

(a) *Subsection (k)(1).* Records which are specifically authorized under criteria established under an Executive Order to be kept secret in the interest of national defense or foreign policy, and which are in fact properly classified according to such Executive Order;

(b) *Subsection (k)(2).* Investigatory records compiled for law enforcement purposes (other than material within the scope of subsection (j)(2) as discussed in §505.13(a)). If any individual is denied any right, privilege, or benefit for which she/he would otherwise be eligible, as a result of the maintenance of such material, the material shall be provided to the individual, unless disclosure of the material would reveal the identity of a source who has been pledged confidentiality;

(c) *Subsection (k)(3).* Records maintained in connection with protection of the President and other VIPs accorded special protection by statute;

(d) *Subsection (k)(4).* Records required by statute to be maintained and used solely as statistical records.

(e) *Subsection (k)(5).* Records compiled solely for the purpose of determining suitability, eligibility, or qualifications for Federal civilian employment, military service, Federal contracts, or access to classified information, but only if disclosure of the material would reveal the identity of a confidential source that furnished information to the Government.

(f) *Subsection (k)(6).* Testing or examination records used solely to determine individual qualifications for appointment or promotion in the Federal service when the disclosure of such would compromise the objectivity or fairness of the testing or examination process.

(g) *Subsection (k)(7).* Evaluation records used to determine potential for promotion in the armed services, but only if disclosure would reveal the identity of a confidential source.

§505.15 Exempt systems of records used.

The BBG is authorized to use exemptions (k)(1), (k)(2), (k)(4), (k)(5) and (k)(6).

PART 506—PART-TIME CAREER EMPLOYMENT PROGRAM

Sec.

AUTHORITY: 5 U.S.C. 3401 (note and 3402).

SOURCE: 44 FR 63098, Nov. 2, 1979, unless otherwise noted.

§506.1 Purpose of program.

Many individuals in society possess great productive potential which goes unrealized because they cannot meet the requirements of a standard workweek. Permanent part-time employment also provides benefits to other individuals in a variety of ways, such as providing older individuals with a gradual transition into retirement, providing employment opportunities to handicapped individuals or others who require a reduced workweek, providing parents opportunities to balance family responsibilities with the need for additional income, providing employment opportunities for women returning to the workforce and assisting students who must finance their own education or vocational training. In view of this, the Broadcasting Board of Governors will operate a part-time career employment program, consistent with the needs of its beneficiaries and its responsibilities.

§ 506.2 Review of positions.

Positions becoming vacant unless excepted as provided by § 506.7, will be reviewed to determine the feasibility of converting them to part-time. Among the criteria which may be used when conducting this review are:

(a) Mission requirements and occupational mix.

(b) Workload fluctuations.

(c) Employment ceilings and budgetary considerations.

(d) Size of workforce, turnover rate and employment trends.

(e) Affirmative action.

§ 506.3 Establishing and converting part-time positions.

Position management and other internal reviews may indicate that positions may be either converted from full-time or initially established as part-time positions. Criteria listed above may be used during these reviews. If a decision is made to convert to or to establish a part-time position, regular position management and classification procedures will be followed.

§ 506.4 Annual goals and timetables.

A Board-wide plan for promoting part-time employment opportunities will be developed annually by the Office of Personnel after consultation with the operating elements. This plan will establish annual goals and set deadlines for achieving these goals.

[44 FR 63098, Nov. 2, 1979, as amended at 51 FR 11015, Apr. 1, 1986]

§ 506.5 Review and evaluation.

The part-time career employment program will be reviewed through semiannual reports submitted by the Director, Office of Personnel to the Associate Director for Management. Regular employment reports will be used to determine levels of part-time employment.

[44 FR 63098, Nov. 2, 1979, as amended at 51 FR 11016, Apr. 1, 1986]

§ 506.6 Publicizing vacancies.

When applicants from outside the Federal service are desired, part-time vacancies may be publicized through various recruiting means, such as:

(a) Federal Job Information Centers.

(b) State Employment Offices.

(c) Broadcasting Board of Governors Vacancy Announcements.

(d) College and University Placement Offices.

§ 506.7 Exceptions.

The Director of the Board and the Associate Director for Management may except positions from inclusion in this program as necessary to carry out the mission of the Board.

PART 507—RULES FOR IMPLEMENTING OPEN MEETINGS UNDER THE SUNSHINE ACT FOR THE BROADCASTING BOARD OF GOVERNORS

Sec.

AUTHORITY: Pub. L. 93–129, 87 Stat. 956, 5 U.S.C. 552b.

SOURCE: 67 FR 76112, Dec. 11, 2002, unless otherwise noted.

§ 507.1 General policies.

The Broadcasting Board of Governors will provide the public with the fullest practical information regarding its decision making process while protecting the rights of individuals and its abilities to carry out its responsibilities.

§ 507.2 Definitions.

The following definitions apply:

(a) The term *agency* includes any establishment in the executive branch of the government headed by a collegial body composed of two or more individual members, a majority of whom are appointed to such position by the President with the advice and consent of the Senate, and any subdivision thereof authorized to act on behalf of the agency. The Broadcasting Board of Governors is a government agency headed by a nine-member board, eight of whom are appointed by the President with the advice and consent of the

Senate, and the ninth being the Secretary of State. Therefore, the Broadcasting Board of Governors is an "agency" under these terms.

(b) The term *meeting* means the deliberation of this Board where such deliberations determine or result in the joint conduct or disposition of official Board business.

(c) The term *member* means an individual who belongs to the Board who has been appointed by the President and confirmed by the Senate or is the Secretary of State.

§ 507.3 Requirement for open meetings.

Members shall not jointly conduct or dispose of agency business other than in accordance with this part. Except as provided in § 507.4 every portion of every meeting of the agency shall be open to public observation.

§ 507.4 Grounds on which meetings may be closed.

The Board shall open every portion of every meeting of the agency for public observation except where the agency determines that such portion or portions of the meeting or the disclosure of such information is likely to:

(a) Disclose matters that are:

(1) Specifically authorized under criteria established by an Executive order to be kept secret in the interests of national defense or foreign policy, and

(2) In fact properly classified pursuant to such Executive order;

(b) Relate solely to the internal personnel rules and practice of the agency;

(c) Disclose matters specifically exempted from disclosure by statute: Provided, that such statute:

(1) Requires that the matters be withheld from the public in such manner as to leave no discretion on the issue, or

(2) Established practical criteria for withholding or refers to particular types of matters to be withheld;

(d) Disclose trade secrets and commercial or financial information obtained from a person and privileged or confidential;

(e) Involve accusing any person of a crime, or formally censuring any person;

(f) Disclose information of a personal nature where disclosure would constitute a clearly unwarranted invasion of personal privacy;

(g) Disclose investigatory records compiled for law enforcement purposes, or information which if written would be contained in such records, but only to the extent that the production of such records or information would:

(1) Interfere with enforcement proceedings,

(2) Deprive a person of a right to a fair trial on an impartial adjudication,

(3) Constitute an unwarranted invasion of personal privacy,

(4) Disclose the identity of a confidential source and, in the case of a record compiled by a criminal law enforcement authority in the course of a criminal investigation, or by an agency conducting a lawful national security intelligence investigation, confidential source,

(5) Disclose investigative techniques and procedures, or

(6) Endanger the life or physical safety of law enforcement personnel;

(h) Disclose information, the premature disclosure of which would be likely to significantly frustrate implementation of a proposed agency action. This shall not apply in any instance where the Board has already disclosed to the public the content or the nature of its proposed action, or where the Board is required by law to make such disclosures on its own initiative prior to taking final Board action on such proposal; or

(i) Specifically concern the Board's issuance of a subpoena, or the Board's participation in a civil action or proceeding, an action in a foreign court or international tribunal, or an arbitration, or the initiation, conduct or disposition by the Board of a particular case of formal agency adjudication, or otherwise involving a determination on the record after opportunity for a hearing.

§ 507.5 Procedures for announcing meetings.

(a) In the case of each meeting, the Board shall make public, at least one week before the meeting, the time, place, and subject matter of the meeting, whether it is to be open or closed to the public, and the name and phone number of the official designated by the Board to respond to requests for information about the meeting. Such announcement shall be made unless a majority of the members of the Board determine by a recorded vote that such meeting must be called at an earlier date, in which case the Board shall make public announcement of the time, place, subject matter of such meeting and whether it is open or closed to the public, at the earliest practical time.

(b) Immediately following the public announcement, the Board will publish it in the FEDERAL REGISTER.

§ 507.6 Procedures for closing meetings.

(a) The closing of a meeting shall occur only when:

(1) A majority of the membership of the Board votes to take such action. A separate vote of the Board members shall be taken with respect to each Board meeting, a portion or portions of which are proposed to be closed to the public pursuant to § 507.4, or with respect to any information which is proposed to be withheld under § 507.4. A single vote may be taken with respect to a series of meetings, a portion or portions of which are proposed to be closed to the public, or with respect to any information concerning such series of meetings, so long as each meeting in such series involves the same particular matters and is scheduled to be held not more than thirty days after the initial meeting in such series. The vote of each Board member participating in such vote shall be recorded and no proxies shall be allowed.

(2) Whenever any person whose interest may be directly affected by a portion of the meeting requests that the Board close such a portion to the public for any of the reasons referred to in § 507.4 (e), (f) or (g), the Board, upon request of any of its Board members, shall take a recorded vote, whether to close such portion of the meeting.

(b) Within one day of any vote taken, the Board shall make publicly available a written copy of such vote reflecting the vote of each member on the question and full written explanation of its action closing the entire or portion of the meeting together with a list of all persons expected to attend the meeting and their affiliation.

(c) The Board shall announce the time, place and subject matter of the meeting at least eight (8) days before the meeting.

(d) For every closed meeting, the Board's Legal Counsel shall publicly certify that, in his or her opinion, the meeting may be closed to the public and shall state each relevant exemptive provision. A copy of such certification, together with a statement from the presiding officer of the meeting setting forth the time and place of the meeting, and the persons present, shall be retained by the Board.

§ 507.7 Reconsideration of opening or closing a meeting.

The time or place of a Board meeting may be changed following the public announcement only if the Board publicly announces such change at the earliest practicable time. The subject matter of a meeting, or the determination of the agency to open or close a meeting, or a portion of a meeting, to the public, may be changed following the public announcement only if a majority of the Board members determines by a recorded vote that Board business so requires and that no earlier announcement of the change was possible, and the Board publicly announces such change and the vote of each member upon such change at the earliest practicable time.

§ 507.8 Recording keeping of closed meetings.

(a) The Board shall maintain an electronic recording of the proceedings of each meeting, or portion of a meeting, closed to the public.

(b) The Board, after review by the Chairman, shall make promptly available to the public in a place easily accessible to the public, a complete transcript or electronic record of the discussion of any item on the agenda, or any item of testimony of any witness received at the Board meeting, except for such item or items of such discussion or testimony as the Board determines to contain information which may be withheld under § 507.4. Copies of such record, disclosing the identity of each speaker, shall be furnished to any person at the actual cost of duplication. The Board shall maintain a complete transcript or electronic copy of each meeting, or portion of a meeting, closed to the public, for a period of at least two years after such meeting, or until one year after the conclusion of any Board proceeding with respect to which the meeting or portion was held, whichever occurs later.

PART 510—SERVICE OF PROCESS

AUTHORITY: 5 U.S.C. 552(a)(1)(A).

§ 510.1 Service of process.

(a) The General Counsel of the Broadcasting Board of Governors or any of his/her designees shall act as agent for the receipt of legal process against the Broadcasting Board of Governors, as well as against employees of the Board to the extent that the process relates to the official functions of the employees.

(b) When accepting service of process for an employee in his/her official capacity, the General Counsel or his/her designee shall endorse on the server's return of process form, registered mail receipt, certified mail receipt, or express mail receipt: "Service accepted in official capacity only."

(c) Process shall be delivered to:

Mailing address: Office of the General Counsel, Broadcasting Board of Governors, 330 Independence Ave., SW., Cohen Building, Washington, DC 20237.

Location: Office of the General Counsel, Broadcasting Board of Governors, 330 Independence Ave., SW., Cohen Building, Room 3349, Washington, DC 20237.

[53 FR 50515, Dec. 16, 1988, as amended at 74 FR 7562, Feb. 18, 2009]

PART 511—FEDERAL TORT CLAIMS PROCEDURE

Sec.

AUTHORITY: 5 U.S.C. 301.

SOURCE: 34 FR 20430, Dec. 31, 1969, unless otherwise noted.

§ 511.1 Definitions.

Board. Board means the Broadcasting Board of Governors.

Act. Act means the Federal Tort Claims Act, as amended, and codified in 28 U.S.C., sections 2671–2680.

§ 511.2 Scope of regulations.

The regulations in this part shall apply only to claims asserted under the Federal Tort Claims Act, as amended, or as incorporated by reference in any appropriation Act or other statutes, for money damages against the United States for injury, loss of property, personal injury, or death caused by the negligent or wrongful act or omission of any employee of the Board while acting within the scope of his/her office or employment, under circumstances where the United States, if a private person, would be liable to the claimant in accordance with the law of the place where the act or omission occurred.

[43 FR 14301, Apr. 4, 1978]

§ 511.3 Exceptions.

Claims not compensable hereunder are listed in 2680 of the Act with the exception that 2680(k) (claims arising in a foreign country) has been removed by 22 U.S.C. 1474(5).

[44 FR 16374, Mar. 19, 1979]

§ 511.4 Administrative claim; when presented.

(a) For the purposes of the provisions of section 2672 of the Act and of this part, a claim shall be deemed to have been presented when the Board receives, in the office designated in paragraph (b) of this section, an executed "Claim for Damage or Injury", Standard Form 95, or other written notification of an incident, accompanied by a claim for money damages in a sum certain, for injury to or loss of property, personal injury or death, alleged to have occurred by reason of the incident. The claimant may, if he/she desires, file a brief with his/her claim setting forth the law or other arguments in support of his/her claim. In cases involving claims by more than one person arising from a single accident or incident, individual claim forms shall be used. A claim which should have been presented to the Board, but which was mistakenly addressed to or filed with another Federal Agency, shall be deemed to have been presented to the Board as of the date the claim is received by the Board. If a claim is mistakenly addressed to or filed with the Board, the Board shall transfer it forthwith to the appropriate Agency.

(b) A claimant shall mail, or deliver his/her claim to the Office of the General Counsel and Congressional Liaison, Broadcasting Board of Governors, 301 4th Street, SW., Washington, DC 20547.

[34 FR 20430, Dec. 31, 1969, as amended at 51 FR 11016, Apr. 1, 1986]

§511.5 Who may file claim.

(a) Claims for loss or damage of property may be filed by the owner of the property, or his/her legal representatives. Claims for personal injury or death may be made by the injured person or a legal representative of the injured or deceased person. The claim, if filed by a legal representative, should show the capacity of the person signing and be accompanied by evidence of this authority to act.

(b) The claim and all other papers requiring the signature of the claimant should be signed by him/her personally or by his/her representative. Signatures should be identical throughout.

§511.6 Board authority to adjust, determine, compromise, and settle claims and limitations upon that authority.

(a) The General Counsel of the Board, or his/her designee, is delegated authority to consider, ascertain, adjust, determine, compromise, and settle claims asserted under the provisions of section 2672 of the Act and under this part.

(b) Limitation on Board authority: An award, compromise, or settlement of a claim by the Board under the provisions of section 2672 of the Act, in excess of $25,000, shall be effected only with the prior written approval of the Attorney General or his/her designee.

§511.7 Investigations.

The Board may request any other Federal agency to investigate a claim filed under section 2672 of the Act, or to conduct a physical or mental examination of the claimant and provide a report of such examination.

§511.8 Limitations.

(a) Pursuant to the provisions of section 2401(b) of title 28 of the United States Code, a tort claim against the United States shall be forever barred unless presented in writing to the Board within two (2) years after such claim accrues.

(b) A suit may not be filed until the claim shall have been finally denied by the Board. Failure of the Board to make final disposition of the claim within six (6) months after it has been presented shall, at the option of the claimant any time thereafter, be deemed a final denial of the claim for purposes of the Act and of this part.

(c) A suit shall not be filed for a sum greater than the amount of the claim presented to the Board, except where the increased amount is based upon newly discovered evidence not reasonably discoverable at the time for presenting the claim to the Board, or upon allegation and proof of intervening facts, relating to amount of the claim.

§511.9 Supporting evidence.

(a) In support of claims for personal injury or death, the claimant should submit a written report by the attending physician. The report should show the nature and extent of injury, the nature and extent of treatment, the effect upon earning capacity, either temporarily or permanently, the degree of permanent disability, if any, the prognosis, and the period of hospitalization, or incapacitation. Itemized bills for medical, hospital, or burial expenses actually incurred should be attached to report.

(b) In support of claims for damage to property which as been or can be economically repaired, the claimant should submit at least two itemized signed statements, or estimates by reliable, disinterested firms or itemized signed receipts if payment has been made.

(c) In support of claims for loss or damage to property which is not economically repairable, the claimant should submit statements of the original cost of the property, date of purchase, and the value of the property before and after the accident together with a statement setting forth the basis used in arriving at such value. Such statements should be from at least two disinterested, competent persons, preferably reputable dealers or other qualified persons familiar with the type of property in question.

§ 511.10 Settlement of claim.

The General Counsel will review the findings from the standpoint of questions of law applicable to the claim and will determine disposition. The General Counsel will make final review for settlement of the claim and will sign SF–1145, Voucher for Payment Under Federal Tort Claims Act, and forward it to the Financial Operations Division for payment of claim. Payment of any award or settlement in the amount of $2,500 or less will be authorized from the appropriation and allotment current for obligation on the date of settlement irrespective of when the cause of action arose. Payment of any award, compromise or settlement in an amount in excess of $2,500, shall be paid in a manner similar to judgments and compromises out of the appropriation provided by section (c), Pub. L. 89–506 (28 U.S.C. 2672).

§ 511.11 Acceptance of award.

The acceptance by the claimant of any award will be final and conclusive on the claimant. The acceptance will constitute a complete release of any claim by reason of the same subject matter against the United States and against the employee whose act or omission resulted in the claim. Adjudication and payment shall likewise be conclusive on all officers of the United States, unless procured by fraud.

§ 511.12 When litigation is involved in claim.

If a claimant does not agree to a settlement of a claim of which is considered fair and equitable by the Board's responsible officials, the claimant, upon the final disposition thereof by the Board, may elect to file suit. Relief from claims which are disallowed may be sought by filing suit in the U.S. District Court for the district where the claimant resides or wherein the act of omission complained of occurred. The failure of the Board to make final disposition of a claim within 6 months after it has been filed shall, pursuant to 28 U.S.C. 2672, and at the option of the claimant at any time thereafter, is deemed a final denial of the claim. If a suit is filed against the Government involving the Board, the Department of Justice will request the Board to furnish the complete file on the case. The Office of the General Counsel will represent the Board in all negotiations with the Department of Justice.

PART 512—COLLECTION OF DEBTS UNDER THE DEBT COLLECTION ACT OF 1982

Subpart A—General Provisions

Sec.

Subpart B—Administrative Offset and Referral to Collection Agencies

Subpart C—Salary Offset

Subpart D—Interest, Penalties, and Administrative Costs

AUTHORITY: 31 U.S.C. 3701; 31 U.S.C. 3711 *et seq.;* 5 U.S.C. 5514; 4 CFR Parts 101–105; 5 CFR Part 550.

SOURCE: 52 FR 43897, Nov. 17, 1987, unless otherwise noted.

Subpart A—General Provisions

§ 512.1 Definitions.

(a) The term *Board* means the Broadcasting Board of Governors.

(b) The term *Board head* means the Director, Broadcasting Board of Governors.

(c) The term *appropriate Board official* or *designee* means the Chief, Financial Operations Division or such other official as may be named in the future by the Director, Broadcasting Board of Governors.

(d) The terms *debt* or *claim* refer to an amount of money which has been determined by an appropriate Board official to be owed to the United States from any person, organization or entity, except another Federal Agency.

(e) A debt is considered *delinquent* if it has not been paid by the date specified in the Board's written notification or applicable contractual agreement, unless other satisfactory arrangements have been made by that date, or at any time thereafter the debtor fails to satisfy obligations under a payment agreement with the Board.

(f) The term *referral for litigation* means referral to the Department of Justice for appropriate legal proceedings.

§ 512.2 Exceptions.

(a) Claims arising from the audit of transportation accounts pursuant to 31 U.S.C. 3726 shall be determined, collected, compromised, terminated, or settled in accordance with the regulations published under 31 U.S.C. 3726 (refer to 41 CFR part 101–41).

(b) Claims arising out of acquisition contracts subject to the Federal Acquisition Regulation (FAR) shall be determined, collected, compromised, terminated or settled in accordance with those regulations (see 48 CFR part 32). If not otherwise provided for in the FAR system, contract claims that have been the subject of a contracting officer's final decision in accordance with section 6(a) of the Contracts Disputes Act of 1978 (41 U.S.C. 605(a)), may be determined, collected, compromised, terminated, or settled under the provisions of this regulation, except no additional review of the debt shall be granted beyond that provided by the contracting officer in accordance with the provisions of section 6 of the Contract Disputes Act of 1978 (41 U.S.C. 605), and the amount of any interest, administrative charge, or penalty charge shall be subject to the limitations, if any, contained in the contract out of which the claim arose.

(c) Claims based in whole or in part on conduct in violation of the antitrust laws, or in regard to which there is an indication of fraud, presentation of a false claim, or misrepresentation on the part of the debtor or any other party having an interest in the claim, shall be referred to the Department of Justice (DOJ) as only the DOJ has the authority to compromise, suspend or terminate collection action on such claims.

(d) Tax claims are excluded from the coverage of this regulation.

§ 512.3 Use of procedures.

Procedures authorized by this regulation (including but not limited to referral to a debt collection agency, administrative offset, or salary offset) may be used singly or in combination, providing the requirements of the applicable law and regulation are satisfied.

§ 512.4 Conformance to law and regulations.

(a) The requirements of applicable law (31 U.S.C. 3701–3719 as amended by

Pub. L. 97–365, (96 Stat. 1749) have been implemented in Government-wide standards:

(1) The regulations of the Office of Personnel Management (5 CFR part 550).

(2) The Federal Claims Collection Standards issued jointly by the General Accounting Office and the Department of Justice (4 CFR parts 101–105), and

(3) The procedures prescribed by the Office of Management and Budget in Circular A–129 of May 9, 1985.

(b) Not every item in the above described standards has been incorporated or referenced in this regulation. To the extent, however, that circumstances arise which are not covered by the terms stated in this regulation, Broadcasting Board of Governors will proceed in any actions taken in accordance with applicable requirements found in the sources referred to in paragraphs (a)(1), (2), and (3) of this section.

§512.5 Other procedures.

Nothing contained in this regulation is intended to require Broadcasting Board of Governors to duplicate administrative proceedings required by contract or other laws or regulations.

§512.6 Informal action.

Nothing in this regulation is intended to preclude utilization of informal administrative actions or remedies which may be available.

§512.7 Return of property.

Nothing contained in this regulation is intended to deter Broadcasting Board of Governors from demanding the return of specific property or from demanding the return of the property or the payment of its value.

§512.8 Omissions not a defense.

The failure of Broadcasting Board of Governors to comply with any provision in this regulation shall not serve as a defense to the debt.

Subpart B—Administrative Offset and Referral to Collection Agencies

§512.9 Demand for payment.

Prior to initiating administrative offset, demand for payment will be made as follows:

(a) Written demands will be made promptly upon the debtor in terms which inform the debtor of the consequences of failure to cooperate. A total of three progressively stronger written demands at not more than 30-day intervals will normally be made unless a response to the first or second demand indicates that further demand would be futile and the debtor's response does not require rebuttal. In determining the timing of demand letters, Broadcasting Board of Governors will give due regard to the need to act promptly so that, as a general rule, debt referrals to the Department of Justice for litigation, where necessary, can be made within one year of the Board's final determination of the fact and the amount of the debt. When necessary to protect the Government's interests (e.g., to prevent the statute of limitations, 28 U.S.C. 2415, from expiring) written demand may be preceded by other appropriate actions under this chapter, including immediate referral for litigation.

(b) The initial demand letter will inform the debtor of: The basis for the indebtedness and the right of the debtor to request review within the Board; the applicable standards for assessing interest, penalties, and administrative costs (Subpart D of this regulation) and; the date by which payment is to be made, which normally will not be more than 30 days from the date that the initial demand letter was mailed or hand delivered. Broadcasting Board of Governors will exercise care to insure that demand letters are mailed or hand-delivered on the same day that they are actually dated.

(c) As appropriate to the circumstances, Broadcasting Board of Governors will include in the demand letters matters relating to alternative methods of payment, the debtor's rights to representation by his respective bargaining unit, policies relating to referral to collection agencies, the

Board's intentions relative to referral of the debt to the Department of Justice for litigation, and, depending on the statutory authority, the debtor's entitlement to consideration of waiver.

(d) Broadcasting Board of Governors will respond promptly to communications from the debtor and will advise debtors who dispute the debt that they must furnish available evidence to support their contention.

§ 512.10 Collection by administrative offset.

(a) Collection by administrative offset will be undertaken in accordance with these regulations on all claims which are liquidated and certain in amount, in every instance where the appropriate Board official determines such collection to be feasible and not otherwise prohibited.

(1) For purpose of this section, the term *administrative offset* has the same meaning as provided in 31 U.S.C. 3716(a)(1).

(2) Whether collection by administrative offset is feasible is a determination to be made by the Board on a case-by-case basis, in the exercise of sound discretion. Broadcasting Board of Governors will consider not only the practicalities of administrative offset, but whether such offset is best suited to protect and further all of the Government's interests. Broadcasting Board of Governors will give consideration to the debtor's financial condition, and is not required to use offset in every instance where there is an available source of funds. Broadcasting Board of Governors will also consider whether offset would tend to substantially disrupt or defeat the purpose of the program authorizing the payments against which offset is contemplated.

(b) Before the offset is made, a debtor shall be provided with the following: written notice of the nature and the amount of the debt and the Board's intention to collect by offset; opportunity to inspect and copy Board records pertaining to the debt; opportunity to obtain review within the Board of the determination of indebtedness; and opportunity to enter into written agreement with the Board to repay the debt. Broadcasting Board of Governors may also make requests to other agencies holding funds payable to the debtor, and process requests for offset that are received from other agencies.

(1) Broadcasting Board of Governors will exercise sound judgment in determining whether to accept a repayment agreement in lieu of offset. The determination will weigh the Government's interest in collecting the debt against fairness to the debtor.

(2) In cases where the procedural requirements specified in this paragraph (b) have previously been provided to the debtor in connection with the same debt under some other statutory or regulatory authority, such as pursuant to an audit allowance, the Board is not required to duplicate those requirements before taking administrative offset.

(3) Broadcasting Board of Governors may not initiate administrative offset to collect a debt more than 10 years after the Government's right to collect the debt first accrued, unless facts material to the Government's right were not known and could not reasonably have been known by the official or officials of the Government who were charged with the responsibility to discover and collect the debt. When the debt first accrued is to be determined according to existent law regarding the accrual of debts (e.g., 28 U.S.C. 2415).

(4) Broadcasting Board of Governors is not authorized by 31 U.S.C. 3716 to use administrative offset with respect to: Debts owed by any State or local Government; debts arising under or payments made under the Social Security Act, the Internal Revenue Code of 1954 or the tariff laws of the United States; or any case in which collection of the type of debt involved by administrative offset is explicitly provided for or prohibited by another statute. Unless otherwise provided by contract or law, debts or payments which are not subject to administrative offset under 31 U.S.C. 3716 may be collected by administrative offset under the common law or other applicable statutory authority.

(5) Broadcasting Board of Governors may effect administrative offset against a payment to be made to a debtor prior to completion of the procedures required by paragraph (b) of

this section if failure to take offset would substantially prejudice the Government's ability to collect the debt, and the time before the payment is to be made does not reasonably permit the completion of those procedures. Amounts recovered by offset but later determined not to be owed to the Government shall be promptly refunded 30 days after the Board has notified the debtor in writing that the debt is not owed. Such written notification will be issued within 15 days after the Board has confirmed through a review of its official records that the debt is not owed.

(c) Type of hearing or review: (1) For purposes of this section, whenever Broadcasting Board of Governors is required to afford a hearing or review within the Board, the Board will provide the debtor with a reasonable opportunity for an oral hearing when: An applicable statute authorizes or requires the Board to consider waiver of the indebtedness involved, the debtor requests waiver of the indebtedness, and the waiver determination turns on an issue of veracity; or the debtor requests reconsideration of the debt and the Board determines that the question of the indebtedness cannot be resolved by review of the documentary evidence. Unless otherwise required by law, an oral hearing under this section is not required to be a formal evidentiary type hearing.

(2) This section does not require an oral hearing with respect to debt collection systems in which determinations of indebtedness or waiver rarely involve issues of veracity and the Board has determined that the review of the written record is ordinarily enough to correct prior mistakes.

(3) In those cases where an oral hearing is not required by this section, the Board will make its determination on the request for waiver or reconsideration based upon a review of the written record.

(d) Appropriate use will be made of the cooperative efforts of other agencies in effecting collection by administrative offset. Broadcasting Board of Governors will not refuse to initiate administrative offset to collect debts owed the United States, unless the requesting agency has not complied with the applicable provisions of these standards.

(e) Collection by offset against a judgment obtained against the United States shall be accomplished in accordance with 31 U.S.C. 3728.

(f) Whenever the creditor agency is not the agency which is responsible for making the payment against which offset is sought, the latter agency shall not initiate the requested offset until it has been provided by the creditor agency with an appropriate written certification that the debtor owes the debt (including the amount) and that full compliance with the provisions of this section has taken place.

(g) When collecting multiple debts by administrative offset, Broadcasting Board of Governors will apply the recovered amounts to those debts in accordance with the best interests of the United States, as determined by the facts and circumstances of the particular case, paying particular attention to the applicable statutes of limitations.

§512.11 Administrative offset against amounts payable from Civil Service Retirement and Disability Fund.

(a) Unless otherwise prohibited by law, Broadcasting Board of Governors may request that monies that are due and payable to a debtor from the Civil Service Retirement and Disability Fund be administratively offset in reasonable amounts in order to collect in one full payments, or a minimal number of payment, debts owed the United States by the debtor. Such requests shall be made to the appropriate officials within the Office of Personnel Management in accordance with such regulations as may be prescribed by the Director of that Office.

(b) When making a request for administrative offset under paragraph (a) of this section, Broadcasting Board of Governors shall include written statements that:

(1) The debtor owes the United States a debt, including the amount of the debt;

(2) The Broadcasting Board of Governors has complied with the applicable statutes, regulations, and procedures of the Office of Personnel Management; and

(3) The Broadcasting Board of Governors has complied with the requirements of § 512.10 of this part, including any required hearing or review.

(c) Once Broadcasting Board of Governors decides to request offset under paragraph (a) of this section, it will make the request as soon as practical after completion of the applicable procedures in order that the Office of Personnel Management may identify the debtor's account in anticipation of the time when the debtor requests or becomes eligible to receive payments from the Fund. This will satisfy any requirement that offset be initiated prior to expiration of the applicable statute of limitations.

(d) If Broadcasting Board of Governors collects part or all of the debt by other means before deductions are made or completed pursuant to paragraph (a) of this section, Broadcasting Board of Governors shall act promptly to modify or terminate its request for offset under paragraph (a) of this section.

(e) This section does not require or authorize the Office of Personnel Management to review the merits of the Broadcasting Board of Governors determination relative to the amount and validity of the debt, its determination on waiver under an applicable statute, or its determination whether to provide an oral hearing.

§ 512.12 Collection in installments.

(a) Whenever feasible, and except as required otherwise by law, debts owed to the United States, together with interest, penalties, and administrative costs as required by this regulation, should be collected in one lump sum. This is true whether the debt is being collected under administrative offset or by another method, including voluntary payment. However, if the debtor is financially unable to pay the indebtedness in one lump sum, payment may be accepted in regular installments. If Broadcasting Board of Governors agrees to accept payment in installments, it will obtain a legally enforceable written agreement from the debtor that specifies all of the terms of the arrangement and which contains a provision accelerating the debt in the event the debtor defaults. The size and frequency of the payments should bear a reasonable relation to the size of the debt and ability to the debtor to pay. If possible the installment payments should be sufficient in size and frequency to liquidate the Government's claim within 3 years.

(b) If the debtor owes more than one debt and designates how a voluntary installment plan is to be applied among those debts, the Board will follow that designation. If no such designation is made, the Board will apply payments to the various debts in accordance with the best interest of the United States as as determined by the facts and circumstances of each case, with particular attention to application statutes of limitation.

§ 512.13 Exploration of compromise.

Broadcasting Board of Governors may attempt to effect compromise in accordance with the standards set forth in part 103 of the Federal Claims Collection Standards (4 CFR part 103).

§ 512.14 Suspending or terminating collection action.

The suspension or termination of collection action shall be made in accordance with the standards set forth in part 104 of the Federal Claims Collection Standard (4 CFR part 104).

§ 512.15 Referrals to the Department of Justice or the General Accounting Office.

Referrals to the Department of Justice or the General Accounting Office shall be made in accordance with the standards set forth in part 105 of the Federal Claims Collection Standards (4 CFR part 105).

§ 512.16 Collection services.

(a) Broadcasting Board of Governors has authority to contract for collection services to recover delinquent debts in accordance with 31 U.S.C. 3718(c) and 4 CFR 102.6.

(b) Contracts with collection agencies will provide that:

(1) The authority to resolve disputes, compromise claims, suspend or terminate collection action, and refer the matter to the Justice Department for litigation will be retained by Broadcasting Board of Governors;

(2) Contractors are subject to 5 U.S.C. 552a, the Privacy Act of 1974, as amended, to the extent specified in 5 U.S.C. 552a(m) and to applicable Federal and State laws and regulations pertaining to debt collection practices, such as the Fair Debt Collection Practices Act, 15 U.S.C. 1692;

(3) The contractor is required to strictly account for all amounts collected;

(4) The contractor must agree that uncollectible accounts shall be returned with appropriate documentation to enable Broadcasting Board of Governors to determine whether to pursue collection through litigation or to terminate collection;

(5) The contractor must agree to provide any data in its files relating to paragraphs (a)(1), (2), and (3) of §105.2 of the Federal Claims Collection Standards (4 CFR part 105) upon returning the account to Broadcasting Board of Governors for subsequent referral to the Department of Justice for litigation.

(c) Broadcasting Board of Governors will not use a collection agency to collect a debt owed by a currently employed or retired Federal employee, if collection by salary or annuity offset is available.

Subpart C—Salary Offset

§512.17 Purpose.

This subpart provides the standards to be followed by Broadcasting Board of Governors in implementing 5 U.S.C. 5514 to recover a debt from the pay of an Board employee or former employee, and establishes the procedural guidelines to recover debts when the employee's creditor and paying agencies are not the same.

[52 FR 43897, Nov. 17, 1987, as amended at 55 FR 3050, Jan. 30, 1990]

§512.18 Scope.

(a) *Coverage.* This subpart applies to Executive agencies, military departments, an agency or court in the judicial branch, an agency of the legislative branch and other independent entities of the Federal Government as defined in 5 CFR 550.1103, under the heading "Agency".

(b) *Applicability.* This subpart and 5 U.S.C. 5514 apply in recovering debts by offset without the employee's consent from the current pay of that employee. Debt collection procedures which are not specified in 5 U.S.C. 5514 and these regulations will be consistent with the Federal Claims Collection Standards (4 CFR parts 101–105).

(1) The procedures contained in this subpart do not apply to debts or claims arising under the Internal Revenue Code of 1954 as amended (26 U.S.C. 1 *et seq.*), the Social Security Act (42 U.S.C. 301 *et seq.*), or the tariff laws of the United States or to any case where collection of a debt is explicitly provided for or prohibited by another statute (e.g., travel advances in 5 U.S.C. 5705).

(2) This subpart does not preclude an employee from requesting a waiver of a salary overpayment under 5 U.S.C. 5584, 10 U.S.C. 2774, or 32 U.S.C. 716, or in any way questioning the amount or validity of a debt by submitting a subsequent claim to the General Accounting Office in accordance with procedures prescribed by the General Accounting Officer, nor does it preclude an employee from requesting waiver when waiver is available under any statutory provision.

[52 FR 43897, Nov. 17, 1987, as amended at 55 FR 3051, Jan. 30, 1990]

§512.19 Definitions.

For purposes of this subpart:

Board means the Broadcasting Board of Governors.

Creditor Agency means the agency to which the debt is owed.

Debt means an amount owed to the United States.

Disposable Pay means that part of current basic pay, special pay, incentive pay, retired pay, retainer pay or authorized pay remaining after the deduction of any amount required to be withheld by law. The Board will exclude deductions described in 5 CFR 581.105 (b) through (f) to determine disposable pay subject to salary offset.

Employee means a current employee of Broadcasting Board of Governors or of another Executive Agency.

Executive Agency means:

(a) An Executive Agency as defined in section 105 of title 5, United States

Code, including the U.S. Postal Service and the U.S. Postal Rate Commission;

(b) A military department as defined in section 102 of title 5, United States Code;

(c) An agency or court in the judicial branch, including a court as defined in section 610 of title 28, United States Code, the District Court for the Northern Mariana Islands, and the Judicial Panel on Multidistrict Litigation;

(d) An agency of the legislative branch, including the U.S. Senate and the U.S. House of Representatives; and

(e) Other independent establishments that are entities of the Federal Government.

FCCS means the Federal Claims Collection Standards jointly published by the Justice Department and the General Accounting Office at 4 CFR parts 101–105.

Paying agency means the agency employing the individual and authorizing the payment of his or her current pay.

Salary offset means an administrative offset to collect a debt under 5 U.S.C. 5514 by deductions at one or more officially established pay intervals from the current pay account of an employee without his or her consent.

Waiver means the cancellation, remission, forgiveness, or non-recovery of a debt allegedly owed by an employee to an agency as permitted or required by U.S.C. 5584, 10 U.S.C. 2774, or 32 U.S.C. 710, 5 U.S.C. 8346(b), or any other law.

[52 FR 43897, Nov. 17, 1987, as amended at 55 FR 3051, Jan. 30, 1990]

§ 512.20 Notification.

(a) Salary offset deductions shall not be made unless the Director, Financial Operations Division of Broadcasting Board of Governors, or such other official as may be named in the future by the Director of Broadcasting Board of Governors, provides to the employee a written notice, 30 calendar days prior to any deduction, stating at a minimum:

(1) The Board's determination that a debt is owed including the nature, origin, and amount of the debt;

(2) The Board's intent to collect the debt by means of deduction from the employee's current disposable pay account;

(3) The amount, frequency and proposed beginning date and duration of the intended deductions;

(4) An explanation of the Board's policy concerning interest, penalties, and administrative costs;

(5) The employee's right to inspect and copy Government records pertaining to the debt;

(6) The opportunity to establish a schedule for the voluntary repayment of the debt or to enter into a written agreement to establish a schedule for repayment in lieu of offset per the requirements of 4 CFR 102.2(e).

(7) The employee's right to a hearing arranged by the Board and conducted by an administrative law judge or, alternatively, an official not under the control of the head of the Board;

(8) The method and time period for filing a petition for a hearing;

(9) That timely filing of the petition will stay the commencement of collection proceedings;

(10) That final decision on the hearing will be issued not later than 60 days after the filing of the petition for hearing unless the employee requests and the hearing officer grants a delay in the proceedings.

(11) That knowingly false, misleading, or frivolous statements, representations or evidence may subject the employee to:

(i) Disciplinary procedures under chapter 75 of title 5, United States Code or any other applicable statutes;

(ii) Penalties under the False Claims Act, sections 3729–3731 of title 31 U.S.C. or any other applicable statutes.

(iii) Criminal penalties under sections 286, 287, 1001, 1002 of title 18 United States Code or any other applicable statutes.

(12) Any other rights or remedies available to the employee, including representation by counsel or his respective bargaining unit, under the statutes or regulations governing the program for which collection is being made.

(13) That amounts paid on or deducted for the debts that are later waived or found not owed to the United States will be promptly refunded to the employee.

(b) Notifications under this section shall be hand delivered with a record made of the delivery, or shall be mailed certified mail with return receipt requested.

(c) No notification hearing, written responses or final decisions under this regulation are required of Broadcasting Board of Governors for any adjustment to pay arising from an employee's election of coverage under a Federal benefit program requiring periodic deductions from pay, if the amount to be recovered was accumulated over four pay periods or less.

§512.21 Hearing.

(a) *Petition for hearing.* (1) A hearing may be requested by filing a written petition with the Director, Financial Operations Division of Broadcasting Board of Governors, or such other official as may be named in the future by the Director of Broadcasting Board of Governors, stating why the employee believes the Board's determination of the existence or amount of the debt is in error.

(2) The petition must be signed by the employee and fully identify and explain with reasonable specificity all the facts, evidence and witnesses which the employee believes support his or her position.

(3) The petition must be filed no later than fifteen (15) calendar days from the date the notification under §512.20(b) was hand delivered or the date of delivery by certified mail.

(4) Where petition is received after the 15 calendar day limit, Broadcasting Board of Governors will accept the petition if the employee can show that the delay was beyond his or her control or because of failure to receive notice.

(5) If the petition is not filed within the time limit, and is not accepted pursuant to paragraph (a)(4) of this section, the employee's right to hearing will be considered waived, and salary offset will be implemented.

(b) *Type of hearing.* (1) The form and content of the hearing will be determined by the hearing official who shall be a person outside the control or authority of Broadcasting Board of Governors.

(2) The employee may represent him or herself, or may be represented by counsel.

(3) The hearing official shall maintain a summary record of the hearing.

(4) The hearing official will prepare a written decision which will state:

(i) The facts purported to evidence nature and origin of the alleged debt;

(ii) The hearing official's analysis, findings, and conclusions relative to:

(A) The employee's and/or the Board's grounds;

(B) The amount and the validity of the alleged debt;

(C) The repayment schedule, if applicable.

(5) The decision of the hearing official shall constitute the final administrative decision of the Board.

§512.22 Deduction from pay.

(a) Deduction by salary offset, from an employee's disposable current pay, shall be subject to the following circumstances:

(1) When funds are available, the Board will collect debts owed the United States in full in one lump-sum. If funds are not available or the debt exceeds 15% of disposable pay for an officially established pay interval, collection will normally be made in installments.

(2) The installments shall not exceed 15% of the disposable pay from which the deduction is made, unless the employee has agreed in writing to a larger amount.

(3) Deduction will commence with the next full pay interval following notice that deductions will commence.

(4) Installment deductions will not be made over a period greater than the anticipated period of employment.

[52 FR 43897, Nov. 17, 1987, as amended at 55 FR 3051, Jan. 30, 1990]

§512.23 Liquidation from final check or recovery from other payment.

(a) If an employee retires or resigns before collection of the debt is completed, offset of the entire remaining balance may be made from a final payment of any nature to such extent as is necessary to liquidate the debt.

(b) Where debt cannot be liquidated by offset from final payment, offset may be made from later payments of any kind due from the United States inclusive of Civil Service Retirement and Disability Fund pursuant to 5

U.S.C. 8347 and 5 CFR 831.1801 *et seq* of this regulation.

[52 FR 43897, Nov. 17, 1987, as amended at 55 FR 3051, Jan. 30, 1990]

§ 512.24 Non-waiver of rights by payments.

An employee's voluntary payment of all or part of a debt being collected under 5 U.S.C. 5514 shall not be construed as a waiver of any rights which the employee may have under 5 U.S.C., or any other provision of contract or law, unless statutory or contractual provisions provide to the contrary.

§ 512.25 Refunds.

(a) Refunds shall be promptly made when:

(1) A debt is waived or otherwise found not to be owed to the United States; or

(2) The employee's paying agency is directed by an administrative or judicial order to refund amounts deducted from his or her current pay.

(b) Refunds do not bear interest unless required or permitted by law or contract.

§ 512.26 Interest, penalties, and administrative costs.

The assessment of interest, penalties and administrative costs shall be in accordance with subpart D of this regulation.

§ 512.27 Recovery when paying agency is not creditor agency.

(a) *Format for request for recovery.* (1) Upon completion of the procedures prescribed under 5 CFR 550.1104 and its own regulations, the creditor agency shall certify the debt in writing to the paying agency.

(2) The creditor agency shall certify in writing that the employee owes the debt, the amount and basis of the debt; the date on which payment is due, the date the Government's right to collect first accrued, and that the creditor agency's regulations implementing section 5514 have been approved by OPM.

(3) If collection must be made in installments, the creditor agency must advise the paying agency of the number of installments to be collected, the amount of each installment, and the commencing date of the first installment.

(b) *Submitting the request for recovery*—(1) *Current employees.* The creditor agency shall submit the debt claim, agreement, or other instruction on the payment schedule to the employee's paying agency.

(2) *Separated employees*—(i) *Employees who are in the process of separating.* If the employee is in the process of separating, the creditor agency will submit its debt claim to the employee's paying agency for collection as provided in §§ 512.22 and 512.23. The paying agency shall certify the total amount of its collection and notify the creditor agency and the employee as provided in paragraph (b)(2)(iii) of this section. Where the paying agency is aware that the employee is entitled to payments from the Civil Service Retirement and Disability Fund, it will send a copy of the certified debt claim to the agency responsible for making such payments as notice that a debt is outstanding. It is the responsibility of the creditor agency for pursuing the claim.

(ii) *Employees who have already separated.* If the employee is already separated and all payments due from his or her former paying agency have been paid, the creditor agency may request that monies which are due and payable to the employee from the Civil Service Retirement and Disability Fund (5 CFR 831.1801) or other similar funds be administratively offset in order to collect the debt (31 U.S.C. 3716 and the FCCS).

(iii) *Employees who transfer from one paying agency to another.* If an employee transfers to a position served by a different paying agency subsequent to the creditor agency's debt claim but before complete collection, the paying agency from which the employee separates shall certify the total of collection made on the debt. One copy of the certification will be supplied to the employee, and another to the creditor agency with notice of the employee's transfer. The original shall be inserted in the employees official personnel folder. The creditor agency shall submit a properly certified claim to the new paying agency before collection can be resumed. The paying agency will then resume collection from the employee's current pay account, and notify the employee and the creditor agency of the resumption. The creditor agency will not need to repeat the due process procedure described by 5 U.S.C. 5514 and 5 CFR 550.1101 *et seq*." Upon settlement or repayment of the debt all records of the debt will be removed from official personnel records.

(c) Processing the debt claim upon receipt by the paying agency:

(1) *Incomplete claims*. If the paying agency receives an improperly completed debt certification, it shall return the request with a notice that procedures under 5 CFR 550.1101 *et seq*. and the creditor agency's own regulations must be completed and a properly completed debt certification form received before action will be taken to effect collection.

(2) *Complete claim*. If the paying agency receives a properly completed debt form, deductions will begin prospectively at the next officially established pay interval. A copy of the debt form will be given to the debtor along with notice of the date deductions will commence.

(3) The paying agency is not required or authorized to review the merits of the creditor agency's determination with respect to the amount or validity of the debt as stated in the debt claim.

[52 FR 43897, Nov. 17, 1987, as amended at 55 FR 3051, Jan. 30, 1990]

Subpart D—Interest, Penalties, and Administrative Costs

§ 512.28 Assessment.

(a) Except as provided in paragraph (h) of this section, or § 512.29, Broadcasting Board of Governors shall assess interest, penalties, and administrative costs on debts owed to the United States pursuant to 31 U.S.C. 3717. Before assessing these charges, Broadcasting Board of Governors will mail or hand deliver a written notice to the debtor. This notice will include a statement of the Board's requirements concerning §§ 512.9 and 512.21.

(b) Interest shall accrue from the date on which notice of the debt is first mailed or hand-delivered to the debtor, using the most current address available to the Board.

(c) The rate of interest assessed shall be the rate of the current value of funds to the United States Treasury (i.e., the Treasury Tax and Loan account rate), as prescribed and published by the Secretary of the Treasury in the FEDERAL REGISTER and the Treasury Fiscal Requirements Manual Bulletins annually or quarterly, in accordance with 31 U.S.C. 3717. The rate of interest as initially assessed shall remain fixed for the duration of the indebtedness. However, in cases where the debtor has defaulted on a repayment agreement and seeks a new agreement, Broadcasting Board of Governors may set a new rate which reflects the current value of funds to the Treasury at the time the agreement is executed. Interest will not be assessed on interest, penalties, or administrative costs required by this section.

(d) Broadcasting Board of Governors shall assess charges to cover administrative costs incurred as a result of a delinquent debt. Calculation of administrative costs shall be based upon actual costs incurred. Administrative costs include costs incurred to obtain credit reports in the case of employee debt or in using a private debt collector in the case of non-employee debt.

(e) Broadcasting Board of Governors shall assess a penalty charge not to exceed 6% per year on any portion of a debt that is delinquent for more than 90 days. This charge need not be calculated until the 91st day of delinquency, but shall accrue from the date that the debt became delinquent.

(f) When a debt is paid in partial or installment payments, amounts received shall be applied first to the outstanding penalty and administrative cost charges, second to accrued interest and third to outstanding principal.

(g) Broadcasting Board of Governors will waive the collection of interest on the debt or any portion of the debt that is paid within 30 days after the date on which interest began to accrue. Broadcasting Board of Governors may extend this 30-day period, on a case-by-case basis, if it reasonably determines such action is appropriate. Broadcasting Board of Governors may also waive in whole or in part the collection of interest, penalties, and administrative costs assessed under this section per the criteria specified in part 103 of the Federal Claims Collection Standards (4 CFR part 103) relating to the compromise of claims or if the Board determines that collection of these charges is not in the best interest of the United States. Waiver under the first sentence of this paragraph is mandatory. Under the second and third sentences, it may be exercised under the following circumstances:

(1) Waiver of interest pending consideration of a request for reconsideration, administrative review, or waiver of the underlying debt under a permissive statute, and

(2) Waiver of interest where Broadcasting Board of Governors has accepted an installment plan under §512.12, there is no indication of fault or lack of good faith on the part of the debtor and the amount of the interest is large enough, in relation to the size of the installments that the debtor can reasonably afford to pay, that the debt will never be repaid.

(h) Where a mandatory waiver or review statute applies, interest and related charges may not be assessed for those periods during which collection must be suspended under §104.2(c)(1) of the Federal Claims Collection Standards (4 CFR part 104).

§512.29 Exemptions.

(a) The provisions of 31 U.S.C. 3717 do not apply—

(1) To debts owned by any State or local government;

(2) To debt arising under contracts which were executed prior to, and were in effect on October 25, 1982;

(3) To debts where an applicable statute, loan agreement, or contract either prohibits such charges or explicitly fixes the charges that apply to the debts arising under the Social Security Act, the Internal Revenue Code of 1954, or the tariff laws of the United States.

(b) However Broadcasting Board of Governors is authorized to assess interest and related charges on debts which are not subject to 31 U.S.C. 3717 to the extent authorized under the common law or other applicable statutory authority.

PART 513—GOVERNMENT DEBARMENT AND SUSPENSION (NONPROCUREMENT) AND GOVERNMENTWIDE REQUIREMENTS FOR DRUG-FREE WORKPLACE (GRANTS)

Subpart A—General

Subpart B—Effect of Action

Subpart C—Debarment

Subpart D—Suspension

Subpart E—Responsibilities of GSA, Board and Participants

Subpart F—Drug-Free Workplace Requirements (Grants)

AUTHORITY: 40 U.S.C. 486 (c); 41 U.S.C. 701 *et seq.;* Sec. 2455, Pub. L. 103–355, 108 Stat. 3327 (31 U.S.C. 6101 note); E. O. 12549, 3 CFR, 1986 Comp., p. 189; E.O. 12689, 3 CFR, 1989 comp., p. 235.

SOURCE: 53 FR 19179, 19204, May 26, 1988, unless otherwise noted.

CROSS REFERENCE: See also Office of Management and Budget notice published at 55 FR 21679, May 25, 1990, and 60 FR 33036, June 26, 1995.

Subpart A—General

§513.100 Purpose.

(a) Executive Order (E.O.) 12549 provides that, to the extent permitted by law, Executive departments and agencies shall participate in a governmentwide system for nonprocurement debarment and suspension. A person who is debarred or suspended shall be excluded from Federal financial and nonfinancial assistance and benefits under Federal programs and activities. Debarment or suspension of a participant in a program by one agency shall have governmentwide effect.

(b) These regulations implement section 3 of E.O. 12549 and the guidelines promulgated by the Office of Management and Budget under section 6 of the E.O. by:

(1) Prescribing the programs and activities that are covered by the governmentwide system;

(2) Prescribing the governmentwide criteria and governmentwide minimum due process procedures that each agency shall use;

(3) Providing for the listing of debarred and suspended participants, participants declared ineligible (see definition of "ineligible" in §513.105), and participants who have voluntarily excluded themselves from participation in covered transactions;

(4) Setting forth the consequences of a debarment, suspension, determination of ineligibility, or voluntary exclusion; and

(5) Offering such other guidance as necessary for the effective implementation and administration of the governmentwide system.

(c) These regulations also implement Executive Order 12689 (3 CFR, 1989 Comp., p. 235) and 31 U.S.C. 6101 note (Public Law 103–355, sec. 2455, 108 Stat. 3327) by—

(1) Providing for the inclusion in the *List of Parties Excluded from Federal Procurement and Nonprocurement Programs* all persons proposed for debarment, debarred or suspended under the Federal Acquisition Regulation, 48 CFR Part 9, subpart 9.4; persons against which governmentwide exclusions have been entered under this part; and persons determined to be ineligible; and

(2) Setting forth the consequences of a debarment, suspension, determination of ineligibility, or voluntary exclusion.

(d) Although these regulations cover the listing of ineligible participants and the effect of such listing, they do not prescribe policies and procedures governing declarations of ineligibility.

[60 FR 33040, 33045, June 26, 1995]

§513.105 Definitions.

The following definitions apply to this part:

Adequate evidence. Information sufficient to support the reasonable belief that a particular act or omission has occurred.

Affiliate. Persons are affiliates of each other if, directly or indirectly, either one controls or has the power to control the other, *or*, a third person controls or has the power to control both. Indicia of control include, but are not limited to: interlocking management or ownership, identity of interests among family members, shared facilities and equipment, common use of employees, or a business entity organized following the suspension or debarment of a person which has the same or similar management, ownership, or principal employees as the suspended, debarred, ineligible, or voluntarily excluded person.

Agency. Any executive department, military department or defense agency or other agency of the executive branch, excluding the independent regulatory agencies.

Civil judgment. The disposition of a civil action by any court of competent jurisdiction, whether entered by verdict, decision, settlement, stipulation, or otherwise creating a civil liability for the wrongful acts complained of; or a final determination of liability under the Program Fraud Civil Remedies Act of 1988 (31 U.S.C. 3801–12).

Conviction. A judgment or conviction of a criminal offense by any court of competent jurisdiction, whether entered upon a verdict or a plea, including a plea of nolo contendere.

Debarment. An action taken by a debarring official in accordance with these regulations to exclude a person from participating in covered transactions. A person so excluded is "debarred."

Debarring official. An official authorized to impose debarment. The debarring official is either:

(1) The agency head, or

(2) An official designated by the agency head.

Indictment. Indictment for a criminal offense. An information or other filing by competent authority charging a criminal offense shall be given the same effect as an indictment.

Ineligible. Excluded from participation in Federal nonprocurement programs pursuant to a determination of ineligibility under statutory, executive order, or regulatory authority, other than Executive Order 12549 and its agency implementing regulations; for exemple, excluded pursuant to the Davis-Bacon Act and its implementing regulations, the equal employment opportunity acts and executive orders, or the environmental protection acts and executive orders. A person is ineligible where the determination of ineligibility affects such person's eligibility to participate in more than one covered transaction.

Legal proceedings. Any criminal proceeding or any civil judicial proceeding to which the Federal Government or a State or local government or quasi-governmental authority is a party. The term includes appeals from such proceedings.

List of Parties Excluded from Federal Procurement and Nonprocurement Programs. A list compiled, maintained and distributed by the General Services Administration (GSA) containing the names and other information about persons who have been debarred, suspended, or voluntarily excluded under Executive Orders 12549 and 12689 and these regulations or 48 CFR part 9, subpart 9.4, persons who have been proposed for debarment under 48 CFR part 9, subpart 9.4, and those persons who have been determined to be ineligible.

Notice. A written communication served in person or sent by certified mail, return receipt requested, or its equivalent, to the last known address of a party, its identified counsel, its agent for service of process, or any partner, officer, director, owner, or joint venturer of the party. Notice, if undeliverable, shall be considered to have been received by the addressee five days after being properly sent to the last address known by the Board.

Participant. Any person who submits a proposal for, enters into, or reasonably may be expected to enter into a covered transaction. This term also includes any person who acts on behalf of or is authorized to commit a participant in a covered transaction as an agent or representative of another participant.

Person. Any individual, corporation, partnership, association, unit of government or legal entity, however organized, except: foreign governments or foreign governmental entities, public international organizations, foreign government owned (in whole or in part) or controlled entities, and entities consisting wholly or partially of foreign governments or foreign governmental entities.

Preponderance of the evidence. Proof by information that, compared with that opposing it, leads to the conclusion that the fact at issue is more probably true than not.

Principal. Officer, director, owner, partner, key employee, or other person within a participant with primary management or supervisory responsibilities; or a person who has a critical influence on or substantive control over a covered transaction, whether or not employed by the participant. Persons who have a critical influence on or substantive control over a covered transaction are:

(1) Principal investigators.

Proposal. A solicited or unsolicited bid, application, request, invitation to consider or similar communication by or on behalf of a person seeking to participate or to receive a benefit, directly or indirectly, in or under a covered transaction.

Respondent. A person against whom a debarment or suspension action has been initiated.

State. Any of the States of the United States, the District of Columbia, the Commonwealth of Puerto Rico, any territory or possession of the United States, or any agency of a State, exclusive of institutions of higher education, hospitals, and units of local government. A State instrumentality will be considered part of the State government if it has a written determination from a State government that such State considers that instrumentality to be an agency of the State government.

Suspending official. An official authorized to impose suspension. The suspending official is either:

(1) The agency head, or

(2) An official designated by the agency head.

Suspension. An action taken by a suspending official in accordance with these regulations that immediately excludes a person from participating in covered transactions for a temporary period, pending completion of an investigation and such legal, debarment, or Program Fraud Civil Remedies Act proceedings as may ensue. A person so excluded is "suspended."

Voluntary exclusion or voluntarily excluded. A status of nonparticipation or limited participation in covered transactions assumed by a person pursuant to the terms of a settlement.

Broadcasting Board of Governors.

[53 FR 19204, 19179, May 26, 1988, as amended at 60 FR 33041, 33045, June 26, 1995]

§513.110 Coverage.

(a) These regulations apply to all persons who have participated, are currently participating or may reasonably be expected to participate in transactions under Federal nonprocurement programs. For purposes of these regulations such transactions will be referred to as "covered transactions."

(1) *Covered transaction.* For purposes of these regulations, a covered transaction is a primary covered transaction or a lower tier covered transaction. Covered transactions at any tier need not involve the transfer of Federal funds.

(i) *Primary covered transaction.* Except as noted in paragraph (a)(2) of this section, a primary covered transaction is any nonprocurement transaction between an agency and a person, regardless of type, including: grants, cooperative agreements, scholarships, fellowships, contracts of assistance, loans, loan guarantees, subsidies, insurance, payments for specified use, donation agreements and any other nonprocurement transactions between a Federal agency and a person. Primary covered transactions also include those transactions specially designated by the U.S. Department of Housing and Urban Development in such agency's regulations governing debarment and suspension.

(ii) *Lower tier covered transaction.* A lower tier covered transaction is:

(A) Any transaction between a participant and a person other than a procurement contract for goods or services, regardless of type, under a primary covered transaction.

(B) Any procurement contract for goods or services between a participant and a person, regardless of type, expected to equal or exceed the Federal procurement small purchase threshold fixed at 10 U.S.C. 2304(g) and 41 U.S.C. 253(g) (currently $25,000) under a primary covered transaction.

(C) Any procurement contract for goods or services between a participant and a person under a covered transaction, regardless of amount, under which that person will have a critical influence on or substantive control over that covered transaction. Such persons are:

(*1*) Principal investigators.

(*2*) Providers of federally-required audit services.

(2) *Exceptions.* The following transactions are not covered:

(i) Statutory entitlements or mandatory awards (but not subtier awards thereunder which are not themselves mandatory), including deposited funds insured by the Federal Government;

(ii) Direct awards to foreign governments or public international organizations, or transactions with foreign governments or foreign governmental entities, public international organizations, foreign government owned (in whole or in part) or controlled entities, entities consisting wholly or partially of foreign governments or foreign governmental entities;

(iii) Benefits to an individual as a personal entitlement without regard to the individual's present responsibility (but benefits received in an individual's business capacity are not excepted);

(iv) Federal employment;

(v) Transactions pursuant to national or agency-recognized emergencies or disasters;

(vi) Incidental benefits derived from ordinary governmental operations; and

(vii) Other transactions where the application of these regulations would be prohibited by law.

(b) *Relationship to other sections.* This section describes the types of transactions to which a debarment or suspension under the regulations will apply. Subpart B, "Effect of Action," 513.200, "Debarment or suspension," sets forth the consequences of a debarment or suspension. Those consequences would obtain only with respect to participants and principals in the covered transactions and activities described in 513.110(a). Sections 513.325, "Scope of debarment," and 513.420, "Scope of suspension," govern the extent to which a specific participant or organizational elements of a participant would be automatically included within a debarment or suspension action, and the conditions under which affiliates or persons associated with a participant may also be brought within the scope of the action.

(c) *Relationship to Federal procurement activities.* In accordance with E.O. 12689 and section 2455 of Public Law 103–355, any debarment, suspension, proposed debarment or other governmentwide exclusion initiated under the Federal Acquisition Regulation (FAR) on or after August 25, 1995 shall be recognized by and effective for Executive Branch agencies and participants as an exclusion under this regulation. Similarly, any debarment, suspension or other governmentwide exclusion initiated under this regulation on or after August 25, 1995 shall be recognized by and effective for those agencies as a debarment or suspension under the FAR.

[53 FR 19179, 19204, May 26, 1988, as amended at 60 FR 33041, 33045, June 26, 1995]

§ 513.115 Policy.

(a) In order to protect the public interest, it is the policy of the Federal Government to conduct business only with responsible persons. Debarment and suspension are discretionary actions that, taken in accordance with Executive Order 12549 and these regulations, are appropriate means to implement this policy.

(b) Debarment and suspension are serious actions which shall be used only in the public interest and for the Federal Government's protection and not for purposes of punishment. Agencies may impose debarment or suspension for the causes and in accordance with the procedures set forth in these regulations.

(c) When more than one agency has an interest in the proposed debarment or suspension of a person, consideration shall be given to designating one agency as the lead agency for making the decision. Agencies are encouraged to establish methods and procedures for coordinating their debarment or suspension actions.

Subpart B—Effect of Action

§ 513.200 Debarment or suspension.

(a) *Primary covered transactions.* Except to the extent prohibited by law, persons who are debarred or suspended shall be excluded from primary covered transactions as either participants or principals throughout the Executive Branch of the Federal Government for the period of their debarment, suspension, or the period they are proposed for debarment under 48 CFR part 9, subpart 9.4. Accordingly, no agency shall enter into primary covered transactions with such excluded persons during such period, except as permitted pursuant to § 513.215.

(b) *Lower tier covered transactions.* Except to the extent prohibited by law, persons who have been proposed for debarment under 48 CFR part 9, subpart 9.4, debarred or suspended shall be excluded from participating as either participants or principals in all lower tier covered transactions (see § 513.110(a)(1)(ii)) for the period of their exclusion.

(c) *Exceptions.* Debarment or suspension does not affect a person's eligibility for—

(1) Statutory entitlements or mandatory awards (but not subtier awards thereunder which are not themselves mandatory), including deposited funds insured by the Federal Government;

(2) Direct awards to foreign governments or public international organizations, or transactions with foreign governments or foreign governmental entities, public international organizations, foreign government owned (in whole or in part) or controlled entities, and entities consisting wholly or partially of foreign governments or foreign governmental entities;

(3) Benefits to an individual as a personal entitlement without regard to the individual's present responsibility (but benefits received in an individual's business capacity are not excepted);

(4) Federal employment;

(5) Transactions pursuant to national or agency-recognized emergencies or disasters;

(6) Incidental benefits derived from ordinary governmental operations; and

(7) Other transactions where the application of these regulations would be prohibited by law.

[60 FR 33041, 33045, June 26, 1995]

§ 513.205 Ineligible persons.

Persons who are ineligible, as defined in § 513.105(i), are excluded in accordance with the applicable statutory, executive order, or regulatory authority.

§ 513.210 Voluntary exclusion.

Persons who accept voluntary exclusions under § 513.315 are excluded in accordance with the terms of their settlements. Broadcasting Board of Governors shall, and participants may, contact the original action agency to ascertain the extent of the exclusion.

§ 513.215 Exception provision.

may grant an exception permitting a debarred, suspended, or voluntarily excluded person, or a person proposed for debarment under 48 CFR part 9, subpart 9.4, to participate in a particular covered transaction upon a written determination by the agency head or an authorized designee stating the reason(s) for deviating from the Presidential policy established by Executive Order 12549 and § 513.200. However, in accordance with the President's stated intention in the Executive Order, exceptions shall be granted only infrequently. Exceptions shall be reported in accordance with § 513.505(a).

[60 FR 33041, 33045, June 26, 1995]

§ 513.220 Continuation of covered transactions.

(a) Notwithstanding the debarment, suspension, proposed debarment under 48 CFR part 9, subpart 9.4, determination of ineligibility, or voluntary exclusion of any person by an agency, agencies and participants may continue covered transactions in existence at the time the person was debarred, suspended, proposed for debarment under 48 CFR part 9, subpart 9.4, declared ineligible, or voluntarily excluded. A decision as to the type of termination action, if any, to be taken should be made only after thorough review to ensure the propriety of the proposed action.

(b) Agencies and participants shall not renew or extend covered transactions (other than no-cost time extensions) with any person who is debarred, suspended, proposed for debarment under 48 CFR part 9, subpart 9.4, ineligible or voluntary excluded, except as provided in § 513.215.

[60 FR 33041, 33045, June 26, 1995]

§ 513.225 Failure to adhere to restrictions.

(a) Except as permitted under § 513.215 or § 513.220, a participant shall not knowingly do business under a covered transaction with a person who is—

(1) Debarred or suspended;

(2) Proposed for debarment under 48 CFR part 9, subpart 9.4; or

(3) Ineligible for or voluntarily excluded from the covered transaction.

(b) Violation of the restriction under paragraph (a) of this section may result in disallowance of costs, annulment or termination of award, issuance of a stop work order, debarment or suspension, or other remedies as appropriate.

(c) A participant may rely upon the certification of a prospective participant in a lower tier covered transaction that it and its principals are not debarred, suspended, proposed for debarment under 48 CFR part 9, subpart 9.4, ineligible, or voluntarily excluded from the covered transaction (See appendix B of these regulations), unless it knows that the certification is erroneous. An agency has the burden of proof that a participant did knowingly do business with a person that filed an erroneous certification.

[60 FR 33041, 33045, June 26, 1995]

Subpart C—Debarment

§ 513.300 General.

The debarring official may debar a person for any of the causes in § 513.30, using procedures established in §§ 513.310 through 513.314. The existence of a cause for debarment, however, does not necessarily require that the person be debarred; the seriousness of the person's acts or omissions and any mitigating factors shall be considered in making any debarment decision.

§ 513.305 Causes for debarment.

Debarment may be imposed in accordance with the provisions of §§ 513.300 through 513.314 for:

(a) Conviction of or civil judgment for:

(1) Commission of fraud or a criminal offense in connection with obtaining, attempting to obtain, or performing a public or private agreement or transaction;

(2) Violation of Federal or State antitrust statutes, including those proscribing price fixing between competitors, allocation of customers between competitors, and bid rigging;

(3) Commission of embezzlement, theft, forgery, bribery, falsification or destruction of records, making false statements, receiving stolen property, making false claims, or obstruction of justice; or

(4) Commission of any other offense indicating a lack of business integrity or business honesty that seriously and directly affects the present responsibility of a person.

(b) Violation of the terms of a public agreement or transaction so serious as to affect the integrity of an agency program, such as:

(1) A willful failure to perform in accordance with the terms of one or more public agreements or transactions;

(2) A history of failure to perform or of unsatisfactory performance of one or more public agreements or transactions; or

(3) A willful violation of a statutory or regulatory provision or requirement applicable to a public agreement or transaction.

(c) Any of the following causes:

(1) A nonprocurement debarment by any Federal agency taken before October 1, 1988, the effective date of these regulations, or a procurement debarment by any Federal agency taken pursuant to 48 CFR subpart 9.4;

(2) Knowingly doing business with a debarred, suspended, ineligible, or voluntarily excluded person, in connection with a covered transaction, except as permitted in § 513.215 or § 513.220;

(3) Failure to pay a single substantial debt, or a number of outstanding debts (including disallowed costs and overpayments, but not including sums owed the Federal Government under the Internal Revenue Code) owed to any Federal agency or instrumentality, provided the debt is uncontested by the debtor or, if contested, provided that the debtor's legal and administrative remedies have been exhausted;

(4) Violation of a material provision of a voluntary exclusion agreement entered into under §513.315 or of any settlement of a debarment or suspension action; or

(5) Violation of any requirement of subpart F of this part, relating to providing a drug-free workplace, as set forth in §513.615 of this part.

(d) Any other cause of so serious or compelling a nature that it affects the present responsibility of a person.

[53 FR 19179, 19204, May 26, 1988, as amended at 54 FR 4950, 4955, Jan. 31, 1989]

§513.310 Procedures.

Broadcasting Board of Governors shall process debarment actions as informally as practicable, consistent with the principles of fundamental fairness, using the procedures in §§513.311 through 513.314.

§513.311 Investigation and referral.

Information concerning the existence of a cause for debarment from any source shall be promptly reported, investigated, and referred, when appropriate, to the debarring official for consideration. After consideration, the debarring official may issue a notice of proposed debarment.

§513.312 Notice of proposed debarment.

A debarment proceeding shall be initiated by notice to the respondent advising:

(a) That debarment is being considered;

(b) Of the reasons for the proposed debarment in terms sufficient to put the respondent on notice of the conduct or transaction(s) upon which it is based;

(c) Of the cause(s) relied upon under §513.305 for proposing debarment;

(d) Of the provisions of §513.311 through §513.314, and any other Broadcasting Board of Governors procedures, if applicable, governing debarment decisionmaking; and

(e) Of the potential effect of a debarment.

§513.313 Opportunity to contest proposed debarment.

(a) *Submission in opposition.* Within 30 days after receipt of the notice of proposed debarment, the respondent may submit, in person, in writing, or through a representative, information and argument in opposition to the proposed debarment.

(b) *Additional proceedings as to disputed material facts.* (1) In actions not based upon a conviction or civil judgment, if the debarring official finds that the respondent's submission in opposition raises a genuine dispute over facts material to the proposed debarment, respondent(s) shall be afforded an opportunity to appear with a representative, submit documentary evidence, present witnesses, and confront any witness the agency presents.

(2) A transcribed record of any additional proceedings shall be made available at cost to the respondent, upon request, unless the respondent and the agency, by mutual agreement, waive the requirement for a transcript.

§513.314 Debarring official's decision.

(a) *No additional proceedings necessary.* In actions based upon a conviction or civil judgment, or in which there is no genuine dispute over material facts, the debarring official shall make a decision on the basis of all the information in the administrative record, including any submission made by the respondent. The decision shall be made within 45 days after receipt of any information and argument submitted by the respondent, unless the debarring official extends this period for good cause.

(b) *Additional proceedings necessary.* (1) In actions in which additional proceedings are necessary to determine disputed material facts, written findings of fact shall be prepared. The debarring official shall base the decision on the facts as found, together with any information and argument submitted by the respondent and any other information in the administrative record.

(2) The debarring official may refer disputed material facts to another official for findings of fact. The debarring official may reject any such findings, in whole or in part, only after specifically determining them to be arbitrary and capricious or clearly erroneous.

(3) The debarring official's decision shall be made after the conclusion of

the proceedings with respect to disputed facts.

(c)(1) *Standard of proof*. In any debarment action, the cause for debarment must be established by a preponderance of the evidence. Where the proposed debarment is based upon a conviction or civil judgment, the standard shall be deemed to have been met.

(2) *Burden of proof*. The burden of proof is on the agency proposing debarment.

(d) *Notice of debarring official's decision*. (1) If the debarring official decides to impose debarment, the respondent shall be given prompt notice:

(i) Referring to the notice of proposed debarment;

(ii) Specifying the reasons for debarment;

(iii) Stating the period of debarment, including effective dates; and

(iv) Advising that the debarment is effective for covered transactions throughout the executive branch of the Federal Government unless an agency head or an authorized designee makes the determination referred to in §513.215.

(2) If the debarring official decides not to impose debarment, the respondent shall be given prompt notice of that decision. A decision not to impose debarment shall be without prejudice to a subsequent imposition of debarment by any other agency.

§513.315 Settlement and voluntary exclusion.

(a) When in the best interest of the Government, Broadcasting Board of Governors may, at any time, settle a debarment or suspension action.

(b) If a participant and the Board agree to a voluntary exclusion of the participant, such voluntary exclusion shall be entered on the Nonprocurement List (see subpart E).

§513.320 Period of debarment.

(a) Debarment shall be for a period commensurate with the seriousness of the cause(s). If a suspension precedes a debarment, the suspension period shall be considered in determining the debarment period.

(1) Debarment for causes other than those related to a violation of the requirements of subpart F of this part generally should not exceed three years. Where circumstances warrant, a longer period of debarment may be imposed.

(2) In the case of a debarment for a violation of the requirements of subpart F of this part (*see* 513.305(c)(5)), the period of debarment shall not exceed five years.

(b) The debarring official may extend an existing debarment for an additional period, if that official determines that an extension is necessary to protect the public interest. However, a debarment may not be extended solely on the basis of the facts and circumstances upon which the initial debarment action was based. If debarment for an additional period is determined to be necessary, the procedures of §§513.311 through 513.314 shall be followed to extend the debarment.

(c) The respondent may request the debarring official to reverse the debarment decision or to reduce the period or scope of debarment. Such a request shall be in writing and supported by documentation. The debarring official may grant such a request for reasons including, but not limited to:

(1) Newly discovered material evidence;

(2) Reversal of the conviction or civil judgment upon which the debarment was based;

(3) Bona fide change in ownership or management;

(4) Elimination of other causes for which the debarment was imposed; or

(5) Other reasons the debarring official deems appropriate.

[53 FR 19179, 19204, May 26, 1988, as amended at 54 FR 4950, 4955, Jan. 31, 1989]

§513.325 Scope of debarment.

(a) *Scope in general*. (1) Debarment of a person under these regulations constitutes debarment of all its divisions and other organizational elements from all covered transactions, unless the debarment decision is limited by its terms to one or more specifically identified individuals, divisions or other organizational elements or to specific types of transactions.

(2) The debarment action may include any affiliate of the participant that is specifically named and given notice of the proposed debarment and

an opportunity to respond (see §§513.311 through 513.314).

(b) *Imputing conduct.* For purposes of determining the scope of debarment, conduct may be imputed as follows:

(1) *Conduct imputed to participant.* The fraudulent, criminal or other seriously improper conduct of any officer, director, shareholder, partner, employee, or other individual associated with a participant may be imputed to the participant when the conduct occurred in connection with the individual's performance of duties for or on behalf of the participant, or with the participant's knowledge, approval, or acquiescence. The participant's acceptance of the benefits derived from the conduct shall be evidence of such knowledge, approval, or acquiescence.

(2) *Conduct imputed to individuals associated with participant.* The fraudulent, criminal, or other seriously improper conduct of a participant may be imputed to any officer, director, shareholder, partner, employee, or other individual associated with the participant who participated in, knew of, or had reason to know of the participant's conduct.

(3) *Conduct of one participant imputed to other participants in a joint venture.* The fraudulent, criminal, or other seriously improper conduct of one participant in a joint venture, grant pursuant to a joint application, or similar arrangement may be imputed to other participants if the conduct occurred for or on behalf of the joint venture, grant pursuant to a joint application, or similar arrangement may be imputed to other participants if the conduct occurred for or on behalf of the joint venture, grant pursuant to a joint application, or similar arrangement or with the knowledge, approval, or acquiescence of these participants. Acceptance of the benefits derived from the conduct shall be evidence of such knowledge, approval, or acquiescence.

Subpart D—Suspension

§513.400 General.

(a) The suspending official may suspend a person for any of the causes in §513.405 using procedures established in §§513.410 through 513.413.

(b) Suspension is a serious action to be imposed only when:

(1) There exists adequate evidence of one or more of the causes set out in §513.405, and

(2) Immediate action is necessary to protect the public interest.

(c) In assessing the adequacy of the evidence, the Board should consider how much information is available, how credible it is given the circumstances, whether or not important allegations are corroborated, and what inferences can reasonably be drawn as a result. This assessment should include an examination of basic documents such as grants, cooperative agreements, loan authorizations, and contracts.

§513.405 Causes for suspension.

(a) Suspension may be imposed in accordance with the provisions of §§513.400 through 513.413 upon adequate evidence:

(1) To suspect the commission of an offense listed in §513.305(a); or

(2) That a cause for debarment under §513.305 may exist.

(b) Indictment shall constitute adequate evidence for purposes of suspension actions.

§513.410 Procedures.

(a) *Investigation and referral.* Information concerning the existence of a cause for suspension from any source shall be promptly reported, investigated, and referred, when appropriate, to the suspending official for consideration. After consideration, the suspending official may issue a notice of suspension.

(b) *Decisionmaking process.* Broadcasting Board of Governors shall process suspension actions as informally as practicable, consistent with principles of fundamental fairness, using the procedures in §513.411 through §513.413.

§513.411 Notice of suspension.

When a respondent is suspended, notice shall immediately be given:

(a) That suspension has been imposed;

(b) That the suspension is based on an indictment, conviction, or other adequate evidence that the respondent has committed irregularities seriously reflecting on the propriety of further Federal Government dealings with the respondent;

(c) Describing any such irregularities in terms sufficient to put the respondent on notice without disclosing the Federal Government's evidence;

(d) Of the cause(s) relied upon under § 513.405 for imposing suspension;

(e) That the suspension is for a temporary period pending the completion of an investigation or ensuing legal, debarment, or Program Fraud Civil Remedies Act proceedings;

(f) Of the provisions of § 513.411 through § 513.413 and any other Broadcasting Board of Governors procedures, if applicable, governing suspension decisionmaking; and

(g) Of the effect of the suspension.

§ 513.412 Opportunity to contest suspension.

(a) *Submission in opposition.* Within 30 days after receipt of the notice of suspension, the respondent may submit, in person, in writing, or through a representative, information and argument in opposition to the suspension.

(b) *Additional proceedings as to disputed material facts.* (1) If the suspending official finds that the respondent's submission in opposition raises a genuine dispute over facts material to the suspension, respondent(s) shall be afforded an opportunity to appear with a representative, submit documentary evidence, present witnesses, and confront any witness the Board presents, unless:

(i) The action is based on an indictment, conviction or civil judgment, or

(ii) A determination is made, on the basis of Department of Justice advice, that the substantial interests of the Federal Government in pending or contemplated legal proceedings based on the same facts as the suspension would be prejudiced.

(2) A transcribed record of any additional proceedings shall be prepared and made available at cost to the respondent, upon request, unless the respondent and the Board, by mutual agreement, waive the requirement for a transcript.

§ 513.413 Suspending official's decision.

The suspending official may modify or terminate the suspension (for example, see § 513.320(c) for reasons for reducing the period or scope of debarment) or may leave it in force. However, a decision to modify or terminate the suspension shall be without prejudice to the subsequent imposition of suspension by any other agency or debarment by any agency. The decision shall be rendered in accordance with the following provisions:

(a) *No additional proceedings necessary.* In actions: based on an indictment, conviction, or civil judgment; in which there is no genuine dispute over material facts; or in which additional proceedings to determine disputed material facts have been denied on the basis of Department of Justice advice, the suspending official shall make a decision on the basis of all the information in the administrative record, including any submission made by the respondent. The decision shall be made within 45 days after receipt of any information and argument submitted by the respondent, unless the suspending official extends this period for good cause.

(b) *Additional proceedings necessary.* (1) In actions in which additional proceedings are necessary to determine disputed material facts, written findings of fact shall be prepared. The suspending official shall base the decision on the facts as found, together with any information and argument submitted by the respondent and any other information in the administrative record.

(2) The suspending official may refer matters involving disputed material facts to another official for findings of fact. The suspending official may reject any such findings, in whole or in part, only after specifically determining them to be arbitrary or capricious or clearly erroneous.

(c) *Notice of suspending official's decision.* Prompt written notice of the suspending official's decision shall be sent to the respondent.

§ 513.415 Period of suspension.

(a) Suspension shall be for a temporary period pending the completion of an investigation or ensuing legal, debarment, or Program Fraud Civil Remedies Act proceedings, unless terminated sooner by the suspending official or as provided in paragraph (b) of this section.

(b) If legal or administrative proceedings are not initiated within 12 months after the date of the suspension notice, the suspension shall be terminated unless an Assistant Attorney General or United States Attorney requests its extension in writing, in which case it may be extended for an additional six months. In no event may a suspension extend beyond 18 months, unless such proceedings have been initiated within that period.

(c) The suspending official shall notify the Department of Justice of an impending termination of a suspension, at least 30 days before the 12-month period expires, to give that Department an opportunity to request an extension.

§513.420 Scope of suspension.

The scope of a suspension is the same as the scope of a debarment (see §513.325), except that the procedures of §§513.410 through 513.413 shall be used in imposing a suspension.

Subpart E—Responsibilities of GSA, Board and Participants

§513.500 GSA responsibilities.

(a) In accordance with the OMB guidelines, GSA shall compile, maintain, and distribute a list of all persons who have been debarred, suspended, or voluntarily excluded by agencies under Executive Order 12549 and these regulations, and those who have been determined to be ineligible.

(b) At a minimum, this list shall indicate:

(1) The names and addresses of all debarred, suspended, ineligible, and voluntarily excluded persons, in alphabetical order, with cross-references when more than one name is involved in a single action;

(2) The type of action;

(3) The cause for the action;

(4) The scope of the action;

(5) Any termination date for each listing; and

(6) The agency and name and telephone number of the agency point of contact for the action.

§513.505 Broadcasting Board of Governors responsibilities.

(a) The Board shall provide GSA with current information concerning debarments, suspension, determinations of ineligibility, and voluntary exclusions it has taken. Until February 18, 1989, the Board shall also provide GSA and OMB with information concerning all transactions in which Broadcasting Board of Governors has granted exceptions under §513.215 permitting participation by debarred, suspended, or voluntarily excluded persons.

(b) Unless an alternative schedule is agreed to by GSA, the Board shall advise GSA of the information set forth in §513.500(b) and of the exceptions granted under §513.215 within five working days after taking such actions.

(c) The Board shall direct inquiries concerning listed persons to the agency that took the action.

(d) Board officials shall check the Nonprocurement List before entering covered transactions to determine whether a participant in a primary transaction is debarred, suspended, ineligible, or voluntarily excluded (Tel. #).

(e) Board officials shall check the Nonprocurement List before approving principals or lower tier participants where Board approval of the principal or lower tier participant is required under the terms of the transaction, to determine whether such principals or participants are debarred, suspended, ineligible, or voluntarily excluded.

§513.510 Participants' responsibilities.

(a) *Certification by participants in primary covered transactions.* Each participant shall submit the certification in appendix A to this part for it and its principals at the time the participant submits its proposal in connection with a primary covered transaction, except that States need only complete such certification as to their principals. Participants may decide the method and frequency by which they determine the eligibility of their principals. In addition, each participant may, but is not required to, check the Nonprocurement List for its principals (Tel. #). Adverse information on the certification will not necessarily result in denial of participation. However, the certification, and any additional information pertaining to the certification submitted by the participant, shall be considered in the administration of covered transactions.

(b) *Certification by participants in lower tier covered transactions.* (1) Each participant shall require participants in lower tier covered transactions to include the certification in appendix B to this part for it and its principals in any proposal submitted in connection with such lower tier covered transactions.

(2) A participant may rely upon the certification of a prospective participant in a lower tier covered transaction that it and its principals are not debarred, suspended, ineligible, or voluntarily excluded from the covered transaction by any Federal agency, unless it knows that the certification is erroneous. Participants may decide the method and frequency by which they determine the eligiblity of their principals. In addition, a participant may, but is not required to, check the Nonprocurement List for its principals and for participants (Tel. #).

(c) *Changed circumstances regarding certification.* A participant shall provide immediate written notice to Broadcasting Board of Governors if at any time the participant learns that its certification was erroneous when submitted or has become erroneous by reason of changed circumstances. Participants in lower tier covered transactions shall provide the same updated notice to the participant to which it submitted its proposals.

Subpart F—Drug-Free Workplace Requirements (Grants)

SOURCE: 55 FR 21688, 21694, May 25, 1990, unless otherwise noted.

§ 513.600 Purpose.

(a) The purpose of this subpart is to carry out the Drug-Free Workplace Act of 1988 by requiring that—

(1) A grantee, other than an individual, shall certify to the Board that it will provide a drug-free workplace;

(2) A grantee who is an individual shall certify to the Board that, as a condition of the grant, he or she will not engage in the unlawful manufacture, distribution, dispensing, possession or use of a controlled substance in conducting any activity with the grant.

(b) Requirements implementing the Drug-Free Workplace Act of 1988 for contractors with the Board are found at 48 CFR subparts 9.4, 23.5, and 52.2.

§ 513.605 Definitions.

(a) Except as amended in this section, the definitions of § 513.105 apply to this subpart.

(b) For purposes of this subpart—

(1) *Controlled substance* means a controlled substance in schedules I through V of the Controlled Substances Act (21 U.S.C. 812), and as further defined by regulation at 21 CFR 1308.11 through 1308.15;

(2) *Conviction* means a finding of guilt (including a plea of nolo contendere) or imposition of sentence, or both, by any judicial body charged with the responsibility to determine violations of the Federal or State criminal drug statutes;

(3) *Criminal drug statute* means a Federal or non-Federal criminal statute involving the manufacture, distribution, dispensing, use, or possession of any controlled substance;

(4) *Drug-free workplace* means a site for the performance of work done in connection with a specific grant at which employees of the grantee are prohibited from engaging in the unlawful manufacture, distribution, dispensing, possession, or use of a controlled substance;

(5) *Employee* means the employee of a grantee directly engaged in the performance of work under the grant, including:

(i) All *direct charge* employees;

(ii) All *indirect charge* employees, unless their impact or involvement is insignificant to the performance of the grant; and,

(iii) Temporary personnel and consultants who are directly engaged in the performance of work under the grant and who are on the grantee's payroll.

This definition does not include workers not on the payroll of the grantee (e.g., volunteers, even if used to meet a matching requirement; consultants or independent contractors not on the payroll; or employees of subrecipients or subcontractors in covered workplaces);

(6) *Federal agency* or *agency* means any United States executive department, military department, government corporation, government controlled corporation, any other establishment in the executive branch (including the Executive Office of the President), or any independent regulatory agency;

(7) *Grant* means an award of financial assistance, including a cooperative agreement, in the form of money, or property in lieu of money, by a Federal agency directly to a grantee. The term grant includes block grant and entitlement grant programs, whether or not exempted from coverage under the grants management government-wide common rule on uniform administrative requirements for grants and cooperative agreements. The term does not include technical assistance that provides services instead of money, or other assistance in the form of loans, loan guarantees, interest subsidies, insurance, or direct appropriations; or any veterans' benefits to individuals, i.e., any benefit to veterans, their families, or survivors by virtue of the service of a veteran in the Armed Forces of the United States;

(8) *Grantee* means a person who applies for or receives a grant directly from a Federal agency (except another Federal agency);

(9) *Individual* means a natural person;

(10) *State* means any of the States of the United States, the District of Columbia, the Commonwealth of Puerto Rico, any territory or possession of the United States, or any agency of a State, exclusive of institutions of higher education, hospitals, and units of local government. A State instrumentality will be considered part of the State government if it has a written determination from a State government that such State considers the instrumentality to be an agency of the State government.

§ 513.610 Coverage.

(a) This subpart applies to any grantee of the Board.

(b) This subpart applies to any grant, except where application of this subpart would be inconsistent with the international obligations of the United States or the laws or regulations of a foreign government. A determination of such inconsistency may be made only by the Board head or his/her designee.

(c) The provisions of subparts A, B, C, D and E of this part apply to matters covered by this subpart, except where specifically modified by this subpart. In the event of any conflict between provisions of this subpart and other provisions of this part, the provisions of this subpart are deemed to control with respect to the implementation of drug-free workplace requirements concerning grants.

§ 513.615 Grounds for suspension of payments, suspension or termination of grants, or suspension or debarment.

A grantee shall be deemed in violation of the requirements of this subpart if the Board head or his or her official designee determines, in writing, that—

(a) The grantee has made a false certification under § 513.630;

(b) With respect to a grantee other than an individual—

(1) The grantee has violated the certification by failing to carry out the requirements of paragraphs (A)(a)–(g) and/or (B) of the certification (Alternate I to appendix C) or

(2) Such a number of employees of the grantee have been convicted of violations of criminal drug statutes for violations occurring in the workplace as to indicate that the grantee has failed to make a good faith effort to provide a drug-free workplace.

(c) With respect to a grantee who is an individual—

(1) The grantee has violated the certification by failing to carry out its requirements (Alternate II to appendix C); or

(2) The grantee is convicted of a criminal drug offense resulting from a violation occurring during the conduct of any grant activity.

§ 513.620 Effect of violation.

(a) In the event of a violation of this subpart as provided in § 513.615, and in accordance with applicable law, the grantee shall be subject to one or more of the following actions:

(1) Suspension of payments under the grant;

(2) Suspension or termination of the grant; and

(3) Suspension or debarment of the grantee under the provisions of this part.

(b) Upon issuance of any final decision under this part requiring debarment of a grantee, the debarred grantee shall be ineligible for award of any grant from any Federal agency for a period specified in the decision, not to exceed five years (*see* § 513.320(a)(2) of this part).

§ 513.625 Exception provision.

The Board head may waive with respect to a particular grant, in writing, a suspension of payments under a grant, suspension or termination of a grant, or suspension or debarment of a grantee if the Board head determines that such a waiver would be in the public interest. This exception authority cannot be delegated to any other official.

§ 513.630 Certification requirements and procedures.

(a)(1) As a prior condition of being awarded a grant, each grantee shall make the appropriate certification to the Federal agency providing the grant, as provided in appendix C to this part.

(2) Grantees are not required to make a certification in order to continue receiving funds under a grant awarded before March 18, 1989, or under a no-cost time extension of such a grant. However, the grantee shall make a one-time drug-free workplace certification for a non-automatic continuation of such a grant made on or after March 18, 1989.

(b) Except as provided in this section, all grantees shall make the required certification for each grant. For mandatory formula grants and entitlements that have no application process, grantees shall submit a one-time certification in order to continue receiving awards.

(c) A grantee that is a State may elect to make one certification in each Federal fiscal year. States that previously submitted an annual certification are not required to make a certification for Fiscal Year 1990 until June 30, 1990. Except as provided in paragraph (d) of this section, this certification shall cover all grants to all State agencies from any Federal agency. The State shall retain the original of this statewide certification in its Governor's office and, prior to grant award, shall ensure that a copy is submitted individually with respect to each grant, unless the Federal agency has designated a central location for submission.

(d)(1) The Governor of a State may exclude certain State agencies from the statewide certification and authorize these agencies to submit their own certifications to Federal agencies. The statewide certification shall name any State agencies so excluded.

(2) A State agency to which the statewide certification does not apply, or a State agency in a State that does not have a statewide certification, may elect to make one certification in each Federal fiscal year. State agencies that previously submitted a State agency certification are not required to make a certification for Fiscal Year 1990 until June 30, 1990. The State agency shall retain the original of this State agency-wide certification in its central office and, prior to grant award, shall ensure that a copy is submitted individually with respect to each grant, unless the Federal agency designates a central location for submission.

(3) When the work of a grant is done by more than one State agency, the certification of the State agency directly receiving the grant shall be deemed to certify compliance for all workplaces, including those located in other State agencies.

(e)(1) For a grant of less than 30 days performance duration, grantees shall have this policy statement and program in place as soon as possible, but in any case by a date prior to the date on which performance is expected to be completed.

(2) For a grant of 30 days or more performance duration, grantees shall have this policy statement and program in place within 30 days after award.

(3) Where extraordinary circumstances warrant for a specific grant, the grant officer may determine a different date on which the policy statement and program shall be in place.

§ 513.635 Reporting of and employee sanctions for convictions of criminal drug offenses.

(a) When a grantee other than an individual is notified that an employee has been convicted for a violation of a criminal drug statute occurring in the workplace, it shall take the following actions:

(1) Within 10 calendar days of receiving notice of the conviction, the grantee shall provide written notice, including the convicted employee's position title, to every grant officer, or other designee on whose grant activity the convicted employee was working, unless a Federal agency has designated a central point for the receipt of such notifications. Notification shall include the identification number(s) for each of the Federal agency's affected grants.

(2) Within 30 calendar days of receiving notice of the conviction, the grantee shall do the following with respect to the employee who was convicted.

(i) Take appropriate personnel action against the employee, up to and including termination, consistent with requirements of the Rehabilitation Act of 1973, as amended; or

(ii) Require the employee to participate satisfactorily in a drug abuse assistance or rehabilitation program approved for such purposes by a Federal, State, or local health, law enforcement, or other appropriate agency.

(b) A grantee who is an individual who is convicted for a violation of a criminal drug statute occurring during the conduct of any grant activity shall report the conviction, in writing, within 10 calendar days, to his or her Federal agency grant officer, or other designee, unless the Federal agency has designated a central point for the receipt of such notices. Notification shall include the identification number(s) for each of the Federal agency's affected grants.

(Approved by the Office of Management and Budget under control number 0991–0002)

APPENDIX A TO PART 513—CERTIFICATION REGARDING DEBARMENT, SUSPENSION, AND OTHER RESPONSIBILITY MATTERS—PRIMARY COVERED TRANSACTIONS

Instructions for Certification

1. By signing and submitting this proposal, the prospective primary participant is providing the certification set out below.

2. The inability of a person to provide the certification required below will not necessarily result in denial of participation in this covered transaction. The prospective participant shall submit an explanation of why it cannot provide the certification set out below. The certification or explanation will be considered in connection with the department or Board's determination whether to enter into this transaction. However, failure of the prospective primary participant to furnish a certification or an explanation shall disqualify such person from participation in this transaction.

3. The certification in this clause is a material representation of fact upon which reliance was placed when the department or Board determined to enter into this transaction. If it is later determined that the prospective primary participant knowingly rendered an erroneous certification, in addition to other remedies available to the Federal Government, the department or Board may terminate this transaction for cause or default.

4. The prospective primary participant shall provide immediate written notice to the department or Board to which this proposal is submitted if at any time the prospective primary participant learns that its certification was erroneous when submitted or has become erroneous by reason of changed circumstances.

5. The terms *covered transaction, debarred, suspended, ineligible, lower tier covered transaction, participant, person, primary covered transaction, principal, proposal, and voluntarily excluded*, as used in this clause, have the meanings set out in the Definitions and Coverage sections of the rules implementing Executive Order 12549. You may contact the department or Board to which this proposal is being submitted for assistance in obtaining a copy of those regulations.

6. The prospective primary participant agrees by submitting this proposal that, should the proposed covered transaction be entered into, it shall not knowingly enter

into any lower tier covered transaction with a person who is proposed for debarment under 48 CFR part 9, subpart 9.4, debarred, suspended, declared ineligible, or voluntarily excluded from participation in this covered transaction, unless authorized by the department or Board entering into this transaction.

7. The prospective primary participant further agrees by submitting this proposal that it will include the clause titled "Certification Regarding Debarment, Suspension, Ineligibility and Voluntary Exclusion-Lower Tier Covered Transaction," provided by the department or Board entering into this covered transaction, without modification, in all lower tier covered transactions and in all solicitations for lower tier covered transactions.

8. A participant in a covered transaction may rely upon a certification of a prospective participant in a lower tier covered transaction that it is not proposed for debarment under 48 CFR part 9, subpart 9.4, debarred, suspended, ineligible, or voluntarily excluded from the covered transaction, unless it knows that the certification is erroneous. A participant may decide the method and frequency by which it determines the eligibility of its principals. Each participant may, but is not required to, check the List of Parties Excluded from Federal Procurement and Nonprocurement Programs.

9. Nothing contained in the foregoing shall be construed to require establishment of a system of records in order to render in good faith the certification required by this clause. The knowledge and information of a participant is not required to exceed that which is normally possessed by a prudent person in the ordinary course of business dealings.

10. Except for transactions authorized under paragraph 6 of these instructions, if a participant in a covered transaction knowingly enters into a lower tier covered transaction with a person who is proposed for debarment under 48 CFR part 9, subpart 9.4, suspended, debarred, ineligible, or voluntarily excluded from participation in this transaction, in addition to other remedies available to the Federal Government, the department or Board may terminate this transaction for cause or default.

Certification Regarding Debarment, Suspension, and Other Responsibility Matters—Primary Covered Transactions

(1) The prospective primary participant certifies to the best of its knowledge and belief, that it and its principals:

(a) Are not presently debarred, suspended, proposed for debarment, declared ineligible, or voluntarily excluded by any Federal department or Board;

(b) Have not within a three-year period preceding this proposal been convicted of or had a civil judgment rendered against them for commission of fraud or a criminal offense in connection with obtaining, attempting to obtain, or performing a public (Federal, State or local) transaction or contract under a public transaction; violation of Federal or State antitrust statutes or commission of embezzlement, theft, forgery, bribery, falsification or destruction of records, making false statements, or receiving stolen property;

(c) Are not presently indicted for or otherwise criminally or civilly charged by a governmental entity (Federal, State or local) with commission of any of the offenses enumerated in paragraph (1)(b) of this certification; and

(d) Have not within a three-year period preceding this application/proposal had one or more public transactions (Federal, State or local) terminated for cause or default.

(2) Where the prospective primary participant is unable to certify to any of the statements in this certification, such prospective participant shall attach an explanation to this proposal.

[60 FR 33042, 33045, June 26, 1995]

Appendix B to Part 513—Certification Regarding Debarment, Suspension, Ineligibility and Voluntary Exclusion—Lower Tier Covered Transactions

Instructions for Certification

1. By signing and submitting this proposal, the prospective lower tier participant is providing the certification set out below.

2. The certification in this clause is a material representation of fact upon which reliance was placed when this transaction was entered into. If it is later determined that the prospective lower tier participant knowingly rendered an erroneous certification, in addition to other remedies available to the Federal Government the department or Board with which this transaction originated may pursue available remedies, including suspension and/or debarment.

3. The prospective lower tier participant shall provide immediate written notice to the person to which this proposal is submitted if at any time the prospective lower tier participant learns that its certification was erroneous when submitted or had become erroneous by reason of changed circumstances.

4. The terms *covered transaction, debarred, suspended, ineligible, lower tier covered transaction, participant, person, primary covered transaction, principal, proposal,* and *voluntarily excluded,* as used in this clause, have the meaning set out in the Definitions and

Coverage sections of rules implementing Executive Order 12549. You may contact the person to which this proposal is submitted for assistance in obtaining a copy of those regulations.

5. The prospective lower tier participant agrees by submitting this proposal that, should the proposed covered transaction be entered into, it shall not knowingly enter into any lower tier covered transaction with a person who is proposed for debarment under 48 CFR part 9, subpart 9.4, debarred, suspended, declared ineligible, or voluntarily excluded from participation in this covered transaction, unless authorized by the department or Board with which this transaction originated.

6. The prospective lower tier participant further agrees by submitting this proposal that it will include this clause titled "Certification Regarding Debarment, Suspension, Ineligibility and Voluntary Exclusion-Lower Tier Covered Transaction," without modification, in all lower tier covered transactions and in all solicitations for lower tier covered transactions.

7. A participant in a covered transaction may rely upon a certification of a prospective participant in a lower tier covered transaction that it is not proposed for debarment under 48 CFR part 9, subpart 9.4, debarred, suspended, ineligible, or voluntarily excluded from covered transactions, unless it knows that the certification is erroneous. A participant may decide the method and frequency by which it determines the eligibility of its principals. Each participant may, but is not required to, check the List of Parties Excluded from Federal Procurement and Nonprocurement Programs.

8. Nothing contained in the foregoing shall be construed to require establishment of a system of records in order to render in good faith the certification required by this clause. The knowledge and information of a participant is not required to exceed that which is normally possessed by a prudent person in the ordinary course of business dealings.

9. Except for transactions authorized under paragraph 5 of these instructions, if a participant in a covered transaction knowingly enters into a lower tier covered transaction with a person who is proposed for debarment under 48 CFR part 9, subpart 9.4, suspended, debarred, ineligible, or voluntarily excluded from participation in this transaction, in addition to other remedies available to the Federal Government, the department or Board with which this transaction originated may pursue available remedies, including suspension and/or debarment.

Certification Regarding Debarment, Suspension, Ineligibility an Voluntary Exclusion—Lower Tier Covered Transactions

(1) The prospective lower tier participant certifies, by submission of this proposal, that neither it nor its principals is presently debarred, suspended, proposed for debarment, declared ineligible, or voluntarily excluded from participation in this transaction by any Federal department or agency.

(2) Where the prospective lower tier participant is unable to certify to any of the statements in this certification, such prospective participant shall attach an explanation to this proposal.

[60 FR 33042, 33045, June 26, 1995]

APPENDIX C TO PART 513—CERTIFICATION REGARDING DRUG-FREE WORKPLACE REQUIREMENTS

Instructions for Certification

1. By signing and/or submitting this application or grant agreement, the grantee is providing the certification set out below.

2. The certification set out below is a material representation of fact upon which reliance is placed when the Board awards the grant. If it is later determined that the grantee knowingly rendered a false certification, or otherwise violates the requirements of the Drug-Free Workplace Act, the Board, in addition to any other remedies available to the Federal Government, may take action authorized under the Drug-Free Workplace Act.

3. For grantees other than individuals, Alternate I applies.

4. For grantees who are individuals, Alternate II applies.

5. Workplaces under grants, for grantees other than individuals, need not be identified on the certification. If known, they may be identified in the grant application. If the grantee does not identify the workplaces at the time of application, or upon award, if there is no application, the grantee must keep the identity of the workplace(s) on file in its office and make the information available for Federal inspection. Failure to identify all known workplaces constitutes a violation of the grantee's drug-free workplace requirements.

6. Workplace identifications must include the actual address of buildings (or parts of buildings) or other sites where work under the grant takes place. Categorical descriptions may be used (e.g., all vehicles of a mass transit authority or State highway department while in operation, State employees in each local unemployment office, performers in concert halls or radio studios).

7. If the workplace identified to the Board changes during the performance of the grant, the grantee shall inform the Board of the

change(s), if it previously identified the workplaces in question (see paragraph five).

8. Definitions of terms in the Nonprocurement Suspension and Debarment common rule and Drug-Free Workplace common rule apply to this certification. Grantees' attention is called, in particular, to the following definitions from these rules:

Controlled substance means a controlled substance in Schedules I through V of the Controlled Substances Act (21 U.S.C. 812) and as further defined by regulation (21 CFR 1308.11 through 1308.15);

Conviction means a finding of guilt (including a plea of nolo contendere) or imposition of sentence, or both, by any judicial body charged with the responsibility to determine violations of the Federal or State criminal drug statutes;

Criminal drug statute means a Federal or non-Federal criminal statute involving the manufacture, distribution, dispensing, use, or possession of any controlled substance;

Employee means the employee of a grantee directly engaged in the performance of work under a grant, including: (i) All *direct charge* employees; (ii) All *indirect charge* employees unless their impact or involvement is insignificant to the performance of the grant; and, (iii) Temporary personnel and consultants who are directly engaged in the performance of work under the grant and who are on the grantee's payroll. This definition does not include workers not on the payroll of the grantee (e.g., volunteers, even if used to meet a matching requirement; consultants or independent contractors not on the grantee's payroll; or employees of subrecipients or subcontractors in covered workplaces.

Certification Regarding Drug-Free Workplace Requirements

Alternate I. (Grantees Other Than Individuals)

A. The grantee certifies that it will or will continue to provide a drug-free workplace by:

(a) Publishing a statement notifying employees that the unlawful manufacture, distribution, dispensing, possession, or use of a controlled substance is prohibited in the grantee's workplace and specifying the actions that will be taken against employees for violation of such prohibition;

(b) Establishing an ongoing drug-free awareness program to inform employees about—

(1) The dangers of drug abuse in the workplace;

(2) The grantee's policy of maintaining a drug-free workplace;

(3) Any available drug counseling, rehabilitation, and employee assistance programs; and

(4) The penalties that may be imposed upon employees for drug abuse violations occurring in the workplace;

(c) Making it a requirement that each employee to be engaged in the performance of the grant be given a copy of the statement required by paragraph (a);

(d) Notifying the employee in the statement required by paragraph (a) that, as a condition of employment under the grant, the employee will—

(1) Abide by the terms of the statement; and

(2) Notify the employer in writing of his or her conviction for a violation of a criminal drug statute occurring in the workplace no later than five calendar days after such conviction;

(e) Notifying the Board in writing, within ten calendar days after receiving notice under paragraph (d)(2) from an employee or otherwise receiving actual notice of such conviction. Employers of convicted employees must provide notice, including position title, to every grant officer or other designee on whose grant activity the convicted employee was working, unless the Federal agency has designated a central point for the receipt of such notices. Notice shall include the identification number(s) of each affected grant;

(f) Taking one of the following actions, within 30 calendar days of receiving notice under paragraph (d)(2), with respect to any employee who is so convicted—

(1) Taking appropriate personnel action against such an employee, up to and including termination, consistent with the requirements of the Rehabilitation Act of 1973, as amended; or

(2) Requiring such employee to participate satisfactorily in a drug abuse assistance or rehabilitation program approved for such purposes by a Federal, State, or local health, law enforcement, or other appropriate agency;

(g) Making a good faith effort to continue to maintain a drug-free workplace through implementation of paragraphs (a), (b), (c), (d), (e) and (f).

B. The grantee may insert in the space provided below the site(s) for the performance of work done in connection with the specific grant:

Place of Performance (Street address, city, county, state, zip code)

____

____

____

Check ☐ if there are workplaces on file that are not identified here.

Alternate II. (Grantees Who Are Individuals)

(a) The grantee certifies that, as a condition of the grant, he or she will not engage in the unlawful manufacture, distribution, dispensing, possession, or use of a controlled substance in conducting any activity with the grant;

(b) If convicted of a criminal drug offense resulting from a violation occurring during the conduct of any grant activity, he or she will report the conviction, in writing, within 10 calendar days of the conviction, to every grant officer or other designee, unless the Federal agency designates a central point for the receipt of such notices. When notice is made to such a central point, it shall include the identification number(s) of each affected grant.

[55 FR 21690, 21694, May 25, 1990]

PART 518—UNIFORM ADMINISTRATIVE REQUIREMENTS FOR GRANTS AND AGREEMENTS WITH INSTITUTIONS OF HIGHER EDUCATION, HOSPITALS, AND OTHER NON-PROFIT ORGANIZATIONS

Subpart A—General

Subpart B—Pre-Award Requirements

Subpart C—Post-Award Requirements

FINANCIAL AND PROGRAM MANAGEMENT

PROPERTY STANDARDS

PROCUREMENT STANDARDS

REPORTS AND RECORDS

TERMINATION AND ENFORCEMENT

Subpart D—After-the-Award Requirements

AUTHORITY: 22 U.S.C. 2658; 31 U.S.C. 503 and 1111; Reorganization Plan No. 2 of 1977, 42 FR 62461, 3 CFR, 1977 Comp. p. 200; E.O. 12048, 43 FR 13361, 3 CFR, 1978 Comp. p. 168.

SOURCE: 59 FR 39440, Aug. 3, 1994, unless otherwise noted.

Subpart A—General

§ 518.1 Purpose.

This part establishes uniform administrative requirements for Federal grants and agreements awarded to institutions of higher education, hospitals, and other non-profit organizations. Federal awarding agencies shall not impose additional or inconsistent requirements, except as provided in §§ 518.4 and 518.14 or unless specifically required by Federal statute or executive order. Non-profit organizations that implement Federal programs for the States are also subject to State requirements.

§518.2 Definitions.

(a) *Accrued expenditures* means the charges incurred by the recipient during a given period requiring the provision of funds for:

(1) Goods and other tangible property received;

(2) Services performed by employees, contractors, subrecipients, and other payees; and,

(3) Other amounts becoming owed under programs for which no current services or performance is required.

(b) *Accrued income* means the sum of:

(1) Earnings during a given period from:

(i) Services performed by the recipient, and

(ii) Goods and other tangible property delivered to purchasers; and

(2) Amounts becoming owed to the recipient for which no current services or performance is required by the recipient.

(c) *Acquisition cost of equipment* means the net invoice price of the equipment, including the cost of modifications, attachments, accessories, or auxiliary apparatus necessary to make the property usable for the purpose for which it was acquired. Other charges, such as the cost of installation, transportation, taxes, duty or protective in-transit insurance, shall be included or excluded from the unit acquisition cost in accordance with the recipient's regular accounting practices.

(d) *Advance* means a payment made by Treasury check or other appropriate payment mechanism to a recipient upon its request either before outlays are made by the recipient or through the use of predetermined payment schedules.

(e) *Award* means financial assistance that provides support or stimulation to accomplish a public purpose. Awards include grants and other agreements in the form of money or property in lieu of money, by the Federal Government to an eligible recipient. The term does not include: technical assistance, which provides services instead of money; other assistance in the form of loans, loan guarantees, interest subsidies, or insurance; direct payments of any kind to individuals; and, contracts which are required to be entered into and administered under procurement laws and regulations.

(f) *Cash contributions* means the recipient's cash outlay, including the outlay of money contributed to the recipient by third parties.

(g) *Closeout* means the process by which a Federal awarding agency determines that all applicable administrative actions and all required work of the award have been completed by the recipient and Federal awarding agency.

(h) *Contract* means a procurement contract under an award or subaward, and a procurement subcontract under a recipient's or subrecipient's contract.

(i) *Cost sharing or matching* means that portion of project or program costs not borne by the Federal Government.

(j) *Date of completion* means the date on which all work under an award is completed or the date on the award document, or any supplement or amendment thereto, on which Federal sponsorship ends.

(k) *Disallowed costs* means those charges to an award that the Federal awarding agency determines to be unallowable, in accordance with the applicable Federal cost principles or other terms and conditions contained in the award.

(l) *Equipment* means tangible nonexpendable personal property including exempt property charged directly to the award having a useful life or more than one year and an acquisition cost of $5,000 or more per unit. However, consistent with recipient policy, lower limits may be established.

(m) *Excess property* means property under the control of any Federal awarding agency that, as determined by the head thereof, is no longer required for its needs or the discharge of its responsibilities.

(n) *Exempt property* means tangible personal property acquired in whole or in part with Federal funds, where the Federal awarding agency has statutory authority to vest title in the recipient without further obligation to the Federal Government. An example of exempt property authority is contained in the Federal Grant and Cooperative Agreement Act (31 U.S.C. 6306), for property acquired under an award to conduct basic or applied research by a non-profit institution or higher education or non-profit organization whose principal purpose is conducting scientific research.

(o) *Federal awarding agency* means the Federal agency that provides an award to the recipient.

(p) *Federal funds authorized* means the total amount of Federal funds obligated by the Federal Government for use by the recipient. This amount may include any authorized carryover of unobligated funds from prior funding periods when permitted by agency regulations or agency implementing instructions.

(q) *Federal share* of real property, equipment, or supplies means that percentage of the property's acquisition costs and any improvement expenditures paid with Federal funds.

(r) *Funding period* means the period of time when Federal funding is available for obligation by the recipient.

(s) *Intangible property and debt instruments* means, but is not limited to, trademarks, copyrights, patents and patent applications and such property as loans, notes and other debt instruments, lease agreements, stock and other instruments of property ownership, whether considered tangible or intangible.

(t) *Obligations* means the amounts of orders placed, contracts and grants awarded, services received and similar transactions during a given period that require payment by the recipient during the same or a future period.

(u) *Outlays or expenditures* means charges made to the project or program. They may be reported on a cash or accrual basis. For reports prepared on a cash basis, outlays are the sum of cash disbursements for direct charges for goods and services, the amount of indirect expense charged, the value of third party in-kind contributions applied and the amount of cash advances and payments made to subrecipients. For reports prepared on an accrual basis, outlays are the sum of cash disbursements for direct charges for goods and services, the amount of indirect expense incurred, the value of in-kind contributions applied, and the net increase (or decrease) in the amounts owed by the recipient for goods and other property received, for services performed by employees, contractors, subrecipients and other payees and other amounts becoming owed under programs for which no current services or performance are required.

(v) *Personal property* means property of any kind except real property. It may be tangible, having physical existence, or intangible, having no physical existence, such as copyrights, patents, or securities.

(w) *Prior approval* means written approval by an authorized official evidencing prior consent.

(x) *Program income* means gross income earned by the recipient that is directly generated by a supported activity or earned as a result of the award (see exclusions in §§518.24 (e) and (h)). Program income includes, but is not limited to, income from fees for services performed, the use or rental of real or personal property acquired under federally-funded projects, the sale of commodities or items fabricated under an award, license fees and royalties on patents and copyrights, and interest on loans made with award funds. Interest earned on advances of Federal funds is not program income. Except as otherwise provided in Federal awarding agency regulations or the terms and conditions of the award, program income does not include the receipt of principal on loans, rebates, credits, discounts, etc., or interest earned on any of them.

(y) *Project costs* means all allowable costs, as set forth in the applicable Federal cost principles, incurred by a recipient and the value of the contributions made by third parties in accomplishing the objectives of the award during the project period.

(z) *Project period* means the period established in the award document during which Federal sponsorship begins and ends.

(aa) *Property* means, unless otherwise stated, real property, equipment, intangible property and debt instruments.

(bb) *Real property* means land, including land improvements, structures and appurtenances thereto, but excludes movable machinery and equipment.

(cc) *Recipient* means an organization receiving financial assistance directly from Federal awarding agencies to carry out a project or program. The term includes public and private institutions of higher education, public and private hospitals, and other quasi-public and private non-profit organizations such as, but not limited to, community action agencies, research institutes, educational associations, and health centers. The term may include commercial organizations, foreign or international organizations (such as agencies of the United Nations) which are recipients, subrecipients, or contractors or subcontractors of recipients or subrecipients at the discretion of the Federal awarding agency. The term does not include government-owned contractor-operated facilities or research centers providing continued support for mission-oriented, large-scale programs that are government-owned or controlled, or are designated as federally-funded research and development centers.

(dd) *Research and development* means all research activities, both basic and applied, and all development activities that are supported at universities, colleges, and other non-profit institutions. "Research" is defined as a systematic study directed toward fuller scientific knowledge or understanding of the subject studied. "Development" is the systematic use of knowledge and understanding gained from research directed toward the production of useful materials, devices, systems, or methods, including design and development of prototypes and processes. The term research also includes activities involving the training of individuals in research techniques where such activities utilize the same facilities as other research and development activities and where such activities are not included in the instruction function.

(ee) *Small awards* means a grant or cooperative agreement not exceeding the small purchase threshold fixed at 41 U.S.C. 403(11) (currently $25,000).

(ff) *Subaward* means an award of financial assistance in the form of money, or property in lieu of money, made under an award by a recipient to an eligible subrecipient or by a subrecipient to a lower tier subrecipient. The term includes financial assistance when provided by any legal agreement, even if the agreement is called a contract, but does not include procurement of goods and services nor does it include any form of assistance which is excluded from the definition of "award" in paragraph (e) of this section.

(gg) *Subrecipient* means the legal entity to which a subaward is made and which is accountable to the recipient for the use of the funds provided. The term may include foreign or international organizations (such as agencies of the United Nations) at the discretion of the Federal awarding agency.

(hh) *Supplies* means all personal property excluding equipment, intangible property, and debt instruments as defined in this section, and inventions of a contractor conceived or first actually reduced to practice in the performance of work under a funding agreement ("subject inventions"), as defined in 37 CFR part 401, "Rights to Inventions Made by Nonprofit Organizations and Small Business Firms Under Government Grants, Contracts, and Cooperative Agreements."

(ii) *Suspension* means an action by a Federal awarding agency that temporarily withdraws Federal sponsorship under an award, pending corrective action by the recipient or pending a decision to terminate the award by the Federal awarding agency. Suspension of an award is a separate action from suspension under Federal agency regulations implementing E.O.'s 12549 and 12689, "Debarment and Suspension."

(jj) *Termination* means the cancellation of Federal sponsorship, in whole or in part, under an agreement at any time prior to the date of completion.

(kk) *Third party in-kind contributions* means the value of non-cash contributions provided by non-Federal third parties. Third party in-kind contributions may be in the form of real property, equipment, supplies and other expendable property, and the value of goods and services directly benefiting and specifically identifiable to the project or program.

(ll) *Unliquidated obligations*, for financial reports prepared on a cash basis, means the amount of obligations incurred by the recipient that have not been paid. For reports prepared on an accrued expenditure basis, they represent the amount of obligations incurred by the recipient for which an outlay has not been recorded.

(mm) *Unobligated balance* means the portion of the funds authorized by the Federal awarding agency that has not been obligated by the recipient and is determined by deducting the cumulative obligations from the cumulative funds authorized.

(nn) *Unrecovered indirect cost* means the difference between the amount awarded and the amount which could have been awarded under the recipient's approved negotiated indirect cost rate.

(oo) *Working capital advance* means a procedure whereby funds are advanced to the recipient to cover its estimated disbursement needs for a given initial period.

§518.3 Effect on other issuances.

For awards subject to this part, all administrative requirements of codified program regulations, program manuals, handbooks and other non-regulatory materials which are inconsistent with the requirements of this part shall be superseded, except to the extent they are required by statute, or authorized in accordance with the deviations provision in §518.4.

§518.4 Deviations.

The Office of Management and Budget (OMB) may grant exceptions for classes of grants or recipients subject to the requirements of this part when exceptions are not prohibited by statute. However, in the interest of maximum uniformity, exceptions from the requirements of this part shall be permitted only in unusual circumstances. Federal awarding agencies may apply more restrictive requirements to a class of recipients when approved by OMB. Federal awarding agencies may apply less restrictive requirements when awarding small awards, except for those requirements which are statutory. Exceptions on a case-by-case basis may also be made by Federal awarding agencies.

§518.5 Subawards.

Unless sections of this part specifically exclude subrecipients from coverage, the provisions of this part shall be applied to subrecipients performing work under awards if such subrecipients are institutions of higher education, hospitals or other non-profit organizations. State and local government subrecipients are subject to the provisions of regulations implementing the grants management common rule, "Uniform Administrative Requirements for Grants and Cooperative Agreements to State and Local Governments," published at 53 FR 9034 (3/11/88).

Subpart B—Pre-Award Requirements

§518.10 Purpose.

Sections 518.11 through 518.17 prescribes forms and instructions and other pre-award matters to be used in applying for Federal awards.

§518.11 Pre-award policies.

(a) Use of Grants and Cooperative Agreements, and Contracts. In each instance, the Federal awarding agency shall decide on the appropriate award instrument (i.e., grant, cooperative agreement, or contract). The Federal Grant and Cooperative Agreement Act (31 U.S.C. 6301–08) governs the use of grants, cooperative agreements and contracts. A grant or cooperative agreement shall be used only when the principal purpose of a transaction is to accomplish a public purpose of support or stimulation authorized by Federal statute. The statutory criterion for choosing between grants and cooperative agreements is that for the latter, "substantial involvement is expected between the executive agency and the State, local government, or other recipient when carrying out the activity contemplated in the agreement." Contracts shall be used when the principal purpose is acquisition of property or services for the direct benefit or use of the Federal Government.

(b) Public Notice and Priority Setting. Federal awarding agencies shall notify the public of its intended funding priorities for discretionary grant programs, unless funding priorities are established by Federal statute.

§ 518.12 Forms for applying for Federal assistance.

(a) Federal awarding agencies shall comply with the applicable report clearance requirements of 5 CFR part 1320, "Controlling Paperwork Burdens on the Public," with regard to all forms used by the Federal awarding agency in place of or as a supplement to the Standard Form 424 (SF–424) series.

(b) Applicants shall use the SF–424 series or those forms and instructions prescribed by the Federal awarding agency.

(c) For Federal programs covered by E.O. 12372, "Intergovernmental Review of Federal Programs," the applicant shall complete the appropriate sections of the SF–424 (Application for Federal Assistance) indicating whether the application was subject to review by the State Single Point of Contact (SPOC). The name and address of the SPOC for a particular State can be obtained from the Federal awarding agency or the *Catalog of Federal Domestic Assistance.* The SPOC shall advise the applicant whether the program for which application is made has been selected by that State for review.

(d) Federal awarding agencies that do not use the SF–424 form should indicate whether the application is subject to review by the State under E.O. 12372.

§ 518.13 Debarment and suspension.

Federal awarding agencies and recipients shall comply with the nonprocurement debarment and suspension rule, implementing E.O.'s 12549 and 12689, "Debarment and Suspension." This rule restricts subawards and contracts with certain parties that are debarred, suspended or otherwise excluded from or ineligible for participation in Federal assistance programs or activities.

§ 518.14 Special award conditions.

(a) Federal awarding agencies may impose additional requirements as needed, if an applicant or recipient:

(1) Has a history of poor performance,

(2) Is not financially stable,

(3) Has a management system that does not meet the standards prescribed in this part,

(4) Has not conformed to the terms and conditions of a previous award, or

(5) Is not otherwise responsible.

(b) Additional requirements may only be imposed provided that such applicant or recipient is notified in writing as to:

(1) The nature of the additional requirements,

(2) The reason why the additional requirements are being imposed,

(3) The nature of the corrective action needed,

(4) The time allowed for completing the corrective actions, and

(5) The method for requesting reconsideration of the additional requirements imposed.

§ 518.15 Metric system of measurement.

The Metric Conversion Act, as amended by the Omnibus Trade and Competitiveness Act (15 U.S.C. 205), declares that the metric system is the preferred measurement system for U.S. trade and commerce. The Act requires each Federal agency to establish a date or dates in consultation with the Secretary of Commerce, when the metric system of measurement will be used in the agency's procurements, grants, and other business-related activities. Metric implementation may take longer where the use of the system is initially impractical or likely to cause significant inefficiencies in the accomplishment of federally-funded activities. Federal awarding agencies shall follow the provisions of E.O. 12770, "Metric Usage in Federal Government Programs."

§ 518.16 Resource Conservation and Recovery Act.

Under the Act, any State agency or agency of a political subdivision of a State which is using appropriated Federal funds must comply with section

6002. Section 6002 requires that preference be given in procurement programs to the purchase of specific products containing recycled materials identified in guidelines developed by the Environmental Protection Agency (EPA) (40 CFR Parts 247–254). Accordingly, State and local institutions of higher education, hospitals, and nonprofit organizations that receive direct Federal awards or other Federal funds shall give preference in their procurement programs funded with Federal funds to the purchase of recycled products pursuant to the EPA guidelines.

§518.17 Certification and representations.

Unless prohibited by statute or codified regulation, each Federal awarding agency is authorized and encouraged to allow recipients to submit certifications and representations required by statute, executive order, or regulation on an annual basis, if the recipients have ongoing and continuing relationships with the agency. Annual certifications and representations shall be signed by responsible officials with the authority to ensure recipients' compliance with the pertinent requirements.

Subpart C—Post-Award Requirements

FINANCIAL AND PROGRAM MANAGEMENT

§518.20 Purpose of financial and program management.

Sections 518.21 through 518.28 prescribe standards for financial management systems, methods for making payments and rules for: satisfying cost sharing and matching requirements, accounting for program income, budget revision approvals, making audits, determining allowability of cost, and establishing fund availability.

§518.21 Standards for financial management systems.

(a) Federal awarding agencies shall require recipients to relate financial data to performance data and develop unit cost information whenever practical.

(b) Recipients' financial management systems shall provide for the following.

(1) Accurate, current and complete disclosure of the financial results of each federally-sponsored project or program in accordance with the reporting requirements set forth in §19.52. If a Federal awarding agency requires reporting on an accrual basis from a recipient that maintains its records on other than an accrual basis, the recipient shall not be required to establish an accrual accounting system. These recipients may develop such accrual data for its reports on the basis of an analysis of the documentation on hand.

(2) Records that identify adequately the source and application of funds for federally-sponsored activities. These records shall contain information pertaining to Federal awards, authorizations, obligations, unobligated balances, assets, outlays, income and interest.

(3) Effective control over and accountability for all funds, property and other assets. Recipients shall adequately safeguard all such assets and assure they are used solely for authorized purposes.

(4) Comparison of outlays with budget amounts for each award. Whenever appropriate, financial information should be related to performance and unit cost data.

(5) Written procedures to minimize the time elapsing between the transfer of funds to the recipient from the U.S. Treasury and the issuance or redemption of checks, warrants or payments by other means for program purposes by the recipient. To the extent that the provisions of the Cash Management Improvement Act (CMIA) (Pub. L. 101–453) govern, payment methods of State agencies, instrumentalities, and fiscal agents shall be consistent with CMIA Treasury-State Agreements or the CMIA default procedures codified at 31 CFR part 205, "Withdrawal of Cash from the Treasury for Advances under Federal Grant and Other Programs."

(6) Written procedures for determining the reasonableness, allocability and allowability of costs in accordance with the provisions of the applicable Federal cost principles and the terms and conditions of the award.

(7) Accounting records including cost accounting records that are supported by source documentation.

(c) Where the Federal Government guarantees or insures the repayment of money borrowed by the recipient, the Federal awarding agency, at its discretion, may require adequate bonding and insurance if the bonding and insurance requirements of the recipient are not deemed adequate to protect the interest of the Federal Government.

(d) The Federal awarding agency may require adequate fidelity bond coverage where the recipient lacks sufficient coverage to protect the Federal Government's interest.

(e) Where bonds are required in the situations described above, the bonds shall be obtained from companies holding certificates of authority as acceptable sureties, as prescribed in 31 CFR part 223, "Surety Companies Doing Business with the United States."

§ 518.22 Payment.

(a) Payment methods shall minimize the time elapsing between the transfer of funds from the United States Treasury and the issuance or redemption of checks, warrants, or payment by other means by the recipients. Payment methods of State agencies or instrumentalities shall be consistent with Treasury-State CMIA agreements or default procedures codified at 31 CFR part 205.

(b)(1) Recipients are to be paid in advance, provided they maintain or demonstrate the willingness to maintain:

(i) Written procedures that minimize the time elapsing between the transfer of funds and disbursement by the recipient, and

(ii) Financial management systems that meet the standards for fund control and accountability as established in section § 518.21.

(2) Cash advances to a recipient organization shall be limited to the minimum amounts needed and be timed to be in accordance with the actual, immediate cash requirements of the recipient organization in carrying out the purpose of the approved program or project. The timing and amount of cash advances shall be as close as is administratively feasible to the actual disbursements by the recipient organization for direct program or project costs and the proportionate share of any allowable indirect costs.

(c) Whenever possible, advances shall be consolidated to cover anticipated cash needs for all awards made by the Federal awarding agency to the recipient.

(1) Advance payment mechanisms include, but are not limited to, Treasury check and electronic funds transfer.

(2) Advance payment mechanisms are subject to 31 CFR part 205.

(3) Recipients shall be authorized to submit requests for advances and reimbursements at least monthly when electronic fund transfers are not used.

(d) Requests for Treasury check advance payment shall be submitted on SF–270, "Request for Advance or Reimbursement," or other forms as may be authorized by OMB. This form is not to be used when Treasury check advance payments are made to the recipient automatically through the use of a predetermined payment schedule or if precluded by special Federal awarding agency instructions for electronic funds transfer.

(e) Reimbursement is the preferred method when the requirements in paragraph (b) cannot be met. Federal awarding agencies may also use this method on any construction agreement, or if the major portion of the construction project is accomplished through private market financing or Federal loans, and the Federal assistance constitutes a minor portion of the project.

(1) When the reimbursement method is used, the Federal awarding agency shall make payment within 30 days after receipt of the billing, unless the billing is improper.

(2) Recipients shall be authorized to submit request for reimbursement at least monthly when electronic funds are not used.

(f) If a recipient cannot meet the criteria for advance payments and the Federal awarding agency has determined that reimbursement is not feasible because the recipient lacks sufficient working capital, the Federal awarding agency may provide cash on a working capital advance basis. Under this procedure, the Federal awarding agency shall advance cash to the recipient to cover its estimated disbursement needs for an initial period generally geared to the awardee's disbursing cycle. Thereafter, the Federal awarding agency shall reimburse the recipient for its actual cash disbursements. The working capital advance method of payment shall not be used for recipients unwilling or unable to provide timely advances to their subrecipient to meet the subrecipient's actual cash disbursements.

(g) To the extent available, recipients shall disburse funds available from repayments to and interest earned on a revolving fund, program income, rebates, refunds, contract settlements, audit recoveries and interest earned on such funds before requesting additional cash payments.

(h) Unless otherwise required by statute, Federal awarding agencies shall not withhold payments for proper charges made by recipients at any time during the project period unless the conditions in paragraphs (h)(1) or (2) of this section apply.

(1) A recipient has failed to comply with the project objectives, the terms and conditions of the award, or Federal reporting requirements.

(2) The recipient or subrecipient is delinquent in a debt to the United States as defined in OMB Circular A-129, "Managing Federal Credit Programs." Under such conditions, the Federal awarding agency may, upon reasonable notice, inform the recipient that payments shall not be made for obligations incurred after a specified date until the conditions are corrected or the indebtedness to the Federal Government is liquidated.

(i) Standards governing the use of banks and other institutions as depositories of funds advanced under awards are as follows:

(1) Except for situations described in paragraph (i)(2) of this section, Federal awarding agencies shall not require separate depository accounts for funds provided to a recipient or establish any eligibility requirements for depositories for funds provided to a recipient. However, recipients must be able to account for the receipt, obligation and expenditure of funds.

(2) Advances of Federal funds shall be deposited and maintained in insured accounts whenever possible.

(j) Consistent with the national goal of expanding the opportunities for women-owned and minority-owned business enterprises, recipients shall be encouraged to use women-owned and minority-owned banks (a bank which is owned at least 50 percent by women or minority group members).

(k) Recipients shall maintain advances of Federal funds in interest bearing accounts, unless the conditions in paragraphs (k)(1), (2) or (3) of this section apply.

(1) The recipient receives less than $120,000 in Federal awards per year.

(2) The best reasonably available interest bearing account would not be expected to earn interest in excess of $250 per year on Federal cash balances.

(3) The depository would require an average or minimum balance so high that it would not be feasible within the expected Federal and non-Federal cash resources.

(l) For those entities where CMIA and its implementing regulations do not apply, interest earned on Federal advances deposited in interest bearing accounts shall be remitted annually to Department of Health and Human Services, Payment Management System, P.O. Box 6021, Rockville, MD 20852. Interest amounts up to $250 per year may be retained by the recipient for administrative expense. In keeping with Electric Funds Transfer rules, (31 CFR part 206), interest should be remitted to the HHS Payment Management System through an electric medium such as the FEDWIRE Deposit system. Recipients which do not have this capability should use a check. State universities and hospitals shall comply with CMIA, as it pertains to interest. If an entity subject to CMIA uses its own funds to pay pre-award costs for discretionary awards without prior written approval from the Federal awarding agency, it waives its right to recover the interest under CMIA.

(m) Except as noted elsewhere in this part, only the following forms shall be authorized for the recipients in requesting advances and reimbursements. Federal agencies shall not require more than an original and two copies of these forms.

(1) SF–270, Request for Advance or Reimbursement. Each Federal awarding agency shall adopt the SF–270 as a standard form for all nonconstruction programs when electronic funds transfer or predetermined advance methods are not used. Federal awarding agencies, however, have the option of using this form for construction programs in lieu of the SF–271, "Outlay Report and Request for Reimbursement for Construction Programs."

(2) SF–271, Outlay Report and Request for Reimbursement for Construction Programs. Each Federal awarding agency shall adopt the SF–271 as the standard form to be used for requesting reimbursement for construction programs. However, a Federal awarding agency may substitute the SF–270 when the Federal awarding agency determines that it provides adequate information to meet Federal needs.

§ 518.23 Cost sharing or matching.

(a) All contributions, including cash and third party in-kind, shall be accepted as part of the recipient's cost sharing or matching when such contributions meet all of the following criteria.

(1) Are verifiable from the recipient's records.

(2) Are not included as contributions for any other federally-assisted project or program.

(3) Are necessary and reasonable for proper and efficient accomplishment of project or program objectives.

(4) Are allowable under the applicable cost principles.

(5) Are not paid by the Federal Government under another award, except where authorized by Federal statute to be used for cost sharing or matching.

(6) Are provided for in the approved budget when required by the Federal awarding agency.

(7) Conform to other provisions of this part, as applicable.

(b) Unrecovered indirect costs may be included as part of cost sharing or matching only with the prior approval of the Federal awarding agency.

(c) Values for recipient contributions of services and property shall be established in accordance with the applicable cost principles. If a Federal awarding agency authorizes recipients to donate buildings or land for construction/facilities acquisition projects or long-term use, the value of the donated property for cost sharing or matching shall be the lesser of paragraph (c) (1) or (2) of this section.

(1) The certified value of the remaining life of the property recorded in the recipient's accounting records at the time of donation.

(2) The current fair market value. However, when there is sufficient justification, the Federal awarding agency may approve the use of the current fair market value of the donated property, even if it exceeds the certified value at the time of donation to the project.

(d) Volunteer services furnished by professional and technical personnel, consultants, and other skilled and unskilled labor may be counted as cost sharing or matching if the service is an integral and necessary part of an approved project or program. Rates for volunteer services shall be consistent with those paid for similar work in the recipient's organization. In those instances in which the required skills are not found in the recipient organization, rates shall be consistent with those paid for similar work in the labor market in which the recipient competes for the kind of services involved. In either case, paid fringe benefits that are reasonable, allowable, and allocable may be included in the valuation.

(e) When an employer other than the recipient furnishes the services of an employee, these services shall be valued at the employee's regular rate of pay (plus an amount of fringe benefits that are reasonable, allowable, and allocable, but exclusive of overhead costs), provided these services are in the same skill for which the employee is normally paid.

(f) Donated supplies may include such items as expendable equipment, office supplies, laboratory supplies or workshop and classroom supplies. Value assessed to donated supplies included in the cost sharing or matching share shall be reasonable and shall not exceed the fair market value of the property at the time of the donation.

(g) The method used for determining cost sharing or matching for donated equipment, buildings and land for which title passes to the recipient may differ according to the purpose of the award, if the conditions in paragraphs (g)(1) or (2) of this section apply.

(1) If the purpose of the award is to assist the recipient in the acquisition of equipment, buildings or land, the total value of the donated property may be claimed as cost sharing or matching.

(2) If the purpose of the award is to support activities that require the use of equipment, buildings or land, normally only depreciation or use charges for equipment and buildings may be made. However, the full value of equipment or other capital assets and fair rental charges for land may be allowed, provided that the Federal awarding agency has approved the charges.

(h) The value of donated property shall be determined in accordance with the usual accounting policies of the recipient, with the following qualifications.

(1) The value of donated land and buildings shall not exceed its fair market value at the time of donation to the recipient as established by an independent appraiser (*e.g.*, certified real property appraiser or General Services Administration representative) and certified by a responsible official of the recipient.

(2) The value of donated equipment shall not exceed the fair market value of equipment of the same age and condition at the time of donation.

(3) The value of donated space shall not exceed the fair rental value of comparable space as established by an independent appraisal of comparable space and facilities in a privately-owned building in the same locality.

(4) The value of loaned equipment shall not exceed its fair rental value.

(5) The following requirements pertain to the recipient's supporting records for in-kind contributions from third parties.

(i) Volunteer services shall be documented and, to the extent feasible, supported by the same methods used by the recipient for its own employees.

(ii) The basis for determining the valuation for personal service, material, equipment, buildings and land shall be documented.

§518.24 Program income.

(a) Federal awarding agencies shall apply the standards set forth in this section in requiring recipient organizations to account for program income related to projects financed in whole or in part with Federal funds.

(b) Except as provided in paragraph (h) of this section, program income earned during the project period shall be retained by the recipient and, in accordance with Federal awarding agency regulations or the terms and conditions of the award, shall be used in one or more of the ways listed in the following.

(1) Added to funds committed to the project by the Federal awarding agency and recipient and used to further eligible project or program objectives.

(2) Used to finance the non-Federal share of the project or program.

(3) Deducted from the total project or program allowable cost in determining the net allowable costs on which the Federal share of costs is based.

(c) When an agency authorizes the disposition of program income as described in paragraphs (b)(1) or (b)(2) of this section, program income in excess of any limits stipulated shall be used in accordance with paragraph (b)(3) of this section.

(d) In the event that the Federal awarding agency does not specify in its regulations or the terms and conditions of the award how program income is to be used, paragraph (b)(3) of this section shall apply automatically to all projects or programs except research. For awards that support research, paragraph (b)(1) of this section shall apply automatically unless the awarding agency indicates in the terms and conditions another alternative on the award or the recipient is subject to special award conditions, as indicated in §518.14.

(e) Unless Federal awarding agency regulations or the terms and conditions of the award provide otherwise, recipients shall have no obligation to the Federal Government regarding program income earned after the end of the project period.

(f) If authorized by Federal awarding agency regulations or the terms and conditions of the award, costs incident to the generation of program income may be deducted from gross income to determine program income, provided these costs have not been charged to the award.

(g) Proceeds from the sale of property shall be handled in accordance with the requirements of the Property Standards (See §§518.30 through 518.37).

(h) Unless Federal awarding agency regulations or the terms and condition of the award provide otherwise, recipients shall have no obligation to the Federal Government with respect to program income earned from license fees and royalties for copyrighted material, patents, patent applications, trademarks, and inventions produced under an award. However, Patent and Trademark Amendments (35 U.S.C. 18) apply to inventions made under an experimental, developmental, or research award.

§518.25 Revision of budget and program plans.

(a) The budget plan is the financial expression of the project or program as approved during the award process. It may include either the Federal and non-Federal share, or only the Federal share, depending upon Federal awarding agency requirements. It shall be related to performance for program evaluation purposes whenever appropriate.

(b) Recipients are required to report deviations from budget and program plans, and request prior approvals for budget and program plan revisions, in accordance with this section.

(c) For nonconstruction awards, recipients shall request prior approvals from Federal awarding agencies for one or more of the following program or budget related reasons.

(1) Change in the scope or the objective of the project or program (even if there is no associated budget revision requiring prior written approval).

(2) Change in a key person specified in the application or award document.

(3) The absence for more than three months, or a 25 percent reduction in time devoted to the project, by the approved project director or principal investigator.

(4) The need for additional Federal funding.

(5) The transfer of amounts budgeted for indirect costs to absorb increases in direct costs, or vice versa, if approval is required by the Federal awarding agency.

(6) The inclusion, unless waived by the Federal awarding agency, of costs that require prior approval in accordance with OMB Circular A–21, "Cost Principles for Institutions of Higher Education," OMB Circular A–122, "Cost Principles for Non-Profit Organizations," or 45 CFR part 74 Appendix E, "Principles for Determining Costs Applicable to Research and Development under Grants and Contracts with Hospitals," or 48 CFR part 31, "Contract Cost Principles and Procedures," as applicable.

(7) The transfer of funds allotted for training allowances (direct payment to trainees) to other categories of expense.

(8) Unless described in the application and funded in the approved awards, the subaward, transfer or contracting out of any work under an award. This provision does not apply to the purchase of supplies, material, equipment or general support services.

(d) No other prior approval requirements for specific items may be imposed unless a deviation has been approved by OMB.

(e) Except for requirements listed in paragraphs (c)(1) and (c)(4) of this section, Federal awarding agencies are authorized, at their option, to waive cost-related and administrative prior written approvals required by this part and OMB Circulars A–21 and A–122. Such waivers may include authorizing recipients to do any one or more of the following:

(1) Incur pre-award costs 90 calendar days prior to award or more than 90 calendar days with the prior approval of the Federal awarding agency. All pre-award costs are incurred at the recipient's risk (i.e., the Federal awarding agency is under no obligation to reimburse such costs if for any reason the recipient does not receive an award

or if the award is less than anticipated and inadequate to cover such costs).

(2) Initiate a one-time extension of the expiration date of the award of up to 12 months unless one or more of the following conditions apply. For one-time extensions, the recipient must notify the Federal awarding agency in writing with the supporting reasons and revised expiration date at least 10 days before the expiration date specified in the award. This one-time extension may not be exercised merely for the purpose of using unobligated balances.

(i) The terms and conditions of award prohibit the extension.

(ii) The extension requires additional Federal funds.

(iii) The extension involves any change in the approved objectives or scope of the project.

(3) Carry forward unobligated balances to subsequent funding periods.

(4) For awards that support research, unless the Federal awarding agency provides otherwise in the award or in the agency's regulations, the prior approval requirements described in paragraph (e) of this section are automatically waived (i.e., recipients need not obtain such prior approvals) unless one of the conditions included in paragraph (e)(2) of this section applies.

(f) The Federal awarding agency may, at its option, restrict the transfer of funds among direct cost categories or programs, functions and activities for awards in which the Federal share of the project exceeds $100,000 and the cumulative amount of such transfers exceeds or is expected to exceed 10 percent of the total budget as last approved by the Federal awarding agency. No Federal awarding agency shall permit a transfer that would cause any Federal appropriation or part thereof to be used for purposes other than those consistent with the original intent of the appropriation.

(g) All other changes to nonconstruction budgets, except for the changes described in paragraph (j) of this section, do not require prior approval.

(h) For construction awards, recipients shall request prior written approval promptly from Federal awarding agencies for budget revisions whether the conditions in paragraphs (h) (1), (2) or (3) of this section apply.

(1) The revision results from changes in the scope or the objective of the project or program.

(2) The need arises for additional Federal funds to complete the project.

(3) A revision is desired which involves specific costs for which prior written approval requirements may be imposed consistent with applicable OMB cost principles listed in §518.27

(i) No other prior approval requirements for specific items may be imposed unless a deviation has been approved by OMB.

(j) When a Federal awarding agency makes an award that provides support for both construction and nonconstruction work, the Federal awarding agency may require the recipient to request prior approval from the Federal awarding agency before making any fund or budget transfers between the two types of work supported.

(k) For both construction and nonconstruction awards, Federal awarding agencies shall require recipients to notify the Federal awarding agency in writing promptly whenever the amount of Federal authorized funds is expected to exceed the needs of the recipient for the project period by more than $5000 or five percent of the Federal award, whichever is greater. This notification shall not be required if an application for additional funding is submitted for a continuation award.

(l) When requesting approval for budget revisions, recipients shall use the budget forms that were used in the application unless the Federal awarding agency indicates a letter of request suffices.

(m) Within 30 calendar days from the date of receipt of the request for budget revisions, Federal awarding agencies shall review the request and notify the recipient whether the budget revisions have been approved. If the revision is still under consideration at the end of 30 calendar days, the Federal awarding agency shall inform the recipient in writing of the date when the recipient may expect the decision.

§518.26 Non-Federal audits.

(a) Recipients and subrecipients that are institutions of higher education or other non-profit organizations (including hospitals) shall be subject to the audit requirements contained in the Single Audit Act Amendments of 1996 (31 U.S.C. 7501–7507) and revised OMB Circular A–133, "Audits of States, Local Governments, and Non-Profit Organizations."

(b) State and local governments shall be subject to the audit requirements contained in the Single Audit Act Amendments of 1996 (31 U.S.C. 7501–7507) and revised OMB Circular A–133, "Audits of States, Local Governments, and Non-Profit Organizations."

(c) For-profit hospitals not covered by the audit provisions of revised OMB Circular A–133 shall be subject to the audit requirements of the Federal awarding agencies.

(d) Commercial organizations shall be subject to the audit requirements of the Federal awarding agency or the prime recipients as incorporated into the award document.

[59 FR 39440, Aug. 3, 1994, as amended at 62 FR 45939, 45941, Aug. 29, 1997]

§ 518.27 Allowable costs.

For each kind of recipient, there is a set of Federal principles for determining allowable costs. Allowability of costs shall be determined in accordance with the cost principles applicable to the entity incurring the costs. Thus, allowability of costs incurred by State, local or federally-recognized Indian tribal governments is determined in accordance with the provisions of OMB Circular A–87, "Cost Principles for State and Local Governments." The allowability of costs incurred by non-profit organizations is determined in accordance with the provisions of OMB Circular A–122, "Cost Principles for Non-Profit Organizations." The allowability of costs incurred by institutions of higher education is determined in accordance with the provisions of OMB Circular A–21, "Cost Principles for Educational Institutions." The allowability of costs incurred by hospitals is determined in accordance with the provisions of Appendix E of 45 CFR part 74, "Principles for Determining Costs Applicable to Research and Development Under Grants and Contracts with Hospitals." The allowability of costs incurred by commercial organizations and those non-profit organizations listed in Attachment C to Circular A–122 is determined in accordance with the provisions of the Federal Acquisition Regulation (FAR) at 48 CFR part 31.

§ 518.28 Period of availability of funds.

Where a funding period is specified, a recipient may charge to the grant only allowable costs resulting from obligations incurred during the funding period and any pre-award costs authorized by the Federal awarding agency.

PROPERTY STANDARDS

§ 518.30 Purpose of property standards.

(a) Sections 518.31 through 518.37 set forth uniform standards governing management and disposition of property furnished by the Federal Government whose cost was charged to a project supported by a Federal award. Federal awarding agencies shall require recipients to observe these standards under awards and shall not impose additional requirements, unless specifically required by Federal statute. The recipient may use its own property management standards and procedures provided it observes the provisions of §§ 518.31 through 518.37.

§ 518.31 Insurance coverage.

Recipients shall, at a minimum, provide the equivalent insurance coverage for real property and equipment acquired with Federal funds as provided to property owned by the recipient. Federally-owned property need not be insured unless required by the terms and conditions of the award.

§ 518.32 Real property.

Each Federal awarding agency shall prescribe requirements for recipients concerning the use and disposition of real property acquired in whole or in part under awards. Unless otherwise provided by statute, such requirements, at a minimum, shall contain the following.

(a) Title to real property shall vest in the recipient subject to the condition that the recipient shall use the real property for the authorized purpose of the project as long as it is needed and shall not encumber the property without approval of the Federal awarding agency.

(b) The recipient shall obtain written approval by the Federal awarding agency for the use of real property in other federally-sponsored projects when the recipient determines that the property is no longer needed for the purpose of the original project. Use in other projects shall be limited to those under federally-sponsored projects (i.e., awards) or programs that have purposes consistent with those authorized for support by the Federal awarding agencies.

(c) When the real property is no longer needed as provided in paragraphs (a) and (b) of this section, the recipient shall request disposition instructions from the Federal awarding agency or its successor Federal awarding agency. The Federal awarding agency shall observe one or more of the following disposition instructions.

(1) The recipient may be permitted to retain title without further obligation to the Federal Government after it compensates the Federal Government for that percentage of the current fair market value of the property attributable to the Federal participation in the project.

(2) The recipient may be directed to sell the property under guidelines provided by the Federal awarding agency and pay the Federal Government for that percentage of the current fair market value of the property attributable to the Federal participation in the project (after deducting actual and reasonable selling and fix-up expenses, if any, from the sales proceeds). When the recipient is authorized or required to sell the property, proper sales procedures shall be established that provide for competition to the extent practicable and result in the highest possible return.

(3) The recipient may be directed to transfer title to the property to the Federal Government or to an eligible third party provided that, in such cases, the recipient shall be entitled to compensation for its attributable percentage of the current fair market value of the property.

§518.33 Federally-owned and exempt property.

(a) Federally-owned property. (1) Title to federally-owned property remains vested in the Federal Government. Recipients shall submit annually an inventory listing of federally-owned property in their custody to the Federal awarding agency. Upon completion of the award or when the property is no longer needed, the recipient shall report the property to the Federal awarding agency for further Federal agency utilization.

(2) If the Federal awarding agency has no further need for the property, it shall be declared excess and reported to the General Services Administration, unless the Federal awarding agency has statutory authority to dispose of the property by alternative methods (*e.g.*, the authority provided by the Federal Technology Transfer Act (15 U.S.C. 3710(I)) to donate research equipment to educational and non-profit organizations in accordance with E.O. 12821, "Improving Mathematics and Science Education in Support of the National Education Goals.") Appropriate instructions shall be issued to the recipient by the Federal awarding agency.

(b) Exempt property. When statutory authority exists, the Federal awarding agency has the option to vest title to property acquired with Federal funds in the recipient without further obligation to the Federal Government and under conditions the Federal awarding agency considers appropriate. Such property is "exempt property." Should a Federal awarding agency not establish conditions, title to exempt property upon acquisition shall vest in the recipient without further obligation to the Federal Government.

§518.34 Equipment.

(a) Title to equipment acquired by a recipient with Federal funds shall vest in the recipient, subject to conditions of this section.

(b) The recipient shall not use equipment acquired with Federal funds to provide services to non-Federal outside organizations for a fee that is less than private companies charge for equivalent services, unless specifically authorized by Federal statute, for as long as the Federal Government retains an interest in the equipment.

(c) The recipient shall use the equipment in the project or program for which it was acquired as long as needed, whether or not the project or program continues to be supported by Federal funds and shall not encumber the property without approval of the Federal awarding agency. When no longer needed for the original project or program, the recipient shall use the equipment in connection with its other federally-sponsored activities, in the following order or priority:

(1) Activities sponsored by the Federal awarding agency which funded the original project, then

(2) Activities sponsored by other Federal awarding agencies.

(d) During the time that equipment is used on the project or program for which it was acquired, the recipient shall make it available for use on other projects or programs if such other use will not interfere with the work on the project or program for which the equipment was originally acquired. First preference for such other use shall be given to other projects or programs sponsored by the Federal awarding agency that financed the equipment; second preference shall be given to projects or programs sponsored by other Federal awarding agencies. If the equipment is owned by the Federal Government, use on other activities not sponsored by the Federal Government shall be permissible if authorized by the Federal awarding agency. User charges shall be treated as program income.

(e) When acquiring replacement equipment, the recipient may use the equipment to be replaced as trade-in or sell the equipment and use the proceeds to offset the costs of the replacement equipment subject to the approval of the Federal awarding agency.

(f) The recipient's property management standards for equipment acquired with Federal funds and federally-owned equipment shall include all of the following.

(1) Equipment records shall be maintained accurately and shall include the following information.

(i) A description of the equipment.

(ii) Manufacturer's serial number, model number, Federal stock number, national stock number, or other identification number.

(iii) Source of the equipment, including the award number.

(iv) Whether title vests in the recipient or the Federal Government.

(v) Acquisition date (or date received, if the equipment was furnished by the Federal Government) and cost.

(vi) Information from which one can calculate the percentage of Federal participation in the cost of the equipment (not applicable to equipment furnished by the Federal Government).

(vii) Location and condition of the equipment and the date the information was reported.

(viii) Unit acquisition cost.

(ix) Ultimate disposition data, including date of disposal and sales price or the method used to determine current fair market value where a recipient compensates the Federal awarding agency for its share.

(2) Equipment owned by the Federal Government shall be identified to indicate Federal ownership.

(3) A physical inventory of equipment shall be taken and the results reconciled with the equipment records at least once every two years. Any differences between quantities determined by the physical inspection and those shown in the accounting records shall be investigated to determine the causes of the difference. The recipient shall, in connection with the inventory, verify the existence, current utilization, and continued need for the equipment.

(4) A control system shall be in effect to insure adequate safeguards to prevent loss, damage, or theft of the equipment. Any loss, damage, or theft of equipment shall be investigated and fully documented; if the equipment was owned by the Federal Government, the recipient shall promptly notify the Federal awarding agency.

(5) Adequate maintenance procedures shall be implemented to keep the equipment in good condition.

(6) Where the recipient is authorized or required to sell the equipment, proper sales procedures shall be established which provide for competition to the

extent practicable and result in the highest possible return.

(g) When the recipient no longer needs the equipment, the equipment may be used for other activities in accordance with the following standards. For equipment with a current per unit fair market value of $5,000 or more, the recipient may retain the equipment for other uses provided that compensation is made to the original Federal awarding agency or its successor. The amount of compensation shall be computed by applying the percentage of Federal participation in the cost of the original project or program to the current fair market value of the equipment. If the recipient has no need for the equipment, the recipient shall request disposition instructions from the Federal awarding agency. The Federal awarding agency shall determine whether the equipment can be used to meet the agency's requirements. If no requirement exists within that agency, the availability of the equipment shall be reported to the General Services Administration by the Federal awarding agency to determine whether a requirement for the equipment exists in other Federal agencies. The Federal awarding agency shall issue instructions to the recipient no later than 120 calendar days after the recipient's request and the following procedures shall govern.

(1) If so instructed or if disposition instructions are not issued within 120 calendar days after the recipient's request, the recipient shall sell the equipment and reimburse the Federal awarding agency an amount computed by applying to the sales proceeds the percentage of Federal participation in the cost of the original project or program. However, the recipient shall be permitted to deduct and retain from the Federal share $500 or ten percent of the proceeds, whichever is less, for the recipient's selling and handling expenses.

(2) If the recipient is instructed to ship the equipment elsewhere, the recipient shall be reimbursed by the Federal Government by an amount which is computed by applying the percentage of the recipient's participation in the cost of the original project or program to the current fair market value of the equipment, plus any reasonable shipping or interim storage costs incurred.

(3) If the recipient is instructed to otherwise dispose of the equipment, the recipient shall be reimbursed by the Federal awarding agency for such costs incurred in its disposition.

(4) The Federal awarding agency may reserve the right to transfer the title to the Federal Government or to a third party named by the Federal Government when such third party is otherwise eligible under existing statutes. Such transfer shall be subject to the following standards.

(i) The equipment shall be appropriately identified in the award or otherwise made known to the recipient in writing.

(ii) The Federal awarding agency shall issue disposition instructions within 120 calendar days after receipt of a final inventory. The final inventory shall list all equipment acquired with grant funds and federally-owned equipment. If the Federal awarding agency fails to issue disposition instructions within the 120 calendar day period, the recipient shall apply the standards of this section, as appropriate.

(iii) When the Federal awarding agency exercises its right to take title, the equipment shall be subject to the provisions for federally-owned equipment.

§518.35 Supplies and other expendable property.

(a) Title to supplies and other expendable property shall vest in the recipient upon acquisition. If there is a residual inventory of unused supplies exceeding $5000 in total aggregate value upon termination or completion of the project or program and the supplies are not needed for any other federally-sponsored project or program, the recipient shall retain the supplies for use on non-Federal sponsored activities or sell them, but shall, in either cases, compensate the Federal Government for its share. The amount of compensation shall be computed in the same manner as for equipment.

(b) The recipient shall not use supplies acquired with Federal funds to provide services to non-Federal outside organizations for a fee that is less than private companies charge for equivalent services, unless specifically authorized by Federal statute as long as the Federal Government retains an interest in the supplies.

§ 518.36 Intangible property.

(a) The recipient may copyright any work that is subject to copyright and was developed, or for which ownership was purchased, under an award. The Federal awarding agency(ies) reserve a royalty-free, nonexclusive and irrevocable right to reproduce, publish, or otherwise use the work for Federal purposes, and to authorize others to do so.

(b) Recipients are subject to applicable regulations governing patents and inventions, including government-wide regulations issued by the Department of Commerce at 37 CFR part 401, "Rights to Inventions Made by Nonprofit Organizations and Small Business Firms Under Government Grants, Contracts and Cooperative Agreements."

(c) Unless waived by the Federal awarding agency, the Federal Government has the right to the following:

(1) Obtain, reproduce, publish or otherwise use the data first produced under an award.

(2) Authorize others to receive, reproduce, publish, or otherwise use such data for Federal purposes.

(d) Title to intangible property and debt instruments acquired under an award or subaward vests upon acquisition in the recipient. The recipient shall use that property for the originally-authorized purpose, and the recipient shall not encumber the property without approval of the Federal awarding agency. When no longer needed for the originally authorized purpose, disposition of the intangible property shall occur in accordance with the provisions of paragraph § 19.34(g).

§ 518.37 Property trust relationship.

Real property, equipment, intangible property and debt instruments that are acquired or improved with Federal funds shall be held in trust by the recipient as trustee for the beneficiaries of the project or program under which the property was acquired or improved. Agencies may require recipients to record liens or other appropriate notices of record to indicate that personal or real property has been acquired or improved with Federal funds and that use and disposition conditions apply to the property.

PROCUREMENT STANDARDS

§ 518.40 Purpose of procurement standards.

Sections 518.41 through 518.48 set forth standards for use by recipients in establishing procedures for the procurement of supplies and other expendable property, equipment, real property and other services with Federal funds. These standards are furnished to ensure that such materials and services are obtained in an effective manner and in compliance with the provisions of applicable Federal statutes and executive orders. No additional procurement standards or requirements shall be imposed by the Federal awarding agencies upon recipients, unless specifically required by Federal statute or executive order or approved by OMB.

§ 518.41 Recipient responsibilities.

The standards contained in this section do not relieve the recipient of the contractual responsibilities arising under its contract(s). The recipient is the responsible authority, without recourse to the Federal awarding agency, regarding the settlement and satisfaction of all contractual and administrative issues arising out of procurements entered into in support of an award or other agreement. This includes disputes, claims, protests of award, source evaluation or other matters of a contractual nature. Matters concerning violation of statute are to be referred to such Federal, State or local authority as may have proper jurisdiction.

§ 518.42 Codes of conduct.

The recipient shall maintain written standards of conduct governing the performance of its employees engaged in the award and administration of contracts. No employee, officer, or agent shall participate in the selection, award, or administration of a contract supported by Federal funds if a real or apparent conflict of interest would be involved. Such a conflict would arise when the employee, officer, or agent, any member of his or her immediate family, his or her partner, or an organization which employs or is about to employ any of the parties indicated herein, has a financial or other interest in the firm selected for an award. The officers, employees, and agents of the recipient shall neither solicit nor accept gratuities, favors, or anything of monetary value from contractors, or parties to subagreements. However, recipients may set standards for situations in which the financial interest is not substantial or the gift is an unsolicited item of nominal value. The standards of conduct shall provide for disciplinary actions to be applied for violations of such standards by officers, employees, or agents of the recipient.

§518.43 Competition.

All procurement transactions shall be conducted in a manner to provide, to the maximum extent practical, open and free competition. The recipient shall be alert to organizational conflicts of interest as well as noncompetitive practices among contractors that may restrict or eliminate competition or otherwise restrain trade. In order to ensure objective contractor performance and eliminate unfair competitive advantage, contractors that develop or draft specifications, requirements, statements of work, invitations for bids and/or requests for proposals shall be excluded from competing for such procurements. Awards shall be made to the bidder or offeror whose bid or offer is responsive to the solicitation and is most advantageous to the recipient, price, quality and other factors considered. Solicitations shall clearly set forth all requirements that the bidder or offeror shall fulfill in order for the bid or offer to be evaluated by the recipient. Any and all bids or offers may be rejected when it is in the recipient's interest to do so.

§518.44 Procurement procedures.

(a) All recipients shall establish written procurement procedures. These procedures shall provide for, at a minimum, that the conditions in paragraphs (a)(1), (2) and (3) of this section apply.

(1) Recipients avoid purchasing unnecessary items.

(2) Where appropriate, an analysis is made of lease and purchase alternatives to determine which would be the most economical and practical procurement for the Federal Government.

(3) Solicitations for goods and services provide for all of the following:

(i) A clear and accurate description of the technical requirements for the material, product or service to be procured. In competitive procurements, such a description shall not contain features which unduly restrict competition.

(ii) Requirements which the bidder/offeror must fulfill and all other factors to be used in evaluating bids or proposals.

(iii) A description, whenever practicable, of technical requirements in terms or functions to be performed or performance required, including the range of acceptable characteristics or minimum acceptable standards.

(iv) The specific features of "brand name or equal" descriptions that bidders are required to meet when such items are included in the solicitation.

(v) The acceptance, to the extent practicable and economically feasible, of products and services dimensioned in the metric system of measurement.

(vi) Preference, to the extent practicable and economically feasible, for products and services that conserve natural resources and protect the environment and are energy efficient.

(b) Positive efforts shall be made by recipient to utilize small businesses, minority-owned firms, and women's business enterprises, whenever possible. Recipients of Federal awards shall take all of the following steps to further this goal.

(1) Ensure that small businesses, minority-owned firms, and women's business enterprises are used to the fullest extent practicable.

(2) Make information on forthcoming opportunities available and arrange timeframes for purchases and contracts to encourage and facilitate participation by small businesses, minority-owned firms, and women's business enterprises.

(3) Consider in the contract process whether firms competing for larger

contracts intend to subcontract with small businesses, minority-owned firms, and women's business enterprises.

(4) Encourage contracting with consortiums of small businesses, minority-owned firms and women's business enterprises when a contract is too large for one of these firms to handle individually.

(5) Use of services and assistance, as appropriate, of such organizations as the Small Business Administration and the Department of Commerce's Minority Business Development Agency in the solicitation and utilization of small businesses, minority-owned firms, and women's business enterprises.

(c) The type of procuring instruments used (*e.g.*, fixed price contracts, cost reimbursable contracts, purchase orders, and incentive contracts) shall be determined by the recipient but shall be appropriate for the particular procurement and for promoting the best interest of the program or project involved. The "cost-plus-a-percentage-of-cost" or "percentage of construction cost" methods of contracting shall not be used.

(d) Contracts shall be made only with responsible contractors who possess the potential ability to perform successfully under the terms and conditions of the proposed procurement. Consideration shall be given to such matters as contractor integrity, record of past performance, financial and technical resources or accessibility to other necessary resources. In certain circumstances, contracts with certain parties are restricted by the implementation of E.O.'s 12549 and 12689, "Debarment and Suspension."

(e) Recipients shall, on request, make available for the Federal awarding agency, pre-award review and procurement documents, such as request for proposals or invitations for bids, independent cost estimates, etc., when any of the following conditions apply.

(1) A recipient's procurement procedures or operation fails to comply with the procurement standards in this part.

(2) The procurement is expected to exceed the small purchase threshold fixed at 41 U.S.C. 403 (11) (currently $25,000) and is to be awarded without competition or only one bid or offer is received in response to a solicitation.

(3) The procurement, which is expected to exceed the small purchase threshold, specifies a "brand name" product.

(4) The proposed award over the small purchase threshold is to be awarded to other than the apparent low bidder under a sealed bid procurement.

(5) A proposed contract modification changes the scope of a contract or increases the contract amount by more than the amount of the small purchase threshold.

§ 518.45 Cost and price analysis.

Some form of cost or price analysis shall be made and documented in the procurement files in connection with every procurement action. Price analysis may be accomplished in various ways, including the comparison of price quotations submitted, market prices and similar indicia, together with discounts. Cost analysis is the review and evaluation of each element of cost to determine reasonableness, allocability and allowability.

§ 518.46 Procurement records.

Procurement records and files for purchases in excess of the small purchase threshold shall include the following at a minimum:

(a) Basis for contractor selection,

(b) Justification for lack of competition when competitive bids or offers are not obtained, and

(c) Basis for award cost or price.

§ 518.47 Contract administration.

A system for contract administration shall be maintained to ensure contractor conformance with the terms, conditions and specifications of the contract and to ensure adequate and timely follow up of all purchases. Recipients shall evaluate contractor performance and document, as appropriate, whether contractors have met the terms, conditions, and specifications of the contract.

§ 518.48 Contract provisions.

The recipient shall include, in addition to provisions to define a sound and complete agreement, the following provisions in all contracts. The following provisions shall also be applied to subcontracts.

(a) Contracts in excess of the small purchase threshold shall contain contractual provisions or conditions that allow for administrative, contractual, or legal remedies in instances in which a contractor violates or breaches the contract terms, and provide for such remedial actions as may be appropriate.

(b) All contracts in excess of the small purchase threshold shall contain suitable provisions for termination by the recipient, including the manner by which termination shall be effected and the basis for settlement. In addition, such contracts shall describe conditions under which the contract may be terminated for default as well as conditions where the contract may be terminated because of circumstances beyond the control of the contractor.

(c) Except as otherwise required by statute, an award that requires the contracting (or subcontracting) for construction or facility improvements shall provide for the recipient to follow its own requirements relating to bid guarantees, performance bonds, and payment bonds unless the construction contract or subcontract exceeds $100,000. For those contracts or subcontracts exceeding $100,000, the Federal awarding agency may accept the bonding policy and requirements of the recipient, provided the Federal awarding agency has made a determination that the Federal Government's interest is adequately protected. If such a determination has not been made, the minimum requirements shall be as follows.

(1) A bid guarantee from each bidder equivalent to five percent of the bid price. The "bid guarantee" shall consist of a firm commitment such as a bid bond, certified check, or other negotiable instrument accompanying a bid as assurance that the bidder shall, upon acceptance of his bid, execute such contractual documents as may be required within the time specified.

(2) A performance bond on the part of the contractor for 100 percent of the contract price. A "performance bond" is one executed in connection with a contract to secure fulfillment of all the contractor's obligations under such contract.

(3) A payment bond on the part of the contractor for 100 percent of the contract price. A "payment bond" is one executed in connection with a contract to assure payment as required by statute of all persons supplying labor and material in the execution of the work provided for in the contract.

(4) Where bonds are required in the situations described herein, the bonds shall be obtained from companies holding certificates of authority as acceptable sureties pursuant to 31 CFR part 223, "Surety Companies Doing Business with the United States."

(d) All negotiated contracts (except those for less than the small purchase threshold) awarded by recipients shall include a provision to the effect that the recipient, the Federal awarding agency, the Comptroller General of the United States, or any of their duly authorized representatives, shall have access to any books, documents, papers and records of the contractor which are directly pertinent to a specific program for the purpose of making audits, examinations, excerpts and transcriptions.

(e) All contracts, including small purchases, awarded by recipients and their contractors shall contain the procurement provisions of Appendix A to this part, as applicable.

Reports and Records

§518.50 Purpose of reports and records.

Sections 518.51 through 518.53 set forth the procedures for monitoring and reporting on the recipient's financial and program performance and the necessary standard reporting forms. They also set forth record retention requirements.

§518.51 Monitoring and reporting program performance.

(a) Recipients are responsible for managing and monitoring each project, program, subaward, function or activity supported by the award. Recipients shall monitor subawards to ensure subrecipients have met the audit requirements as delineated in §518.26.

(b) The Federal awarding agency shall prescribe the frequency with which the performance reports shall be submitted. Except as provided in § 518.51(f), performance reports shall not be required more frequently than quarterly or, less frequently than annually. Annual reports shall be due 90 calendar days after the grant year; quarterly or semi-annual reports shall be due 30 days after the reporting period. The Federal awarding agency may require annual reports before the anniversary dates of multiple year awards in lieu of these requirements. The final performance reports are due 90 calendar days after the expiration or termination of the award.

(c) If inappropriate, a final technical or performance report shall not be required after completion of the project.

(d) When required, performance reports shall generally contain, for each award, brief information on each of the following.

(1) A comparison of actual accomplishments with the goals and objectives established for the period, the findings of the investigator, or both. Whenever appropriate and the output of programs or projects can be readily quantified, such quantitative data should be related to cost data for computation of unit costs.

(2) Reasons why established goals were not met, if appropriate.

(3) Other pertinent information including, when appropriate, analysis and explanation of cost overruns or high unit costs.

(e) Recipients shall not be required to submit more than the original and two copies of performance reports.

(f) Recipients shall immediately notify the Federal awarding agency of developments that have a significant impact on the award-supported activities. Also, notification shall be given in the case of problems, delays, or adverse conditions which materially impair the ability to meet the objectives of the award. This notification shall include a statement of the action taken or contemplated, and any assistance needed to resolve the situation.

(g) Federal awarding agencies may make site visits, as needed.

(h) Federal awarding agencies shall comply with clearance requirements of 5 CFR part 1320 when requesting performance data from recipients.

§ 518.52 Financial reporting.

(a) The following forms or such other forms as may be approved by OMB are authorized for obtaining financial information from recipients.

(1) SF–269 or SF–269A, Financial Status Report.

(i) Each Federal awarding agency shall require recipients to use the SF–269 or SF–269A to report the status of funds for all nonconstruction projects or programs. A Federal awarding agency may, however, have the option of not requiring the SF–269 or SF–269A when the SF–270, Request for Advance or Reimbursement, or SF–272, Report of Federal Cash Transactions, is determined to provide adequate information to meet its needs, except that a final SF–269 or SF–269A shall be required at the completion of the project when the SF–270 is used only for advances.

(ii) The Federal awarding agency shall prescribe whether the report shall be on a cash or accrual basis. If the Federal awarding agency requires accrual information and the recipient's accounting records are not normally kept on the accrual basis, the recipient shall not be required to convert its accounting system, but shall develop such accrual information through best estimates based on an analysis of the documentation on hand.

(iii) The Federal awarding agency shall determine the frequency of the Financial Status Report for each project or program, considering the size and complexity of the particular project or program. However, the report shall not be required more frequently than quarterly or less frequently than annually. A final report shall be required at the completion of the agreement.

(iv) The Federal awarding agency shall require recipients to submit the SF–269 or SF–269A (an original and no more than two copies) no later than 30 days after the end of each specified reporting period for quarterly and semiannual reports, and 90 calendar days for annual and final reports. Extensions of reporting due dates may be approved by the Federal awarding agency upon request of the recipient.

(2) SF-272, Report of Federal Cash Transactions.

(i) When funds are advanced to recipients the Federal awarding agency shall require each recipient to submit the SF-272 and, when necessary, its continuation sheet, SF-272a. The Federal awarding agency shall use this report to monitor cash advanced to recipients and to obtain disbursement information for each agreement with the recipients.

(ii) Federal awarding agencies may require forecasts of Federal cash requirements in the "Remarks" section of the report.

(iii) When practical and deemed necessary, Federal awarding agencies may require recipients to report in the "Remarks" section the amount of cash advances received in excess of three days. Recipients shall provide short narrative explanations of actions taken to reduce the excess balances.

(iv) Recipients shall be required to submit not more than the original and two copies of the SF-272 15 calendar days following the end of each quarter. The Federal awarding agencies may require a monthly report from those recipients receiving advances totaling $1 million or more per year.

(v) Federal awarding agencies may waive the requirement for submission of the SF-272 for any one of the following reasons:

(A) When monthly advances do not exceed $25,000 per recipient, provided that such advances are monitored through other forms contained in this section;

(B) If, in the Federal awarding agency's opinion, the recipient's accounting controls are adequate to minimize excessive Federal advances; or,

(C) When the electronic payment mechanisms provide adequate data.

(b) When the Federal awarding agency needs additional information or more frequent reports, the following shall be observed.

(1) When additional information is needed to comply with legislative requirements, Federal awarding agencies shall issue instructions to require recipients to submit such information under the "Remarks" section of the reports.

(2) When a Federal awarding agency determines that a recipient's accounting system does not meet the standards in §518.21, additional pertinent information to further monitor awards may be obtained upon written notice to the recipient until such time as the system is brought up to standard. The Federal awarding agency, in obtaining this information, shall comply with report clearance requirements of 5 CFR part 1320.

(3) Federal awarding agencies are encouraged to shade out any line item on any report if not necessary.

(4) Federal awarding agencies may accept the identical information from the recipients in machine readable format or computer printouts or electronic outputs in lieu of prescribed formats.

(5) Federal awarding agencies may provide computer or electronic outputs to recipients when such expedites or contributes to the accuracy of reporting.

§518.53 Retention and access requirements for records.

(a) This section sets forth requirements for record retention and access to records for awards to recipients. Federal awarding agencies shall not impose any other record retention or access requirements upon recipients.

(b) Financial records, supporting documents, statistical records, and all other records pertinent to an award shall be retained for a period of three years from the date of submission of the final expenditure report or, for awards that are renewed quarterly or annually, from the date of the submission of the quarterly or annual financial report, as authorized by the Federal awarding agency. The only exceptions are the following.

(1) If any litigation, claim, or audit is started before the expiration of the 3-year period, the records shall be retained until all litigation, claims or audit findings involving the records have been resolved and final action taken.

(2) Records for real property and equipment acquired with Federal funds shall be retained for 3 years after final disposition.

(3) When records are transferred to or maintained by the Federal awarding agency, the 3-year retention requirement is not applicable to the recipient.

(4) Indirect cost rate proposals, cost allocations plans, etc. as specified in paragraph § 518.53(g).

(c) Copies of original records may be substituted for the original records if authorized by the Federal awarding agency.

(d) The Federal awarding agency shall request transfer of certain records to its custody from recipients when it determines that the records possess long term retention value. However, in order to avoid duplicate recordkeeping, a Federal awarding agency may make arrangements for recipients to retain any records that are continuously needed for joint use.

(e) The Federal awarding agency, the Inspector General, Comptroller General of the United States, or any of their duly authorized representatives, have the right of timely and unrestricted access to any books, documents, papers, or other records of recipients that are pertinent to the awards, in order to make audits, examinations, excerpts, transcripts and copies of such documents. This right also includes timely and reasonable access to a recipient's personnel for the purpose of interview and discussion related to such documents. The rights of access in this paragraph are not limited to the required retention period, but shall last as long as records are retained.

(f) Unless required by statute, no Federal awarding agency shall place restrictions on recipients that limit public access to the records of recipients that are pertinent to an award, except when the Federal awarding agency can demonstrate that such records shall be kept confidential and would have been exempted from disclosure pursuant to the Freedom of Information Act (5 U.S.C. 552) if the records had belonged to the Federal awarding agency.

(g) Indirect cost rate proposals, cost allocations plans, etc. Paragraphs (g)(1) and (g)(2) of this section apply to the following types of documents, and their supporting records: indirect cost rate computations or proposals, cost allocation plans, and any similar accounting computations of the rate at which a particular group of costs is chargeable (such as computer usage chargeback rates or composite fringe benefit rates).

(1) If submitted for negotiation. If the recipient submits to the Federal awarding agency or the subrecipient submits to the recipient the proposal, plan, or other computation to form the basis for negotiation of the rate, then the 3-year retention period for its supporting records starts on the date of such submission.

(2) If not submitted for negotiation. If the recipient is not required to submit to the Federal awarding agency or the subrecipient is not required to submit to the recipient the proposal, plan, or other computation for negotiation purposes, then the 3-year retention period for the proposal, plan, or other computation and its supporting records starts at the end of the fiscal year (or other accounting period) covered by the proposal, plan, or other computation.

TERMINATION AND ENFORCEMENT

§ 518.60 Purpose of termination and enforcement.

Sections 518.61 and 518.62 set forth uniform suspension, termination and enforcement procedures.

§ 518.61 Termination.

(a) Awards may be terminated in whole or in part only if the conditions in paragraphs (a)(1), (2) or (3) of this section apply.

(1) By the Federal awarding agency, if a recipient materially fails to comply with the terms and conditions of an award.

(2) By the Federal awarding agency with the consent of the recipient, in which case the two parties shall agree upon the termination conditions, including the effective date and, in the case of partial termination, the portion to be terminated.

(3) By the recipient upon sending to the Federal awarding agency written notification setting forth the reasons for such termination, the effective date, and, in the case of partial termination, the portion to be terminated.

However, if the Federal awarding agency determines in the case of partial termination that the reduced or modified portion of the grant will not accomplish the purposes for which the grant was made, it may terminate the grant in its entirety under either paragraphs (a)(1) or (2) of this section.

(b) If costs are allowed under an award, the responsibilities of the recipient referred to in §518.71(a), including those for property management as applicable, shall be considered in the termination of the award, and provision shall be made for continuing responsibilities of the recipient after termination, as appropriate.

§518.62 Enforcement.

(a) Remedies for noncompliance. If a recipient materially fails to comply with the terms and conditions of an award, whether stated in a Federal statute, regulation, assurance, application, or notice of award, the Federal awarding agency may, in addition to imposing any of the special conditions outlined in §518.14, take one or more of the following actions, as appropriate in the circumstances.

(1) Temporarily withhold cash payments pending correction of the deficiency by the recipient or more severe enforcement action by the Federal awarding agency.

(2) Disallow (that is, deny both use of funds and any applicable matching credit for) all or part of the cost of the activity or action not in compliance.

(3) Wholly or partly suspend or terminate the current award.

(4) Without further awards for the project or program.

(5) Take other remedies that may be legally available.

(b) Hearings and appeals. In taking an enforcement action, the awarding agency shall provide the recipient an opportunity for hearing, appeal, or other administrative proceeding to which the recipient is entitled under any statute or regulation applicable to the action involved.

(c) Effects of suspension and termination. Costs of a recipient resulting from obligations incurred by the recipient during a suspension or after termination of an award are not allowable unless the awarding agency expressly authorizes them in the notice of suspension or termination or subsequently. Other recipient costs during suspension or after termination which are necessary and not reasonably avoidable are allowable if the conditions in paragraphs (c) (1) or (2) of this section apply.

(1) The costs result from obligations which were properly incurred by the recipient before the effective date of suspension or termination, are not in anticipation of it, and in the case of a termination, are noncancellable.

(2) The costs would be allowable if the award were not suspended or expired normally at the end of the funding period in which the termination takes effect.

(d) Relationship to debarment and suspension. The enforcement remedies identified in this section, including suspension and termination, do not preclude a recipient from being subject to debarment and suspension under E.O.s 12549 and 12689 and the Federal awarding agency implementing regulations (see §518.13).

Subpart D—After-the-Award Requirements

§518.70 Purpose.

Sections 518.71 through 518.73 contain closeout procedures and other procedures for subsequent disallowances and adjustments.

§518.71 Closeout procedures.

(a) Recipients shall submit, within 90 calendar days after the date of completion of the award, all financial, performance, and other reports as required by the terms and conditions of the award. The Federal awarding agency may approve extensions when requested by the recipient.

(b) Unless the Federal awarding agency authorizes an extension, a recipient shall liquidate all obligations incurred under the award not later than 90 calendar days after the funding period or the date of completion as specified in the terms and conditions of the award or in agency implementing instructions.

(c) The Federal awarding agency shall make prompt payments to a recipient for allowable reimbursable costs under the award being closed out.

(d) The recipient shall promptly refund any balances of unobligated cash that the Federal awarding agency has advanced or paid and that is not authorized to be retained by the recipient for use in other projects. OMB Circular A–129 governs unreturned amounts that become delinquent debts.

(e) When authorized by the terms and conditions of the award, the Federal awarding agency shall make a settlement for any upward or downward adjustments to the Federal share of costs after closeout reports are received.

(f) The recipient shall account for any real and personal property acquired with Federal funds or received from the Federal Government in accordance with §§ 518.31 through 518.37.

(g) In the event a final audit has not been performed prior to the closeout of an award, the Federal awarding agency shall retain the right to recover an appropriate amount after fully considering the recommendations on disallowing costs resulting from the final audit.

§ 518.72 Subsequent adjustments and continuing responsibilities.

(a) The closeout of an award does not affect any of the following.

(1) The right of the Federal awarding agency to disallow costs and recover funds on the basis of a later audit or other review.

(2) The obligation of the recipient to return any funds due as a result of later refunds, corrections, or other transactions.

(3) Audit requirements in § 518.26.

(4) Property management requirements in §§ 518.31 through 518.37.

(5) Records retention as required in § 518.53.

(b) After closeout of an award, a relationship created under an award may be modified or ended in whole or in part with the consent of the Federal awarding agency and the recipient, provided the responsibilities of the recipient referred to in § 518.73(a), including those for property management as applicable, are considered and provisions made for continuing responsibilities of the recipient, as appropriate.

§ 518.73 Collection of amounts due.

(a) Any funds paid to a recipient in excess of the amount to which the recipient is finally determined to be entitled under the terms and conditions of the award constitute a debt to the Federal Government. If not paid within a reasonable period after the demand for payment, the Federal awarding agency may reduce the debt by the provisions of paragraphs (a) (1), (2) or (3) of this section.

(1) Making an administrative offset against other requests for reimbursements.

(2) Withholding advance payments otherwise due to the recipient.

(3) Taking over action permitted by statute.

(b) Except as otherwise provided by law, the Federal awarding agency shall charge interest on an overdue debt in accordance with 4 CFR chapter II, "Federal Claims Collection Standards."

APPENDIX A TO PART 518—CONTRACT PROVISIONS

All contracts, awarded by a recipient including small purchases, shall contain the following provisions as applicable:

1. *Equal Employment Opportunity*—All contracts shall contain a provision requiring compliance with E.O. 11246, "Equal Employment Opportunity," as amended by E.O. 11375, "Amending Executive Order 11246 Relating to Equal Employment Opportunity," and as supplemented by regulations at 41 CFR part 60, "Office of Federal Contract Compliance Programs, Equal Employment Opportunity, Department of Labor."

2. *Copeland "Anti-Kickback" Act (18 U.S.C. 874 and 40 U.S.C. 276c)*—All contracts and subgrants in excess of $2,000 for construction or repair awarded by recipients and subrecipients shall include a provision for compliance with the Copeland "Anti-Kickback" Act (18 U.S.C. 874), as supplemented by Department of Labor regulations (29 CFR part 3, "Contractors and Subcontractors on Public Building or Public Work Financed in Whole or in part by Loans or Grants from the United States"). The Act provides that each contractor or subrecipient shall be prohibited from inducing, by any means, any person employed in the construction, completion, or repair of public work, to give up any part of the compensation to which he is otherwise

entitled. The recipient shall report all suspected or reported violations to the Federal awarding agency.

3. *Davis-Bacon Act, as amended (40 U.S.C. 276a to a-7)*—When required by Federal program legislation, all construction contracts awarded by the recipients and subrecipients of more than $2,000 shall include a provision for compliance with the Davis-Bacon Act (40 U.S.C. 276a to a-7) and as supplemented by Department of Labor regulations (29 CFR part 5, "Labor Standards Provisions Applicable to Contracts Governing Federally Financed and Assisted Construction"). Under this Act, contractors shall be required to pay wages to laborers and mechanics at a rate not less than the minimum wages specified in a wage determination made by the Secretary of Labor. In addition, contractors shall be required to pay wages not less than once a week. The recipient shall place a copy of the current prevailing wage determination issued by the Department of Labor in each solicitation and the award of a contract shall be conditioned upon the acceptance of the wage determination. The recipient shall report all suspected or reported violations to the Federal awarding agency.

4. *Contract Work Hours and Safety Standards Act (40 U.S.C. 327-333)*—Where applicable, all contracts awarded by recipients in excess of $2,000 for construction contracts and in excess of $2,500 for other contracts that involve the employment of mechanics or laborers shall include a provision for compliance with Sections 102 and 107 of the Contract Work Hours and Safety Standards Act (40 U.S.C. 327-333), as supplemented by Department of Labor regulations (29 CFR part 5). Under Section 102 of the Act, each contractor shall be required to compute the wages of every mechanic and laborer on the basis of a standard work week of 40 hours. Work in excess of the standard work week is permissible provided that the worker is compensated at a rate of not less than 1½ times the basic rate of pay for all hours worked in excess of 40 hours in the work week. Section 107 of the Act is applicable to construction work and provides that no laborer or mechanic shall be required to work in surroundings or under working conditions which are unsanitary, hazardous or dangerous. These requirements do not apply to the purchases of supplies or materials or articles ordinarily available on the open market, or contracts for transportation or transmission of intelligence.

5. *Rights to Inventions Made Under a Contract or Agreement*—Contracts or agreements for the performance of experimental, developmental, or research work shall provide for the right of the Federal Government and the recipient in any resulting invention in accordance with 37 CFR part 401, "Rights to Inventions Made by Nonprofit Organizations and Small Business Firms Under Government Grants, Contracts and Cooperative Agreements," and any implementing regulations issued by the awarding agency.

6. *Clean Air Act (42 U.S.C. 7401 et seq.) and the Federal Water Pollution Control Act (33 U.S.C. 1251 et seq.), as amended*—Contracts and subgrants of amounts in excess of $100,000 shall contain a provision that requires the recipient to agree to comply with all applicable standards, orders or regulations issued pursuant to the Clean Air Act (42 U.S.C. 7401 *et seq.*) and the Federal Water Pollution Control Act as amended (33 U.S.C. 1251 *et seq.*). Violations shall be reported to the Federal awarding agency and the Regional Office of the Environmental Protection Agency (EPA).

7. *Byrd Anti-Lobbying Amendment (31 U.S.C. 1352)*—Contractors who apply or bid for an award of $100,000 or more shall file the required certification. Each tier certifies to the tier above that it will not and has not used Federal appropriated funds to pay any person or organization for influencing or attempting to influence an officer or employee of any agency, a member of Congress, officer or employee of Congress, or an employee of a member of Congress in connection with obtaining any Federal contract, grant or any other award covered by 31 U.S.C. 1352. Each tier shall also disclose any lobbying with non-Federal funds that takes place in connection with obtaining any Federal award. Such disclosures are forwarded from tier to tier up to the recipient.

8. *Debarment and Suspension (E.O.s 12549 and 12689)*—No contract shall be made to parties listed on the General Services Administration's List of Parties Excluded from Federal Procurement or Nonprocurement Programs in accordance with E.O.s 12549 and 12689, "Debarment and Suspension" and 49 CFR part 29. This list contains the names of parties debarred, suspended, or otherwise excluded by agencies, and contractors declared ineligible under statutory or regulatory authority other than E.O. 12549. Contractors with awards that exceed the small purchase threshold shall provide the required certification regarding its exclusion status and that of its principal employees.

PART 519—NEW RESTRICTIONS ON LOBBYING

Subpart A—General

Sec.

Subpart B—Activities by Own Employees

AUTHORITY: Sec. 319, Public Law 101–121 (31 U.S.C. 1352); 41 U.S.C. 701 *et seq.*

SOURCE: 55 FR 6737, 6750, Feb. 26, 1990, unless otherwise noted.

CROSS REFERENCE: See also Office of Management and Budget notice published at 54 FR 52306, December 20, 1989.

Subpart A—General

§ 519.100 Conditions on use of funds.

(a) No appropriated funds may be expended by the recipient of a Federal contract, grant, loan, or cooperative ageement to pay any person for influencing or attempting to influence an officer or employee of any agency, a Member of Congress, an officer or employee of Congress, or an employee of a Member of Congress in connection with any of the following covered Federal actions: the awarding of any Federal contract, the making of any Federal grant, the making of any Federal loan, the entering into of any cooperative agreement, and the extension, continuation, renewal, amendment, or modification of any Federal contract, grant, loan, or cooperative agreement.

(b) Each person who requests or receives from an agency a Federal contract, grant, loan, or cooperative agreement shall file with that agency a certification, set forth in appendix A, that the person has not made, and will not make, any payment prohibited by paragraph (a) of this section.

(c) Each person who requests or receives from an agency a Federal contract, grant, loan, or a cooperative agreement shall file with that agency a disclosure form, set forth in appendix B, if such person has made or has agreed to make any payment using nonappropriated funds (to include profits from any covered Federal action), which would be prohibited under paragraph (a) of this section if paid for with appropriated funds.

(d) Each person who requests or receives from an agency a commitment providing for the United States to insure or guarantee a loan shall file with that agency a statement, set forth in appendix A, whether that person has made or has agreed to make any payment to influence or attempt to influence an officer or employee of any agency, a Member of Congress, an officer or employee of Congress, or an employee of a Member of Congress in connection with that loan insurance or guarantee.

(e) Each person who requests or receives from an agency a commitment providing for the United States to insure or guarantee a loan shall file with that agency a disclosure form, set forth in appendix B, if that person has made or has agreed to make any payment to influence or attempt to influence an officer or employee of any agency, a Member of Congress, an officer or employee of Congress, or an employee of a Member of Congress in connection with that loan insurance or guarantee.

§ 519.105 Definitions.

For purposes of this part:

(a) *Agency,* as defined in 5 U.S.C. 552(f), includes Federal executive departments and agencies as well as independent regulatory commissions and Government corporations, as defined in 31 U.S.C. 9101(1).

(b) *Covered Federal action* means any of the following Federal actions:

(1) The awarding of any Federal contract;

(2) The making of any Federal grant;

(3) The making of any Federal loan;

(4) The entering into of any cooperative agreement; and,

(5) The extension, continuation, renewal, amendment, or modification of

any Federal contract, grant, loan, or cooperative agreement.

Covered Federal action does not include receiving from an agency a commitment providing for the United States to insure or guarantee a loan. Loan guarantees and loan insurance are addressed independently within this part.

(c) *Federal contract* means an acquisition contract awarded by an agency, including those subject to the Federal Acquisition Regulation (FAR), and any other acquisition contract for real or personal property or services not subject to the FAR.

(d) *Federal cooperative agreement* means a cooperative agreement entered into by an agency.

(e) *Federal grant* means an award of financial assistance in the form of money, or property in lieu of money, by the Federal Government or a direct appropriation made by law to any person. The term does not include technical assistance which provides services instead of money, or other assistance in the form of revenue sharing, loans, loan guarantees, loan insurance, interest subsidies, insurance, or direct United States cash assistance to an individual.

(f) *Federal loan* means a loan made by an agency. The term does not include loan guarantee or loan insurance.

(g) *Indian tribe* and *tribal organization* have the meaning provided in section 4 of the Indian Self-Determination and Education Assistance Act (25 U.S.C. 450B). Alaskan Natives are included under the definitions of Indian tribes in that Act.

(h) *Influencing or attempting to influence* means making, with the intent to influence, any communication to or appearance before an officer or employee or any agency, a Member of Congress, an officer or employee of Congress, or an employee of a Member of Congress in connection with any covered Federal action.

(i) *Loan guarantee* and *loan insurance* means an agency's guarantee or insurance of a loan made by a person.

(j) *Local government* means a unit of government in a State and, if chartered, established, or otherwise recognized by a State for the performance of a governmental duty, including a local public authority, a special district, an intrastate district, a council of governments, a sponsor group representative organization, and any other instrumentality of a local government.

(k) *Officer or employee of an agency* includes the following individuals who are employed by an agency:

(1) An individual who is appointed to a position in the Government under title 5, U.S. Code, including a position under a temporary appointment;

(2) A member of the uniformed services as defined in section 101(3), title 37, U.S. Code;

(3) A special Government employee as defined in section 202, title 18, U.S. Code; and,

(4) An individual who is a member of a Federal advisory committee, as defined by the Federal Advisory Committee Act, title 5, U.S. Code appendix 2.

(l) *Person* means an individual, corporation, company, association, authority, firm, partnership, society, State, and local government, regardless of whether such entity is operated for profit or not for profit. This term excludes an Indian tribe, tribal organization, or any other Indian organization with respect to expenditures specifically permitted by other Federal law.

(m) *Reasonable compensation* means, with respect to a regularly employed officer or employee of any person, compensation that is consistent with the normal compensation for such officer or employee for work that is not furnished to, not funded by, or not furnished in cooperation with the Federal Government.

(n) *Reasonable payment* means, with respect to perfessional and other technical services, a payment in an amount that is consistent with the amount normally paid for such services in the private sector.

(o) *Recipient* includes all contractors, subcontractors at any tier, and subgrantees at any tier of the recipient of funds received in connection with a Federal contract, grant, loan, or cooperative agreement. The term excludes an Indian tribe, tribal organization, or any other Indian organization with respect to expenditures specifically permitted by other Federal law.

(p) *Regularly employed* means, with respect to an officer or employee of a person requesting or receiving a Federal contract, grant, loan, or cooperative agreement or a commitment providing for the United States to insure or guarantee a loan, an officer or employee who is employed by such person for at least 130 working days within one year immediately preceding the date of the submission that initiates agency consideration of such person for receipt of such contract, grant, loan, cooperative agreement, loan insurance commitment, or loan guarantee commitment. An officer or employee who is employed by such person for less than 130 working days within one year immediately preceding the date of the submission that initiates agency consideration of such person shall be considered to be regularly employed as soon as he or she is employed by such person for 130 working days.

(q) *State* means a State of the United States, the District of Columbia, the Commonwealth of Puerto Rico, a territory or possession of the United States, an agency or instrumentality of a State, and a multi-State, regional, or interstate entity having governmental duties and powers.

§ 519.110 Certification and disclosure.

(a) Each person shall file a certification, and a disclosure form, if required, with each submission that initiates agency consideration of such person for:

(1) Award of a Federal contract, grant, or cooperative agreement exceeding $100,000; or

(2) An award of a Federal loan or a commitment providing for the United States to insure or guarantee a loan exceeding $150,000.

(b) Each person shall file a certification, and a disclosure form, if required, upon receipt by such person of:

(1) A Federal contract, grant, or cooperative agreement exceeding $100,000; or

(2) A Federal loan or a commitment providing for the United States to insure or guarantee a loan exceeding $150,000,

Unless such person previously filed a certification, and a disclosure form, if required, under paragraph (a) of this section.

(c) Each person shall file a disclosure form at the end of each calendar quarter in which there occurs any event that requires disclosure or that materially affects the accuracy of the information contained in any disclosure form previously filed by such person under paragraphs (a) or (b) of this section. An event that materially affects the accuracy of the information reported includes:

(1) A cumulative increase of $25,000 or more in the amount paid or expected to be paid for influencing or attempting to influence a covered Federal action; or

(2) A change in the person(s) or individual(s) influencing or attempting to influence a covered Federal action; or,

(3) A change in the officer(s), employee(s), or Member(s) contacted to influence or attempt to influence a covered Federal action.

(d) Any person who requests or receives from a person referred to in paragraphs (a) or (b) of this section:

(1) A subcontract exceeding $100,000 at any tier under a Federal contract;

(2) A subgrant, contract, or subcontract exceeding $100,000 at any tier under a Federal grant;

(3) A contract or subcontract exceeding $100,000 at any tier under a Federal loan exceeding $150,000; or,

(4) A contract or subcontract exceeding $100,000 at any tier under a Federal cooperative agreement,

Shall file a certification, and a disclosure form, if required, to the next tier above.

(e) All disclosure forms, but not certifications, shall be forwarded from tier to tier until received by the person referred to in paragraphs (a) or (b) of this section. That person shall forward all disclosure forms to the agency.

(f) Any certification or disclosure form filed under paragraph (e) of this section shall be treated as a material representation of fact upon which all receiving tiers shall rely. All liability arising from an erroneous representation shall be borne solely by the tier filing that representation and shall not be shared by any tier to which the erroneous representation is forwarded. Submitting an erroneous certification or disclosure constitutes a failure to file the required certification or disclosure, respectively. If a person fails to file a required certification or disclosure, the United States may pursue all available remedies, including those authorized by section 1352, title 31, U.S. Code.

(g) For awards and commitments in process prior to December 23, 1989, but not made before that date, certifications shall be required at award or commitment, covering activities occurring between December 23, 1989, and the date of award or commitment. However, for awards and commitments in process prior to the December 23, 1989 effective date of these provisions, but not made before December 23, 1989, disclosure forms shall not be required at time of award or commitment but shall be filed within 30 days.

(h) No reporting is required for an activity paid for with appropriated funds if that activity is allowable under either subpart B or C.

Subpart B—Activities by Own Employees

§ 519.200 Agency and legislative liaison.

(a) The prohibition on the use of appropriated funds, in § 519.100 (a), does not apply in the case of a payment of reasonable compensation made to an officer or employee of a person requesting or receiving a Federal contract, grant, loan, or cooperative agreement if the payment is for agency and legislative liaison activities not directly related to a covered Federal action.

(b) For purposes of paragraph (a) of this section, providing any information specifically requested by an agency or Congress is allowable at any time.

(c) For purposes of paragraph (a) of this section, the following agency and legislative liaison activities are allowable at any time only where they are not related to a specific solicitation for any covered Federal action:

(1) Discussing with an agency (including individual demonstrations) the qualities and characteristics of the person's products or services, conditions or terms of sale, and service capabilities; and,

(2) Technical discussions and other activities regarding the application or adaptation of the person's products or services for an agency's use.

(d) For purposes of paragraph (a) of this section, the following agencies and legislative liaison activities are allowable only where they are prior to formal solicitation of any covered Federal action:

(1) Providing any information not specifically requested but necessary for an agency to make an informed decision about initiation of a covered Federal action;

(2) Technical discussions regarding the preparation of an unsolicited proposal prior to its official submission; and,

(3) Capability presentations by persons seeking awards from an agency pursuant to the provisions of the Small Business Act, as amended by Public Law 95–507 and other subsequent amendments.

(e) Only those activities expressly authorized by this section are allowable under this section.

§ 519.205 Professional and technical services.

(a) The prohibition on the use of appropriated funds, in § 519.100 (a), does not apply in the case of a payment of reasonable compensation made to an officer or employee of a person requesting or receiving a Federal contract, grant, loan, or cooperative agreement or an extension, continuation, renewal, amendment, or modification of a Federal contract, grant, loan, or cooperative agreement if payment is for professional or technical services rendered directly in the preparation, submission, or negotiation of any bid, proposal, or application for that Federal contract, grant, loan, or cooperative agreement or for meeting requirements imposed by or pursuant to law as a condition for receiving that Federal contract, grant, loan, or cooperative agreement.

(b) For purposes of paragraph (a) of this section, "professional and technical services" shall be limited to advice and analysis directly applying any professional or technical discipline. For example, drafting of a legal document accompanying a bid or proposal by a lawyer is allowable. Similarly, technical advice provided by an engineer on the performance or operational capability of a piece of equipment rendered directly in the negotiation of a contract is allowable. However, communications with the intent to influence made by a professional (such as a licensed lawyer) or a technical person (such as a licensed accountant) are not allowable under this section unless they provide advice and analysis directly applying their professional or technical expertise and unless the advice or analysis is rendered directly and solely in the preparation, submission or negotiation of a covered Federal action. Thus, for example, communications with the intent to influence made by a lawyer that do not provide legal advice or analysis directly and solely related to the legal aspects of his or her client's proposal, but generally advocate one proposal over another are not allowable under this section because the lawyer is not providing professional legal services. Similarly, communications with the intent to influence made by an engineer providing an engineering analysis prior to the preparation or submission of a bid or proposal are not allowable under this section since the engineer is providing technical services but not directly in the preparation, submission or negotiation of a covered Federal action.

(c) Requirements imposed by or pursuant to law as a condition for receiving a covered Federal award include those required by law or regulation, or reasonably expected to be required by law or regulation, and any other requirements in the actual award documents.

(d) Only those services expressly authorized by this section are allowable under this section.

§ 519.210 Reporting.

No reporting is required with respect to payments of reasonable compensation made to regularly employed officers or employees of a person.

Subpart C—Activities by Other than Own Employees

§ 519.300 Professional and technical services.

(a) The prohibition on the use of appropriated funds, in § 519.100 (a), does not apply in the case of any reasonable payment to a person, other than an officer or employee of a person requesting or receiving a covered Federal action, if the payment is for professional or technical services rendered directly in the preparation, submission, or negotiation of any bid, proposal, or application for that Federal contract, grant, loan, or cooperative agreement or for meeting requirements imposed by or pursuant to law as a condition for receiving that Federal contract, grant, loan, or cooperative agreement.

(b) The reporting requirements in § 519.110 (a) and (b) regarding filing a disclosure form by each person, if required, shall not apply with respect to professional or technical services rendered directly in the preparation, submission, or negotiation of any commitment providing for the United States to insure or guarantee a loan.

(c) For purposes of paragraph (a) of this section, "professional and technical services" shall be limited to advice and analysis directly applying any professional or technical discipline. For example, drafting or a legal document accompanying a bid or proposal by a lawyer is allowable. Similarly, technical advice provided by an engineer on the performance or operational capability of a piece of equipment rendered directly in the negotiation of a contract is allowable. However, communications with the intent to influence made by a professional (such as a licensed lawyer) or a technical person (such as a licensed accountant) are not allowable under this section unless they provide advice and analysis directly applying their professional or technical expertise and unless the advice or analysis is rendered directly and solely in the preparation, submission or negotiation of a covered Federal action. Thus, for example, communications with the intent to influence made by a lawyer that do not provide legal advice or analysis directly and solely related to the legal aspects of his or her client's proposal, but generally advocate one proposal over another are not allowable under this section because the lawyer is not providing professional legal services. Similarly, communications with the intent to influence made by an engineer providing an engineering analysis prior to the preparation or submission of a bid or proposal are not allowable under this section since the engineer is providing technical services but not directly in the preparation, submission or negotiation of a covered Federal action.

(d) Requirements imposed by or pursuant to law as a condition for receiving a covered Federal award include those required by law or regulation, or reasonably expected to be required by law or regulation, and any other requirements in the actual award documents.

(e) Persons other than officers or employees of a person requesting or receiving a covered Federal action include consultants and trade associations.

(f) Only those services expressly authorized by this section are allowable under this section.

Subpart D—Penalties and Enforcement

§ 519.400 Penalties.

(a) Any person who makes an expenditure prohibited herein shall be subject to a civil penalty of not less than $10,000 and not more than $100,000 for each such expenditure.

(b) Any person who fails to file or amend the disclosure form (see appendix B) to be filed or amended if required herein, shall be subject to a civil penalty of not less than $10,000 and not more than $100,000 for each such failure.

(c) A filing or amended filing on or after the date on which an administrative action for the imposition of a civil penalty is commenced does not prevent the imposition of such civil penalty for a failure occurring before that date. An administrative action is commenced with respect to a failure when an investigating official determines in writing to commence an investigation of an allegation of such failure.

(d) In determining whether to impose a civil penalty, and the amount of any such penalty, by reason of a violation by any person, the agency shall consider the nature, circumstances, extent, and gravity of the violation, the effect on the ability of such person to continue in business, any prior violations by such person, the degree of culpability of such person, the ability of the person to pay the penalty, and such other matters as may be appropriate.

(e) First offenders under paragraphs (a) or (b) of this section shall be subject to a civil penalty of $10,000, absent aggravating circumstances. Second and subsequent offenses by persons shall be subject to an appropriate civil penalty between $10,000 and $100,000, as determined by the agency head or his or her designee.

(f) An imposition of a civil penalty under this section does not prevent the United States from seeking any other remedy that may apply to the same conduct that is the basis for the imposition of such civil penalty.

§ 519.405 Penalty procedures.

Agencies shall impose and collect civil penalties pursuant to the provisions of the Program Fraud and Civil Remedies Act, 31 U.S.C. sections 3803 (except subsection (c)), 3804, 3805, 3806, 3807, 3808, and 3812, insofar as these provisions are not inconsistent with the requirements herein.

§ 519.410 Enforcement.

The head of each agency shall take such actions as are necessary to ensure that the provisions herein are vigorously implemented and enforced in that agency.

Subpart E—Exemptions

§ 519.500 Secretary of Defense.

(a) The Secretary of Defense may exempt, on a case-by-case basis, a covered Federal action from the prohibition whenever the Secretary determines, in writing, that such an exemption is in the national interest. The Secretary shall transmit a copy of each such written exemption to Congress immediately after making such a determination.

(b) The Department of Defense may issue supplemental regulations to implement paragraph (a) of this section.

Subpart F—Agency Reports

§ 519.600 Semi-annual compilation.

(a) The head of each agency shall collect and compile the disclosure reports (see appendix B) and, on May 31 and November 30 of each year, submit to the Secretary of the Senate and the Clerk of the House of Representatives a report containing a compilation of the information contained in the disclosure reports received during the six-month period ending on March 31 or September 30, respectively, of that year.

(b) The report, including the compilation, shall be available for public inspection 30 days after receipt of the report by the Secretary and the Clerk.

(c) Information that involves intelligence matters shall be reported only to the Select Committee on Intelligence of the Senate, the Permanent Select Committee on Intelligence of the House of Representatives, and the Committees on Appropriations of the Senate and the House of Representatives in accordance with procedures agreed to by such committees. Such information shall not be available for public inspection.

(d) Information that is classified under Executive Order 12356 or any successor order shall be reported only to the Committee on Foreign Relations of the Senate and the Committee on Foreign Affairs of the House of Representatives or the Committees on Armed Services of the Senate and the House of Representatives (whichever such committees have jurisdiction of matters involving such information) and to the Committees on Appropriations of the Senate and the House of Representatives in accordance with procedures agreed to by such committees. Such information shall not be available for public inspection.

(e) The first semi-annual compilation shall be submitted on May 31, 1990, and shall contain a compilation of the disclosure reports received from December 23, 1989 to March 31, 1990.

(f) Major agencies, designated by the Office of Management and Budget (OMB), are required to provide machine-readable compilations to the Secretary of the Senate and the Clerk of the House of Representatives no later than with the compilations due on May 31, 1991. OMB shall provide detailed specifications in a memorandum to these agencies.

(g) Non-major agencies are requested to provide machine-readable compilations to the Secretary of the Senate and the Clerk of the House of Representatives.

(h) Agencies shall keep the originals of all disclosure reports in the official files of the agency.

§ 519.605 Inspector General report.

(a) The Inspector General, or other official as specified in paragraph (b) of this section, of each agency shall prepare and submit to Congress each year, commencing with submission of the President's Budget in 1991, an evaluation of the compliance of that agency with, and the effectiveness of, the requirements herein. The evaluation may include any recommended changes that may be necessary to strengthen or improve the requirements.

(b) In the case of an agency that does not have an Inspector General, the agency official comparable to an Inspector General shall prepare and submit the annual report, or, if there is no such comparable official, the head of the agency shall prepare and submit the annual report.

(c) The annual report shall be submitted at the same time the agency submits its annual budget justifications to Congress.

(d) The annual report shall include the following: All alleged violations relating to the agency's covered Federal actions during the year covered by the report, the actions taken by the head of the agency in the year covered by the report with respect to those alleged violations and alleged violations in previous years, and the amounts of civil penalties imposed by the agency in the year covered by the report.

APPENDIX A TO PART 519—CERTIFICATION REGARDING LOBBYING

Certification for Contracts, Grants, Loans, and Cooperative Agreements

The undersigned certifies, to the best of his or her knowledge and belief, that:

(1) No Federal appropriated funds have been paid or will be paid, by or on behalf of the undersigned, to any person for influencing or attempting to influence an officer or employee of an agency, a Member of Congress, an officer or employee of Congress, or an employee of a Member of Congress in connection with the awarding of any Federal contract, the making of any Federal grant, the making of any Federal loan, the entering into of any cooperative agreement, and the extension, continuation, renewal, amendment, or modification of any Federal contract, grant, loan, or cooperative agreement.

(2) If any funds other than Federal appropriated funds have been paid or will be paid to any person for influencing or attempting to influence an officer or employee of any agency, a Member of Congress, an officer or employee of Congress, or an employee of a Member of Congress in connection with this Federal contract, grant, loan, or cooperative agreement, the undersigned shall complete and submit Standard Form-LLL, "Disclosure Form to Report Lobbying," in accordance with its instructions.

(3) The undersigned shall require that the language of this certification be included in the award documents for all subawards at all tiers (including subcontracts, subgrants, and contracts under grants, loans, and cooperative agreements) and that all subrecipients shall certify and disclose accordingly.

This certification is a material representation of fact upon which reliance was placed when this transaction was made or entered into. Submission of this certification is a prerequisite for making or entering into this transaction imposed by section 1352, title 31, U.S. Code. Any person who fails to file the required certification shall be subject to a civil penalty of not less than $10,000 and not more than $100,000 for each such failure.

Statement for Loan Guarantees and Loan Insurance

The undersigned states, to the best of his or her knowledge and belief, that:

If any funds have been paid or will be paid to any person for influencing or attempting to influence an officer or employee of any agency, a Member of Congress, an officer or employee of Congress, or an employee of a Member of Congress in connection with this commitment providing for the United States to insure or guarantee a loan, the undersigned shall complete and submit Standard Form-LLL, "Disclosure Form to Report Lobbying," in accordance with its instructions.

Submission of this statement is a prerequisite for making or entering into this transaction imposed by section 1352, title 31, U.S. Code. Any person who fails to file the required statement shall be subject to a civil penalty of not less than $10,000 and not more than $100,000 for each such failure.

APPENDIX B TO PART 519—DISCLOSURE FORM TO REPORT LOBBYING

DISCLOSURE OF LOBBYING ACTIVITIES

Approved by OMB 0348-0046

Complete this form to disclose lobbying activities pursuant to 31 U.S.C. 1352
(See reverse for public burden disclosure.)

1. Type of Federal Action:
☐ a. contract
b. grant
c. cooperative agreement
d. loan
e. loan guarantee
f. loan insurance

2. Status of Federal Action:
☐ a. bid/offer/application
b. initial award
c. post-award

3. Report Type:
☐ a. initial filing
b. material change
For Material Change Only:
year ______ quarter ____
date of last report ________

4. Name and Address of Reporting Entity:
☐ Prime ☐ Subawardee
Tier ____, *if known*:

Congressional District, *if known*:

5. If Reporting Entity in No. 4 is Subawardee, Enter Name and Address of Prime:

Congressional District, *if known*:

6. Federal Department/Agency:

7. Federal Program Name/Description:

CFDA Number, *if applicable*: ________

8. Federal Action Number, *if known*:

9. Award Amount, *if known*:
$

10. a. Name and Address of Lobbying Entity
(if individual, last name, first name, MI):

b. Individuals Performing Services *(including address if different from No. 10a)*
(last name, first name, MI):

(attach Continuation Sheet(s) SF-LLL-A, if necessary)

11. Amount of Payment *(check all that apply)*:
$ ____________ ☐ actual ☐ planned

12. Form of Payment *(check all that apply)*:
☐ a. cash
☐ b. in-kind; specify: nature ____________
value ____________

13. Type of Payment *(check all that apply)*:
☐ a. retainer
☐ b. one-time fee
☐ c. commission
☐ d. contingent fee
☐ e. deferred
☐ f. other; specify: ____________

14. Brief Description of Services Performed or to be Performed and Date(s) of Service, including officer(s), employee(s), or Member(s) contacted, for Payment Indicated in Item 11:

(attach Continuation Sheet(s) SF-LLL-A, if necessary)

15. Continuation Sheet(s) SF-LLL-A attached: ☐ Yes ☐ No

16. Information requested through this form is authorized by title 31 U.S.C. section 1352. This disclosure of lobbying activities is a material representation of fact upon which reliance was placed by the tier above when this transaction was made or entered into. This disclosure is required pursuant to 31 U.S.C. 1352. This information will be reported to the Congress semi-annually and will be available for public inspection. Any person who fails to file the required disclosure shall be subject to a civil penalty of not less than $10,000 and not more than $100,000 for each such failure.

Signature: ____________
Print Name: ____________
Title: ____________
Telephone No.: ____________ **Date:** ____________

Federal Use Only:

Authorized for Local Reproduction
Standard Form - LLL

INSTRUCTIONS FOR COMPLETION OF SF-LLL, DISCLOSURE OF LOBBYING ACTIVITIES

This disclosure form shall be completed by the reporting entity, whether subawardee or prime Federal recipient, at the initiation or receipt of a covered Federal action, or a material change to a previous filing, pursuant to title 31 U.S.C. section 1352. The filing of a form is required for each payment or agreement to make payment to any lobbying entity for influencing or attempting to influence an officer or employee of any agency, a Member of Congress, an officer or employee of Congress, or an employee of a Member of Congress in connection with a covered Federal action. Use the SF-LLL-A Continuation Sheet for additional information if the space on the form is inadequate. Complete all items that apply for both the initial filing and material change report. Refer to the implementing guidance published by the Office of Management and Budget for additional information.

1. Identify the type of covered Federal action for which lobbying activity is and/or has been secured to influence the outcome of a covered Federal action.
2. Identify the status of the covered Federal action.
3. Identify the appropriate classification of this report. If this is a followup report caused by a material change to the information previously reported, enter the year and quarter in which the change occurred. Enter the date of the last previously submitted report by this reporting entity for this covered Federal action.
4. Enter the full name, address, city, state and zip code of the reporting entity. Include Congressional District, if known. Check the appropriate classification of the reporting entity that designates if it is, or expects to be, a prime or subaward recipient. Identify the tier of the subawardee, e.g., the first subawardee of the prime is the 1st tier. Subawards include but are not limited to subcontracts, subgrants and contract awards under grants.
5. If the organization filing the report in item 4 checks "Subawardee", then enter the full name, address, city, state and zip code of the prime Federal recipient. Include Congressional District, if known.
6. Enter the name of the Federal agency making the award or loan commitment. Include at least one organizational level below agency name, if known. For example, Department of Transportation, United States Coast Guard.
7. Enter the Federal program name or description for the covered Federal action (item 1). If known, enter the full Catalog of Federal Domestic Assistance (CFDA) number for grants, cooperative agreements, loans, and loan commitments.
8. Enter the most appropriate Federal identifying number available for the Federal action identified in item 1 (e.g., Request for Proposal (RFP) number; Invitation for Bid (IFB) number; grant announcement number; the contract, grant, or loan award number; the application/proposal control number assigned by the Federal agency). Include prefixes, e.g., "RFP-DE-90-001."
9. For a covered Federal action where there has been an award or loan commitment by the Federal agency, enter the Federal amount of the award/loan commitment for the prime entity identified in item 4 or 5.
10. (a) Enter the full name, address, city, state and zip code of the lobbying entity engaged by the reporting entity identified in item 4 to influence the covered Federal action.

    (b) Enter the full names of the individual(s) performing services, and include full address if different from 10 (a). Enter Last Name, First Name, and Middle Initial (MI).
11. Enter the amount of compensation paid or reasonably expected to be paid by the reporting entity (item 4) to the lobbying entity (item 10). Indicate whether the payment has been made (actual) or will be made (planned). Check all boxes that apply. If this is a material change report, enter the cumulative amount of payment made or planned to be made.
12. Check the appropriate box(es). Check all boxes that apply. If payment is made through an in-kind contribution, specify the nature and value of the in-kind payment.
13. Check the appropriate box(es). Check all boxes that apply. If other, specify nature.
14. Provide a specific and detailed description of the services that the lobbyist has performed, or will be expected to perform, and the date(s) of any services rendered. Include all preparatory and related activity, not just time spent in actual contact with Federal officials. Identify the Federal official(s) or employee(s) contacted or the officer(s), employee(s), or Member(s) of Congress that were contacted.
15. Check whether or not a SF-LLL-A Continuation Sheet(s) is attached.
16. The certifying official shall sign and date the form, print his/her name, title, and telephone number.

Public reporting burden for this collection of information is estimated to average 30 mintues per response, including time for reviewing instructions, searching existing data sources, gathering and maintaining the data needed, and completing and reviewing the collection of information. Send comments regarding the burden estimate or any other aspect of this collection of information, including suggestions for reducing this burden, to the Office of Management and Budget, Paperwork Reduction Project (0348-0046), Washington, D.C. 20503.

DISCLOSURE OF LOBBYING ACTIVITIES
CONTINUATION SHEET

Approved by OMB
0348-0046

Reporting Entity: ______________________ Page _____ of _____

Authorized for Local Reproduction
Standard Form - LLL-A

PART 521—IMPLEMENTATION OF THE PROGRAM FRAUD CIVIL REMEDIES ACT

AUTHORITY: 22 U.S.C. 2658; 31 U.S.C. 3801–3812.

SOURCE: 56 FR 25028, June 3, 1991, unless otherwise noted.

§521.1 Basis and purpose.

(a) *Basis*. This part implements the Program Fraud Civil Remedies Act of 1986, Public Law 99–509, sections 6101–6104, 100 Stat. 1874 (October 21, 1986), codified at 31 U.S.C. 3801–3812. The Act requires each authority head to promulgate regulations necessary to implement the provisions of the statute (31 U.S.C. 3809).

(b) *Purpose*. (1) This part establishes administrative procedures for imposing civil penalties and assessments against persons who make, submit, or present, or cause to be made, submitted, or presented, false, fictitious, or fraudulent claims or written statements to the Broadcasting Board of Governors or to its agents, and

(2) Specifies the hearing and appeal rights of persons subject to allegations of liability for such penalties and assessments.

(c) *Special considerations abroad*. Where a party, witness or material evidence in a proceeding under these regulations is located abroad, the investigating official, reviewing official or ALJ, as the case may be, may adjust the provisions below for service, filing of documents, time limitations, and related matters to meet special problems arising out of that location.

§521.2 Definitions.

ALJ means an Administrative Law Judge in the Broadcasting Board of Governors appointed pursuant to 5 U.S.C. 3105 or detailed to the Broadcasting Board of Governors pursuant to 5 U.S.C. 3344.

Benefit means, in the context of "statement," anything of value, including but not limited to any advantage, preference, privilege, license, permit, favorable decision, ruling, status, or loan guarantee.

Claim means any request, demand, or submission—

(1) Made to the Broadcasting Board of Governors for property, services or money (including money representing grants, loans, insurance or benefits);

(2) Made to a recipient of property, services or money from the Broadcasting Board of Governors, or to a party to a contract with the Broadcasting Board of Governors—

(i) For property or services if the United States—

(A) Provided such property or services;

(B) Provided any portion of the funds for the purchase of such property or services; or

(C) Will reimburse such recipient or party for the purchase of such property or services; or

(ii) For the payment of money (including money representing grants, loans, insurance, or benefits) if the United States—

(A) Provided any portion of the money requested or demanded; or

(B) Will reimburse such recipient or party for any portion of the money paid on such request or demand; or

(3) Made to the Broadcasting Board of Governors which has the effect of decreasing an obligation to pay or account for property, services, or money.

Complaint means the administrative complaint served by the reviewing official on the defendant under §521.7.

Defendant means any person alleged in a complaint under §521.7 to be liable for a civil penalty or assessment under § 521.3.

Director means Director of the Broadcasting Board of Governors.

Government means the United States Government.

Individual means a natural person.

Initial decision means the written decision of the ALJ required by § 521.10 or § 521.37, and includes a revised initial decision issued following a remand or a motion for reconsideration.

Investigating Official means the Inspector General for the Broadcasting Board of Governors or an officer or employee of the Office of Inspector General designated by the Inspector General and serving in a position for which the rate of basic pay is not less than the minimum rate of basic pay for grade GS–16 under the General Schedule.

Knows or has reason to know means that a person, with respect to a claim or statement—

(1) Has the actual knowledge that the claim or statement is false, fictitious, or fraudulent;

(2) Acts in deliberate ignorance of the truth or falsity of the claim or statement; or

(3) Acts in reckless disregard of the truth or falsity of the claim or statement.

Makes, wherever it appears, shall include the terms *presents, submits and causes to be made, presented, or submitted.* As the context requires, *making* or *made* shall likewise include the corresponding forms of such terms.

Person means any individual, partnership, corporation, association, or private organization and includes the plural of that term.

Representative means an attorney who is a member in good standing of the bar of any State, Territory, or possession of the United States or the District of Columbia or the Commonwealth of Puerto Rico.

Reviewing official means the General Counsel of the Broadcasting Board of Governors or his designee who is:

BBG means the Broadcasting Board of Governors.

(1) Not subject to supervision by, or required to report to, the investigating official;

(2) Not employed in the organizational unit of the Broadcasting Board of Governors in which the investigating official is employed; and

(3) Is serving in a position for which the rate of basic pay is not less than the minimum rate of basic pay for grade GS–16 under the General Schedule.

Statement means any representation, certification, affirmation, document, record, or accounting or bookkeeping entry made—

(1) With respect to a claim or to obtain the approval or payment of a claim (including relating to eligibility to make a claim); or

(2) With respect to (including relating to eligibility for)—

(i) A contract with, or a bid or proposal for a contract with; or

(ii) A grant, loan, or benefit from, the Broadcasting Board of Governors, or any State, political subdivision of a State, or other party, if the United States Government provides any portion of the money or property under such contract or for such grant, loan, or benefit, or if the Government will reimburse such State, political subdivision, or party for any portion of the money or property under such contract or for such grant, loan, or benefit.

BBG means the Broadcasting Board of Governors.

§ 521.3 Basis for civil penalties and assessments.

(a) *Claims.* (1) Any person who makes claim that the person knows or has reason to know—

(i) Is false, fictitious, or fraudulent;

(ii) Includes or is supported by any written statement which asserts a material fact which is false, fictitious, or fraudulent;

(iii) Includes or is supported by any written statement that—

(A) Omits a material fact;

(B) Is false, fictitious, or fraudulent as a result of such omission; and

(C) Is a statement in which the person making such statement has a duty to include such material fact; or

(iv) Is for payment for the provision of property or services which the person has not provided as claimed; shall be subject, in addition to any other remedy that may be prescribed by law, to a civil penalty of not more than $5,000 for each such claim.

(2) Each voucher, invoice, claim form, or other individual request or demand for property, services, or money constitutes a separate claim.

(3) A claim shall be considered made to the Broadcasting Board of Governors, a recipient, or party when such claim is actually made to an agent, fiscal intermediary, or other entity, including any State or political subdivision thereof, acting for or on behalf of the Broadcasting Board of Governors or such recipient or party.

(4) Each claim for property, services, or money is subject to a civil penalty regardless of whether such property, services, or money is actually delivered or paid.

(5) If the Government has made any payment (including transferred property or provided services) on a claim, a person subject to a civil penalty under paragraph (a)(1) of this section shall also be subject to an assessment of not more than twice the amount of such claim or that portion thereof that is determined to be in violation of paragraph (a)(1) of this section. Such assessment shall be in lieu of damages sustained by the Government because of such claim.

(b) *Statement.* (1) Any person who makes, a written statement that—

(i) The person knows or has reason to know—

(A) Asserts a material fact which is false, fictitious, or fraudulent; or

(B) Is false, fictitious, or fraudulent because it omits a material fact that the person making the statement has a duty to include in such statement; and

(ii) Contains or is accompanied by an express certification or affirmation of the truthfulness and accuracy of the contents of the statement, shall be subject, in addition to any other remedy that may be prescribed by law, to a civil penalty of not more than $5,000 for each such statement.

(2) Each written representation, certification, or affirmation constitutes a separate statement.

(3) A statement shall be considered made to the Broadcasting Board of Governors when such statement is actually made to an agent, fiscal intermediary, or other entity, including any State or political subdivision thereof, acting for or on behalf of the Broadcasting Board of Governors.

(c) No proof of specific intent to defraud is required to establish liability under this section.

(d) In any case in which it is determined that more than one person is liable for making a claim or statement under this section, each such person may be held liable for a civil penalty under this section.

(e) In any case in which it is determined that more than one person is liable for making a claim under this section on which the Government has made payment (including transferred property or provided services), an assessment may be imposed against any such person or jointly and severally against any combination of such persons.

§521.4 Investigation.

(a) If an investigating official concludes that a subpoena pursuant to the authority conferred by 31 U.S.C. 3804(a) is warranted—

(1) The subpoena so issued shall notify the person to whom it is addressed of the authority under which the subpoena is issued, and shall identify the records or documents sought;

(2) The investigating official may designate a person to act on his or her behalf to receive the documents sought; and

(3) The person receiving such subpoena shall be required to tender to the investigating official or the person designated to receive the documents a certification that the documents sought have been produced, or that such documents are not available and the reasons therefore, or that such documents, suitably identified, have been withheld based upon the assertion of an identified privilege.

(b) If the investigating official concludes that an action under the Program Fraud Civil Remedies Act may be warranted, the investigating official shall submit a report containing the findings and conclusions of such investigation to the reviewing official.

(c) Nothing in this section shall preclude or limit an investigating official's discretion to refer allegations directly to the Department of Justice for suit under the False Claims Act or other civil relief, or to defer or postpone a report or referral to the reviewing official to avoid interference with a criminal investigation or prosecution.

(d) Nothing in this section modifies any responsibility of an investigating official to report violations of criminal law to the Attorney General.

§ 521.5 Review by the reviewing official.

(a) If, based on the report of the investigating official under § 521.4(b), the reviewing official determines that there is adequate evidence to believe that a person is liable under § 521.3 of this part, the reviewing official shall transmit to the Attorney General a written notice of the reviewing official's intention to issue a complaint under § 521.7.

(b) Such notice shall include—

(1) A statement of the reviewing official's reasons for issuing a complaint;

(2) A statement specifying the evidence that supports the allegations of liability;

(3) A description of the claims or statements upon which the allegations of liability are based;

(4) An estimate of the amount of money or the value of property, services, or other benefits requested or demanded in violation of § 521.3 of this part;

(5) A statement of any exculpatory or mitigating circumstances that may relate to the claims or statements known by the reviewing official or the investigating official; and

(6) A statement that there is a reasonable prospect of collecting an appropriate amount of penalties and assessments.

§ 521.6 Prerequisites for issuing a complaint.

(a) The reviewing official may issue a complaint under § 521.7 only if:

(1) The Department of Justice approves the issuance of a complaint in a written statement described in 31 U.S.C. 3803(b)(1); and

(2) In the case of allegations of liability under § 521.3(a) with respect to a claim, the reviewing official determines that, with respect to such claim or a group of related claims submitted at the same time such claim is submitted (as defined in paragraph (b) of this section), the amount of money or the value of property or services demanded or requested in violation of § 521.3(a) does not exceed $150,000.

(b) For the purposes of this section, a related group of claims submitted at the same time shall include only those claims arising from the same transaction (e.g., grant, loan, application, or contract) that are submitted simultaneously as part of a single request, demand, or submission.

(c) Nothing in this section shall be construed to limit the reviewing official's authority to join in a single complaint against a person's claims that are unrelated or were not submitted simultaneously, regardless of the amount of money, or the value of property or services, demanded or requested.

§ 521.7 Complaint.

(a) On or after the date the Department of Justice approves the issuance of a complaint in accordance with 31 U.S.C. 3803(b)(1), the reviewing official may serve a complaint on the defendant, as provided in § 521.8.

(b) The complaint shall state:

(1) Allegations of liability against the defendant including the statutory basis for liability, an identification of the claims or statements that are the basis for the alleged liability, and the reasons why liability allegedly arises from such claims or statements;

(2) The maximum amount of penalties and assessments for which the defendant may be held liable;

(3) Instructions for filing an answer to request a hearing, including a specific statement of the defendant's right to request a hearing by filing an answer and to be represented by a representative; and

(4) That failure to file an answer within 30 days of service of the complaint will result in the imposition of the maximum amount of penalties and assessment without right to appeal, as provided in § 521.10.

(c) At the same time the reviewing official serves the complaint, he or she shall serve the defendant with a copy of these regulations.

§521.8 Service of complaint.

(a) Service of a complaint must be made by certified or registered mail or by delivery in any manner authorized by rule 4(d) of the Federal Rules of Civil Procedure. Service is complete upon receipt.

(b) Proof of service, stating the name and address of the person on whom the complaint was served, and the manner and date of service, may be made by:

(1) Affidavit of the individual serving the complaint by delivery;

(2) A United States Postal Service return receipt card acknowledging receipt; or

(3) Written acknowledgment of receipt by the defendant or the defendant's representative.

(4) In case of service abroad authenticated in accordance with the Convention on the Service Abroad of Judicial and Extra Judicial Documents in Civil or Commercial Matters.

§521.9 Answer.

(a) The defendant may request a hearing by filing an answer with the reviewing official within 30 days of service of the complaint. An answer shall be deemed to be a request for a hearing.

(b) In the answer, the defendant:

(1) Shall admit or deny each of the allegations of liability made in the complaint;

(2) Shall state any defense on which the defendant intends to rely;

(3) May state any reasons why the defendant contends that the penalties and assessments should be less than the statutory maximum; and

(4) Shall state the name, address, and telephone number of the person authorized by the defendant to act as defendant's representative, if any.

(c) If the defendant is unable to file an answer meeting the requirements of paragraph (b) of this section within the time provided, the defendant may, before the expiration of 30 days from service of the complaint, file with the reviewing official a general answer denying liability and requesting a hearing, and a request for an extension of time within which to file an answer meeting the requirements of paragraph (b) of this section. The reviewing official shall file promptly with the ALJ the complaint, the general answer denying liability, and the request for an extension of time as provided in §521.11. For good cause shown, the ALJ may grant the defendant up to 30 additional days within which to file an answer meeting the requirements of paragraph (b) of this section.

§521.10 Default upon failure to file an answer.

(a) If the defendant does not file an answer within the time prescribed in §521.9(a), the reviewing official may refer the complaint to the ALJ.

(b) Upon the referral of the complaint, the ALJ shall promptly serve on defendant in the manner prescribed in §521.8, a notice that an initial decision will be issued under this section.

(c) If the defendant fails to answer, the ALJ shall assume the facts alleged in the complaint to be true, and, if such facts establish liability under §521.3, the ALJ shall issue an initial decision imposing the maximum amount of penalties and assessments allowed under the statute.

(d) Except as otherwise provided in this section, by failing to file a timely answer, the defendant waives any right to further review of the penalties and assessments imposed under paragraph (c) of this section, and the initial decision shall become final and binding upon the parties 30 days after it is issued.

(e) If, before such an initial decision becomes final, the defendant files a motion with the ALJ seeking to reopen on the grounds that extraordinary circumstances prevented the defendant from filing an answer, the initial decision shall be stayed pending the ALJ's decision on the motion.

(f) If, on such motion, the defendant can demonstrate extraordinary circumstances excusing the failure to file a timely answer, the ALJ shall withdraw the initial decision in paragraph (c) of this section, if such a decision has been issued, and shall grant the defendant an opportunity to answer the complaint.

(g) A decision of the ALJ denying defendant's motion under paragraph (e) of this section is not subject to reconsideration under §521.38.

(h) The defendant may appeal to the Director the decision denying a motion to reopen by filing a notice of appeal with the Director within 15 days after the ALJ denies the motion. The timely filing of a notice of appeal shall stay the initial decision until the Director decides the issue.

(i) If the defendant files a timely notice of appeal with the Director, the ALJ shall forward the record of the proceeding to the Director.

(j) The Director shall decide expeditiously whether extraordinary circumstances excuse the defendant's failure to file a timely answer based solely on the record before the ALJ.

(k) If the Director decides that extraordinary circumstances excused the defendant's failure to file a timely answer, the Director shall remand the case to the ALJ with instructions to grant the defendant an opportunity to answer.

(l) If the Director decides that the defendant's failure to file a timely answer is not excused, the Director shall reinstate the initial decision of the ALJ, which shall become final and binding upon the parties 30 days after the Director issues such decision.

§ 521.11 Referral of complaint and answer to the ALJ.

Upon receipt of an answer, the reviewing official shall file the complaint and answer with the ALJ.

§ 521.12 Notice of hearing.

(a) When the ALJ receives the complaint and answer, the ALJ shall promptly serve a notice of hearing upon the defendant in the manner prescribed by § 521.8. At the same time, the ALJ shall send a copy of such notice to the representative for the Government.

(b) Such notice shall include:

(1) The tentative time and place, and the nature of the hearing;

(2) The legal authority and jurisdiction under which the hearing is to be held;

(3) The matters of fact and law to be asserted;

(4) A description of the procedures for the conduct of the hearing;

(5) The name, address, and telephone number of the representative of the Government and of the defendant, if any; and

(6) Such other matters as the ALJ deems appropriate.

§ 521.13 Parties to the hearing.

(a) The parties to the hearing shall be the defendant and the Broadcasting Board of Governors.

(b) Pursuant to 31 U.S.C. 3730(c)(5), a private plaintiff under the False Claims Act may participate in these proceedings to the extent authorized by the provisions of that Act.

§ 521.14 Separation of functions.

(a) The investigating official, the reviewing official, and any employee or agent of the Broadcasting Board of Governors who takes part in investigating, preparing, or presenting a particular case may not, in such case or a factually related case:

(1) Participate in the hearing as the ALJ;

(2) Participate or advise in the initial decision or the review of the initial decision by the Director, except as a witness or representative in public proceedings; or

(3) Make the collection of penalties and assessments under 31 U.S.C. 3806.

(b) The ALJ shall not be responsible to, or subject to, the supervision or direction of the investigating official or the reviewing official.

(c) Except as provided in paragraph (a) of this section, the representative for the Government may be employed anywhere in the Broadcasting Board of Governors, including in the offices of either the investigating official or the reviewing official.

§ 521.15 Ex Parte contacts.

No party or person (except employees of the ALJ's office) shall communicate in any way with the ALJ on any matter at issue in a case, unless on notice and opportunity for all parties to participate. This provision does not prohibit a person or party from inquiring about the status of a case or asking routine questions concerning administrative functions or procedures.

§521.16 Disqualification of reviewing official or ALJ.

(a) A reviewing official or ALJ in a particular case may disqualify himself or herself at any time.

(b) A party may file with the ALJ a motion for disqualification of a reviewing official or ALJ. Such motion shall be accompanied by an affidavit alleging personal bias or other reason for disqualification.

(c) Such motion and affidavit shall be filed promptly upon the party's discovery of reasons requiring disqualification, or such objections shall be deemed waived.

(d) Such affidavit shall state specific facts that support the party's belief that personal bias or other reason for disqualification exists and the time and circumstances of the party's discovery of such facts. It shall be accompanied by a certificate of the representative of record that it is made in good faith.

(e) Upon the filing of such a motion and affidavit, the ALJ shall proceed no further in the case until he or she resolves the matter of disqualification in accordance with paragraph (f) of this section.

(f)(1) If the ALJ determines that the reviewing official is disqualified, the ALJ shall dismiss the complaint without prejudice.

(2) If the ALJ disqualifies himself or herself, the case shall be reassigned promptly to another ALJ.

(3) If the ALJ denies a motion to disqualify, the Director may determine the matter only as part of his or her review of the initial decision upon appeal, if any.

§521.17 Rights of parties.

Except as otherwise limited by this part, all parties may:

(a) Be accompanied, represented, and advised by a representative;

(b) Participate in any conference held by the ALJ;

(c) Conduct discovery;

(d) Agree to stipulations of fact or law, which shall be made part of the record;

(e) Present evidence relevant to the issues at the hearing;

(f) Present and cross-examine witnesses;

(g) Present oral arguments at the hearing as permitted by the ALJ; and

(h) Submit written briefs and proposed findings of fact and conclusions of law after the hearing.

§521.18 Authority of the ALJ.

(a) The ALJ shall conduct a fair and impartial hearing, avoid delay, maintain order, and assure that a record of the proceeding is made.

(b) The ALJ may:

(1) Set and change the date, time and place of the hearing upon reasonable notice to the parties;

(2) Continue or recess the hearing in whole or in part for a reasonable period of time;

(3) Hold conferences to identify or simplify the issues, or to consider other matters that may aid in the expeditious disposition of the proceeding;

(4) Administer oaths and affirmations;

(5) Issue subpoenas to be served within the United States requiring the attendance of witnesses and the production of documents at depositions or at hearings. Subpoenas to be served outside the jurisdiction of the United States shall state on their face the authority therefore;

(6) Rule on motions and other procedural matters;

(7) Regulate the scope and time of discovery;

(8) Regulate the course of the hearing and the conduct of representatives and parties;

(9) Examine witnesses;

(10) Receive, rule on, exclude, or limit evidence;

(11) Upon motion of a party, take official notice of facts;

(12) Upon motion of a party, decide cases, in whole or in part, by summary judgment where there is no disputed issue of material fact;

(13) Conduct any conference, argument, or hearing on motions in person or by telephone; and

(14) Exercise such other authority as is necessary to carry out the responsibilities of the ALJ under this part.

(c) The ALJ does not have the authority to find treaties and other international agreements or Federal Statutes or regulations invalid.

§ 521.19 Prehearing conferences.

(a) The ALJ may schedule prehearing conferences as appropriate.

(b) Upon the motion of any party, the ALJ shall schedule at least one prehearing conference at a reasonable time in advance of the hearing.

(c) The ALJ may use prehearing conferences to discuss the following:

(1) Simplification of the issues;

(2) The necessity or desirability of amendments to the pleadings, including the need for a more definite statement;

(3) Stipulations and admissions of fact or as to the contents and authenticity of documents;

(4) Whether the parties can agree to submission of the case on a stipulated record;

(5) Whether a party chooses to waive appearance at an oral hearing and to submit only documentary evidence (subject to the objection of other parties) and written argument;

(6) Limitation of the number of witnesses;

(7) Scheduling dates for the exchange of witness lists and of proposed exhibits;

(8) Discovery;

(9) The time and place for the hearing; and

(10) Such other matters as may tend to expedite the fair and just disposition of the proceedings.

(d) The ALJ shall issue an order containing all matters agreed upon by the parties or ordered by the ALJ at a prehearing conference.

§ 521.20 Disclosure of documents.

(a) Upon written request to the reviewing official, the defendant may review any relevant and material documents, transcripts, records, and other materials that relate to the allegations set out in the complaint and upon which the findings and conclusions of the investigating official under § 521.4(b) are based, unless such documents are subject to a privilege under Federal law. Upon payment of fees for duplication, the defendant may obtain copies of such documents.

(b) Upon written request to the reviewing official, the defendant also may obtain a copy of all exculpatory information in the possession of the reviewing official or investigating official relating to the allegations in the complaint, even if it is contained in a document that would otherwise be privileged. If the document would otherwise be privileged, only that portion containing exculpatory information must be disclosed.

(c) The notice sent to the Attorney General from the reviewing official as described in § 521.5 is not discoverable under any circumstances.

(d) The defendant may file a motion to compel disclosure of the doucment subject to the provisions of this section. Such a motion may only be filed with the ALJ following the filing of an answer pursuant to § 521.9.

§ 521.21 Discovery.

(a) The following types of discovery are authorized:

(1) Requests for production of documents for inspection and copying;

(2) Requests for admissions of the authenticity of any relevant document or the truth of any relevant fact;

(3) Written interrogatories; and

(4) Depositions.

(b) For the purpose of this section and § 521.22 and § 521.23, the term "documents" includes information, documents, reports, answers, records, accounts, papers, and other data and documentary evidence. Nothing contained herein shall be interpreted to require the creation of a document.

(c) Unless mutually agreed to by the parties, discovery is available only as ordered by the ALJ. The ALJ shall regulate the timing of discovery.

(d) *Motions for discovery.* (1) A party seeking discovery may file a motion with the ALJ. Such a motion shall be accompanied by a copy of the requested discovery, or in the case of depositions, a summary of the scope of the proposed deposition.

(2) Within ten days of service a party may file an opposition to the motion and/or a motion for protective order as provided § 521.24.

(3) The ALJ may grant a motion for discovery only if the ALJ finds that the discovery sought:

(i) Is necessary for the expeditious, fair, and reasonable consideration of the issues;

(ii) Is not unduly costly or burdensome;

(iii) Will not unduly delay the proceeding; and

(iv) Does not seek privileged information.

(4) The burden of showing that discovery should be allowed is on the party seeking discovery.

(5) The ALJ may grant discovery subject to a protective order under §521.24.

(e) *Deposition.* (1) If a motion for deposition is granted, the ALJ shall issue a subpoena for the deponent, which may require the deponent to produce documents. The subpoena shall specify the time and place at which the deposition will be held.

(2) The party seeking to depose shall serve the subpoena in the manner prescribed in §521.8.

(3) The deponent may file with the ALJ a motion to quash the subpoena or a motion for a protective order within ten days of service.

(4) The party seeking to depose shall provide for the taking of a verbatim transcript of the deposition which it shall make available to all other parties for inspection and copying.

(f) Each party shall bear its own costs of discovery.

§521.22 Exchange of witness lists, statements and exhibits.

(a) At least 15 days before the hearing or at such other time as may be ordered by the ALJ, the parties shall exchange witness lists, copies of prior statements of proposed witnesses, and copies of proposed hearing exhibits, including copies of any written statements that the party intends to offer in lieu of live testimony in accordance with §521.33(b). At the time the above documents are exchanged, any party that intends to rely on the transcript of deposition testimony in lieu of live testimony at the hearing, if permitted by the ALJ, shall provide each party with a copy of the specific pages of the transcript it intends to introduce into evidence.

(b) If a party objects, the ALJ shall not admit into evidence the testimony of any witness whose name does not appear on the witness list or any exhibit not provided to the opposing party as provided above, unless the ALJ finds good cause for the failure or that there is no prejudice to the objecting party.

(c) Unless another party objects within the time set by the ALJ, documents exchanged in accordance with paragraph (a) of this section shall be deemed to be authentic for the purpose of admissibility at the hearing.

§521.23 Subpoenas for attendance at hearing.

(a) A party wishing to procure the appearance and testimony of any individual at the hearing may request that the ALJ issue a subpoena.

(b) A subpoena requiring the attendance and testimony of an individual may also require the individual to produce documents at the hearing.

(c) A party seeking a subpoena shall file a written request therefor not less than 15 days before the date fixed for the hearing unless otherwise allowed by the ALJ for good cause shown. Such request shall specify any documents to be produced and shall designate the witnesses and describe the address and location thereof with sufficient particularity to permit such witnesses to be found.

(d) The subpoena shall specify the time and place at which the witness is to appear and any documents the witness is to produce.

(e) The party seeking the subpoena shall serve it in the manner prescribed in §521.8. A subpoena on a party or upon an individual under the control of a party may be served by first class mail.

(f) A party or individual to whom the subpoena is directed may file with the ALJ a motion to quash the subpoena within ten days after service or on or before the time specified in the subpoena for compliance if it is less than ten days after service.

§521.24 Protective order.

(a) A party or a prospective witness or deponent may file a motion for a protective order with respect to discovery sought by an opposing party or, with respect to the hearing, seeking to limit the availability or disclosure of evidence.

(b) In issuing a protective order, the ALJ may make any order which justice requires to protect a party or person from annoyance, embarrassment, oppression, or undue burden or expense, including one or more of the following:

(1) That the discovery not be had;

(2) That the discovery may be had only on specified terms and conditions, including a designation of the time or place;

(3) That the discovery may be had only through a method of discovery other than that requested;

(4) That certain matters not be inquired into, or that the scope of discovery be limited to certain matters;

(5) That discovery be conducted with no one present except persons designated by the ALJ;

(6) That the contents of discovery or evidence be sealed;

(7) That a deposition after being sealed be opened only by order of the ALJ;

(8) That a trade secret or other confidential research, development, commercial information, or facts pertaining to any criminal investigation, proceeding or other administrative investigation not be disclosed or be disclosed only in a designated way; or

(9) That the parties simultaneously file specified documents or information enclosed in sealed envelopes to be opened as directed by the ALJ.

§ 521.25 Fees.

The party requesting a subpoena shall pay the cost of the fee and mileage of any witness subpoenaed in the amounts that would be payable to a witness in a proceeding in the United States District Court. A check for witness fees and mileage shall accompany the subpoena when served, except that when a subpoena is issued on behalf of the Broadcasting Board of Governors, a check for witness fees and mileage need not accompany the subpoena.

§ 521.26 Form, filing and service of papers.

(a) *Form.* (1) Documents filed with the ALJ shall include an original and two copies.

(2) Every pleading and paper filed in the proceeding shall contain a caption setting forth the title of the action, the case number assigned by the ALJ, and a designation of the paper (e.g., motion to quash subpoena), and shall be in English or accompanied by an English translation.

(3) Every pleading and paper shall be signed by, and shall contain the address and telephone number of, the party or the person on whose behalf the paper was filed, or his or her representative.

(4) Papers are considered filed when they are mailed. Date of mailing may be established by a certificate from the party or its representative or by proof that the document was sent by certified or registered mail.

(b) *Service.* A party filing a document with the ALJ shall, at the time of filing, serve a copy of such document on every other party. Service upon any party of any document other than those required to be served as prescribed in § 521.8, shall be made by delivering a copy or by placing a copy of the document in the United States mail, postage prepaid, and addressed to the party's last known address. When a party is represented by a representative, service shall be made upon such representative in lieu of the actual party.

(c) *Proof of service.* A certificate of the individual serving the document by personal delivery or by mail, setting forth the manner of service, shall be proof of service.

§ 521.27 Computation of time.

(a) In computing any period of time under this part or in an order issued hereunder, the time begins with the day following the act, event, or default, and includes the last day of the period, unless it is a Saturday, Sunday, or legal holiday observed by the Federal Government, in which event it includes the next business day.

(b) When the period of time allowed is less than seven days, intermediate Saturdays, Sundays, and legal holidays observed by the Federal Government shall be excluded from the computation.

(c) Where a document has been served or issued by placing it in the mail, an additional five days will be added to the time permitted for any response.

§ 521.28 Motions.

(a) Any application to the ALJ for an order or ruling shall be by motion. Motions shall state the relief sought, the authority relied upon, and the facts alleged, and shall be filed with the ALJ and served on all other parties.

(b) Except for motions made during a prehearing conference or at the hearing, all motions shall be in writing. The ALJ may require that oral motions be reduced to writing.

(c) Within 15 days after a written motion is served, or such other time as may be fixed by the ALJ, any party may file a response to such motion.

(d) The ALJ may not grant a written motion before the time for filing responses thereto has expired, except upon consent of the parties or following a hearing on the motion, but may overrule or deny such motion without awaiting a response.

(e) The ALJ shall make a reasonable effort to dispose of all outstanding motions prior to the beginning of the hearing.

§ 521.29 Sanctions.

(a) The ALJ may sanction a person, including any party or representative for:

(1) Failing to comply with an order, rule, or procedure governing the proceeding;

(2) Failing to prosecute or defend an action; or

(3) Engaging in other misconduct that interferes with the speedy, orderly, or fair conduct of the hearing.

(b) Any such sanction, including but not limited to those listed in paragraphs (c), (d), and (e) of this section, shall reasonably relate to the severity and nature of the failure or misconduct.

(c) When a party fails to comply with an order, including an order for taking a deposition, the production of evidence within the party's control, or a request for admission, the ALJ may:

(1) Draw an inference in favor of the requesting party with regard to the information sought;

(2) In the case of requests for admission, deem each matter of which an admission is requested to be admitted;

(3) Prohibit the party failing to comply with such order from introducing evidence concerning, or otherwise relying upon, testimony relating to the information sought; and

(4) Strike any part of the pleadings or other submissions of the party failing to comply with such request.

(d) If a party fails to prosecute or defend an action under this part commenced by service of a notice of hearing, the ALJ may dismiss the action or may issue an initial decision imposing penalties and assessments.

(e) The ALJ may refuse to consider any motion, request, response, brief or other document which is not filed in a timely fashion.

§ 521.30 The hearing and burden of proof.

(a) The ALJ shall conduct a hearing on the record in order to determine whether the defendant is liable for a civil penalty or assessment under § 521.3, and if so, the appropriate amount of any such civil penalty or assessment considering any aggravating or mitigating factors.

(b) The Broadcasting Board of Governors shall prove defendant's liability and any aggravating factors by a preponderance of the evidence.

(c) The defendant shall prove any affirmative defenses and any mitigating factors by a preponderance of the evidence.

(d) The hearing shall be open to the public unless otherwise ordered by the ALJ for good cause shown.

§ 521.31 Determining the amount of penalties and assessments.

(a) In determining an appropriate amount of civil penalties and assessments, the ALJ and the Director, upon appeal, should evaluate any circumstances that mitigate or aggravate the violation and should articulate in their opinions the reasons that support the penalties and assessments they impose. Because of the intangible costs of fraud, the expense of investigating such conduct, and the need to deter others who might be similarly tempted, ordinarily double damages and a significant civil penalty should be imposed.

(b) Although not exhaustive, the following factors are among those that may influence the ALJ and the Director in determining the amount of penalties and assessments to impose with respect to the misconduct (i.e., the false, fictitious, or fraudulent claims or statements) charged in the complaint:

(1) The number of false, fictitious, or fraudulent claims or statements;

(2) The time period over which such claims or statements were made;

(3) The degree of the defendant's culpability with respect to the misconduct;

(4) The amount of money or the value of the property, services, or benefit falsely claimed;

(5) The value of the Government's actual loss as a result of the misconduct, including foreseeable consequential damages and the costs of investigation;

(6) The relationship of the amount imposed as civil penalties to the amount of the Government's loss;

(7) The potential or actual impact of the misconduct upon national defense, public health or safety, or public confidence in the management of Government programs and operations, including particularly the impact on the intended beneficiaries of such programs;

(8) Whether the defendant has engaged in a pattern of the same or similar misconduct;

(9) Whether the defendant attempted to conceal the misconduct;

(10) The degree to which the defendant has involved others in the misconduct or in concealing it;

(11) Where the misconduct of employees of agents is imputed to the defendant, the extent to which the defendant's practices fostered or attempted to preclude such misconduct;

(12) Whether the defendant cooperated in or obstructed an investigation of the misconduct;

(13) Whether the defendant assisted in identifying and prosecuting other wrongdoers;

(14) The complexity of the program or transaction, and the degree of the defendant's sophistication with respect to it, including the extent of defendant's prior participation in the program or in similar transactions;

(15) Whether the defendant has been found, in any criminal, civil, or administrative proceeding, to have engaged in similar misconduct or to have dealt dishonestly with the Government of the United States or of a State, directly or indirectly; and

(16) The need to deter the defendant and others from engaging in the same or similar misconduct.

(c) Nothing in this section shall be construed to limit the ALJ or the Director from considering any other factors that in any given case may mitigate or aggravate the offense for which penalties and assessments are imposed.

§ 521.32 Location of hearing.

(a) The hearing may be held:

(1) In any judicial district of the United States in which the defendant resides or transacts business;

(2) In any judicial district of the United States in which the claim or statement in issue was made; or

(3) In such other place as may be agreed upon by the defendant and the ALJ.

(b) Each party shall have the opportunity to present arguments with respect to the location of the hearing.

(c) The hearing shall be held at the place and at the time ordered by the ALJ.

§ 521.33 Witnesses.

(a) Except as provided in paragraph (b) of this section, testimony at the hearing shall be given orally by witnesses under oath or affirmation.

(b) At the discretion of the ALJ, testimony may be admitted in the form of a written statement or deposition. Any such written statement must be provided to all other parties along with the last known address of such witness, in a manner which allows sufficient time for other parties to subpoena such witness for cross-examination at the hearing. Prior written statements of witnesses proposed to testify at the hearing and deposition transcripts shall be exchanged as provided in § 521.22(a).

(c) The ALJ shall exercise reasonable control over the mode and order of interrogating witnesses and presenting evidence so as to

(1) Make the interrogation and presentation effective for the ascertainment of the truth,

(2) Avoid needless consumption of time, and

(3) Protect witnesses from harassment or undue embarrassment.

(d) The ALJ shall permit the parties to conduct such cross-examination as may be required for a full and true disclosure of the facts.

(e) At the discretion of the ALJ, a witness may be cross-examined on matters relevant to the proceeding without regard to the scope of his or her direct examination. To the extent permitted by the ALJ, cross-examination on matters outside the scope of direct examination shall be conducted in the manner of direct examination and may proceed by leading questions only if the witness is a hostile witness, an adverse party, or a witness identified with an adverse party.

(f) Upon motion of any party, the ALJ shall order witnesses excluded so that they cannot hear the testimony of other witnesses. This rule does not authorize exclusion of:

(1) A party who is an individual;

(2) In the case of a party that is not an individual, an officer or employee of the party appearing for the entity pro se or designated by the party's representative; or

(3) An individual whose presence is shown by a party to be essential to the presentation of its case, including an individual employed by the Government engaged in assisting the representative for the Government.

§521.34 Evidence.

(a) The ALJ shall determine the admissibility of evidence.

(b) Except as provided in this part, the ALJ shall not be bound by the Federal Rules of Evidence. However, the ALJ may apply the Federal Rules of Evidence, where appropriate (e.g., to exclude unreliable evidence).

(c) The ALJ shall exclude irrelevant and immaterial evidence.

(d) Although relevant, evidence may be excluded if its probative value is substantially outweighed by the danger of unfair prejudice, confusion of the issues, or by consideration of undue delay or needless presentation of cumulative evidence.

(e) Although relevant, evidence may be excluded if it is privileged under Federal law.

(f) Evidence concerning offers of compromise or settlement shall be inadmissible to the extent provided in Rule 408 of the Federal Rules of Evidence.

(g) The ALJ shall permit the parties to introduce rebuttal witnesses and evidence.

(h) All documents and other evidence offered or taken for the record shall be open to examination by all parties, unless otherwise ordered by the ALJ pursuant to §521.24.

§521.35 The record.

(a) The hearing will be recorded and transcribed. Transcripts may be obtained following the hearing from the ALJ at a cost not to exceed the actual cost of duplication.

(b) The transcript of testimony, exhibits and other evidence admitted at the hearing, and all papers and requests filed in the proceeding constitute the record for the decision by the ALJ and the Director.

(c) The record of the hearing may be inspected and copied (upon payment of a reasonable fee) by anyone, unless otherwise ordered by the ALJ pursuant to §521.24.

§521.36 Post-hearing briefs.

The ALJ may require the parties to file post-hearing briefs. In any event, any party may file a post-hearing brief. The ALJ shall fix the time for filing briefs, at a time not exceeding 60 days from the date the parties receive the transcript of the hearing or, if applicable, the stipulated record. Such briefs may be accompanied by proposed findings of fact and conclusions of law. The ALJ may permit the parties to file reply briefs.

§521.37 Initial decision.

(a) The ALJ shall issue an initial decision based only on the record, which shall contain findings of fact, conclusions of law, and the amount of any penalties and assessments imposed.

(b) The findings of fact shall include a finding on each of the following issues:

(1) Whether the claims or statements identified in the complaint, or any portion thereof, violate § 521.3;

(2) If the person is liable for penalties or assessments, the appropriate amount of any such penalties or assessments, considering any mitigating or aggravating factors that he or she finds in the case, such as those described in § 521.31.

(c) The ALJ shall promptly serve the initial decision on all parties within 90 days after the time for submission of post-hearing briefs and reply briefs (if permitted) has expired. The ALJ shall at the same time serve all parties with a statement describing the right of any defendant determined to be liable for a civil penalty or assessment to file a motion for reconsideration with the ALJ or a notice of appeal with the Director. If the ALJ fails to meet the deadline contained in this paragraph, he or she shall notify the parties of the reason for the delay and shall set a new deadline.

(d) Unless the initial decision of the ALJ is timely appealed to the Director, or a motion for reconsideration of the initial decision is timely filed, the initial decision shall constitute the final decision of the Director and shall be final and binding on the parties 30 days after it is issued by the ALJ.

§ 521.38 Reconsideration of initial decision.

(a) Except as provided in paragraph (d) of this section, any party may file a motion for reconsideration of the initial decision within 20 days of receipt of the initial decision. If service was made by mail, receipt will be presumed to be five days from the date of mailing in the absence of contrary proof.

(b) Every such motion must set forth the matters claimed to have been erroneously decided and the nature of the alleged errors. Such motion shall be accompanied by a supporting brief.

(c) Responses to such motions shall be allowed only upon request of the ALJ.

(d) No party may file a motion for reconsideration of an initial decision that has been revised in response to a previous motion for reconsideration.

(e) The ALJ may dispose of a motion for reconsideration by denying it or by issuing a revised initial decision.

(f) If the ALJ denies a motion for reconsideration, the initial decision shall constitute the final decision of the Director and shall be final and binding on the parties 30 days after the ALJ denies the motion, unless the initial decision is timely appealed to the Director in accordance with § 521.39.

(g) If the ALJ issues a revised initial decision, that decision shall constitute the final decision of the Director and shall be final and binding on the parties 30 days after it is issued, unless it is timely appealed to the Director in accordance with § 521.39.

§ 521.39 Appeal to the Broadcasting Board of Governors Director.

(a) Any defendant who has filed a timely answer and who is determined in an initial decision to be liable for a civil penalty or assessment may appeal such decision to the Broadcasting Board of Governors Director by filing a notice of appeal with the Broadcasting Board of Governors Director in accordance with this section.

(b)(1) No notice of appeal may be filed until the time period for filing a motion for reconsideration under § 521.38 has expired.

(2) If a motion for reconsideration is timely filed, a notice of appeal may be filed within 30 days after the ALJ denies the motion or issues a revised initial decision, whichever applies.

(3) If no motion for reconsideration is timely filed, a notice of appeal must be filed within 30 days after the ALJ issues the initial decision.

(4) The Director may extend the initial 30-day period for an additional 30 days if the defendant files with the Director a request for an extension within the initial 30-day period and shows good cause.

(c) If the defendant files a timely notice of appeal with the Director, and the time for filing motions for reconsideration under § 521.38 has expired, the ALJ shall forward the record of the proceeding to the Director.

(d) A notice of appeal shall be accompanied by a written brief specifying exceptions to the initial decisions and reasons supporting the exceptions.

(e) The representative for the Government may file a brief in opposition to exceptions within 30 days of receiving the notice of appeal and accompanying brief.

(f) There is no right to appear personally before the Director.

(g) There is no right to appeal any interlocutory ruling by the ALJ.

(h) In reviewing the initial decision, the Director shall not consider any objection that was not raised before the ALJ unless a demonstration is made of extraordinary circumstances causing the failure to raise the objection.

(i) If any party demonstrates to the satisfaction of the Director that additional evidence not presented at such hearing is material and that there were reasonable grounds for the failure to present such evidence at such hearing, the Director shall remand the matter to the ALJ for consideration of such additional evidence.

(j) The Director may affirm, reduce, reverse, compromise, remand, or settle any penalty or assessment determined by the ALJ in an initial decision.

(k) The Director shall promptly serve each party to the appeal with a copy of her/his decision and a statement describing the right of any person determined to be liable for a penalty or assessment to seek judicial review.

(l) Unless a petition for review is filed as provided in 31 U.S.C. 3805 after a defendant has exhausted all administrative remedies under this part and within 60 days after the date on which the Director serves the defendant with a copy of her/his decision, a determination that a defendant is liable under § 521.3 is final and is not subject to judicial review.

§ 521.40 Stays ordered by the Department of Justice.

If at any time the Attorney General or an Assistant Attorney General designated by the Attorney General transmits to the Director a written finding that continuation of the administrative process described in this part with respect to a claim or statement may adversely affect any pending or potential criminal or civil action related to such claim or statement, the Director shall stay the process immediately. The Director may order the process resumed only upon receipt of the written authorization of the Attorney General.

§ 521.41 Stay pending appeal.

(a) An initial decision is stayed automatically pending disposition of a motion for reconsideration or of an appeal to the Director.

(b) No administrative stay is available following a final decision of the Director.

§ 521.42 Judicial review.

Section 3805 of title 31, United States Code, authorizes judicial review by an appropriate United States District Court of a final decision of the Director imposing penalties or assessments under this part and specifies the procedures for such.

§ 521.43 Collection of civil penalties and assessments.

Sections 3806 and 3808(b) of title 31, United States Code, authorize actions for collection of civil penalties and assessments imposed under this part and specify the procedures for such actions.

§ 521.44 Right to administrative offset.

The amount of any penalty or assessment which has become final, or for which a judgment has been entered under § 521.42 or § 521.43, or any amount agreed upon in a compromise or settlement under § 521.46, may be collected by administrative offset under 31 U.S.C. 3716, except that an administrative offset may not be made under the subsection against a refund of an overpayment of Federal taxes, then or later owing by the United States to the defendant.

§ 521.45 Deposit in Treasury of United States.

All amounts collected pursuant to this part shall be deposited as miscellaneous receipts in the Treasury of the United States, except as provided in 31 U.S.C. 3806(g).

§ 521.46 Compromise or settlement.

(a) Parties may make offers of compromise or settlement at any time.

(b) The reviewing official has the exclusive authority to compromise or settle a case under this part at any time after the date on which the reviewing official is permitted to issue a complaint and before the date on which the ALJ issues an initial decision.

(c) The Director has exclusive authority to compromise or settle a case under this part at any time after the date on which the ALJ issues an initial decision, except during pendency of any review under § 521.42 or during the pendency of any action to collect penalties and assessments under § 521.43.

(d) The Attorney General has exclusive authority to compromise or settle a case under this part during the pendency of any review under § 521.42 or of any action to recover penalties and assessments under 31 U.S.C. 3806.

(e) The investigating official may recommend settlement terms to the reviewing official, the Director, or the Attorney General, as appropriate. The reviewing official may recommend settlement terms to the Director, or the Attorney General, as appropriate.

(f) Any compromise or settlement must be in writing.

§ 521.47 Limitations.

(a) The notice of hearing with respect to a claim or statement must be served in the manner specified in § 521.8 within 6 years after the date on which such claim or statement is made.

(b) If the defendant fails to file a timely answer, service of a notice under § 521.10(b) shall be deemed notice of hearing for purposes of this section.

(c) The statute of limitations may be extended by agreement of the parties.

PART 530—ENFORCEMENT OF NONDISCRIMINATION ON THE BASIS OF HANDICAP IN PROGRAMS OR ACTIVITIES CONDUCTED BY THE BROADCASTING BOARD OF GOVERNORS

Sec.

AUTHORITY: 29 U.S.C. 794.

SOURCE: 51 FR 22890, 22896, June 23, 1986, unless otherwise noted.

§ 530.101 Purpose.

This part effectuates section 119 of the Rehabilitation, Comprehensive Services, and Developmental Disabilities Amendments of 1978, which amended section 504 of the Rehabilitation Act of 1973 to prohibit discrimination on the basis of handicap in programs or activities conducted by Executive agencies or the United States Postal Service.

§ 530.102 Application.

This part applies to all programs or activities conducted by the Board.

§ 530.103 Definitions.

For purposes of this part, the term—

Assistant Attorney General means the Assistant Attorney General, Civil Rights Division, United States Department of Justice.

Auxiliary aids means services or devices that enable persons with impaired sensory, manual, or speaking skills to have an equal opportunity to participate in, and enjoy the benefits of, programs or activities conducted by the Board. For example, auxiliary aids useful for persons with impaired vision include readers, brailled materials, audio recordings, telecommunications devices and other similar services and devices. Auxiliary aids useful for persons with impaired hearing include telephone handset amplifiers, telephones compatible with hearing aids, telecommunication devices for deaf persons (TDD's), interpreters, notetakers, written materials, and other similar services and devices.

Complete complaint means a written statement that contains the complainant's name and address and describes the Board's alleged discriminatory action in sufficient detail to inform the Board of the nature and date of the alleged violation of section 504. It shall be signed by the complainant or by someone authorized to do so on his or her behalf. Complaints filed on behalf of classes or third parties shall describe or identify (by name, if possible) the alleged victims of discrimination.

Facility means all or any portion of buildings, structures, equipment, roads, walks, parking lots, rolling stock or other conveyances, or other real or personal property.

Handicapped person means any person who has a physical or mental impairment that substantially limits one or more major life activities, has a record of such an impairment, or is regarded as having such an impairment.

As used in this definition, the phrase:

(1) *Physical or mental impairment* includes—

(i) Any physiological disorder or condition, cosmetic disfigurement, or anatomical loss affecting one or more of the following body systems: Neurological; musculoskeletal; special sense organs; respiratory, including speech organs; cardiovascular; reproductive; digestive; genitourinary; hemic and lymphatic; skin; and endocrine; or

(ii) Any mental or psychological disorder, such as mental retardation, organic brain syndrome, emotional or mental illness, and specific learning disabilities. The term *physical or mental impairment* includes, but is not limited to, such diseases and conditions as orthopedic, visual, speech, and hearing impairments, cerebral palsy, epilepsy, muscular dystrophy, multiple sclerosis, cancer, heart disease, diabetes, mental retardation, emotional illness, and drug addiction and alocoholism.

(2) *Major life activities* includes functions such as caring for one's self, performing manual tasks, walking, seeing, hearing, speaking, breathing, learning, and working.

(3) *Has a record of such an impairment* means has a history of, or has been misclassified as having, a mental or physical impairment that substantially limits one or more major life activities.

(4) *Is regarded as having an impairment* means—

(i) Has a physical or mental impairment that does not substantially limit major life activities but is treated by the Board as constituting such a limitation;

(ii) Has a physical or mental impairment that substantially limits major life activities only as a result of the attitudes of others toward such impairment; or

(iii) Has none of the impairments defined in paragraph (1) of this definition but is treated by the Board as having such an impairment.

Historic preservation programs means programs conducted by the Board that have preservation of historic properties as a primary purpose.

Historic properties means those properties that are listed or eligible for listing in the National Register of Historic Places or properties designated as historic under a statute of the appropriate State or local government body.

Qualified handicapped person means—

(1) With respect to preschool, elementary, or secondary education services provided by the Board, a handicapped person who is a member of a class of persons otherwise entitled by statute, regulation, or Board policy to receive education services from the Board.

(2) With respect to any other Board program or activity under which a person is required to perform services or to achieve a level of accomplishment, a handicapped person who meets the essential eligibility requirements and who can acheive the purpose of the program or activity without modifications in the program or activity that the Board can demonstrate would result in a fundamental alteration in its nature;

(3) With respect to any other program or activity, a handicapped person who meets the essential eligibility requirements for participation in, or receipt of benefits from, that program or activity; and

(4) *Qualified handicapped person* is defined for purposes of employment in 29 CFR 1613.702(f), which is made applicable to this part by § 530.140.

Section 504 means section 504 of the Rehabilitation Act of 1973 (Pub. L. 93–112, 87 Stat. 394 (29 U.S.C. 794)), as amended by the Rehabilitation Act Amendments of 1974 (Pub. L. 93–516, 88 Stat. 1617), and the Rehabilitation,

Comprehensive Services, and Developmental Disabilities Amendments of 1978 (Pub. L. 95–602, 92 Stat. 2955). As used in this part, section 504 applies only to programs or activities conducted by Executive agencies and not to federally assisted programs.

Substantial impairment means a significant loss of the integrity of finished materials, design quality, or special character resulting from a permanent alteration.

§§ 530.104–530.109 [Reserved]

§ 530.110 Self-evaluation.

(a) The Board shall, by August 24, 1987, evaluate its current policies and practices, and the effects thereof, that do not or may not meet the requirements of this part, and, to the extent modification of any such policies and practices is required, the Board shall proceed to make the necessary modifications.

(b) The Board shall provide an opportunity to interested persons, including handicapped persons or organizations representing handicapped persons, to participate in the self-evaluation process by submitting comments (both oral and written).

(c) The Board shall, until three years following the completion of the self-evaluation, maintain on file and make available for public inspection:

(1) A description of areas examined and any problems identified, and

(2) A description of any modifications made.

§ 530.111 Notice.

The Board shall make available to employees, applicants, participants, beneficiaries, and other interested persons such information regarding the provisions of this part and its applicability to the programs or activities conducted by the Board, and make such information available to them in such manner as the head of the Board finds necessary to apprise such persons of the protections against discrimination assured them by section 504 and this regulation.

§§ 530.112–530.129 [Reserved]

§ 530.130 General prohibitions against discrimination.

(a) No qualified handicapped person shall, on the basis of handicap, be excluded from participation in, be denied the benefits of, or otherwise be subjected to discrimination under any program or activity conducted by the Board.

(b)(1) The Board, in providing any aid, benefit, or service, may not, directly or through contractual, licensing, or other arrangements, on the basis of handicap—

(i) Deny a qualified handicapped person the opportunity to participate in or benefit from the aid, benefit, or service;

(ii) Afford a qualified handicapped person an opportunity to participate in or benefit from the aid, benefit, or service that is not equal to that afforded others;

(iii) Provide a qualified handicapped person with an aid, benefit, or service that is not as effective in affording equal opportunity to obtain the same result, to gain the same benefit, or to reach the same level of achievement as that provided to others;

(iv) Provide different or separate aid, benefits, or services to handicapped persons or to any class of handicapped persons than is provided to others unless such action is necessary to provide qualified handicapped persons with aid, benefits, or services that are as effective as those provided to others;

(v) Deny a qualified handicapped person the opportunity to participate as a member of planning or advisory boards; or

(vi) Otherwise limit a qualified handicapped person in the enjoyment of any right, privilege, advantage, or opportunity enjoyed by others receiving the aid, benefit, or service.

(2) The Board may not deny a qualified handicapped person the opportunity to participate in programs or activities that are not separate or different, despite the existence of permissibly separate or different programs or activities.

(3) The Board may not, directly or through contractual or other

arrangments, utilize criteria or methods of administration the purpose or effect of which would—

(i) Subject qualified handicapped persons to discrimination on the basis of handicap; or

(ii) Defeat or substantially impair accomplishment of the objectives of a program or activity with respect to handicapped persons.

(4) The Board may not, in determining the site or location of a facility, make selections the purpose or effect of which would—

(i) Exclude handicapped persons from, deny them the benefits of, or otherwise subject them to discrimination under any program or activity conducted by the Board; or

(ii) Defeat or substantially impair the accomplishment of the objectives of a program or activity with respect to handicapped persons.

(5) The Board, in the selection of procurement contractors, may not use criteria that subject qualified handicapped persons to discrimination on the basis of handicap.

(6) The Board may not administer a licensing or certification program in a manner that subjects qualified handicapped persons to discrimination on the basis of handicap, nor may the Board establish requirements for the programs or activities of licensees or certified entities that subject qualified handicapped persons to discrimination on the basis of handicap. However, the programs or activities of entities that are licensed or certified by the Board are not, themselves, covered by this part.

(c) The exclusion of nonhandicapped persons from the benefits of a program limited by Federal statute or Executive order to handicapped persons or the exclusion of a specific class of handicapped persons from a program limited by Federal statute or Executive order to a different class of handicapped persons is not prohibited by this part.

(d) The Board shall administer programs and activities in the most integrated setting appropriate to the needs of qualified handicapped persons.

§§ 530.131–530.139 [Reserved]

§ 530.140 Employment.

No qualified handicapped person shall, on the basis of handicap, be subjected to discrimination in employment under any program or activity conducted by the Board. The definitions, requirements, and procedures of section 501 of the Rehabilitation Act of 1973 (29 U.S.C. 791), as established by the Equal Employment Opportunity Commission in 29 CFR part 1613, shall apply to employment in federally conducted programs or activities.

§§ 530.141–530.148 [Reserved]

§ 530.149 Program accessibility: Discrimination prohibited.

Except as otherwise provided in § 530.150, no qualified handicapped person shall, because the Board's facilities are inaccessible to or unusable by handicapped persons, be denied the benefits of, be excluded from participation in, or otherwise be subjected to discrimination under any program or activity conducted by the Board.

§ 530.150 Program accessibility: Existing facilities.

(a) *General.* The Board shall operate each program or activity so that the program or activity, when viewed in its entirety, is readily accessible to and usable by handicapped persons. This paragraph does not—

(1) Necessarily require the Board to make each of its existing facilities accessible to and usable by handicapped persons;

(2) In the case of historic preservation programs, require the Board to take any action that would result in a substantial impairment of significant historic features of an historic property; or

(3) Require the Board to take any action that it can demonstrate would result in a fundamental alteration in the nature of a program or activity or in undue financial and administrative burdens. In those circumstances where Board personnel believe that the proposed action would fundamentally alter the program or activity or would

result in undue financial and administrative burdens, the Board has the burden of proving that compliance with § 530.150(a) would result in such alteration or burdens. The decision that compliance would result in such alteration or burdens must be made by the Board head or his or her designee after considering all Board resources available for use in the funding and operation of the conducted program or activity, and must be accompanied by a written statement of the reasons for reaching that conclusion. If an action would result in such an alteration or such burdens, the Board shall take any other action that would not result in such an alteration or such burdens but would nevertheless ensure that handicapped persons receive the benefits and services of the program or activity.

(b) *Methods*—(1) *General.* The Board may comply with the requirements of this section through such means as redesign of equipment, reassignment of services to accessible buildings, assignment of aides to beneficiaries, home visits, delivery of services at alternate accessible sites, alteration of existing facilities and construction of new facilities, use of accessible rolling stock, or any other methods that result in making its programs or activities readily accessible to and usable by handicapped persons. The Board is not required to make structural changes in existing facilities where other methods are effective in achieving compliance with this section. The Board, in making alterations to existing buildings, shall meet accessibility requirements to the extent compelled by the Architectural Barriers Act of 1968, as amended (42 U.S.C. 4151–4157), and any regulations implementing it. In choosing among available methods for meeting the requirements of this section, the Board shall give priority to those methods that offer programs and activities to qualified handicapped persons in the most integrated setting appropriate.

(2) *Historic preservation programs.* In meeting the requirements of § 530.150(a) in historic preservation programs, the Board shall give priority to methods that provide physical access to handicapped persons. In cases where a physical alteration to an historic property is not required because of § 530.150(a)(2) or (a)(3), alternative methods of achieving program accessibility include—

(i) Using audio-visual materials and devices to depict those portions of an historic property that cannot otherwise be made accessible;

(ii) Assigning persons to guide handicapped persons into or through portions of historic properties that cannot otherwise be made accessible; or

(iii) Adopting other innovative methods.

(c) *Time period for compliance.* The Board shall comply with the obligations established under this section by October 21, 1986, except that where structural changes in facilities are undertaken, such changes shall be made by August 22, 1989, but in any event as expeditiously as possible.

(d) *Transition plan.* In the event that structural changes to facilities will be undertaken to achieve program accessibility, the Board shall develop, by February 23, 1987, a transition plan setting forth the steps necessary to complete such changes. The Board shall provide an opportunity to interested persons, including handicapped persons or organizations representing handicapped persons, to participate in the development of the transition plan by submitting comments (both oral and written). A copy of the transition plan shall be made available for public inspection. The plan shall, at a minimum—

(1) Identify physical obstacles in the Board's facilities that limit the accessibility of its programs or activities to handicapped persons;

(2) Describe in detail the methods that will be used to make the facilities accessible;

(3) Specify the schedule for taking the steps necessary to achieve compliance with this section and, if the time period of the transition plan is longer than one year, identify steps that will be taken during each year of the transition period; and

(4) Indicate the official responsible for implementation of the plan.

§ 530.151 Program accessibility: New construction and alterations.

Each building or part of a building that is constructed or altered by, on behalf of, or for the use of the Board shall be designed, constructed, or altered so as to be readily accessible to and usable by handicapped persons. The definitions, requirements, and standards of the Architectural Barriers Act (42 U.S.C. 4151–4157), as established in 41 CFR 101–19.600 to 101–19.607, apply to buildings covered by this section.

§§ 530.152–530.159 [Reserved]

§ 530.160 Communications.

(a) The Board shall take appropriate steps to ensure effective communication with applicants, participants, personnel of other Federal entities, and members of the public.

(1) The Board shall furnish appropriate auxiliary aids where necessary to afford a handicapped person an equal opportunity to participate in, and enjoy the benefits of, a program or activity conducted by the Board.

(i) In determining what type of auxiliary aid is necessary, the Board shall give primary consideration to the requests of the handicapped person.

(ii) The Board need not provide individually prescribed devices, readers for personal use or study, or other devices of a personal nature.

(2) Where the Board communicates with applicants and beneficiaries by telephone, telecommunication devices for deaf person (TDD's) or equally effective telecommunication systems shall be used.

(b) The Board shall ensure that interested persons, including persons with impaired vision or hearing, can obtain information as to the existence and location of accessible services, activities, and facilities.

(c) The Board shall provide signage at a primary entrance to each of its inaccessible facilities, directing users to a location at which they can obtain information about accessible facilities. The international symbol for accessibility shall be used at each primary entrance of an accessible facility.

(d) This section does not require the Board to take any action that it can demonstrate would result in a fundamental alteration in the nature of a program or activity or in undue financial and adminstrative burdens. In those circumstances where Board personnel believe that the proposed action would fundamentally alter the program or activity or would result in undue financial and administrative burdens, the Board has the burden of proving that compliance with § 530.160 would result in such alteration or burdens. The decision that compliance would result in such alteration or burdens must be made by the Board head or his or her designee after considering all Board resources available for use in the funding and operation of the conducted program or activity, and must be accompanied by a written statement of the reasons for reaching that conclusion. If an action required to comply with this section would result in such an alteration or such burdens, the Board shall take any other action that would not result in such an alteration or such burdens but would nevertheless ensure that, to the maximum extent possible, handicapped persons receive the benefits and services of the program or activity.

§§ 530.161–530.169 [Reserved]

§ 530.170 Compliance procedures.

(a) Except as provided in paragraph (b) of this section, this section applies to all allegations of discrimination on the basis of handicap in programs or activities conducted by the Board.

(b) The Board shall process complaints alleging violations of section 504 with respect to employment according to the procedures established by the Equal Employment Opportunity Commission in 29 CFR part 1613 pursuant to section 501 of the Rehabilitation Act of 1973 (29 U.S.C. 791).

(c) The Director, Office of Equal Employment Opportunity and Civil Rights, shall be responsible for coordinating implementation of this section. Complaints may be sent to Director, Office of Equal Employment Opportunity and Civil Rights, Broadcasting Board of Governors, 301 4th Street NW., Washington, DC 20547.

(d) The Board shall accept and investigate all complete complaints for which it has jurisdiction. All complete complaints must be filed within 180 days of the alleged act of discrimination. The Board may extend this time period for good cause.

(e) If the Board receives a complaint over which it does not have jurisdiction, it shall promptly notify the complainant and shall make reasonable efforts to refer the complaint to the appropriate government entity.

(f) The Board shall notify the Architectural and Transportation Barriers Compliance Board upon receipt of any complaint alleging that a building or facility that is subject to the Architectural Barriers Act of 1968, as amended (42 U.S.C. 4151–4157), or section 502 of the Rehabilitation Act of 1973, as amended (29 U.S.C. 792), is not readily accessible to and usable by handicapped persons.

(g) Within 180 days of the receipt of a complete complaint for which it has jurisdiction, the Board shall notify the complainant of the results of the investigation in a letter containing—

(1) Findings of fact and conclusions of law;

(2) A description of a remedy for each violation found; and

(3) A notice of the right to appeal.

(h) Appeals of the findings of fact and conclusions of law or remedies must be filed by the complainant within 90 days of receipt from the Board of the letter required by § 530.170(g). The Board may extend this time for good cause.

(i) Timely appeals shall be accepted and processed by the head of the Board.

(j) The head of the Board shall notify the complainant of the results of the appeal within 60 days of the receipt of the request. If the head of the Board determines that additional information is needed from the complainant, he or she shall have 60 days from the date of receipt of the additional information to make his or her determination on the appeal.

(k) The time limits cited in paragraphs (g) and (j) of this section may be extended with the permission of the Assistant Attorney General.

(l) The Board may delegate its authority for conducting complaint investigations to other Federal agencies, except that the authority for making the final determination may not be delegated to another agency.

[51 FR 22890, 22896, June 23, 1986, as amended at 51 FR 22890, June 23, 1986]

§§ 530.171–530.999 [Reserved]

PARTS 531–599 [RESERVED]

CHAPTER VII—OVERSEAS PRIVATE INVESTMENT CORPORATION

SUBCHAPTER A—ADMINISTRATIVE PROVISIONS

SUBCHAPTER A—ADMINISTRATIVE PROVISIONS

PARTS 700–704 [RESERVED]

PART 705—EMPLOYEE ETHICAL CONDUCT STANDARDS AND FINANCIAL DISCLOSURE REGULATIONS

AUTHORITY: 5 U.S.C. 7301.

§ 705.101 Cross-reference to employee ethical conduct standards and financial disclosure regulations.

Employees of the Overseas Private Investment Corporation (OPIC) should refer to the executive branch-wide Standards of Ethical Conduct at 5 CFR part 2635, the OPIC regulation at 5 CFR 4301.101 which supplements the executive branch-wide standards, and the executive branch-wide financial disclosure regulation at 5 CFR part 2634.

[58 FR 33320, June 17, 1993]

PART 706—INFORMATION DISCLOSURE UNDER THE FREEDOM OF INFORMATION ACT

Subpart A—General

Subpart B—Obtaining OPIC Records

Subpart C—Fees for Requests for Non-Public Records

Subpart D—Processing of Requests for Non-Public Records

AUTHORITY: 5 U.S.C. 552, Pub. L. 114–185.

SOURCE: 82 FR 20434, May 2, 2017, unless otherwise noted.

Subpart A—General

§ 706.1 Description.

This part contains the rules that the Overseas Private Investment Corporation ("OPIC") follows in processing requests for records under the Freedom of Information Act ("FOIA"), 5 U.S.C. 552 as amended. These rules should be read together with the FOIA and the Uniform Freedom of Information Fee Schedule and Guidelines published by the Office of Management and Budget. Requests made by individuals for records about themselves under the Privacy Act of 1974, 5 U.S.C. 552a, are processed in accordance with OPIC's Privacy Act regulations at 22 CFR part 707 as well as under this subpart.

§ 706.2 Policy.

It is OPIC's policy to make its records available to the public to the greatest extent possible, in keeping with the spirit of the FOIA. This policy includes providing reasonably segregable information from records that also contain information that may be withheld under the FOIA. However, implementation of this policy also reflects OPIC's view that the soundness and viability of many of its programs depend in large measure upon full and reliable commercial, financial, technical and business information received from applicants for OPIC assistance and that the willingness of those applicants to provide such information depends on OPIC's ability to hold it in confidence. Consequently, except as provided by law and in this part, information provided to OPIC in confidence will not be disclosed without the submitter's consent.

§ 706.3 Scope.

This part applies to all agency records in OPIC's possession and control. This part does not compel OPIC to create records or to ask outside parties to provide documents in order to satisfy a FOIA request. OPIC may, however, in its discretion and in consultation with a FOIA requester, create a new record as a partial or complete response to a FOIA request. In responding to requests for information, OPIC will ordinarily consider only those records within its possession and control as of the date of OPIC's search. If any other date is used, OPIC will inform the requester of that date. A record that is excluded from the requirements of the FOIA pursuant to 5 U.S.C. 552(c), is not considered responsive to a request.

§ 706.4 Preservation and transfer of records.

(a) *Preservation of records.* OPIC preserves all correspondence pertaining to the requests that it receives under this part, as well as copies of all requested records, until disposition or destruction is authorized pursuant to title 44 of the United States Code or the General Records Schedule 4.2 of the National Archives and Records Administration. Records that are identified as responsive to a request will not be disposed of or destroyed while they are the subject of a pending request, appeal, or lawsuit under the FOIA.

(b) *Transfer of records to the National Archives.* Under the Records Disposal Act, 44 U.S.C. Chapter 33, OPIC is required to transfer legal custody and control of records with permanent historical value to the National Archives. OPIC's Finance Project and Insurance Contract Case files generally do not qualify as records with permanent historical value. OPIC will not transfer these files except when the National Archives determines that an individual project or case is especially significant or unique. If the National Archives receives a FOIA request for records that have been transferred it will respond to the request in accordance with its own FOIA regulations.

§ 706.5 Other rights and services.

Nothing in this subpart shall be construed to entitle any person, as of right, to any service or to the disclosure of any record to which such person is not entitled under the FOIA.

Subpart B—Obtaining OPIC Records

§ 706.10 Publicly available records.

Records that the FOIA requires agencies to make available for public inspection in an electronic format may be accessed through OPIC's FOIA Web site at *www.opic.gov/foia.* Records identified as of interest to the public and appropriate for public disclosure are also available, along with an index. These include annual reports and financial statements, program handbooks, press releases, application forms, claims information, and annual FOIA reports. OPIC will review and update its Web site of posted records on an ongoing basis. Persons seeking information are encouraged to visit OPIC's Web site to see what information is already available before submitting a request; OPIC's FOIA Office and FOIA Public Liaison are available to assist individuals in locating records.

§ 706.11 Requesting non-public records.

(a) *General information*—(1) *How to submit.* To make a request for records a requester must submit a written request to OPIC's FOIA Office either by mail to Overseas Private Investment Corporation, 1100 New York Avenue NW., Washington, DC 20527 or electronic mail to *FOIA@opic.gov.* The envelope or subject line should read "Freedom of Information Request" to ensure proper routing. The request is considered received by OPIC upon actual receipt by OPIC's FOIA Office.

(2) *Records about oneself.* A requester who is making a request for records about himself or herself must verify his or her identity by providing a notarized statement or a statement under 28 U.S.C. 1746, a law that permits statements to be made under penalty of perjury as a substitute for notarization, stating that the requester is the person he or she claims to be.

(3) *Records about a third party.* Where a request for records pertains to a third party, a requester may receive greater access by submitting a notarized authorization signed by that individual, a declaration by that individual made in compliance with the requirements set

forth in 28 U.S.C. 1746 authorizing disclosure of the records to the requester, proof of guardianship, or proof that the individual is deceased (*e.g.*, a copy of a death certificate or an obituary). OPIC may require a requester to supply additional information if necessary in order to verify that a particular individual has consented to disclosure.

(b) *Description of records sought*. Requesters must describe the records sought in sufficient detail to enable OPIC personnel to locate them with a reasonable amount of effort. To the extent possible, requesters should include specific information that may assist OPIC in identifying the requested records, such as the project name, contract number, date or date range, country, title, name, author, recipient, subject matter of the record, or reference number. In general, requesters should include as much detail as possible about the specific records or the types of records sought. Before submitting their requests, requesters may contact OPIC's FOIA Office or FOIA Public Liaison to discuss the records they seek and to receive assistance in describing the records. If a requester fails to reasonably describe the records sought, OPIC will inform the requester what additional information is needed or why the request is otherwise insufficient. Requesters who are attempting to reformulate or modify such a request may discuss their request with the FOIA Office or FOIA Public Liaison. If a request does not reasonably describe the records sought, OPIC's response to the request may be delayed.

(c) *Format*. Requests may state a preferred format for released records including electronic formats. The records will be provided in the preferred format if the record is readily reproducible in that format. If you do not state a preference, you will receive any released records in the format most convenient to OPIC.

(d) *Requester information*. Requests must include the requester's name and contact information, such as phone number, email address, or mailing address, to assist OPIC in communicating with them and providing the released records.

(e) *Fees*. You should state your willingness to pay fees under these regulations or, alternately, your willingness to pay up to a specified limit. If you believe that you qualify for a partial or total fee waiver under 706.24 you should request a waiver and provide justification as required by 706.24. If your request does not contain a statement of your willingness to pay fees or a request for a fee waiver, OPIC will consider your request an agreement to pay up to $25.00 in fees.

Subpart C—Fees for Requests of Non-Public Records.

§ 706.20 In general.

OPIC will charge for processing requests under the FOIA in accordance with the provisions of this section and with the OMB Guidelines. For purposes of assessing fees, the FOIA establishes three categories of requests: Commercial use requests, non-commercial scientific or educational institutions or news media requests, and all other requests. OPIC will inform requesters as to which category their request has been placed into. Different fees are assessed depending on the category. Requesters may seek a fee waiver. OPIC will consider requests for fee waiver in accordance with the requirements in § 706.24. To resolve any fee issues that arise under this section, OPIC may contact a requester for additional information. OPIC will ensure that searches, review, and duplication are conducted in the most efficient and the least expensive manner. OPIC ordinarily will collect all applicable fees before sending copies of records to a requester. Requesters must pay fees by check or money order made payable to the Treasury of the United States.

§ 706.21 Types of fees.

(a) Direct costs are those expenses that OPIC expends in searching for and duplicating (and, in the case of commercial-use requests, reviewing) records in order to respond to a FOIA request. For example, direct costs include the salary of the employee performing the work (*i.e.*, the basic rate of pay for the employee, plus 16 percent of that rate to cover benefits) and the cost of operating computers and other electronic equipment. Direct costs do not include overhead expenses such as the costs of space, and of heating or lighting a facility.

(b) Duplication is reproducing a copy of a record or of the information contained in it, necessary to respond to a FOIA request. Copies can take the form of paper, audiovisual materials, or electronic records, among others.

(c) Review is the examination of a record located in response to a request in order to determine whether any portion of it is exempt from disclosure. Review time includes processing any record for disclosure, such as doing all that is necessary to prepare the record for disclosure, including the process of redacting the record and marking the appropriate exemptions. Review costs are properly charged even if a record ultimately is not disclosed. Review time also includes time spent both obtaining and considering any formal objection to disclosure made by a confidential commercial information submitter under §706.33(c) of this subpart, but it does not include time spent resolving general legal or policy issues regarding the application of exemptions.

(d) Search is the process of looking for and retrieving records or information responsive to a request. Search time includes page-by-page or line-by-line identification of information within records; and the reasonable efforts expended to locate and retrieve information from electronic records.

§ 706.22 Request categories.

(a) A Commercial Use request is a request that asks for information for a use or a purpose that furthers a commercial, trade, or profit interest, which can include furthering those interests through litigation. OPIC's decision to place a requester in the commercial use category will be made on a case-by-case basis based on the requester's intended use of the information.

(b) An Educational Use request is one made on behalf of an educational institution, defined as any school that operates a program of scholarly research. A requester in this category must show that the request is made in connection with his or her role at the educational institution. OPIC may request verification from the requester that the request is in furtherance of scholarly research.

(1) *Example 1.* A request from a professor of geology at a university for records relating to soil erosion, written on letterhead of the Department of Geology, would be presumed to be from an educational institution.

(2) *Example 2.* A request from the same professor of geology seeking drug information from the Food and Drug Administration in furtherance of a murder mystery he is writing would not be presumed to be an institutional request, regardless of whether it was written on institutional stationery.

(3) *Example 3.* A student who makes a request in furtherance of their coursework or other school-sponsored activities and provides a copy of a course syllabus or other reasonable documentation to indicate the research purpose for the request, would qualify as part of this fee category.

(c) A Noncommercial Scientific Institution Use request is a request made on behalf of a noncommercial scientific institution, defined as an institution that is not operated on a "commercial" basis, as defined in paragraph (a) of this section, and that is operated solely for the purpose of conducting scientific research, the results of which are not intended to promote any particular product or industry. A requester in this category must show that the request is authorized by and is made under the auspices of a qualifying institution and that the records are sought to further scientific research and not for a commercial use.

(d) A News Media Request is a request made by a representative of the news media in that capacity. A representative of the news media is defined as any person or entity that gathers information of potential interest to a segment of the public, uses its editorial skills to turn the raw materials into a distinct work, and distributes that work to an audience. The term "news" means information that is about current events or that would be of current interest to the public. Examples of news media entities include television or radio stations that broadcast news to the public at large and publishers of periodicals that disseminate news and make their products available through a variety of means to the general public. A request for records that supports the news-dissemination function of the requester shall not be considered to be for a commercial use. "Freelance" journalists who demonstrate a solid basis for expecting publication through a news media entity shall be considered as a representative of the news media. A publishing contract would provide the clearest evidence that publication is expected; however, OPIC shall also consider a requester's past publication record in making this determination.

(e) All other requests include any requests that do not qualify under one of the above categories.

§ 706.23 Fees charged.

(a) *Fees.* In responding to FOIA requests, OPIC will charge the following fees unless a waiver or reduction of fees has been granted under § 706.24 of this subpart. Because the fee amounts provided below already account for the direct costs associated with a given fee type, OPIC should not add any additional costs to charges calculated under this section.

(1) *Search.* (i) Requests made by educational institutions, noncommercial scientific institutions, or representatives of the news media are not subject to search fees. Search fees will be charged to all other requests, subject to the restrictions of paragraph (b) of this section. Fees for time spent searching is properly charged even if no responsive records are located or if all responsive records are determined to be entirely exempt from disclosure.

(ii) For each quarter hour spent by personnel searching for requested records, including electronic searches that do not require new programming, the fees will be as follows: Professional—$13.75; and administrative—$7.50.

(iii) Requesters will be charged the direct costs associated with conducting any search that requires the creation of a new program to locate the requested records. Before incurring such costs, OPIC will notify the requester and the requester must agree to pay.

(iv) For requests that require the retrieval of records stored at a Federal Records Center operated by the National Archives and Records Administration (NARA), additional costs shall be charged in accordance with the Transactional Billing Rate Schedule established by NARA.

(2) *Duplication.* Duplication fees will be charged to all requesters, subject to the restrictions of paragraph (b) of this section. OPIC will honor a requester's preference for receiving a record in a particular form or format where it is readily reproducible in the form or format requested. Where photocopies are supplied, OPIC will provide one copy per request at a cost of $0.10 per page. For copies of records produced on tapes, disks, or other electronic media, OPIC will charge the direct costs of producing the copy, including operator time. Where paper documents must be scanned in order to comply with a requester's preference to receive the records in an electronic format, the requester must also pay the direct costs associated with scanning those materials. For other forms of duplication, OPIC will charge the direct costs.

(3) *Review.* Review fees will be charged to requesters who make commercial use requests. Review fees will be assessed in connection with the initial review of the record, *i.e.*, the review conducted by OPIC to determine whether an exemption applies to a particular record or portion of a record. No charge will be made for review at the administrative appeal stage of exemptions applied at the initial review stage. However, if the appellate authority determines that a particular exemption no longer applies, any costs associated with the re-review of the records in order to consider the use of other exemptions may be assessed as review fees. Review fees will be charged at the same rates as those charged for a search under paragraph (a)(1)(ii) of this section.

(b) *Restrictions on charging fees.* (1) No search fees will be charged for educational use requests, noncommercial scientific use requests, or news media requests as defined in Section 706.22.

(2) Fees charged when OPIC exceeds time limits.

(i) When OPIC fails to comply with the time limits in which to respond to a request, it may not charge search fees, or, in the instances of requests from requesters described in paragraph (b)(1) of this section, may not charge duplication fees, except as described in (b)(2)(ii) through (iv) of this section.

(ii) If OPIC has determined that unusual circumstances as defined by the FOIA apply and OPIC provided timely written notice to the requester in accordance with the FOIA, a failure to comply with the time limit shall be excused for an additional ten days.

(iii) If OPIC has determined that unusual circumstances, as defined by the FOIA, apply and more than 5,000 pages are necessary to respond to the request, OPIC may charge all applicable fees incurred in processing the request if the following steps are taken:

(A) OPIC has provided timely written notice of unusual circumstances to the requester in accordance with the FOIA; and

(B) OPIC has discussed with the requester via written mail, email, or telephone (or made not less than three good-faith attempts to do so) how the requester could effectively limit the scope of the request in accordance with 5 U.S.C. 552(a)(6)(B)(ii).

(iv) If a court has determined that exceptional circumstances exist, as defined by the FOIA, a failure to comply with the time limits shall be excused for the length of time provided by the court order.

(3) No search or review fees will be charged for a quarter-hour period unless more than half of that period is required for search or review.

(4) Except for requesters seeking records for a commercial use, OPIC will provide without charge:

(i) The first 100 pages of duplication (or the cost equivalent for other media); and

(ii) The first two hours of search.

(5) If, after deducting free entitlements, the total fee calculated under this section is $25.00 or less, no fee will be charged.

(c) *Notice of anticipated fees in excess of $25.00.* (1) When OPIC determines or estimates that the fees to be assessed in accordance with this section will exceed $25.00, OPIC will notify the requester of the actual or estimated amount of the fees, including a breakdown of fees for search, review, and duplication, unless the requester has indicated a willingness to pay fees as high as those anticipated. If only a portion of the fee can be estimated readily, OPIC will advise the requester accordingly. If the request is for noncommercial use, the notice will specify that the requester is entitled to the statutory entitlements of 100 pages of duplication at no charge, and if the requester is charged search fees, two hours of search time at no charge, and will advise the requester whether those entitlements have been provided.

(2) If OPIC notifies the requester that the actual or estimated fees are in excess of $25.00, the request will not be considered received and further work will not be completed until the requester commits in writing to pay the actual or estimated total fee, or designates some amount of fees the requester is willing to pay, or in the case of a noncommercial use requester who has not yet been provided with the requester's statutory entitlements, designates that the requester seeks only that which can be provided by the statutory entitlements. The requester must provide the commitment or designation in writing, and must, when applicable, designate an exact dollar amount the requester is willing to pay. OPIC is not required to accept payments in installments.

(3) If the requester has indicated a willingness to pay some designated amount of fees, but OPIC estimates that the total fee will exceed that amount, the processing of the request will be tolled when OPIC notifies the requester of the estimated fees in excess of the amount the requester has indicated a willingness to pay. OPIC will inquire whether the requester wishes to revise the amount of fees the requester is willing to pay or modify the request. Once the requester responds, OPIC's time to respond will resume from where it was at the date of the notification.

(4) OPIC's FOIA Office or FOIA Public Liaison is available to assist any requester in reformulating a request to meet the requester's needs at a lower cost.

(d) *Charges for other services.* Although not required to provide special services, if OPIC chooses to do so as a matter of administrative discretion, the direct costs of providing the service will be charged. Examples of such services include certifying that records are true copies, providing multiple copies of the same document, or sending records by means other than first class mail.

(e) *Charging interest.* OPIC may charge interest on any unpaid bill starting on the thirty-first day following the billing date. Interest charges will be assessed at the rate provided in 31 U.S.C. 3717 and will accrue from the billing date until payment is received by OPIC. OPIC will follow the provisions of the Debt Collection Act of 1982 (Pub. L. 97–365, 96 Stat. 1749), as amended, and its administrative procedures, including the use of consumer reporting agencies, collection agencies, and offset.

(f) *Aggregating requests.* If OPIC reasonably believes that a requester or a group of requesters acting in concert is attempting to divide a single request into a series of requests for the purpose of avoiding fees, OPIC may aggregate those requests and charge accordingly. OPIC may presume that multiple requests of this type made within a 30-day period have been made in order to avoid fees. For requests separated by a longer period, OPIC will aggregate them only where there is a reasonable basis for determining that aggregation is warranted in view of all the circumstances involved. Multiple requests involving unrelated matters will not be aggregated.

(g) *Advance payments.* (1) For requests other than those described in paragraphs (g)(2) and (3) of this section OPIC will not require the requester to make an advance payment before work is commenced or continued on a request. Payment owed for work already completed (*i.e.*, payment before copies are sent to a requester) is not an advance payment.

(2) When OPIC determines or estimates that a total fee to be charged under this section will exceed $250.00, it may require that the requester make an advance payment up to the amount of the entire anticipated fee before beginning to process the request. OPIC may elect to process the request prior to collecting fees when it receives a satisfactory assurance of full payment from a requester with a history of prompt payment.

(3) Where a requester has previously failed to pay a properly charged FOIA fee to any agency within thirty calendar days of the billing date, OPIC may require that the requester pay the full amount due, plus any applicable interest on that prior request. OPIC may also require that the requester make an advance payment of the full amount of any anticipated fee before OPIC begins to process a new request or continues to process a pending request or any pending appeal. Where OPIC has a reasonable basis to believe that a requester has misrepresented his or her identity in order to avoid paying outstanding fees, it may require that the requester provide proof of identity.

(4) In cases in which OPIC requires advance payment, OPIC's response time will be tolled and further work will not be completed until the required payment is received. If the requester does not pay the advance payment within thirty calendar days after the date of OPIC's fee letter, OPIC may administratively close the request.

(h) *Other statutes specifically providing for fees.* The fee schedule of this section does not apply to fees charged under any statute that specifically requires an agency to set and collect fees for particular types of records. In instances where records responsive to a request are subject to a statutorily-based fee schedule program, OPIC will inform the requester of the contact information for that program.

§ 706.24 Requirements for waiver or reduction of fees.

(a) Requesters may seek a waiver of fees by submitting a written application demonstrating how disclosure of the requested information is in the public interest because it is likely to contribute significantly to public understanding of the operations and activities of the government and is not primarily in the interest of the requester.

(b) OPIC will furnish records responsive to a request without charge or at a reduced rate when it determines, based on all available information, that the factors described in paragraphs (b)(1)–(3) of this section are satisfied.

(1) Disclosure of the requested information would shed light on the operations or activities of the government. The subject of the request must concern identifiable operations or activities of the Federal government, with a connection that is direct and clear, not remote or attenuated.

(2) Disclosure of the requested information is likely to contribute significantly to public understanding of those operations or activities. This factor is satisfied when the following criteria are met:

(i) Disclosure of the requested records must be meaningfully informative about government operations or activities. The disclosure of information that already is in the public domain, in either the same or a substantially identical form, would not be meaningfully informative if nothing new would be added to the public's understanding.

(ii) The disclosure must contribute to the understanding of a reasonably broad audience of persons interested in the subject, as opposed to the individual understanding of the requester. A requester's expertise in the subject area as well as his or her ability and intention to effectively convey information to the public shall be considered. It shall ordinarily be presumed that a representative of the news media satisfies this consideration.

(3) The disclosure must not be primarily in the commercial interest of the requester. To determine whether disclosure of the requested information is primarily in the commercial interest of the requester, OPIC will consider the following factors:

(i) OPIC shall identify whether the requester has any commercial interest that would be furthered by the requested disclosure. A commercial interest includes any commercial, trade, or profit interest. Requesters shall be given an opportunity to provide explanatory information regarding this consideration.

(ii) If there is a commercial interest, OPIC will determine whether that is the primary interest furthered by the request. A waiver or reduction of fees is justified when the requirements of paragraphs (b)(1) and (2) of this section are satisfied and any commercial interest is not the primary interest furthered by the request. OPIC will ordinarily presume that when a news media requester has satisfied factors in paragraphs (b)(1) and (2) of this section, the request is not primarily in the commercial interest of the requester. Disclosure to data brokers or others who merely compile and market government information for direct economic return will not be presumed to primarily serve the public interest.

(c) Where only some of the records to be released satisfy the requirements for a waiver of fees, a waiver shall be granted for those records.

(d) Requests for a waiver or reduction of fees should be made when the request is first submitted to OPIC and should address the criteria referenced above. A requester may submit a fee waiver request at a later time so long as the underlying record request is pending or on administrative appeal. When a requester who has committed to pay fees subsequently asks for a waiver of those fees and that waiver is denied, the requester will be required to pay any costs incurred up to the date the fee waiver request was received.

Subpart D—Processing of Requests for Non-Public Records

§ 706.30 Responsibility for responding to requests.

(a) *Authority to grant or deny requests.* The OPIC President and CEO or designee is authorized to grant or to deny any requests for records.

(b) *Consultation, referral, and coordination.* When reviewing records responsive to a request, OPIC will determine whether another agency of the Federal Government is better able to determine whether the record is exempt from disclosure under the FOIA. As to any such record, OPIC will proceed in one of the following ways:

(1) *Consultation.* When records originated with OPIC, but contain within

them information of interest to another agency or other Federal Government office, OPIC will typically consult with that other entity prior to making a release determination.

(2) *Referral*. (i) When OPIC believes that a different agency is best able to determine whether to disclose the record, OPIC will typically refer the responsibility for responding to the request regarding that record to that agency. Ordinarily, the agency that originated the record is presumed to be the best agency to make the disclosure determination. However, if OPIC and the originating agency jointly agree that OPIC is in the best position to respond regarding the record, then the record may be handled as a consultation.

(ii) Whenever OPIC refers any part of the responsibility for responding to a request to another agency, it will document the referral, maintain a copy of the record that it refers, and notify the requester of the referral, informing the requester of the name(s) of the agency to which the record was referred, including that agency's FOIA contact information.

(3) *Coordination*. The standard referral procedure is not appropriate where disclosure of the identity of the agency to which the referral would be made could harm an interest protected by an applicable exemption, such as the exemptions that protect personal privacy or national security interests. For example, if in responding to a request for records on a living third party, OPIC locates within its files records originating with a law enforcement agency, and if the existence of that law enforcement interest in the third party was not publicly known, then to disclose that law enforcement interest could cause an unwarranted invasion of the personal privacy of the third party. Similarly, if OPIC locates within its files material originating with an Intelligence Community agency, and the involvement of that agency in the matter is classified and not publicly acknowledged, then to disclose or give attribution to the involvement of that Intelligence Community agency could cause national security harms. In such instances, in order to avoid harm to an interest protected by an applicable exemption, OPIC should coordinate with the originating agency to seek its views on the disclosability of the record. The release determination for the record that is the subject of the coordination should then be conveyed to the requester by OPIC.

(c) *Classified information*. On receipt of any request involving a record containing information that has been classified or may be appropriate for classification by another agency under any applicable executive order concerning the classification of records, OPIC must refer the responsibility for responding to the request to the agency that classified the information, or that should consider the information for classification. Whenever OPIC's record contains information that has been derivatively classified (for example, when it contains information classified by another agency), OPIC must refer the responsibility for responding to that portion of the request to the agency that classified the underlying information.

(d) *Timing of responses to consultations and referrals*. All consultations and referrals will be handled according to the date that the first agency received the perfected FOIA request.

(e) *Agreements regarding consultations and referrals*. OPIC may establish agreements with other agencies to eliminate the need for consultations or referrals with respect to particular types of records.

§ 706.31 Timing of responses to requests.

(a) *In general*. OPIC ordinarily will process requests according to their order of receipt within their appropriate track under paragraph (b) of this section. The response time will commence on the date that the request is received by the FOIA Office, but in any event not later than ten working days after the request is first received by OPIC. Any time tolled under subparagraph (c) of this section does not count against OPIC's response time.

(b) *Multitrack processing*. OPIC has a track for requests that are granted expedited processing, in accordance with the standards set forth in paragraph (f) of this section. Non-expedited requests will be placed into a "simple" or "complex" track based on the estimated amount of work or time needed to process the request. OPIC will consider the number of records requested, the number of pages involved in processing the request, and the need for consultations or referrals. OPIC will advise the requester into which track the request falls and, when appropriate, will offer requesters the opportunity to narrow or modify the request so that it can be placed in a different track.

(c) *Tolling of response time.* OPIC may toll its response time once to seek clarification of a request in accordance with § 706.11(b) or as needed to resolve fee issues in accordance with §§ 706.22(c) and 706.23(d) of this part. The response time will resume upon OPIC's receipt of the requester's clarification or upon resolution of the fee issue.

(d) *Unusual circumstances.* Whenever the statutory time limits for processing cannot be met because of "unusual circumstances" as defined in the FOIA, and OPIC extends the time limits on that basis, OPIC will notify the requester in writing of the unusual circumstances involved and of the date by which OPIC estimates processing of the request will be completed. Where the extension exceeds ten working days, the requester will be provided an opportunity to modify the request or agree to an alternative time period for processing the original or modified request. OPIC will make its FOIA Office and its FOIA Public Liaison available for this purpose and will notify the requester of the availability of the Office of Government Services (OGIS) dispute resolution services.

(e) *Aggregating requests.* For the purposes of satisfying unusual circumstances under the FOIA, OPIC may aggregate requests in cases where it reasonably appears that multiple requests, submitted either by a requester or by a group of requesters acting in concert, constitute a single request that would otherwise involve unusual circumstances. OPIC will not aggregate multiple requests that involve unrelated matters.

(f) *Expedited processing.* (1) Requests and appeals will be processed on an expedited basis whenever it is determined that they involve:

(i) Circumstances in which the lack of expedited processing could reasonably be expected to pose an imminent threat to the life or physical safety of an individual;

(ii) An urgency to inform the public about an actual or alleged Federal government activity, if made by a person who is primarily engaged in disseminating information;

(2) A request for expedited processing may be made at any time.

(3) A requester who seeks expedited processing must submit a statement, certified to be true and correct, explaining in detail the basis for making the request for expedited processing. For example, under paragraph (f)(1)(ii) of this section, a requester who is not a full-time member of the news media must establish that the requester is a person whose primary activity or occupation is information dissemination, though it need not be the requester's sole occupation. Such a requester also must establish a particular urgency to inform the public about the government activity involved in the request—one that extends beyond the public's right to know about government activity generally. The existence of numerous articles published on a given subject can be helpful in establishing the requirement that there be an "urgency to inform" the public on the topic. OPIC may waive the formal certification requirement in its administrative discretion.

(4) OPIC shall notify the requester within ten calendar days of the receipt of a request for expedited processing of its decision whether to grant or deny expedited processing. If expedited processing is granted, the request shall be given priority, placed in the processing track for expedited requests, and shall be processed as soon as practicable. If OPIC denies expedited processing, any appeal of that decision which complies with the procedures set forth in § 706.34 of this subpart shall be acted on expeditiously.

§ 706.32 Responses to requests.

(a) *In general.* To the extent practicable, OPIC will communicate electronically with requesters who have access to the internet.

(b) *Acknowledgments of requests.* If a request will take longer than ten days to process, OPIC will send the requester an acknowledgment letter that assigns the request an individualized tracking number. The letter will include a brief description of the records sought to allow requesters to more easily keep track of requests.

(c) *Grants of requests.* OPIC will notify the requester in writing if it makes a determination to grant a request in full or in part. The notice will inform the requester of any fees charged under § 706.22 of this part and of the availability of the FOIA Public Liaison to offer assistance. OPIC will disclose the requested records to the requester promptly upon payment of any applicable fees.

(d) *Adverse determinations of requests.* OPIC will notify the requester in writing if it makes an adverse determination denying a request in any respect. Adverse determinations, or denials of requests, include decisions that: The requested record is exempt, in whole or in part; the request does not reasonably describe the records sought; the information requested is not a record subject to the FOIA; the requested record does not exist, cannot be located, or has been destroyed; or the requested record is not readily reproducible in the form or format sought by the requester. Adverse determinations also include denials involving fees or fee waiver matters or denials of requests for expedited processing.

(e) *Content of denial letter.* The denial letter will be signed by the person responsible for the denial, and will include:

(1) The name and title or position of the person responsible for the denial;

(2) A brief statement of the reasons for the denial, including any FOIA exemptions applied;

(3) An estimate of the volume of any records or information withheld, for example, by providing the number of pages or some other reasonable form of estimation. This estimation is not required if the volume is otherwise indicated by deletions marked on records that are disclosed in part, or if providing an estimate would harm an interest protected by an applicable exemption;

(4) A brief description of the types of information withheld and the reasons for doing so. A description and explanation are not required if providing it would harm an interest protected by an applicable exemption;

(5) A statement that the denial may be appealed under Section 706.34(a) of this subpart, and a description of the appeal requirements;

(6) A statement notifying the requester of the assistance available from OPIC's FOIA Public Liaison and dispute resolution services offered by OGIS; and

(7) Notice of any fees charged under § 706.23 of this part.

(f) *Markings on released documents.* Records disclosed in part must be marked clearly to show the amount of information deleted and the exemption under which the deletion was made unless doing so would harm an interest protected by an applicable exemption. If technically feasible, the location of the information deleted will be indicated on the record.

(g) *Notice of record exclusions.* (1) In the event that OPIC identifies records that may be subject to exclusion from the requirements of the FOIA pursuant to 5 U.S.C. 552(c), the agency will confer with the Department of Justice, Office of Information Policy, to obtain approval to apply the exclusion.

(2) OPIC will maintain an administrative record of the process of invocation and approval of the exclusion by OIP.

§ 706.33 Confidential commercial information.

(a) *Definitions*—(1) *Confidential commercial information* means commercial or financial information obtained by the agency from a submitter that may be protected from disclosure under Exemption 4 of the FOIA. Exemption 4 protects certain:

(i) Trade secrets as defined under FOIA law; or

(ii) Commercial or financial information that is privileged or confidential as defined under FOIA law.

(2) *Submitter* means any person or entity, including a corporation, State, or foreign government, but not including another Federal Government entity, that provides confidential commercial

information to the Federal government, directly or indirectly.

(b) *Designation of confidential commercial information.* All submitters may designate, by appropriate markings, any portions of their submissions that they consider to be protected from disclosure under the FOIA. These markings will be considered by OPIC in responding to a FOIA request but such markings (or the absence of such markings) will not be dispositive as to whether the marked information is ultimately released. Unless otherwise requested and approved these markings will be considered no longer applicable ten years after submission or five years after the close of the associated project, whichever is later.

(c) *When notice to submitters is required.* (1) Except as provided in paragraph (d) of this section, OPIC's FOIA Office will use reasonable efforts to notify a submitter in writing whenever:

(i) The requested information has been designated in good faith by the submitter as confidential commercial information protected from disclosure under Exemption 4; or

(ii) OPIC has reason to believe that the requested information may be protected from disclosure under Exemption 4, but has not yet determined whether the information is protected from disclosure.

(2) This notification will describe the nature and scope of the request, advise the submitter of its right to submit written objections in response to the request, and provide a reasonable time for response. The notice will either describe the commercial information requested or include copies of the requested records or portions of records containing the information. In cases involving a voluminous number of submitters, notice may be made by posting or publishing the notice in a place or manner reasonably likely to inform the submitters of the proposed disclosure, instead of sending individual notifications.

(d) *Exceptions to submitter notice requirements.* The notice requirements of this section shall not apply if:

(1) OPIC determines that the information is exempt under the FOIA, and therefore will not be disclosed;

(2) The information has been lawfully published or has been officially made available to the public;

(3) Disclosure of the information is required by a statute other than the FOIA or by a regulation issued in accordance with the requirements of Executive Order 12600 of June 23, 1987; or

(4) The designation made by the submitter under paragraph (b) of this section appears obviously frivolous. In such case, OPIC will give the submitter written notice of any final decision to disclose the information within a reasonable number of days prior to a specified disclosure date.

(e) *Opportunity to object to disclosure.*

(1) OPIC will specify a reasonable time period within which the submitter must respond to the notice referenced above.

(2) If a submitter has any objections to disclosure, it should provide OPIC with a detailed written statement that specifies all grounds for withholding the particular information under any exemption of the FOIA. In setting forth such grounds, the submitter should explain the basis of its belief that the nondisclosure of any item of information requested is mandated or permitted by law. In order to rely on Exemption 4 as a basis for nondisclosure, the submitter shall explain why the information is considered a trade secret or commercial or financial information that is privileged or confidential as defined under FOIA law.

(3) A submitter who fails to respond within the time period specified in the notice shall be considered to have no objection to disclosure of the information. OPIC is not required to consider any information received after the date of any disclosure decision. Any information provided by a submitter under this subpart may itself be subject to disclosure under the FOIA.

(4) The period for providing OPIC with objections to disclosure of information may be extended by OPIC upon receipt of a written request for an extension from the submitter. Such written request shall set forth the date upon which any objections are expected to be completed and shall provide reasonable justification for the extension. In its discretion, OPIC may permit more than one extension.

(f) *Analysis of objections.* OPIC will consider a submitter's objections and specific grounds for nondislosure in deciding whether to disclose the requested information.

(g) *Notice of intent to disclose.* If OPIC decides to disclosure information over the objection of a submitter, OPIC will notify the submitter of its determination at least five working days prior to release of the information. The notification will include:

(1) A statement of the reasons why each of the submitter's disclosure objections was not sustained;

(2) A description of the information to be disclosed, or a copy thereof; and

(3) A specified disclosure date, which shall be a reasonable time subsequent to the notice.

(h) *Notice of FOIA lawsuit.* Whenever a requester files a FOIA lawsuit seeking to compel the disclosure of confidential commercial information, OPIC will promptly notify the submitter.

(i) *Requester notification.* OPIC will notify a requester whenever it provides the submitter with notice and an opportunity to object to disclosure; whenever it notifies the submitter of its intent to disclose the requested information; and whenever a submitter files a lawsuit to prevent the disclosure of the information.

§ 706.34 Administrative appeals.

(a) *Requirements for making an appeal.* A requester may appeal any adverse determinations to OPIC's Vice President and General Counsel at *FOIA@opic.gov* or 1100 New York Avenue NW., Washington, DC 20527. Examples of adverse determinations are provided in Section 706.06(c) of this subpart. The requester must make the appeal in writing and it must be postmarked, or in the case of electronic submissions, transmitted, within ninety calendar days after the date of the response. The appeal should clearly identify OPIC's determination that is being appealed and the assigned request number. The requester should mark both the appeal letter and envelope, or subject line of the electronic transmission, "Freedom of Information Act Appeal."

(b) *Adjudication of appeals.* OPIC's Vice President and General Counsel or his/her designee will render a written decision within twenty working days after the date of OPIC's receipt of the appeal, unless an extension of up to ten working days is deemed necessary due to unusual circumstances. The requester will be notified in writing of any extension.

(c) *Decisions on appeals.* A decision that upholds the initial determination will contain a written statement that identifies the reasons for the affirmance, including any FOIA exemptions applied, and will provide the requester with notification of the statutory right to file a lawsuit and the ability to request dispute resolution from the Office of Government Information Services. If an initial determination is remanded or modified on appeal the requester will be notified in writing. OPIC's FOIA Office will then process the request in accordance with that appeal determination and respond directly to the requester. If an appeal is granted in whole or in part, the information will be made available promptly, provided the requirements of Section 706.23 regarding payment of fees are satisfied.

(d) *Engaging in dispute resolution services provided by OGIS.* Dispute resolution is a voluntary process. If OPIC agrees to participate in the dispute resolution services provided by OGIS, it will actively engage as a partner to the process in an attempt to resolve the dispute.

(e) *When appeal is required.* Before seeking court review, a requester generally must first submit a timely administrative appeal.

PART 707—ACCESS TO AND SAFEGUARDING OF PERSONAL INFORMATION IN RECORDS OF THE OVERSEAS PRIVATE INVESTMENT CORPORATION

Subpart A—General

Subpart B—Requests for Access to Records; Amendment of Records, Accounting of Disclosures; Notice of Court Ordered Disclosures

Subpart C—Exceptions

AUTHORITY: 5 U.S.C. 552a.

SOURCE: 79 FR 8614, Feb. 13, 2014, unless otherwise noted.

Subpart A—General

§ 707.11 Scope and purpose.

This part applies to all records in systems of records maintained by OPIC that are retrievable by an individual's name or personal identifier. The rules in this part describe the procedures by which individuals may request access to records about themselves, request amendment or correction of those records, or request an accounting of disclosures of records by OPIC. These rules should be read in conjunction with the Privacy Act of 1974, 5 U.S.C. 552a, which provides additional information about records maintained on individuals.

§ 707.12 Definitions.

As used in this part:

(a) *Individual* means a citizen of the United States or an alien lawfully admitted for permanent residence;

(b) *Maintain* includes maintain, collect, use, or disseminate;

(c) *Record* means any item, collection, or grouping of information about an individual that is maintained by an agency, including, but not limited to, his education, financial transactions, medical history, and criminal or employment history and that contains his name, or the identifying number, symbol, or other identifying particular assigned to the individual, such as a finger or voice print or photograph;

(d) *System of records* mean a group of any records under the control of OPIC from which information is retrieved by the name of the individual or by some identifying number, symbol, or other identifying particular assigned to the individual;

(e) *Statistical record* means a record in a system of records maintained for statistical research or reporting purposes only and not used in whole or in part in making any determination about an identifiable individual, except as provided by 13 U.S.C. 8;

(f) *Routine use* means, with respect to the disclosure of a record, the use of such record for a purpose which is compatible with the purpose for which it was collected.

§ 707.13 Preservation of records.

OPIC preserves all correspondence pertaining to the requests that it receives under this part, as well as copies of all requested records, until disposition or destruction is authorized pursuant to title 44 of the United States Code or the General Records Schedule 14 of the National Archives and Records Administration. Records that are identified as responsive to a request will not be disposed of or destroyed while they are the subject of a pending request, appeal, or lawsuit under the Privacy Act.

Subpart B—Requests for Access to Records; Amendment of Records, Accounting of Disclosures; Notice of Court Ordered Disclosures

§ 707.21 Requests for access to or copies of records.

(a) *How to submit*. An individual may request access to or copies of records maintained by OPIC that are retrieved by an individual's personal identifier. To make a request for records a requester must submit a written request to the Director of Human Resources Management either by mail or delivery to Overseas Private Investment Corporation, 1100 New York Avenue NW., Washington, DC 20527 or electronic mail to *Privacy@opic.gov*. The envelope or subject line should read "Privacy Act Request" to ensure proper routing. Access to records maintained by OPIC will be provided only by appointment. No officer or employee of OPIC shall provide an individual with any records under this part until a written request as described in paragraph (b) of this section is provided and the identity of the individual is verified as described in paragraph (c) of this section.

(b) *Information to include*. All requests under this section must:

(1) Be in writing and be signed by the requester. Unless the requester is a current officer or employee of OPIC, the letter must also be duly acknowledged before a notary public or other authorized public official or signed under 28 U.S.C. 1746, a law that permits statements to be made under penalty of perjury as a substitute for notarization;

(2) Provide information sufficient to verify the identity of the requester, including the requester's full name, current address, date of birth, place of birth, or the system of record identification name or number. Also include a clearly legible copy of a valid form of identification. If the request is being made by a parent or guardian on behalf of another, also include the same information for the individual who is the subject of the request along with a court order, birth certificate, or similar document proving the guardianship. OPIC will review the sufficiency of identity evidence under paragraph (c) of this section;

(3) Provide information sufficient to accurately identify the records or information so that OPIC staff can locate the records with a reasonable amount of effort. At minimum this should include the full name, the system of record identification name, or the system identification number for the individual who is the subject of the records. Provision of a social security number is optional. If possible, also include a description of the records as well as providing a record creation time range and the name of the systems that should be searched. A description of OPIC's system of records can be located in the "Privacy Act Compilation" published by the National Archives and Records Administration's Office of the Federal Register. Each system of records is also published in the FEDERAL REGISTER;

(4) Specify whether the individual wishes access to or copies of the information pertaining to him. If access is requested, provide at least one preferred date and hour for which an appointment is requested during regular business hours as provided in paragraph (a) of this section. OPIC encourages appointments to be made at least one week in advance and for a requester to provide at least three preferred appointment times; and

(5) Include an agreement to pay fees or an agreement to pay fees up to a specified amount under § 707.27. A request that does not include an agreement to pay fees will be considered an agreement to pay fees up to $25.00.

(c) *Verification of identity*. Prior to providing any requested information about an individual, the Director of Human Resources Management shall verify the identity of the individual. If the requester is acting as the guardian of the individual who is the subject of the records, the Director will also verify the identity of the individual who is the subject of the records, the relationship between the requester and the subject individual, and that the requester is acting on behalf of the subject individual. In order to verify identity, the Director shall require the individual to provide reasonable proof of identity such as a valid driver's license, identification card, passport, employee identification card, or any other identifying information. The Director shall deny any request where she determines, at her sole discretion, that the evidence offered to verify the identity of an individual is insufficient to conclusively establish the identity of the individual.

(d) *Release of records*. Originals and record copies will not be released from the files of OPIC. Individuals will not be permitted to disturb any record files or to remove records from designated place of examination. If copies were requested in the request letter, copies will be furnished upon payment of the fees prescribed in § 707.27.

(e) *Denial of request.* If the Director of Human Resources Management declines any request submitted under this section, the denial will be made in writing and contain a brief description of the denial. Denials include a determination that an individual has not provided adequate evidence to verify identity under paragraph (c) of this section, a determination that the record cannot be located, and a withholding of a record in whole or in part. In the event of a denial, the requester may file a written appeal within thirty days of the date of notification, following the procedures in § 707.25.

§ 707.22 Requests to permit access of records to an individual other than the individual to whom the record pertains.

(a) *Access by an authorized individual.* An individual requester who wishes to be accompanied by another individual when reviewing records pertaining to the requester must provide OPIC with a signed, written statement authorizing discussion of the information contained in the records in the presence of the accompanying individual. Both parties will be required to verify their identity under § 707.21(c) before access is granted.

(b) *Release to an authorized individual.* An individual requester who wishes to have copies of records pertaining to the requester released to another individual must provide OPIC with a written statement authorizing release of the information contained in the records to the other individual. The identity of the individual to whom the record pertains must be verified under § 707.21(c) before release is authorized.

(c) *Access or release to parent or guardian.* Guardians will be provided access or copies under the provisions of § 707.21.

§ 707.23 Requests for amendment of records.

(a) *How to submit.* Unless a record is not subject to amendment, per paragraphs (g) and (h) of this section, an individual may request an amendment of a record to correct information the individual believes is not accurate, relevant, timely, or complete. The request must be in writing, labeled "Privacy Act Request," and should be addressed to the Director of Human Resources Management. The request may either be mailed to OPIC or delivered to the receptionist at 1100 New York Avenue NW., Washington, DC 20527, during regular business hours, between 8:45 a.m. and 5:30 p.m., Monday through Friday, excluding public holidays. The request will be considered received when actually delivered to or, if mailed, when it is actually received by the Director of Human Resources Management.

(b) *Information to include.* All requests under this section must:

(1) Be in writing and be signed by the requester. Unless the requester is a current officer or employee of OPIC, the letter must also be duly acknowledged before a notary public or other authorized public official or signed under 28 U.S.C. 1746, a law that permits statements to be made under penalty of perjury as a substitute for notarization;

(2) Provide information sufficient to verify the identity of the requester, including the requester's full name, current address, date of birth, place of birth, or the system of record identification name or number. Also include a clearly legible copy of a valid form of identification. If the request is being made by a parent or guardian on behalf of another, also include the same information for the individual who is the subject of the request along with a court order, birth certificate, or similar document proving the guardianship. OPIC will review the sufficiency of identity evidence under paragraph (c) of this section;

(3) Provide information sufficient to accurately identify each record so that OPIC staff can locate the record and information with a reasonable amount of effort. At minimum this should include the full name, the system of record identification name, or the system record identification number for the individual who is the subject of the records and the name for each system that you believe the record is located in. Provision of a social security number is optional. If possible, you should also include a description of the records and provide a record creation

time range. A description of OPIC's systems of records can be located in the "Privacy Act Compilation" published by the National Archives and Records Administration's Office of the Federal Register. Each system of records is also published in the FEDERAL REGISTER;

(4) Specify the correction requested; and

(5) Detail the basis for the requester's belief that the records and information are not accurate, relevant, timely, or complete. This includes providing substantial and reliable evidence sufficient to permit OPIC to determine whether an amendment is in order.

(c) *Verification of identity*. Prior to amending information about an individual, the Director of Human Resources Management shall verify the identity of the requesting individual. If the requester is acting as the guardian of the individual who is the subject of the records, the Director will also verify the identity of the individual who is the subject of the records, the relationship between the requester and the subject individual, and that the requester is acting on behalf of the subject individual. In order to verify identity, the Director shall require the individual to provide reasonable proof of identity such as a valid driver's license, identification card, passport, employee identification card, or any other identifying information. The Director shall deny any request where she determines, at her sole discretion, that the evidence offered to verify the identity of an individual is insufficient to conclusively establish the identity of the individual.

(d) *Acknowledgment of request*. If a request will take longer than ten (10) business days to process, OPIC will send the requester an acknowledgment letter. Any request that Director of Human Resources Management determines does not describe records or information in enough detail to permit the staff to promptly locate the records; does not describe the correction requested in enough detail to permit the staff to make a correction; or does not reasonably specify the amendment requested or its basis will be returned without prejudice to the requester and treated as not received.

(e) *Determination*. The Director of Human Resources Management will provide a determination on a request under this section within thirty (30) days from receipt.

(1) *Amendment*. The Director of Human Resources Management will notify the requester in writing if the amendment is made and provide the individual an opportunity to request a copy of the amended record.

(2) *Denial*. The Director of Human Resources Management will notify the requester in writing if she denies any portion of a request made under this section. The denial will include a brief explanation of the reason for the refusal and the right of the individual to file an appeal within thirty (30) days, following the procedures in § 707.25. In the event an appeal is denied, a requester may file a statement of disagreement with OPIC as described in § 707.25(c).

(f) *Notification of amendment*. Within thirty (30) days of the amendment or correction of a record or the filing of a statement of disagreement, OPIC will notify all persons, organizations, or agencies to which it previously disclosed the record, if an accounting of that disclosure was made. If an individual has filed a statement of disagreement, OPIC will attach a copy of it to the disputed record whenever the record is disclosed in the future and may also attach a concise statement of its reasons for denying the request to amend or correct.

(g) *Records not subject to amendment*. The following records are not subject to amendment:

(1) Transcripts of testimony given under oath or written statements made under oath;

(2) Transcripts of grand jury proceedings, judicial proceedings, or quasi-judicial proceedings, which are the official record of those proceedings;

(3) Presentence records that originated with the courts; and

(4) Records in systems of records that have been exempted from amendment and correction under the Privacy Act, 5 U.S.C. 552a(j) or (k) or by notice published in the FEDERAL REGISTER.

(h) *No amendment permitted*. No part of these rules shall be construed to permit:

(1) The alteration of evidence presented in the course of judicial, quasi-judicial, or quasi-legislative proceedings;

(2) Collateral attack upon any matter which has been the subject of judicial or quasi-judicial action; or

(3) An amendment or correction which would be in violation of an existing statute, executive order, or regulation.

§ 707.24 Requests for an accounting of record disclosures.

(a) *How to submit.* Unless an accounting of disclosures is not required to be kept under paragraph (e) of this section, an individual may request an accounting of all disclosures OPIC has made of a record, maintained in a system of records and about the individual, to another person, organization, or agency. The request must be in writing, labeled "Privacy Act Request," and should be addressed to the Director of Human Resources Management. The request may either be mailed to OPIC or delivered to the receptionist at 1100 New York Avenue NW., Washington, DC 20527, during regular business hours, between 8:45 a.m. and 5:30 p.m., Monday through Friday, excluding public holidays. The request will be considered received when actually delivered to or, if mailed, when it is actually received by the Director of Human Resources Management.

(b) *Information to include.* All requests under this section must:

(1) Be in writing and be signed by the requester. Unless the requester is a current officer or employee of OPIC, the letter must also be duly acknowledged before a notary public or other authorized public official or signed under 28 U.S.C. 1746, a law that permits statements to be made under penalty of perjury as a substitute for notarization;

(2) Provide information sufficient to verify the identity of the requester, including the requester's full name, current address, date of birth, place of birth, or the system of record identification name or number. Also include a clearly legible copy of a valid form of identification. If the request is being made by a parent or guardian on behalf of another, also include the same information for the individual who is the subject of the request along with a court order, birth certificate, or similar document proving the guardianship. OPIC will review the sufficiency of identity evidence under paragraph (c) of this section;

(3) Provide information sufficient to accurately identify the records or information so that OPIC staff can locate the records with a reasonable amount of effort. At minimum this should include the full name, the system of record identification name, or the system record identification number for the individual who is the subject of the records and the name for each system that you believe the record is located in. Provision of a social security number is optional. If possible, you should also include a description of the records and provide a time range. A description of OPIC's system of records can be located in the "Privacy Act Compilation" published by the National Archives and Records Administration's Office of the Federal Register. Each system of records is also published in the FEDERAL REGISTER;

(4) Include an agreement to pay fees or an agreement to pay fees up to a specified amount under § 707.27. A request that does not include an agreement to pay fees will be considered an agreement to pay fees up to $25.00.

(c) *Verification of identity.* Prior to providing any requested information about an individual, the Director of Human Resources Management shall verify the identity of the requesting individual. If the requester is acting as the guardian of the individual who is the subject of the records, the Director will also verify the identity of the individual who is the subject of the records, the relationship between the requester and the subject individual, and that the requester is acting on behalf of the subject individual. In order to verify identity, the Director shall require the individual to provide reasonable proof of identity such as a valid driver's license, identification card, passport, employee identification card, or any other identifying information. The Director shall deny any request where she determines, at her sole discretion, that the evidence offered to verify the identity of an individual is insufficient to conclusively *establish* the identity of the individual.

(d) *Determination.* The Director of Human Resources Management will provide a requester with one of the following:

(1) *Provision of accounting of disclosures.* If the request is granted, the Director of Human Resources Management will provide the individual with an accounting containing the date, nature, and purpose of each disclosure, as well as the name and address of the person, organization, or agency to which the disclosure was made.

(2) *Denial.* The Director of Human Resources Management will notify the individual in writing if she denies any portion of a request made under this section. The denial will include a brief explanation of the reason for the refusal and the right of the individual to request a review thereof under the provisions of § 707.25.

(e) *Disclosures where an accounting of disclosures is not required.* OPIC need not provide an accounting of disclosures where:

(1) The disclosures are of the type for which accountings are not kept. For example, disclosures made to employees within the agency; or

(2) The disclosure was made in response to a written request from a law enforcement agency for authorized law enforcement purposes.

§ 707.25 Appeals.

An individual may appeal a denial made under §§ 707.21 through 707.23 within thirty (30) days of the notification of such denial.

(a) *How to submit.* The appeal must be in writing, labeled "Privacy Act Appeal," and should be addressed to the Executive Vice President. The request may either be mailed to OPIC or delivered to the receptionist at 1100 New York Avenue NW., Washington, DC 20527, during regular business hours, between 8:45 a.m. and 5:30 p.m., Monday through Friday, excluding public holidays.

(b) *Information to include.* All requests under this section must:

(1) Be in writing and be signed by the requester;

(2) Be clearly labeled "PRIVACY ACT APPEAL" on both the letter and the envelope;

(3) Clearly reference the determination being appealed; and

(4) Provide support for your information, including documentation provided in the initial determination and any additional information.

(b) *Appeal determination.* The Executive Vice President will advise the individual of OPIC's determination within thirty (30) business days. If the Executive Vice President is unable to provide a determination within thirty business days, the individual will be advised in writing of the reason before the expiry of the thirty business days.

(1) *Overturn initial determination.* If the Executive Vice President grants the appeal and overturns the initial determination in whole or part, the individual will be notified in writing and the requested action taken promptly along with any other steps OPIC would have taken had the initial determination come to the same result as the appeal.

(2) *Uphold initial determination.* If the Executive Vice President denies the appeal and upholds the initial determination in whole or in part, the individual will be notified in writing and provided with an explanation. In cases where a denial of amendment or correction is upheld, the individual will also be notified of the ability to file a statement of disagreement under paragraph (c) of this section.

(c) *Statement of disagreement.* If an individual is denied a request to amend a record in whole or in part and that denial is upheld on appeal, the individual may file a statement of disagreement. Statements of disagreement must be concise, clearly identify each part of any record that is disputed, and should be no longer than one typed page for each fact disputed. The statement of disagreement will be placed in the system of records that contains the disputed record and the record will be marked to indicate that a statement of disagreement has been filed. The statement of disagreement will be attached to any future releases of the disputed record and may be accompanied by a concise statement from OPIC explaining its denial.

§ 707.26 Notification of court-ordered disclosures.

(a) Except in cases under paragraph (c) of this section, when a record pertaining to an individual is required to be disclosed by court order, OPIC will make reasonable efforts to provide notice of this to the individual. If OPIC cannot locate the individual, notice will be deemed sufficient for this part if it is mailed to the individual's last known address. The notice will contain a copy of the order and a description of the information disclosed.

(b) Notice will be given within a reasonable time after OPIC's receipt of the order, unless the order is not a matter of public record. In those cases, the notice will be given only after the order becomes public.

(c) Notice is not required if disclosure is made from an exempt system of records.

§ 707.27 Fees.

(a) The fees to be charged for making copies of any records provided to an individual under this part are ten (10) cents per page. No fees will be charged for search or review.

(b) At its discretion, OPIC may grant a request for special services such as mailing copies by means other than first class mail or providing document certification. All special services provided to the requester will be provided at cost.

(c) OPIC considers any request under the Privacy Act to be an authorization to incur up to $25.00 in fees unless a request states otherwise.

(d) OPIC may condition access to records or copies of records upon full payment of any fees due.

(e) All payments under this part must be in the form of a check or bank draft denominated in U.S. currency. Checks should be made payable to the order of the United States Treasury and mailed or hand delivered to OPIC at 1100 New York Avenue NW., Washington, DC 20527.

Subpart C—Exceptions

§ 707.31 Specific exemptions.

The provisions of 5 U.S.C. 552a(c)(3), (d), (e)(1), (e)(4)(G), (H) and (I) and (f) shall not apply to any system of records maintained by OPIC that is—

(a) Subject to the provisions of 5 U.S.C. 552(b)(1);

(b) Composed of Investigatory material compiled for law enforcement purposes other than those specified in 5 U.S.C. 552a(j)(2);

(c) Required by statute to be maintained and used solely as statistical records;

(d) Composed of investigatory material compiled solely for the purpose of determining suitability, eligibility or qualifications for Federal civilian employment, military service, Federal contracts or access to classified information, but only to the extent that OPIC may determine, in its sole discretion, that the disclosure of such material would reveal the identity of the source who, subsequent to September 27, 1975, furnished information to the Government under an express promise that the identity of the source would be held in confidence or, prior to such date, under an implied promise to such effect; and

(e) Composed of testing or examination materials used solely to determine individual qualifications for appointment or promotion in the Federal service and OPIC determines, in its sole discretion, that disclosure of such materials would compromise the fairness of the testing or examination process.

§ 707.32 Special exemption.

Nothing in this part shall allow an individual access to any information compiled in reasonable anticipation of a civil action or proceeding.

§ 707.33 Other rights and services.

Nothing in this part shall be construed to entitle any person, as of right, to any service or to the disclosure of any record to which such person is not entitled under the Privacy Act.

PART 708—SUNSHINE REGULATIONS

Sec.

708.6 Records of closed meetings.

AUTHORITY: 5 U.S.C. 552b.

SOURCE: 42 FR 13110, Mar. 9, 1977, unless otherwise noted.

§708.1 Purpose and applicability.

The purpose of this part is to effectuate the provisions of the Government in the Sunshine Act. This part applies to the deliberations of a quorum of the Directors of the Corporation required to take action on behalf of the Corporation where such deliberations determine or result in the joint conduct or disposition of official Corporation business, but does not apply to deliberations to take action to open or close a meeting or to release or withhold information under §708.5. Any deliberation to which this part applies is hereinafter in this part referred to as a meeting of the Board of Directors.

§708.2 Open meeting policy.

(a) It is the policy of the Corporation to provide the public with the fullest practicable information regarding the decisionmaking process of the Board of Directors of the Corporation while protecting the rights of individuals and the ability of the Corporation to carry out its responsibilities. In order to effect this policy, every meeting of the Board of Directors shall be open to public observation and will only be closed to public observation if justified under one of the provisions of §708.5. The public is invited to observe and listen to all meetings of the Board of Directors, or portions thereof, open to public observation, but may not participate or record any of the discussions by means of electronic or other devices or cameras. Documents being considered at meetings of the Board of Directors may be obtained subject to the procedures and exemptions set forth in part 706 of this chapter.

(b) Directors of the Corporation shall not jointly conduct or dispose of agency business other than in accordance with this part. This prohibition shall not prevent Directors from considering individually business that is circulated to them sequentially in writing.

(c) The Secretary of the Corporation shall be responsible for assuring that ample space, sufficient visibility, and adequate acoustics are provided for public observation of meetings of the Board of Directors.

§708.3 Scheduling of a meeting.

A decision to hold a meeting of the Board of Directors should be made as provided in the By-laws of the Corporation and at least eight days prior to the scheduled meeting date in order for the Secretary of the Corporation to give the public notice required by §708.4. However in special cases, a majority of the Directors may decide to hold a meeting less than eight days prior to the scheduled meeting date if they determine by a recorded vote that Corporation business requires such meeting at such earlier date. After public announcement of a meeting of the Board of Directors under the provisions of §708.4, the subject matter thereof, or the determination to open or close a meeting, or portion thereof, may only be changed if a majority of the Directors determines by a recorded vote that business so requires and that no earlier announcement of the change is possible.

§708.4 Public announcement.

(a) Except to the extent that such information is exempt from disclosure under the provisions of §708.5, in the case of each meeting of the Board of Directors, the Secretary shall make public announcement at least one week before the meeting, of the time, place, and subject matter of the meeting, whether it is to be open or closed to the public, and the name and telephone number of the official designated by the Corporation to respond to requests for information about the meeting. Such announcement shall be made unless a majority of the Directors determines by a recorded vote that Corporation business requires that such meeting be called at an earlier date, in which case the Secretary shall make public announcement of the time, place, and subject matter of such meeting, and whether open or closed to the public, at the earliest practicable time.

(b) The time or place of a meeting may be changed following the public announcement required by paragraph (a) of this section only if the Secretary publicly announces such change at the earliest practicable time. The subject matter of a meeting, or the determination of the Corporation to open or close a meeting, or portion of a meeting, to the public, may be changed following the public announcement required by this section only if (1) a majority of the Directors determines by a recorded vote that business so requires and that no earlier announcement of the change was possible, and (2) the Secretary publicly announces such change and the vote of each Director upon such change at the earliest practicable time.

(c) The *earliest practicable time*, as used in this subsection, means as soon as possible, which should in few, if any, instances be later than the commencement of the meeting or portion in question.

(d) The Secretary shall use reasonable means to assure that the public is fully informed of the public announcements required by this section. Such public announcements may be made by posting notices in the public areas of the Corporation's headquarters and mailing notices to the persons on a list maintained for those who want to receive such announcements.

(e) Immediately following each public announcement required by this section, notice of the time, place, and subject matter of a meeting, whether the meeting is open or closed, any change in one of the preceding announcements, and the name and telephone number of the official designated by the Corporation to respond to requests for information about the meeting shall also be submitted by the Secretary for publication in the FEDERAL REGISTER.

§ 708.5 Closed meetings.

(a) Meetings of the Board of Directors will be closed to public observation where the Corporation properly determines, according to the procedures set forth in paragraph (c) of this section, that such portion or portions of the meeting or disclosure of such information is likely to:

(1) Disclose matters that are (i) specifically authorized under criteria established by an Executive order to be kept secret in the interests of national defense or foreign policy and are (ii) in fact properly classified pursuant to such Executive order;

(2) Relate solely to the internal personnel rules and practices of an agency;

(3) Disclose matters specifically exempted from disclosure by statute (other than 5 U.S.C. 552), *Provided*, That such statute (i) requires that the matters be withheld from the public in such a manner as to leave no discretion on the issue, or (ii) establishes particular criteria for withholding or refers to particular types of matters to be withheld;

(4) Disclose the trade secrets and commercial or financial information obtained from a person and privileged or confidential;

(5) Involve accusing any person of a crime, or formally censuring any person;

(6) Disclose information of a personal nature where disclosure would constitute a clearly unwarranted invasion of personal privacy;

(7) Disclose investigatory records compiled for law enforcement purposes, or information which if written would be contained in such records, but only to the extent that the production of such records or information would (i) interfere with enforcement proceedings, (ii) deprive a person of a right to a fair trial or an impartial adjudication, (iii) constitute an unwarranted invasion of personal privacy, (iv) disclose the identity of a confidential source and, in the case of a record compiled by a criminal law enforcement authority in the course of a criminal investigation, or by an agency conducting a lawful national security intelligence investigation, confidential information furnished only by the confidential source, (v) disclose investigative techniques and procedures, or (vi) endanger the life or physical safety of law enforcement personnel;

(8) Disclose information the premature disclosure of which would be likely to significantly frustrate implementation of a proposed agency action, except in any instance where the Corporation has already disclosed to the public the content or nature of its proposed action, or where the Corporation is required by law to make such disclosure on its own initiative prior to taking final Corporation action on such proposal; or

(9) Specifically concern the Corporation's participation in a civil action or proceeding, an action in a foreign court or international tribunal, or an arbitration, or the initiation, conduct, or disposition by the Corporation of a particular case of formal Corporation adjudication pursuant to the procedures in 5 U.S.C. 554 or otherwise involving a determination on the record after opportunity for a hearing.

(b) Meetings of the Board of Directors shall not be closed pursuant to paragraph (a) of this section when the Corporation finds that the public interest requires that they be open.

(c)(1) Action to close a meeting, or portion thereof, pursuant to the exemptions defined in paragraph (a) of this section may be initiated by the President or any Director of the Corporation by presentation of a request for closure to the Board of Directors. The person initiating the request for closure shall give the Board of Directors a statement specifying the extent of the proposed closure, the relevant exemptive provisions and the circumstances pertinent to such request, and how the public interest will be served by closure. Such statement shall also be given to the General Counsel of the Corporation to serve as a basis for the certification the General Counsel may determine can be issued in accordance with § 708.6. The General Counsel's determination shall be given to the Board of Directors. Action to close a meeting, or portion thereof, shall be taken only when a majority of the entire membership of the Board of Directors votes to take such action. A separate vote of the Board of Directors shall be taken with respect to each meeting of the Board of Directors a portion or portions of which are proposed to be closed to the public or with respect to any information which is proposed to be withheld. A single vote may be taken with respect to a series of meetings, a portion or portions of which are proposed to be closed to the public, or with respect to any information which is proposed to be withheld. A single vote may be taken with respect to a series of meetings, a portion or portions of which are proposed to be closed to the public, or with respect to any information concerning such series of meetings, so long as each meeting in such series involves the same particular matters and is scheduled to be held no more than thirty days after the initial meeting in such series. The vote of each Director participating in such vote shall be recorded and no proxies shall be allowed.

(2) Whenever any person whose interests may be directly affected by a portion of a meeting requests that the Corporation close such portion to the public for any of the reasons referred to in paragraph (a)(5), (a)(6), or (a)(7) of this section, the Corporation, upon request of any one of its Directors, shall vote by recorded vote whether to close such meeting.

(3) Within one day of any vote taken pursuant to paragraph (c)(1) or (c)(2) of this section, the Secretary shall make publicly available a written copy of such vote reflecting the vote of each member on the question. If a portion of a meeting is to be closed to the public, the Secretary shall, by the close of the business day next succeeding the day of the vote taken pursuant to paragraph (c)(1) or (c)(2) of this section, make publicly available a full written explanation of the Corporation's action closing the portion together with a list of all persons expected to attend the meeting and their affiliation. The information required by this subparagraph shall be disclosed except to the extent that it is exempt from disclosure under the provisions of paragraph (a) of this section.

§ 708.6 Records of closed meetings.

(a) For every meeting of the Board of Directors closed pursuant to § 708.5, the General Counsel of the Corporation shall publicly certify prior to such meeting that, in his or her opinion, the meeting may be closed to the public and shall state each relevant exemptive provision. A copy of such certification, together with a statement from the presiding officer of the meeting setting forth the time and place of the meeting, and the persons present, shall be retained by the Secretary as part of the transcript, recording, or minutes required by paragraph (b) of this section.

(b) The Secretary shall maintain a complete transcript or electronic recording adequate to record fully the proceedings of each meeting, or portion of a meeting, closed to the public, except that in the case of a meeting, or portion of a meeting, closed to the public pursuant to §708.5(a)(9), the Secretary shall maintain either such a transcript or recording, or a set of minutes. Such minutes shall fully and clearly describe all matters discussed and shall provide a full and accurate summary of any actions taken, and the reasons therefor, including a description of each of the views expressed on any item and the record of any roll-call vote (reflecting the vote of each member on the question). All documents considered in connection with any Corporation action shall be identified in such minutes.

(c) The Secretary shall maintain a complete verbatim copy of the transcript, a complete copy of the minutes, or a complete electronic recording of each meeting, or portion of a meeting, closed to the public, for a period of at least two years after such meeting, or until one year after the conclusion of the proceeding of the Board of Directors with respect to which the meeting or portion was held, whichever occurs later.

(d) Within ten days of receipt of a request for information (excluding Saturdays, Sundays, and legal public holidays), the Corporation shall make available to the public, in the Office of Secretary of the Corporation, Washington, DC, the transcript, electronic recording, or minutes (as required by paragraph (b) of this section) of the discussion of any item on the agenda, or of any item of the testimony of any witness received at the meeting, except for such item or items of such discussion or testimony as the Secretary determines to contain information which may be withheld under the provisions of §708.5. Copies of such transcript, or minutes, or a transcription of such recording disclosing the identify of each speaker, shall be furnished to any person at the actual cost of duplication or transcription.

(e) The determination of the Secretary to withhold information pursuant to paragraph (d) of this section may be appealed to the President of the Corporation, in his or her capacity as administrative head of the Corporation. The President will make a determination to withhold or release the requested information within twenty days from the date of receipt of the request for review (excluding Saturdays, Sundays, and legal public holidays).

PART 709—FOREIGN CORRUPT PRACTICES ACT OF 1977

Sec.

AUTHORITY: Sec. 237(1), Foreign Assistance Act of 1961, added by Pub. L. 95–268.

SOURCE: 43 FR 36064, Aug. 15, 1978, unless otherwise noted.

§709.1 Authority and purpose.

(a) These regulations are issued under the general powers of the Overseas Private Investment Corporation (“OPIC”) and pursuant to section 237(1) of the Foreign Assistance Act of 1961, added by Pub. L. 95–268.[1] The Board of

[1] Section 237(1) of that Act states:

(1) No payment may be made under any insurance or reinsurance which is issued under this title on or after the date of enactment of this subsection for any loss occurring with respect to a project, if the preponderant cause of such loss was an act by the investor seeking payment under this title, by a person possessing majority ownership and control of the investor at the time of the act, or by any agent of such investor or controlling person, and a court of the United States has entered a final judgment that such act constituted a violation under the Foreign Corrupt Practices Act of 1977.

(2) Not later than 120 days after the date of enactment of this subsection, the Corporation shall adopt regulations setting forth appropriate conditions under which any person convicted under the Foreign Corrupt Practices Act of 1977 for an offense related to a project insured or otherwise supported by the Corporation shall be suspended, for a period of not more than 5 years, from eligibility to receive any insurance, reinsurance,

Directors of OPIC has authorized the President of OPIC to issue these regulations and to amend them as the President shall deem appropriate.

(b) These regulations prescribe the procedure under which individuals and companies may be suspended, as mandated by section 237(1) of the Foreign Assistance Act of 1961, as amended, from eligibility for OPIC services because of conviction under the Foreign Corrupt Practices Act of 1977 (Pub. L. 95–213) of an offense related to an OPIC-supported project.

(c) The purposes of the suspensions provided herein are to carry out the statutory requirements of Section 237(1) of the Foreign Assistance Act of 1961, as amended, to protect the interest of the United States and to foster full and free competition in international commerce.

(d) The specific provisions of law under which OPIC operates and the general powers conferred on OPIC give OPIC broad discretion in the conduct of its programs. The issuance of these regulations is not to be construed as in any way limiting or derogating from the discretion of OPIC to determine whether or not to support the investment of a particular entity in a particular case.

§ 709.2 Applicability.

These regulations take effect on the date of publication in the FEDERAL REGISTER and govern eligibility for OPIC services for which OPIC has not previously obligated itself.

§ 709.3 Definitions

(a) The *Act* means the Foreign Corrupt Practices Act of 1977.

(b) *Entity* means any individual, association, company, corporation, concern, partnership, or person.

(c) *Offense* means any act or omission to act which has been found by a United States court of competent jurisdiction to constitute, with respect to a particular entity, a violation of the Act, of section 13(b)(2), 13(b)(3) or 30A of the Securities Exchange Act of 1934 (which were added in 1977 by the Act), or of any other provision of law derived from the Act.

(d) *Suspension* means the designation of an entity as ineligible to receive OPIC services through a suspension determination.

(e) *Suspension determination* means a determination by the President of OPIC pursuant to these regulations that an entity is ineligible to receive OPIC services.

guaranty, loan or other financial support authorized by this title.

§ 709.4 Cause for suspension of entities from eligibility.

Any entity which has been convicted of an offense related to a project insured or otherwise supported by OPIC may be suspended from eligibility for additional OPIC services for a period of not more than 5 years pursuant to a suspension determination.

§ 709.5 Procedure.

(a) Upon receipt of an application for OPIC services from any entity which OPIC has reason to believe may have been convicted under the Act the OPIC General Counsel shall ascertain whether a conviction has been entered against such entity under the Act and, if so, whether it was entered for an offense related to a project insured or otherwise supported by OPIC. If such an offense is found, the General Counsel shall advise the President of such finding and any known circumstances indicating that suspension would not be in the national interest of the United States. If, after reviewing the submission from the General Counsel, the President determines that national interest considerations are not great enough to preclude suspension, OPIC shall furnish the subject entity with a written notice (1) specifying the offense and stating that suspension for the maximum duration is being considered and (2) inviting the subject entity to submit to OPIC any evidence of facts or circumstances which it deems appropriate to indicate that a suspension should not be imposed or that the duration of the suspension should be less than the maximum. Such notice shall further state that the subject entity must provide such evidence within 30 days of the date of such written notice or any extension of time granted in writing by OPIC. The General Counsel shall promptly review any evidence submitted by the subject entity and report his findings and recommendations to the President. The President shall determine whether the subject entity shall be suspended and, if so, the President shall issue a suspension determination specifying the duration of such suspension. Notice of such suspension determination shall be forwarded by registered mail to the subject entity and any entity so notified shall be advised that such suspension may be reduced as provided in section 5(b) or voided as provided in section 8.

(b) The duration of any suspension may be reduced by the President at any time for good cause, including the submission by the suspended entity of an application for relief, supported by evidence and setting forth appropriate grounds for granting such relief, such as the institution of measures designed to preclude the recurrence of the actions with respect to which the suspension was initially imposed. Notice of each such reduction shall be forwarded to the suspended entity by registered mail.

(c) The duration of any suspension may be increased by the President at any time for good cause, subject to providing the subject entity with notice and opportunity to submit evidence in accordance with section 5(a). In no event shall any such increase result in a period of suspension exceeding 5 years with respect to any single conviction.

§ 709.6 Suspension duration criteria.

Factors which the President may consider in setting or amending the duration of any suspension imposed pursuant to these regulations include, but are not limited to, the following:

(a) Whether the offense with respect to which suspension has been imposed or is being considered was committed with the knowledge or consent of the board of directors or other group or officer or individual responsible for the overall management of the subject entity;

(b) Whether or not such offense was committed under pressure of extortion, political intervention, or other duress exerted by the government, or any official of the government, of the country in which such offense was committed;

(c) Quantitative factors relating to the seriousness of the offense, such as the amounts of any improper payments and the frequency with which, and period of time over which, they were made;

(d) The purpose of any such offense;

(e) Whether such offense violated the laws of the country in which it was committed;

(f) The extent to which the offense was related to the establishment or operation of a project supported by OPIC; and

(g) Any factors relating to the effect of suspension on the national interest of the United States.

§ 709.7 Effect of suspension.

(a) Any entity suspended pursuant to a suspension determination shall not, for the duration of such suspension, and subject to the provisions of section 7(b), be eligible to receive any additional insurance, reinsurance, guaranty, loan, or other financial support from OPIC.

(b) Suspended entities:

(1) May be retained on the OPIC mailing list only for the purpose of receiving informational mailings;

(2) May register projects with OPIC but may not submit project applications to OPIC;

(3) May continue to deal with OPIC with respect to agreements entered with OPIC prior to the suspension and may amend or be granted modifications of such agreements, including loan reschedulings and refinancings;

(4) May not be invited to participate in OPIC-sponsored investment missions or other similar activities; and

(5) May not receive indirectly, or beneficially, whether through the purchase of project participations, the use of intermediary entities or other such devices, any OPIC services which they would not be entitled to receive directly, and may not be the beneficiary of financial support advanced by a third party where such support, in turn, is guaranteed or insured by OPIC; provided, however that such suspended entity shall be entitled to all benefits and payments accruing to holders of negotiable instruments guaranteed by

OPIC and acquired by such suspended entity pursuant to a public offering thereof by the original or any subsequent holder thereof.

§ 709.8 Procedure for voiding suspensions.

Upon receipt by OPIC from the subject entity of notice of the entry of a final judgment of reversal of the conviction or convictions on which a suspension was based, and subject to verification thereof by the General Counsel and to a finding by the General Counsel that no other convictions under the act are outstanding, the President shall void such suspension

PART 710—ADMINISTRATIVE ENFORCEMENT PROCEDURES OF POST-EMPLOYMENT RESTRICTIONS

AUTHORITY: 18 U.S.C. 207(j).

SOURCE: 45 FR 5685, Jan. 24, 1980, unless otherwise noted.

§ 710.1 General.

The following procedures are hereby established with respect to the administrative enforcement of restrictions on post-employment activities (18 U.S.C. 207(a), (b) or (c) and implementing regulations (44 FR 19987 and 19988, April 3, 1979) published by the Office of Government Ethics.

§ 710.2 Action on receipt of information regarding violation.

On receipt of information regarding a possible violation of the statutory or regulatory post-employment restrictions by a former OPIC employee and after determining that such information does not appear to be frivolous, the President of OPIC or the President's designee shall provide such information to the Director of the Office of Government Ethics and to the Criminal Division, Department of Justice. Any investigation or administrative action shall be coordinated with the Department of Justice to avoid prejudicing possible criminal proceedings. If the Department of Justice informs OPIC that it does not intend to institute criminal proceedings, such coordination shall no longer be required and OPIC shall be free to pursue administrative action.

§ 710.3 Initiation of administrative disciplinary proceeding.

Whenever the President of OPIC or the President's designee determines after appropriate review that there is reasonable cause to believe that a former OPIC employee had violated the statutory or regulatory post-employment restrictions, an administrative disciplinary proceeding shall be initiated.

§ 710.4 Notice.

The President of OPIC or the President's designee shall initiate an administrative disciplinary hearing by providing the former OPIC employee with notice of an intention to institute a proceeding and an opportunity for a hearing. Notice must include:

(a) A statement of allegations and the basis thereof sufficiently detailed to enable the former employee to prepare an adequate defense;

(b) Notification of the right to a hearing; and

(c) An explanation of the method by which a hearing may be requested.

§ 710.5 Failure to request hearing.

The President of OPIC may take appropriate action referred to in § 710.13 in the case of any former OPIC employee who has failed to make a written request to OPIC for a hearing within 30 days after receiving adequate notice.

§ 710.6 Appointment and qualifications of examiner.

When a former OPIC employee after receiving adequate notice requests a hearing, a presiding official (hereinafter referred to as "examiner") shall be appointed by the President of OPIC to make an initial decision. The examiner shall be a responsible person who is a member of the bar of a State or of the District of Columbia, who is impartial and who has not participated in any manner in the decision to initiate the proceedings. The examiner may or may not be an OPIC employee.

§ 710.7 Time, date and place of hearing.

The examiner shall establish a reasonable time, date and place to conduct the hearing. In establishing a date, the examiner shall give due regard to the former employee's need for:

(a) Adequate time to prepare a defense properly; and

(b) An expeditious resolution of allegations that may be damaging to the individual's reputation.

§ 710.8 Rights of parties at hearing.

A hearing shall include, at a minimum, the following rights for both parties to:

(a) Represent oneself or be represented by counsel;

(b) Introduce and examine witnesses and submit physical evidence (including the use of interrogatories);

(c) Confront and cross-examine adverse witnesses;

(d) Present oral argument; and

(e) Receive a transcript or recording of the proceedings on request.

§ 710.9 Burden of proof.

In any hearing under this part, OPIC shall have the burden of proof and must establish substantial evidence of a violation of the statutory or post-employment restrictions.

§ 710.10 Findings.

The examiner shall make a determination exclusively on matters of record in the proceeding and shall set forth in the written decision all findings of fact and conclusions of law relevant to the matters in issue.

§ 710.11 Appeal.

(a) Within 20 days of the date of the initial decision, either party may appeal the decision to the President of OPIC. The President's decision on such appeal shall be based solely on the record of the proceedings or those portions thereof cited by the parties to limit the issues.

(b) If the President modifies or reverses the examiner's decision, the President shall specify such findings of fact and conclusions of law as are different from those of the examiner.

(c) The decision of the President on appeal, shall constitute final administrative decision. An initial decision of the examiner which has not been appealed during the 20-day period provided shall become a final administrative decision on the twenty-first day.

§ 710.12 Finding of violation.

The President of OPIC shall take appropriate action referred to in § 710.13 in the case of an individual who is found in violation of the statutory or regulatory post-employment restrictions, after a final administrative decision.

§ 710.13 Appropriate action.

Appropriate action includes:

(a) Prohibiting the individual from making, on behalf of any other person (except the United States), any formal or informal appearance before, or with the intent to influence, any oral or written communication to, OPIC on any matter or business for a period not to exceed five years, which may be accomplished by directing OPIC employees to refuse to participate in any such appearance or to accept any such communication.

(b) Taking other appropriate disciplinary action.

[45 FR 5685, Jan. 24, 1980; 49 FR 18295, Apr. 30, 1984]

§ 710.14 Judicial review.

Any person found to have participated in a violation of statutory or regulatory post-employment restrictions (18 U.S.C. 207(a), (b) or (c) or the regulations compiled at 44 FR 19987 and 19988, April 3, 1979) may seek judicial review of the administrative determination.

§710.15 Delegation of authority.

The functions of the President of OPIC specified in §§710.2, 710.4 and 710.5 of this part are delegated to the General Counsel of OPIC. An examiner shall be delegated authority on an *ad hoc* basis.

PART 711—ENFORCEMENT OF NONDISCRIMINATION ON THE BASIS OF HANDICAP IN PROGRAMS OR ACTIVITIES CONDUCTED BY THE OVERSEAS PRIVATE INVESTMENT CORPORATION

AUTHORITY: 29 U.S.C. 794.

SOURCE: 53 FR 25882, 25885, July 8, 1988, unless otherwise noted.

§711.101 Purpose.

The purpose of this regulation is to effectuate section 119 of the Rehabilitation, Comprehensive Services, and Developmental Disabilities Amendments of 1978, which amended section 504 of the Rehabilitation Act of 1973 to prohibit discrimination on the basis of handicap in programs or activities conducted by Executive agencies or the United States Postal Service.

§711.102 Application.

This regulation (§§711.101–711.170) applies to all programs or activities conducted by the agency, except for programs or activities conducted outside the United States that do not involve individuals with handicaps in the United States.

§711.103 Definitions.

For purposes of this regulation, the term—

Assistant Attorney General means the Assistant Attorney General, Civil Rights Division, United States Department of Justice.

Auxiliary aids means services or devices that enable persons with impaired sensory, manual, or speaking skills to have an equal opportunity to participate in, and enjoy the benefits of, programs or activities conducted by the agency. For example, auxiliary aids useful for persons with impaired vision include readers, Brailled materials, audio recordings, and other similar services and devices. Auxiliary aids useful for persons with impaired hearing include telephone handset amplifiers, telephones compatible with hearing aids, telecommunication devices for deaf persons (TDD's), interpreters, notetakers, written materials, and other similar services and devices.

Complete complaint means a written statement that contains the complainant's name and address and describes the agency's alleged discriminatory action in sufficient detail to inform the agency of the nature and date of the alleged violation of section 504. It shall be signed by the complainant or by someone authorized to do so on his or her behalf. Complaints filed on behalf of classes or third parties shall describe or identify (by name, if possible) the alleged victims of discrimination.

Facility means all or any portion of buildings, structures, equipment, roads, walks, parking lots, rolling stock or other conveyances, or other real or personal property.

Historic preservation programs means programs conducted by the agency that have preservation of historic properties as a primary purpose.

Historic properties means those properties that are listed or eligible for listing in the National Register of Historic Places or properties designated as historic under a statute of the appropriate State or local government body.

Individual with handicaps means any person who has a physical or mental impairment that substantially limits one or more major life activities, has a record of such an impairment, or is regarded as having such an impairment.

As used in this definition, the phrase:

(1) *Physical or mental impairment* includes—

(i) Any physiological disorder or condition, cosmetic disfigurement, or anatomical loss affecting one or more of the following body systems: Neurological; musculoskeletal; special sense organs; respiratory, including speech organs; cardiovascular; reproductive; digestive; genitourinary; hemic and lymphatic; skin; and endocrine; or

(ii) Any mental or psychological disorder, such as mental retardation, organic brain syndrome, emotional or mental illness, and specific learning disabilities. The term *physical or mental impairment* includes, but is not limited to, such diseases and conditions as orthopedic, visual, speech, and hearing impairments, cerebral palsy, epilepsy, muscular dystrophy, multiple sclerosis, cancer, heart disease, diabetes, mental retardation, emotional illness, and drug addiction and alcoholism.

(2) *Major life activities* includes functions such as caring for one's self, performing manual tasks, walking, seeing, hearing, speaking, breathing, learning, and working.

(3) *Has a record of such an impairment* means has a history of, or has been misclassified as having, a mental or physical impairment that substantially limits one or more major life activities.

(4) *Is regarded as having an impairment* means—

(i) Has a physical or mental impairment that does not substantially limit major life activities but is treated by the agency as constituting such a limitation;

(ii) Has a physical or mental impairment that substantially limits major life activities only as a result of the attitudes of others toward such impairment; or

(iii) Has none of the impairments defined in paragraph (1) of this definition but is treated by the agency as having such an impairment.

Qualified individual with handicaps means—

(1) With respect to preschool, elementary, or secondary education services provided by the agency, an individual with handicaps who is a member of a class of persons otherwise entitled by statute, regulation, or agency policy to receive education services from the agency;

(2) With respect to any other agency program or activity under which a person is required to perform services or to achieve a level of accomplishment, an individual with handicaps who meets the essential eligibility requirements and who can achieve the purpose of the program or activity without modifications in the program or activity that the agency can demonstrate would result in a fundamental alteration in its nature;

(3) With respect to any other program or activity, an individual with handicaps who meets the essential eligibility requirements for participation in, or receipt of benefits from, that program or activity; and

(4) *Qualified handicapped person* as that term is defined for purposes of employment in 29 CFR 1613.702(f), which is made applicable to this regulation by § 711.140.

Section 504 means section 504 of the Rehabilitation Act of 1973 (Pub. L. 93–112, 87 Stat. 394 (29 U.S.C. 794)), as amended by the Rehabilitation Act Amendments of 1974 (Pub. L. 93–516, 88 Stat. 1617); the Rehabilitation, Comprehensive Services, and Developmental Disabilities Amendments of 1978 (Pub. L. 95–602, 92 Stat. 2955); and the Rehabilitation Act Amendments of 1986 (Pub. L. 99–506, 100 Stat. 1810). As used in this regulation, section 504 applies only to programs or activities conducted by Executive agencies and not to federally assisted programs.

Substantial impairment means a significant loss of the integrity of finished materials, design quality, or special character resulting from a permanent alteration.

§§711.104–711.109 [Reserved]

§711.110 Self-evaluation.

(a) The agency shall, by September 6, 1989, evaluate its current policies and practices, and the effects thereof, that do not or may not meet the requirements of this regulation and, to the extent modification of any such policies and practices is required, the agency shall proceed to make the necessary modifications.

(b) The agency shall provide an opportunity to interested persons, including individuals with handicaps or organizations representing individuals with handicaps, to participate in the self-evaluation process by submitting comments (both oral and written).

(c) The agency shall, for at least three years following completion of the self-evaluation, maintain on file and make available for public inspection:

(1) A description of areas examined and any problems identified; and

(2) A description of any modifications made.

§711.111 Notice.

The agency shall make available to employees, applicants, participants, beneficiaries, and other interested persons such information regarding the provisions of this regulation and its applicability to the programs or activities conducted by the agency, and make such information available to them in such manner as the head of the agency finds necessary to apprise such persons of the protections against discrimination assured them by section 504 and this regulation.

§§711.112–711.129 [Reserved]

§711.130 General prohibitions against discrimination.

(a) No qualified individual with handicaps shall, on the basis of handicap, be excluded from participation in, be denied the benefits of, or otherwise be subjected to discrimination under any program or activity conducted by the agency.

(b)(1) The agency, in providing any aid, benefit, or service, may not, directly or through contractual, licensing, or other arrangements, on the basis of handicap—

(i) Deny a qualified individual with handicaps the opportunity to participate in or benefit from the aid, benefit, or service;

(ii) Afford a qualified individual with handicaps an opportunity to participate in or benefit from the aid, benefit, or service that is not equal to that afforded others;

(iii) Provide a qualified individual with handicaps with an aid, benefit, or service that is not as effective in affording equal opportunity to obtain the same result, to gain the same benefit, or to reach the same level of achievement as that provided to others;

(iv) Provide different or separate aid, benefits, or services to individuals with handicaps or to any class of individuals with handicaps than is provided to others unless such action is necessary to provide qualified individuals with handicaps with aid, benefits, or services that are as effective as those provided to others;

(v) Deny a qualified individual with handicaps the opportunity to participate as a member of planning or advisory boards;

(vi) Otherwise limit a qualified individual with handicaps in the enjoyment of any right, privilege, advantage, or opportunity enjoyed by others receiving the aid, benefit, or service.

(2) The agency may not deny a qualified individual with handicaps the opportunity to participate in programs or activities that are not separate or different, despite the existence of permissibly separate or different programs or activities.

(3) The agency may not, directly or through contractual or other arrangements, utilize criteria or methods of administration the purpose or effect of which would—

(i) Subject qualified individuals with handicaps to discrimination on the basis of handicap; or

(ii) Defeat or substantially impair accomplishment of the objectives of a program or activity with respect to individuals with handicaps.

(4) The agency may not, in determining the site or location of a facility, make selections the purpose or effect of which would—

(i) Exclude individuals with handicaps from, deny them the benefits of, or otherwise subject them to discrimination under any program or activity conducted by the agency; or

(ii) Defeat or substantially impair the accomplishment of the objectives of a program or activity with respect to individuals with handicaps.

(5) The agency, in the selection of procurement contractors, may not use criteria that subject qualified individuals with handicaps to discrimination on the basis of handicap.

(6) The agency may not administer a licensing or certification program in a manner that subjects qualified individuals with handicaps to discrimination on the basis of handicap, nor may the agency establish requirements for the programs or activities of licensees or certified entities that subject qualified individuals with handicaps to discrimination on the basis of handicap. However, the programs or activities of entities that are licensed or certified by the agency are not, themselves, covered by this regulation.

(c) The exclusion of nonhandicapped persons from the benefits of a program limited by Federal statute or Executive order to individuals with handicaps or the exclusion of a specific class of individuals with handicaps from a program limited by Federal statute or Executive order to a different class of individuals with handicaps is not prohibited by this regulation.

(d) The agency shall administer programs and activities in the most integrated setting appropriate to the needs of qualified individuals with handicaps.

§§ 711.131–711.139 [Reserved]

§ 711.140 Employment.

No qualified individual with handicaps shall, on the basis of handicap, be subject to discrimination in employment under any program or activity conducted by the agency. The definitions, requirements, and procedures of section 501 of the Rehabilitation Act of 1973 (29 U.S.C. 791), as established by the Equal Employment Opportunity Commission in 29 CFR part 1613, shall apply to employment in federally conducted programs or activities.

§§ 711.141–711.148 [Reserved]

§ 711.149 Program accessibility: Discrimination prohibited.

Except as otherwise provided in § 711.150, no qualified individual with handicaps shall, because the agency's facilities are inaccessible to or unusable by individuals with handicaps, be denied the benefits of, be excluded from participation in, or otherwise be subjected to discrimination under any program or activity conducted by the agency.

§ 711.150 Program accessibility: Existing facilities.

(a) *General.* The agency shall operate each program or activity so that the program or activity, when viewed in its entirety, is readily accessible to and usable by individuals with handicaps. This paragraph does not—

(1) Necessarily require the agency to make each of its existing facilities accessible to and usable by individuals with handicaps;

(2) In the case of historic preservation programs, require the agency to take any action that would result in a substantial impairment of significant historic features of an historic property; or

(3) Require the agency to take any action that it can demonstrate would result in a fundamental alteration in the nature of a program or activity or in undue financial and administrative burdens. In those circumstances where agency personnel believe that the proposed action would fundamentally alter the program or activity or would result in undue financial and administrative burdens, the agency has the burden of proving that compliance with § 711.150(a) would result in such alteration or burdens. The decision that compliance would result in such alteration or burdens must be made by the agency head or his or her designee after considering all agency resources available for use in the funding and operation of the conducted program or activity, and must be accompanied by a written statement of the reasons for reaching that conclusion. If an action would result in such an alteration or such burdens, the agency shall take any other action that would not result

in such an alteration or such burdens but would nevertheless ensure that individuals with handicaps receive the benefits and services of the program or activity.

(b) *Methods*—(1) *General.* The agency may comply with the requirements of this section through such means as redesign of equipment, reassignment of services to accessible buildings, assignment of aides to beneficiaries, home visits, delivery of services at alternate accessible sites, alteration of existing facilities and construction of new facilities, use of accessible rolling stock, or any other methods that result in making its programs or activities readily accessible to and usable by individuals with handicaps. The agency is not required to make structural changes in existing facilities where other methods are effective in achieving compliance with this section. The agency, in making alterations to existing buildings, shall meet accessibility requirements to the extent compelled by the Architectural Barriers Act of 1968, as amended (42 U.S.C. 4151–4157), and any regulations implementing it. In choosing among available methods for meeting the requirements of this section, the agency shall give priority to those methods that offer programs and activities to qualified individuals with handicaps in the most integrated setting appropriate.

(2) *Historic preservation programs.* In meeting the requirements of §711.150(a) in historic preservation programs, the agency shall give priority to methods that provide physical access to individuals with handicaps. In cases where a physical alteration to an historic property is not required because of §711.150(a) (2) or (3), alternative methods of achieving program accessibility include—

(i) Using audio-visual materials and devices to depict those portions of an historic property that cannot otherwise be made accessible;

(ii) Assigning persons to guide individuals with handicaps into or through portions of historic properties that cannot otherwise be made accessible; or

(iii) Adopting other innovative methods.

(c) *Time period for compliance.* The agency shall comply with the obligations established under this section by November 7, 1988, except that where structural changes in facilities are undertaken, such changes shall be made by September 6, 1991, but in any event as expeditiously as possible.

(d) *Transition plan.* In the event that structural changes to facilities will be undertaken to achieve program accessibility, the agency shall develop, by March 6, 1989, a transition plan setting forth the steps necessary to complete such changes. The agency shall provide an opportunity to interested persons, including individuals with handicaps or organizations representing individuals with handicaps, to participate in the development of the transition plan by submitting comments (both oral and written). A copy of the transition plan shall be made available for public inspection. The plan shall, at a minimum—

(1) Identify physical obstacles in the agency's facilities that limit the accessibility of its programs or activities to individuals with handicaps;

(2) Describe in detail the methods that will be used to make the facilities accessible;

(3) Specify the schedule for taking the steps necessary to achieve compliance with this section and, if the time period of the transition plan is longer than one year, identify steps that will be taken during each year of the transition period; and

(4) Indicate the official responsible for implementation of the plan.

§711.151 Program accessibility: New construction and alterations.

Each building or part of a building that is constructed or altered by, on behalf of, or for the use of the agency shall be designed, constructed, or altered so as to be readily accessible to and usable by individuals with handicaps. The definitions, requirements, and standards of the Architectural Barriers Act (42 U.S.C. 4151–4157), as established in 41 CFR 101–19.600 to 101–19.607, apply to buildings covered by this section.

§§ 711.152–711.159 [Reserved]

§ 711.160 Communications.

(a) The agency shall take appropriate steps to ensure effective communication with applicants, participants, personnel of other Federal entities, and members of the public.

(1) The agency shall furnish appropriate auxiliary aids where necessary to afford an individual with handicaps an equal opportunity to participate in, and enjoy the benefits of, a program or activity conducted by the agency.

(i) In determining what type of auxiliary aid is necessary, the agency shall give primary consideration to the requests of the individual with handicaps.

(ii) The agency need not provide individually prescribed devices, readers for personal use or study, or other devices of a personal nature.

(2) Where the agency communicates with applicants and beneficiaries by telephone, telecommunication devices for deaf persons (TDD's) or equally effective telecommunication systems shall be used to communicate with persons with impaired hearing.

(b) The agency shall ensure that interested persons, including persons with impaired vision or hearing, can obtain information as to the existence and location of accessible services, activities, and facilities.

(c) The agency shall provide signage at a primary entrance to each of its inaccessible facilities, directing users to a location at which they can obtain information about accessible facilities. The international symbol for accessibility shall be used at each primary entrance of an accessible facility.

(d) This section does not require the agency to take any action that it can demonstrate would result in a fundamental alteration in the nature of a program or activity or in undue financial and administrative burdens. In those circumstances where agency personnel believe that the proposed action would fundamentally alter the program or activity or would result in undue financial and administrative burdens, the agency has the burden of proving that compliance with § 711.160 would result in such alteration or burdens. The decision that compliance would result in such alteration or burdens must be made by the agency head or his or her designee after considering all agency resources available for use in the funding and operation of the conducted program or activity and must be accompanied by a written statement of the reasons for reaching that conclusion. If an action required to comply with this section would result in such an alteration or such burdens, the agency shall take any other action that would not result in such an alteration or such burdens but would nevertheless ensure that, to the maximum extent possible, individuals with handicaps receive the benefits and services of the program or activity.

§§ 711.161–711.169 [Reserved]

§ 711.170 Compliance procedures.

(a) Except as provided in paragraph (b) of this section, this section applies to all allegations of discrimination on the basis of handicap in programs and activities conducted by the agency.

(b) The agency shall process complaints alleging violations of section 504 with respect to employment according to the procedures established by the Equal Employment Opportunity Commission in 29 CFR part 1613 pursuant to section 501 of the Rehabilitation Act of 1973 (29 U.S.C. 791).

(c) The Director of Personnel shall be responsible for coordinating implementation of this section. Complaints may be sent to Overseas Private Investment Corporation, 1615 M Street, NW., Washington, DC 20527, Attention: Director of Personnel.

(d) The agency shall accept and investigate all complete complaints for which it has jurisdiction. All complete complaints must be filed within 180 days of the alleged act of discrimination. The agency may extend this time period for good cause.

(e) If the agency receives a complaint over which it does not have jurisdiction, it shall promptly notify the complainant and shall make reasonable efforts to refer the complaint to the appropriate Government entity.

(f) The agency shall notify the Architectural and Transportation Barriers Compliance Board upon receipt of any complaint alleging that a building or facility that is subject to the Architectural Barriers Act of 1968, as amended (42 U.S.C. 4151–4157), is not readily accessible to and usable by individuals with handicaps.

(g) Within 180 days of the receipt of a complete complaint for which it has jurisdiction, the agency shall notify the complainant of the results of the investigation in a letter containing—

(1) Findings of fact and conclusions of law;

(2) A description of a remedy for each violation found; and

(3) A notice of the right to appeal.

(h) Appeals of the findings of fact and conclusions of law or remedies must be filed by the complainant within 90 days of receipt from the agency of the letter required by § 711.170(g). The agency may extend this time for good cause.

(i) Timely appeals shall be accepted and processed by the head of the agency.

(j) The head of the agency shall notify the complainant of the results of the appeal within 60 days of the receipt of the request. If the head of the agency determines that additional information is needed from the complainant, he or she shall have 60 days from the date of receipt of the additional information to make his or her determination on the appeal.

(k) The time limits cited in paragraphs (g) and (j) of this section may be extended with the permission of the Assistant Attorney General.

(l) The agency may delegate its authority for conducting complaint investigations to other Federal agencies, except that the authority for making the final determination may not be delegated to another agency.

[53 FR 25882, 25885, July 8, 1988, as amended 53 FR 25883, July 8, 1988]

§§ 711.171–711.999 [Reserved]

PART 712—NEW RESTRICTIONS ON LOBBYING

Subpart A—General

Subpart B—Activities by Own Employees

Subpart C—Activities by Other Than Own Employees

Subpart D—Penalties and Enforcement

Subpart E—Exemptions

Subpart F—Agency Reports

AUTHORITY: Section 319, Public Law 101–121 (31 U.S.C. 1352).

CROSS REFERENCE: See also Office of Management and Budget notice published at 54 FR 52306, December 20, 1989.

SOURCE: 55 FR 6737, 6750, Feb. 26, 1990, unless otherwise noted.

Subpart A—General

§ 712.100 Conditions on use of funds.

(a) No appropriated funds may be expended by the recipient of a Federal contract, grant, loan, or cooperative ageement to pay any person for influencing or attempting to influence an officer or employee of any agency, a Member of Congress, an officer or employee of Congress, or an employee of a Member of Congress in connection with any of the following covered Federal actions: the awarding of any Federal contract, the making of any Federal grant, the making of any Federal loan, the entering into of any cooperative agreement, and the extension, continuation, renewal, amendment, or modification of any Federal contract, grant, loan, or cooperative agreement.

(b) Each person who requests or receives from an agency a Federal contract, grant, loan, or cooperative agreement shall file with that agency a certification, set forth in appendix A, that the person has not made, and will not make, any payment prohibited by paragraph (a) of this section.

(c) Each person who requests or receives from an agency a Federal contract, grant, loan, or a cooperative agreement shall file with that agency a disclosure form, set forth in appendix B, if such person has made or has agreed to make any payment using nonappropriated funds (to include profits from any covered Federal action), which would be prohibited under paragraph (a) of this section if paid for with appropriated funds.

(d) Each person who requests or receives from an agency a commitment providing for the United States to insure or guarantee a loan shall file with that agency a statement, set forth in appendix A, whether that person has made or has agreed to make any payment to influence or attempt to influence an officer or employee of any agency, a Member of Congress, an officer or employee of Congress, or an employee of a Member of Congress in connection with that loan insurance or guarantee.

(e) Each person who requests or receives from an agency a commitment providing for the United States to insure or guarantee a loan shall file with that agency a disclosure form, set forth in appendix B, if that person has made or has agreed to make any payment to influence or attempt to influence an officer or employee of any agency, a Member of Congress, an officer or employee of Congress, or an employee of a Member of Congress in connection with that loan insurance or guarantee.

§712.105 Definitions.

For purposes of this part:

(a) *Agency*, as defined in 5 U.S.C. 552(f), includes Federal executive departments and agencies as well as independent regulatory commissions and Government corporations, as defined in 31 U.S.C. 9101(1).

(b) *Covered Federal action* means any of the following Federal actions:

(1) The awarding of any Federal contract;

(2) The making of any Federal grant;

(3) The making of any Federal loan;

(4) The entering into of any cooperative agreement; and,

(5) The extension, continuation, renewal, amendment, or modification of any Federal contract, grant, loan, or cooperative agreement.

Covered Federal action does not include receiving from an agency a commitment providing for the United States to insure or guarantee a loan. Loan guarantees and loan insurance are addressed independently within this part.

(c) *Federal contract* means an acquisition contract awarded by an agency, including those subject to the Federal Acquisition Regulation (FAR), and any other acquisition contract for real or personal property or services not subject to the FAR.

(d) *Federal cooperative agreement* means a cooperative agreement entered into by an agency.

(e) *Federal grant* means an award of financial assistance in the form of money, or property in lieu of money, by the Federal Government or a direct appropriation made by law to any person. The term does not include technical assistance which provides services instead of money, or other assistance in the form of revenue sharing, loans, loan guarantees, loan insurance, interest subsidies, insurance, or direct United States cash assistance to an individual.

(f) *Federal loan* means a loan made by an agency. The term does not include loan guarantee or loan insurance.

(g) *Indian tribe* and *tribal organization* have the meaning provided in section 4 of the Indian Self-Determination and Education Assistance Act (25 U.S.C. 450B). Alaskan Natives are included under the definitions of Indian tribes in that Act.

(h) *Influencing or attempting to influence* means making, with the intent to influence, any communication to or appearance before an officer or employee or any agency, a Member of Congress, an officer or employee of Congress, or an employee of a Member of Congress in connection with any covered Federal action.

(i) *Loan guarantee* and *loan insurance* means an agency's guarantee or insurance of a loan made by a person.

(j) *Local government* means a unit of government in a State and, if chartered, established, or otherwise recognized by a State for the performance of a governmental duty, including a local public authority, a special district, an intrastate district, a council of governments, a sponsor group representative organization, and any other instrumentality of a local government.

(k) *Officer or employee of an agency* includes the following individuals who are employed by an agency:

(1) An individual who is appointed to a position in the Government under title 5, U.S. Code, including a position under a temporary appointment;

(2) A member of the uniformed services as defined in section 101(3), title 37, U.S. Code;

(3) A special Government employee as defined in section 202, title 18, U.S. Code; and,

(4) An individual who is a member of a Federal advisory committee, as defined by the Federal Advisory Committee Act, title 5, U.S. Code appendix 2.

(l) *Person* means an individual, corporation, company, association, authority, firm, partnership, society, State, and local government, regardless of whether such entity is operated for profit or not for profit. This term excludes an Indian tribe, tribal organization, or any other Indian organization with respect to expenditures specifically permitted by other Federal law.

(m) *Reasonable compensation* means, with respect to a regularly employed officer or employee of any person, compensation that is consistent with the normal compensation for such officer or employee for work that is not furnished to, not funded by, or not furnished in cooperation with the Federal Government.

(n) *Reasonable payment* means, with respect to perfessional and other technical services, a payment in an amount that is consistent with the amount normally paid for such services in the private sector.

(o) *Recipient* includes all contractors, subcontractors at any tier, and subgrantees at any tier of the recipient of funds received in connection with a Federal contract, grant, loan, or cooperative agreement. The term excludes an Indian tribe, tribal organization, or any other Indian organization with respect to expenditures specifically permitted by other Federal law.

(p) *Regularly employed* means, with respect to an officer or employee of a person requesting or receiving a Federal contract, grant, loan, or cooperative agreement or a commitment providing for the United States to insure or guarantee a loan, an officer or employee who is employed by such person for at least 130 working days within one year immediately preceding the date of the submission that initiates agency consideration of such person for receipt of such contract, grant, loan, cooperative agreement, loan insurance commitment, or loan guarantee commitment. An officer or employee who is employed by such person for less than 130 working days within one year immediately preceding the date of the submission that initiates agency consideration of such person shall be considered to be regularly employed as soon as he or she is employed by such person for 130 working days.

(q) *State* means a State of the United States, the District of Columbia, the Commonwealth of Puerto Rico, a territory or possession of the United States, an agency or instrumentality of a State, and a multi-State, regional, or interstate entity having governmental duties and powers.

§ 712.110 Certification and disclosure.

(a) Each person shall file a certification, and a disclosure form, if required, with each submission that initiates agency consideration of such person for:

(1) Award of a Federal contract, grant, or cooperative agreement exceeding $100,000; or

(2) An award of a Federal loan or a commitment providing for the United States to insure or guarantee a loan exceeding $150,000.

(b) Each person shall file a certification, and a disclosure form, if required, upon receipt by such person of:

(1) A Federal contract, grant, or cooperative agreement exceeding $100,000; or

(2) A Federal loan or a commitment providing for the United States to insure or guarantee a loan exceeding $150,000,

Unless such person previously filed a certification, and a disclosure form, if required, under paragraph (a) of this section.

(c) Each person shall file a disclosure form at the end of each calendar quarter in which there occurs any event that requires disclosure or that materially affects the accuracy of the information contained in any disclosure form previously filed by such person under paragraphs (a) or (b) of this section. An event that materially affects the accuracy of the information reported includes:

(1) A cumulative increase of $25,000 or more in the amount paid or expected to be paid for influencing or attempting to influence a covered Federal action; or

(2) A change in the person(s) or individual(s) influencing or attempting to influence a covered Federal action; or,

(3) A change in the officer(s), employee(s), or Member(s) contacted to influence or attempt to influence a covered Federal action.

(d) Any person who requests or receives from a person referred to in paragraphs (a) or (b) of this section:

(1) A subcontract exceeding $100,000 at any tier under a Federal contract;

(2) A subgrant, contract, or subcontract exceeding $100,000 at any tier under a Federal grant;

(3) A contract or subcontract exceeding $100,000 at any tier under a Federal loan exceeding $150,000; or,

(4) A contract or subcontract exceeding $100,000 at any tier under a Federal cooperative agreement,

Shall file a certification, and a disclosure form, if required, to the next tier above.

(e) All disclosure forms, but not certifications, shall be forwarded from tier to tier until received by the person referred to in paragraphs (a) or (b) of this section. That person shall forward all disclosure forms to the agency.

(f) Any certification or disclosure form filed under paragraph (e) of this section shall be treated as a material representation of fact upon which all receiving tiers shall rely. All liability arising from an erroneous representation shall be borne solely by the tier filing that representation and shall not be shared by any tier to which the erroneous representation is forwarded. Submitting an erroneous certification or disclosure constitutes a failure to file the required certification or disclosure, respectively. If a person fails to file a required certification or disclosure, the United States may pursue all available remedies, including those authorized by section 1352, title 31, U.S. Code.

(g) For awards and commitments in process prior to December 23, 1989, but not made before that date, certifications shall be required at award or commitment, covering activities occurring between December 23, 1989, and the date of award or commitment. However, for awards and commitments in process prior to the December 23, 1989 effective date of these provisions, but not made before December 23, 1989, disclosure forms shall not be required at time of award or commitment but shall be filed within 30 days.

(h) No reporting is required for an activity paid for with appropriated funds if that activity is allowable under either subpart B or C.

Subpart B—Activities by Own Employees

§ 712.200 Agency and legislative liaison.

(a) The prohibition on the use of appropriated funds, in § 712.100 (a), does not apply in the case of a payment of reasonable compensation made to an officer or employee of a person requesting or receiving a Federal contract, grant, loan, or cooperative agreement if the payment is for agency and legislative liaison activities not directly related to a covered Federal action.

(b) For purposes of paragraph (a) of this section, providing any information specifically requested by an agency or Congress is allowable at any time.

(c) For purposes of paragraph (a) of this section, the following agency and legislative liaison activities are allowable at any time only where they are not related to a specific solicitation for any covered Federal action:

(1) Discussing with an agency (including individual demonstrations) the qualities and characteristics of the person's products or services, conditions or terms of sale, and service capabilities; and,

(2) Technical discussions and other activities regarding the application or adaptation of the person's products or services for an agency's use.

(d) For purposes of paragraph (a) of this section, the following agencies and legislative liaison activities are allowable only where they are prior to formal solicitation of any covered Federal action:

(1) Providing any information not specifically requested but necessary for an agency to make an informed decision about initiation of a covered Federal action;

(2) Technical discussions regarding the preparation of an unsolicited proposal prior to its official submission; and,

(3) Capability presentations by persons seeking awards from an agency pursuant to the provisions of the Small Business Act, as amended by Public Law 95–507 and other subsequent amendments.

(e) Only those activities expressly authorized by this section are allowable under this section.

§712.205 Professional and technical services.

(a) The prohibition on the use of appropriated funds, in §712.100 (a), does not apply in the case of a payment of reasonable compensation made to an officer or employee of a person requesting or receiving a Federal contract, grant, loan, or cooperative agreement or an extension, continuation, renewal, amendment, or modification of a Federal contract, grant, loan, or cooperative agreement if payment is for professional or technical services rendered directly in the preparation, submission, or negotiation of any bid, proposal, or application for that Federal contract, grant, loan, or cooperative agreement or for meeting requirements imposed by or pursuant to law as a condition for receiving that Federal contract, grant, loan, or cooperative agreement.

(b) For purposes of paragraph (a) of this section, "professional and technical services" shall be limited to advice and analysis directly applying any professional or technical discipline. For example, drafting of a legal document accompanying a bid or proposal by a lawyer is allowable. Similarly, technical advice provided by an engineer on the performance or operational capability of a piece of equipment rendered directly in the negotiation of a contract is allowable. However, communications with the intent to influence made by a professional (such as a licensed lawyer) or a technical person (such as a licensed accountant) are not allowable under this section unless they provide advice and analysis directly applying their professional or technical expertise and unless the advice or analysis is rendered directly and solely in the preparation, submission or negotiation of a covered Federal action. Thus, for example, communications with the intent to influence made by a lawyer that do not provide legal advice or analysis directly and solely related to the legal aspects of his or her client's proposal, but generally advocate one proposal over another are not allowable under this section because the lawyer is not providing professional legal services. Similarly, communications with the intent to influence made by an engineer providing an engineering analysis prior to the preparation or submission of a bid or proposal are not allowable under this section since the engineer is providing technical services but not directly in the preparation, submission or negotiation of a covered Federal action.

(c) Requirements imposed by or pursuant to law as a condition for receiving a covered Federal award include those required by law or regulation, or reasonably expected to be required by law or regulation, and any other requirements in the actual award documents.

(d) Only those services expressly authorized by this section are allowable under this section.

§ 712.210 Reporting.

No reporting is required with respect to payments of reasonable compensation made to regularly employed officers or employees of a person.

Subpart C—Activities by Other Than Own Employees

§ 712.300 Professional and technical services.

(a) The prohibition on the use of appropriated funds, in § 712.100 (a), does not apply in the case of any reasonable payment to a person, other than an officer or employee of a person requesting or receiving a covered Federal action, if the payment is for professional or technical services rendered directly in the preparation, submission, or negotiation of any bid, proposal, or application for that Federal contract, grant, loan, or cooperative agreement or for meeting requirements imposed by or pursuant to law as a condition for receiving that Federal contract, grant, loan, or cooperative agreement.

(b) The reporting requirements in § 712.110 (a) and (b) regarding filing a disclosure form by each person, if required, shall not apply with respect to professional or technical services rendered directly in the preparation, submission, or negotiation of any commitment providing for the United States to insure or guarantee a loan.

(c) For purposes of paragraph (a) of this section, "professional and technical services" shall be limited to advice and analysis directly applying any professional or technical discipline. For example, drafting or a legal document accompanying a bid or proposal by a lawyer is allowable. Similarly, technical advice provided by an engineer on the performance or operational capability of a piece of equipment rendered directly in the negotiation of a contract is allowable. However, communications with the intent to influence made by a professional (such as a licensed lawyer) or a technical person (such as a licensed accountant) are not allowable under this section unless they provide advice and analysis directly applying their professional or technical expertise and unless the advice or analysis is rendered directly and solely in the preparation, submission or negotiation of a covered Federal action. Thus, for example, communications with the intent to influence made by a lawyer that do not provide legal advice or analysis directly and solely related to the legal aspects of his or her client's proposal, but generally advocate one proposal over another are not allowable under this section because the lawyer is not providing professional legal services. Similarly, communications with the intent to influence made by an engineer providing an engineering analysis prior to the preparation or submission of a bid or proposal are not allowable under this section since the engineer is providing technical services but not directly in the preparation, submission or negotiation of a covered Federal action.

(d) Requirements imposed by or pursuant to law as a condition for receiving a covered Federal award include those required by law or regulation, or reasonably expected to be required by law or regulation, and any other requirements in the actual award documents.

(e) Persons other than officers or employees of a person requesting or receiving a covered Federal action include consultants and trade associations.

(f) Only those services expressly authorized by this section are allowable under this section.

Subpart D—Penalties and Enforcement

§ 712.400 Penalties.

(a) Any person who makes an expenditure prohibited herein shall be subject to a civil penalty of not less than $10,000 and not more than $100,000 for each such expenditure.

(b) Any person who fails to file or amend the disclosure form (see appendix B) to be filed or amended if required herein, shall be subject to a civil penalty of not less than $10,000 and not more than $100,000 for each such failure.

(c) A filing or amended filing on or after the date on which an administrative action for the imposition of a civil penalty is commenced does not prevent the imposition of such civil penalty for a failure occurring before that date. An administrative action is commenced with respect to a failure when an investigating official determines in writing to commence an investigation of an allegation of such failure.

(d) In determining whether to impose a civil penalty, and the amount of any such penalty, by reason of a violation by any person, the agency shall consider the nature, circumstances, extent, and gravity of the violation, the effect on the ability of such person to continue in business, any prior violations by such person, the degree of culpability of such person, the ability of the person to pay the penalty, and such other matters as may be appropriate.

(e) First offenders under paragraphs (a) or (b) of this section shall be subject to a civil penalty of $10,000, absent aggravating circumstances. Second and subsequent offenses by persons shall be subject to an appropriate civil penalty between $10,000 and $100,000, as determined by the agency head or his or her designee.

(f) An imposition of a civil penalty under this section does not prevent the United States from seeking any other remedy that may apply to the same conduct that is the basis for the imposition of such civil penalty.

§712.405 Penalty procedures.

Agencies shall impose and collect civil penalties pursuant to the provisions of the Program Fraud and Civil Remedies Act, 31 U.S.C. sections 3803 (except subsection (c)), 3804, 3805, 3806, 3807, 3808, and 3812, insofar as these provisions are not inconsistent with the requirements herein.

§712.410 Enforcement.

The head of each agency shall take such actions as are necessary to ensure that the provisions herein are vigorously implemented and enforced in that agency.

Subpart E—Exemptions

§712.500 Secretary of Defense.

(a) The Secretary of Defense may exempt, on a case-by-case basis, a covered Federal action from the prohibition whenever the Secretary determines, in writing, that such an exemption is in the national interest. The Secretary shall transmit a copy of each such written exemption to Congress immediately after making such a determination.

(b) The Department of Defense may issue supplemental regulations to implement paragraph (a) of this section.

Subpart F—Agency Reports

§712.600 Semi-annual compilation.

(a) The head of each agency shall collect and compile the disclosure reports (see appendix B) and, on May 31 and November 30 of each year, submit to the Secretary of the Senate and the Clerk of the House of Representatives a report containing a compilation of the information contained in the disclosure reports received during the six-month period ending on March 31 or September 30, respectively, of that year.

(b) The report, including the compilation, shall be available for public inspection 30 days after receipt of the report by the Secretary and the Clerk.

(c) Information that involves intelligence matters shall be reported only to the Select Committee on Intelligence of the Senate, the Permanent Select Committee on Intelligence of the House of Representatives, and the Committees on Appropriations of the Senate and the House of Representatives in accordance with procedures agreed to by such committees. Such information shall not be available for public inspection.

(d) Information that is classified under Executive Order 12356 or any successor order shall be reported only to the Committee on Foreign Relations of the Senate and the Committee on Foreign Affairs of the House of Representatives or the Committees on Armed Services of the Senate and the House of Representatives (whichever such committees have jurisdiction of matters involving such information) and to the Committees on Appropriations of the Senate and the House of Representatives in accordance with procedures agreed to by such committees. Such information shall not be available for public inspection.

(e) The first semi-annual compilation shall be submitted on May 31, 1990, and shall contain a compilation of the disclosure reports received from December 23, 1989 to March 31, 1990.

(f) Major agencies, designated by the Office of Management and Budget (OMB), are required to provide machine-readable compilations to the Secretary of the Senate and the Clerk of the House of Representatives no later than with the compilations due on May 31, 1991. OMB shall provide detailed specifications in a memorandum to these agencies.

(g) Non-major agencies are requested to provide machine-readable compilations to the Secretary of the Senate and the Clerk of the House of Representatives.

(h) Agencies shall keep the originals of all disclosure reports in the official files of the agency.

§ 712.605 Inspector General report.

(a) The Inspector General, or other official as specified in paragraph (b) of this section, of each agency shall prepare and submit to Congress each year, commencing with submission of the President's Budget in 1991, an evaluation of the compliance of that agency with, and the effectiveness of, the requirements herein. The evaluation may include any recommended changes that may be necessary to strengthen or improve the requirements.

(b) In the case of an agency that does not have an Inspector General, the agency official comparable to an Inspector General shall prepare and submit the annual report, or, if there is no such comparable official, the head of the agency shall prepare and submit the annual report.

(c) The annual report shall be submitted at the same time the agency submits its annual budget justifications to Congress.

(d) The annual report shall include the following: All alleged violations relating to the agency's covered Federal actions during the year covered by the report, the actions taken by the head of the agency in the year covered by the report with respect to those alleged violations and alleged violations in previous years, and the amounts of civil penalties imposed by the agency in the year covered by the report.

Appendix A to Part 712—Certification Regarding Lobbying

Certification for Contracts, Grants, Loans, and Cooperative Agreements

The undersigned certifies, to the best of his or her knowledge and belief, that:

(1) No Federal appropriated funds have been paid or will be paid, by or on behalf of the undersigned, to any person for influencing or attempting to influence an officer or employee of an agency, a Member of Congress, an officer or employee of Congress, or an employee of a Member of Congress in connection with the awarding of any Federal contract, the making of any Federal grant, the making of any Federal loan, the entering into of any cooperative agreement, and the extension, continuation, renewal, amendment, or modification of any Federal contract, grant, loan, or cooperative agreement.

(2) If any funds other than Federal appropriated funds have been paid or will be paid to any person for influencing or attempting to influence an officer or employee of any agency, a Member of Congress, an officer or employee of Congress, or an employee of a Member of Congress in connection with this Federal contract, grant, loan, or cooperative agreement, the undersigned shall complete and submit Standard Form-LLL, "Disclosure Form to Report Lobbying," in accordance with its instructions.

(3) The undersigned shall require that the language of this certification be included in the award documents for all subawards at all tiers (including subcontracts, subgrants, and contracts under grants, loans, and cooperative agreements) and that all subrecipients shall certify and disclose accordingly.

This certification is a material representation of fact upon which reliance was placed when this transaction was made or entered into. Submission of this certification is a prerequisite for making or entering into this transaction imposed by section 1352, title 31, U.S. Code. Any person who fails to file the required certification shall be subject to a civil penalty of not less than $10,000 and not more than $100,000 for each such failure.

Statement for Loan Guarantees and Loan Insurance

The undersigned states, to the best of his or her knowledge and belief, that:

If any funds have been paid or will be paid to any person for influencing or attempting to influence an officer or employee of any agency, a Member of Congress, an officer or employee of Congress, or an employee of a Member of Congress in connection with this commitment providing for the United States to insure or guarantee a loan, the undersigned shall complete and submit Standard Form-LLL, "Disclosure Form to Report Lobbying," in accordance with its instructions.

Submission of this statement is a prerequisite for making or entering into this transaction imposed by section 1352, title 31, U.S. Code. Any person who fails to file the required statement shall be subject to a civil penalty of not less than $10,000 and not more than $100,000 for each such failure.

APPENDIX B TO PART 712—DISCLOSURE FORM TO REPORT LOBBYING

DISCLOSURE OF LOBBYING ACTIVITIES

Approved by OMB 0348-0046

Complete this form to disclose lobbying activities pursuant to 31 U.S.C. 1352
(See reverse for public burden disclosure.)

1. Type of Federal Action:
☐ a. contract
b. grant
c. cooperative agreement
d. loan
e. loan guarantee
f. loan insurance

2. Status of Federal Action:
☐ a. bid/offer/application
b. initial award
c. post-award

3. Report Type:
☐ a. initial filing
b. material change

For Material Change Only:
year _______ quarter _____
date of last report _________

4. Name and Address of Reporting Entity:
☐ Prime ☐ Subawardee
Tier _____ , *if known*:

Congressional District, *if known*:

5. If Reporting Entity in No. 4 is Subawardee, Enter Name and Address of Prime:

Congressional District, *if known*:

6. Federal Department/Agency:

7. Federal Program Name/Description:

CFDA Number, *if applicable*: _____________

8. Federal Action Number, *if known*:

9. Award Amount, *if known*:
$

10. a. Name and Address of Lobbying Entity
(if individual, last name, first name, MI):

b. Individuals Performing Services *(including address if different from No. 10a)*
(last name, first name, MI):

(attach Continuation Sheet(s) SF-LLL-A, if necessary)

11. Amount of Payment *(check all that apply)*:
$ _________________ ☐ actual ☐ planned

12. Form of Payment *(check all that apply)*:
☐ a. cash
☐ b. in-kind; specify: nature _________________
value _________________

13. Type of Payment *(check all that apply)*:
☐ a. retainer
☐ b. one-time fee
☐ c. commission
☐ d. contingent fee
☐ e. deferred
☐ f. other; specify: ___________________

14. Brief Description of Services Performed or to be Performed and Date(s) of Service, including officer(s), employee(s), or Member(s) contacted, for Payment Indicated in Item 11:

(attach Continuation Sheet(s) SF-LLL-A, if necessary)

15. Continuation Sheet(s) SF-LLL-A attached: ☐ Yes ☐ No

16. Information requested through this form is authorized by title 31 U.S.C. section 1352. This disclosure of lobbying activities is a material representation of fact upon which reliance was placed by the tier above when this transaction was made or entered into. This disclosure is required pursuant to 31 U.S.C. 1352. This information will be reported to the Congress semi-annually and will be available for public inspection. Any person who fails to file the required disclosure shall be subject to a civil penalty of not less than $10,000 and not more than $100,000 for each such failure.

Signature: ______________________
Print Name: ______________________
Title: ______________________
Telephone No.: ______________ **Date:** ______________

Federal Use Only:

Authorized for Local Reproduction
Standard Form - LLL

INSTRUCTIONS FOR COMPLETION OF SF-LLL, DISCLOSURE OF LOBBYING ACTIVITIES

This disclosure form shall be completed by the reporting entity, whether subawardee or prime Federal recipient, at the initiation or receipt of a covered Federal action, or a material change to a previous filing, pursuant to title 31 U.S.C. section 1352. The filing of a form is required for each payment or agreement to make payment to any lobbying entity for influencing or attempting to influence an officer or employee of any agency, a Member of Congress, an officer or employee of Congress, or an employee of a Member of Congress in connection with a covered Federal action. Use the SF-LLL-A Continuation Sheet for additional information if the space on the form is inadequate. Complete all items that apply for both the initial filing and material change report. Refer to the implementing guidance published by the Office of Management and Budget for additional information.

1. Identify the type of covered Federal action for which lobbying activity is and/or has been secured to influence the outcome of a covered Federal action.
2. Identify the status of the covered Federal action.
3. Identify the appropriate classification of this report. If this is a followup report caused by a material change to the information previously reported, enter the year and quarter in which the change occurred. Enter the date of the last previously submitted report by this reporting entity for this covered Federal action.
4. Enter the full name, address, city, state and zip code of the reporting entity. Include Congressional District, if known. Check the appropriate classification of the reporting entity that designates if it is, or expects to be, a prime or subaward recipient. Identify the tier of the subawardee, e.g., the first subawardee of the prime is the 1st tier. Subawards include but are not limited to subcontracts, subgrants and contract awards under grants.
5. If the organization filing the report in item 4 checks "Subawardee", then enter the full name, address, city, state and zip code of the prime Federal recipient. Include Congressional District, if known.
6. Enter the name of the Federal agency making the award or loan commitment. Include at least one organizational level below agency name, if known. For example, Department of Transportation, United States Coast Guard.
7. Enter the Federal program name or description for the covered Federal action (item 1). If known, enter the full Catalog of Federal Domestic Assistance (CFDA) number for grants, cooperative agreements, loans, and loan commitments.
8. Enter the most appropriate Federal identifying number available for the Federal action identified in item 1 (e.g., Request for Proposal (RFP) number; Invitation for Bid (IFB) number; grant announcement number; the contract, grant, or loan award number; the application/proposal control number assigned by the Federal agency). Include prefixes, e.g., "RFP-DE-90-001."
9. For a covered Federal action where there has been an award or loan commitment by the Federal agency, enter the Federal amount of the award/loan commitment for the prime entity identified in item 4 or 5.
10. (a) Enter the full name, address, city, state and zip code of the lobbying entity engaged by the reporting entity identified in item 4 to influence the covered Federal action.

    (b) Enter the full names of the individual(s) performing services, and include full address if different from 10 (a). Enter Last Name, First Name, and Middle Initial (MI).
11. Enter the amount of compensation paid or reasonably expected to be paid by the reporting entity (item 4) to the lobbying entity (item 10). Indicate whether the payment has been made (actual) or will be made (planned). Check all boxes that apply. If this is a material change report, enter the cumulative amount of payment made or planned to be made.
12. Check the appropriate box(es). Check all boxes that apply. If payment is made through an in-kind contribution, specify the nature and value of the in-kind payment.
13. Check the appropriate box(es). Check all boxes that apply. If other, specify nature.
14. Provide a specific and detailed description of the services that the lobbyist has performed, or will be expected to perform, and the date(s) of any services rendered. Include all preparatory and related activity, not just time spent in actual contact with Federal officials. Identify the Federal official(s) or employee(s) contacted or the officer(s), employee(s), or Member(s) of Congress that were contacted.
15. Check whether or not a SF-LLL-A Continuation Sheet(s) is attached.
16. The certifying official shall sign and date the form, print his/her name, title, and telephone number.

Public reporting burden for this collection of information is estimated to average 30 mintues per response, including time for reviewing instructions, searching existing data sources, gathering and maintaining the data needed, and completing and reviewing the collection of information. Send comments regarding the burden estimate or any other aspect of this collection of information, including suggestions for reducing this burden, to the Office of Management and Budget, Paperwork Reduction Project (0348-0046), Washington, D.C. 20503.

DISCLOSURE OF LOBBYING ACTIVITIES
CONTINUATION SHEET

Approved by OMB
0348-0046

Reporting Entity: ______________________________ **Page** _____ **of** _____

Authorized for Local Reproduction
Standard Form - LLL-A

PART 713—PRODUCTION OF NONPUBLIC RECORDS AND TESTIMONY OF OPIC EMPLOYEES IN LEGAL PROCEEDINGS

AUTHORITY: 5 U.S.C. 301; 5 U.S.C. 552; 5 U.S.C. 552a; 5 U.S.C. 702; 18 U.S.C. 207; 18 U.S.C. 641; 22 U.S.C. 2199(d); 28 U.S.C. 1821.

SOURCE: 64 FR 8241, Feb. 19, 1999, unless otherwise noted.

§713.1 What does this part prohibit?

This part prohibits the release of nonpublic records for legal proceedings or the appearance of an OPIC employee to testify in legal proceedings except as provided in this part. Any person possessing nonpublic records may release them or permit their disclosure or release only as provided in this part.

(a) *Duty of OPIC employees.* (1) If you are an OPIC employee and you are served with a subpoena requiring you to appear as a witness or to produce records, you must promptly notify the Vice-president/General Counsel in the Department of Legal Affairs. The Vice-President/General Counsel has the authority to instruct OPIC employees to refuse to appear as a witness or to withhold nonpublic records. The Vice-President/General Counsel may let an OPIC employee provide testimony, including expert or opinion testimony, if the Vice-President/General Counsel determines that the need for the testimony clearly outweighs contrary considerations.

(2) If a court or other appropriate authority orders or demands from you expert or opinion testimony or testimony beyond authorized subjects contrary to the Vice-President/General Counsel's instructions, you must immediately notify the Vice-President/General Counsel of the order and then respectfully decline to comply with the order. You must decline to answer questions on the grounds that this part forbids such disclosure. You should produce a copy of this part, request an opportunity to consult with the Vice-President/General Counsel, and explain that providing such testimony without approval may expose you to disciplinary or other adverse action.

(b) *Duty of persons who are not OPIC employees.* (1) If you are not an OPIC employee but have custody of nonpublic records, as defined at §713.10, and you are served with a subpoena requiring you to produce records or to testify as a witness, you must promptly notify OPIC of the subpoena. Also, you must notify the issuing court or authority and the person or entity for whom the subpoena was issued of the contents of this part. Provide notice to OPIC by sending a copy of the subpoena to the Vice-President/General Counsel, OPIC, 1100 New York Avenue, NW, Washington, DC 20527. After reviewing notice, OPIC may advise the issuing court or authority and the person or entity for whom the subpoena was issued that this part applies and, in addition, may intervene, attempt to have the subpoena quashed or withdrawn, or register appropriate objections.

(2) After you notify the Vice-President/General Counsel of the subpoena, respond to the subpoena by appearing at the time and place stated in the subpoena, unless otherwise directed by the Vice President/General Counsel. Unless otherwise authorized by the Vice-President/General Counsel, decline to produce any records or give any testimony, basing your refusal on this part. If the issuing court or authority orders the disclosure of records or orders you to testify, decline to produce records or testify and advise the Vice-President/General Counsel.

(c) *Penalties.* Anyone who discloses nonpublic records or gives testimony related to those records, except as expressly authorized by OPIC or as ordered by a federal court after OPIC has had the opportunity to be heard, may face the penalties provided in 18 U.S.C. 641 and other applicable laws. Also, former OPIC employees, in addition to the prohibition contained in this part, are subject to the restrictions and penalties of 18 U.S.C. 207.

§ 713.2 When does this part apply?

This part applies if you want to obtain nonpublic records or testimony of an OPIC employee for a legal proceeding. It does not apply to records that OPIC is required to release, records which OPIC discretionarily releases under the Freedom of Information Act (FOIA), records that OPIC releases to federal or state investigatory agencies, records that OPIC is required to release pursuant to the Privacy Act, 5 U.S.C. 552a, or records that OPIC releases under any other applicable authority.

[79 FR 8619, Feb. 13, 2014]

§ 713.3 How do I request nonpublic records or testimony?

To request nonpublic records or the testimony of an OPIC employee, you must submit a written request as described in § 713.4 to the Vice-President/General Counsel of OPIC. If you serve a subpoena on OPIC or an OPIC employee before submitting a written request and receiving a final determination, OPIC will oppose the subpoena on the grounds that you failed to follow the requirements of this part.

[79 FR 8619, Feb. 13, 2014]

§ 713.4 What must my written request contain?

Your written request for records or testimony must include:

(a) The caption of the legal proceeding, docket number, and name of the court or other authority involved.

(b) A copy of the complaint or equivalent document setting forth the assertions in the case and any other pleading or document necessary to show relevance.

(c) A list of categories of records sought, a detailed description of how the information sought is relevant to the issues in the legal proceeding, and a specific description of the substance of the testimony or records sought.

(d) A statement as to how the need for the information outweighs the need to maintain the confidentiality of the information and outweighs the burden on OPIC to produce the records or provide testimony.

(e) A statement indicating that the information sought is not available from another source, such as the requestor's own books and records, other persons or entities, or the testimony of someone other than an OPIC employee, such as retained experts.

(f) A description of all prior decisions, orders, or pending motions in the case that bear upon the relevance of the records or testimony you want.

(g) The name, address, and telephone number of counsel to each party in the case.

(h) An estimate of the amount of time you anticipate that you and other parties will need with each OPIC employee for interviews, depositions, and/or testimony.

§ 713.5 When should I make my request?

Submit your request at least 45 days before the date you need the records or testimony. If you want your request processed in a shorter time, you must explain why you could not submit the request earlier and why you need such expedited processing. OPIC retains full discretion to grant, deny, or propose a new completion date on any request for expedited processing. If you are requesting the testimony of an OPIC employee, OPIC expects you to anticipate your need for the testimony in sufficient time to obtain it by deposition. The Vice-President/General Counsel may well deny a request for testimony at a legal proceeding unless you explain why you could not have used deposition testimony instead. The Vice-President/General Counsel will determine the location of a deposition, taking into consideration OPIC's interest in minimizing the disruption for an OPIC employee's work schedule and the costs and convenience of other persons attending the deposition.

[79 FR 8619, Feb. 13, 2014]

§ 713.6 Where should I send my request?

Send your request or subpoena for records or testimony to the attention of the Vice-President/General Counsel, OPIC, 1100 New York Avenue NW, Washington, DC 20527.

§713.7 What will OPIC do with my request?

(a) *Factors OPIC will consider.* OPIC may consider various factors in reviewing a request for nonpublic records or testimony of OPIC employees, including:

(1) Whether disclosure would assist or hinder OPIC in performing its statutory duties or use OPIC resources unreasonably, including whether responding to the request will interfere with OPIC employees' ability to do their work.

(2) Whether disclosure is necessary to prevent the perpetration of a fraud or other injustice in the matter.

(3) Whether you can get the records or testimony you want from sources other than OPIC.

(4) Whether the request is unduly burdensome.

(5) Whether disclosure would violate a statute, executive order, or regulation, such as the Privacy Act, 5 U.S.C. 552a.

(6) Whether disclosure would reveal confidential, sensitive or privileged information, trade secrets or similar, confidential commercial or financial information, or would otherwise be inappropriate for release and, if so, whether a confidentiality agreement or protective order as provided in §713.9(a) can adequately limit the disclosure.

(7) Whether the disclosure would interfere with law enforcement proceedings, compromise constitutional rights, or hamper OPIC programs or other OPIC operations.

(8) Whether the disclosure could result in OPIC's appearing to favor one litigant over another.

(9) Any other factors OPIC determines to be relevant to the interests of OPIC.

(b) *Review of your request.* OPIC will process your request in the order it is received. OPIC will try to respond to your request within 45 days, but this may vary, depending on the scope of your request.

(c) *Final determination.* the Vice-President/General Counsel makes the final determination on requests for nonpublic records or OPIC employee testimony. All final determinations are in the sole discretion of the Vice-President/General Counsel. The Vice-President/General Counsel will notify you and the court or other authority of the final determination of your request. In considering your request, the Vice-President/General Counsel may contact you to inform you of the requirements of this part, ask that the request or subpoena be modified or withdrawn, or may try to resolve the request or subpoena informally without issuing a final determination.

§713.8 If my request is granted, what fees apply?

(a) *Generally.* You must pay any fees associated with complying with your request, including copying fees for records and witness fees for testimony. The Vice-President/General Counsel may condition the production of records or appearance for testimony upon advance payment of a reasonable estimate of the fees.

(b) *Fees for records.* You must pay all fees for searching, reviewing and duplicating records produced in response to your request. The fees will be the same as those charged by OPIC under its Freedom of Information Act regulations, 22 CFR Part 706, Subpart B, §706.26.

(c) *Witness fees.* Your must pay the fees, expenses, and allowances prescribed by the court's rules for attendance by a witness. If no such fees are prescribed, the local federal district court rule concerning witness fees, for the federal district court closest to where the witness appears, will apply. For testimony by current OPIC employees, you must pay witness fees, allowances, and expenses to the Vice-President/General Counsel by check made payable to the "Overseas Private Investment Corporation" within 30 days from receipt of OPIC's billing statement. For the testimony of a former OPIC employee, you must pay witness fees, allowances, and expenses directly to the former employee, in accordance with 28 U.S.C. 1821 or other applicable statutes.

(d) *Certification of records.* OPIC may authenticate or certify records to facilitate their use as evidence. If you require authenticated records, you must request certified copies at least 45 days before the date they will be needed.

Send your request to the Vice-President/General Counsel. OPIC will charge you a certification fee of $5.00 per document.

(e) *Waiver of fees.* A waiver or reduction of any fees in connection with the testimony, production, or certification or authentication of records may be granted in the discretion of the Vice-President/General Counsel. Waivers will not be granted routinely. If you request a waiver, your request for records or testimony must state the reasons why a waiver should be granted.

§ 713.9 If my request is granted, what restrictions may apply?

(a) *Records.* The Vice-President/General Counsel may impose conditions or restrictions on the release of nonpublic records, including a requirement that you obtain a protective order or execute a confidentiality agreement with the other parties in the legal proceeding that limits access to and any further disclosure of the nonpublic records. The terms of a confidentiality agreement or protective order must be acceptable to the Vice-President/General Counsel. In cases where protective orders or confidentiality agreements have already been executed, OPIC may condition the release of nonpublic records on an amendment to the existing protective order or confidentiality agreement.

(b) *Testimony.* The Vice-President/General Counsel may impose conditions or restrictions on the testimony of OPIC employees, including, for example, limiting the areas of testimony or requiring you and the other parties to the legal proceeding to agree that the transcript of the testimony will be kept under seal or will only be used or made available in the particular legal proceeding for which you requested the testimony. The Vice-President/General Counsel may also require you to provide a copy of the transcript of the testimony to OPIC at your expense.

§ 713.10 Definitions.

For purposes of this part:

Legal proceedings means any matter before any federal, state or foreign administrative or judicial authority, including courts, agencies, commissions, boards, grand juries, or other tribunals, involving such proceedings as lawsuits, licensing matters, hearings, trials, discovery, investigations, mediation or arbitration. When OPIC is a party to a legal proceeding, it will be subject to the applicable rules of civil procedure governing production of documents and witnesses; however testimony and/or production of documents by OPIC employees, as defined, will still be subject to this part.

Nonpublic records means any OPIC records which are exempt from disclosure by statute or under Part 706, OPIC's regulations implementing the provisions of the Freedom of Information Act. For example, this may include records created in connection with OPIC's receipt, evaluation and action on actual and proposed OPIC finance projects and insurance policies (whether such projects or policies were cancelled or not), including all reports, internal memoranda, opinions, interpretations, and correspondence, whether prepared by OPIC employees or by persons under contract, as well as confidential business information submitted by parties seeking to do business with OPIC. Whether OPIC has actually chosen in practice to apply any exemption to specific documents is irrelevant to the question of whether they are "nonpublic" for the purposes of this Part.

OPIC employee means current and former officials, members of the Board of Directors, officers, directors, employees and agents of the Overseas Private Investment Corporation, including contract employees, consultants and their employees. This definition does not include persons who are no longer employed by OPIC and are retained or hired as expert witnesses or agree to testify about general matters, matters available to the public, or matters with which they had no specific involvement or responsibility during their employment.

Subpoena means any order, subpoena for records or other tangible things or for testimony, summons, notice or legal process issued in a legal proceeding.

Testimony means any written or oral statements made by an individual in connection with a legal proceeding, including personal appearances in court or at depositions, interviews in person or by telephone, responses to written interrogatories or other written statements such as reports, declarations, affidavits, or certifications or any response involving more than the delivery of records.

PARTS 714–799 [RESERVED]

CHAPTER IX—FOREIGN SERVICE GRIEVANCE BOARD

PART 900 [RESERVED]

PART 901—GENERAL

Subpart A—Purpose and Scope

Subpart B—Meanings of Terms as Used in This Chapter

AUTHORITY: Secs. 610, 1101, 1102, 1105, and 1106 of the Foreign Service Act of 1980, Pub. L. 96–465 (22 U.S.C. 4131, 4132, 4135, and 4136), as amended.

SOURCE: 50 FR 31353, Aug. 2, 1985, unless otherwise noted.

Subpart A—Purpose and Scope

§ 901.1 Purpose and scope.

The regulations contained in this chapter establish the internal organization of the Foreign Service Grievance Board and prescribe its procedures in:

(a) Determining its jurisdiction in cases involving grievances and separation for cause proceedings;

(b) Compiling a record in such cases;

(c) Conducting hearings in such cases, when required or deemed necessary; and

(d) Deciding such cases, or otherwise disposing of them, so as to ensure the fullest measure of due process for the members of the Foreign Service.

Subpart B—Meanings of Terms As Used in This Chapter

§ 901.10 Act.

Act means the Foreign Service Act of 1980 (Pub. L. 96–465, October 17, 1980), as amended.

[56 FR 55458, Oct. 28, 1991]

§ 901.11 Agency.

Agency means the Department of State, the Agency for International Development, the U.S. Information Agency, the Department of Agriculture, or the Department of Commerce, if the Agency employs the individual appearing in a case before the Board and/or has control over the act, omission, or condition forming the subject matter of such case.

§ 901.12 Board.

Board means the Foreign Service Grievance Board, including any designated panel or member thereof.

§ 901.13 Executive secretary.

Executive secretary means the executive secretary of the Board or his or her designee.

§ 901.14 Service.

Service means the Foreign Service of the United States.

§ 901.15 Exclusive representative.

Exclusive representative means any labor organization which is certified as the exclusive representative of the bargaining unit of which the grievant or charged employee is a member.

§ 901.16 Grievant.

Grievant means anyone who has filed a grievance and who is a member of the Service and is a citizen of the United States, or for the purposes of § 901.18(a)(7) a former member of the Service, or in the case of death of the member, the surviving spouse or, if none, another member of the family.

§ 901.17 Charged employee.

Charged employee means a member of the Senior Foreign Service or a member of the Service assigned to a salary class who has been proposed for separation for cause under section 610(a)(2) of the Act.

§ 901.18 Grievance.

(a) *Grievance* means any act, omission, or condition subject to the control of an Agency which is alleged to deprive a member of the Service who is a citizen of the United States of a right or benefit authorized by law or regulation or is otherwise a source of concern or dissatisfaction to the member, including but not limited to:

(1) Complaints against separation of a member allegedly contrary to law or regulation or predicated upon alleged inaccuracy, omission, error or falsely prejudicial character of information in any part of the official personnel record of the member;

(2) Other alleged violation, misinterpretation or misapplication of applicable law, regulation, collective bargaining agreement or published post or agency policy affecting the terms and conditions of the employment or career status of the member;

(3) Allegedly wrongful disciplinary action against the member;

(4) Dissatisfaction with respect to the working environment of the member;

(5) Alleged inaccuracy, omission, error, or falsely prejudicial character of information in the official personnel record of the member which is or could be prejudicial to the member;

(6) Action alleged to be in the nature of reprisal or other interference with freedom of action in connection with participation by a member in a grievance; and

(7) Alleged denial of an allowance, premium pay or other financial benefit to which the member claims entitlement under applicable laws or regulations.

(b) The scope of grievances described above may be modified by written agreement between an Agency and its exclusive representative.

(c) The term *grievance* does not include:

(1) Complaints against an individual assignment of a member under chapter 5 of the Act, other than an assignment which is alleged to be contrary to law or regulation;

(2) The judgment of a selection board (established under section 602 of the Act) or a tenure board (established under section 306(b) of the Act) or any other equivalent body established by laws or regulations which similarly evaluates the performance of members of the Service on a comparative basis, including a merit promotion selecting official, except that alleged procedural violations of law, regulation or collective bargaining agreement or prohibited personnel practice(s) arising under these procedures are grievable;

(3) The expiration of a limited appointment, termination of a limited appointment under section 611 of the Act, or the denial of a limited career extension or denial of a renewal of a limited career extension under section 607(b) of the Act; or

(4) Pursuant to section 1109 of the Act, any complaint or appeal where a specific statutory hearing procedure exists other than procedures for considering prohibited personnel practice charges before the Merit Systems Protection Board or Special Counsel (5 U.S.C. 1206).

(5) Non-adoption of a member suggestion or disapproval of a quality salary increase, performance award, or any other kind of honorary discretionary award, except where such action is alleged to be contrary to law, regulation or collective bargaining agreement; and

(6) The content of published agency policy which is not contrary to law, regulation or collective bargaining agreement.

(d) For the purposes of these regulations, the written complaint concerning any act, omission, or condition specified above may be referred to as the "grievance".

[50 FR 31353, Aug. 2, 1985, as amended at 56 FR 55458, Oct. 28, 1991]

§901.19 Labor organization.

Labor organization means any employee organization accorded recognition as the exclusive employee representative under section 1002(11) of the Act. For the Department of State and the Agency for International Development (AID), the exclusive employee representative is the American Foreign Service Association; for the U.S. Information Agency (USIA), the exclusive employee representative is the American Federation of Government Employees, Local 1812 (AFL-CIO).

§901.20 Party.

Party means—

(a) The grievant/charged employee;

(b) The Agency or Agencies employing the grievant/charged employee and/

or having control over the act, omission, or condition leading to appearance before the Board; or

(c) The exclusive representative if it has achieved party status under §903.4.

A Party may act through its duly designated representative.

[50 FR 31353, Aug. 2, 1985, as amended at 56 FR 55458, Oct. 28, 1991]

§901.21 Record of proceedings.

Record of proceedings means the case file maintained by the Board on each grievance case, or separation for cause proceeding.

§901.22 Representative.

Representative means the person(s) identified in writing to the Board as assisting the party or parties in the presentation of the case.

PART 902—ORGANIZATION

Sec.

AUTHORITY: Secs. 1105 and 1106 of the Foreign Service Act of 1980, Pub. L. 96–465 (22 U.S.C. 4135 and 4136), as amended.

§902.1 Chairperson and deputy chairperson.

The chairperson presides over meetings of the Board. The chairperson shall select one of the Board members as deputy. In the absence of the chairperson, the deputy chairperson, or in his or her absence, another member designated by the chairperson, may act for him or her.

[50 FR 31354, Aug. 2, 1985]

§902.2 Board operations.

(a) The Board may operate either as a whole, or through panels or individual members designated by the chairperson.

(b) When operating as a whole, the Board may not act in the absence of a quorum. A majority of the members shall constitute a quorum. The Board will act by a majority vote of those present. Amendments to these regulations and Board policies adopted pursuant to §910.3 shall be adopted by the Board operating as a whole.

(c) Board panels and presiding members of panels shall be designated by the chairperson subject only to the provisions of §906.4.

[50 FR 31354, Aug. 2, 1985, as amended at 56 FR 55459, Oct. 28, 1991]

§902.3 Board staff.

The chairperson shall select the Board's executive secretary and other staff provided for in the Act. The executive secretary and staff shall be responsible only to the Board through the chairperson.

[50 FR 31354, Aug. 2, 1985]

PART 903—INITIATION AND DOCUMENTATION OF CASES

Sec.

AUTHORITY: Secs. 610, 1104, and 1106–1109 of the Foreign Service Act of 1980, Pub. L. 96–465 (22 U.S.C. 4010, 4134, and 4136–4139), as amended.

SOURCE: 50 FR 31354, Aug. 2, 1985, unless otherwise noted.

§903.1 Initiation of cases.

(a) Grievances submitted to the Board shall be in writing, and shall explain the nature of the grievance, and the remedy sought; shall contain all the documentation furnished to the Agency and the Agency's final review; and shall be timely filed in accordance with applicable regulations.

(b) A member whose grievance is not resolved satisfactorily under Agency procedures, the representative of the grievant, or the exclusive representative (on behalf of a grievant who is a member of the bargaining unit), shall be entitled to file a grievance with the Board no later than 60 days after receiving the Agency decision. In the event that an Agency has not provided its decision within 90 days of filing with the Agency, the grievant, the representative of the grievant, or the exclusive representative (on the grievant's behalf) shall be entitled to file a grievance with the Board no later than 150 days after the date of filing with the Agency. The Board may extend or waive for good cause shown the time limits stated in this section, and may permit or request the views of the parties with respect to whether good cause has been shown for such an extension.

(c) Separation for cause proceedings against a charged employee shall be initiated before the Board by submission of a statement of the acts or behavior considered by the Agency to warrant separation.

§ 903.2 Record of proceedings.

Upon receipt of initial documents relating to a case, a record of proceedings shall be established, and all material received or obtained by the Board in connection with the case shall be placed in it unless the Board excludes such material under § 903.3. The parties and the exclusive representative, if any, shall have access to the record of proceedings. Classified portions of the record of proceedings may be reviewed by the parties and the exclusive representative, if any, under conditions prescribed by the Board to ensure appropriate security.

§ 903.3 Rulings on materials.

The Board may at any stage of the proceedings exclude materials from the record of proceedings at the request of a party or on its own initiative, on the grounds that such materials are irrelevant, immaterial or unduly repetitive.

§ 903.4 Participation of exclusive representative.

(a) Upon the initiation of a case, the executive secretary shall ascertain from the Agency, the grievant/charged employee and any labor organization which has been certified as the exclusive representative of employees of the Agency, whether the relevant position occupied by the grievant/charged employee is part of the bargaining unit for which the labor organization is the exclusive representative. If a substantial dispute exists as to whether that position is part of the bargaining unit, and if the Board determines that resolution of that dispute is necessary for determining the status of the labor organization in a case, the Board shall notify the parties and the labor organization, who may request the Foreign Service Labor Relations Board to make a final determination of that dispute. If the Foreign Service Labor Relations Board determines that the grievant or charged employee is a member of a bargaining unit represented by an exclusive representative, the executive secretary shall promptly send a copy of the papers filed with the Board to the exclusive representative.

(b) The exclusive representative has the right to intervene as a party to the case if such exclusive representative gives timely notice to the Board in writing of its decision to intervene as a party. Notice shall be considered to be timely if given prior to or at the prehearing conference, or, in a case to be decided under part 907 of this chapter, if given within 10 days of receipt of a notice from the Board of the Board's intent to close the record of proceedings.

(c) An exclusive representative which has not intervened under paragraph (b) of this section may be permitted to intervene as a party upon written application. In ruling upon the application, the Board shall consider whether granting the application will unduly delay or prejudice the adjudication of the rights of the original parties, and may place conditions on the exclusive representative's participation to avoid such delay or prejudice.

§ 903.5 Service of documents.

Any party submitting documents to the Board in connection with a case shall send a copy to the other parties and to the exclusive representative, if any. The Board shall send copies of its correspondence concerning the case to the parties and the exclusive representative, if any.

§ 903.6 Interrogatories.

Each party shall be entitled to serve interrogatories upon another party, and have such interrogatories answered by the other party unless the Board finds such interrogatories irrelevant, immaterial, or unduly repetitive. Parties shall follow procedures established by the Board concerning the use of interrogatories.

§ 903.7 Acknowledgment.

Each case received shall be acknowledged in writing by the executive secretary of the Board. If in the judgment of the executive secretary additional documentation or information is needed, he or she may request such materials.

§ 903.8 Withdrawal.

A case may be withdrawn at any time by written notification to the Board from the party initiating the case. A case may be determined by the Board to have lapsed when the grievant fails to respond in writing to two successive written Board inquiries within any deadline fixed for such response. The Board may permit the reopening of lapsed cases upon a showing of good cause and may permit or request the views of the parties as to whether good cause has been shown.

§ 903.9 Access to records.

(a) If a party is denied access to any Agency record prior to or during the consideration of a case by the Agency, the party may protest such denial before the Board in connection with the case.

(b) In considering a case, the Board shall have access to any Agency record as follows:

(1) the Board shall request access to any Agency record which the grievant/charged employee requests to substantiate his or her grievance or defense to a charge if the Board determines that such record may be relevant and material to the case.

(2) the Board may request access to any other Agency record which the Board determines may be relevant and material to the case.

(3) An Agency shall make available to the Board any Agency record requested under paragraphs (b)(1) and (2) of this section unless the head or deputy head or such Agency personally certifies in writing to the Board that disclosure of the record to the Board and the parties would adversely affect the foreign policy or national security of the United States or that such disclosure is prohibited by law. If such a certification is made with respect to any record, the Agency shall supply to the Board a summary or extract of such record unless the reasons specified in the preceding sentence preclude such a summary or extract.

(c) If the Board determines that an Agency record, or a summary or extract of a record, made available to the Board under paragraph (b) of this section is relevant and material to the case, the Agency concerned shall make such record, summary, or extract, as the case may be, available to the parties.

(d) In considering a case, the Board may take into account the fact that the parties or the Board were denied access to any Agency record which the Board determines is or may be relevant and material to the case.

(e) The parties in any case decided by the Board shall have access to the record of proceedings and the decision of the Board.

§ 903.10 Access to witnesses.

The grievant or grievant's representative, or charged employee or his representative, shall be given access to witnesses employed by the foreign affairs agencies. In the event that the agency of the grievant determines that the requests for access are excessive, it may so notify the Board, which shall rule on the relevance and materiality of the potential testimony and may order that access be granted to any or all of the potential witnesses. It shall be the responsibility of the grievant to advise the agency of the agency witnesses to be interviewed and to request administrative leave.

PART 904—JURISDICTION AND PRELIMINARY DETERMINATIONS

Sec.

AUTHORITY: Secs. 1101, 1104, 1108, and 1109 of the Foreign Service Act of 1980, Pub. L. 96–465 (22 U.S.C. 4131, 4134, 4138, and 4139), as amended.

§ 904.1 General.

The Board's jurisdiction extends to any grievance, and to any separation for cause proceeding initiated pursuant to section 610(a)(2) of the Act.

[50 FR 31355, Aug. 2, 1985]

§ 904.2 Preliminary determinations.

(a) If an Agency, in its final review, has questioned whether a complaint constitutes a grievance, the Board will make a preliminary determination of its jurisdiction unless the Board concludes that resolution of the question of jurisdiction should be deferred until the Board has compiled a record of proceedings or held a hearing on the merits of the case.

(b) The Board may also make a preliminary determination on any question raised by a Party concerning the timeliness of a grievance, the election of other remedies under § 904.3, or any other issue whose resolution might avoid the necessity of further proceedings.

(c) Before making a preliminary determination under this section, the Board shall obtain the views of the other parties and transmit those views to all parties.

(d) Where an issue presented for preliminary determination under this section is contested by a party or would result in the termination of a case, a panel of three members of the Board shall decide the issue.

[50 FR 31355, Aug. 2, 1985, as amended at 56 FR 55459, Oct. 28, 1991]

§ 904.3 Relationship to other remedies.

(a) A grievant may not file a grievance with the Board if the grievant has formally requested, prior to filing a grievance, that the matter or matters which are the basis of the grievance be considered or resolved and relief provided under another provision of law, regulation, or executive order, and the matter has been carried to final decision under such provision on its merits or is still under consideration. This provision shall not apply to grievants who have filed a prohibited personnel practice charge before the Special Counsel for the Merit Systems Protection Board.

(b) If a grievant is not prohibited from filing a grievance under paragraph (a) of this section, the grievant may file with the Board a grievance which is also eligible for consideration, resolution, and relief as a prohibited personnel practice complaint under the provisions of law relating to the Merit Systems Protection Board or Special Counsel, or under a regulation or executive order. An election of remedies under this section shall be final upon the acceptance of jurisdiction by the Board.

[50 FR 31355, Aug. 2, 1985]

§ 904.4 Suspension of agency actions.

(a) If the Board determines that the agency is considering involuntary separation of the Grievant, disciplinary action against the Grievant, or recovery from the Grievant of alleged overpayment of salary, expenses, or allowances, which is related to a grievance pending before the Board, and that such action should be suspended, the agency shall suspend such action until the Board has ruled on the grievance. Notwithstanding such suspension of action, the head of the agency concerned or a chief of mission or principal officer may exclude the Grievant from official premises or from the performance of specified functions when such exclusion is determined in writing to be essential to the functioning of the post or office to which the Grievant is assigned.

(b) Notwithstanding paragraph (a) of this section, the Board shall not determine that action to suspend without pay a Grievant shall be suspended if the head of an agency or his designee has determined that there is reasonable cause to believe that a Grievant has committed a job-related crime for which a sentence of imprisonment may be imposed and has taken action to suspend the Grievant without pay pending a final resolution of the underlying matter. For this purpose, reasonable cause to believe that a member has committed a crime for which a sentence of imprisonment may be imposed shall be defined as a member of the Service having been convicted of, and sentence of imprisonment having been imposed for a job-related crime.

(c) The Board shall expedite its decisions on requested suspensions of proposed Agency actions. The Board may permit or require argument with respect to such requests by the Parties and Exclusive Representative, if any.

[56 FR 55459, Oct. 28, 1991]

PART 905—BURDEN OF PROOF

AUTHORITY: Secs. 610 and 1106 of the Foreign Service Act of 1980, Pub. L. 96-465 (22 U.S.C. 4010 and 4136), as amended.

§905.1 Grievances other than disciplinary actions.

(a) In all grievances other than those concerning disciplinary actions, the grievant has the burden of establishing, by a preponderance of the evidence, that the grievance is meritorious.

(b) Where a grievant establishes that an evaluation contained falsely prejudicial material which may have been a substantial factor in an agency action, and the question is presented whether the agency would have taken the same action had the evaluation not contained that material, the burden will shift to the agency to establish, by a preponderance of the evidence, that it would have done so.

(c) Where a grievant establishes that a procedural error occurred which is of such a nature that it may have been a substantial factor in an agency action with respect to the grievant, and the question is presented whether the agency would have taken the same action had the procedural error not occurred, the burden will shift to the agency to establish, by a preponderance of the evidence, that it would have done so.

[50 FR 31356, Aug. 2, 1985]

§905.2 Disciplinary grievances.

In grievances over disciplinary actions, the agency has the burden of establishing by a preponderance of the evidence that the disciplinary action was justified, provided, however, that in a grievance concerning suspension without pay pursuant to section 610(a)(3) of the Act, the Board's determination of the grievance shall be limited to:

(a) Whether the required procedures have been followed; and

(b) Whether there exists reasonable cause to believe a crime has been committed for which a sentence of imprisonment may be imposed and there is a nexus between the conduct and the efficiency of the Service.

For this purpose, reasonable cause to believe that a member has committed a crime for which a sentence of imprisonment may be imposed shall be defined as a member of the Service having been convicted of, and sentence of imprisonment having been imposed for, a job-related crime.

[56 FR 55459, Oct. 28, 1991]

§905.3 Separation for cause.

In separation for cause cases, the agency has the burden of establishing, by a preponderance of the evidence, that the proposed separation is for such cause as will promote the efficiency of the service.

[50 FR 31356, Aug. 2, 1985]

PART 906—HEARINGS

AUTHORITY: Secs. 610 and 1106 of the Foreign Service Act of 1980, Pub. L. 96-465 (22 U.S.C. 4010 and 4136), as amended.

SOURCE: 50 FR 31356, Aug. 2, 1985, unless otherwise noted.

§906.1 Decision whether to hold a hearing.

After deciding either to accept jurisdiction over a grievance or to postpone decision of that question under §904.2(a) of this chapter, the Board will make an initial determination of whether a hearing shall be held in accordance with part 906 of this chapter, or whether the grievance shall be resolved without a hearing in accordance with part 907 of this chapter. The Board may reconsider its decision as to holding a hearing upon the written request of any party or on its own initiative.

§ 906.2 Mandatory hearing.

The Board shall conduct a hearing—(a) At the request of the grievant in any case which involves disciplinary action or a grievant's retirement from the Service for expiration of time-in-class or based on relative performance, or (b) In any case which in the judgment of the Board can best be resolved by a hearing or presentation of oral argument. The Board shall also conduct a hearing in separation for cause proceedings unless the charged employee waives in writing his or her right to such hearing.

§ 906.3 Notification.

When the Board orders a hearing, the executive secretary shall so notify the parties in writing. The parties shall be given reasonable notice of the date and place selected by the Board for the hearing.

§ 906.4 Hearing panels and members.

Unless the Board and the parties agree otherwise, all hearings shall be held before a panel of at least three members.

§ 906.5 Prehearing conferences.

(a) The Board may in its discretion order a prehearing conference of the parties (which may be presided over by any member) for the purpose of considering:

(1) Simplification or clarification of the issues;

(2) Serving of interrogatories;

(3) Stipulations, admissions, agreements on documents, matters already on record, or similar agreements which will avoid the necessity of proving facts or issues not in dispute;

(4) Identification of witnesses the parties may wish to call and the intended scope of their testimony; limitation on the number of witnesses; and arrangement for the appearance of witnesses;

(5) Avoidance of irrelevant, immaterial, or unduly repetitive testimony;

(6) The possibility of disposition of the case through agreement;

(7) The order of presentation at the hearing and the allocation of the burden of proof; and

(8) Such other matters as may aid in the disposition of the case.

(b) The parties authorized to attend the hearing may attend the prehearing conference.

(c) The results of the conference shall be summarized in writing by the Board and made a part of the record of proceedings. Copies of the summary shall be sent to the parties. The parties may submit comments or corrections on the summary.

§ 906.6 Powers of presiding member.

In connection with the hearing, the presiding member shall, as appropriate:

(a) Fix the time and place of the hearing;

(b) Order further conferences;

(c) Regulate the course of the hearing;

(d) Administer oaths and affirmations;

(e) Dispose of procedural requests and similar matters;

(f) Rule on admissibility of testimony and exhibits;

(g) Exclude any person from the hearing for behavior that obstructs the hearing;

(h) Authorize and set the time for the filing of briefs or other documents;

(i) Grant continuances and extensions of time;

(j) Reopen the record;

(k) Take any other action in the course of the proceedings consistent with the purpose of this part.

§ 906.7 Conduct of hearing.

(a) *Authorized attendance.* The parties and, as determined by the Board, a reasonable number of representatives of the parties are entitled to be present at the hearing. The Board may, after considering the views of the parties and of any other individuals connected with the grievance, decide that a hearing should be open to others. No person shall be permitted to attend the hearing when classified material is being discussed unless that person possesses the appropriate security clearance.

(b) *Procedure.* Hearings shall be conducted by the presiding member so as to assure a full and fair proceeding. The Board shall not be limited by the legal rules of evidence. However, the presiding member shall exclude irrelevant, immaterial, or unduly repetitive evidence. The Board may require the parties to designate one of their representatives as principal spokesperson.

(c) *Order of presentation.* In cases involving disciplinary action, including separation for cause cases, the Agency will ordinarily present its case first and will retain that order of precedence throughout the hearing. In other cases the grievant will ordinarily present his or her case first and will retain that order of precedence throughout the hearing.

(d) *Evidence.* Subject to the presiding member's rulings on the relevancy, materiality, and repetitious nature of evidence, the parties may offer such evidence, including interrogatories, depositions and Agency records as they desire. The shall produce such additional evidence as the presiding member shall consider relevant and material. Where deemed appropriate by the Board, the parties may be supplied only with a summary or extract of classified material (also see §903.9 of this chapter).

(e) *Testimony.* Testimony at a hearing shall be given under oath or affirmation.

(f) *Transcript.* A verbatim transcript shall be made of any hearing and shall be part of the record of proceedings.

§ 906.8 Witnesses.

(a) *General.* Each party shall be entitled to examine and cross-examine witnesses at the hearing or by deposition. A party wishing to take the deposition of a witness shall give the other parties reasonable notice of the time and place of the deposition and of the identity of the witness.

(b) *Availability.* Upon request of the Board or upon request of the grievant/charged employee deemed relevant and material by the Board, an Agency shall promptly make available at the hearing or by deposition any witness under its control, supervision or responsibility. If the Board determines that the actual presence of such witness at the hearing is required for just resolution of the case, the witness shall be made available at the hearing, with necessary costs and travel expenses paid by the Agency which is a party to the hearing.

(c) *Notice.* The parties are responsible for notifying their witnesses and for arranging for their appearance at the time and place set for the hearing. The Board may preclude a witness from testifying because of the failure of the party responsible for witness' appearance to comply with this section.

§ 906.9 Failure of party to appear.

The hearing may proceed in the absence of any party who, after due notice and without good cause, fails to be present or obtain an adjournment.

PART 907—PROCEDURE WHEN HEARING IS NOT HELD

AUTHORITY: Sec. 1106 of the Foreign Service Act of 1980, Pub. L. 96–465 (22 U.S.C. 4136), as amended.

§ 907.1 General.

(a) In a case in which a hearing is not required under §906.1 of this chapter, the Board may request in writing that specified documents or other evidence be furnished to it and/or may authorize the executive secretary to obtain such additional documents or other evidence as may be necessary to understand and decide the case.

(b) Each party will be offered the opportunity to review and to supplement, by written submissions, the record of proceedings, prior to the date fixed by the Board for closing of the Record. The Board shall then consider the case and make a decision based on that Record. This may include the ordering of a hearing in accordance with part 906.

[50 FR 31357, Aug. 2, 1985]

PART 908—REMEDIES

AUTHORITY: Secs. 1106 and 1107 of the Foreign Service Act of 1980, Pub. L. 96–465 (22 U.S.C. 610, 4010, 4136, and 4137).

§ 908.1 Board orders.

If the Board finds that a grievance is meritorious, the Board shall have the authority to direct the Agency:

(a) To correct any official personnel record relating to the grievant which the Board finds to be inaccurate or erroneous, to have an omission, or to contain information of a falsely prejudicial character;

(b) To reverse a decision denying the grievant compensation or any other perquisite of employment authorized by laws or regulations when the Board finds that such decision was arbitrary, capricious, or contrary to laws or regulations;

(c) To retain in the Service a member whose separation would be in consequence of the matter by which the member is aggrieved;

(d) To reinstate the grievant, and to grant the grievant back pay, where it is established that the separation or suspension without pay of the employee was unjustified or unwarranted under the Back Pay Act (5 U.S.C. 5596(b)(1));

(e) To take any corrective action deemed appropriate by the Board provided it is not contrary to law or collective bargaining agreement.

[50 FR 31357, Aug. 2, 1985, as amended at 56 FR 55459, Oct. 28, 1991]

§ 908.2 Attorney fees.

(a) If the Board finds that a grievance is meritorious or that an Agency has not established the cause for separation of a charged employee in a hearing before the Board pursuant to section 610 of the Act, the Board shall have the authority to direct the Agency to pay reasonable attorney fees to the same extent and in the same manner as such fees may be required by the Merit Systems Protection Board under 5 U.S.C. 7701(g).

(b) Requests for attorney fees, accompanied by supporting documentation, must be filed with the Board within thirty (30) days of the date of the Board's decision.

[56 FR 55459, Oct. 28, 1991]

§ 908.3 Board recommendations.

(a) If the Board finds that the grievance is meritorious and that remedial action should be taken that relates directly to promotion, tenure, or assignment of the Grievant or to other remedial action not otherwise provided for in this section, or if the Board finds that the evidence in a grievance proceeding warrants disciplinary action against any employee of an Agency, it shall make an appropriate recommendation to the head of the concerned Agency.

(b) The head of the Agency shall make a written decision on the recommendation of the Board within 30 days after receiving the recommendation and shall implement the recommendation of the Board except to the extent that the head of the Agency rejects the recommendation in whole or in part on the basis of a determination that implementation of the recommendation would be contrary to law or would adversely affect the foreign policy or national security of the United States. If the head of the Agency rejects the recommendation in whole or in part, the decision shall specify the reasons for such action. Copies of the decision shall be served on the other parties. Pending the decision of the head of the Agency, there shall be no ex parte communication concerning the grievance between the head of the Agency and any person involved in the proceedings of the Board. The head of the Agency shall, however, have access to the entire Record of the Proceedings of the Board.

(c) A recommendation under this section shall, for the purposes of section 1110 of the Act, be considered a final action upon the expiration of a 30-day period referred to in paragraph (b) of this section, except to the extent that it is rejected by the head of the Agency by an appropriate written decision.

(d)(1) If the head of the Agency makes a written decision under paragraph (b) of this section rejecting a recommendation in whole or in part on the basis of a determination that implementing such recommendation would be contrary to law, the head of the Agency shall, within the 30-day period referred to in paragraph (b) of this section:

(i) Submit a copy of such decision to the Board; and

(ii) Request that the Board reconsider its recommendation or, if less than the entirety is rejected, that the Board reconsider the portion rejected.

(2) Within 30 days after receiving such a request, the Board shall, after reviewing the head of the Agency's decision, make a recommendation to the head of the agency confirming, modifying, or vacating its original recommendation or, if less than the entirety was rejected, the portion involved. Reconsideration shall be limited to the question of whether implementing the Board's original recommendation, either in whole or in part, as applicable, would be contrary to law.

(e) A Board recommendation made under the preceding paragraph (d)(2) of this section shall be considered a final action for the purpose of section 1110 of the Act, and shall be implemented by the head of the Agency.

(f) The provisions of paragraphs (c), (d), and (e) of this section shall not apply with respect to any grievance in which the Board has issued a final decision pursuant to section 1107 of the Act before December 22, 1987.

[50 FR 31357, Aug. 2, 1985. Redesignated and amended at 56 FR 55459, Oct. 28, 1991]

PART 909—DECISIONMAKING

Sec.

AUTHORITY: Secs. 1106 and 1107, Foreign Service Act of 1980 (Pub. L. 96–465; 22 U.S.C. 4136 and 4137).

SOURCE: 50 FR 31358, Aug. 2, 1985, unless otherwise noted.

§909.1 Basis.

Decisions of the Board shall be based upon the record of proceedings, shall be in writing, shall include findings of fact, and shall include a statement of the reasons for the decision.

§909.2 Board order.

Where the Board's decision imposes action on an Agency the decision shall be in the form of a remedial order addressed to the designated official of the Agency. A copy of the decision shall be supplied to each party.

§909.3 Board recommendation.

Where the Board's decision is a recommendation, it shall be directed to the head of the Agency. A copy of the decision shall be supplied to each party.

§909.4 Other decision.

Where the Board's decision requires no action by an Agency, the decision shall be forwarded to the grievant. A copy of the decision shall be supplied to each party.

§909.5 Time limits for compliance.

Orders of the Board and recommendations which are not rejected in accordance with §908.2 of this chapter shall be complied with within any time limits for compliance established by the Board's decision, unless the Board extends the time limit on a showing of good cause.

§909.6 Summaries of Board decisions.

The Board may, from time to time, issue such summaries and expurgated versions of its decisions as it may consider necessary to permit the Agencies, the exclusive representative organization(s), and the members of the Service to become aware of the general nature of the cases it has received and their manner of disposition, without invading the privacy of the grievants.

PART 910—MISCELLANEOUS

Sec.

AUTHORITY: Secs. 1106, 1107, 1110, and 2401 of the Foreign Service Act of 1980, Pub. L. 96–465 (22 U.S.C. 4136, 4137, 4140, and 4172).

§910.1 Requests to reopen cases.

The Board may reconsider any decision upon the presentation of newly discovered or previously unavailable material evidence.

[50 FR 31358, Aug. 2, 1985. Redesignated at 56 FR 55460, Oct. 28, 1991]

§910.2 Ex parte communications.

(a) "Ex parte communications" are oral or written communications between the Board or its staff and an interested party to a proceeding which are made without providing the other parties a chance to participate.

(b) Ex parte communications concerning the merits of any matter which has or may come before the Board for adjudication or which would otherwise contravene the rules regarding written submissions are prohibited until the Board renders a final decision. Any communication made in contravention of this rule shall be made a part of the record and an opportunty for rebuttal allowed. If the communication was oral, a memorandum stating the substance of the discussion shall be placed in the record.

(c) This rule does not apply to communications concerning such matters as the status of a case, the methods for transmitting evidence to the Board, and other procedural matters which do not concern the merits of any matter before the Board for adjudication and which do not otherwise contravene the rules regarding written submissions.

[50 FR 31358, Aug. 2, 1985. Redesignated at 56 FR 55460, Oct. 28, 1991]

§910.3 Board policy statements.

The Board may publish statements regarding policies it has established as to its operations and procedures.

[50 FR 31358, Aug. 2, 1985. Redesignated at 56 FR 55460, Oct. 28, 1991]

§910.4 Confidentiality; Record of grievances awarded.

(a) To the maximum extent practicable, the Board will make every effort to preserve the confidentiality of the identity of the grievant or charged employee.

(b) The records of the Board shall be maintained by the Board under appropriate safeguards to preserve confidentiality and shall be separate from all records of the Agencies; provided, however, that records of all grievances awarded in favor of the Grievant in which the grievance concerns gross misconduct by a supervisor shall be separately maintained by the Board and the procedures regarding confidentiality and disclosure of such records shall be as provided in section 1107(e) of the Foreign Service Act of 1980, as amended; and provided further, that the Board shall not make a finding of gross misconduct without first providing the supervisor whose conduct is at issue notice and an opportunity to respond.

[50 FR 31358, Aug. 2, 1985. Redesignated and amended at 56 FR 55460, Oct. 28, 1991]

§910.5 Judicial review.

Any aggrieved party may obtain judicial review of a final action of an Agency head or the Board on any grievance in the district courts of the United States in accordance with the standards set forth in chapter 7 of title 5 of the United States Code. 5 U.S.C. 706 shall apply without limitation or exception.

[50 FR 31358, Aug. 2, 1985. Redesignated at 56 FR 55460, Oct. 28, 1991]

§910.6 Pending grievances.

Any grievance pending before the Board prior to February 15, 1981 shall be resolved under the provisions of the Foreign Service Act of 1946 as amended, and the regulations promulgated thereunder.

[50 FR 31358, Aug. 2, 1985. Redesignated at 56 FR 55460, Oct. 28, 1991]

PART 911—IMPLEMENTATION DISPUTES

Sec.

AUTHORITY: Sec. 1014 of the Foreign Service Act of 1980, Pub. L. 96–465 (22 U.S.C. 4114), as amended.

SOURCE: 50 FR 31359, Aug. 2, 1985, unless otherwise noted.

§911.1 Definition.

An implementation dispute is any dispute between the agency and the exclusive representative, as provided in regulations adopted as a result of collective bargaining between the agencies and the employee representatives. Such a dispute, also referred to as an institutional dispute, is one which directly concerns the rights and obligations of an agency and an exclusive representative toward each other or the rights or obligations between an agency and one or more employees as set forth in a collective bargaining agreement.

§911.2 Filing complaint.

If the dispute is not satisfactorily resolved at the agency level, the moving party may file a complaint within 45 calendar days from the date of the response (or in any case must file within 90 days of filing the implementation dispute) with the Board in writing and with specificity as to the nature of the violation.

§911.3 Procedure.

Implementation disputes shall be handled by the Board in accordance with the procedures set forth in parts 901–910 of this chapter.

§911.4 Effect of Board decision.

The action of the Board shall be final and binding and shall be implemented by the parties, unless an exception is filed with the Foreign Service Labor Relations Board within 30 days after receipt of the Grievance Board action.

§911.5 Arbitrability of determination.

Questions that cannot be resolved by the parties as to whether a complaint is subject to this procedure may be referred by either party to the Grievance Board for a threshold determination.

§911.6 Finality of choice.

An alleged violation of an institutional right as reflected in a collective bargaining agreement may be filed under these procedures or as an unfair labor practice, but not both.

§911.7 Review.

Resolution of disputes under this section shall not be subject to judicial review.

PARTS 912–999 [RESERVED]

CHAPTER X—INTER-AMERICAN FOUNDATION

PART 1000 [RESERVED]

PART 1001—EMPLOYEE RESPONSIBILITIES AND CONDUCT

AUTHORITY: 5 U.S.C. 7301.

§ 1001.1 Cross-references to employee ethical conduct standards and financial disclosure regulations.

Directors and other employees of the Inter-American Foundation should refer to the Standards of Ethical Conduct for Employees of the Executive Branch at 5 CFR part 2635, the Inter-American Foundation regulations at 5 CFR part 7301 which supplement the executive branch standards, and the executive branch financial disclosure regulations at 5 CFR part 2634.

[59 FR 3772, Jan. 27, 1994]

PART 1002—AVAILABILITY OF RECORDS

AUTHORITY: 5 U.S.C. 552, and 31 U.S.C. 483(a).

SOURCE: 37 FR 8375, Apr. 26, 1972, unless otherwise noted.

§ 1002.1 Introduction.

(a) It is the policy of the Inter-American Foundation that information about its operations, procedures, and records be freely available to the public in accordance with the provisions of the Freedom of Information Act.

(b) The Foundation will make the fullest possible disclosure of its information and identifiable records consistent with the provisions of this Act and the regulations in this part.

§ 1002.2 Definitions.

As used in this part, the following words have the meaning set forth below:

Act. "Act" means the Act of June 5, 1967, sometimes referred to as the "Freedom of Information Act" or the Public Information Section of the Administrative Procedure Act, as amended, Pub. L. 90–23, 81 Stat. 54, and codified at 5 U.S.C. 552.

Foundation. "Foundation" means the Inter-American Foundation.

President. "President" means the President of the Foundation.

Records. The word "records" includes all books, papers, or other documentary materials made or received by the Foundation in connection with the transaction of its business which have been preserved or are appropriate for preservation by the Foundation as evidence of the organization, functions, policies, decisions, procedures, operations, or other activities, or because of the informational value of data contained therein. Library or other material acquired and preserved solely for reference or exhibition purposes, and stocks of publications and processed documents are not included within the definition of the word "records."

§ 1002.3 Access to Foundation records.

Any person desiring to have access to Foundation records should call or apply in person between the hours of 9 a.m. and 5 p.m. on weekdays (holidays excluded) at the Foundation offices at 901 N. Stuart St., 10th Floor, Arlington, VA 22203. Requests for access should be made to the General Counsel, Office of the General Counsel () at the Foundation offices. If request is made for copies of any record, the General Counsel's Office will assist the person making such request in seeing that such copies are provided according to the rules in this part.

[37 FR 8375, Apr. 26, 1972, as amended at 71 FR 63235, Oct. 30, 2006]

§ 1002.4 Written requests.

In order to facilitate the processing of written requests, every petitioner should:

(a) Address his request to:

General Counsel, Inter-American Foundation, 901 N. Stuart St., 10th Floor, Arlington, VA 22203.

(b) Identify the desired record by name or brief description, or number, and date, as applicable. The identification should be specific enough so that a record can be readily identified and found;

(c) Include a check or money order to the order of the "Inter-American Foundation" covering the appropriate search and copying fees, or request a determination of fee;

(d) Allow a reasonable amount of time for reply. Furnishing the requested information will involve search and retrieval of records, copying and mailing;

(e) Blanket requests or requests for "the entire file of" or "all matters relating to" a specified subject will not be accepted.

[37 FR 8375, Apr. 26, 1972, as amended at 71 FR 63236, Oct. 30, 2006]

§ 1002.5 Records available at the Foundation.

The General Counsel's Office will make available, to the extent not authorized to be withheld, the following works or classes of information:

(a) A copy of Agency regulations, including a copy of title 22 of the Code of Federal Regulations, or of any other title of the Code in which Agency regulations may have been published;

(b) Final unclassified reports;

(c) Copies of grants, loans, or other agreements in force;

(d) Personnel information affecting the public;

(e) Procurement information affecting the public;

(f) Contracts;

(g) Reimbursable agreements with other agencies.

[37 FR 8375, Apr. 26, 1972, as amended at 71 FR 63236, Oct. 30, 2006]

§ 1002.6 Records of other Departments and Agencies.

Requests for records that have been originated by or are primarily the concern of another U.S. Department or Agency will be forwarded to the particular Department of Agency involved, and the petitioner notified. In response to requests for records or publications published by the Government Printing Office or other Government printing activity, the Foundation will refer the petitioner to the appropriate sales office and refund any fee payments therefor which accompany the request.

§ 1002.7 Fees.

Except as otherwise specifically provided by the Foundation, a fee will be levied for all searches for, or copies of, records. These fees will be computed so as to recover the full cost of searching and copying.

(a) *Advance payment and deposits.* When the amount of a fee can be readily computed (as, for example, when a specified number of copy pages are requested) advance payment will be required. When the amount cannot be readily computed (as, for example, when an unknown amount of stafftime must be used in complying with a request), the General Counsel may require payment of a reasonable deposit before undertaking to collect the requested records. At the earliest practicable time, the General Counsel will determine the full amount of the fee and, before complying fully with the request, will require payment of any balance due or refund any overpayment.

(b) *Schedule of fees.* The following fees apply for services rendered to the public:

(1) Searching for records and collateral assistance, per hour or fraction thereof	$5.00
(2) Making copies (Xerox or comparable) per page	0.40

Should a situation arise which is not covered by the above schedule, the fee to be charged will include all direct and indirect costs of the service, including but not limited to materials, labor, and the like. The amount of the fee including charges, if any, for records printed by contractors or grantees will be determined by the A&F Director.

(c) *Revision of schedule.* The fee schedule will be revised from time to time, without notice, to assure recovery of the cost of rendering information services to any person. The revised schedule will be available without charge.

[37 FR 8375, Apr. 26, 1972, as amended at 71 FR 63236, Oct. 30, 2006]

§ 1002.8 Exemptions.

The Act authorizes exemption from disclosure of records and information concerning matters that are:

(a) Specifically required by Executive order to be exempt from disclosure in the interest of the national defense or foreign policy;

(b) Related solely to the internal personnel rules and practices by the Foundation;

(c) Specifically exempted from disclosure by statute;

(d) Trade secrets and commercial or financial information obtained from any person which is privileged or confidential;

(e) Interagency or intra-agency memoranda or letters which would not be available by law to a private party in litigation with the Foundation;

(f) Personnel and medical files and similar files the disclosure of which would constitute an unwarranted invasion of personal privacy;

(g) Investigatory files (including security investigation files and files concerning the conduct of employees) compiled for law enforcement purposes except to the extent available by law to a private party.

The Foundation will not honor requests for exempt records or information.

§ 1002.9 Denial of records; review.

If a request for records is denied, the person who made the request is entitled to have the denial reviewed by the Foundation President as promptly as circumstances permit. If the President determines that the withholding is improper, he will direct in writing that the requested records be made available in accordance with these regulations. If he determines that the withholding is proper, he will so notify such person in writing, and his determination will constitute the final Foundation decision.

PART 1003—RULES SAFEGUARDING PERSONAL INFORMATION IN IAF RECORDS

Sec.

AUTHORITY: 5 U.S.C. 552a.

SOURCE: 41 FR 19211, May 11, 1976, unless otherwise noted.

§ 1003.1 General policies, conditions of disclosure, accounting of certain disclosures, and definitions.

(a) The Inter-American Foundation will safeguard an individual against an invasion of personal privacy. Except as otherwise provided by law or regulation its officials and employees will:

(1) Permit an individual to determine what records pertaining to him or her will be collected, maintained, used, or disseminated by the Inter-American Foundation.

(2) Permit an individual to prevent records pertaining to him or her, obtained by the Inter-American Foundation for a particular purpose, from being used or made available for another purpose without his or her consent.

(3) Permit an individual to gain access to information pertaining to him or her in the Inter-American Foundation records, to have a copy made of all or any portion thereof, and to correct or amend such records.

(4) Collect, maintain, use or disseminate any record of identifiable personal information in a manner that assures that such action is for a necessary and lawful purpose, that the information is correct and accurate for its intended use, and that adequate safeguards are provided to prevent misuse of such information.

(5) Permit exemptions from records requirements provided in 5 U.S.C. 552a only where an important public policy need for such exemption has been determined pursuant to specific statutory authority.

(b) The Inter-American Foundation will not disclose any record contained in a system of records by any means of communication to any person or any other agency except by written request of or prior written consent of the individual to whom the record pertains unless such disclosure is:

(1) To those officers and employees of the agency which maintains the record and who have a need for the record in the performance of their duties;

(2) Required under 5 U.S.C. 552;

(3) For a routine use of the record compatible with the purpose for which it was collected;

(4) To the Bureau of the Census for purposes of planning or carrying out a census or survey or related activity pursuant to title 13, United States Code;

(5) To a recipient who has provided the Inter-American Foundation with advance adequate written assurance that the record will be used solely as a statistical research or reporting record, and the record is to be transferred in a form that is not individually identifiable;

(6) To the National Archives of the United States as a record which has sufficient historical or other value to warrant its continued preservation by the U.S. Government, or for evaluation by the Administrator of General Services or designee to determine whether the record has such value;

(7) To another agency or to an instrumentality of any governmental jurisdiction within or under the control of the United States for a civil or criminal law enforcement activity if the activity is authority by law, and if the head of the agency or instrumentality has made a written request to the Inter-American foundation specifying the particular portion desired and the law enforcement activity for which the record is sought;

(8) To a person pursuant to a showing of compelling circumstances affecting the health or safety of an individual if upon such disclosure notification is transmitted to the last known address of such individual;

(9) To either House of Congress, or, to the extent of matter within its jurisdiction, any committee or subcommittee thereof, any joint committee of Congress or subcommittee of any such joint committee;

(10) To the Comptroller General, or any authorized representatives in the course of the performance of the duties of the General Accounting Office; or

(11) Pursuant to the order of a court of competent jurisdiction.

(c) With respect to each system of records (i.e., a group of records from which information is retrieved by the name of the individual or by some identifying number, symbol, or other identifying particular assigned to the individual) under Inter-American foundation control the Inter-American Foundation will (except for disclosures made under paragraph (b) (1) or (2) of this section) keep an accurate accounting as follows:

(1) For each disclosure of a record to any person or to another agency made under paragraph (b) of this section, maintain information consisting of the date, nature, and purpose of each disclosure, and the name and address of the person or agency to whom the disclosure is made;

(2) Retain the accounting made under paragraph (c)(1) of this section for at least 5 years or the life of the record, whichever is longer, after the disclosures for which the accounting is made;

(3) Except for disclosures made under paragraph (b)(7) of this section, make the accounting under paragraph (c)(1) of this section available to the individual named in the record at his or her request; and

(4) Inform any person or other agency about any correction or notation of dispute made by the agency of any record that has been disclosed to the person or agency if an accounting of the disclosure was made.

(d) The parent of any minor, or the legal guardian of any individual who has been declared incompetent due to physical or mental incapacity or age by a court of competent jurisdiction, may act on behalf of the individual.

(e) Section 552a(e), title 5, United States Code, provided that:

(1) Any officer or employee of the Inter-American Foundation, who by virtue of his or her employment or official position, has possession of, or access to, Inter-American Foundation records which contain individually identifiable information the disclosure of which is prohibited by 5 U.S.C. 552a and who knowing that disclosure of the specific material is so prohibited, willfully discloses the material in any manner to any person or agency not entitled to receive it, shall be guilty of

a misdemeanor and fined not more than $5,000.

(2) Any officer or employee of the Inter-American Foundation who willfully maintains a system of records without meeting the notice requirements of 5 U.S.C. 552a(e)(4) shall be guilty of a misdemeanor and fined not more than $5,000.

(3) Any person who knowingly and willfully requests or obtains any record concerning an individual from the Inter-American Foundation under false pretenses shall be guilty of a misdemeanor and fined not more than $5,000.

§ 1003.2 Definitions.

The following definitions apply:

(a) The term *agency* includes any executive department, military department, Government corporation, Government controlled corporation, or other establishment in the executive branch of the government (including the Executive Office of the President), or any independent regulatory agency.

(b) The term *individual* means a citizen of the United States or an alien lawfully admitted for permanent residence.

(c) The term *maintain* includes maintain, collect, use, or disseminate.

(d) The term *record* means any item, collection, or grouping of information about an individual that is maintained by an agency, including, but not limited to, his or her educational, financial transactions, medical history, and criminal or employment history and that contains his or her name, or the identifying number, symbol, or other identifying particular assigned to the individual, such as a finger or voice print or a photograph.

(e) The term *system of records* means a group of any records under the control of any agency from which information is retrieved by the name of the individual or by some identifying number, symbol, or other identifying particular assigned to the individual.

(f) The term *statistical record* means a record in a system of records maintained for statistical research or reporting purposes only and not used in whole or in part in making any determination about an identifiable individual except as provided by section 8 of title 13, United States Code.

(g) The term *routine use* means, with respect to the disclosure or a record, the use of such record for a purpose which is compatible with the purpose for which it was collected.

§ 1003.3 Access to records.

(a) Except as otherwise provided by law or regulation any individual upon request may gain access to his or her record or to any information pertaining to him or her which is contained in any system or records maintained by the Inter-American Foundation. The individual will be permitted, and upon his or her request, a person of his or her own choosing permitted to accompany him or her, to review the record and have a copy made of all or any portion thereof in a form comprehensible to him or her. The Inter-American foundation will require, however, a written statement from the individual authorizing discussion of that individual's record in the accompanying person's presence.

(b) Any individual may request amendment of any Inter-American Foundation record pertaining to him or her. Not later than 10 days (excluding Saturdays, Sundays, and legal public holidays) after the date of receipt of such request, the Inter-American Foundation will acknowledge in writing such receipt. The Inter-American Foundation will also promptly either:

(1) Correct any part thereof which the individual believes is not accurate, relevant, timely, or complete; or

(2) Inform the individual of the Inter-American Foundation's refusal to amend the record in accordance with his or her request, the reason for the refusal, the procedures by which the individual may request a review of that refusal by the Administrator or designee, and the name and address of such official.

(c) Any individual who disagrees with the Inter-American Foundation's refusal to amend his or her record may request a review of such refusal. The Inter-American Foundation will complete such review not later than 30 days (excluding Saturdays, Sundays, and legal public holidays) from the date on which the individual requests such review and make a final determination unless, for good cause shown, the Administrator extends such 30-day period. If, after review, the Administrator or designee also refuses to amend the record in accordance with the request the individual will be advised of the right to file with the Inter-American Foundation a concise statement setting forth the reasons for his or her disagreement with the Inter-American Foundation's refusal, and also advised of the provisions for judicial review of the reviewing official's determination (5 U.S.C. 552a(g)(1)(A)).

(d) In any disclosure, containing information about which the individual has filed a statement of disagreement, occurring after the filing of the statement under paragraph (c) of this section, the Inter-American Foundation will clearly note any part of the record which is disputed and provide copies of the statement (and, if the Inter-American Foundation deems it appropriate, copies also of a concise statement of the Inter-American Foundation's reasons for not making the amendments requested) to persons or other agencies to whom the disputed record has been disclosed.

(e) Nothing in 5 U.S.C. 552a, however, allows an individual access to any information compiled in reasonable anticipation of a civil action or proceeding.

[41 FR 19211, May 11, 1976, as amended at 42 FR 37368, July 21, 1977]

§ 1003.4 Inter-American Foundation system of records requirements.

(a) The Inter-American Foundation will maintain in its records any such information about an individual as is relevant and necessary to accomplish a purpose of the Inter-American Foundation required to be accomplished by statute or Executive order of the President.

(b) The Inter-American Foundation will collect information to the greatest extent practicable directly from the subject individual when the information may result in adverse determinations about an individual's rights, benefits, and privileges under Federal programs.

(c) The Inter-American Foundation will inform each individual whom it asks to supply information, on the form which it uses to collect the information or on a separate form that can be retained by the individual of:

(1) The authority (whether granted by statute or Executive order of the President) which authorizes the solicitation of the information and whether disclosure of such information is mandatory or voluntary;

(2) The principal purpose or purposes for which the information is intended to be used;

(3) The routine uses which may be made of the information, as published pursuant to paragraph (d)(4) of this section; and

(4) The effects on him or her, if any, of not providing all or any part of the requested information.

(d) Subject to the provisions of paragraph (k) of this section, the Inter-American Foundation will publish in the FEDERAL REGISTER at least annually a notice of the existence and character of its system of records. This notice will include:

(1) The name and location of the system or systems;

(2) The categories of individuals on whom records are maintained in the system or systems;

(3) The categories of records maintained in the system or systems;

(4) Each routine use of the records contained in the system or systems, including the categories of users and the purpose of such use;

(5) The policies and practices of the Inter-American Foundation regarding storage, retrievability, access controls, retention, and disposal of the records;

(6) The title and business address of the Inter-American Foundation official or officials responsible for the system or systems of records;

(7) The Inter-American Foundation procedures whereby an individual can be notified at his or her request if the system or systems of records contain a record pertaining to him or her;

(8) The Inter-American Foundation procedures whereby an individual can be notified at his or her request how he or she can gain access to any record pertaining to him or her contained in the system or systems of records, and how he or she can contest its content; and

(9) The categories of sources of records in the system or systems.

(e) All records used by the Inter-American Foundation in making any determination about any individual will be maintained with the accuracy, relevance, timeliness, and completeness reasonably necessary to assure fairness to the individual in the determination.

(f) Before disseminating any record about any individual to any person other than an agency the Inter-American Foundation will make reasonable efforts to assure that such records are accurate, complete, timely, and relevant for Inter-American Foundation purposes unless the dissemination is required pursuant to 5 U.S.C. 552.

(g) The Inter-American Foundation will maintain no record describing how any individual exercises rights guaranteed by the First Amendment unless expressly authorized by statute or by the individual about whom the record is maintained or unless pertinent to and within the scope of an authorized law enforcement activity.

(h) The Inter-American Foundation will make reasonable efforts to serve notice on an individual when any record on such individuals is made available to any person under compulsory legal process when such process becomes a matter of public record.

(i) The Inter-American Foundation will establish rules of conduct for persons involved in the design, development, operation, or maintenance of any system of records, or in maintaining any record. Each such person will be instructed regarding such rules and the requirements of 5 U.S.C. 552a. The instruction will include any other rules and procedures adopted pursuant to 5 U.S.C. 552a, and the penalties it provides for noncompliance.

(j) The Inter-American Foundation will establish appropriate administrative, technical, and physical safeguards to insure the security and confidentiality of records and to protect against any anticipated threats or hazards to their security or integrity which could result in substantial harm, embarrassment, inconvenience, or unfairness to any individual on whom information is maintained.

(k) At least 30 days prior to the publication of a notice in the FEDERAL REGISTER at least annually regarding the routine use of the records contained in the Inter-American Foundation system or systems of records including the categories of users and the purpose of such use, pursuant to paragraph (d)(4) of this section, the Inter-American Foundation will also:

(1) Publish a notice in the FEDERAL REGISTER of any new use or intended use of the information in the system or systems; and

(2) Provide an opportunity for interested persons to submit written data, views, or arguments to the Inter-American Foundation.

§ 1003.5 Access to personal information from Inter-American Foundation records.

(a) The Inter-American Foundation will promulgate regulations, as necessary, to insure compliance with the provisions of 5 U.S.C. 552a, developed in accordance with the provisions of 5 U.S.C. 553, as applicable.

(b) Any individual will be notified upon request if any Inter-American Foundation system of records named contains a record pertaining to him or her. Such request must be in writing over the signature of the requester. The request must contain a reasonable description of the Inter-American Foundation system or systems of records meant, as described at least annually by notice published in the FEDERAL REGISTER describing the existence and character of the Inter-American Foundation's system or systems of records. The request should be made to the Executive Officer, Inter-American Foundation, 1515 Wilson Boulevard, Rosslyn, Virginia 22209. Personal contacts should normally be made during the regular duty hours of the office concerned, which are 8:30 a.m. to 4:00 p.m. Monday through Friday. Identification of the individual requesting the information will be required consisting of name, signature, address, and claim, insurance or other identifying file number, if any, as a minimum.

(c) The department or staff office having jurisdiction over the records involved will establish appropriate disclosure procedures and will notify the individual requesting disclosure of his or her record or information pertaining to him or her of the time, place and conditions under which the Inter-American Foundation will comply to the extent permitted by law and Inter-American Foundation regulation. Special procedures will be established by the department or staff office concerned governing the disclosure to an individual of medical records, including psychological records pertaining to him or her.

(d) The department or staff office having jurisdiction over the records involved will also establish procedures for reviewing a request from an individual concerning the amendment of any record or information pertaining to the individual for making a determination on the request, for an appeal within the Inter-American Foundation of an initial adverse Inter-American Foundation determination, and for whatever additional means may be necessary for each individual to be able to exercise fully his or her rights under 5 U.S.C. 552a.

(e) Fees to be charged, if any, to any individual for making copies of his or her record, excluding the cost of any search for and review of the record, will be as follows:

(1) Photocopy reproductions from all types of copying processes, each reproduction image, $0.05.

(2) Where the Inter-American Foundation undertakes to perform for a requester or for any other person services which are very clearly not required to be performed under section 552a, title 5, United States Code, either voluntarily or because such services are required by some other law (e.g., the formal certification of records as true copies, attestation under the seal of the Inter-American Foundation, etc.), the question of charging fees for such services will be determined by the official or designee authorized to release the information under § 1.556, in the light of the Federal user charge statute, 31 U.S.C. 483a, and any other applicable law.

§ 1003.6 Administrative review.

(a) Upon denial of a request, the responsible Inter-American Foundation official or designated employee will inform the requester in writing of the denial, cite the reason or reasons and the Inter-American Foundation regulations upon which the denial is based, and advise that the denial may be appealed to the Administrator.

(b) The final agency decision in such appeals will be made by the Administrator or Deputy Administrator.

§ 1003.7 Judicial review.

Any person may file a complaint against the Inter-American Foundation in the appropriate U.S. district court, as provided in 5 U.S.C. 552a(g), whenever the Inter-American Foundation:

(a) Makes a determination not to amend an individual's record in accordance with his or her request, or fails to make such review in conformity with that section;

(b) Refuses to comply with an individual request;

(c) Fails to maintain any record concerning any individual with such accuracy, relevance, timeliness, and completeness as is necessary to assure fairness in any determination relating to the qualifications, character, rights, or opportunities of, or benefits to the individual that may be made on the basis of such record, and consequently a determination is made which is adverse to the individual; or

(d) Fails to comply under any other provision of 5 U.S.C. 552a, or any Inter-American Foundation regulation promulgated thereunder, in such a way as to have an adverse effect on an individual.

§ 1003.8 Exemptions.

No Inter-American Foundation records system or systems as such are exempted from the provisions of 5 U.S.C. 552a as permitted under certain conditions by 5 U.S.C. 552a (j) and (k).

§ 1003.9 Mailing lists.

An individual's name and address may not be sold or rented by the Inter-American Foundation unless such action is specifically authorized by law. This section does not require the withholding of names and addresses otherwise permitted to be made public.

§ 1003.10 Reports.

(a) The Administrator or designee will provide adequate advance notice to Congress and the Office of Management and Budget of any proposal to establish or alter any Inter-American Foundation system or systems of records, as required by 5 U.S.C. 552a(o). This will permit an evaluation of the probable or potential effect of such proposal on the privacy and other personal or property rights of individuals or the disclosure of information relating to such individuals, and its effect on the preservation of the constitutional principles of federalism and separation of powers.

(b) If at any time an Inter-American Foundation system or systems of records is determined to be exempt from the application of 5 U.S.C. 552a in accordance with the provisions of 5 U.S.C. 552a (j) and (k), the number of records contained in such system or systems will be separately listed and reported to the Office of Management and Budget in accordance with the then prevailing guidelines and instructions of that agency.

PART 1004—RULES FOR IMPLEMENTING OPEN MEETINGS WITHIN THE INTER-AMERICAN FOUNDATION

AUTHORITY: 5 U.S.C. 552b.

SOURCE: 71 FR 63237, Oct. 30, 2006, unless otherwise noted.

§ 1004.1 General policies.

The Inter-American Foundation (IAF) will, in accordance with the Government in the Sunshine Act, 5 U.S.C. 552b, provide the public with the fullest practical information regarding its decisionmaking processes while protecting the rights of individuals and its ability to carry out its responsibilities.

§ 1004.2 Definitions.

The following definitions apply:

(a) *Agency* includes any executive department, military department, government corporation, government controlled corporation other establishment in the executive branch of the government (including the Executive Office of the President) or any independent regulatory agency, and is headed by a collegial body composed of two or more individual members, a majority of whom are appointed to such position by the President with the advice and consent of the Senate, and any subdivision thereof authorized to act on behalf of the agency. The Inter-American Foundation is a government corporation headed by a nine-member Board of Directors, all of whom are appointed by the President with the advice and consent of the Senate, and is therefore an "agency" under these terms.

(b) *Meeting* means the deliberation of this Board of Directors where such deliberation determines or results in the joint conduct or disposition of official IAF business, but does not include deliberations required or permitted by subsection 1004.6 or 1004.7.

(c) *Member* means an individual who belongs to the IAF Board of Directors.

(d) *Public Observation* means attendance at any meeting but does not include participation, or attempted participation, in such meeting in any matter.

§ 1004.3 Requirement of open meetings.

Members shall not jointly conduct or dispose of agency business other than in accordance with this section. Except as provided in § 1004.4 every portion of every meeting of the agency shall be open to public observation.

§ 1004.4 Grounds on which meetings may be closed.

The IAF shall open every portion of every meeting of the agency for public observation. Except in a case where the agency finds that the public interest requires otherwise, this requirement does not apply where the agency determines that such portion or portions of its meeting or the disclosure of such information is likely to:

(a) Disclose matters that are:

(1) Specifically authorized under criteria established by an Executive order to be kept secret in the interests of national defense or foreign policy, and

(2) In fact, properly classified pursuant to such Executive order;

(b) Relate solely to the internal personnel rules and practice of the agency;

(c) Disclose matters specifically exempted from disclosure by statute, provided that such statute:

(1) Requires that the matters be withheld from the public in such manner as to have no discretion on the issue, or

(2) Establishes practical criteria for withholding or refers to particular types of matters to be withheld;

(d) Disclose trade secrets and commercial or financial information obtained from a person and privileged or confidential;

(e) Involve accusing any person of a crime, or formally censuring any person;

(f) Disclose information of a personal nature where disclosure would constitute a clearly unwarranted invasion of personal privacy;

(g) Disclose investigatory records compiled for law enforcement purposes, or information which if written would be contained in such records, but only to the extent that the production of such records or information would:

(1) Interfere with enforcement proceedings,

(2) Deprive a person of a right to a fair trial of an impartial adjudication,

(3) Constitute an unwarranted invasion of personal privacy,

(4) Disclose the identity of a confidential source and, in the case of a record compiled by a criminal law enforcement authority in the course of a criminal investigation, or by an agency conducting a lawful national security intelligence investigation, information furnished by a confidential source,

(5) Disclose investigative techniques and procedures, or

(6) Endanger the life or physical safety of law enforcement personnel;

(h) Disclose information contained in or related to examination, operating or condition reports prepared by, on behalf of, or for the use of an agency responsible for the regulation or supervision of financial institutions;

(i) Disclose information the premature disclosure of which would be likely to significantly frustrate implementation of a proposed agency action. This shall not apply in any instance where the IAF has already disclosed to the public the content or nature of its proposed action or where the IAF is required by law to make such disclosure of its own initiative prior to taking final IAF action on such proposal;

(j) Specifically concern the IAF's issuance of subpoena, or the IAF's participation in a civil action or proceeding, an action in a foreign court or international tribunal, or an arbitration, or the initiation, conduct, or disposition by the IAF of a particular case of formal agency adjudication pursuant to the procedures in section 554 of this title or otherwise involving a determination on the record after opportunity for a hearing.

NOTE TO § 1004.4: The requirements of §§ 1004.5 and 1004.6 shall not apply to any information pertaining to those meetings exempted under this section.

§ 1004.5 Procedures for announcing meetings.

(a) In the case of each meeting, the IAF shall make public, at least one week before the meeting, of the time, place and subject matter of the meeting, whether it is to be open or closed to the public, and the name and phone number of the official designated by the IAF to respond to requests for information about the meeting. Such announcement shall be made unless a majority of the Board of Directors of the IAF determines by a recorded vote that the IAF requires that such a meeting be called at an earlier date, in which case the IAF shall make public announcement of the time, place and subject matter of such meeting and whether open or closed to the public, at the earliest practical time.

(b) Immediately following the public announcement, the IAF will submit notice for publication in the FEDERAL REGISTER.

(c) The IAF shall also make public the announcement by other reasonable means, accessible to the public.

§ 1004.6 Procedures for closing meetings.

(a) The closing of a meeting or a portion of a meeting shall occur only when:

(1) A majority of the membership of the IAF Board votes to take such action. That vote shall determine whether or not any portion or portions of a meeting or portions of a series of meetings may be closed to public observation for any of the reasons provided in § 1004.4 and whether or not the public interest nevertheless requires that portion of the meeting or meetings remain open. A single vote may be taken with respect to a series of meetings, a portion or portions of which are proposed to be closed to the public, or with respect to any information concerning such series of meetings, so long as each meeting in such series involves the same particular matters and is scheduled to be held no more than thirty days after the initial meeting in such series. The vote of each Board member participating in such vote shall be recorded and no proxies shall be allowed.

(2) Whenever any person whose interests may be directly affected by a portion of a meeting requests that the IAF close such portion to the public for any of the reasons referred to in § 1004.4 the IAF, upon request of any one of its Board members, shall take a recorded vote, whether to close such portion of the meeting.

(b) Within one day of any vote taken pursuant to this Section, the IAF shall make publicly available a written copy of such vote reflecting the vote of each member on the question and full written explanation of its action closing the entire or portion of the meeting together with a list of persons expecting to attend the meeting and their affiliation.

(c) The IAF shall, subject to change, announce the time, place and subject matter of the meeting at least 7 days before the meeting.

(d) For every closed meeting pursuant to § 1004.4, the General Counsel of the IAF shall publicly certify prior to a Board of Directors' vote on closing the meeting, that, in his or her opinion, the meeting may be closed to the public and shall state each relevant exemptive provision. A copy of such certification, together with a statement from the presiding officer of the meeting setting forth the time and place of the meeting, and the persons present, shall be retained by the IAF.

§ 1004.7 Reconsideration of opening or closing of meeting.

The time or place of a Board meeting may be changed, without vote, following public announcement. The IAF will announce any such change at the earliest practicable time. The subject matter of a meeting, or the determination of the agency to open or close a meeting, or portion of a meeting, to the public, may be changed only if a majority of the Board of Directors determines by a recorded vote that IAF business so requires and that no earlier announcement of the change was possible, and the IAF publicly announces such change and the vote of each member upon such change at the earliest practicable time.

§ 1004.8 Transcripts, recording of closed meetings.

(a) The IAF shall maintain a complete transcript or electronic recording adequate to record fully the proceedings of each meeting, or portion of a meeting, closed to the public, except that in the case of a meeting, or portion of a meeting, closed to the public pursuant to paragraph (d), (h), or (j) of § 1004.4, the IAF shall maintain either such a transcript or recording, or a set of minutes. Such records shall fully and clearly describe all matters discussed and shall provide a full and accurate summary of any actions taken, and the reasons therefore, including a description of each of the views expressed on any item and the record of any roll call vote (reflecting the vote of each member on the question). All documents considered in connection with any action shall be identified in such records.

(b) The IAF, after review by the General Counsel shall make promptly available to the public, in a place easily accessible to the public, the transcript or electronic recording or minutes of the discussion of any time on the agenda, or any item of the testimony of any witness received at the Board meeting, except for such item or items of such discussion or testimony as the IAF determines to contain information which may be withheld under §1004.4. Copies of such transcript, or a transcription of such recording disclosing the identity of each speaker, shall be furnished to any person at the actual cost of duplication or transcription. The IAF shall maintain a complete verbatim copy of the transcript, a complete copy of the minutes or a complete electronic recording of each meeting, or portion of a meeting, closed to the public, for a period of at least two years after such meeting, or until one year after the conclusion or any IAF proceedings with respect to which the meeting or portion was held, whichever occurs later.

PART 1005—ENFORCEMENT OF NONDISCRIMINATION ON THE BASIS OF HANDICAP IN PROGRAMS OR ACTIVITIES CONDUCTED BY THE INTER-AMERICAN FOUNDATION

Sec.

AUTHORITY: 29 U.S.C. 794.

SOURCE: 51 FR 22890, 22896, June 23, 1986, unless otherwise noted.

§1005.101 Purpose.

This part effectuates section 119 of the Rehabilitation, Comprehensive Services, and Developmental Disabilities Amendments of 1978, which amended section 504 of the Rehabilitation Act of 1973 to prohibit discrimination on the basis of handicap in programs or activities conducted by Executive agencies or the United States Postal Service.

§1005.102 Application.

This part applies to all programs or activities conducted by the agency.

§1005.103 Definitions.

For purposes of this part, the term—

Assistant Attorney General means the Assistant Attorney General, Civil Rights Division, United States Department of Justice.

Auxiliary aids means services or devices that enable persons with impaired sensory, manual, or speaking skills to have an equal opportunity to participate in, and enjoy the benefits of, programs or activities conducted by the agency. For example, auxiliary aids useful for persons with impaired vision include readers, brailled materials, audio recordings, telecommunications devices and other similar services and devices. Auxiliary aids useful for persons with impaired hearing include telephone handset amplifiers, telephones compatible with hearing aids, telecommunication devices for deaf persons (TDD's), interpreters, notetakers, written materials, and other similar services and devices.

Complete complaint means a written statement that contains the complainant's name and address and describes the agency's alleged discriminatory action in sufficient detail to inform the agency of the nature and date of the alleged violation of section 504. It shall be signed by the complainant or by someone authorized to do so on his or her behalf. Complaints filed on behalf of classes or third parties shall describe or identify (by name, if possible) the alleged victims of discrimination.

Facility means all or any portion of buildings, structures, equipment, roads, walks, parking lots, rolling stock or other conveyances, or other real or personal property.

Handicapped person means any person who has a physical or mental impairment that substantially limits one or more major life activities, has a record of such an impairment, or is regarded as having such an impairment.

As used in this definition, the phrase:

(1) *Physical or mental impairment* includes—

(i) Any physiological disorder or condition, cosmetic disfigurement, or anatomical loss affecting one or more of the following body systems: Neurological; musculoskeletal; special sense organs; respiratory, including speech organs; cardiovascular; reproductive; digestive; genitourinary; hemic and lymphatic; skin; and endocrine; or

(ii) Any mental or psychological disorder, such as mental retardation, organic brain syndrome, emotional or mental illness, and specific learning disabilities. The term *physical or mental impairment* includes, but is not limited to, such diseases and conditions as orthopedic, visual, speech, and hearing impairments, cerebral palsy, epilepsy, muscular dystrophy, multiple sclerosis, cancer, heart disease, diabetes, mental retardation, emotional illness, and drug addiction and alocoholism.

(2) *Major life activities* includes functions such as caring for one's self, performing manual tasks, walking, seeing, hearing, speaking, breathing, learning, and working.

(3) *Has a record of such an impairment* means has a history of, or has been misclassified as having, a mental or physical impairment that substantially limits one or more major life activities.

(4) *Is regarded as having an impairment* means—

(i) Has a physical or mental impairment that does not substantially limit major life activities but is treated by the agency as constituting such a limitation;

(ii) Has a physical or mental impairment that substantially limits major life activities only as a result of the attitudes of others toward such impairment; or

(iii) Has none of the impairments defined in paragraph (1) of this definition but is treated by the agency as having such an impairment.

Historic preservation programs means programs conducted by the agency that have preservation of historic properties as a primary purpose.

Historic properties means those properties that are listed or eligible for listing in the National Register of Historic Places or properties designated as historic under a statute of the appropriate State or local government body.

Qualified handicapped person means—

(1) With respect to preschool, elementary, or secondary education services provided by the agency, a handicapped person who is a member of a class of persons otherwise entitled by statute, regulation, or agency policy to receive education services from the agency.

(2) With respect to any other agency program or activity under which a person is required to perform services or to achieve a level of accomplishment, a handicapped person who meets the essential eligibility requirements and who can acheive the purpose of the program or activity without modifications in the program or activity that the agency can demonstrate would result in a fundamental alteration in its nature;

(3) With respect to any other program or activity, a handicapped person who meets the essential eligibility requirements for participation in, or receipt of benefits from, that program or activity; and

(4) *Qualified handicapped person* is defined for purposes of employment in 29 CFR 1613.702(f), which is made applicable to this part by § 1005.140.

Section 504 means section 504 of the Rehabilitation Act of 1973 (Pub. L. 93–112, 87 Stat. 394 (29 U.S.C. 794)), as amended by the Rehabilitation Act Amendments of 1974 (Pub. L. 93–516, 88 Stat. 1617), and the Rehabilitation, Comprehensive Services, and Developmental Disabilities Amendments of 1978 (Pub. L. 95–602, 92 Stat. 2955). As used in this part, section 504 applies only to programs or activities conducted by Executive agencies and not to federally assisted programs.

Substantial impairment means a significant loss of the integrity of finished materials, design quality, or special character resulting from a permanent alteration.

§§ 1005.104–1005.109 [Reserved]

§ 1005.110 Self-evaluation.

(a) The agency shall, by August 24, 1987, evaluate its current policies and practices, and the effects thereof, that do not or may not meet the requirements of this part, and, to the extent modification of any such policies and practices is required, the agency shall proceed to make the necessary modifications.

(b) The agency shall provide an opportunity to interested persons, including handicapped persons or organizations representing handicapped persons, to participate in the self-evaluation process by submitting comments (both oral and written).

(c) The agency shall, until three years following the completion of the self-evaluation, maintain on file and make available for public inspection:

(1) A description of areas examined and any problems identified, and

(2) A description of any modifications made.

§ 1005.111 Notice.

The agency shall make available to employees, applicants, participants, beneficiaries, and other interested persons such information regarding the provisions of this part and its applicability to the programs or activities conducted by the agency, and make such information available to them in such manner as the head of the agency finds necessary to apprise such persons of the protections against discrimination assured them by section 504 and this regulation.

§§ 1005.112–1005.129 [Reserved]

§ 1005.130 General prohibitions against discrimination.

(a) No qualified handicapped person shall, on the basis of handicap, be excluded from participation in, be denied the benefits of, or otherwise be subjected to discrimination under any program or activity conducted by the agency.

(b)(1) The agency, in providing any aid, benefit, or service, may not, directly or through contractual, licensing, or other arrangements, on the basis of handicap—

(i) Deny a qualified handicapped person the opportunity to participate in or benefit from the aid, benefit, or service;

(ii) Afford a qualified handicapped person an opportunity to participate in or benefit from the aid, benefit, or service that is not equal to that afforded others;

(iii) Provide a qualified handicapped person with an aid, benefit, or service that is not as effective in affording equal opportunity to obtain the same result, to gain the same benefit, or to reach the same level of achievement as that provided to others;

(iv) Provide different or separate aid, benefits, or services to handicapped persons or to any class of handicapped persons than is provided to others unless such action is necessary to provide qualified handicapped persons with aid, benefits, or services that are as effective as those provided to others;

(v) Deny a qualified handicapped person the opportunity to participate as a member of planning or advisory boards; or

(vi) Otherwise limit a qualified handicapped person in the enjoyment of any right, privilege, advantage, or opportunity enjoyed by others receiving the aid, benefit, or service.

(2) The agency may not deny a qualified handicapped person the opportunity to participate in programs or activities that are not separate or different, despite the existence of permissibly separate or different programs or activities.

(3) The agency may not, directly or through contractual or other arrangments, utilize criteria or methods of administration the purpose or effect of which would—

(i) Subject qualified handicapped persons to discrimination on the basis of handicap; or

(ii) Defeat or substantially impair accomplishment of the objectives of a program or activity with respect to handicapped persons.

(4) The agency may not, in determining the site or location of a facility, make selections the purpose or effect of which would—

(i) Exclude handicapped persons from, deny them the benefits of, or otherwise subject them to discrimination under any program or activity conducted by the agency; or

(ii) Defeat or substantially impair the accomplishment of the objectives of a program or activity with respect to handicapped persons.

(5) The agency, in the selection of procurement contractors, may not use criteria that subject qualified handicapped persons to discrimination on the basis of handicap.

(6) The agency may not administer a licensing or certification program in a manner that subjects qualified handicapped persons to discrimination on the basis of handicap, nor may the agency establish requirements for the programs or activities of licensees or certified entities that subject qualified handicapped persons to discrimination on the basis of handicap. However, the programs or activities of entities that are licensed or certified by the agency are not, themselves, covered by this part.

(c) The exclusion of nonhandicapped persons from the benefits of a program limited by Federal statute or Executive order to handicapped persons or the exclusion of a specific class of handicapped persons from a program limited by Federal statute or Executive order to a different class of handicapped persons is not prohibited by this part.

(d) The agency shall administer programs and activities in the most integrated setting appropriate to the needs of qualified handicapped persons.

§§ 1005.131–1005.139 [Reserved]

§ 1005.140 Employment.

No qualified handicapped person shall, on the basis of handicap, be subjected to discrimination in employment under any program or activity conducted by the agency. The definitions, requirements, and procedures of section 501 of the Rehabilitation Act of 1973 (29 U.S.C. 791), as established by the Equal Employment Opportunity Commission in 29 CFR part 1613, shall apply to employment in federally conducted programs or activities.

§§ 1005.141–1005.148 [Reserved]

§ 1005.149 Program accessibility: Discrimination prohibited.

Except as otherwise provided in § 1005.150, no qualified handicapped person shall, because the agency's facilities are inaccessible to or unusable by handicapped persons, be denied the benefits of, be excluded from participation in, or otherwise be subjected to discrimination under any program or activity conducted by the agency.

§ 1005.150 Program accessibility: Existing facilities.

(a) *General.* The agency shall operate each program or activity so that the program or activity, when viewed in its entirety, is readily accessible to and usable by handicapped persons. This paragraph does not—

(1) Necessarily require the agency to make each of its existing facilities accessible to and usable by handicapped persons;

(2) In the case of historic preservation programs, require the agency to take any action that would result in a substantial impairment of significant historic features of an historic property; or

(3) Require the agency to take any action that it can demonstrate would result in a fundamental alteration in the nature of a program or activity or in undue financial and administrative burdens. In those circumstances where agency personnel believe that the proposed action would fundamentally alter the program or activity or would result in undue financial and administrative burdens, the agency has the burden of proving that compliance with § 1005.150(a) would result in such alteration or burdens. The decision that compliance would result in such alteration or burdens must be made by the agency head or his or her designee after considering all agency resources available for use in the funding and operation of the conducted program or activity, and must be accompanied by a written statement of the reasons for reaching that conclusion. If an action would result in such an alteration or such burdens, the agency shall take any other action that would not result in such an alteration or such burdens

but would nevertheless ensure that handicapped persons receive the benefits and services of the program or activity.

(b) *Methods*—(1) *General.* The agency may comply with the requirements of this section through such means as redesign of equipment, reassignment of services to accessible buildings, assignment of aides to beneficiaries, home visits, delivery of services at alternate accessible sites, alteration of existing facilities and construction of new facilities, use of accessible rolling stock, or any other methods that result in making its programs or activities readily accessible to and usable by handicapped persons. The agency is not required to make structural changes in existing facilities where other methods are effective in achieving compliance with this section. The agency, in making alterations to existing buildings, shall meet accessibility requirements to the extent compelled by the Architectural Barriers Act of 1968, as amended (42 U.S.C. 4151–4157), and any regulations implementing it. In choosing among available methods for meeting the requirements of this section, the agency shall give priority to those methods that offer programs and activities to qualified handicapped persons in the most integrated setting appropriate.

(2) *Historic preservation programs.* In meeting the requirements of § 1005.150(a) in historic preservation programs, the agency shall give priority to methods that provide physical access to handicapped persons. In cases where a physical alteration to an historic property is not required because of § 1005.150(a)(2) or (a)(3), alternative methods of achieving program accessibility include—

(i) Using audio-visual materials and devices to depict those portions of an historic property that cannot otherwise be made accessible;

(ii) Assigning persons to guide handicapped persons into or through portions of historic properties that cannot otherwise be made accessible; or

(iii) Adopting other innovative methods.

(c) *Time period for compliance.* The agency shall comply with the obligations established under this section by October 21, 1986, except that where structural changes in facilities are undertaken, such changes shall be made by August 22, 1989, but in any event as expeditiously as possible.

(d) *Transition plan.* In the event that structural changes to facilities will be undertaken to achieve program accessibility, the agency shall develop, by February 23, 1987, a transition plan setting forth the steps necessary to complete such changes. The agency shall provide an opportunity to interested persons, including handicapped persons or organizations representing handicapped persons, to participate in the development of the transition plan by submitting comments (both oral and written). A copy of the transition plan shall be made available for public inspection. The plan shall, at a minimum—

(1) Identify physical obstacles in the agency's facilities that limit the accessibility of its programs or activities to handicapped persons;

(2) Describe in detail the methods that will be used to make the facilities accessible;

(3) Specify the schedule for taking the steps necessary to achieve compliance with this section and, if the time period of the transition plan is longer than one year, identify steps that will be taken during each year of the transition period; and

(4) Indicate the official responsible for implementation of the plan.

§ 1005.151 Program accessibility: New construction and alterations.

Each building or part of a building that is constructed or altered by, on behalf of, or for the use of the agency shall be designed, constructed, or altered so as to be readily accessible to and usable by handicapped persons. The definitions, requirements, and standards of the Architectural Barriers Act (42 U.S.C. 4151–4157), as established in 41 CFR 101–19.600 to 101–19.607, apply to buildings covered by this section.

§§ 1005.152–1005.159 [Reserved]

§ 1005.160 Communications.

(a) The agency shall take appropriate steps to ensure effective communication with applicants, participants, personnel of other Federal entities, and members of the public.

(1) The agency shall furnish appropriate auxiliary aids where necessary to afford a handicapped person an equal opportunity to participate in, and enjoy the benefits of, a program or activity conducted by the agency.

(i) In determining what type of auxiliary aid is necessary, the agency shall give primary consideration to the requests of the handicapped person.

(ii) The agency need not provide individually prescribed devices, readers for personal use or study, or other devices of a personal nature.

(2) Where the agency communicates with applicants and beneficiaries by telephone, telecommunication devices for deaf person (TDD's) or equally effective telecommunication systems shall be used.

(b) The agency shall ensure that interested persons, including persons with impaired vision or hearing, can obtain information as to the existence and location of accessible services, activities, and facilities.

(c) The agency shall provide signage at a primary entrance to each of its inaccessible facilities, directing users to a location at which they can obtain information about accessible facilities. The international symbol for accessibility shall be used at each primary entrance of an accessible facility.

(d) This section does not require the agency to take any action that it can demonstrate would result in a fundamental alteration in the nature of a program or activity or in undue financial and adminstrative burdens. In those circumstances where agency personnel believe that the proposed action would fundamentally alter the program or activity or would result in undue financial and administrative burdens, the agency has the burden of proving that compliance with § 1005.160 would result in such alteration or burdens. The decision that compliance would result in such alteration or burdens must be made by the agency head or his or her designee after considering all agency resources available for use in the funding and operation of the conducted program or activity, and must be accompanied by a written statement of the reasons for reaching that conclusion. If an action required to comply with this section would result in such an alteration or such burdens, the agency shall take any other action that would not result in such an alteration or such burdens but would nevertheless ensure that, to the maximum extent possible, handicapped persons receive the benefits and services of the program or activity.

§§ 1005.161–1005.169 [Reserved]

§ 1005.170 Compliance procedures.

(a) Except as provided in paragraph (b) of this section, this section applies to all allegations of discrimination on the basis of handicap in programs or activities conducted by the agency.

(b) The agency shall process complaints alleging violations of section 504 with respect to employment according to the procedures established by the Equal Employment Opportunity Commission in 29 CFR part 1613 pursuant to section 501 of the Rehabilitation Act of 1973 (29 U.S.C. 791).

(c) The General Counsel, Inter-American Foundation, shall be responsible for coordinating implementation of this section. Complaints may be sent to 901 N. Stuart St., 10th Floor, Arlington, VA 22203.

(d) The agency shall accept and investigate all complete complaints for which it has jurisdiction. All complete complaints must be filed within 180 days of the alleged act of discrimination. The agency may extend this time period for good cause.

(e) If the agency receives a complaint over which it does not have jurisdiction, it shall promptly notify the complainant and shall make reasonable efforts to refer the complaint to the appropriate government entity.

(f) The agency shall notify the Architectural and Transportation Barriers Compliance Board upon receipt of any complaint alleging that a building or facility that is subject to the Architectural Barriers Act of 1968, as amended (42 U.S.C. 4151–4157), or section 502 of the Rehabilitation Act of 1973, as amended (29 U.S.C. 792), is not readily accessible to and usable by handicapped persons.

(g) Within 180 days of the receipt of a complete complaint for which it has jurisdiction, the agency shall notify the complainant of the results of the investigation in a letter containing—

(1) Findings of fact and conclusions of law;

(2) A description of a remedy for each violation found; and

(3) A notice of the right to appeal.

(h) Appeals of the findings of fact and conclusions of law or remedies must be filed by the complainant within 90 days of receipt from the agency of the letter required by §1005.170(g). The agency may extend this time for good cause.

(i) Timely appeals shall be accepted and processed by the head of the agency.

(j) The head of the agency shall notify the complainant of the results of the appeal within 60 days of the receipt of the request. If the head of the agency determines that additional information is needed from the complainant, he or she shall have 60 days from the date of receipt of the additional information to make his or her determination on the appeal.

(k) The time limits cited in paragraphs (g) and (j) of this section may be extended with the permission of the Assistant Attorney General.

(l) The agency may delegate its authority for conducting complaint investigations to other Federal agencies, except that the authority for making the final determination may not be delegated to another agency.

[51 FR 22890, 22896, June 23, 1986, as amended at 51 FR 22891, June 23, 1986; 71 FR 63236, Oct. 30, 2006]

§§ 1005.171–1005.999 [Reserved]

PART 1006—GOVERNMENTWIDE DEBARMENT AND SUSPENSION (NONPROCUREMENT)

Sec.

Subpart A—General

Subpart B—Covered Transactions

Subpart C—Responsibilities of Participants Regarding Transactions

Doing Business With Other Persons

Subpart H—Debarment

Subpart I—Definitions

Subpart J [Reserved]

AUTHORITY: Sec. 2455, Pub. L. 103–355, 108 Stat. 3327 (31 U.S.C. 6101 note); E.O. 12549, 3 CFR, 1986 Comp., p. 189; E.O. 12689, 3 CFR, 1989 Comp., p. 235.

§ 1006.25 How is this part organized?

(a) This part is subdivided into ten subparts. Each subpart contains information related to a broad topic or specific audience with special responsibilities, as shown in the following table:

In subpart . . .	You will find provisions related to . . .
A	general information about this rule.
B	the types of Inter-American Foundation transactions that are covered by the Governmentwide nonprocurement suspension and debarment system.
C	the responsibilities of persons who participate in covered transactions.
D	the responsibilities of Inter-American Foundation officials who are authorized to enter into covered transactions.
E	the responsibilities of Federal agencies for the *Excluded Parties List System* (Disseminated by the General Services Administration).
F	the general principles governing suspension, debarment, voluntary exclusion and settlement.
G	suspension actions.
H	debarment actions.
I	definitions of terms used in this part.
J	[Reserved]

(b) The following table shows which subparts may be of special interest to you, depending on who you are:

If you are . . .	See subpart(s) . . .
(1) a participant or principal in a nonprocurement transaction.	A, B, C, and I.
(2) a respondent in a suspension action	A, B, F, G and I.
(3) a respondent in a debarment action	A, B, F, H and I.
(4) a suspending official	A, B, D, E, F, G and I.
(5) a debarring official	A, B, D, E, F, H and I.
(6) a (n) Inter-American Foundation official authorized to enter into a covered transaction.	A, B, D, E and I.
(7) Reserved	J.

§ 1006.50 How is this part written?

(a) This part uses a "plain language" format to make it easier for the general public and business community to use. The section headings and text, often in the form of questions and answers, must be read together.

(b) Pronouns used within this part, such as "I" and "you," change from subpart to subpart depending on the audience being addressed. The pronoun "we" always is the Inter-American Foundation.

(c) The "Covered Transactions" diagram in the appendix to this part shows the levels or "tiers" at which the Inter-American Foundation enforces an exclusion under this part.

§ 1006.75 Do terms in this part have special meanings?

This part uses terms throughout the text that have special meaning. Those terms are defined in Subpart I of this part. For example, three important terms are—

(a) *Exclusion or excluded*, which refers only to discretionary actions taken by a suspending or debarring official under this part or the Federal Acquisition Regulation (48 CFR part 9, subpart 9.4);

(b) *Disqualification or disqualified*, which refers to prohibitions under specific statutes, executive orders (other than Executive Order 12549 and Executive Order 12689), or other authorities. Disqualifications frequently are not subject to the discretion of an agency official, may have a different scope than exclusions, or have special conditions that apply to the disqualification; and

(c) *Ineligibility or ineligible*, which generally refers to a person who is either excluded or disqualified.

Subpart A—General

§ 1006.100 What does this part do?

This part adopts a governmentwide system of debarment and suspension for Inter-American Foundation nonprocurement activities. It also provides for reciprocal exclusion of persons who have been excluded under the Federal Acquisition Regulation, and provides for the consolidated listing of all persons who are excluded, or disqualified by statute, executive order, or other legal authority. This part satisfies the requirements in section 3 of Executive Order 12549, "Debarment and Suspension" (3 CFR 1986 Comp., p. 189), Executive Order 12689, "Debarment and Suspension" (3 CFR 1989 Comp., p. 235) and 31 U.S.C. 6101 note (Section 2455, Public Law 103–355, 108 Stat. 3327).

§ 1006.105 Does this part apply to me?

Portions of this part (see table at § 1006.25(b)) apply to you if you are a(n)—

(a) Person who has been, is, or may reasonably be expected to be, a participant or principal in a covered transaction;

(b) Respondent (a person against whom the Inter-American Foundation has initiated a debarment or suspension action);

(c) Inter-American Foundation debarring or suspending official; or

(d) Inter-American Foundation official who is authorized to enter into covered transactions with non-Federal parties.

§ 1006.110 What is the purpose of the nonprocurement debarment and suspension system?

(a) To protect the public interest, the Federal Government ensures the integrity of Federal programs by conducting business only with responsible persons.

(b) A Federal agency uses the nonprocurement debarment and suspension system to exclude from Federal programs persons who are not presently responsible.

(c) An exclusion is a serious action that a Federal agency may take only to protect the public interest. A Federal agency may not exclude a person or commodity for the purposes of punishment.

§ 1006.115 How does an exclusion restrict a person's involvement in covered transactions?

With the exceptions stated in §§ 1006.120, 1006.315, and 1006.420, a person who is excluded by the Inter-American Foundation or any other Federal agency may not:

(a) Be a participant in a(n) Inter-American Foundation transaction that is a covered transaction under subpart B of this part;

(b) Be a participant in a transaction of any other Federal agency that is a covered transaction under that agency's regulation for debarment and suspension; or

(c) Act as a principal of a person participating in one of those covered transactions.

§ 1006.120 May we grant an exception to let an excluded person participate in a covered transaction?

(a) The Inter-American Foundation Debarring Official may grant an exception permitting an excluded person to participate in a particular covered transaction. If the Inter-American Foundation Debarring Official grants an exception, the exception must be in writing and state the reason(s) for deviating from the governmentwide policy in Executive Order 12549.

(b) An exception granted by one agency for an excluded person does not extend to the covered transactions of another agency.

§ 1006.125 Does an exclusion under the nonprocurement system affect a person's eligibility for Federal procurement contracts?

If any Federal agency excludes a person under its nonprocurement common rule on or after August 25, 1995, the excluded person is also ineligible to participate in Federal procurement transactions under the FAR. Therefore, an exclusion under this part has reciprocal effect in Federal procurement transactions.

§ 1006.130 Does exclusion under the Federal procurement system affect a person's eligibility to participate in nonprocurement transactions?

If any Federal agency excludes a person under the FAR on or after August 25, 1995, the excluded person is also ineligible to participate in nonprocurement covered transactions under this part. Therefore, an exclusion under the FAR has reciprocal effect in Federal nonprocurement transactions.

§ 1006.135 May the Inter-American Foundation exclude a person who is not currently participating in a nonprocurement transaction?

Given a cause that justifies an exclusion under this part, we may exclude any person who has been involved, is currently involved, or may reasonably be expected to be involved in a covered transaction.

§ 1006.140 How do I know if a person is excluded?

Check the *Excluded Parties List System (EPLS)* to determine whether a person is excluded. The General Services Administration (GSA) maintains the *EPLS* and makes it available, as detailed in subpart E of this part. When a Federal agency takes an action to exclude a person under the nonprocurement or procurement debarment and suspension system, the agency enters the information about the excluded person into the *EPLS.*

§ 1006.145 Does this part address persons who are disqualified, as well as those who are excluded from nonprocurement transactions?

Except if provided for in Subpart J of this part, this part—

(a) Addresses disqualified persons only to—

(1) Provide for their inclusion in the *EPLS;* and

(2) State responsibilities of Federal agencies and participants to check for disqualified persons before entering into covered transactions.

(b) Does not specify the—

(1) Inter-American Foundation transactions for which a disqualified person is ineligible. Those transactions vary on a case-by-case basis, because they depend on the language of the specific

statute, Executive order, or regulation that caused the disqualification;

(2) Entities to which the disqualification applies; or

(3) Process that the agency uses to disqualify a person. Unlike exclusion, disqualification is frequently not a discretionary action that a Federal agency takes.

Subpart B—Covered Transactions

§ 1006.200 What is a covered transaction?

A covered transaction is a nonprocurement or procurement transaction that is subject to the prohibitions of this part. It may be a transaction at—

(a) The primary tier, between a Federal agency and a person (see appendix to this part); or

(b) A lower tier, between a participant in a covered transaction and another person.

§ 1006.205 Why is it important if a particular transaction is a covered transaction?

The importance of a covered transaction depends upon who you are.

(a) As a participant in the transaction, you have the responsibilities laid out in Subpart C of this part. Those include responsibilities to the person or Federal agency at the next higher tier from whom you received the transaction, if any. They also include responsibilities if you subsequently enter into other covered transactions with persons at the next lower tier.

(b) As a Federal official who enters into a primary tier transaction, you have the responsibilities laid out in subpart D of this part.

(c) As an excluded person, you may not be a participant or principal in the transaction unless—

(1) The person who entered into the transaction with you allows you to continue your involvement in a transaction that predates your exclusion, as permitted under § 1006.310 or § 1006.415; or

(2) A(n) Inter-American Foundation official obtains an exception from the Inter-American Foundation Debarring Official to allow you to be involved in the transaction, as permitted under § 1006.120.

§ 1006.210 Which nonprocurement transactions are covered transactions?

All nonprocurement transactions, as defined in § 1006.970, are covered transactions unless listed in § 1006.215. (See appendix to this part.)

§ 1006.215 Which nonprocurement transactions are not covered transactions?

The following types of nonprocurement transactions are not covered transactions:

(a) A direct award to—

(1) A foreign government or foreign governmental entity;

(2) A public international organization;

(3) An entity owned (in whole or in part) or controlled by a foreign government; or

(4) Any other entity consisting wholly or partially of one or more foreign governments or foreign governmental entities.

(b) A benefit to an individual as a personal entitlement without regard to the individual's present responsibility (but benefits received in an individual's business capacity are not excepted). For example, if a person receives social security benefits under the Supplemental Security Income provisions of the Social Security Act, 42 U.S.C. 1301 *et seq.*, those benefits are not covered transactions and, therefore, are not affected if the person is excluded.

(c) Federal employment.

(d) A transaction that the Inter-American Foundation needs to respond to a national or agency-recognized emergency or disaster.

(e) A permit, license, certificate, or similar instrument issued as a means to regulate public health, safety, or the environment, unless the Inter-American Foundation specifically designates it to be a covered transaction.

(f) An incidental benefit that results from ordinary governmental operations.

(g) Any other transaction if the application of an exclusion to the transaction is prohibited by law.

§ 1006.220 Are any procurement contracts included as covered transactions?

(a) Covered transactions under this part—

(1) Do not include any procurement contracts awarded directly by a Federal agency; but

(2) Do include some procurement contracts awarded by non-Federal participants in nonprocurement covered transactions (see appendix to this part).

(b) Specifically, a contract for goods or services is a covered transaction if any of the following applies:

(1) The contract is awarded by a participant in a nonprocurement transaction that is covered under § 1006.210, and the amount of the contract is expected to equal or exceed $25,000.

(2) The contract requires the consent of a(n) Inter-American Foundation official. In that case, the contract, regardless of the amount, always is a covered transaction, and it does not matter who awarded it. For example, it could be a subcontract awarded by a contractor at a tier below a nonprocurement transaction, as shown in the appendix to this part.

(3) The contract is for federally-required audit services.

§ 1006.225 How do I know if a transaction in which I may participate is a covered transaction?

As a participant in a transaction, you will know that it is a covered transaction because the agency regulations governing the transaction, the appropriate agency official, or participant at the next higher tier who enters into the transaction with you, will tell you that you must comply with applicable portions of this part.

Subpart C—Responsibilities of Participants Regarding Transactions

DOING BUSINESS WITH OTHER PERSONS

§ 1006.300 What must I do before I enter into a covered transaction with another person at the next lower tier?

When you enter into a covered transaction with another person at the next lower tier, you must verify that the person with whom you intend to do business is not excluded or disqualified. You do this by:

(a) Checking the *EPLS;* or

(b) Collecting a certification from that person if allowed by this rule; or

(c) Adding a clause or condition to the covered transaction with that person.

§ 1006.305 May I enter into a covered transaction with an excluded or disqualified person?

(a) You as a participant may not enter into a covered transaction with an excluded person, unless the Inter-American Foundation grants an exception under § 1006.120.

(b) You may not enter into any transaction with a person who is disqualified from that transaction, unless you have obtained an exception under the disqualifying statute, Executive order, or regulation.

§ 1006.310 What must I do if a Federal agency excludes a person with whom I am already doing business in a covered transaction?

(a) You as a participant may continue covered transactions with an excluded person if the transactions were in existence when the agency excluded the person. However, you are not required to continue the transactions, and you may consider termination. You should make a decision about whether to terminate and the type of termination action, if any, only after a thorough review to ensure that the action is proper and appropriate.

(b) You may not renew or extend covered transactions (other than no-cost time extensions) with any excluded person, unless the Inter-American Foundation grants an exception under § 1006.120.

§ 1006.315 May I use the services of an excluded person as a principal under a covered transaction?

(a) You as a participant may continue to use the services of an excluded person as a principal under a covered transaction if you were using the services of that person in the transaction before the person was excluded. However, you are not required to continue using that person's services as a principal. You should make a decision about whether to discontinue that person's services only after a thorough review to ensure that the action is proper and appropriate.

(b) You may not begin to use the services of an excluded person as a principal under a covered transaction unless the Inter-American Foundation grants an exception under § 1006.120.

§ 1006.320 Must I verify that principals of my covered transactions are eligible to participate?

Yes, you as a participant are responsible for determining whether any of your principals of your covered transactions is excluded or disqualified from participating in the transaction. You may decide the method and frequency by which you do so. You may, but you are not required to, check the *EPLS*.

§ 1006.325 What happens if I do business with an excluded person in a covered transaction?

If as a participant you knowingly do business with an excluded person, we may disallow costs, annul or terminate the transaction, issue a stop work order, debar or suspend you, or take other remedies as appropriate.

§ 1006.330 What requirements must I pass down to persons at lower tiers with whom I intend to do business?

Before entering into a covered transaction with a participant at the next lower tier, you must require that participant to—

(a) Comply with this subpart as a condition of participation in the transaction. You may do so using any method(s), unless § 1006.440 requires you to use specific methods.

(b) Pass the requirement to comply with this subpart to each person with whom the participant enters into a covered transaction at the next lower tier.

DISCLOSING INFORMATION—PRIMARY TIER PARTICIPANTS

§ 1006.335 What information must I provide before entering into a covered transaction with the Inter-American Foundation?

Before you enter into a covered transaction at the primary tier, you as the participant must notify the Inter-American Foundation office that is entering into the transaction with you, if you know that you or any of the principals for that covered transaction:

(a) Are presently excluded or disqualified;

(b) Have been convicted within the preceding three years of any of the offenses listed in § 1006.800(a) or had a civil judgment rendered against you for one of those offenses within that time period;

(c) Are presently indicted for or otherwise criminally or civilly charged by a governmental entity (Federal, State or local) with commission of any of the offenses listed in § 1006.800(a); or

(d) Have had one or more public transactions (Federal, State, or local) terminated within the preceding three years for cause or default.

§ 1006.340 If I disclose unfavorable information required under § 1006.335, will I be prevented from participating in the transaction?

As a primary tier participant, your disclosure of unfavorable information about yourself or a principal under § 1006.335 will not necessarily cause us to deny your participation in the covered transaction. We will consider the information when we determine whether to enter into the covered transaction. We also will consider any additional information or explanation that you elect to submit with the disclosed information.

§ 1006.345 What happens if I fail to disclose information required under § 1006.335?

If we later determine that you failed to disclose information under § 1006.335 that you knew at the time you entered into the covered transaction, we may—

(a) Terminate the transaction for material failure to comply with the terms and conditions of the transaction; or

(b) Pursue any other available remedies, including suspension and debarment.

§ 1006.350 What must I do if I learn of information required under § 1006.335 after entering into a covered transaction with the Inter-American Foundation?

At any time after you enter into a covered transaction, you must give immediate written notice to the Inter-American Foundation office with which you entered into the transaction if you learn either that—

(a) You failed to disclose information earlier, as required by § 1006.335; or

(b) Due to changed circumstances, you or any of the principals for the transaction now meet any of the criteria in § 1006.335.

DISCLOSING INFORMATION—LOWER TIER PARTICIPANTS

§ 1006.355 What information must I provide to a higher tier participant before entering into a covered transaction with that participant?

Before you enter into a covered transaction with a person at the next higher tier, you as a lower tier participant must notify that person if you know that you or any of the principals are presently excluded or disqualified.

§ 1006.360 What happens if I fail to disclose the information required under § 1006.355?

If we later determine that you failed to tell the person at the higher tier that you were excluded or disqualified at the time you entered into the covered transaction with that person, we may pursue any available remedies, including suspension and debarment.

§ 1006.365 What must I do if I learn of information required under § 1006.355 after entering into a covered transaction with a higher tier participant?

At any time after you enter into a lower tier covered transaction with a person at a higher tier, you must provide immediate written notice to that person if you learn either that—

(a) You failed to disclose information earlier, as required by § 1006.355; or

(b) Due to changed circumstances, you or any of the principals for the transaction now meet any of the criteria in § 1006.355.

Subpart D—Responsibilities of Inter-American Foundation Officials Regarding Transactions

§ 1006.400 May I enter into a transaction with an excluded or disqualified person?

(a) You as an agency official may not enter into a covered transaction with an excluded person unless you obtain an exception under § 1006.120.

(b) You may not enter into any transaction with a person who is disqualified from that transaction, unless you obtain a waiver or exception under the statute, Executive order, or regulation that is the basis for the person's disqualification.

§ 1006.405 May I enter into a covered transaction with a participant if a principal of the transaction is excluded?

As an agency official, you may not enter into a covered transaction with a participant if you know that a principal of the transaction is excluded, unless you obtain an exception under § 1006.120.

§ 1006.410 May I approve a participant's use of the services of an excluded person?

After entering into a covered transaction with a participant, you as an agency official may not approve a participant's use of an excluded person as a principal under that transaction, unless you obtain an exception under § 1006.120.

§ 1006.415 What must I do if a Federal agency excludes the participant or a principal after I enter into a covered transaction?

(a) You as an agency official may continue covered transactions with an excluded person, or under which an excluded person is a principal, if the transactions were in existence when the person was excluded. You are not required to continue the transactions, however, and you may consider termination. You should make a decision about whether to terminate and the type of termination action, if any, only after a thorough review to ensure that the action is proper.

(b) You may not renew or extend covered transactions (other than no-cost time extensions) with any excluded person, or under which an excluded person is a principal, unless you obtain an exception under § 1006.120.

§ 1006.420 May I approve a transaction with an excluded or disqualified person at a lower tier?

If a transaction at a lower tier is subject to your approval, you as an agency official may not approve—

(a) A covered transaction with a person who is currently excluded, unless you obtain an exception under § 1006.120; or

(b) A transaction with a person who is disqualified from that transaction, unless you obtain a waiver or exception under the statute, Executive order, or regulation that is the basis for the person's disqualification.

§ 1006.425 When do I check to see if a person is excluded or disqualified?

As an agency official, you must check to see if a person is excluded or disqualified before you—

(a) Enter into a primary tier covered transaction;

(b) Approve a principal in a primary tier covered transaction;

(c) Approve a lower tier participant if agency approval of the lower tier participant is required; or

(d) Approve a principal in connection with a lower tier transaction if agency approval of the principal is required.

§ 1006.430 How do I check to see if a person is excluded or disqualified?

You check to see if a person is excluded or disqualified in two ways:

(a) You as an agency official must check the *EPLS* when you take any action listed in § 1006.425.

(b) You must review information that a participant gives you, as required by § 1006.335, about its status or the status of the principals of a transaction.

§ 1006.435 What must I require of a primary tier participant?

You as an agency official must require each participant in a primary tier covered transaction to—

(a) Comply with subpart C of this part as a condition of participation in the transaction; and

(b) Communicate the requirement to comply with Subpart C of this part to persons at the next lower tier with whom the primary tier participant enters into covered transactions.

§ 1006.440 What method do I use to communicate those requirements to participants?

To communicate the requirements to participants, you must include a term or condition in the transaction requiring the participant's compliance with Subpart C of this part and requiring them to include a similar term or condition in lower tier covered transactions.

§ 1006.445 What action may I take if a primary tier participant knowingly does business with an excluded or disqualified person?

If a participant knowingly does business with an excluded or disqualified person, you as an agency official may refer the matter for suspension and debarment consideration. You may also disallow costs, annul or terminate the transaction, issue a stop work order, or take any other appropriate remedy.

§ 1006.450 What action may I take if a primary tier participant fails to disclose the information required under § 1006.335?

If you as an agency official determine that a participant failed to disclose information, as required by § 1006.335, at the time it entered into a covered transaction with you, you may—

(a) Terminate the transaction for material failure to comply with the terms and conditions of the transaction; or

(b) Pursue any other available remedies, including suspension and debarment.

§ 1006.455 What may I do if a lower tier participant fails to disclose the information required under § 1006.355 to the next higher tier?

If you as an agency official determine that a lower tier participant failed to disclose information, as required by § 1006.355, at the time it entered into a covered transaction with a participant at the next higher tier, you may pursue any remedies available to you, including the initiation of a suspension or debarment action.

Subpart E—Excluded Parties List System

§ 1006.500 What is the purpose of the Excluded Parties List System (EPLS)?

The *EPLS* is a widely available source of the most current information about persons who are excluded or disqualified from covered transactions.

§ 1006.505 Who uses the EPLS?

(a) Federal agency officials use the *EPLS* to determine whether to enter into a transaction with a person, as required under § 1006.430.

(b) Participants also may, but are not required to, use the *EPLS* to determine if—

(1) Principals of their transactions are excluded or disqualified, as required under § 1006.320; or

(2) Persons with whom they are entering into covered transactions at the next lower tier are excluded or disqualified.

(c) The *EPLS* is available to the general public.

§ 1006.510 Who maintains the EPLS?

In accordance with the OMB guidelines, the General Services Administration (GSA) maintains the *EPLS*. When a Federal agency takes an action to exclude a person under the nonprocurement or procurement debarment and suspension system, the agency enters the information about the excluded person into the *EPLS*.

§ 1006.515 What specific information is in the EPLS?

(a) At a minimum, the *EPLS* indicates—

(1) The full name (where available) and address of each excluded or disqualified person, in alphabetical order, with cross references if more than one name is involved in a single action;

(2) The type of action;

(3) The cause for the action;

(4) The scope of the action;

(5) Any termination date for the action;

(6) The agency and name and telephone number of the agency point of contact for the action; and

(7) The Dun and Bradstreet Number (DUNS), or other similar code approved by the GSA, of the excluded or disqualified person, if available.

(b)(1) The database for the *EPLS* includes a field for the Taxpayer Identification Number (TIN) (the social security number (SSN) for an individual) of an excluded or disqualified person.

(2) Agencies disclose the SSN of an individual to verify the identity of an individual, only if permitted under the Privacy Act of 1974 and, if appropriate, the Computer Matching and Privacy Protection Act of 1988, as codified in 5 U.S.C. 552(a).

§ 1006.520 Who places the information into the EPLS?

Federal officials who take actions to exclude persons under this part or officials who are responsible for identifying disqualified persons must enter the following information about those persons into the *EPLS*:

(a) Information required by § 1006.515(a);

(b) The Taxpayer Identification Number (TIN) of the excluded or disqualified person, including the social security number (SSN) for an individual, if the number is available and may be disclosed under law;

(c) Information about an excluded or disqualified person, generally within five working days, after—

(1) Taking an exclusion action;

(2) Modifying or rescinding an exclusion action;

(3) Finding that a person is disqualified; or

(4) Finding that there has been a change in the status of a person who is listed as disqualified.

§ 1006.525 Whom do I ask if I have questions about a person in the EPLS?

If you have questions about a person in the *EPLS*, ask the point of contact for the Federal agency that placed the person's name into the *EPLS*. You may find the agency point of contact from the *EPLS*.

§ 1006.530 Where can I find the EPLS?

(a) You may access the *EPLS* through the Internet, currently at *http://epls.arnet.gov*.

(b) As of November 26, 2003, you may also subscribe to a printed version. However, we anticipate discontinuing the printed version. Until it is discontinued, you may obtain the printed version by purchasing a yearly subscription from the Superintendent of Documents, U.S. Government Printing Office, Washington, DC 20402, or by calling the Government Printing Office Inquiry and Order Desk at (202) 783–3238.

Subpart F—General Principles Relating to Suspension and Debarment Actions

§ 1006.600 How do suspension and debarment actions start?

When we receive information from any source concerning a cause for suspension or debarment, we will promptly report and investigate it. We refer the question of whether to suspend or debar you to our suspending or debarring official for consideration, if appropriate.

§ 1006.605 How does suspension differ from debarment?

Suspension differs from debarment in that—

A suspending official . . .	A debarring official . . .
(a) Imposes suspension as a temporary status of ineligibility for procurement and nonprocurement transactions, pending completion of an investigation or legal proceedings.	Imposes debarment for a specified period as a final determination that a person is not presently responsible.
(b) Must— (1) Have *adequate evidence* that there may be a cause for debarment of a person; and. (2) Conclude that *immediate action* is necessary to protect the Federal interest.	Must conclude, based on a *preponderance of the evidence*, that the person has engaged in conduct that warrants debarment.
(c) Usually imposes the suspension *first*, and then promptly notifies the suspended person, giving the person an opportunity to contest the suspension and have it lifted.	Imposes debarment *after* giving the respondent notice of the action and an opportunity to contest the proposed debarment.

§ 1006.610 What procedures does the Inter-American Foundation use in suspension and debarment actions?

In deciding whether to suspend or debar you, we handle the actions as informally as practicable, consistent with principles of fundamental fairness.

(a) For suspension actions, we use the procedures in this subpart and subpart G of this part.

(b) For debarment actions, we use the procedures in this subpart and subpart H of this part.

§ 1006.615 How does the Inter-American Foundation notify a person of a suspension or debarment action?

(a) The suspending or debarring official sends a written notice to the last known street address, facsimile number, or e-mail address of—

(1) You or your identified counsel; or

(2) Your agent for service of process, or any of your partners, officers, directors, owners, or joint venturers.

(b) The notice is effective if sent to any of these persons.

§ 1006.620 Do Federal agencies coordinate suspension and debarment actions?

Yes, when more than one Federal agency has an interest in a suspension or debarment, the agencies may consider designating one agency as the lead agency for making the decision. Agencies are encouraged to establish methods and procedures for coordinating their suspension and debarment actions.

§ 1006.625 What is the scope of a suspension or debarment?

If you are suspended or debarred, the suspension or debarment is effective as follows:

(a) Your suspension or debarment constitutes suspension or debarment of all of your divisions and other organizational elements from all covered transactions, unless the suspension or debarment decision is limited—

(1) By its terms to one or more specifically identified individuals, divisions, or other organizational elements; or

(2) To specific types of transactions.

(b) Any affiliate of a participant may be included in a suspension or debarment action if the suspending or debarring official—

(1) Officially names the affiliate in the notice; and

(2) Gives the affiliate an opportunity to contest the action.

§ 1006.630 May the Inter-American Foundation impute conduct of one person to another?

For purposes of actions taken under this rule, we may impute conduct as follows:

(a) *Conduct imputed from an individual to an organization.* We may impute the fraudulent, criminal, or other improper conduct of any officer, director, shareholder, partner, employee, or other individual associated with an organization, to that organization when the improper conduct occurred in connection with the individual's performance of duties for or on behalf of that organization, or with the organization's knowledge, approval or acquiescence. The organization's acceptance of the benefits derived from the conduct is evidence of knowledge, approval or acquiescence.

(b) *Conduct imputed from an organization to an individual, or between individuals.* We may impute the fraudulent, criminal, or other improper conduct of any organization to an individual, or from one individual to another individual, if the individual to whom the improper conduct is imputed either participated in, had knowledge of, or reason to know of the improper conduct.

(c) *Conduct imputed from one organization to another organization.* We may impute the fraudulent, criminal, or other improper conduct of one organization to another organization when the improper conduct occurred in connection with a partnership, joint venture, joint application, association or similar arrangement, or when the organization to whom the improper conduct is imputed has the power to direct, manage, control or influence the activities of the organization responsible for the improper conduct. Acceptance of the benefits derived from the conduct is evidence of knowledge, approval or acquiescence.

§ 1006.635 May the Inter-American Foundation settle a debarment or suspension action?

Yes, we may settle a debarment or suspension action at any time if it is in the best interest of the Federal Government.

§ 1006.640 May a settlement include a voluntary exclusion?

Yes, if we enter into a settlement with you in which you agree to be excluded, it is called a voluntary exclusion and has governmentwide effect.

§ 1006.645 Do other Federal agencies know if the Inter-American Foundation agrees to a voluntary exclusion?

(a) Yes, we enter information regarding a voluntary exclusion into the *EPLS.*

(b) Also, any agency or person may contact us to find out the details of a voluntary exclusion.

Subpart G—Suspension

§ 1006.700 When may the suspending official issue a suspension?

Suspension is a serious action. Using the procedures of this subpart and subpart F of this part, the suspending official may impose suspension only when that official determines that—

(a) There exists an indictment for, or other adequate evidence to suspect, an offense listed under § 1006.800(a), or

(b) There exists adequate evidence to suspect any other cause for debarment listed under § 1006.800(b) through (d); and

(c) Immediate action is necessary to protect the public interest.

§ 1006.705 What does the suspending official consider in issuing a suspension?

(a) In determining the adequacy of the evidence to support the suspension, the suspending official considers how much information is available, how credible it is given the circumstances, whether or not important allegations are corroborated, and what inferences can reasonably be drawn as a result. During this assessment, the suspending official may examine the basic documents, including grants, cooperative agreements, loan authorizations, contracts, and other relevant documents.

(b) An indictment, conviction, civil judgment, or other official findings by Federal, State, or local bodies that determine factual and/or legal matters, constitutes adequate evidence for purposes of suspension actions.

(c) In deciding whether immediate action is needed to protect the public interest, the suspending official has wide discretion. For example, the suspending official may infer the necessity for immediate action to protect the public interest either from the nature of the circumstances giving rise to a cause for suspension or from potential business relationships or involvement with a program of the Federal Government.

§ 1006.710 When does a suspension take effect?

A suspension is effective when the suspending official signs the decision to suspend.

§ 1006.715 What notice does the suspending official give me if I am suspended?

After deciding to suspend you, the suspending official promptly sends you a Notice of Suspension advising you—

(a) That you have been suspended;

(b) That your suspension is based on—

(1) An indictment;

(2) A conviction;

(3) Other adequate evidence that you have committed irregularities which seriously reflect on the propriety of further Federal Government dealings with you; or

(4) Conduct of another person that has been imputed to you, or your affiliation with a suspended or debarred person;

(c) Of any other irregularities in terms sufficient to put you on notice without disclosing the Federal Government's evidence;

(d) Of the cause(s) upon which we relied under § 1006.700 for imposing suspension;

(e) That your suspension is for a temporary period pending the completion of an investigation or resulting legal or debarment proceedings;

(f) Of the applicable provisions of this subpart, Subpart F of this part, and any other Inter-American Foundation procedures governing suspension decision making; and

(g) Of the governmentwide effect of your suspension from procurement and nonprocurement programs and activities.

§ 1006.720 How may I contest a suspension?

If you as a respondent wish to contest a suspension, you or your representative must provide the suspending official with information in opposition to the suspension. You may do this orally or in writing, but any information provided orally that you consider important must also be submitted in writing for the official record.

§ 1006.725 How much time do I have to contest a suspension?

(a) As a respondent you or your representative must either send, or make rrangements to appear and present, the information and argument to the suspending official within 30 days after you receive the Notice of Suspension.

(b) We consider the notice to be received by you—

(1) When delivered, if we mail the notice to the last known street address, or five days after we send it if the letter is undeliverable;

(2) When sent, if we send the notice by facsimile or five days after we send it if the facsimile is undeliverable; or

(3) When delivered, if we send the notice by e-mail or five days after we send it if the e-mail is undeliverable.

§ 1006.730 What information must I provide to the suspending official if I contest a suspension?

(a) In addition to any information and argument in opposition, as a respondent your submission to the suspending official must identify—

(1) Specific facts that contradict the statements contained in the Notice of Suspension. A general denial is insufficient to raise a genuine dispute over facts material to the suspension;

(2) All existing, proposed, or prior exclusions under regulations implementing E.O. 12549 and all similar actions taken by Federal, state, or local agencies, including administrative agreements that affect only those agencies;

(3) All criminal and civil proceedings not included in the Notice of Suspension that grew out of facts relevant to the cause(s) stated in the notice; and

(4) All of your affiliates.

(b) If you fail to disclose this information, or provide false information, the Inter-American Foundation may seek further criminal, civil or administrative action against you, as appropriate.

§ 1006.735 Under what conditions do I get an additional opportunity to challenge the facts on which the suspension is based?

(a) You as a respondent will not have an additional opportunity to challenge the facts if the suspending official determines that—

(1) Your suspension is based upon an indictment, conviction, civil judgment, or other finding by a Federal, State, or local body for which an opportunity to contest the facts was provided;

(2) Your presentation in opposition contains only general denials to information contained in the Notice of Suspension;

(3) The issues raised in your presentation in opposition to the suspension are not factual in nature, or are not material to the suspending official's initial decision to suspend, or the official's decision whether to continue the suspension; or

(4) On the basis of advice from the Department of Justice, an office of the United States Attorney, a State attorney general's office, or a State or local prosecutor's office, that substantial interests of the government in pending or contemplated legal proceedings based on the same facts as the suspension would be prejudiced by conducting fact-finding.

(b) You will have an opportunity to challenge the facts if the suspending official determines that—

(1) The conditions in paragraph (a) of this section do not exist; and

(2) Your presentation in opposition raises a genuine dispute over facts material to the suspension.

(c) If you have an opportunity to challenge disputed material facts under this section, the suspending official or designee must conduct additional proceedings to resolve those facts.

§ 1006.740 Are suspension proceedings formal?

(a) Suspension proceedings are conducted in a fair and informal manner. The suspending official may use flexible procedures to allow you to present matters in opposition. In so doing, the suspending official is not required to follow formal rules of evidence or procedure in creating an official record upon which the official will base a final suspension decision.

(b) You as a respondent or your representative must submit any documentary evidence you want the suspending official to consider.

§ 1006.745 How is fact-finding conducted?

(a) If fact-finding is conducted—

(1) You may present witnesses and other evidence, and confront any witness presented; and

(2) The fact-finder must prepare written findings of fact for the record.

(b) A transcribed record of fact-finding proceedings must be made, unless you as a respondent and the Inter-American Foundation agree to waive it in advance. If you want a copy of the transcribed record, you may purchase it.

§ 1006.750 What does the suspending official consider in deciding whether to continue or terminate my suspension?

(a) The suspending official bases the decision on all information contained in the official record. The record includes—

(1) All information in support of the suspending official's initial decision to suspend you;

(2) Any further information and argument presented in support of, or opposition to, the suspension; and

(3) Any transcribed record of fact-finding proceedings.

(b) The suspending official may refer disputed material facts to another official for findings of fact. The suspending official may reject any resulting findings, in whole or in part, only after specifically determining them to be arbitrary, capricious, or clearly erroneous.

§ 1006.755 When will I know whether the suspension is continued or terminated?

The suspending official must make a written decision whether to continue, modify, or terminate your suspension within 45 days of closing the official record. The official record closes upon the suspending official's receipt of final submissions, information and findings of fact, if any. The suspending official may extend that period for good cause.

§ 1006.760 How long may my suspension last?

(a) If legal or debarment proceedings are initiated at the time of, or during your suspension, the suspension may continue until the conclusion of those proceedings. However, if proceedings are not initiated, a suspension may not exceed 12 months.

(b) The suspending official may extend the 12 month limit under paragraph (a) of this section for an additional 6 months if an office of a U.S. Assistant Attorney General, U.S. Attorney, or other responsible prosecuting official requests an extension in writing. In no event may a suspension exceed 18 months without initiating proceedings under paragraph (a) of this section.

(c) The suspending official must notify the appropriate officials under paragraph (b) of this section of an impending termination of a suspension at least 30 days before the 12 month period expires to allow the officials an opportunity to request an extension.

Subpart H—Debarment

§ 1006.800 What are the causes for debarment?

We may debar a person for—

(a) Conviction of or civil judgment for—

(1) Commission of fraud or a criminal offense in connection with obtaining, attempting to obtain, or performing a public or private agreement or transaction;

(2) Violation of Federal or State antitrust statutes, including those proscribing price fixing between competitors, allocation of customers between competitors, and bid rigging;

(3) Commission of embezzlement, theft, forgery, bribery, falsification or destruction of records, making false statements, tax evasion, receiving stolen property, making false claims, or obstruction of justice; or

(4) Commission of any other offense indicating a lack of business integrity or business honesty that seriously and directly affects your present responsibility;

(b) Violation of the terms of a public agreement or transaction so serious as to affect the integrity of an agency program, such as—

(1) A willful failure to perform in accordance with the terms of one or more public agreements or transactions;

(2) A history of failure to perform or of unsatisfactory performance of one or more public agreements or transactions; or

(3) A willful violation of a statutory or regulatory provision or requirement applicable to a public agreement or transaction;

(c) Any of the following causes:

(1) A nonprocurement debarment by any Federal agency taken before October 1, 1988, or a procurement debarment by any Federal agency taken pursuant to 48 CFR part 9, subpart 9.4, before August 25, 1995;

(2) Knowingly doing business with an ineligible person, except as permitted under § 1006.120;

(3) Failure to pay a single substantial debt, or a number of outstanding debts (including disallowed costs and overpayments, but not including sums owed the Federal Government under the Internal Revenue Code) owed to any Federal agency or instrumentality, provided the debt is uncontested by the debtor or, if contested, provided that the debtor's legal and administrative remedies have been exhausted;

(4) Violation of a material provision of a voluntary exclusion agreement entered into under § 1006.640 or of any settlement of a debarment or suspension action; or

(5) Violation of the provisions of the Drug-Free Workplace Act of 1988 (41 U.S.C. 701); or

(d) Any other cause of so serious or compelling a nature that it affects your present responsibility.

§ 1006.805 What notice does the debarring official give me if I am proposed for debarment?

After consideration of the causes in § 1006.800 of this subpart, if the debarring official proposes to debar you, the official sends you a Notice of Proposed Debarment, pursuant to § 1006.615, advising you—

(a) That the debarring official is considering debarring you;

(b) Of the reasons for proposing to debar you in terms sufficient to put you on notice of the conduct or transactions upon which the proposed debarment is based;

(c) Of the cause(s) under § 1006.800 upon which the debarring official relied for proposing your debarment;

(d) Of the applicable provisions of this subpart, Subpart F of this part, and any other Inter-American Foundation procedures governing debarment; and

(e) Of the governmentwide effect of a debarment from procurement and nonprocurement programs and activities.

§ 1006.810 When does a debarment take effect?

A debarment is not effective until the debarring official issues a decision. The debarring official does not issue a decision until the respondent has had an opportunity to contest the proposed debarment.

§ 1006.815 How may I contest a proposed debarment?

If you as a respondent wish to contest a proposed debarment, you or your representative must provide the debarring official with information in opposition to the proposed debarment. You may do this orally or in writing, but any information provided orally that you consider important must also be submitted in writing for the official record.

§ 1006.820 How much time do I have to contest a proposed debarment?

(a) As a respondent you or your representative must either send, or make arrangements to appear and present, the information and argument to the debarring official within 30 days after you receive the Notice of Proposed Debarment.

(b) We consider the Notice of Proposed Debarment to be received by you—

(1) When delivered, if we mail the notice to the last known street address, or five days after we send it if the letter is undeliverable;

(2) When sent, if we send the notice by facsimile or five days after we send it if the facsimile is undeliverable; or

(3) When delivered, if we send the notice by e-mail or five days after we send it if the e-mail is undeliverable.

§ 1006.825 What information must I provide to the debarring official if I contest a proposed debarment?

(a) In addition to any information and argument in opposition, as a respondent your submission to the debarring official must identify—

(1) Specific facts that contradict the statements contained in the Notice of Proposed Debarment. Include any information about any of the factors listed in § 1006.860. A general denial is insufficient to raise a genuine dispute over facts material to the debarment;

(2) All existing, proposed, or prior exclusions under regulations implementing E.O. 12549 and all similar actions taken by Federal, State, or local agencies, including administrative

agreements that affect only those agencies;

(3) All criminal and civil proceedings not included in the Notice of Proposed Debarment that grew out of facts relevant to the cause(s) stated in the notice; and

(4) All of your affiliates.

(b) If you fail to disclose this information, or provide false information, the Inter-American Foundation may seek further criminal, civil or administrative action against you, as appropriate.

§ 1006.830 Under what conditions do I get an additional opportunity to challenge the facts on which a proposed debarment is based?

(a) You as a respondent will not have an additional opportunity to challenge the facts if the debarring official determines that—

(1) Your debarment is based upon a conviction or civil judgment;

(2) Your presentation in opposition contains only general denials to information contained in the Notice of Proposed Debarment; or

(3) The issues raised in your presentation in opposition to the proposed debarment are not factual in nature, or are not material to the debarring official's decision whether to debar.

(b) You will have an additional opportunity to challenge the facts if the debarring official determines that—

(1) The conditions in paragraph (a) of this section do not exist; and

(2) Your presentation in opposition raises a genuine dispute over facts material to the proposed debarment.

(c) If you have an opportunity to challenge disputed material facts under this section, the debarring official or designee must conduct additional proceedings to resolve those facts.

§ 1006.835 Are debarment proceedings formal?

(a) Debarment proceedings are conducted in a fair and informal manner. The debarring official may use flexible procedures to allow you as a respondent to present matters in opposition. In so doing, the debarring official is not required to follow formal rules of evidence or procedure in creating an official record upon which the official will base the decision whether to debar.

(b) You or your representative must submit any documentary evidence you want the debarring official to consider.

§ 1006.840 How is fact-finding conducted?

(a) If fact-finding is conducted—

(1) You may present witnesses and other evidence, and confront any witness presented; and

(2) The fact-finder must prepare written findings of fact for the record.

(b) A transcribed record of fact-finding proceedings must be made, unless you as a respondent and the Inter-American Foundation agree to waive it in advance. If you want a copy of the transcribed record, you may purchase it.

§ 1006.845 What does the debarring official consider in deciding whether to debar me?

(a) The debarring official may debar you for any of the causes in § 1006.800. However, the official need not debar you even if a cause for debarment exists. The official may consider the seriousness of your acts or omissions and the mitigating or aggravating factors set forth at § 1006.860.

(b) The debarring official bases the decision on all information contained in the official record. The record includes—

(1) All information in support of the debarring official's proposed debarment;

(2) Any further information and argument presented in support of, or in opposition to, the proposed debarment; and

(3) Any transcribed record of fact-finding proceedings.

(c) The debarring official may refer disputed material facts to another official for findings of fact. The debarring official may reject any resultant findings, in whole or in part, only after specifically determining them to be arbitrary, capricious, or clearly erroneous.

§ 1006.850 What is the standard of proof in a debarment action?

(a) In any debarment action, we must establish the cause for debarment by a preponderance of the evidence.

(b) If the proposed debarment is based upon a conviction or civil judgment, the standard of proof is met.

§ 1006.855 Who has the burden of proof in a debarment action?

(a) We have the burden to prove that a cause for debarment exists.

(b) Once a cause for debarment is established, you as a respondent have the burden of demonstrating to the satisfaction of the debarring official that you are presently responsible and that debarment is not necessary.

§ 1006.860 What factors may influence the debarring official's decision?

This section lists the mitigating and aggravating factors that the debarring official may consider in determining whether to debar you and the length of your debarment period. The debarring official may consider other factors if appropriate in light of the circumstances of a particular case. The existence or nonexistence of any factor, such as one of those set forth in this section, is not necessarily determinative of your present responsibility. In making a debarment decision, the debarring official may consider the following factors:

(a) The actual or potential harm or impact that results or may result from the wrongdoing.

(b) The frequency of incidents and/or duration of the wrongdoing.

(c) Whether there is a pattern or prior history of wrongdoing. For example, if you have been found by another Federal agency or a State agency to have engaged in wrongdoing similar to that found in the debarment action, the existence of this fact may be used by the debarring official in determining that you have a pattern or prior history of wrongdoing.

(d) Whether you are or have been excluded or disqualified by an agency of the Federal Government or have not been allowed to participate in State or local contracts or assistance agreements on a basis of conduct similar to one or more of the causes for debarment specified in this part.

(e) Whether you have entered into an administrative agreement with a Federal agency or a State or local government that is not governmentwide but is based on conduct similar to one or more of the causes for debarment specified in this part.

(f) Whether and to what extent you planned, initiated, or carried out the wrongdoing.

(g) Whether you have accepted responsibility for the wrongdoing and recognize the seriousness of the misconduct that led to the cause for debarment.

(h) Whether you have paid or agreed to pay all criminal, civil and administrative liabilities for the improper activity, including any investigative or administrative costs incurred by the government, and have made or agreed to make full restitution.

(i) Whether you have cooperated fully with the government agencies during the investigation and any court or administrative action. In determining the extent of cooperation, the debarring official may consider when the cooperation began and whether you disclosed all pertinent information known to you.

(j) Whether the wrongdoing was pervasive within your organization.

(k) The kind of positions held by the individuals involved in the wrongdoing.

(l) Whether your organization took appropriate corrective action or remedial measures, such as establishing ethics training and implementing programs to prevent recurrence.

(m) Whether your principals tolerated the offense.

(n) Whether you brought the activity cited as a basis for the debarment to the attention of the appropriate government agency in a timely manner.

(o) Whether you have fully investigated the circumstances surrounding the cause for debarment and, if so, made the result of the investigation available to the debarring official.

(p) Whether you had effective standards of conduct and internal control systems in place at the time the questioned conduct occurred.

(q) Whether you have taken appropriate disciplinary action against the individuals responsible for the activity which constitutes the cause for debarment.

(r) Whether you have had adequate time to eliminate the circumstances within your organization that led to the cause for the debarment.

(s) Other factors that are appropriate to the circumstances of a particular case.

§ 1006.865 How long may my debarment last?

(a) If the debarring official decides to debar you, your period of debarment will be based on the seriousness of the cause(s) upon which your debarment is based. Generally, debarment should not exceed three years. However, if circumstances warrant, the debarring official may impose a longer period of debarment.

(b) In determining the period of debarment, the debarring official may consider the factors in § 1006.860. If a suspension has preceded your debarment, the debarring official must consider the time you were suspended.

(c) If the debarment is for a violation of the provisions of the Drug-Free Workplace Act of 1988, your period of debarment may not exceed five years.

§ 1006.870 When do I know if the debarring official debars me?

(a) The debarring official must make a written decision whether to debar within 45 days of closing the official record. The official record closes upon the debarring official's receipt of final submissions, information and findings of fact, if any. The debarring official may extend that period for good cause.

(b) The debarring official sends you written notice, pursuant to § 1006.615 that the official decided, either—

(1) Not to debar you; or

(2) To debar you. In this event, the notice:

(i) Refers to the Notice of Proposed Debarment;

(ii) Specifies the reasons for your debarment;

(iii) States the period of your debarment, including the effective dates; and

(iv) Advises you that your debarment is effective for covered transactions and contracts that are subject to the Federal Acquisition Regulation (48 CFR chapter 1), throughout the executive branch of the Federal Government unless an agency head or an authorized designee grants an exception.

§ 1006.875 May I ask the debarring official to reconsider a decision to debar me?

Yes, as a debarred person you may ask the debarring official to reconsider the debarment decision or to reduce the time period or scope of the debarment. However, you must put your request in writing and support it with documentation.

§ 1006.880 What factors may influence the debarring official during reconsideration?

The debarring official may reduce or terminate your debarment based on—

(a) Newly discovered material evidence;

(b) A reversal of the conviction or civil judgment upon which your debarment was based;

(c) A bona fide change in ownership or management;

(d) Elimination of other causes for which the debarment was imposed; or

(e) Other reasons the debarring official finds appropriate.

§ 1006.885 May the debarring official extend a debarment?

(a) Yes, the debarring official may extend a debarment for an additional period, if that official determines that an extension is necessary to protect the public interest.

(b) However, the debarring official may not extend a debarment solely on the basis of the facts and circumstances upon which the initial debarment action was based.

(c) If the debarring official decides that a debarment for an additional period is necessary, the debarring official must follow the applicable procedures in this subpart, and subpart F of this part, to extend the debarment.

Subpart I—Definitions

§ 1006.900 Adequate evidence.

Adequate evidence means information sufficient to support the reasonable belief that a particular act or omission has occurred.

§ 1006.905 Affiliate.

Persons are *affiliates* of each other if, directly or indirectly, either one controls or has the power to control the other or a third person controls or has the power to control both. The ways we use to determine control include, but are not limited to—

(a) Interlocking management or ownership;

(b) Identity of interests among family members;

(c) Shared facilities and equipment;

(d) Common use of employees; or

(e) A business entity which has been organized following the exclusion of a person which has the same or similar management, ownership, or principal employees as the excluded person.

§ 1006.910 Agency.

Agency means any United States executive department, military department, defense agency, or any other agency of the executive branch. Other agencies of the Federal government are not considered "agencies" for the purposes of this part unless they issue regulations adopting the governmentwide Debarment and Suspension system under Executive orders 12549 and 12689.

§ 1006.915 Agent or representative.

Agent or representative means any person who acts on behalf of, or who is authorized to commit, a participant in a covered transaction.

§ 1006.920 Civil judgment.

Civil judgment means the disposition of a civil action by any court of competent jurisdiction, whether by verdict, decision, settlement, stipulation, other disposition which creates a civil liability for the complained of wrongful acts, or a final determination of liability under the Program Fraud Civil Remedies Act of 1988 (31 U.S.C. 3801–3812).

§ 1006.925 Conviction.

Conviction means—

(a) A judgment or any other determination of guilt of a criminal offense by any court of competent jurisdiction, whether entered upon a verdict or plea, including a plea of nolo contendere; or

(b) Any other resolution that is the functional equivalent of a judgment, including probation before judgment and deferred prosecution. A disposition without the participation of the court is the functional equivalent of a judgment only if it includes an admission of guilt.

§ 1006.930 Debarment.

Debarment means an action taken by a debarring official under subpart H of this part to exclude a person from participating in covered transactions and transactions covered under the Federal Acquisition Regulation (48 CFR chapter 1). A person so excluded is debarred.

§ 1006.935 Debarring official.

(a) *Debarring official* means an agency official who is authorized to impose debarment. A debarring official is either—

(1) The agency head; or

(2) An official designated by the agency head.

(b) [Reserved]

§ 1006.940 Disqualified.

Disqualified means that a person is prohibited from participating in specified Federal procurement or nonprocurement transactions as required under a statute, Executive order (other than Executive Orders 12549 and 12689) or other authority. Examples of disqualifications include persons prohibited under—

(a) The Davis-Bacon Act (40 U.S.C. 276(a));

(b) The equal employment opportunity acts and Executive orders; or

(c) The Clean Air Act (42 U.S.C. 7606), Clean Water Act (33 U.S.C. 1368) and Executive Order 11738 (3 CFR, 1973 Comp., p. 799).

§ 1006.945 Excluded or exclusion.

Excluded or exclusion means—

(a) That a person or commodity is prohibited from being a participant in covered transactions, whether the person has been suspended; debarred; proposed for debarment under 48 CFR part 9, subpart 9.4; voluntarily excluded; or

(b) The act of excluding a person.

§ 1006.950 Excluded Parties List System

Excluded Parties List System (EPLS) means the list maintained and disseminated by the General Services Administration (GSA) containing the names and other information about persons who are ineligible. The *EPLS* system includes the printed version entitled, "List of Parties Excluded or Disqualified from Federal Procurement and Nonprocurement Programs," so long as published.

§ 1006.955 Indictment.

Indictment means an indictment for a criminal offense. A presentment, information, or other filing by a competent authority charging a criminal offense shall be given the same effect as an indictment.

§ 1006.960 Ineligible or ineligibility.

Ineligible or ineligibility means that a person or commodity is prohibited from covered transactions because of an exclusion or disqualification.

§ 1006.965 Legal proceedings.

Legal proceedings means any criminal proceeding or any civil judicial proceeding, including a proceeding under the Program Fraud Civil Remedies Act (31 U.S.C. 3801–3812), to which the Federal Government or a State or local government or quasi-governmental authority is a party. The term also includes appeals from those proceedings.

§ 1006.970 Nonprocurement transaction.

(a) *Nonprocurement transaction* means any transaction, regardless of type (except procurement contracts), including, but not limited to the following:

(1) Grants.

(2) Cooperative agreements.

(3) Scholarships.

(4) Fellowships.

(5) Contracts of assistance.

(6) Loans.

(7) Loan guarantees.

(8) Subsidies.

(9) Insurances.

(10) Payments for specified uses.

(11) Donation agreements.

(b) A nonprocurement transaction at any tier does not require the transfer of Federal funds.

§ 1006.975 Notice.

Notice means a written communication served in person, sent by certified mail or its equivalent, or sent electronically by e-mail or facsimile. (See § 1006.615.)

§ 1006.980 Participant.

Participant means any person who submits a proposal for or who enters into a covered transaction, including an agent or representative of a participant.

§ 1006.985 Person.

Person means any individual, corporation, partnership, association, unit of government, or legal entity, however organized.

§ 1006.990 Preponderance of the evidence.

Preponderance of the evidence means proof by information that, compared with information opposing it, leads to the conclusion that the fact at issue is more probably true than not.

§ 1006.995 Principal.

Principal means—

(a) An officer, director, owner, partner, principal investigator, or other person within a participant with management or supervisory responsibilities related to a covered transaction; or

(b) A consultant or other person, whether or not employed by the participant or paid with Federal funds, who—

(1) Is in a position to handle Federal funds;

(2) Is in a position to influence or control the use of those funds; or,

(3) Occupies a technical or professional position capable of substantially influencing the development or outcome of an activity required to perform the covered transaction.

§ 1006.1000 Respondent.

Respondent means a person against whom an agency has initiated a debarment or suspension action.

§ 1006.1005 State.

(a) *State* means—

(1) Any of the states of the United States;

(2) The District of Columbia;

(3) The Commonwealth of Puerto Rico;

(4) Any territory or possession of the United States; or

(5) Any agency or instrumentality of a state.

(b) For purposes of this part, *State* does not include institutions of higher education, hospitals, or units of local government.

§ 1006.1010 Suspending official.

(a) *Suspending official* means an agency official who is authorized to impose suspension. The suspending official is either:

(1) The agency head; or

(2) An official designated by the agency head.

(b) [Reserved]

§ 1006.1015 Suspension.

Suspension is an action taken by a suspending official under subpart G of this part that immediately prohibits a person from participating in covered transactions and transactions covered under the Federal Acquisition Regulation (48 CFR chapter 1) for a temporary period, pending completion of an agency investigation and any judicial or administrative proceedings that may ensue. A person so excluded is suspended.

§ 1006.1020 Voluntary exclusion or voluntarily excluded.

(a) *Voluntary exclusion* means a person's agreement to be excluded under the terms of a settlement between the person and one or more agencies. Voluntary exclusion must have governmentwide effect.

(b) *Voluntarily excluded* means the status of a person who has agreed to a voluntary exclusion.

Subpart J [Reserved]

APPENDIX TO PART 1006—COVERED TRANSACTIONS

COVERED TRANSACTIONS

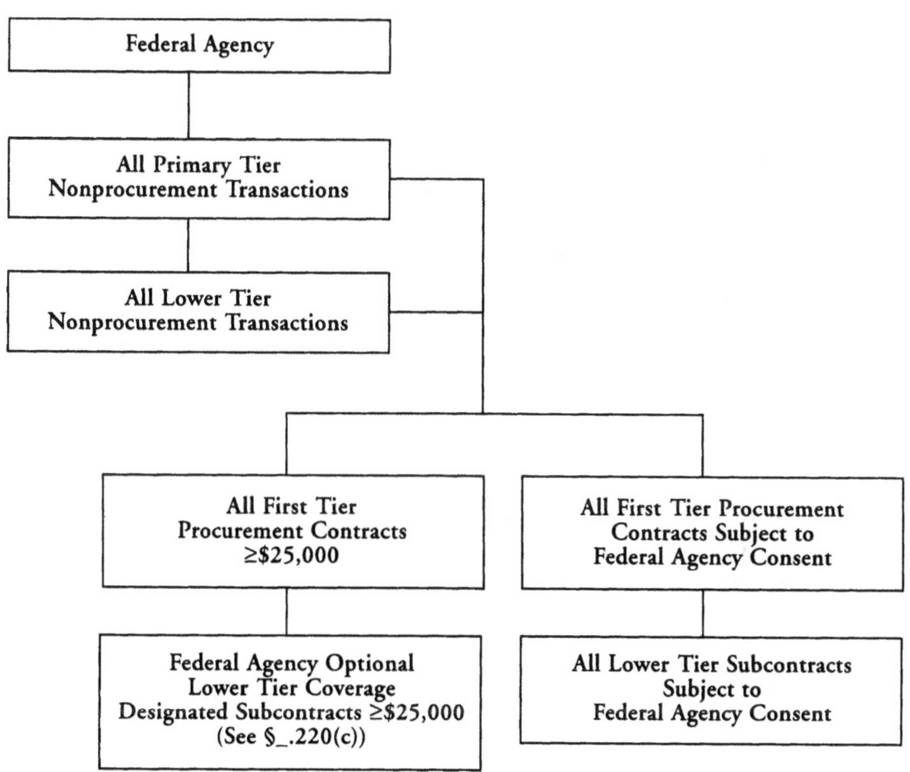

PART 1007—SALARY OFFSET

AUTHORITY: 5 U.S.C. 5514, E.O. 12107, 3 CFR, 1978 Comp., p. 264; 5 CFR part 550, subpart K, and 22 U.S.C. 290f(e)(11).

SOURCE: 57 FR 2837, Jan. 24, 1992, unless otherwise noted.

§ 1007.1 Purpose and scope.

(a) This regulation provides procedures for the collection by administrative offset of a federal employee's salary without his/her consent to satisfy certain debts owed to the federal government. These regulations apply to all federal employees who owe debts to the Inter-American Foundation (IAF) and to current employees of the Inter-American Foundation who owe debts to other federal agencies. This regulation does not apply when the employee consents to recovery from his/her current pay account.

(b) This regulation does not apply to debts or claims arising under:

(1) The Internal Revenue Code of 1954, as amended, 26 U.S.C. 1 *et seq.;*

(2) The Social Security Act, 42 U.S.C. 301 *et seq.;*

(3) The tariff laws of the United States; or

(4) Any case where a collection of a debt by salary offset is explicitly provided for or prohibited by another statute.

(c) This regulation does not apply to any adjustment to pay arising out of an employee's selection of coverage or a change in coverage under a federal benefits program requiring periodic deductions from pay if the amount to be recovered was accumulated over four pay periods or less.

(d) This regulation does not preclude the compromise, suspension, or termination of collection action where appropriate under the standards implementing the Federal Claims Collection Act, 31 U.S.C. 3711 *et seq.*, 4 CFR parts 101 through 105, 45 CFR part 1177.

(e) This regulation does not preclude an employee from requesting waiver of an overpayment under 5 U.S.C. 5584, 10 U.S.C. 2774 or 32 U.S.C. 716 or in any way questioning the amount or validity of the debt by submitting a subsequent claim to the General Accounting Office. This regulation does not preclude an employee from requesting a waiver pursuant to other statutory provisions applicable to the particular debt being collected.

(f) Matters not addressed in these regulations should be reviewed in accordance with the Federal Claims Collection Standards at 4 CFR 101.1 *et seq.*

§ 1007.2 Definitions.

For the purposes of the part, the following definitions will apply:

Agency means an executive agency as defined at 5 U.S.C. 105 including the U.S. Postal Service, the U.S. Postal Commission, a military department as defined at 5 U.S.C. 102, an agency or court in the judicial branch, an agency of the legislative branch including the U.S. Senate and House of Representatives and other independent establishments that are entities of the Federal government.

Creditor Agency means the agency to which the debt is owed.

Debt means an amount owed to the United States from sources which include loans insured or guaranteed by the United States and all other amounts due the United States from fees, leases, rents, royalties, services, sales of real or personal property, overpayments, penalties, damages, interests, fines, forfeitures (except those arising under the Uniform Code of Military Justice), and all other similar sources.

Disposable pay means the amount that remains from an employee's federal pay after the required deductions for social security, federal, state or local income tax, health insurance premiums, retirement contributions, life insurance premiums, federal employment taxes, and any other deductions that are required to be withheld by law.

Hearing official means an individual responsible for conducting any hearing with respect to the existence or amount of a debt claimed and who renders a decision on the basis of such hearing. A hearing official may not be under the supervision or control of the President of the Inter-American Foundation.

Paying Agency means the agency that employs the individual who owes the debt and authorizes the payment of his/her current pay.

President means the President of the Inter-American Foundation or the President's designee.

Salary offset means an administrative offset to collect a debt pursuant to 5 U.S.C. 5514 by deduction(s) at one or more officially established pay intervals from the current pay account of an employee without his/her consent.

§ 1007.3 Applicability.

(a) These regulations are to be followed when:

(1) The Inter-American Foundation is owed a debt by an individual currently employed by another federal agency;

(2) The Inter-American Foundation is owed a debt by an individual who is a current employee of the Inter-American Foundation; or

(3) The Inter-American Foundation employs an individual who owes a debt to another federal agency.

§ 1007.4 Notice requirements.

(a) Deductions shall not be made unless the employee is provided with written notice, signed by the President, of the debt at least 30 days before salary offset commences.

(b) The written notice shall contain:

(1) A statement that the debt is owed and an explanation of its nature and amount;

(2) The agency's intention to collect the debt by deducting from the employee's current disposable pay account;

(3) The amount, frequency, proposed beginning date, and duration of the intended deduction(s);

(4) An explanation of interest, penalties, and administrative charges, including a statement that such charges will be assessed unless excused in accordance with the Federal Claims Collections Standards at 4 CFR 101.1 *et seq.;*

(5) The employee's right to inspect, request, and receive a copy of government records relating to the debt;

(6) The opportunity to establish a written schedule for the voluntary repayment of the debt;

(7) The right to a hearing conducted by an impartial hearing official;

(8) The methods and time period for petitioning for hearings;

(9) A statement that the timely filing of a petition for a hearing will stay the commencement of collection proceedings;

(10) A statement that a final decision on the hearing will be issued not later than 60 days after the filing of the petition requesting the hearing unless the employee requests and the hearing official grants a delay in the proceedings;

(11) A statement that knowingly false or frivolous statements, representations, or evidence may subject the employee to appropriate disciplinary procedures;

(12) A statement of other rights and remedies available to the employee under statutes or regulations governing the program for which the collection is being made; and

(13) Unless there are contractual or statutory provisions to the contrary, a statement that amounts paid on or deducted for the debt which are later waived or found not owed to the United States will be promptly refunded to the employee.

§ 1007.5 Hearing.

(a) *Request for hearing.* (1) An employee must file a petition for a hearing in accordance with the instructions outlined in the agency's notice to offset.

(2) A hearing may be requested by filing a written petition addressed to the President of the Inter-American Foundation stating why the employee disputes the existence or amount of the debt. The petition for a hearing must be received by the President no later than fifteen (15) calendar days after the date of the notice to offset unless the employee can show good cause for failing to meet the deadline date.

(b) *Hearing procedures.* (1) The hearing will be presided over by an impartial hearing official.

(2) The hearing shall conform to procedures contained in the Federal Claims Collection Standards, 4 CFR 102.3(c). The burden shall be on the employee to demonstrate that the existence or the amount of the debt is in error.

§ 1007.6 Written decision.

(a) The hearing official shall issue a written opinion no later than 60 days after the hearing.

(b) The written opinion will include: a statement of the facts presented to demonstrate the nature and origin of the alleged debt; the hearing official's analysis, findings and conclusions; the amount and validity of the debt, and the repayment schedule.

§ 1007.7 Coordinating offset with another Federal agency.

(a) *The Inter-American Foundation as the creditor agency.* (1) When the President determines that an employee of another federal agency owes a delinquent debt to the Inter-American Foundation, the President shall as appropriate:

(i) Arrange for a hearing upon the proper petitioning by the employee;

(ii) Certify to the paying agency in writing that the employee owes the debt, the amount and basis of the debt, the date on which payment is due, the date the Government's right to collect the debt accrued, and that Foundation regulations for salary offset have been approved by the Office of Personnel Management;

(iii) If collection must be made in installments, the President must advise the paying agency of the amount or percentage of disposable pay to be collected in each installment;

(iv) Advise the paying agency of the actions taken under 5 U.S.C. 5514(b) and provide the dates on which action was taken unless the employee has consented to salary offset in writing or signed a statement acknowledging receipt of procedures required by law. The written consent or acknowledgment must be sent to the paying agency;

(v) If the employee is in the process of separating, the Foundation must submit its debt claim to the paying agency as provided in this part. The paying agency must certify any amounts already collected, notify the employee, and send a copy of the certification and notice of the employee's separation to the Inter-American Foundation. If the paying agency is aware that the employee is entitled to payments from the Civil Service Retirement and Disability Fund or similar payments, it must certify to the agency responsible for making such payments the amount of the debt and that the provisions of 5 CFR 550.1108 have been followed; and

(vi) If the employee has already separated and all the payments due from the paying agency have been paid, the President may request unless otherwise prohibited, that money payable to the employee from the Civil Service Retirement and Disability Fund or other similar funds be collected by administrative offset.

(b) *The Foundation as the paying agency.* (1) Upon receipt of a properly certified debt claim from another agency, deductions will be scheduled to begin at the next established pay interval. The employee must receive written notice that the Inter-American Foundation has received a certified debt claim from the creditor agency, the amount of the debt, the date salary offset will begin, and the amount of the deduction(s). The Inter-American Foundation shall not review the merits of the creditor agency's determination of the validity or the amount of the certified claim.

(2) If the employee transfers to another agency after the creditor agency has submitted its debt claim to the Inter-American Foundation and before the debt is collected completely, the Inter-American Foundation must certify the total amount collected. One copy of the certification must be furnished to the employee. A copy must be furnished to the creditor agency with notice of the employee's transfer.

§ 1007.8 Procedures for salary offset.

(a) Deductions to liquidate an employee's debt will be by the method and in the amount stated in the President's notice of intention to offset as provided in § 1007.4. Debts will be collected in one lump sum where possible. If the employee is financially unable to pay in one lump sum, collection must be made in installments.

(b) Debts will be collected by deduction at officially established pay intervals from an employee's current pay account unless alternative arrangements for repayment are made.

(c) Installment deductions will be made over a period not greater than the anticipated period of employment. The size of installment deductions must bear a reasonable relationship to the size of the debt and the employee's ability to pay. The deduction for the pay interval for any period must not exceed 15% of disposable pay unless the employee has agreed in writing to a deduction of a greater amount.

(d) Unliquidated debts may be offset against any financial payment due to a separated employee including but not limited to final salary or leave payments in accordance with 31 U.S.C. 3716.

§ 1007.9 Refunds.

(a) The Inter-American Foundation will refund promptly any amounts deducted to satisfy debts owed to the IAF when the debt is waived, found not owed to the IAF, or when directed by an administrative or judicial order.

(b) The creditor agency will promptly return any amounts deducted by IAF to satisfy debts owed to the creditor agency when the debt is waived, found not owed, or when directed by an administrative or judicial order.

(c) Unless required by law, refunds under this subsection shall not bear interest.

§ 1007.10 Statute of limitations.

If a debt has been outstanding for more than 10 years after the agency's right to collect the debt first accrued, the agency may not collect by salary offset unless facts material to the Government's right to collect were not known and could not reasonably have been known by the official or officials who were charged with the responsibility for discovery and collection of such debts.

§ 1007.11 Non-waiver of rights.

An employee's involuntary payment of all or any part of a debt collected under these regulations will not be construed as a waiver of any rights that employee may have under 5 U.S.C. 5514 or any other provision of contract or law unless there are statutes or contract(s) to the contrary.

§ 1007.12 Interest, penalties, and administrative costs.

Charges may be assessed for interest, penalties, and administrative costs in accordance with the Federal Claims Collection Standards, 4 CFR 102.13.

PART 1008—GOVERNMENTWIDE REQUIREMENTS FOR DRUG-FREE WORKPLACE (FINANCIAL ASSISTANCE)

Subpart A—Purpose and Coverage

Sec.

Subpart B—Requirements for Recipients Other Than Individuals

Subpart C—Requirements for Recipients Who Are Individuals

Subpart D—Responsibilities of Inter-American Foundation Awarding Officials

Subpart E—Violations of This Part and Consequences

Subpart F—Definitions

AUTHORITY: 41 U.S.C. 701 *et seq.*

SOURCE: 68 FR 66590, Nov. 26, 2003, unless otherwise noted.

Subpart A—Purpose and Coverage

§ 1008.100 What does this part do?

This part carries out the portion of the Drug-Free Workplace Act of 1988 (41 U.S.C. 701 *et seq.*, as amended) that applies to grants. It also applies the provisions of the Act to cooperative agreements and other financial assistance awards, as a matter of Federal Government policy.

§ 1008.105 Does this part apply to me?

(a) Portions of this part apply to you if you are either—

(1) A recipient of an assistance award from the Inter-American Foundation; or

(2) A(n) Inter-American Foundation awarding official. (See definitions of award and recipient in §§ 1008.605 and 1008.660, respectively.)

(b) The following table shows the subparts that apply to you:

If you are . . .	see subparts . . .
(1) A recipient who is not an individual	A, B and E.
(2) A recipient who is an individual	A, C and E.
(3) A(n) Inter-American Foundation awarding official	A, D and E.

§ 1008.110 Are any of my Federal assistance awards exempt from this part?

This part does not apply to any award that the Inter-American Foundation President or designee determines that the application of this part would be inconsistent with the international obligations of the United States or the laws or regulations of a foreign government.

§ 1008.115 Does this part affect the Federal contracts that I receive?

It will affect future contract awards indirectly if you are debarred or suspended for a violation of the requirements of this part, as described in § 1008.510(c). However, this part does not apply directly to procurement contracts. The portion of the Drug-Free Workplace Act of 1988 that applies to Federal procurement contracts is carried out through the Federal Acquisition Regulation in chapter 1 of Title 48 of the Code of Federal Regulations (the drug-free workplace coverage currently is in 48 CFR part 23, subpart 23.5).

Subpart B—Requirements for Recipients Other Than Individuals

§ 1008.200 What must I do to comply with this part?

There are two general requirements if you are a recipient other than an individual.

(a) First, you must make a good faith effort, on a continuing basis, to maintain a drug-free workplace. You must agree to do so as a condition for receiving any award covered by this part. The specific measures that you must take in this regard are described in more detail in subsequent sections of this subpart. Briefly, those measures are to—

(1) Publish a drug-free workplace statement and establish a drug-free awareness program for your employees (see §§ 1008.205 through 1008.220); and

(2) Take actions concerning employees who are convicted of violating drug statutes in the workplace (see § 1008.225).

(b) Second, you must identify all known workplaces under your Federal awards (see § 1008.230).

§ 1008.205 What must I include in my drug-free workplace statement?

You must publish a statement that—

(a) Tells your employees that the unlawful manufacture, distribution, dispensing, possession, or use of a controlled substance is prohibited in your workplace;

(b) Specifies the actions that you will take against employees for violating that prohibition; and

(c) Lets each employee know that, as a condition of employment under any award, he or she:

(1) Will abide by the terms of the statement; and

(2) Must notify you in writing if he or she is convicted for a violation of a criminal drug statute occurring in the workplace and must do so no more

than five calendar days after the conviction.

§ 1008.210 To whom must I distribute my drug-free workplace statement?

You must require that a copy of the statement described in § 1008.205 be given to each employee who will be engaged in the performance of any Federal award.

§ 1008.215 What must I include in my drug-free awareness program?

You must establish an ongoing drug-free awareness program to inform employees about—

(a) The dangers of drug abuse in the workplace;

(b) Your policy of maintaining a drug-free workplace;

(c) Any available drug counseling, rehabilitation, and employee assistance programs; and

(d) The penalties that you may impose upon them for drug abuse violations occurring in the workplace.

§ 1008.220 By when must I publish my drug-free workplace statement and establish my drug-free awareness program?

If you are a new recipient that does not already have a policy statement as described in § 1008.205 and an ongoing awareness program as described in § 1008.215, you must publish the statement and establish the program by the time given in the following table:

If . . .	then you . . .
(a) The performance period of the award is less than 30 days	must have the policy statement and program in place as soon as possible, but before the date on which performance is expected to be completed.
(b) The performance period of the award is 30 days or more ...	must have the policy statement and program in place within 30 days after award.
(c) You believe there are extraordinary circumstances that will require more than 30 days for you to publish the policy statement and establish the awareness program.	may ask the Inter-American Foundation awarding official to give you more time to do so. The amount of additional time, if any, to be given is at the discretion of the awarding official.

§ 1008.225 What actions must I take concerning employees who are convicted of drug violations in the workplace?

There are two actions you must take if an employee is convicted of a drug violation in the workplace:

(a) First, you must notify Federal agencies if an employee who is engaged in the performance of an award informs you about a conviction, as required by § 1008.205(c)(2), or you otherwise learn of the conviction. Your notification to the Federal agencies must_

(1) Be in writing;

(2) Include the employee's position title;

(3) Include the identification number(s) of each affected award;

(4) Be sent within ten calendar days after you learn of the conviction; and

(5) Be sent to every Federal agency on whose award the convicted employee was working. It must be sent to every awarding official or his or her official designee, unless the Federal agency has specified a central point for the receipt of the notices.

(b) Second, within 30 calendar days of learning about an employee's conviction, you must either_

(1) Take appropriate personnel action against the employee, up to and including termination, consistent with the requirements of the Rehabilitation Act of 1973 (29 U.S.C. 794), as amended; or

(2) Require the employee to participate satisfactorily in a drug abuse assistance or rehabilitation program approved for these purposes by a Federal, State or local health, law enforcement, or other appropriate agency.

§ 1008.230 How and when must I identify workplaces?

(a) You must identify all known workplaces under each Inter-American Foundation award. A failure to do so is a violation of your drug-free workplace requirements. You may identify the workplaces_

(1) To the Inter-American Foundation official that is making the award, either at the time of application or upon award; or

(2) In documents that you keep on file in your offices during the performance of the award, in which case you must make the information available for inspection upon request by Inter-American Foundation officials or their designated representatives.

(b) Your workplace identification for an award must include the actual address of buildings (or parts of buildings) or other sites where work under the award takes place. Categorical descriptions may be used (*e.g.*, all vehicles of a mass transit authority or State highway department while in operation, State employees in each local unemployment office, performers in concert halls or radio studios).

(c) If you identified workplaces to the Inter-American Foundation awarding official at the time of application or award, as described in paragraph (a)(1) of this section, and any workplace that you identified changes during the performance of the award, you must inform the Inter-American Foundation awarding official.

Subpart C—Requirements for Recipients Who Are Individuals

§ 1008.300 What must I do to comply with this part if I am an individual recipient?

As a condition of receiving a(n) Inter-American Foundation award, if you are an individual recipient, you must agree that—

(a) You will not engage in the unlawful manufacture, distribution, dispensing, possession, or use of a controlled substance in conducting any activity related to the award; and

(b) If you are convicted of a criminal drug offense resulting from a violation occurring during the conduct of any award activity, you will report the conviction:

(1) In writing.

(2) Within 10 calendar days of the conviction.

(3) To the Inter-American Foundation awarding official or other designee for each award that you currently have, unless § 1008.301 or the award document designates a central point for the receipt of the notices. When notice is made to a central point, it must include the identification number(s) of each affected award.

§ 1008.301 [Reserved]

Subpart D—Responsibilities of Inter-American Foundation Awarding Officials

§ 1008.400 What are my responsibilities as a(n) Inter-American Foundation awarding official?

As a(n) Inter-American Foundation awarding official, you must obtain each recipient's agreement, as a condition of the award, to comply with the requirements in—

(a) Subpart B of this part, if the recipient is not an individual; or

(b) Subpart C of this part, if the recipient is an individual.

Subpart E—Violations of this Part and Consequences

§ 1008.500 How are violations of this part determined for recipients other than individuals?

A recipient other than an individual is in violation of the requirements of this part if the Inter-American Foundation President or designee determines, in writing, that—

(a) The recipient has violated the requirements of subpart B of this part; or

(b) The number of convictions of the recipient's employees for violating criminal drug statutes in the workplace is large enough to indicate that the recipient has failed to make a good faith effort to provide a drug-free workplace.

§ 1008.505 How are violations of this part determined for recipients who are individuals?

An individual recipient is in violation of the requirements of this part if the Inter-American Foundation President or designee determines, in writing, that—

(a) The recipient has violated the requirements of subpart C of this part; or

(b) The recipient is convicted of a criminal drug offense resulting from a violation occurring during the conduct of any award activity.

§ 1008.510 What actions will the Federal Government take against a recipient determined to have violated this part?

If a recipient is determined to have violated this part, as described in § 1008.500 or § 1008.505, the Inter-American Foundation may take one or more of the following actions—

(a) Suspension of payments under the award;

(b) Suspension or termination of the award; and

(c) Suspension or debarment of the recipient under 22 CFR part 1006, for a period not to exceed five years.

§ 1008.515 Are there any exceptions to those actions?

The Inter-American Foundation may waive with respect to a particular award, in writing, a suspension of payments under an award, suspension or termination of an award, or suspension or debarment of a recipient if the Inter-American Foundation determines that such a waiver would be in the public interest. This exception authority cannot be delegated to any other official.

Subpart F—Definitions

§ 1008.605 Award.

Award means an award of financial assistance by the Inter-American Foundation or other Federal agency directly to a recipient.

(a) The term award includes:

(1) A Federal grant or cooperative agreement, in the form of money or property in lieu of money.

(2) A block grant or a grant in an entitlement program, whether or not the grant is exempted from coverage under the Governmentwide rule [Agency-specific CFR citation] that implements OMB Circular A–102 (for availability, see 5 CFR 1310.3) and specifies uniform administrative requirements.

(b) The term award does not include:

(1) Technical assistance that provides services instead of money.

(2) Loans.

(3) Loan guarantees.

(4) Interest subsidies.

(5) Insurance.

(6) Direct appropriations.

(7) Veterans' benefits to individuals (*i.e.*, any benefit to veterans, their families, or survivors by virtue of the service of a veteran in the Armed Forces of the United States).

(c) Notwithstanding paragraph (a)(2) of this section, this paragraph is not applicable for the Inter-American Foundation.

§ 1008.610 Controlled substance.

Controlled substance means a controlled substance in schedules I through V of the Controlled Substances Act (21 U.S.C. 812), and as further defined by regulation at 21 CFR 1308.11 through 1308.15.

§ 1008.615 Conviction.

Conviction means a finding of guilt (including a plea of nolo contendere) or imposition of sentence, or both, by any judicial body charged with the responsibility to determine violations of the Federal or State criminal drug statutes.

§ 1008.620 Cooperative agreement.

Cooperative agreement means an award of financial assistance that, consistent with 31 U.S.C. 6305, is used to enter into the same kind of relationship as a grant (see definition of grant in § 1008.650), except that substantial involvement is expected between the Federal agency and the recipient when carrying out the activity contemplated by the award. The term does not include cooperative research and development agreements as defined in 15 U.S.C. 3710a.

§ 1008.625 Criminal drug statute.

Criminal drug statute means a Federal or non-Federal criminal statute involving the manufacture, distribution, dispensing, use, or possession of any controlled substance.

§ 1008.630 Debarment.

Debarment means an action taken by a Federal agency to prohibit a recipient from participating in Federal Government procurement contracts and covered nonprocurement transactions. A recipient so prohibited is debarred, in accordance with the Federal Acquisition Regulation for procurement contracts (48 CFR part 9, subpart 9.4) and the common rule, Government-wide Debarment and Suspension (Nonprocurement), that implements Executive Order 12549 and Executive Order 12689.

§ 1008.635 Drug-free workplace.

Drug-free workplace means a site for the performance of work done in connection with a specific award at which employees of the recipient are prohibited from engaging in the unlawful manufacture, distribution, dispensing, possession, or use of a controlled substance.

§ 1008.640 Employee.

(a) *Employee* means the employee of a recipient directly engaged in the performance of work under the award, including—

(1) All direct charge employees;

(2) All indirect charge employees, unless their impact or involvement in the performance of work under the award is insignificant to the performance of the award; and

(3) Temporary personnel and consultants who are directly engaged in the performance of work under the award and who are on the recipient's payroll.

(b) This definition does not include workers not on the payroll of the recipient (*e.g.*, volunteers, even if used to meet a matching requirement; consultants or independent contractors not on the payroll; or employees of subrecipients or subcontractors in covered workplaces).

§ 1008.645 Federal agency or agency.

Federal agency or agency means any United States executive department, military department, government corporation, government controlled corporation, any other establishment in the executive branch (including the Executive Office of the President), or any independent regulatory agency.

§ 1008.650 Grant.

Grant means an award of financial assistance that, consistent with 31 U.S.C. 6304, is used to enter into a relationship—

(a) The principal purpose of which is to transfer a thing of value to the recipient to carry out a public purpose of support or stimulation authorized by a law of the United States, rather than to acquire property or services for the Federal Government's direct benefit or use; and

(b) In which substantial involvement is not expected between the Federal agency and the recipient when carrying out the activity contemplated by the award.

§ 1008.655 Individual.

Individual means a natural person.

§ 1008.660 Recipient.

Recipient means any individual, corporation, partnership, association, unit of government (except a Federal agency) or legal entity, however organized, that receives an award directly from a Federal agency.

§ 1008.665 State.

State means any of the States of the United States, the District of Columbia, the Commonwealth of Puerto Rico, or any territory or possession of the United States.

§ 1008.670 Suspension.

Suspension means an action taken by a Federal agency that immediately prohibits a recipient from participating in Federal Government procurement contracts and covered nonprocurement transactions for a temporary period, pending completion of an investigation and any judicial or administrative proceedings that may ensue. A recipient so prohibited is suspended, in accordance with the Federal Acquisition Regulation for procurement contracts (48 CFR part 9, subpart 9.4) and the common rule, Government-wide Debarment and Suspension (Nonprocurement), that implements Executive Order 12549 and Executive Order 12689. Suspension of a recipient is a distinct and separate action from suspension of an award or suspension of payments under an award.

PARTS 1009–1099 [RESERVED]

CHAPTER XI—INTERNATIONAL BOUNDARY AND WATER COMMISSION, UNITED STATES AND MEXICO, UNITED STATES SECTION

PART 1100—EMPLOYEE RESPONSIBILITIES AND CONDUCT

AUTHORITY: 5 U.S.C. 7301.

SOURCE: 71 FR 25934, May 3, 2006, unless otherwise noted.

§ 1100.1 Cross-references to employee ethical conduct standards, financial disclosure and financial interests regulations and other conduct rules.

Employees of the United States Section of the International Boundary and Water Commission are subject to the executive branch standards of ethical conduct contained in 5 CFR part 2635, the executive branch financial disclosure regulations contained in 5 CFR part 2634, and the executive branch financial interests regulations contained in 5 CFR part 2640, as well as the executive branch employee responsibilities and conduct regulations contained in 5 CFR part 735.

PART 1101—PRIVACY ACT OF 1974

AUTHORITY: Privacy Act of 1974 (Pub. L. 93–579, as amended, 5 U.S.C. 552a).

SOURCE: 57 FR 24945, June 12, 1992, unless otherwise noted.

§ 1101.1 Purpose and scope.

The purpose of these regulations is to prescribe responsibilities, rules, guidelines, and policies and procedures to implement the Privacy Act of 1974 (Pub. L. 93–579, as amended; 5 U.S.C. 552a) to assure that personal information about individuals collected by the United States Section is limited to that which is legally authorized and necessary and is maintained in a manner which precludes unwarranted intrusions upon individual privacy. Further, these regulations establish procedures by which an individual can: (a) Determine if the United States Section maintains records or a system of records which includes a record pertaining to the individual and (b) gain access to a record pertaining to him or her for the purpose of review, amendment or correction.

§ 1101.2 Definitions.

For the purpose of these regulations:

(a) *Act* means the Privacy Act of 1974.

(b) *Agency* is defined to include any executive department, military department, Government corporation, Government controlled corporation or other establishment in the executive branch of the Government (including the Executive Office of the President, or any independent regulatory agency) (5 U.S.C. 552)).

(c) *Commission* means the International Boundary and Water Commission, United States and Mexico.

(d) *Commissioner* means head of the United States Section, International Boundary and Water Commission, United States and Mexico.

(e) *Individual* means a citizen of the United States or an alien lawfully admitted for permanent residence.

(f) *Maintain* includes maintain, collect, use, or disseminate.

(g) *Record* means any item, collection, or grouping of information about an individual that is maintained by an agency, including, but not limited to, his education, financial transactions, medical history, and criminal or employment history and that contains his name, or the identifying number, symbol, or other identifying particular assigned to the individual, such as a finger or voice print or a photograph.

(h) *Routine use* means, with respect to the disclosure of a record, the use of such record for a purpose which is compatible with the purpose for which it is collected.

(i) *Section* means the United States Section, International Boundary and Water Commission, United States and Mexico.

(j) *Statistical record* means a record in a system of records maintained for statistical research or reporting purposes only and not used in whole or in part in making any determination about an identifiable individual, except as provided by 13 U.S.C. 8 (Census data).

(k) *System of records* means a group of any records under the control of any agency from which information is retrieved by the name of the individual or by some identifying number, symbol, or other identifying particular assigned to the individual.

§ 1101.3 General policy: Collection and use of personal information.

(a) Heads of Divisions, Branches, and the projects shall ensure that all Section personnel subject to their supervision are advised of the provisions of the Act, including the criminal penalties and civil liabilities provided therein, and that Section personnel are made aware of their responsibilities to protect the security of personal information, to assure its accuracy, relevance, timeliness and completeness, to avoid unauthorized disclosure either orally or in writing, and to ensure that no system of records concerning individuals, no matter how small or specialized, is maintained without public notice.

(b) Section personnel shall:

(1) Collect no information of a personal nature from individuals unless authorized to collect it to achieve a function or carry out a responsibility or function of the Section.

(2) Collect from individuals only that information which is necessary to Section responsibilities or functions;

(3) Collect information, wherever possible, directly from the individual to whom it relates;

(4) Inform individuals from whom information is collected of the authority for collection, the purpose thereof, the uses that will be made of the information, and the effects, both legal and practical, of not furnishing the information;

(5) Neither collect, maintain, use nor disseminate information concerning an individual's religious or political beliefs or activities or his membership in associations or organizations, unless (i) the individual has volunteered such information for his own benefit; (ii) the information is expressly authorized by statute to be collected, maintained, used or disseminated; or (iii) the activities involved are pertinent to and within the scope of an authorized investigation or adjudication activity;

(6) Advise an individual's supervisors of the existence or contemplated development of any system of records which retrieves information about individuals by individual identified;

(7) Maintain an accounting of all disclosures of information to other than Section personnel;

(8) Disclose no information concerning individuals to other than Section personnel except when authorized by the Act or pursuant to a routine use published in the FEDERAL REGISTER;

(9) Maintain and process information concerning individuals with care in order to ensure that no inadvertent disclosure of the information is made to other than Section personnel; and

(10) Call to the attention of the PA Officer any information in a system maintained by the Section which is not authorized to be maintained under the provisions of the Act, including information on First Amendment activities, information that is inaccurate, irrelevant or so incomplete as to risk unfairness to the individual concerned.

(c) The system of records maintained by the Section shall be reviewed annually by the PA Officer to ensure compliance with the provisions of the Act.

(d) Information which may be used in making determinations about an individual's rights, benefits, and privileges shall, to the greatest extent practicable, be collected directly from that individual. In deciding whether collection of information from an individual, as opposed to a third party source, is practicable, the following criteria, among others, may be considered:

(1) Whether the nature of the information sought is such that it can only be obtained from a third party;

(2) Whether the cost of collecting the information from the individual is unreasonable when compared with the cost of collecting it from a third party;

(3) Whether there is a risk that information requested from the third parties, if inaccurate, could result in an adverse determination to the individual concerned;

(4) Whether the information, if supplied by the individual, would have to be verified by a third party; or

(5) Whether provisions can be made for verification by the individual of information collected from third parties.

(e) Employees whose duties require handling of records subject to the Act shall, at all times, take care to protect the integrity, security and confidentiality of these records.

(f) No employee of the section may alter or destroy a record subject to the Act unless (1) such alteration or destruction is properly undertaken in the course of the employee's regular duties or (2) such alteration or destruction is required by a decision of the Commissioner or the decision of a court of competent jurisdiction.

§ 1101.4 Reports on new systems of records; computer matching programs.

(a) Before establishing any new systems of records, or making any significant change in a system of records, the Section shall provide adequate advance notice to:

(1) The Committee on Government Operations of the House of Representatives;

(2) The Committee on Governmental Affairs of the Senate; and

(3) The Office of Management and Budget.

(b) Before participating in any computerized information "matching program," as that term is defined by 5 U.S.C. 552a(a)(8) the Section will comply with the provisions of 5 U.S.C. 552a(o), and will provide adequate advance notice as described in § 1101.4(a) above.

§ 1101.5 Security, confidentiality and protection of records.

(a) The Act requires that records subject to the Act be maintained with appropriate administrative, technical and physical safeguards to ensure the security and confidentiality of records and to protect against any anticipated threats or hazards to their security or integrity which could result in substantial harm, embarrassment, inconvenience or unfairness to any individual on whom information is maintained.

(b) When maintained in manual form (typed, printed, handwritten, etc.) records shall be maintained, at a minimum, subject to the following safeguards, or safeguards affording comparable protection:

(1) Areas in which the records are maintained or regularly used shall be posted with an appropriate warning stating that access to the records is limited to authorized persons. The warning shall also summarize the requirements of § 1101.3 and state that the Act contains a criminal penalty for the unauthorized dislosure of records to which it applies.

(2) During working hours: (i) The area in which the records are maintained or regularly used shall be occupied by authorized personnel or (ii) access to the records shall be restricted by their storage in locked metal file cabinets or a locked room.

(3) During non-working hours, access to the records shall be restricted by their storage in locked metal file cabinets or a locked room.

(4) Where a locked room is the method of security provided for a system, that security shall be supplemented by: (i) Providing lockable file cabinets or containers for the records or (ii) changing the lock or locks for the room so that they may not be opened with a master key. For purposes of this paragraph, a master key is a key which may be used to open rooms other than the room containing records subject to the Act, unless those rooms are utilized by officials or employees authorized to have access to the records subject to the Act.

(5) Personnel handling personal information during routine use will ensure that the information is properly controlled to prevent unintentional or unauthorized disclosure. Such information will be used, held, or stored only

where facilities or conditions are adequate to prevent unauthorized or unintentional disclosure.

(c) When the records subject to the Act are maintained in computerized form, safeguards shall be utilized based on those recommended in the National Bureau of Standard's booklet "Computer Security Guidelines for Implementing the Privacy Act of 1974" (May 30, 1975), and any supplements thereto, which are adequate and appropriate to assuring the integrity of the records.

§ 1101.6 Requests for access to records.

(a) Any individual may submit an inquiry to the Section to ascertain whether a system of records contains a record pertaining to him or her.

(b) The inquiry should be made either in person or by mail addressed to the PA Officer, United States Section, International Boundary and Water Commission, 4171 North Mesa, Suite C–310, El Paso, TX 79902–1422. The PA Officer shall provide assistance to the individual making the inquiry to assure the timely identification of the appropriate systems of records. The office of the PA Officer is located in Suite C–316 and is open to an individual between the hours of 8 a.m. and 4:30 p.m., Monday through Friday (excluding holidays).

(c) Inquiries submitted by mail should be marked "PRIVACY ACT REQUEST" on the bottom left-hand corner of the envelope.

(d) The letter should state that the request is being made under the Privacy Act.

(e) Inquiries concerning whether a system of records contains a record pertaining to an individual should contain the following:

(1) Name, address and telephone number (optional) of the individual making the inquiry;

(2) Name, address and telephone number (optional) of the individual to whom the record pertains, if the inquiring individual is either the parent of a minor or the legal guardian of the individual to whom a record pertains;

(3) A certified or authenticated copy of documents establishing parentage or guardianship;

(4) Whether the individual to whom the record pertains is a citizen of the United States or an alien lawfully admitted for permanent residence into the United States;

(5) Name of the system of records, as published in the FEDERAL REGISTER;

(6) Location of the system of records, as published in the FEDERAL REGISTER;

(7) Such additional information as the individual believes will or might assist the Section in responding to the inquiry and in verifying the individual's identity (for example: date of birth, place of birth, names of parents, place of work, dates of employment, position title, etc.);

(8) Date of inquiry; and

(9) Signature of the requester.

The Section reserves the right to require compliance with the identification procedures appearing at paragraph (f) of this section where conditions warrant.

(f) The requirement for identification of individuals seeking access to records are as follows:

(1) In person: Each individual making a request in person shall be required to present satisfactory proof of identity. The means of proof, in the order of preference and priority, are:

(i) A document bearing the individual's photograph (for example, driver's license, passport or military or civilian identification card);

(ii) A document bearing the individual's signature, preferably issued for participation in a federally sponsored program (for example, Social Security card, unemployment insurance book, employer's identification card, national credit card and professional, craft or union membership card); and

(iii) A document bearing either the photograph or the signature of the individual, preferably issued for participation in a federally sponsored program (for example, Medicaid card). In the event the individual can provide no suitable documentation of identity, the Section will require a signed statement asserting the individual's identity and stipulating that the individual understands the penalty provision of 5 U.S.C. 552a(i)(3).

(2) Not in person: If the individual making a request does not appear in person before the PA Officer, a certificate of a notary public or equivalent

officer empowered to administer oaths must accompany the request.

(3) Parents of minors and legal guardians: An individual acting as the parent of a minor or the legal guardian of the individual or an heir or legal representative of a deceased person to whom a record pertains shall establish his or her personal identity in the manner prescribed in either paragraph (f)(1) or (2) of this section. In addition, such individual shall establish his or her identity in the representative capacity of parent or legal guardian. In the case of the parent of a minor, the proof of identity shall be a certified or authenticated copy of the minor's birth certificate. In the case of a legal guardian of an individual who has been declared incompetent due to physical or mental incapacity or age by a court of competent jurisdiction, the proof of identity shall be a certified or authenticated copy of the court's order. A parent or legal guardian may act only for a living individual, not for a decedent. A parent or legal guardian may be accompanied during personal access to a record by another individual, provided the requirements of paragraph (f) of §1101.7 are satisfied. In the case of an heir or legal representative of a deceased person the proof of identity shall be a certified copy of the Will, if any; the order of a court of competent jurisdiction admitting the Will to probate; the order of a court of competent jurisdiction appointing an executor, executrix, or administrator; a letter of administration; or any other documentary evidence which establishes the identity of the individual as an heir or legal representative of a deceased person.

(g) When the provisions of this part are alleged to have the effect of impeding an individual in exercising his or her right to access, the Section will consider, from an individual making a request, alternative suggestions regarding proof of identity and access to records.

(h) An inquiry which is not addressed as specified in paragraph (b) of this section or which is not marked as specified in paragraph (c) of this section will be so addressed and marked by the Section's personnel and forwarded immediately to the PA Officer. An inquiry which is not properly addressed by the individual will not be deemed to have been "received" for purposes of measuring time periods for response until forwarding of the inquiry to the PA Officer has been effected. In each instance when an inquiry so forwarded is received, the PA Officer shall notify the individual that his or her inquiry was improperly addressed and the date when the inquiry was received at the proper address.

(i) Each inquiry received shall be acted upon promptly by the PA Officer. Although there is no fixed time when an agency must respond to a request for access to records under the Act, every effort will be made to respond within ten (10) days (excluding Saturdays, Sundays and holidays) of the date of receipt. If a response cannot be made within ten (10) days, the PA Officer shall send an acknowledgment during that period providing information on the status of the inquiry and asking for such further information as may be necessary to process the inquiry. Every effort will be made to provide the requested records within thirty (30) days.

(j) An individual shall not be required to state a reason or otherwise justify his or her inquiry.

§1101.7 Disclosure of records to individuals who are subjects of those records.

(a) Each request received shall be acted upon promptly by the PA Officer. Every effort will be made to respond within ten (10) days (excluding Saturdays, Sundays, and holidays) of the date of receipt. If a response cannot be made within ten (10) days due to unusual circumstances, the PA Officer shall send an acknowledgment during that period providing information on the status of the request and asking for such further information as may be necessary to process the request. Every effort will be made to provide the requested records within thirty (30) days. "Unusual circumstances" shall include circumstances where a search for and collection of requested records from inactive storage, field facilities or other establishments are required, cases where a voluminous amount of data is involved, instances where information on other individuals must be separated or expunged from the particular record, and cases where consultations with other agencies having a substantial interest in the determination of the request are necessary.

(b) Grant of access:

(1) Notification.

(i) An individual shall be granted access to a record pertaining to him or her except where the record is subject to an exemption under the Act and these rules.

(ii) The PA Officer shall notify the individual of such determination and provide the following information:

(A) The methods of access, as set forth in paragraph (b)(2) of this section;

(B) The place at which the records may be inspected;

(C) The earliest date on which the record may be inspected and the period of time that the records will remain available for inspection. In no event shall the earliest date be later than thirty (30) days from the date of notification;

(D) The estimated date by which a copy of the record could be mailed and the estimate of fees pursuant to § 1101.11. In no event shall be estimated date be later than thirty (30) days from the date of notification;

(E) The fact that the individual, if he or she wishes, may be accompanied by another individual during the personal access, subject to the procedures set forth in paragraph (f) of this section; and

(F) Any additional requirements needed to grant access to a specific record.

(2) Method of access: The following methods of access to records by an individual may be available depending on the circumstances of a given situation:

(i) Inspection in person may be made in the office specified by the PA Officer, between the hours of 8 a.m. and 4:30 p.m., Monday through Friday (excluding holidays);

(ii) Transfer of records to a Federal facility more convenient to the individual may be arranged, but only if the PA Officer determines that a suitable facility is available, that the individual's access can be properly supervised at that facility, and that transmittal of the records to that facility will not unduly interfere with operations of the section or involve unreasonable costs, in terms of both money and manpower; and

(iii) Copies may be mailed at the request of the individual, subject to payment of the fees prescribed in § 1101.11. The Section, at its own initiative, may elect to provide a copy by mail, in which case no fee will be charged to the individual.

(c) Access to medical records: Upon advice by a physician that release of medical information directly to the requester could have an adverse effect on the requester, the Section may attempt to arrange an acceptable alternative. This will normally involve release of such information to a physician named by the requester, with the requester's written consent. (Note that release to any third party, including a physician or family member, must comply with the provisions of § 1101.8 of this part.)

(d) The Section shall supply such other information and assistance at the time of access to make the record intelligible to the individual.

(e) The Section reserves the right to limit access to copies and abstracts of original records, rather than the original records. This election would be appropriate, for example, when the record is in an automated data media such as tape of disc, when the record contains information on other individuals, and when deletion of information is permissible under exemptions (for example 5, U.S.C. 552(k)(1)). In no event shall original records of the Section be made available to the individual except under the immediate supervision of the PA Officer or his designee. Title 18 U.S.C. 2701(a) makes it a crime to conceal, mutilate, obliterate, or destroy a record filed in a public office, or to attempt to do any of the foregoing.

(f) Any individual who requests access to a record pertaining to that individual may be accompanied by another individual of his or her choice. "Accompanied" includes discussion of the record in the presence of the other individual. The individual to whom the record pertains shall authorize the presence of the other individual in writing and shall include the name of the other individual, a specific description of the record to which access is sought, and the date and the signature of the individual to whom the record pertains. The other individual shall sign the authorization in the presence of the PA Officer or his designee. An individual shall not be required to state a reason or otherwise justify his or her decision to be accompanied by another individual during the personal access to a record.

(g) Initial denial of access:

(1) Grounds. Access by an individual to a record which pertains to that individual will be denied only upon a determination by the PA Officer that:

(i) The record is subject to an exemption under the Act and these rules;

(ii) The record is information compiled in reasonable anticipation of a civil action or proceeding;

(iii) The provisions of § 1101.7(c) pertaining to medical records have been temporarily invoked; or

(iv) The individual unreasonably has failed to comply with the procedural requirements of these rules.

(2) Notification. The PA Officer shall give notice of denial of access of records to the individual in writing and shall include the following information:

(i) The PA Officer's name and title or position;

(ii) The date of denial;

(iii) The reasons for the denial, including citation to the appropriate section of the Act and these rules;

(iv) The individual's opportunities for further administrative consideration, including the identity and address of the responsible official;

(v) If stated to be administratively final within the Section, the individual's right to judicial review under 5 U.S.C. 552a(g) (1) and (5).

(3) Administrative review: When an initial denial of a request is issued by the PA Officer, the individual's opportunities for further consideration shall be as follows:

(i) As to denial under paragraph (g)(1)(i) of this section, the sole procedure is a petition for the issuance, amendment, or repeal of a rule under 5 U.S.C. 553(e). Such petition shall be filed with the Commissioner, United States Section, International Boundary and Water Commission, 4171 North Mesa, Suite C–310, El Paso, TX 79902–1422. If the exception was determined by another agency, the PA Officer will provide the individual with the name and address of the other agency and any relief sought by the individual shall be that provided by the regulations of the other agency. Within the Section, no such denial is administratively final until such a petition has been filed by the individual and disposed of on the merits by the Commissioner.

(ii) As to denial under paragraphs (g)(1), (ii), (iii) or (iv) of this section, the individual may file for review with the Commissioner, as indicated in the PA Officer's initital denial notification.

(h) If a request is partially granted and partially denied, the PA Officer shall follow the appropriate procedures of this section as to the records within the grant and the records within the denial.

§ 1101.8 Disclosure of records to third-parties.

(a) The Section will not disclose any information about an individual to any person other than the individual except in the following instances:

(1) Upon written request by the individual about whom the information is maintained;

(2) With prior written consent of the individual about whom the information is maintained;

(3) To the parent(s) of a minor child, or the legal guardian of an incompetent person, when said parent(s) or legal guardian act(s) on behalf of said minor or incompetent person.

(4) When permitted under 5 U.S.C. 552a(b) (1) through (11) which provides as follows:

(i) To those officers and employees of the agency which maintains the record who have a need for the record in the performance of their duties;

(ii) Required under 5 U.S.C. 552 of the U.S. Code;

(iii) For a routine use as defined in the Act at 5 U.S.C. 552a(a)(7);

(iv) To the Bureau of the Census for purposes of planning or carrying out a census or survey or related activity pursuant to the provisions of title 13 of the U.S. Code;

(v) To a recipient who has provided the agency with advance adequate written assurance that the record will be used solely as a statistical research or reporting record, and the record is to be transferred in a form that is not individually identifiable;

(vi) To the National Archives of the United States as a record which has sufficient historical or other value to warrant its continued preservation by the United States Government, or for evaluation by the Administrator of General Services or his designee to determine whether the record has such value;

(vii) To another agency or to an instrumentality of any governmental jurisdiction within or under the control of the United States for a civil or criminal law enforcement activity if the activity is authorized by law, if the head of the agency or instrumentality has made a written request to the agency which maintains the record specifying the particular portion desired and the law enforcement activity for which the record is sought;

(viii) To a person pursuant to a showing of compelling circumstances affecting the health or safety of an individual if upon such disclosure notification is transmitted to the last known address of such individual;

(ix) To either House of Congress, or, to the extent of matter within its jurisdiction, any committee or subcommittee thereof, any joint committee of Congress or subcommittee of any such joint committee, and to a Congressman who is acting on behalf of his constituent;

(x) To the Comptroller General, or any of his authorized representatives, in the course of the performance of the duties of the General Accounting Office; or

(xi) Pursuant to the order of a court of competent jurisdiction;

(5) When required by the Act and not covered explicitly by the provisions of 5 U.S.C. 552a(b). These situations include the following:

(i) Dissemination of a corrected or amended record or notation of a disagreement statement (5 U.S.C. 552a(c)(4));

(ii) Disclosure of records to an individual to whom they pertain (5 U.S.C. 552a(d));

(iii) Civil actions by an individual (5 U.S.C. 552a(g));

(iv) Release of records or information to the Privacy Protection Study Commission (Section 5 of Pub. L. 93–579);

(v) Fulfill the needs of Office of Management and Budget to provide continuing oversight and assistance to the section in implementation of the Act (Section 6 of Pub. L. 93–579).

§ 1101.9 Exemptions.

The following are exempt from disclosure under 5 U.S.C. 552a (j) and (k):

(a) Any record originated by another agency which has determined that the record is exempt. If a request encompasses such a record, the Section will advise the requester of its existence, and of the name and address of the source agency.

(b) Records specifically authorized under criteria established by an executive order to be kept secret in the interest of national defense or foreign policy, and which are, in fact, properly classified pursuant to such executive order.

(c) Those systems of records listed as exempt in the Notice of Records of the FEDERAL REGISTER, including: Certificates of Medical Examination; Occupational Health and Injury Files; and Investigative Records.

§ 1101.10 Accounting for disclosures.

(a) Each system manager shall establish a system of accounting for all disclosures of records, either orally or in writing made outside the Section, unless otherwise exempted under this section. Accounting procedures may be established in the least expensive and most convenient form that will permit the PA Officer to advise individuals promptly upon request of the persons or agencies to which records concerning them have been disclosed. Accounting of disclosures made under 5 U.S.C. 552a(b)(7) relating to civil or criminal law enforcement activities shall not be made available to the individual named in the record.

(b) Accounting records, at a minimum, shall include the date, nature, and purpose of each disclosure of a record and the name and address of the person or agency to whom the disclosure was made. Accounting records shall be maintained for at least five years or the life of the record, whichever is longer.

(c) Accounting is not required to be kept for disclosure made within the Section or disclosures made pursuant to the Freedom of Information Act.

(d) If an accounting of the disclosure was made, the PA Officer shall inform any person or other agency about any correction or notation of dispute made by the Section in accordance with 5 U.S.C. 552a(d) of any record that has been disclosed to the person or agency.

§ 1101.11 Fees.

(a) Under the Act, fees can only be charged for the cost of copying records. No fees may be charged for the time it takes to search for the records or for the time it takes to determine if any exemptions apply. The Section will not charge a fee for the first copy of an individual's personnel record.

(b) The Section will charge a fee of $0.10 per page for copies of documents which are identified by an individual and reproduced at the individual's request for retention, except that there will be no charge for requests involving costs of $1.00 or less, but the copying fees for contemporaneous request by the same individual shall be aggregated to determine the total fee.

(c) Special and additional services provided at the request of the individual, such as certification or authentication, will be charged to the individual in accordance with other published regulations of the Section pursuant to statute (for example, 22 CFR part 1102—Freedom of Information Act.)

(d) Remittances shall be in the form of either a personal check or bank draft drawn on a bank in the United States, a postal money order, or cash. Remittance shall be made payable to the order of the U.S. Section, International Boundary and Water Commission, and delivered to or mailed to the PA Officer, United States Section, International Boundary and Water Commission, 4171 North Mesa, Suite C–310, El Paso, TX 79902–1422. The Section will assume no responsibility for cash sent by mail.

(e) A receipt for fees paid will be given only upon request.

§ 1101.12 Request to correct or amend a record.

(a) Any individual may submit a request for correction of or amendment to a record to the Section. The request should be made either in person or by mail addressed to the PA Officer who processed the individual's request for access to the record, and to whom is delegated authority to make initial determinations on requests for correction or amendment.

(b) Since the request, in all cases, will follow a request for access under § 1101.6, the individual's identity will be established by his or her signature on the request.

(c) A request for correction or amendment should be in writing. The envelope containing the request should be marked "Privacy Act Amendment Request" on the lower left hand corner. The request should include the following:

(1) First, the letter should state that it is a request to amend a record under the Privacy Act of 1974.

(2) Second, the request should identify the specific record and the specific information in the record for which an amendment is being sought.

(3) Third, the request should state why the information is not accurate, relevant, timely, or complete. Supporting evidence may be included with the request.

(4) Fourth, the request should state what new or additional information, if any, should be included in place of the erroneous information. Evidence of the validity of new or additional information should be included. If the information in the file is wrong and needs to be removed rather than supplemented or corrected, the request should make this clear.

(5) Fifth, the request should include the name, address, and telephone number (optional) of the requester.

§ 1101.13 Agency review of request to correct or amend a record.

(a) (1) Not later than ten (10) days (excluding Saturdays, Sundays and holidays) after receipt of a request to correct or amend a record, the PA Officer shall send an acknowledgment providing an estimate of time within which action will be taken on the request and asking for such further information as may be necessary to process the request. The estimate of time may take into account unusual circumstances as described in § 1101.7(a). No acknowledgment will be sent if the request can be reviewed, processed and the individual notified of the results of review (either compliance or denial) within ten (10) days (excluding Saturdays, Sundays and holidays). Requests filed in person will be acknowledged in writing at the time submitted.

(2) Promptly after acknowledging receipt of a request, or after receiving such further information as might have been requested, or after arriving at a decision within ten (10) days, the PA Officer shall either:

(i) Make the requested correction or amendment and advise the individual in writing of such action, providing either a copy of the corrected or amended record or a statement as to the means whereby the correction or amendment was effected in cases where a copy cannot be provided (for example, erasure of information from a record maintained only in an electronic data bank); or

(ii) Inform the individual in writing that his or her request is denied and provide the following information:

(A) The PA Officer's name, title and position;

(B) The date of denial;

(C) The reasons for the denial, including citation to the appropriate sections of the Act and these rules;

(D) The procedures for appeal of the denial as set forth in § 1101.14.

The term promptly in this paragraph means within thirty (30) days (excluding Saturdays, Sundays and holidays). If the PA Officer cannot make the determination within thirty (30) days, the individual will be advised in writing of the reason therefor and of the estimated date by which the determination will be made.

(b) Whenever an individual's record is corrected or amended pursuant to a request by that individual, the PA Officer shall notify all persons and agencies to which copies of the record had been disclosed prior to its correction or amendment, if an accounting of such disclosure required by the Act was made. The notification shall require a receipt agency maintaining the record to acknowledge receipt of the notification, to correct or amend the record, and to apprise any agency or person to which it has disclosed the record of the substance of the correction or amendment.

(c) The following criteria will be considered by the PA Officer in reviewing a request for correction or amendment.

(1) The sufficiency of the evidence submitted by the individual;

(2) The factual accuracy of the information;

(3) The relevance and necessity of the information in terms of purpose for which it was collected.

(4) The timeliness and currency of the information in light of the purpose for which it was collected;

(5) The completeness of the information in terms of the purpose for which it was collected;

(6) The degree of possibility that denial of the request could unfairly result in determinations adverse to the individual;

(7) The character of the record sought to be corrected or amended; and

(8) The propriety and feasibility of complying with the specific means of correction or amendment requested by the individual.

(d) The Section will not undertake to gather evidence for the individual, but does reserve the right to verify the evidence which the individual submits.

(e) Correction or amendment of a record requested by an individual will be denied only upon a determination by the PA Officer that:

(1) The individual has failed to establish, by a preponderance of the evidence, the propriety of the correction or amendment in light of the criteria set forth in paragraph (c) of this section;

(2) The record sought to be corrected or amended was compiled in a terminated judicial, quasi-judicial or quasi-legislative proceeding to which the individual was a party or participant;

(3) The record sought to be corrected or amended is the subject of a pending

judicial, quasi-judicial or quasi-legislative proceeding to which the individual is a party or participant;

(4) The correction or amendment would violate a duly enacted statute or promulgated regulation; or

(5) The individual unreasonably has failed to comply with the procedural requirements of these rules.

(f) If a request is partially granted and partially denied, the PA Officer shall follow the appropriate procedures of this section as to the records within the grant and the records within the denial.

§ 1101.14 Appeal of agency decision not to correct or amend a record.

(a) An appeal of the initial refusal to amend a record under § 1101.13 may be requested by the individual who submitted the request. The appeal must be requested in writing, and state that the appeal is being made under the Privacy Act of 1974, it should identify the denial that is being appealed and the records that were withheld, it should include the requester's name and address and telephone number (optional), and it should be signed by the individual making the request. It should be received by the Section within sixty (60) calendar days of the date the individual is informed of the PA Officer's refusal to amend a record in whole or in part. The request should be addressed and sent via certified mail to the Commissioner, United States Section, International Boundary and Water Commission, 4171 North Mesa, suite C–310, El Paso, TX 79902–1422. The processing of appeals will be facilitated if the words "PRIVACY APPEAL" appear in capital letters on both the envelope and the top of the appeal papers. An appeal not addressed and marked as provided herein will be marked by Section personnel when it is so identified and will be forwarded immediately to the Commissioner.

(b) The time for decision on the appeal begins on the date the appeal is received by the Commissioner. The appeal should include any documentation, information or statements advanced for the amendment of the record.

(c) There shall be a written record of the reason for the final determination. The final determination will be made not later than thirty (30) days (excluding Saturdays, Sundays and holidays) from the date the Commissioner receives the appeal; unless, for good cause shown, the Commissioner extends such determination beyond the thirty (30) day period.

(d) When the final determination is that the record should be amended in accordance with the individual's request, the Commissioner shall direct the office responsible for the record to comply. The office responsible for the record shall:

(1) Amend the record as directed;

(2) If a distribution of the record has been made, advise all previous recipients of the record of the amendment and its substance;

(3) So advise the individual in writing.

(e) When the final decision is that the request of the individual to amend the record is refused, the Commissioner shall advise the individual:

(1) Of the refusal and the reasons for it;

(2) Of his or her right to file a concise statement of the reasons for disagreeing with the decision of the Section;

(3) Of the procedures for filing the statement of disagreement;

(4) That the statement which is filed will be made available to anyone to whom the record is subsequently disclosed together with, at the discretion of the Section, a brief statement by the Section summarizing its reasons for refusing to amend the record;

(5) That prior recipients of the disputed record will be provided a copy of any statement of dispute to the extent that an accounting of disclosures was maintained; and

(6) Of his or her right to seek judicial review of the Section's refusal to amend the record.

(f) When the final determination is to refuse to amend a record and the individual has filed a statement under paragraph (e)(2) of this section, the Section will clearly annotate the record so that the fact that the record is disputed is apparent to anyone who may subsequently have access to use or disclose it. When information that is the subject of a statement of dispute filed by an individual is subsequently disclosed, the Section will note that the information is disputed and provide a copy of the individual's statement. The Section may also include a brief summary of the reasons for not making a correction when disclosing disputed information. Such statements will normally be limited to the reasons given to the individual for not amending the record. Copies of the Section's statement shall be treated as part of the individual's record for granting access; however, it will not be subject to amendment by the individual under these rules.

(g) An appeal will be decided on the basis of the individual's appeal papers and the record submitted by the PA officer. No personal appearance or hearings on appeals will be allowed.

§ 1101.15 Judicial review.

After having exhausted all administrative remedies set forth in § 1101.7(g)(3) or § 1101.14, a requester may bring a civil action against the Section, in a United States District Court of proper venue, within two years of the final administrative decision which the requester seeks to challenge.

§ 1101.16 Criminal penalties.

(a) Under the provisions of the Act, it is a Federal crime for any person to knowingly and willfully request or obtain information from a Federal agency, including this Section, by false pretenses.

(b) It is also a crime for any officer or employee of the Section to knowingly and willfully:

(1) Make an unauthorized disclosure; or

(2) Fail to publish public notice of a system of records as required by 5 U.S.C. 552a(e)(4).

§ 1101.17 Annual report to Congress.

(a) On or before August 1 of each calendar year the Commissioner shall submit a report covering the preceding calendar year to the Speaker of the House of Representatives and the President of the Senate for referral to the appropriate committees of the Congress. The report shall include:

(1) The U.S. Section's point of contact responsible for implementing the Privacy Act of 1974;

(2) The number of active systems, new systems published, systems deleted, systems automated, either in whole or part, number of existing systems for which new routine uses were established, number of existing systems for which new exemptions were claimed, number of existing systems from which exemptions were deleted, and number of public comments received by the agency of publication of rules or notices;

(3) Total number of requests for access, number of requests wholly or partially granted, number of requests totally denied, number of requests for which no record was found, number of appeals of denials of access, number of appeals in which denial was upheld, number of appeals in which denial was overturned either in whole or part, number of requests to amend records in system, number of amendment requests wholly or partially granted, number of amendment requests totally denied, number of appeals of denials of amendment requests, number of appeals in which denial was upheld, number in which denial was overturned either in whole or in part, whether the U.S. Section denied an individual access to his or her records in a system of record on any basis other than a Privacy Act exemption under 5 U.S.C. 552(j) or (k), and the legal justification for the denial, number of instances in which individuals litigated the results of appeals of access or amendment, and the results of such litigation, and a statement of our involvement in matching programs;

(4) Any other information which will indicate the U.S. Section's effort to comply with the objectives of the Act, to include any problems encountered, with recommendations for solving thereof;

(5) And, a copy of these regulations.

PART 1102—FREEDOM OF INFORMATION ACT

Sec.

AUTHORITY: 5 U.S.C. 552 (Pub. L. 90–23, as amended by Pub. L. 93–502 and 99–570).

SOURCE: 55 FR 35898, Sept. 4, 1990, unless otherwise noted.

§1102.1 Purpose.

The purpose of this part is to prescribe rules, guidelines and procedures to implement the Freedom of Information Act (FOIA), 5 U.S.C. 552, as amended on November 21, 1974, by Public Law 93–502, and on October 27, 1986, by Public Law 99–570.

§1102.2 Definitions.

Act means the Freedom of Information Act, 5 U.S.C. 552, as amended.

Commercial-use request refers to a request from or on behalf of one who seeks information for a cause or purpose that furthers the commercial, trade, or profit interests of the requester or person on whose behalf the request is made. In determining whether a requester properly belongs in this category, the Section will consider how the requester will use the documents.

Commissioner means head of the United States Section, International Boundary and Water Commission, United States and Mexico.

Direct costs means those expenditures which the Section actually incurs in searching for and duplicating (and in the case of commercial requesters, reviewing) documents to respond to a FOIA request. Direct costs include, for example, the salary of the employee performing work (the basic rate of pay for the employee plus 16 percent of that rate to cover benefits) and the cost of operating duplicating machinery. Not included in direct costs are overhead expenses such as costs of space, and heating or lighting the facility where the records are stored.

Disclose or disclosure means making records available, on request for examination and copying, or furnishing a copy of records.

Duplication refers to the process of making a copy of a document in response to a FOIA request. Such copies can take the form of paper, microform, audiovisual materials, or machine-readable documentation. The Section will provide a copy of the material in a form that is usable by the requester unless it is administratively burdensome to do so.

Educational institution refers to a preschool, a public or private elementary or secondary school, an institution of graduate higher education, an institution of undergraduate higher education, an institution of professional education, and an institution of vocational education, which operates a program or programs of scholarly research.

Noncommercial scientific institution refers to an institution that is not operated on a "commercial" basis as that term is referenced above, and which is operated solely for the purpose of conducting scientific research the results of which are not intended to promote any particular product or industry.

Person or *Requester* includes any individual, firm, corporation, organization or other entity.

Records and/or *information* are defined as all books, papers, manuals, maps, photographs, or other documentary materials, regardless of physical form or characteristics, made or received by the Section under Federal law or in connection with the transaction of public business or in carrying out its treaty responsibilities and obligations, and preserved or appropriate for preservation by the Section as evidence of the organization, functions, policies, decisions, procedures, operations, or other activities of the Government or because of the information value of the data in them, but does not include books, magazines or other material acquired solely for library purposes and through other sources, and does not include analyses, computations, or compilations of information not extant at the time of the request. The term "records" does not include objects or articles such as structures, furniture, paintings, sculptures, three-dimensional models, vehicles, and equipment.

Representative of the news media refers to any person actively gathering news for an entity that is organized and operated to publish or broadcast news to the public. The term "news" means information that is about current events or that would be of current interest to the public. Examples of news media include television or radio stations broadcasting to the public at large, and publishers of periodicals (but only those instances when they can qualify as disseminators of "news") who make their products available for purchase or subscription by the general public. In the case of "freelance" journalists, they may be regarded as working for a news organization if they can demonstate a solid basis for expecting publication through that organization even though not actually employed by it.

Request means a letter or other written communication seeking records or information under the Freedom of Information Act.

Review refers to the process of examining documents located in response to a request that is for commercial use to determine if any portion of that document is permitted to be withheld, and processing any document for disclosure (i.e., doing all that is necessary to excise them and otherwise prepare them for release). It does not include time spent resolving general legal or policy issues regarding the application of exemptions.

Search includes all time spent looking for material that is responsive to a request, including page-by-page or line-by-line identification of material within documents. Searches should be performed in the most efficient and least expensive manner so as to minimize costs for both the Section and the requester; for example, line-by-line searches should not be undertaken when it would be more efficient to duplicate the entire document. Note that such activity should be distinguished from "review" of material in determining whether the material is exempt from disclosure. Searches may be done manually or by computer using existing programming.

The *Section* means United States Section, International Boundary and Water Commission, United States and Mexico.

All terms used in this part which are defined in 5 U.S.C. 552 shall have the same meaning herein.

§ 1102.3 Procedures for requesting access to records or information.

(a) A request for any information or records shall be addressed to the FOIA Officer, United States Section, International Boundary and Water Commission, 4171 North Mesa, suite C–310, El Paso, TX 79902–1422. The envelope and the letter shall be clearly marked "Freedom of Information Request" or "Request for Records," or the equivalent, to distinguish it from other mail to the Section. If the request is not so marked and addressed, the 10-day time limit described in the Act will not begin to run until the request has been received by the FOIA Officer in the normal course of business. In each instance where a request is received in the normal course of business, the FOIA Officer shall notify the requester that its request was improperly addressed and the date the request was received.

(b) In order for the Section to locate records or information and make them available, it is necessary that it be able to identify the specific record or information sought. Persons wishing to inspect or obtain copies of records or information should, therefore, seek to identify them as fully and accurately as possible. In cases where requests are submitted which are not sufficient to permit identification, the FOIA Officer will endeavor to assist the persons seeking the records or information in filling in necessary details. In most cases, however, persons seeking records or information will find that time taken in trying to identify materials in the beginning is well worth their while in enabling the Section to respond promptly to their request.

(c) A person submitting a request should—

(1) Indicate the specific event or action, if any or if known, to which the request has reference.

(2) Designate the Division, Branch, or Project Office of the Section which may be responsible for or may have

produced the record or information requested.

(3) Furnish the date of the record or information or the date or period to which it refers or relates, if known.

(4) Name the character of record or information, such as a contract, an application, or a report.

(5) List the Section's personnel who may have prepared or have knowledge of the record or information.

(6) Furnish the reference material such as newspapers or publications which are known to have made a reference to the record or information desired.

(7) If the request relates to a matter in pending litigation or one which has been litigated, supply the Court location and case style and number.

(8) Describe, when the request includes more than one record or source of information, specifically each record or information so that availability may be separately determined.

(9) Clearly indicate whether the request is an initial request or an appeal from a denial of a record or information previously requested.

(10) Identify, when the request concerns a matter about the Section's personnel, the person as follows: First name, middle name or initial, and surname; date and place of birth; and social security account number, if known.

(d) No particular format is needed for the request, except that it:

(1) Must be in writing;

(2) Must describe the records or information sought with sufficient detail to permit identification;

(3) Should state a limitation of the fees the requester is willing to pay, if any; and

(4) Must include the name, address, and telephone number (optional) of the person submitting the request.

§ 1102.4 Fees.

(a) The following shall be applicable with respect to services rendered to members of the public under this subpart:

(1) Fee schedule.

(i) Searching for records, per hour or fraction thereof per individual:

Professional $18.00
Clerical $9.00

Includes the salary of the category of employee who actually performs the search, plus an additional 16% of that rate to cover benefits.

(ii) The cost for computer searches will be calculated based on the salary of the category of employee who actually performs the computer search, plus 16% of that rate to cover benefits, plus the direct costs of the central processing unit, input-output devices, and memory capacity of the actual computer configuration.

(iii) Reproduction fees:

Pages no larger than 8½ by 14 inches when reproduced by routine electrostatic copying: $0.10 per page.

Pages requiring reduction, enlargement, or other special services will be billed at direct cost to the Section.

Reproduction by other than routine electrostatic copying will be billed at direct cost to the Section.

(iv) Certification of each record as a true copy—$1.00

(v) Certification of each record as a true copy under official seal—$1.50

(vi) For each signed statement of negative result of search for record—$1.00

(vii) For each signed statement of nonavailability of record—$1.00

(viii) Duplication of architectural photographs and drawings:

Available tracing or reproducible, per square foot $0.10
If intermediate nagative and reproducible required $2.00;
Plus tracing per square foot $1.00

(ix) *Postage and handling.* It will be up to the person requesting the records or information to designate how the material will be mailed or shipped. In the absence of such instructions no records or information will be sent to a foreign address, and records and information will be sent to domestic addresses utilizing first class certified mail, return receipt requested and will be billed at direct cost to the Section.

(2) Only requesters who are seeking documents for commercial use will be charged for time spent reviewing records to determine whether thay are exempt from mandatory disclosure. The cost for review will be calculated based on the salary of the category of the employee who actually performed the review plus 16% of the rate to cover

benefits. Charges will be assessed only for the initial review (i.e., review undertaken the first time in order to analyze the applicability of specific exemption(s) to a particular record or portion of record) and not review at the administrative appeal level of the exemption(s) already applied.

(3) If records requested under this part are stored elsewhere than the headquarters of the U.S. Section, IBWC, 4171 North Mesa, EL Paso, TX, the special cost of returning such records to the headquarters shall be include in the search costs. These costs will be computed at the actual costs of transportation of either a person or the requested record between the place where the record is stored and the Section headquarters when, for time or other reasons, it is not feasible to rely on Government mail service.

(4) When no specific fee has been established for a service, or the request for a service does not fall under one of the above categories due to the amount or size or type thereof, the FOIA Officer is authorized to establish an appropriate fee, pursuant to the criteria established in Office of Management and Budget Circular No. A–25, entitled "User Charges."

(b) Where it is anticipated that the fees chargeable under this part will amount to more than $25 and the requester has not indicated in advance her/his willingness to pay fees as high as anticipated, the requester shall be promptly notified of the amount of the anticipated fees or such portion thereof as can readily be estimated. The notice or request for an advance deposit shall extend an offer to the requester to confer with knowledgeable Section personnel in an attempt to reformulate the request in a manner which will reduce the fees and meet the needs of the requester. Dispatch of such notice or request shall suspend the running of the period for response by the Section until a reply is received from the requester.

(c) Search costs are due and payable even if the record which was requested cannot be located after all reasonable efforts have been made, or if the Section determines that a record which has been requested, but which is exempt from disclosure under this part, is to be withheld.

(d) The Section will begin assessing interest charges on an unpaid bill starting the 31st day following the day on which the billing was sent. The accrual of interest will be stayed upon receipt of the fee, rather than upon its processing by the Section. Interest will at the rate precribed in section 3717 of title 31 U.S.C.

(e) A requester may not file multiple requests at the same time, each seeking portions of a document or documents, solely in order to avoid payment of fees. When the Section reasonably believes that a requester or a group of requesters acting in concert is attempting to break a request down into a series of requests for the purpose of evading the assessment of fees, the Section will aggregate any such requests and charge accordingly.

(f) The Section will not require a requester to make an advance payment, i.e., payment before work is commenced or continued on a request, unless:

(1) The Section estimates or determines that allowable charges that a requester may be required to pay are likely to exceed $250. Then the Section will notify the requester of the likely costs and obtain satisfactory assurance of full payment where the requester has a history of prompt payment of FOIA fees, or require an advance payment of an amount up to the full estimated charges in the case of requesters with no history of payment; or

(2) Requesters who have previously failed to pay fees charged in a timely fashion (i.e., within 30 days of the date of the billing), the Section will require such requesters to pay the full amount owed plus any applicable interest as provided above or demonstrate that they have, in fact, paid the fee, and to make an advance payment of the full amount of the estimated fee before the agency begins to process new requests or pending requests from such requesters.

When the Section acts under paragraph (f) (1) or (2) of this section, the administrative time limit prescribed in subsection (a)(6) of the FOIA (i.e., 10 working days from receipt of initial requests plus permissible extensions of that time limit) will begin only after the Section has received payments described above.

(g) In accordance with the provisions and authorities of the Debt Collection Act of 1982 (Pub. L. 97–365), the Section reserves the right to disclose information to consumer reporting agencies and to use collection agencies, where appropriate, to encourage repayment.

(h) No fees under $10 will be billed by the Section because the cost of collection would be greater than the fee.

(i) Requester should pay fees by check or money order made out to the U.S. Section, International Boundary and Water Commission, and mailed to the Finance and Accounting Office, United States Section, International Boundary and Water Commission, 4171 North Mesa, suite C–310, El Paso, TX 79902–1422.

§ 1102.5 Categories of requesters for fee purposes.

There are four categories of requesters: Commercial use requesters; educational and non-commercial scientific institutions; representatives of the news media; and all other requesters. The Act prescribes specific levels of fees for each of these categories. The Section will take into account information provided by requesters in determining their eligibility for inclusion in one of these categories is as defined in § 1102.2. It is in the requester's best interest to provide as much information as possible to demonstrate inclusion within a non-commercial category of fee treatment.

(a) The Section will assess charges which recover the full direct costs of searching for, reviewing for release, and duplicating the records sought for commercial use. Commercial use requesters are entitled to neither two hours of free search time nor 100 free pages of reproduction of documents.

(b) The Section will provide documents to educational and non-commercial scientific institutions for the cost of reproduction alone, excluding charges for the first 100 pages. To be eligible for inclusion in this category, requesters must show that the request being made is authorized by, and under the auspices of, a qualifying institution and that the records are not sought for a commercial use, but are sought in furtherance of scholarly (if the request is from an educational institution) or scientific (if the request is from a non-commercial scientific institution) research.

(c) The Section will provide documents to representatives of the news media for the cost of reproduction alone, excluding charges for the first 100 pages. To be eligible for inclusion in this category; a requester must meet the criteria in § 1102.2(m), and the request must not be made for a commercial use. In reference to this class of requesters, a request for records supporting the news dissemination function of the requester shall not be considered to be a request that is for a commercial use.

(d) The Section will charge requesters who do not fit into any of the categories above fees which recover the full reasonable direct cost of searching for and reproducing records that are responsive to the request, except that the first 100 pages of reproduction and the first two hours of search time shall be furnished without charge. Moreover, requests from record subjects for records about themselves will continue to be treated under the fee provisions of the Privacy Act of 1974 which permit fees only for reproduction.

(e) In making determinations under this section, the Section may take into account whether requesters who previously were granted (b), (c), or (d) status under the Act did in fact use the requested records for purposes compatible with the status accorded them.

§ 1102.6 Fee waivers and appeals.

(a) Waiver or reduction of any fee provided for in § 1102.4 may be made upon a determination by the FOIA Officer, United States Section, International Boundary and Water Commission, 4171 North Mesa, suite C–310, El Paso, TX 79902–1422. The Section shall furnish documents without charge or at a reduced charge provided that: Disclosure of the information is in the public interest because it is likely to contribute significantly to public understanding of the operations or activities of the Government, and is not primarily in the commercial interest of the requester. Requests for a waiver or reduction of fees shall be considered on a case-by-case basis.

(1) In order to determine whether disclosure of the information is in the public interest because it is likely to contribute significantly to public understanding of the operations or activities of the Government, the Section will consider the following four factors:

(i) The subject of the request: Whether the subject of the requested records concerns the operations or activities of the Government;

(ii) The informative value of the information to be disclosed: Whether the disclosure is likely to contribute to an understanding of Government operations or activities;

(iii) The contribution to an understanding of the subject by the general public likely to result from disclosure: Whether disclosure of the requested information will contribute to public understanding; and

(iv) The significance of the contribution to public understanding: Whether the disclosure is likely to contribute significantly to public understanding of Government operations or activities.

(2) In order to determine whether disclosure of the information is not primarily in the commercial interest of the requester, the Section will consider the following two factors:

(i) The existence and magnitude of a commercial interest: Whether the requester has a commercial interest that would be furthered by the requested disclosure; and, if so

(ii) The primary interest in disclosure: Whether the magnitude of the identified commercial interest of the requester is sufficiently large, in comparison with the public interest in disclosure, that disclosure is primarily in the commercial interest of the requester.

(b) The Section will not consider waiver or reduction of fees for requesters (persons or organizations) from whom unpaid fees remain due to the Section for another information access request.

(c)(1) The Section's decision to refuse to waive or reduce fees as requested under paragraph (a) of this section may be appealed to the Commissioner, United States Section, International Boundary and Water Commission, 4171 North Mesa, Suite C–310, El Paso, TX 79902–1422. Appeals should contain as much information and documentation as possible to support the request for a waiver or reduction of fees.

(2) Appeals will be reviewed by the Commissioner, who may consult with other officials of the Section as appropriate. The requester will be notified within thirty working days from the date on which the Section received the appeal.

§ 1102.7 The Section's determination and appeal procedures.

Upon receipt of any request for records of information under the Act the following guidelines shall be followed:

(a) The FOIA Officer will determine within 10 days (excepting Saturdays, Sundays, and legal holidays) after receipt of any such request whether to comply with such request and will immediately notify the person making such request of such determination, the reasons therefore, and of the right to such person to appeal to the Commissioner any adverse determination.

(b) All appeals should be addressed to the Commissioner, United States Section, International Boundary and Water Commission, 4171 North Mesa, Suite, C–310, El Paso, TX 79902–1422, and should be clearly identified as such on the envelope and in the letter of appeal by using the marking "Freedom of Information Appeal" or "Appeal for Records" or the equivalent. Failure to properly address an appeal may defer the date of receipt by the Section to take into account the time reasonably required to forward the appeal to the Commissioner. In each instance when an appeal is incorrectly addressed to the Commissioner, he shall notify the person making the appeal that his appeal was improperly addressed and of the date the appeal was received by the Commissioner. The Commissioner will make a determination with respect to any appeal within 20 days (excepting Saturdays, Sundays, and legal holidays) after the receipt of an appeal. If on appeal the denial or the request is in whole or in part upheld, the Commissioner will notify the person making such request of the provisions for judicial review under the Act. An appeal must be in writing and filed within 30 days from receipt of the initial determination (in cases of denials of an entire request), or from receipt of any records being made available pursuant to the initial determination (in case of partial denials). In those cases where a request or appeal is not addressed to the proper official, the time limitations stated above will be computed from the receipt of the request or appeal by the proper official.

(c) In unusual circumstances, as set forth in paragraph (d) of this section, the time limits for responding to the original request or the appeal may be extended by not more than an additional 10 working days by written notice to the person making a request. This notice must be sent within either 10- or 20-day time limit and will specify the reason for the extension and the date on which determination is expected to be dispatched. The extension may be invoked only once during the consideration of a request either during the initial consideration period or during the consideration of an appeal, but not both.

(d) The unusual circumstances are:

(1) The need to search for and collect the requested records from field facilities or other establishments that are separate from the office processing the request.

(2) The need to search for, collect, and appropriately examine a voluminous amount of separate and distinct records which are demanded in a single request; or

(3) The need for consultation, which shall be conducted with all practicable speed, with another agency having a substantial interest in the determination of the requestor among two or more components of the agency having substantial subject-matter interest therein.

(e) If the FOIA Officer receives a request which is of proper concern to an agency or entity outside the Section, it will be returned to the person making the request, advising the requester to refer it to the appropriate agency or entity if requester desires, and providing the requester with the name or title, address and other appropriate information. An information copy of the request and the letter of referral will be forwarded promptly to the agency or entity outside the Section that may expect the request. In the event the FOIA Officer receives a request to make available a record or provide information which is of interest to more than one agency (Federal, State, municipal, or legal entity created thereby), the FOIA Officer will retain and act upon the request if the Section is one of the interest agencies and if its interest in the record is paramount.

(f) The Commissioner's determination on an appeal shall be in writing and when it denies records in whole or in part, the letter to the person making a request shall include:

(1) Notation of the specific exemption or exemptions of the Act authorizing the withholding.

(2) A statement that the decision is final for the Section.

(3) Advice that judicial review of the denial is available in the district in which the person making the request resides or has his principal place of business, the district in which the Section's records are situated, or the District of Columbia.

(4) The names and titles or positions of each official responsible for the denial of a request.

When appropriate, the written determination may also state how an exemption applied in that particular case, and, when relevant, why a discretionary rebase is not appropriate.

(g) In those cases where it is necessary to find and examine records before the legality or appropriateness of their disclosure can be determined, and where after diligent effort this has not been achieved within the required period, the FOIA Officer may advise the person making the request that a determination to presently deny the request has been made because the records or information have not been found or examined, that the determination will be considered when the search or examination is completed and the time within which completion is expected, but that the person making the request may immediately file an administrative appeal to the Commissioner.

§ 1102.8 Exemptions.

(a) 5 U.S.C. 552(b) provides that the requirements of the FOIA do not apply to matters that are:

(1) *Classified documents.* Specifically authorized under criteria established by an Executive order to be kept secret in the interest of national defense or foreign policy and that are, in fact, properly classified under the Executive order.

(2) *Internal personnel rules and practices.* Related solely to the internal personnel rules and practices of an agency.

(3) *Information exempt under other laws.* Specifically exempted from disclosure by statute, provided that the statute—

(i) Requires that the matters be withheld from the public in such a manner as to leave no discretion on the issue or

(ii) Establishes particular criteria for withholding or refers to particular types of matters to be withheld.

(4) *Confidential business information.* Trade secrets and commercial or financial information obtained from a person and privileged or confidential.

(5) *Internal government communications.* Interagency or intra-agency memorandums or letters which would not be available by law to a party other than an agency in litigation with the agency.

(6) *Personal privacy.* Personnel, medical, and similar files the disclosure of which would constitute a clearly unwarranted invasion of personal privacy.

(7) *Law enforcement.* Records or information compiled for law enforcement purposes, but only to the extent that the production of such law enforcement records or information:

(i) Could reasonably be expected to interfere with enforcement proceedings;

(ii) Would deprive a person of a right to a fair trial or an impartial adjudication;

(iii) Could reasonably be expected to constitute an unwarranted invasion of personal privacy;

(iv) Could reasonably be expected to disclose the identity of a confidential source, including a State, local, or foreign agency or authority or any private institution which furnished information on a confidential basis, and, in the case of a record or information compiled by a criminal law enforcement authority in the course of a criminal investigation, or by an agency conducting a lawful national security intelligence investigation information furnished by a confidential source;

(v) Would disclose techniques and procedures for law enforcement investigations or prosecutions, or would disclose guidelines for law enforcement investigations or prosecutions if such disclosure could reasonably be expected to risk circumvention of the law; or

(vi) Could reasonably be expected to endanger the life or physical safety of any individual.

(8) *Financial institutions.* Contained in or related to examination, operating, or condition reports prepared by, on behalf of, or for the use of an agency responsible for the regulation or supervision of financial institutions.

(9) *Geological information.* Geological and geophysical information and data, including maps, concerning wells.

(b) The Section will provide any reasonably segregable portion of a record to a requester after deletion of the portions that are exempt under this section.

(c) The section will invoke no exemption under this section if the requested records are available to the requester under the Privacy Act of 1974 and its implementing regulations.

(d) Whenever a request is made which involves access to records described in paragraph (a)(7)(i) of this section and

(1) The investigation or proceeding involves a possible violation of criminal law, and

(2) There is reason to believe that the subject of the investigation or proceeding is not aware of its pendency, and disclosure of the existence of the records could reasonably be expected to interfere with enforcement proceedings, the agency may, during only such time as that circumstance continues, treat the records as not subject to the requirements of this section.

§ 1102.9 Annual report to Congress.

(a) On or before March 1 of each calendar year the Commissioner shall submit a report covering the preceding calendar year to the Speaker of the

House of Representatives and President of the Senate for referral to the appropriate committees of the Congress. The report shall include:

(1) The number of determinations made by the section not to comply with request for records made to the section under the Act and this part and the reasons for each such determination.

(2) The number of appeals made by persons under the Act and this part, the result of such appeals, and the reason for the action upon each appeal that results in a denial of information.

(3) The names and titles or positions of each person responsible for the denial of records requested under the Act, and the number of instances of participation for each.

(4) The results of each proceeding conducted pursuant to 552(1)(4)(F) of the Act, including a report of the disciplinary action taken against the officer or employee who was primarily responsible for improperly withholding records or an explanation of why disciplinary action was not taken.

(5) A copy of this part.

(6) A copy of the fee schedule and the total amount of fees collected by the section for making records available under the Act.

(7) Such other information as indicates efforts to administer fully the Act.

(b) A copy of each such report to the Congress made pursuant to paragraph (a) of this section will be made available for public inspection and copying in the office of the FOIA Officer, United States Section, International Boundary and Water Commission, 4171 North Mesa, Suite C–310, El Paso, TX 79902–1422.

§ 1102.10 Examination of records.

When a request to examine records is approved by the FOIA Officer, every reasonable effort will be made to provide facilities for the purpose of such examination. "On the spot" copying will be available if the FOIA Officer decides there will be no interference with ordinary activities or routine business of the section.

PART 1103—ENFORCEMENT OF NONDISCRIMINATION ON THE BASIS OF HANDICAP IN PROGRAMS OR ACTIVITIES CONDUCTED BY INTERNATIONAL BOUNDARY AND WATER COMMISSION, UNITED STATES AND MEXICO, UNITED STATES SECTION

AUTHORITY: 29 U.S.C. 794.

SOURCE: 51 FR 4577, Feb. 5, 1986, unless otherwise noted.

§ 1103.101 Purpose.

This part effectuates section 119 of the Rehabilitation, Comprehensive Services, and Developmental Disabilities Amendments of 1978, which amended section 504 of the Rehabilitation Act of 1973 to prohibit discrimination on the basis of handicap in programs or activities conducted by Executive agencies or the United States Postal Service.

§ 1103.102 Application.

This part applies to all programs or activities conducted by the agency.

§ 1103.103 Definitions.

For purposes of this part, the term—

Assistant Attorney General means the Assistant Attorney General, Civil Rights Division, United States Department of Justice.

Auxiliary aids means services or devices that enable persons with impaired sensory, manual, or speaking skills to have an equal opportunity to participate in, and enjoy the benefits of, programs or activities conducted by the agency. For example, auxiliary aids useful for persons with impaired vision include readers, Brailled materials, audio recordings, telecommunications devices and other similar services and devices. Auxiliary aids useful for persons with impaired hearing include telephone handset amplifiers, telephones compatible with hearing aids, telecommunication devices for deaf persons (TDD's), interpreters, notetakers, written materials, and other similar services and devices.

Complete complaint means a written statement that contains the complainant's name and address and describes the agency's alleged discriminatory action in sufficient detail to inform the agency of the nature and date of the alleged violation of section 504. It shall be signed by the complainant or by someone authorized to do so on his or her behalf. Complaints filed on behalf of classes or third parties shall describe or identify (by name, if possible) the alleged victims of discrimination.

Facility means all or any portion of buildings, structures, equipment, roads, walks, parking lots, rolling stock or other conveyances, or other real or personal property.

Handicapped person means any person who has a physical or mental impairment that substantially limits one or more major life activities, has a record of such an impairment, or is regarded as having such an impairment.

As used in this definition, the phrase:

(1) *Physical or mental impairment* includes—

(i) Any physiological disorder or condition, cosmetic disfigurement, or anatomical loss affecting one of more of the following body systems: Neurological; musculoskeletal; special sense organs; respiratory, including speech organs; cardiovascular; reproductive; digestive; genitourinary; hemic and lymphatic; skin; and endocrine; or

(ii) Any mental or psychological disorder, such as mental retardation, organic brain syndrome, emotional or mental illness, and specific learning disabilities. The term *physical or mental impairment* includes, but is not limited to, such diseases and conditions as orthopedic, visual, speech, and hearing impairments, cerebral palsy, epilepsy, muscular dystrophy, multiple sclerosis, cancer, heart disease, diabetes, mental retardation, emotional illness, and drug addition and alcholism.

(2) *Major life activities* includes functions such as caring for one's self, performing manual tasks, walking, seeing, hearing, speaking, breathing, learning, and working.

(3) *Has a record of such an impairment* means has a history of, or has been misclassified as having, a mental or physical impairment that substantially limits one or more major life activities.

(4) *Is regarded as having an impairment* means—

(i) Has a physical or mental impairment that does not substantially limit major life activities but is treated by the agency as constituting such a limitation;

(ii) Has a physical or mental impairment that substantially limits major life activities only as a result of the attitudes of others toward such impairment; or

(iii) Has none of the impairments defined in paragraph (1) of this definition but is treated by the agency as having such an impairment.

Qualified handicapped person means—

(1) With respect to any agency program or activity under which a person is required to perform services or to achieve a level of accomplishment, a handicapped person who meets the essential eligibility requirements and who can achieve the purpose of the program or activity without modifications in the program or activity that the agency can demonstrate would result in a fundamental alteration in its nature; or

(2) With respect to any other program or activity, a handicapped person who meets the essential eligibility requirements for participation in, or receipt of benefits from, that program or activity.

(3) *Qualified handicapped person* is defined for purposes of employment in 29 CFR 1613.702(f), which is made applicable to this part by § 1103.140.

Section 504 means section 504 of the Rehabilitation Act of 1973 (Pub. L. 93–112, 87 Stat. 394 (29 U.S.C. 794)), as amended by the Rehabilitation Act Amendments of 1974 (Pub. L. 93–516, 88 Stat. 1617), and the Rehabilitation, Comprehensive Services, and Developmental Disabilities Amendments of 1978 (Pub. L. 95–602, 92 Stat. 2955). As used in this part, section 504 applies only to programs or activities conducted by Executive agencies and not to federally assisted programs.

[51 FR 4577, Feb. 5, 1986; 51 FR 7543, Mar. 5, 1986]

§§ 1103.104–1103.109 [Reserved]

§ 1103.110 Self-evaluation.

(a) The agency shall, by April 9, 1987, evaluate its current policies and practices, and the effects thereof, that do not or may not meet the requirements of this part, and, to the extent modification of any such policies and practices is required, the agency shall proceed to make the necessary modifications.

(b) The agency shall provide an opportunity to interested persons, including handicapped persons or organizations representing handicapped persons, to participate in the self-evaluation process by submitting comments (both oral and written).

(c) The agency shall, until three years following the completion of the self-evaluation, maintain on file and make available for public inspections:

(1) A description of areas examined and any problems identified, and

(2) A description of any modifications made.

§ 1103.111 Notice.

The agency shall make available to employees, applicants, participants, beneficiaries, and other interested persons such information regarding the provisions of this part and its applicability to the programs or activities conducted by the agency, and make such information available to them in such manner as the head of the agency finds necessary to apprise such persons of the protections against discrimination assured them by section 504 and this regulation.

§§ 1103.112–1103.129 [Reserved]

§ 1103.130 General prohibitions against discrimination.

(a) No qualified handicapped person shall, on the basis of handicap, be excluded from participation in, be denied the benefits of, or otherwise be subjected to discrimination under any program or activity conducted by the agency.

(b)(1) The agency, in providing any aid, benefit, or service, may not, directly or through contractual, licensing, or other arrangements, on the basis of handicap—

(i) Deny a qualified handicapped person the opportunity to participate in or benefit from the aid, benefit, or service;

(ii) Afford a qualfied handicapped person an opportunity to participate in or benefit from the aid, benefit, or service that is not equal to that afforded others;

(iii) Provide a qualified handicapped person with an aid, benefit, or service that is not as effective in affording equal opportunity to obtain the same result, to gain the same benefit, or to reach the same level of achievement as that provided to others;

(iv) Provide different or separate aid, benefits, or services to handicapped persons or to any class of handicapped persons than is provided to others unless such action is necessary to provide qualified handicapped persons with aid, benefits, or services that are as effective as those provided to others;

(v) Deny a qualified handicapped person the opportunity to participate as a member of planning or advisory boards; or

(vi) Otherwise limit a qualified handicapped person in the enjoyment of any right, privilege, advantage, or opportunity enjoyed by others receiving the aid, benefit, or service.

(2) The agency may not deny a qualified handicapped person the opportunity to participate in programs or activities that are not separate or different, despite the existence of permissibly separate or different programs or activities.

(3) The agency may not, directly or through contractual or other arrangements, utilize criteria or methods of

administration the purpose or effect of which would—

(i) Subject qualified handicapped persons to discrimination on the basis of handicap; or

(ii) Defeat or substantially impair accomplishment of the objectives of a program or activity with respect to handicapped persons.

(4) The agency may not, in determining the site or location of a facility, make selections the purpose or effect of which would—

(i) Exclude handicapped persons from, deny them the benefits of, or otherwise subject them to discrimination under any program or activity conducted by the agency; or

(ii) Defeat or substantially impair the accomplishment of the objectives of a program or activity with respect to handicapped persons.

(5) The agency, in the selection of procurement contractors, may not use criteria that subject qualified handicapped persons to discrimination on the basis of handicap.

(c) The exclusion of nonhandicapped persons from the benefits of a program limited by Federal statute or Executive order to handicapped persons or the exclusion of a specific class of handicapped persons from a program limited by Federal statute or Executive order to a different class of handicapped persons is not prohibited by this part.

(d) The agency shall administer programs and activities in the most integrated setting appropriate to the needs of qualified handicapped persons.

§§ 1103.131–1103.139 [Reserved]

§ 1103.140 Employment.

No qualified handicapped person shall, on the basis of handicap, be subjected to discrimination in employment under any program or activity conducted by the agency. The definitions, requirements, and procedures of section 501 of the Rehabilitation Act of 1973 (29 U.S.C. 791), as established by the Equal Employment Opportunity Commission in 29 CFR part 1613, shall apply to employment in federally conducted programs or activities.

§§ 1103.141–1103.148 [Reserved]

§ 1103.149 Program accessibility: Discrimination prohibited.

Except as otherwise provided in § 1103.150, no qualified handicapped person shall, because the agency's facilities are inaccessible to or unusable by handicapped persons, be denied the benefits of, be excluded from participation in, or otherwise be subjected to discrimination under any program or activity conducted by the agency.

§ 1103.150 Program accessibility: Existing facilities.

(a) *General.* The agency shall operate each program or activity so that the program or activity, when viewed in its entirety, is readily accessible to and usable by handicapped persons. This paragraph does not—

(1) Necessarily require the agency to make each of its existing facilities accessible to and usable by handicapped persons; or

(2) Require the agency to take any action that it can demonstrate would result in a fundamental alteration in the nature of a program or activity or in undue financial and administrative burdens. In those circumstances where agency personnel believe that the proposed action would fundamentally alter the program or activity or would result in undue financial and administrative burdens, the agency has the burden of proving that compliance with § 1103.150(a) would result in such alteration or burdens. The decision that compliance would result in such alteration or burdens must be made by the agency head or his or her designee after considering all agency resources available for use in the funding and operation of the conducted program or activity, and must be accompanied by a written statement of the reasons for reaching that conclusion. If an action would result in such an alteration or such burdens, the agency shall take any other action that would not result in such an alteration or such burdens but would nevertheless ensure that handicapped persons receive the benefits and services of the program or activity.

(b) *Methods.* The agency may comply with the requirements of this section through such means as redesign of equipment, reassignment of services to accessible buildings, assignment of aides to beneficiaries, home visits, delivery of services at alternate accessible sites, alteration of existing facilities and construction of new facilities, use of accessible rolling stock, or any other methods that result in making its programs or activities readily accessible to and usable by handicapped persons. The agency is not required to make structural changes in existing facilities where other methods are effective in achieving compliance with this section. The agency, in making alterations to existing buildings, shall meet accessibility requirements to the extent compelled by the Architectural Barriers Act of 1968, as amended (42 U.S.C. 4151–4157), and any regulations implementing it. In choosing among available methods for meeting the requirements of this section, the agency shall give priority to those methods that offer programs and activities to qualified handicapped persons in the most integrated setting appropriate.

(c) *Time period for compliance.* The agency shall comply with the obligations established under this section by June 6, 1986, except that where structural changes in facilities are undertaken, such changes shall be made by April 7, 1989, but in any event as expeditiously as possible.

(d) *Transition plan.* In the event that structural changes to facilities will be undertaken to achieve program accessibility, the agency shall develop, by October 7, 1986, a transition plan setting forth the steps necessary to complete such changes. The agency shall provide an opportunity to interested persons, including handicapped persons or organizations representing handicapped persons, to participate in the development of the transition plan by submitting comments (both oral and written). A copy of the transition plan shall be made available for public inspection. The plan shall, at a minimum—

(1) Identify physical obstacles in the agency's facilities that limit the accessibility of its programs or activities to handicapped persons;

(2) Describe in detail the methods that will be used to make the facilities accessible;

(3) Specify the schedule for taking the steps necessary to achieve compliance with this section and, if the time period of the transition plan is longer than one year, identify steps that will be taken during each year of the transition period; and

(4) Indicate the official responsible for implementation of the plan.

[51 FR 4577, Feb. 5, 1986; 51 FR 7543, Mar. 5, 1986]

§ 1103.151 Program accessibility: New construction and alterations.

Each building or part of a building that is constructed or altered by, on behalf of, or for the use of the agency shall be designed, constructed, or altered so as to be readily accessible to and usable by handicapped persons. The definitions, requirements, and standards of the Architectural Barriers Act (42 U.S.C. 4151–4157), as established in 41 CFR 101–19.600 to 101–19.607, apply to buildings covered by this section.

§§ 1103.152–1103.159 [Reserved]

§ 1103.160 Communications.

(a) The agency shall take appropriate steps to ensure effective communication with applicants, participants, personnel of other Federal entities, and members of the public.

(1) The agency shall furnish appropriate auxiliary aids where necessary to afford a handicapped person an equal opportunity to participate in, and enjoy the benefits of, a program or activity conducted by the agency.

(i) In determining what type of auxiliary aid is necessary, the agency shall give primary consideration to the requests of the handicapped person.

(ii) The agency need not provide individually prescribed devices, readers for personal use or study, or other devices of a personal nature.

(2) Where the agency communicates with applicants and beneficiaries by telephone, telecommunication devices for deaf persons (TDD's) or equally effective telecommunication systems shall be used.

(b) The agency shall ensure that interested persons, including persons with impaired vision or hearing, can obtain information as to the existence and location of accessible services, activities, and facilities.

(c) The agency shall provide signage at a primary entrance to each of its inaccessible facilities, directing users to a location at which they can obtain information about accessible facilities. The international symbol for accessibility shall be used at each primary entrance of an accessible facility.

(d) This section does not require the agency to take any action that it can demonstrate would result in a fundamental alteration in the nature of a program or activity or in undue financial and administrative burdens. In those circumstances where agency personnel believe that the proposed action would fundamentally alter the program or activity or would result in undue financial and administrative burdens, the agency has the burden of proving that compliance with § 1103.160 would result in such alteration or burdens. The decision that compliance would result in such alteration or burdens must be made by the agency head or his or her designee after considering all agency resources available for use in the funding and operation of the conducted program or activity, and must be accompanied by a written statement of the reasons for reaching that conclusion. If an action required to comply with this section would result in such an alteration or such burdens, the agency shall take any other action that would not result in such an alteration or such burdens but would nevertheless ensure that, to the maximum extent possible, handicapped persons receive the benefits and services of the program or activity.

§§ 1103.161–1103.169 [Reserved]

§ 1103.170 Compliance procedures.

(a) Except as provided in paragraph (b) of this section, this section applies to all allegations of discrimination on the basis of handicap in programs or activities conducted by the agency.

(b) The agency shall process complaints alleging violations of section 504 with respect to employment according to the procedures established by the Equal Employment Opportunity Commission in 29 CFR part 1613 pursuant to section 501 of the Rehabilitation Act of 1973 (29 U.S.C. 791).

(c) Director, Equal Employment Opportunity shall be responsible for coordinating implementation of this section. Complaints may be sent to Director, Equal Employment Opportunity, International Boundary and Water Commission, United States and Mexico, United States Section, The Commons, Building C, Suite 310, 4171 North Mesa, El Paso, Texas 79902.

(d) The agency shall accept and investigate all complete complaints for which it has jurisdiction. All complete complaints must be filed within 180 days of the alleged act of discrimination. The agency may extend this time period for good cause.

(e) If the agency receives a complaint over which it does not have jurisdiction, it shall promptly notify the complainant and shall make reasonable efforts to refer the complaint to the appropriate government entity.

(f) The agency shall notify the Architectural and Transportation Barriers Compliance Board upon receipt of any complaint alleging that a building or facility that is subject to the Architectural Barriers Act of 1968, as amended (42 U.S.C. 4151–4157), or section 502 of the Rehabilitation Act of 1973, as amended (29 U.S.C. 792), is not readily accessible to and usable by handicapped persons.

(g) Within 180 days of the receipt of a complete complaint for which it has jurisdiction, the agency shall notify the complainant of the results of the investigation in a letter containing—

(1) Findings of fact and conclusions of law;

(2) A description of a remedy for each violation found;

(3) A notice of the right to appeal.

(h) Appeals of the findings of fact and conclusions of law or remedies must be filed by the complainant within 90 days of receipt from the agency of the letter required by § 1103.170(g). The agency may extend this time for good cause.

(i) Timely appeals shall be accepted and processed by the head of the agency.

(j) The head of the agency shall notify the complainant of the results of the appeal within 60 days of the receipt of the request. If the head of the agency determines that additional information is needed from the complainant, he or she shall have 60 days from the date of receipt of the additional information to make his or her determination on the appeal.

(k) The time limits cited in paragraphs (g) and (j) of this section may be extended with the permission of the Assistant Attorney General.

(l) The agency may delegate its authority for conducting complaint investigations to other Federal agencies, except that the authority for making the final determination may not be delegated to another agency.

[51 FR 4577, Feb. 5, 1986, as amended at 51 FR 4577, Feb. 5, 1986]

§§ 1103.171–1103.999 [Reserved]

PART 1104—PROTECTION OF ARCHAEOLOGICAL RESOURCES

AUTHORITY: Pub. L. 96–95, 93 Stat. 721 (16 U.S.C. 470aa–11) (Sec. 10(a).) Related Authority: Pub. L. 59–209, 34 Stat. 225 (16 U.S.C. 432, 433); Pub. L. 86–523, 74 Stat. 220, 221 (16 U.S.C. 469), as amended, 88 Stat. 174 (1974); Pub. L. 89–665, 80 Stat. 915 (16 U.S.C. 470a-t), as amended, 84 Stat. 204 (1970), 87 Stat. 139 (1973), 90 Stat. 1320 (1976), 92 Stat. 3467 (1978), 94 Stat. 2987 (1980); Pub. L. 95–341, 92 Stat. 469 (42 U.S.C. 1996).

SOURCE: 56 FR 21590, May 10, 1991, unless otherwise noted.

§ 1104.1 Purpose.

(a) The regulations in this part implement provisions of the Archaeological Resources Protection Act of 1979 (16 U.S.C. 470aa–11) by establishing the definitions, standards, and procedures to be followed by the Commissioner in providing protection for archaeological resources, located on public lands through permits authorizing excavation and/or removal of archaeological resources, through civil penalties for unauthorized excavation and/or removal, through provisions for the preservation of archaeological resource collections and data, and through provisions for ensuring confidentiality of information about archaeological resources when disclosure would threaten the archaeological resources.

(b) The regulations in this part do not impose any new restrictions on activities permitted under other laws, authorities, and regulations relating to mining, mineral leasing, reclamation, and other multiple uses of the public lands.

§ 1104.2 Definitions.

As used for purposes of this part:

(a) *Archaeological resource* means any material remains of human life or activities which are at least 100 years of age, and which are of archaeological interest.

(1) *Of archaeological interest* means capable of providing scientific or humanistic understandings of past human behavior, cultural adaptation, and related topics through the application of scientific or scholarly techniques such as controlled observation, contextual measurement, controlled collection, analysis, interpretation and explanation.

(2) *Material remains* means physical evidence of human habitation, occupation, use, or activity, including the site, location, or context in which such evidence is situated.

(3) The following classes of material remains (and illustrative examples), if they are at least 100 years of age, are of archaeological interest and shall be

considered archaeological resources unless determined otherwise pursuant to paragraph (a)(4) or (a)(5) of this section:

(i) Surface or subsurface structures, shelters, facilities, or features (including, but not limited to, domestic structures, storage structures, cooking structures, ceremonial structures, artificial mounds, earthworks, fortifications, canals, reservoirs, horticultural/agricultural gardens or fields, bedrock mortars or grinding surfaces, rock alignments, cairns, trails, borrow pits, cooking pits, refuse pits, burial pits or graves, hearths, kilns, post molds, wall trenches, middens);

(ii) Surface or subsurface artifact concentrations or scatters;

(iii) Whole or fragmentary tools, implements, containers, weapons and weapon projectiles, clothing, and ornaments (including, but not limited to, pottery and other ceramics, cordage, basketry and other weaving, bottles and other glassware, bone, ivory, shell, metal, wood, hide, feathers, pigments, and flaked, ground, or pecked stone);

(iv) By-products, waste products, or debris resulting from manufacture or use of human-made or natural materials;

(v) Organic waste (including but not limited to, vegetable and animal remains, coprolites);

(vi) Human remains (including, but not limited to, bone, teeth, mummified flesh, burials, cremations);

(vii) Rock carvings, rock paintings, intaglios and other works of artistic or symbolic representation;

(viii) Rockshelters and caves or portions thereof containing any of the above material remains;

(ix) All portions of shipwrecks (including but not limited to, armaments, apparel, tackle, cargo);

(x) Any portion or piece of any of the foregoing.

(4) The following material remains shall not be considered of archaeological interest, and shall not be considered to be archaeological resources for purposes of the Act and this part, unless found in a direct physical relationship with archaeological resources as defined in this section:

(i) Paleontological remains;

(ii) Coins, bullets, and unworked minerals and rocks.

(5) The Commissioner may determine that certain material remains, in specified areas under the Commissioner's jurisdiction, and under specified circumstances, are not or are no longer of archaeological interest and are not to be considered archaeological resources under this part. Any determination made pursuant to this subparagraph shall be documented. Such Determination shall in no way affect the Commissioner's obligations under other applicable laws or regulations.

(b) *Arrowhead* means any projectile point which appears to have been designed for use with an arrow.

(c) *Commissioner* means the head of the United States Section, International Boundary and Water Commission, United States and Mexico, and his delegate.

(d) *Public lands* means lands to which the United States of America holds fee title, and which are under the control of the U.S. Section, International Boundary and Water Commission, United States and Mexico.

(e) *Indian tribe* as defined in the Act means any Indian tribe, band, nation, or other organized group or community. In order to clarify this statutory definition for purposes of this part, *Indian tribe* means:

(1) Any tribal entity which is included in the annual list of recognized tribes published in the FEDERAL REGISTER by the Secretary of the Interior pursuant to 25 CFR part 54;

(2) Any other tribal entity acknowledged by the Secretary of the Interior pursuant to 25 CFR part 54 since the most recent publication of the annual list;

(f) *Person* means an individual, corporation, partnership, trust, institution, association, or any other private entity, or any officer, employee, agent, department, or instrumentality of the United States, or of any Indian tribe, or of any State or political subdivision thereof.

(g) *State* means any of the fifty states, the District of Columbia, Puerto Rico, Guam, and the Virgin Islands.

(h) *Act* means the Archaeological Resources Protection Act of 1979 (16 U.S.C. 470aa–11.), as amended.

§ 1104.3 Prohibited acts.

(a) No person may excavate, remove, damage, or otherwise alter or deface any archaeological resource located on public lands unless such activity is pursuant to a permit issued under § 1104.7 or exempted by § 1104.4(b) of this part.

(b) No person may sell, purchase, exchange, transport, or receive any archaeological resource, if such resource was excavated or removed in violation of:

(1) The prohibitions contained in paragraph (a) of this section; or

(2) Any provision, rule, regulation, ordinance, or permit in effect under any other provision of Federal law.

§ 1104.4 Permit requirements and exceptions.

(a) Any person proposing to excavate and/or remove archaeological resources from public lands, and to carry out activities associated with such excavation and/or removal, shall apply to the Commissioner for a permit for the proposed work, and shall not begin the proposed work until a permit has been issued. The Commissioner may issue a permit to any qualified person, subject to appropriate terms and conditions, provided that the person applying for a permit meets conditions in § 1104.7(a) of this part.

(b) Exceptions:

(1) No permit shall be required under this part for any person conducting activities on the public lands under other permits, leases, licenses, or entitlements for use, when those activities are exclusively for purposes other than the excavation and/or removal of archaeological resources, even though those activities might incidentally result in the disturbance of archaeological resources. General earth-moving excavation conducted under a permit or other authorization shall not be construed to mean excavation and/or removal as used in this part. This exception does not, however, affect the Commissioner's responsibility to comply with other authorities which protect archaeological resources prior to approving permits, leases, licenses, or entitlements for use; any excavation and/or removal of archaeological resources required for compliance with those authorities shall be conducted in accordance with the permit requirements of this part.

(2) No permit shall be required under this part for any person collecting for private purposes any rock, coin, bullet, or mineral which is not an archaeological resource as defined in this part, provided that such collecting does not result in disturbance of any archaeological resource.

(3) No permit shall be required under section 3 of the Act of June 8, 1906 (16 U.S.C. 432) for any archaeological work for which a permit is issued under this part.

(c) Persons carrying out official agency duties under the Commissioner's direction, associated with the management of archaeological resources, need not follow the permit application procedures of § 1104.5. However, the Commissioner shall insure that provisions of §§ 1104.7 and 1104.8 have been met by other documented means, and that any official duties which might result in harm to or destruction of any Indian tribal religious or cultural site, as determined by the Commissioner, have been the subject of consideration under § 1104.6.

(d) Upon the written request of the Governor of any State, on behalf of the State or its educational institutions, the Commissioner shall issue a permit, subject to the provisions of §§ 1104.4(b)(5), 1104.6, 1104.7(a) (3), (4), (5), (6), and (7), 1104.8, 1104.9, 1104.11, and 1104.12(a) to such Governor or to such designee as the Governor deems qualified to carry out the intent of the Act, for purposes of conducting archaeological research, excavating and/or removing archaeological resources, and safeguarding and preserving any materials and data collected in a university, museum, or other scientific or educational institution approved by the Commissioner.

(e) Under other statutory, regulatory, or administrative authorities governing the use of public lands, authorizations may be required for activities which do not require a permit under this part. Any person wishing to conduct on public lands any activities related to but believed to fall outside the scope of this part should consult with the Commissioner, for the purpose of determining whether any authorization is required, prior to beginning such activities.

§ 1104.5 Application for permits and information collection.

(a) Any person may apply to the Commissioner for a permit to excavate and/or remove archaeological resources from public lands and to carry out activities associated with such excavation and/or removal.

(b) Each application for a permit shall include:

(1) The nature and extent of the work proposed, including how and why it is proposed to be conducted, proposed time of performance, locational maps, and proposed outlet for public written dissemination of the results.

(2) The name and address of the individual(s) proposed to be responsible for conducting the work, institutional affiliation, if any, and evidence of education, training, and experience in accord with the minimal qualifications listed in § 1104.7(a).

(3) The name and address of the individual(s), if different from the individual(s) named in paragraph (b)(2) of this section, proposed to be responsible for carrying out the terms and conditions of the permit.

(4) Evidence of the applicant's ability to initiate, conduct, and complete the proposed work, including evidence of logistical support and laboratory facilities.

(5) Where the application is for the excavation and/or removal of archaeological resources on public lands, the names of the university, museum, or other scientific or educational institution in which the applicant proposes to store all collections, and copies of records, data, photographs, and other documents derived from the proposed work. Applicants shall submit written certification, signed by an authorized official of the institution, of willingness to assume curatorial responsibility for the collections, records, data, photographs and other documents and to safeguard and preserve these materials as property of the United States.

(c) The Commissioner may require additional information, pertinent to land management responsibilities, to be included in the application for permit and shall so inform the applicant.

(d) Paperwork Reduction Act. The information collection requirement contained in § 1104.5 of these regulations has been approved by the Office of Management and Budget under 44 U.S.C. 3501 *et seq.* and assigned clearance number 1024–0037. The purpose of the information collection is to meet statutory and administrative requirements in the public interest. The information will be used to assist the Commissioner in determining that applicants for permits are qualified, that the work proposed would further archaeological knowledge, that archaeological resources and associated records and data will be properly preserved, and that the permitted activity would not conflict with the management of the public lands involved. Response to the information requirement is necessary in order for an applicant to obtain a benefit.

§ 1104.6 Notification to Indian tribes of possible harm to, or destruction of, sites on public lands having religious or cultural importance.

(a) If the issuance of a permit under this part may result in harm to, or destruction of, any Indian tribal religious or cultural site on public lands, as determined by the Commissioner, at least 30 days before issuing such a permit the Commissioner shall notify any Indian tribe which may consider the site as having religious or cultural importance. Such notice shall not be deemed a disclosure to the public for purposes of section 9 of the Act.

(1) Notice by the Commissioner to any Indian tribe shall be sent to the chief executive officer or other designated official of the tribe. Indian tribes are encouraged to designate a tribal official to be the focal point for any notification and discussion between the tribe and the Commissioner.

(2) The Commissioner may provide notice to any other Native American group that is known by the Commissioner to consider sites potentially affected as being of religious or cultural importance.

(3) Upon request during the 30-day period, the Commissioner may meet with official representatives of any Indian

tribe or group to discuss their interests, including ways to avoid or mitigate potential harm or destruction such as excluding sites from the permit area. Any mitigation measures which are adopted shall be incorporated into the terms and conditions of the permit under § 1104.8.

(4) When the Commissioner determines that a permit applied for under this part must be issued immediately because of an imminent threat of loss or destruction of an archaeological resource, the Commissioner shall so notify the appropriate tribe.

(b)(1) In order to identify sites of religious or cultural importance, the Commissioner shall seek to identify all Indian tribes having aboriginal or historic ties to the lands under the Commissioner's jurisdiction and seek to determine, from the chief executive officer or other designated official of any such tribe, the location and nature of specific sites of religious or cultural importance so that such information may be on file for land management purposes. Information on site eligible for or included in the National Register of Historic Places may be withheld from public disclosure pursuant to section 304 of the Act of October 15, 1966, as amended (16 U.S.C. 470w–3).

(2) If the Commissioner becomes aware of a Native American group that is not an Indian tribe as defined in this part but has aboriginal or historic ties to public lands under the Commissioner's jurisdiction, the Commissioner may seek to communicate with official representatives of that group to obtain information on sites they may consider to be of religious or cultural importance.

(3) The Commissioner may enter into agreement with any Indian tribe or other Native American group for determining locations for which such tribe or group wishes to receive notice under this section.

§ 1104.7 Issuance of permits.

(a) The Commissioner may issue a permit, for a specified period of time appropriate to the work to be conducted, upon determining that:

(1) The applicant is appropriately qualified, as evidenced by training, education, and/or experience, and possesses demonstrable competence in archaeological theory and methods, and in collecting, handling, analyzing, evaluating, and reporting archaeological data, relative to the type and scope of the work proposed, and also meets the following minimum qualifications:

(i) A graduate degree in anthropology or archaeology, or equivalent training and experience;

(ii) The demonstrated ability to plan, equip, staff, organize, and supervise activity of the type and scope proposed;

(iii) The demonstrated ability to carry research to completion, as evidenced by timely completion of theses, research reports, or similar documents;

(iv) Completion of at least 16 months of professional experience and/or specialized training in archaeological field, laboratory, or library research, administration, or management, including at least 4 months experience and/or specialized training in the kind of activity the individual proposes to conduct under authority of a permit; and

(v) Applicants proposing to engage in historical archaeology should have had at least one year of experience in research concerning archaeological resources of the prehistoric period.

(2) The proposed work is to be undertaken for the purpose of furthering archaeological knowledge in the public interest, which may include but need not be limited to, scientific or scholarly research, and preservation of archaeological data;

(3) The proposed work, including time, scope, location, and purpose, is not inconsistent with any management plan or established policy, objectives, or requirements applicable to the management of the public lands concerned;

(4) Where the proposed work consists of archaeological survey and/or data recovery undertaken in accordance with other approved uses of the public lands, and the proposed work has been agreed to in writing by the Commissioner pursuant to section 106 of the National Historic Preservation Act (16 U.S.C. 470f), paragraphs (a)(2) and (a)(3) of this section shall be deemed satisfied by the prior approval;

(5) Evidence is submitted to the Commissioner that any university, museum, or other scientific or educational institution proposed in the application as the repository possesses adequate curatorial capability for safeguarding and preserving the archaeological resources and all associated records; and

(6) The applicant has certified that, not later than 90 days after the date the final report is submitted to the Commissioner, the following will be delivered to the appropriate official of the approved university, museum, or other scientific or educational institution, which shall be named in the permit:

(i) All artifacts, samples, collections, and copies of records, data, photographs, and other documents resulting from work conducted under the requested permit where the permit is for the excavation and/or removal of archaeological resources from public lands.

(b) When the area of the proposed work would cross jurisdictional boundaries, so that permit applications must be submitted to more than one Federal agency, the Commissioner shall coordinate the review and evaluation of applications and the issuance of permits.

§ 1104.8 Terms and conditions of permits.

(a) In all permits issued, the Commissioner shall specify:

(1) The nature and extent of work allowed and required under the permit, including the time, duration, scope, location, and purpose of the work;

(2) The name of the individual(s) responsible for conducting the work and, if different, the name of the individual(s) responsible for carrying out the terms and conditions of the permit;

(3) The name of any university, museum, or other scientific or educational institutions in which any collected materials and data shall be deposited; and

(4) Reporting requirements.

(b) The Commissioner may specify such terms and conditions as deemed necessary, consistent with this part, to protect public safety and other values and/or resources, to secure work areas, to safeguard other legitimate land uses, and to limit activities incidental to work authorized under a permit.

(c) Initiation of work or other activities under the authority of a permit signifies the permittee's acceptance of the terms and conditions of the permit.

(d) The permittee shall not be released from requirements of a permit until all outstanding obligations have been satisifed, whether or not the term of the permit has expired.

(e) The permittee may request that the Commissioner extend or modify a permit.

(f) The permittee's performance under any permit issued for a period greater than 1 year shall be subject to review by the Commissioner, at least annually.

§ 1104.9 Suspension and revocation of permits.

(a) *Suspension or revocation for cause.* (1) The Commissioner may suspend a permit issued pursuant to this part upon determining that the permittee has failed to meet any of the terms and conditions of the permit or has violated any prohibition of the Act or § 1104.3. The Commissioner shall provide written notice to the permittee of the suspension, the cause thereof, and the requirements which must be met before the suspension will be removed.

(2) The Commissioner may revoke a permit upon assessment of a civil penalty under § 1104.14 upon the permittee's conviction under section 6 of the Act, or upon determining that the permittee has failed after notice under this section to correct the situation which led to suspension of the permit.

(b) *Suspension or revocation for management purposes.* The Commissioner may suspend or revoke a permit, without liability to the United States, its agents, or employees, when continuation of work under the permit would be in conflict with management requirements not in effect when the permit was issued. The Commissioner shall provide written notice to the permittee stating the nature of and basis for the suspension or revocation.

§ 1104.10 Appeals relating to permits.

Any affected person may appeal permit issuance, denial of permit issuance, suspension, revocation, and terms and conditions of a permit.

§ 1104.11 Relationship to section 106 of the National Historic Preservation Act.

Issuance of a permit in accordance with the Act and this part does not constitute an undertaking requiring compliance with section 106 of the Act of October 15, 1966 (16 U.S.C. 470f). However, the mere issuance of such a permit does not excuse the Commissioner from compliance with section 106 where otherwise required.

§ 1104.12 Custody of archaeological resources.

(a) Archaeological resources excavated or removed from the public lands remain the property of the United States.

(b) The Commissioner may provide for the exchange of archaeological resources among suitable universities, museums, or other scientific or educational institutions, when such resources have been excavated or removed from public lands under the authority of a permit issued by the Commissioner.

§ 1104.13 Determination of archaeological or commercial value and cost of restoration and repair.

(a) *Archaeological value.* For purposes of this part, the archaeological value of any archaeological resource involved in a violation of the prohibitions in § 1104.3 of this part or conditions of a permit issued pursuant to this part shall be the value of the information associated with the archaeological resource. This value shall be appraised in terms of the costs of the retrieval of the scientific information which would have been obtainable prior to the violation. These costs may include, but need not be limited to, the cost of preparing a research design, conducting field work, carrying out laboratory analysis, and preparing reports as would be necessary to realize the information potential.

(b) *Commercial value.* For purposes of this part, the commercial value of any archaeological resource involved in a violation of the prohibitions in § 1104.3 of this part or conditions of a permit issued pursuant to this part shall be its fair market value. Where the violation has resulted in damage to the archaeological resource, the fair market value should be determined using the condition of the archaeological resource prior to the violation, to the extent that its prior condition can be ascertained.

(c) *Cost of restoration and repair.* For purposes of this part, the cost of restoration and repair of archaeological resources damaged as a result of a violation of prohibitions or conditions pursuant to this part, shall be the sum of the costs already incurred for emergency restoration or repair work, plus those costs projected to be necessary to complete restoration and repair, which may include, but need not be limited to, the costs of the following:

(1) Reconstruction of the archaeological resource;

(2) Stabilization of the archaeological resource;

(3) Ground contour reconstruction and surface stabilization;

(4) Research necessary to carry out reconstruction or stabilization;

(5) Physical barriers or other protective devices, necessitated by the disturbance of the archaeological resource, to protect it from further disturbance;

(6) Examination and analysis of the archaeological resource including recording remaining archaeological information, where necessitated by disturbance, in order to salvage remaining values which cannot be otherwise conserved;

(7) Reinterment of human remains in accordance with religious custom and State, local, or tribal law, where appropriate, as determined by the Commissioner;

(8) Preparation of reports relating to any of the above activities.

§ 1104.14 Assessment of civil penalties.

(a) The Commissioner may assess a civil penalty against any person who has violated any prohibition contained in § 1104.3 or who has violated any term or condition included in a permit issued in accordance with the Act and this part.

(b) *Notice of violation.* The Commissioner shall serve a notice of violation upon any person believed to be subject to a civil penalty, either in person or by registered or certified mail (return receipt requested). The Commissioner shall include in the notice:

(1) A concise statement of the facts believed to show a violation;

(2) A specific reference to the provision(s) of this part or to a permit issued pursuant to this part allegedly violated;

(3) The amount of penalty proposed to be assessed, including any initial proposal to mitigate or remit where appropriate, or a statement that notice of a proposed penalty amount will be served after the damages associated with the alleged violation have been ascertained;

(4) Notification of the right to file a petition for relief pursuant to paragraph (d) of this section, or to await the Commissioner's notice of assessment, and to request a hearing in accordance with paragraph (g) of this section. The notice shall also inform the person of the right to seek judicial review of any final administrative decision assessing a civil penalty.

(c) The person served with a notice of violation shall have 45 calendar days from the date of its service (or the date of service of a proposed penalty amount, if later) in which to respond. During this time the person may:

(1) Seek informal discussions with the Commissioner;

(2) File a petition for relief in accordance with paragraph (d) of this section;

(3) Take no action and await the Commissioner's notice of assessment;

(4) Accept in writing or by payment the proposed penalty, or any mitigation or remission offered in the notice. Acceptance of the proposed penalty or mitigation or remission shall be deemed a waiver of the notice of assessment and of the right to request a hearing under paragraph (g) of this section.

(d) *Petition for relief.* The person served with a notice of violation may request that no penalty be assessed or that the amount be reduced, by filing a petition for relief with the Commissioner within 45 calendar days of the date of service of the notice of violation (or of a proposed penalty amount, if later). The petition shall be in writing and signed by the person served with the notice of violation. If the person is a corporation, the petition must be signed by an officer authorized to sign such documents. The petition shall set forth in full the legal or factual basis for the requested relief.

(e) *Assessment of penalty.* (1) The Commissioner shall assess a civil penalty upon expiration of the period for filing a petition for relief, upon completion of review of any petition filed, or upon completion of informal discussions, whichever is later.

(2) The Commissioner shall take into consideration all available information, including information provided pursuant to paragraphs (c) and (d) of this section or furnished upon further request by the Commissioner.

(3) If the facts warrant a conclusion that no violation has occurred, the Commissioner shall so notify the person served with a notice of violation, and no penalty shall be assessed.

(4) Where the facts warrant a conclusion that a violation has occurred, the Commissioner shall determine a penalty amount in accordance with § 1104.15.

(f) *Notice of assessment.* The Commissioner shall notify the person served with a notice of violation of the penalty amount assessed by serving a written notice of assessment, either in person or by registered or certified mail (return receipt requested). The Commissioner shall include in the notice of assessment:

(1) The facts and conclusions from which it was determined that a violation did occur;

(2) The basis in § 1104.15 for determining the penalty amount assessed and/or any offer to mitigate or remit the penalty; and

(3) Notification of the right to request a hearing, including the procedures to be followed, and to seek judicial review of any final administrative decision assessing a civil penalty.

(g) *Hearings.* (1) Except where the right to request a hearing is deemed to have been waived as provided in paragraph (c)(4) of this section, the person served with a notice of assessment may file a written request for a hearing with the adjudicatory body specified in the notice. The person shall enclose with the request for hearing a copy of the notice of assessment, and shall deliver the request as specified in the notice of assessment, personally or by registered or certified mail (return receipt requested).

(2) Failure to deliver a written request for a hearing within 45 days of the date of service of the notice of assessment shall be deemed a waiver of the right to a hearing.

(3) Any hearing conducted pursuant to this section shall be held in accordance with 5 U.S.C. 554. In any such hearing, the amount of civil penalty assessed shall be determined in accordance with this part, and shall not be limited by the amount assessed by the Commissioner under paragraph (f) of this section or any offer of mitigation or remission made by the Commissioner.

(h) *Final administrative decision.* (1) Where the person served with a notice of violation has accepted the penalty pursuant to paragraph (c)(4) of this section, the notice of violation shall constitute the final administrative decision;

(2) Where the person served with a notice of assessment has not filed a timely request for a hearing pursuant to paragraph (g)(1) of this section, the notice of assessment shall constitute the final administrative decision;

(3) Where the person served with a notice of assessment has filed a timely request for a hearing pursuant to paragraph (g)(1) of this section, the decision resulting from the hearing or any applicable administrative appeal therefrom shall constitute the final administrative decision.

(i) *Payment of penalty.* (1) The person assessed a civil penalty shall have 45 calendar days from the date of issuance of the final administrative decision in which to make full payment of the penalty assessed, unless a timely request for appeal has been filed with a United States District Court as provided in section 7(b)(1) of the Act.

(2) Upon failure to pay the penalty, the Commissioner may request the Attorney General to institute a civil action to collect the penalty in a United States District Court for any district in which the person assessed a civil penalty is found, resides, or transacts business. Where the Commissioner is not represented by the Attorney General, a civil action may be initiated directly by the Commissioner.

(j) *Other remedies not waived.* Assessment of a penalty under this section shall not be deemed a waiver of the right to pursue other available legal or administrative remedies.

§ 1104.15 Civil penalty amounts.

(a) *Maximum amount of penalty.* (1) Where the person being assessed a civil penalty has not committed any previous violation of any prohibition in § 1104.3 or of any term or condition included in a permit issued pursuant to this part, the maximum amount of the penalty shall be the full cost of restoration and repair of archaeological resources damaged plus the archaeological or commercial value of archaeological resources destroyed or not recovered.

(2) Where the person being assessed a civil penalty has committed any previous violation of any prohibition in § 1104.3 or of any term or condition included in a permit issued pursuant to this part, the maximum amount of the penalty shall be double the cost of restoration and repair plus double the archaeological or commercial value of archaeological resources destroyed or not recovered.

(3) Violations limited to the removal of arrowheads located on the surface of the ground shall not be subject to the penalties prescribed in this section.

(b) *Determination of penalty amount, mitigation, and remission.* The Commissioner may assess a penalty amount less than the maximum amount of penalty and may offer to mitigate or remit the penalty.

(1) Determination of the penalty amount and/or a proposal to mitigate or remit the penalty may be based upon any of the following factors:

(i) Agreement by the person being assessed a civil penalty to return to the Commissioner archaeological resources removed from public lands;

(ii) Agreement by the person being assessed a civil penalty to assist the Commissioner in activity to preserve, restore, or otherwise contribute to the protection and study of archaeological resources on public lands;

(iii) Agreement by the person being assessed a civil penalty to provide information which will assist in the detection, prevention, or prosecution of violations of the Act or this part;

(iv) Demonstration of hardship or inability to pay, provided that this factor shall only be considered when the person being assessed a civil penalty has not been found to have previously violated the regulations in this part;

(v) Determination that the person being assessed a civil penalty did not willfully commit the violation;

(vi) Determination that the proposed penalty would constitute excessive punishment under the circumstances;

(vii) Determination of other mitigating circumstances appropriate to consideration in reaching a fair and expeditious assessment.

(2) When the penalty is for a violation which may have had an effect on a known Indian tribal religious or cultural site on public lands, the Commissioner should consult with and consider the interests of the affected tribe(s) prior to proposing to mitigate or remit the penalty.

§ 1104.16 Other penalties and rewards.

(a) Section 6 of the Act contains criminal prohibitions and provisions for criminal penalties. Section 8(b) of the Act provides that archaeological resources, vehicles, or equipment involved in a violation may be subject to forfeiture.

(b) Section 8(a) of the Act provides for rewards to be made to persons who furnish information which leads to conviction for a criminal violation or to assessment of a civil penalty. The Commissioner may certify to the Secretary of the Treasury that a person is eligible to receive payment. Officers and employees of Federal, State, or local government who furnish information or render service in the performance of their official duties, and persons who have provided information under § 1104.15(b)(1)(iii) shall not be certified eligible to receive payment of rewards.

§ 1104.17 Confidentiality of archaeological resource information.

(a) The Commissioner shall not make available to the public, under subchapter II of chapter 5 of title 5 of the United States Code or any other provision of law, information concerning the nature and location of any archaeological resource, with the following exceptions:

(1) The Commissioner may make information available, provided that the disclosure will further the purposes of the Act and this part, or the Act of June 27, 1960, as amended (16 U.S.C. 469–469c), without risking harm to the archaeological resource or to the site in which it is located.

(2) The Commissioner shall make information available, when the Governor of any State has submitted to the Commissioner a written request for information, concerning the archaeological resources within the requesting Governor's State, provided that the request includes:

(i) The specific archaeological resource or area about which information is sought;

(ii) The purpose for which the information is sought; and

(iii) The Governor's written commitment to adequately protect the confidentiality of the information.

§ 1104.18 Report to the Secretary of the Interior.

The Commissioner, when requested by the Secretary of the Interior, shall submit such information as is necessary to enable the Secretary to comply with section 13 of the Act.

PARTS 1105–1199 [RESERVED]

CHAPTER XII—UNITED STATES INTERNATIONAL DEVELOPMENT COOPERATION AGENCY

PART 1200 [RESERVED]

PART 1201—PUBLIC INFORMATION

AUTHORITY: Sec. 621, 22 U.S.C. 2381, as amended; 5 U.S.C. 552.

CROSS REFERENCE: The regulations establishing procedures under the Freedom of Information Act for the United States International Development Cooperation Agency are codified in 22 CFR 212.1 through 212.51, prescribed jointly by the United States International Development Cooperation Agency and the Agency for International Development.

[45 FR 20790, Mar. 31, 1980]

PART 1202—REGULATIONS TO IMPLEMENT THE PRIVACY ACT OF 1974

AUTHORITY: Sec. 621, 22 U.S.C. 2381, as amended; 5 U.S.C. 552a.

CROSS REFERENCE— The regulations establishing procedures by which an individual may obtain notification of the existence of agency records pertaining to that individual, gain access to those records, request an amendment to those records, and appeal adverse decisions to requests for amendment or correction of agency records are codified as 22 CFR 215.1 through 215.14, prescribed jointly by the United States International Development Cooperation Agency and the Agency for International Development.

[45 FR 20791, Mar. 31, 1980]

PART 1203—EMPLOYEE RESPONSIBILITIES AND CONDUCT

Subpart A—General Provisions

Subpart B—Ethical and Other Conduct and Responsibilities of Employees

Subpart C—Ethical and Other Conduct and Responsibilities of Special Government Employees

Subpart D—Statements of Employment and Financial Interests

AUTHORITY: E.O. 11222 of May 8, 1965, as amended; 5 CFR 735.104.

SOURCE: 43 FR 18976, May 2, 1978; 45 FR 18922, Mar. 24, 1980, unless otherwise noted.

Subpart A—General Provisions

§ 1203.735–101 Purpose.

The maintenance of the highest standards of honesty, integrity, impartiality, and conduct by Government employees and special Government employees is essential to assure the proper performance of the Government business and the maintenance of confidence by citizens in their Government. The avoidance of misconduct and conflicts of interest on the part of Government employees and special Government employees through informed judgment is indispensable to the maintenance of these standards. To accord with these concepts the regulations in this part prescribe standards of conduct and responsibilities for employees and special Government employees and require statements reporting employment and financial interests.

NOTE: These regulations are codified in State 3 FAM 620, AID Handbook 24, and ICA MOA V-A 550.

§ 1203.735–102 Definitions.

(a) *Agency* means the United States International Development Cooperation Agency (IDCA).

(b) *Employee* means an officer or employee at home or abroad, of an agency named in paragraph (a) of this section, but does not include a special Government employee or a member of the Army, Navy, Air Force, Marine Corps, Coast Guard, National Oceanic and Atmospheric Administration, or Public Health Service.

(c) *Executive order* means Executive Order 11222 of May 8, 1965, as amended.

(d) *Person* means an individual, a corporation, a company, an association, a firm, a partnership, a society, a joint stock company, or any other organization or institution.

(e) *Special Government employee* means an officer or employee of an agency who is retained, designated, appointed, or employed to perform, with or without compensation, for not to exceed 130 days during any period of 365 consecutive days, temporary duties either on a full-time or intermittent basis.

(f) *Member of an employee's family* means a spouse, minor child, or other member of an employee's immediate household. For the purpose of these regulations *member of an employee's immediate or in-law household* means those blood relations who are residents of the employee's household.

(g) *Counselor* means the agency's Counselor on Ethical Conduct and Conflicts of Interest.

§ 1203.735–103 Interpretation and advisory service.

(a) Counseling services on employee responsibilities and conduct are available in each agency. These services are to be coordinated by a Counselor appointed by the agency head. The Counselor for IDCA is the General Counsel. The Counselor serves as the agency's designee to the Civil Service Commission on matters covered by the regulations in this part and is responsible for coordination of the agency's counseling services under paragraph (b) of this section and for assuring that counseling and interpretations on questions of conflicts of interest and other matters covered by these sections are available to deputy counselors designated under paragraph (b) of this section.

(b) Each agency head may designate deputy counselors for the agency's employees and special Government employees. Deputy Counselors designated under this section must be qualified and in a position to give authoritative advice and guidance to each employee and special Government employee who seeks advice and guidance on questions of conflicts of interest and on other matters covered by the regulations in this part. A Washington employee or special Government employee should address any inquiries concerning the regulations in this part to the Counselor. At missions abroad the chief of each agency's establishment designates an officer, preferably the legal officer where one is available, to provide counseling services under the guidance of the Counselor; a single officer may serve all agencies. An employee or special Government employee serving abroad should submit inquiries to the officer designated.

(c) Each agency shall periodically notify its employees and special Government employees of the availability of counseling services and how and when these services are available. A new employee or special Government employee shall be notified at the time of entrance on duty.

§ 1203.735-104 Applicability to detailed employees.

All the regulations of subparts A, B, and D of this part are applicable to an employee of another U.S. Government agency who may be serving on detail or assignment, formally or informally, on a reimbursable or nonreimbursable basis through a Participating Agency Service Agreement or otherwise, with an agency named in § 1203.735-102(a). However, disciplinary action shall be taken against such an employee only by the employing agency.

§ 1203.735-105 Disciplinary action.

A violation of the regulations in this part by an employee or special Government employee may be cause for appropriate disciplinary action, including separation for cause, which may be in addition to any penalty prescribed by law.

Subpart B—Ethical and Other Conduct and Responsibilities of Employees

§ 1203.735-201 General.

(a) *Proscribed actions.* An employee shall avoid any action, whether or not specifically prohibited by the regulations in this part, which might result in, or create the appearance of:

(1) Using public office for private gain;

(2) Giving preferential treatment to any person;

(3) Impeding Government efficiency or economy;

(4) Losing independence or impartiality;

(5) Making a Government decision outside official channels; or

(6) Affecting adversely the confidence of the public in the integrity of the Government.

(b) *Applicability to members of families of employees.* A U.S. citizen employee shall take care that certain responsibilities placed on the employee are also observed by members of the employee's family. These are the restrictions in regard to: Acceptance of gifts (§§ 1203.735-202 and 1203.735-203); economic and financial activities abroad (§ 1203.735-206); teaching, lecturing, and writing (§ 1203.735-204(c)); participation in activities of private organizations (§ 1203.735-211(c)); and political activities abroad (§ 1203.735-211(g)).

§ 1203.735-202 Gifts, entertainment, and favors.

(a) *Acceptance prohibited.* Except as provided in paragraphs (b), (c), and (d) of this section, an employee shall not solicit or accept, directly or indirectly, any gift, gratuity, favor, entertainment, loan, or any other thing of monetary value, from a person who:

(1) Has, or is seeking to obtain, contractual or other business or financial relations with the employee's agency;

(2) Conducts operations or activities that are regulated by the employee's agency;

(3) Has interests that may be substantially affected by the performance or nonperformance of the employee's official duty; or

(4) Appears to be offering the gift with the hope or expectation of obtaining advantage or preferment in dealing with the U.S. Government for any purpose.

(b) *Acceptance permitted.* The provisions of paragraph (a) of this section do not apply to:

(1) Gifts, gratuities, favors, entertainments, loans, or any other thing of monetary value received on account of close family or personal relationships when the circumstances make it clear that it is that relationship rather than the business of the persons concerned which is the motivating factor;

(2) Acceptance of loans from banks or other financial institutions on customary terms to finance proper and usual activities of employees, such as home mortgage loans;

(3) Acceptance of unsolicited advertising or promotional material, such as pens, pencils, note pads, calendars, and other items of nominal intrinsic value;

(4) Acceptance of rates and discounts offered to employees as a class.

(c) *Acceptance permitted for IDCA employees.* For IDCA employees the provisions of paragraph (a) of this section do not apply to: Acceptance of food and refreshments of nominal value on infrequent occasions in the ordinary course of a luncheon or dinner meeting or other meeting or on an inspection tour where an employee may properly be in attendance.

(d) *Acceptance permitted for AID employees.* For AID employees the provisions of paragraph (a) of this section do not apply in the following situations:

(1) Acceptance of food, refreshments, or entertainment of nominal value on infrequent occasions offered in the ordinary course of luncheons, dinners, or other meetings and gatherings hosted by foreign governments or agencies and officials thereof, embassies, and international organizations, where the primary purpose of the function is representational or social, rather than the transaction of business. Where the primary purpose of the function is the transaction of business, acceptance is not permitted, except if there is justification and reporting in accordance with paragraph (d)(4) of this section.

(2) Participation in widely attended lunches, dinners, and similar gatherings sponsored by industrial, technical, and professional associations for the discussion of matters of mutual interest to Government and industry.

(3) Acceptance of food, refreshments, or entertainment in the unusual situation where the employee, by virtue of the location of the person, firm, corporation, or other entity, or the regulations governing its dining facilities, finds it inconvenient or impracticable not to accept the offer. Each case of acceptance shall be reported in accordance with the requirement of paragraph (d)(4) of this section. In no other case shall employees accept food, refreshments, or entertainment from private corporations, entities, firms, or individual contractors at occasions which are other than widely attended functions whose purposes are unrelated to Agency business.

(4) In exceptional circumstances where acceptance of food, refreshments, or entertainment is not authorized by paragraphs (d) (1), (2), and (3) of this section, but where, in the judgment of the individual concerned, the Government's interest would be served by such acceptance directly or indirectly from any foreign government, agency, or official thereof or a private person, firm, corporation, or other entity which is engaged or is endeavoring to engage in business transactions of any sort with AID, an employee may accept the offer: *Provided,* That a report of the circumstances, together with the employee's statement as to how the Government's interests were served, will be made within 48 hours to the employee's supervisor, or, if the employee is serving abroad, or on temporary duty abroad, to the Mission Director.

(e) *Gifts to superiors.* An employee shall for a gift to an official superior, make a donation as a gift to an official superior, or accept a gift from an employee receiving less pay than the employee (5 U.S.C. 7351). However, this paragraph does not prohibit a voluntary gift of nominal value or donation in a nominal amount made on a special occasion such as marriage, illness, or retirement.

(f) *Neither this section nor § 1203.735–204* precludes an employee from receipt of bona fide reimbursement, unless prohibited by law, for expenses of travel and such other necessary subsistence as is compatible with this part for which no Government payment or reimbursement is made. However, this paragraph does not allow an employee to be reimbursed, or payment to be made on the employee's behalf, for excessive personal living expenses, gifts, entertainment, or other personal benefits, nor does it allow an employee to be reimbursed by a person for travel on official business under agency orders when reimbursement is proscribed by Decision B–128527 of the Comptroller General dated March 7, 1967.

§ 1203.735–203 Gifts from foreign governments.

An employee shall not accept a gift, present, decoration, or other thing from a foreign government unless authorized by Congress as provided by the Constitution and in 5 U.S.C. 7342, and the regulations promulgated thereunder pursuant to E.O. 11320, 31 FR 15789. These regulations are set forth in part 3 of this title (as added, 32 FR 6569, Apr. 28, 1967), and in 3 FAM 621.

§ 1203.735–204 Outside employment and other activity.

(a) An employee shall not engage in outside employment or other outside activity not compatible with the full and proper discharge of the duties and responsibilities of Government employment. Incompatible activities include but are not limited to:

(1) Acceptance of a fee, compensation, gift, payment of expense, or any other thing of monetary value in circumstances in which acceptance may result in, or create the appearance of, conflicts of interest; or

(2) Outside employment which tends to impair the employee's mental or physical capacity to perform Government duties and responsibilities in an acceptable manner.

(b) An employee shall not receive any salary or anything of monetary value from a private source as compensation for the employee's services to the Government (18 U.S.C. 209).

(c) Employees are encouraged to engage in teaching, lecturing, and writing that is not prohibited by law, the Executive order, this part, or the agency regulations. However, an employee shall not, either for or without compensation, engage in teaching, lecturing, or writing including teaching, lecturing, or writing for the purpose of the special preparation of a person or class of persons for an examination of the Civil Service Commission or Board of Examiners for the Foreign Service, that is dependent on information obtained as a result of Government employment, except when that information has been made available to the general public or will be made available on request or when the agency head gives written authorization for use of nonpublic information on the basis that the use is in the public interest. In addition, an employee who is a Presidential appointee covered by section 401(a) of the Executive order shall not receive compensation or anything of monetary value for any consultation, lecture, discussion, writing, or appearance the subject matter of which is devoted substantially to the responsibilities, programs, or operations of the employee's agency, or which draws substantially on official data or ideas which have not become part of the body of public information. Employees are referred to the detailed rules of their agency with respect to clearance and acceptance of compensation (See AID Handbook 18)

(d) [Reserved]

(e) An employee shall not render any services, whether or not compensated, to any foreign government, state, province, or semigovernmental agency, or municipality of any foreign government, or to any international organization of states. However, this shall not prevent the rendering of such services by employees acting on behalf of the United States. Nor shall this provision prevent the rendering of services to an international organization of states when otherwise consistent with law and when authorized by the appropriate officer. The appropriate officer for IDCA is the Assistant Director for Administration.

(f) [Reserved]

(g) This section does not preclude an employee from:

(1) Participation in the activities of national or State political parties not proscribed by law.

(2) Participation in the affairs of or acceptance of an award for a meritorious public contribution or achievement given by a charitable, religious, professional, social, fraternal, nonprofit educational and recreational, public service, or civic organization.

§ 1203.735–205 Financial interests.

(a) An employee shall not: (1) Have a direct or indirect financial interest that conflicts substantially, or appears to conflict substantially with the employee's Government duties and responsibilities; or

(2) Engage in, directly or indirectly, a financial transaction as a result of, or primarily relying on, information obtained through Government employment.

(b) This section does not preclude an employee from having a financial interest or engaging in financial transactions to the same extent as a private citizen not employed by the Government so long as it is not prohibited by law or the regulations in this part.

(c) Pursuant to the provision of 18 U.S.C. 208(b) the following described financial interests of an employee are hereby exempted from the requirements of 18 U.S.C. 208(a) and 208(b)(1) as being too remote or too inconsequential to affect the integrity of the services of an employee. The exemption applies to the financial interests held directly by an employee, by the employee's spouse or minor child whether individually or jointly with the employee, or by an employee and any partner or partners as joint assets of the partnership:

(1) Investments in State and local government bonds; and stocks, bonds, or policies in a mutual fund, investment company, bank or insurance company, provided that in the case of a mutual fund, investment company, or bank, the fair value of such stock or bond holding does not exceed one percent of the value of the reported assets of the mutual fund, investment company, or bank. In the case of a mutual fund or investment company, this exemption applies only where the assets of the fund or company are diversified; it does not apply where the fund or company specializes in a particular industry or commodity.

(2) Interest in an investment club or other group organized for the purpose of investing in equity or debt securities: *Provided*, That the fair value of the interest involved does not exceed $10,000 and that the interest does not exceed one-fourth of the total assets of the investment club or group. Where an employee covered by this exemption is a member of a group organized for the purpose of investing in equity or debt securities, the interest of the employee in any enterprise in which the group holds securities shall be based upon the employee's equity share of the holdings of the group in that enterprise.

(3) If an employee, or the employee's spouse or minor child has a present beneficial interest or a vested remainder interest under a trust, the ownership of stocks, bonds, or other corporate securities under the trust will be exempt to the same extent as provided in paragraphs (c)(1) and (2) of this section for the direct ownership of such securities. The ownership of bonds other than corporate bonds, or of shares in a mutual fund or regulated investment company, under the trust will be equally exempt and to the same extent as under paragraphs (c) (1) and (2) of this section.

(4) If an employee is an officer, director, trustee, or employee of an educational institution, or if the employee is negotiating for, or has an arrangement concerning prospective employment with such an institution, a direct financial interest which the institution has in any matter will not itself be exempt, but any financial interest that the institution may have in the matter through its holdings of securities issued by business entities will be exempt: *Provided*, The employee is not serving as a member of the investment committee of the institution or is not otherwise advising it on its investment portfolio.

(5) An employee may continue to participate in a bona fide pension, retirement, group life, health or accident insurance plan, or other employee welfare or benefit plan that is maintained by a business or nonprofit organization by which the employee was formerly employed. Such financial interest in that organization will be exempt, except to the extent that the welfare or benefit plan is a profit-sharing or stock-bonus plan and the employee's financial interest thereunder exceeds $10,000. This exemption extends also to any financial interests that the organization may have in other business activities.

(d) Nothing in this part shall be deemed to prohibit an employee from acting, with or without compensation, as agent or attorney for the employee's parents, spouse, child, or any person for whom, or for any estate for which, the employee is serving as guardian, executor, administrator, trustee, or other personal fiduciary, except in those matters in which the employee has participated personally and substantially as a Government employee, through decision, approval, disapproval, recommendation, the rendering of advice, investigation, or otherwise, or which are the subject of the employee's official responsibility, as defined in 18 U.S.C. 202(b): *Provided*, The head of the employee's division approves in writing.

§ 1203.735–206 Economic and financial activities of employees abroad.

(a) *Prohibitions in any foreign country.* A U.S. citizen employee abroad is specifically prohibited from engaging in the activities listed below in any foreign country.

(1) Speculation in currency exchange.

(2) Transactions at exchange rates differing from local legally available rates, unless such transactions are duly authorized in advance by the agency.

(3) Sales to unauthorized persons (whether at cost or for profit) of currency acquired at preferential rates through diplomatic or other restricted arrangements.

(4) Transactions which entail the use, without official sanction, of the diplomatic pouch.

(5) Transfers of funds on behalf of blocked nationals, or otherwise in violation of U.S. foreign funds and assets control.

(6) Independent and unsanctioned private transactions which involve an employee as an individual in violation of applicable control regulations of foreign governments.

(7) Acting as an intermediary in the transfer of private funds from persons in one country to persons in another country, including the United States.

(8) Permitting use of one's official title in any private business transactions or in advertisements for business purposes.

(b)–(c) [Reserved]

(d) *Business activities of non-U.S. citizen employees.* A non-U.S citizen employee abroad may engage in outside business activities with the prior approval of the head of the overseas establishment on the basis of the standards expressed in § 1203.735–204(a).

§ 1203.735–207 Use of Government property.

An employee shall not directly or indirectly use, or allow the use of Government property of any kind, including property leased to the Government, for other than officially approved activities. An employee has a positive duty to protect and conserve Government property, including equipment, supplies, and other property entrusted or issued to the employee.

§ 1203.735–208 Misuse of information.

For the purpose of furthering a private interest, an employee shall not, except as provided in § 1203.735–204(c) directly or indirectly use, or allow the use of, official information obtained through or in connection with Government employment which has not been made available to the general public.

§ 1203.735–209 Indebtedness.

An employee shall pay each just financial obligation in a proper and timely manner, especially one imposed by law such as Federal, State, or local taxes. For the purpose of this section, a *just financial obligation* means one acknowledged by the employee or reduced to judgement by a court or one imposed by law such as Federal, State, or local taxes, and "in a proper and timely manner" means in a manner which the agency determines does not, under the circumstances, reflect adversely on the Government as the employer. In the event of dispute between an employee and an alleged creditor, this section does not require an agency to determine the validity or amount of the disputed debt.

§ 1203.735–210 Gambling, betting, and lotteries.

An employee shall not participate, while on Government-owned or leased property or while on duty for the Government, in any gambling activity including the operation of a gambling device, in conducting a lottery or pool, in a game for money or property, or in selling or purchasing a numbers slip or ticket. However, this section does not preclude activities:

(a) Necessitated by an employee's law enforcement duties; or

(b) Under section 3 of Executive Order 10927 and similar agency-approved activities.

§ 1203.735–211 Activities relating to private organizations and politics.

(a) *Definition.* For the purpose of this section, the term *private organization* denotes any group of persons or associations organized for any purpose whatever, except an organization established by the Government of the United States, or officially participated in by IDCA.

(b) *Participation in activities of employee organizations.* An employee may join or refrain from joining employee organizations or associations without interference, coercion, restraint, or fear of discrimination or reprisal.

(c) *Participation in activities of private organizations.* In participating in the program and activities of any private organization, an employee shall make clear that the employee's agency has no official connection with such organization and does not necessarily sponsor or sanction the viewpoints which it may express.

(d) *Legal restrictions on membership in certain organizations.* An employee shall not have membership in any organization that advocates the overthrow of our constitutional form of Government in the United States, knowing that such organization so advocates (5 U.S.C. 7311, 18 U.S.C. 1918).

(e) *Private organizations concerned with foreign policy or other matters of concern to agencies.* (1) Limitation on participation. When a private organization is concerned primarily with foreign policy or international relations or other matters of concern to an employee's agency, an employee shall limit connection therewith as follows: Unless specifically permitted to do so, the employee may not serve as advisor, officer, director, teacher, sponsor, committee chairman, or in any other official capacity or permit the employee's name to be used on a letterhead, in a publication, in an announcement or news story, or at a public meeting, regardless of whether the employee's official title or connection is mentioned. The provisions of this section are not intended to prohibit the normal and active participation of an employee in professional organizations such as the American Political Science Association, the American Economic Association, the American Foreign Service Association, and similar organizations, since such participation is in the interest of both the employee and the Government. Employees are expected, however, to exercise discretion in such activities and are held personally accountable for any improper use of their relationship with IDCA.

(2) Request for special permission. Special permission to assume or continue a connection prohibited by paragraph (e)(1) of this section may be granted in cases where the public interest will not be adversely affected. To request such permission, or to determine whether the provisions are applicable to a particular case, the employee shall address a memorandum setting forth all of the circumstances to the appropriate officer. The appropriate officer for IDCA is the Assistant Director for Administration.

(3) Application to senior officers. Because of the prominence resulting from their official positions, chiefs of mission and other senior officers should recognize the particular bearing of the provisions of paragraph (e)(1) of this section upon their activities. They should restrict association with any organizations involving foreign nations and the United States to simple membership and should not accept even honorary office in such organizations except with the specific prior approval as provided in paragraph (e)(2) of this section.

(f) *Private organizations not concerned with foreign policy.* When the purpose and program of the organization do not fall primarily within the field of foreign policy or international relations, the employee's activity is limited only to the following extent:

(1) The employee's official title or connection may be used to identify the employee, as in a civic association election, but may not be used on a letterhead, in a publication, or otherwise so as to employ the prestige of the U.S. Government to enhance that of the organization or to imply official sponsorship.

(2) When the employee is a representative of an association consisting of IDCA employees, or of a group of such employees, the employee's connection with the agency may be freely used so long as there is no implication of official sponsorship beyond that which may have been officially approved.

(g) *Political activities abroad.* A U.S. citizen employee shall not engage in any form of political activity in any foreign country.

(h) *Activities relating to U.S. politics.* The law (5 U.S.C. 7324, formerly the Hatch Act) provides in summary that it is unlawful for any Federal employee of the executive branch to use the employee's official authority or influence for the purpose of interfering with an election or affecting the result thereof, or to take any active part in political management or in political campaigns. These restrictions do not in any way affect the right of a Federal employee (1) to vote as the employee chooses; (2) to express personal political opinions, except as part of a campaign; (3) to make or refrain from making contributions to political organizations, provided contributions are not made in a Federal building or to another Federal officer or employee (see 18 U.S.C. 602, 603, 607, and 608); (4) to participate in local, nonpartisan activities.

§ 1203.735–212 Wearing of uniforms.

(a) An employee of the Foreign Service may not wear any uniform except as may be authorized by law or as a military commander may require civilians to wear in a theater of military operations (22 U.S.C. 803). When an employee is authorized by law or required by a military commander of the United States to wear a uniform, care shall be taken that the uniform is worn only at authorized times and for authorized purposes.

(b) Conventional attire worn by chauffeurs, elevator operators, and other miscellaneous employees are not considered uniforms within the meaning of this section except that, for ICA, MOA VII 917.2b prohibits the purchase from Agency funds of uniforms or any item of personal wearing apparel other than special protective clothing.

§ 1203.735–213 Recommendations for employment.

(a) *Making recommendations in official capacity.* In general, an employee shall not, in the employee's official capacity, make any recommendations in connection with the employment of persons unless the position concerned are with the Government of the United States and the recommendations are made in response to an inquiry from a Government official authorized to employ persons or to investigate applicants for employment. A principal officer in answer to a letter of inquiry from outside the U.S. Government concerning a former employee assigned to the post, may state the length of time the person was employed at the post and the fact that the former employee performed duties in a satisfactory manner, if such is the case. Also, an AID Mission Director may provide names of persons or firms from which a cooperating government may select an employee or firm to be used in some phase of the AID program.

(b) *Making personal recommendations.* An employee may make a personal recommendation in connection with the employment of any person, including present or former employees, their spouses and/or members of their families, except for employment in a position of trust or profit under the government of the country to which the employee is accredited or assigned (22 U.S.C. 806(b)): *Provided,* That the employee does not divulge any information concerning the person derived from official sources. When a letter of introduction or recommendation is written by an employee, precautionary measures should be taken to prevent its being construed as official correspondence and used by an unscrupulous individual to impress American or foreign officials. Accordingly, official stationery should not be used for this purpose. The letter may, however, show the recommending employee's status as an employee of the U. S. Government. Every personal letter of recommendation shall contain a statement clearly indicating that the letter constitutes a personal recommendation and is not to be construed as an official recommendation by the Government of the United States.

§ 1203.735–214 Transmitting communications and gifts.

(a) *Correspondence.* In corresponding with anyone other than the proper official of the United States with regard to the public affairs of a foreign government, an employee shall use discretion and judgment to ensure that neither the United States nor the employee will be embarrassed or placed in a compromising position (22 U.S.C. 806(a)).

(b) *Communications.* An employee shall not act as an agent for the transmission of communications from private persons or organizations in foreign countries to the President or to

Federal, State, or municipal officials in the United States. A chief of mission may, however, accept communications of this nature and forward them to the Department of State for such further action as may be appropriate, whenever the chief of mission determines it to be clearly in the public interest to do so.

(c) *Gifts*. An employee shall not act as an agent for the transmission of gifts from persons or organizations in foreign countries to the President or to Federal, State, or municipal officials of the United States. However, principal officers may, according to regulations prescribed by the President, accept, and forward to the Office of Protocol of the Department of State, gifts made to the United States or to any political subdivision thereof by the Government to which they are accredited or from which they hold exequaturs. Employees shall not, without the approval of the Secretary of State, transmit gifts from persons or organizations in the United States to heads or other officials of foreign states.

§ 1203.735–215 General conduct prejudicial to the Government.

(a) An employee shall not engage in criminal, infamous, dishonest, immoral, or notoriously disgraceful conduct, or other conduct prejudicial to the Government.

(b) An employee abroad is also obligated to obey the laws of the country in which the employee is present.

(c) An employee shall observe the requirements of courtesy, consideration, and promptness in dealing with or serving the public.

§ 1203.735–216 Miscellaneous statutory provisions.

Each employee shall become acquainted with each statute that relates to the employee's ethical and other conduct as an agency employee of and of the Government.

(a) The attention of employees is directed to the following statutory provisions:

(1) House Concurrent Resolution 175, 85th Congress, 2d session, 72 Stat. B12, the "Code of Ethics for Government Service."

(2) Chapter 11 of title 18, United States Code, relating to bribery, graft, and conflicts of interest, as appropriate to the employees concerned.

(3) The prohibition against lobbying with appropriated funds (18 U.S.C. 1913).

(4) The prohibitions against disloyalty and striking (5 U.S.C. 7311, 18 U.S.C. 1918).[1]

(5) The prohibitions against (i) the disclosure of classified information (18 U.S.C. 798, 50 U.S.C. 783); and (ii) the disclosure of confidential information (18 U.S.C. 1905).

(6) The provision relating to the habitual use of intoxicants to excess (5 U.S.C. 7352).

(7) The prohibition against the misuse of a Government vehicle (31 U.S.C. 638a(c)).

(8) The prohibition against the misuse of the franking privilege (18 U.S.C. 1719).

(9) The prohibition against the use of deceit in an examination or personnel action in connection with Government employment (18 U.S.C. 1917).

(10) The prohibition against fraud or false statements in a Government matter (18 U.S.C. 1001).

(11) The prohibition against mutilating or destroying a public record (18 U.S.C. 2071).

(12) The prohibition against counterfeiting and forging transportation requests (18 U.S.C. 508).

(13) The prohibition against (i) embezzlement of Government money or property (18 U.S.C. 641); (ii) failing to account for public money (18 U.S.C. 643); and (iii) embezzlement of the money or property of another person in the possession of an employee by reason of the employee's employment (18 U.S.C. 654).

(14) The prohibition against unauthorized use of documents relating to claims from or by the Government (18 U.S.C. 285).

(15) The prohibition against political activities in subchapter III of chapter 73 of title 5, United States Code and 18 U.S.C. 602, 603, 607, and 608.

[1] The Courts have stricken from the Code any prohibition against assertion of the right to strike on the basis that such an assertion is a protected right under the First Amendment to the Constitution.

(16) The prohibition against an employee acting as the agent of a foreign principal registered under the Foreign Agents Registration Act (18 U.S.C. 219).

(17) The prohibition against discrimination because of politics, race, religion, or color (22 U.S.C. 807).

(18) The prohibition against officers or employees accepting any honorarium in excess of $2,000 or honoraria aggregating more than $25,000 in any calendar year (sec. 112, Pub. L. 94–283, 90 Stat. 494 (2 U.S.C. 441i)).

(b) The attention of consular officers is directed to the following statutory provisions:

(1) The provisions relating to the duty to account for fees received (22 U.S.C. 9, 812, 1194), liability for exaction of excessive fees (22 U.S.C. 1182, 1189), and liability for failure to collect proper fees (22 U.S.C. 1190).

(2) The provisions relating to liability for failure to give bond and for embezzlement (22 U.S.C. 1179), liability for embezzlement of fees or effects of American citizens (22 U.S.C. 1198), and liability for falsely certifying as to the ownership of property (22 U.S.C. 1200).

(3) The prohibition against profiting from dealings with discharged seamen (22 U.S.C. 1187).

(4) The provision relating to liability for failure to collect the wages of discharged seamen (46 U.S.C. 683).

§ 1203.735–217 Requesting exceptions from certain statutory prohibitions.

(a) Any employee desiring a written advance determination that the prohibitions of 18 U.S.C. 208(a) do not apply will prepare a written request addressed to an appropriate agency official. For purposes of this section, the appropriate agency official is: The Deputy Under Secretary for Management for State, the Administrator for AID, and the Director for ICA. The request will describe the particular matter giving rise to the conflict of interest, the nature and extent of the employee's anticipated participation in the particular matter, and the exact nature and amount of the financial interest related to the particular matter.

(b) The employee will forward the request to the appropriate agency official through the immediate supervisor and the assistant agency head in charge of the organizational agency component to which the employee is assigned, or will be assigned in the case of a new employee. The assistant agency head will forward the written request to the appropriate agency official through the agency's Counselor. The Counselor shall attach a written opinion to the request, prepare a recommended written determination in final form for signature by the appropriate agency official, and shall forward all documents to that official.

(c) The determination of the appropriate agency official will be sent to the employee by the Counselor. If the appropriate agency official grants the requested exception, the original written advance determination will be sent to the employee. A duplicate original shall be retained among the appropriate agency records under the control of the Counselor.

Subpart C—Ethical and Other Conduct and Responsibilities of Special Government Employees

§ 1203.735–301 Conflicts of interest.

Special Government employees are subject to the conflicts of interest statutes (18 U.S.C. 202). An explanation of these conflicts of interest statutes their effects upon special Government employees and guidelines for obtaining and utilizing the services of special Government employees are in appendix C of chapter 735 of the Federal Personnel Manual. A special Government employee shall not have a direct or indirect financial interest that conflicts substantially, or appears to conflict substantially, with Government duties and responsibilities.

§ 1203.735–302 Use of Government employment.

A special Government employee shall not use Government employment for a purpose that is, or gives the appearance of being, motivated by the desire for private gain for the employee or another person, particularly one with whom the employee has family, business, or financial ties.

§ 1203.735–303 Use of inside information.

(a) A special Government employee shall not use inside information obtained as a result of Government employment for private gain for the employee or another person either by direct action on the employee's part or by counsel, recommendation, or suggestion to another person, particularly one with whom the employee has family, business, or financial ties. For the purpose of this section, "inside information" means information obtained under Government authority which has not become part of the body of public information.

(b) A special Government employee may engage in teaching, lecturing, or writing that is not prohibited by law, Executive Order 11222 or the restrictions in this part; however, a special Government employee shall not, either for or without compensation, engage in teaching, lecturing, or writing that is dependent on information obtained as a result of his Government employment, except when that information has been made available to the general public or will be made available, or when the head of the agency gives written authoritzation for the use of nonpublic information on the basis that the use is in the public interest. A special Government employee who wishes to request the agency head to authorize the use of nonpublic information should submit such request through the Counselor. The request should contain complete information concerning the nonpublic information which the employee wishes to disclose and should contain in addition an indication of the intended use of such information and how disclosure of it would be in the public interest.

§ 1203.735–304 Coercion.

A special Government employee shall not use Government employment to coerce, or give the appearance of coercing, a person to provide financial benefit to the employee or another person, particularly one with whom the employee has family, business, or financial ties.

§ 1203.735–305 Gifts, entertainment, and favors.

(a) Except as provided in paragraph (b) of this section, a special Government employee, while so employed or in connection with Government employment, shall not receive or solicit from a person having business with the employee's agency anything of value as a gift, gratuity, loan, entertainment, or favor for the employee or another person, particularly one with whom the employee has family, business or financial ties.

(b) The exceptions to the prohibition against the acceptance of gifts which have been granted to employees in § 1203.735–202 (b), (c), and (d) are also applicable to special Government employees.

(c) A special Government employee shall not accept a gift, present, decoration, or other thing from a foreign government unless authorized by Congress as provided by the Constitution and in 5 U.S.C. 7342, and the regulations promulgated thereunder pursuant to E.O. 11320; 31 FR 15789. These regulations are set forth in part 3 of this title (as added, 32 FR 6569, April 28, 1967), and in 3 FAM 621.

(d) A special Government employee shall avoid any action, whether or not specifically prohibited by these sections on special Government employees, which might result in, or create the appearance of:

(1) Using public office for private gain;

(2) Giving preferential treatment to any person;

(3) Impeding Government efficiency or economy;

(4) Losing independence or impartiality;

(5) Making a Government decision outside official channels; or

(6) Affecting adversely the confidence of the public in the integrity of the Government.

§ 1203.735–306 Miscellaneous statutory provisions.

Each special Government employee shall become acquainted with each statute that relates to the employee's ethical and other conduct as a special Government employee of an agency and of the Government. The attention of special Government employees is directed to the statutes listed in § 1203.735–216.

Subpart D—Statements of Employment and Financial Interests

§ 1203.735–401 Employees required to submit statements.

The following employees of IDCA shall submit statements of employment and financial interests:

(a) All special Government employees including experts or consultants serving on a full-time or intermittent basis, except when waived under § 1203.735–402(c).

(b) Employees paid at a level of the Executive Schedule in subchapter II of chapter 53 of title 5, United States Code, except as provided in § 1203.735–402(b).

(c) Except as provided in § 1203.735–402, employees classified at GS–13, FSO–4, FSR–5, FSS–2, AD–13, FC–5, or above, who are in positions hereby identified either as positions the basic duties of which impose upon the incumbent the responsibility for a Government decision or taking a Government action in regard to:

(1) Contracting or procurement;

(2) Administering or monitoring grants or subsidies;

(3) Regulating or auditing private or other non-Federal enterprise;

(4) Other activities where the decision or action has an economic impact on the interests of any non-Federal enterprise, or as positions which have duties and responsibilities which require the incumbent to report employment and financial interests in order to avoid involvement in a possible conflict of interest situation and carry out the purpose of law, Executive order, and the agency's regulations:

STATE

Director General; of the Foreign Service and the Director of Personnel; Director of the Policy Planning Staff; Inspector General; Director, FSI; Special Assistant to Secretary; Deputy Secretary, Under Secretaries, or Deputy Under Secretary; Deputy Assistant Secretary and others at this level or above; Assistant Legal Adviser for Management; Director, Office of Operations; Office Director; Country Director; Division Chief in Bureau of Economic and Business Affairs, in the Office of Operations, (O/OPR), or in the Office of Foreign Buildings; Executive Director; Deputy Chief of Mission; Principal Officer; Economic Counselor; Commercial Counselor; Administrative Counselor; Civil Air Attache; Petroleum Officer; Minerals Officer; Contracting Specialist; Procurement Specialist; Despatch Agent; Traffic Manager; and Traffic Management Specialist.

ICA

Deputy Director, Associate Directors, Directors and Deputy Directors of Offices or Services, Executive or Special Assistants to the Director; Chief Inspector; Associate Chief Inspector; Commissioner General, Deputy Commissioner General, Staff Director (Advisory Commission), Director of Engineering and Technical Operations; Director of Audio-Visual Procurement and Production; Country Public Affairs Officer, Deputy Country Public Affairs Officer, Public Affairs Counselor, Deputy Public Affairs Counselor, Director or Manager of Regional Service Center, Radio Relay Station, Radio Program Center or Radio Relay Station Construction Site, Administrative Officer or Executive Officer at a post abroad, Administrative Officer, Executive Officer and Business Manager (occupational codes 301, 340, 341, and 1101, or FAS code 200); Contracting Specialist and Procurement Specialist (occupational code 1102, or FAS codes 210 and 211); Auditor and Accountant (occupational code 510, or FAS code 207); General Counsel, Deputy General Counsel, or Attorney (occupational code 905, or FAS code 512).

AID

(1) AID/W: Deputy Assistant Administrators, Associate Assistant Administrators, Deputy Associate Assistant Administrators; Heads and Deputy Heads of Offices, Staffs, and Divisions; Desk Officers and Deputy Desk Officers.

(2) Overseas: Mission Directors, Deputy Directors, Assistant Directors, AID Representatives, Aid Affairs Officers, Chairman, Development Assistance Committee; U.S. Representative to Development Assistance Committee; Development Coordination Officer.

(3) Any person serving as chief of an operational branch responsible for housing, loans, guarantees, or other commercial type transactions with the public.

(4) In addition, employees in AID/W or overseas whose positions fall within the following series or position titles (occupational code given in parenthesis): Economist Series (0110); International Cooperation Series (0136); Auditor General (0301.21); Supervisory Housing Development Officer (0301.31); Chief, Housing and Urban Development (0301.35);

Contract Compliance Specialist (0301.48); Director for Regional Activities (0340.08); Development Officer (0340.09); Regional Development Officer (0340.10); Executive Officer (0341.01); Deputy Executive Officer (0341.02); Regional Executive Officer (0341.03); Administrative Officer (0341.05); Executive Officer—Administrative Support (0341.15); Executive Officer, Operations (0341.16); Executive Officer, Real Property (0341.18); Executive Officer, Personnel (0341.19); General Services Officer (0342.01); Assistant General Services Officer (0342.03); Assistant General Services Officer, Property and Supply (0342.20); Assistant General Services Officer, Procurement (0342.23); Assistant General Services Officer, Housing (0342.25); Program Officer (0345.01); Deputy Program Officer (0345.02); Food and Agriculture Officer (0401.01); Deputy Food and Agriculture Officer (0401.02); Budget and Accounting Series (0504); Financial Management Series (0505); Accounting Series (0510); Budget Administration Series (0560); General Attorney Series (0905); General Business and Industry Series (1101); Contract and Procurement Series (1102); Property Disposal Series (1104); Purchasing Series (1105); Trade Specialist Series (1140); Private Resources Development Series (1150); Financial Analysis Series (1160); General Investigating Series (1810); Criminal Investigating Series (1811); Import Specialist Series (1889); General Supply Series (2001); Supply Program Management Series (2003).

§ 1203.735–402 Employees not required to submit statements.

(a) Employees in positions that meet the criteria in paragraph (c) of § 1203.735–401 may be excluded from the reporting requirement when the agency head or designee determines that:

(1) The duties of the position are such that the likelihood of the incumbent's involvement in a conflict-of-interest situation is remote;

(2) The duties of the position are at such a level of responsibility that the submission of a statement of employment and financial interests is not necessary because of the degree of supervision and review over incumbent or the inconsequential effect on the integrity of the Government.

(b) A statement of employment and financial interests is not required by the regulations in this part from an agency head, or a full-time member of a committee, board, or commission appointed by the President. These employees are subject to separate reporting requirements under section 401 of Executive Order 11222.

(c) Special Government employees not required to submit statements. An agency head may waive the requirement of this section for the submission of a statement of employment and financial interest in the case of a special Government employee who is not a consultant or an expert when the agency finds that the duties of the position held by that special Government employee are of a nature and at such a level of responsibility that the submission of the statement by the incumbent is not necessary to protect the integrity of the Government. For the purpose of this paragraph, "consultant" and "expert" have the meanings given those terms by chapter 304 of the Federal Personnel Manual, but do not include a physician, dentist, or allied medical specialist whose services are procured to provide care and service to patients.

§ 1203.735–403 Employee's complaint on filing requirement.

Each employee shall have the opportunity for review through agency grievance procedure of the employee's complaint that the employee's position has been improperly included within § 1203.735–401 as one requiring the submission of a statement of employment and financial interests. Employees are reminded that they may obtain counseling pursuant to § 1203.735–103 prior to filing a complaint.

§ 1203.735–404 Time and place of submission, and forms.

(a) An employee or special Government employee shall submit a statement to the Counselor (in the case of a State employee, through the employee's Bureau) no later than:

(1) Ninety days after the effective date of this part if the employee has entered on duty on or before that effective date; or

(2) At least 10 days prior to entrance on duty, if the employee enters on duty after that effective date; except that an employee or special Government employee who enters on duty within 90 days of the effective date of this part may submit such statement within 90 days after entrance on duty.

(b) Only the original of the statement or supplement thereto required by this part shall be submitted. The individual submitting a statement should retain a copy for the individual's own records.

§ 1203.735–405 Information required.

(a) *Employees.* Employees' statement of employment and financial interests required by the regulations in this part shall be submitted on the form, "Confidential Statement of Employment and Financial Interests (for use by Government Employees)", Form OF–106, and shall contain all the information therein required.

(b) *Special Government employees.* All special Government employees shall submit statements of employment and financial interest on the form, "Confidential Statement of Employment and Financial Interests (for use by Special Government Employees)", Form AID 4–450 for IDCA, and shall contain all the information therein required.

(c) *Interests of employee's relatives.* The interest of a member of an employee's family is considered to be an interest of the employee. The term "member of an employee's family" is defined in § 1203.735–102(f).

(d) *Information not known by employees.* If any information required to be included on a statement of employment and financial interests or supplementary statement, including holdings placed in trust, is not known to the employee but is known to another person, the employee shall request that other person to submit information in the employee's behalf.

(e) *Interests not required to be reported.* An employee need not disclose those financial interests described in § 1203.735–205(c) as being too remote or too inconsequential to affect the integrity of employees' services.

(f) *Information not required.* The regulations in this part do not require an employee to submit on a statement of employment and financial interests or supplementary statement any information relating to the employee's connection with, or interest in, a professional society or a charitable, religious, social, fraternal, recreational, public service, civic, or political organization or a similar organization not conducted as a business enterprise. For the purpose of this section, educational and other institutions doing research and development or related work involving grants or money from or contracts with the Government are deemed "business enterprises" and are required to be included in an employee's statement of employment and financial interests.

§ 1203.735–406 Submission of position description.

Each Statement of Employment and Financial Interests or annual supplement thereto must be accompanied by a full description of the employee's principal governmental duties. The description should be particularly detailed in regard to those duties which might possibly be an element in a conflict of interest. If the statement indicates that the employee has no outside employment or financial interests, the employee need not submit a description of duties. For a special Government employee, the employing office shall submit the description.

§ 1203.735–407 Supplementary statements.

(a) Employees, as defined in paragraphs (b) and (c) of § 1203.735–401, shall report changes in, or additions to, the information contained in their statements of employment and financial interests in supplementary statements as of June 30 each year. If no changes or additions occur, a negative report is required.

(b) All special Government employees, as defined in paragraph (a) of § 1203.735–401, shall submit a current statement at the time their appointments are extended. A supplementary report indicating any changes in, or additions to the information already submitted will be accepted in lieu of a full submission. If there are no changes or additions, a negative report is required.

(c) Notwithstanding the filing of reports required by this section, each employee shall at all times avoid acquiring a financial interest that could result, or taking an action that would result, in a violation of the conflicts-of-interest provisions of section 208 of title 18, United States Code, or subpart B of this part.

(d) An employee is also to keep current the employee's description of principal duties as to changes or additions which might possibly be an element in a conflict of interest. The employing office shall submit descriptions of changes in the principal duties of a special Government employee as they occur.

§ 1203.735–408 Review of statements and determination as to conflicts of interest.

(a) On the basis of the Statement of Employment and Financial Interests submitted by each employee or special Government employee, or on the basis of information received from other sources, the Counselor shall determine, in the light of the duties which that employee or special Government employee is or will be performing, whether any conflicts of interest, real or apparent, are indicated. The Counselor shall make this determination based on the applicable statutes, the Executive order, and the applicable regulations of the Civil Service Commission, and of the agency.

(b) Where the Counselor's determination in a particular case is that a conflict of interest, real or apparent, is indicated, the Counselor shall initiate informal discussions with the employee or special Government employee concerned. These discussions shall have as their objectives:

(1) Providing the individual with a full opportunity to explain the conflict or appearance of conflict; and

(2) Arriving at an agreement (acceptable to the Counselor, the individual and the individual's immediate superior) whereby the conflict of interest may be removed or avoided. Such an agreement may include, but is not limited to: (i) Changes in assigned duties; (ii) divestiture of the financial or employment interest creating the conflict or apparent conflict; or (iii) disqualification for a particular assignment.

(c) Where an acceptable agreement cannot be obtained pursuant to paragraph (b) of this section, the Counselor shall present findings and recommendations to the officer designated by the agency head, who shall decide which remedy is most appropriate to remove or correct that conflict or apparent conflict. Remedial action under this paragraph may include disciplinary action, including separation for cause, or any of the actions enumerated in paragraph (b)(2) of this section and shall be effective in accordance with applicable laws, Executive orders, and regulations.

(d) Written summaries of all agreements and decisions arrived at pursuant to paragraph (b) or (c) of this section shall be placed in the Counselor's files. Copies shall also be made available to the employee or special Government employee concerned.

§ 1203.735–409 Confidentiality of employees' statements.

An agency shall hold each statement of employment and financial interests, and each supplementary statement, in confidence. To insure this confidentiality only the Counselor and Deputy Counselors are authorized to review and retain the statements. The Counselor and Deputy Counselors are responsible for maintaining the statements in confidence and shall not allow access to, or allow information to be disclosed from, a statement except to carry out the purpose of this part. An agency may not disclose information from a statement except as the Civil Service Commission or the agency head may determine for good cause shown.

§ 1203.735–410 Effect of employees' statements on other requirements.

The statements of employment and financial interests and supplementary statements required for employees are in addition to, and not in substitution for, or in derogation of, any similar requirement imposed by law, order, or regulation. The submission of a statement or supplementary statement by an employee does not permit the employee or any other person to participate in a matter in which the employee or the other person's participation is prohibited by law, order, or regulation. Save with respect to those financial interests excepted from the conflict of interest prohibitions of 18 U.S.C. 208(a) pursuant to a written advance determination under § 1203.735–217 or exempted by the provisions of § 1203.735–205(c), an employee must disqualify himself or herself from participating in any matter in which the employee has a financial interest.

§ 1203.735–411 Disqualification procedures.

(a) Where an employee is prohibited from participating in a matter because of a conflicting financial interest that is not exempt under § 1203.735–205(c) or has not been specifically excepted by the appropriate agency official pursuant to § 1203.735–217 in advance of the employee's participation in the particular matter, the employee shall conduct himself or herself in accordance with the following provisions:

(1) The employee shall promptly disclose the financial interest in such matter to the employee's immediate superior. The superior will thereupon relieve the employee of duty and responsibility in the matter.

(2) In foreign posts, it may be impossible or highly impracticable for an employee, who has a disqualifying financial interest, to assign the matter for official action to anyone other than a subordinate. In this event, the employee must instruct the subordinate to report fully and directly to the immediate superior to whom the employee himself or herself would normally report. The employee must concurrently direct such subordinate to take such action as may be appropriate in the matter, and without thereafter revealing to the disqualified employee in any way any aspect of the particular matter.

(b) Nothing herein precludes the employee from disposing of such disqualifying financial interest, thereby wholly eliminating the conflict of interest. In some circumstances, where the employee may not obtain an exception under § 1203.735–217, or may not disqualify himself or herself and refer or assign the matter to another employee, the performance of duty may even require divestiture.

(c) Where a supervisor has reason to believe that a subordinate employee may have a conflicting financial interest, the supervisor should discuss the matter with the employee. If the supervisor finds that a conflict of interest does exist, the supervisor must relieve the subordinate employee of duty and responsibility in the particular matter.

(d) The obligation to avoid conflicts of interest is upon each employee. It is a continuing obligation calling for alert vigilance.

(e) Notwithstanding any other provision of this part to the contrary, if an employee's holdings rise in value above the amount exempted by § 1203.735–205(c), then the statutory and regulation prohibitions apply in a conflict of interest situation.

PARTS 1204–1299 [RESERVED]

CHAPTER XIII—MILLENNIUM CHALLENGE CORPORATION

PART 1300—ORGANIZATION AND FUNCTIONS OF THE MILLENNIUM CHALLENGE CORPORATION

AUTHORITY: 5 U.S.C. 552, as amended.

SOURCE: 72 FR 49192, Aug. 28, 2007, unless otherwise noted.

§ 1300.1 Purpose.

This part describes the organization, functions and operation of the Millennium Challenge Corporation (MCC). MCC is a government corporation (as defined in 5 U.S.C. 103) established by the Millennium Challenge Act of 2003 (Pub. L. 108–199, 118 Stat. 211.) Information about MCC is available from its Web site, *http://www.mcc.gov.*

§ 1300.2 Organization.

(a) MCC's Board consists of: (1) The Secretary of State, the Secretary of the Treasury, the Administrator of the United States Agency for International Development, the United States Trade Representative; and the Chief Executive Officer of the Corporation; and (2) four other individuals with relevant international experience from the private sector; appointed by the President with the advice and consent of the Senate.

(b) MCC's staff is comprised of the following administrative units:

(1) The Office of the Chief Executive Officer;

(2) The Department of Accountability;

(3) The Department of Administration and Finance;

(4) The Department of Congressional and Public Affairs;

(5) The Department of Operations;

(6) The Department of Policy and International Relations; and

(7) The Office of the General Counsel.

§ 1300.3 Functions.

(a) MCC provides United States assistance for global development; and

(b) Provides such assistance in a manner that promotes economic growth and the elimination of extreme poverty and strengthens good governance, economic freedom, and investments in people.

§ 1300.4 Operations.

In exercising its functions, duties, and responsibilities, MCC utilizes:

(a) MCC staff, consisting of specialized offices performing specialized, administrative, legal and financial work for the Board.

(b) Rules published in the FEDERAL REGISTER and codified in this title of the Code of Federal Regulations.

(c) Meetings of the Board of Directors conducted pursuant to the Government in the Sunshine Act or voting by notation as provided in section 1300.5(b).

§ 1300.5 Quorum and voting requirements.

(a) *Quorum requirements.* A majority of the members of the Board shall constitute a quorum, which shall include at least one private sector member of the Board.

(b) *Voting.* The Board votes on items of business in meetings conducted pursuant to the Government in the Sunshine Act.

§ 1300.6 Office location.

The principal offices of the Millennium Challenge Corporation are located at 875 Fifteenth Street, NW., Washington, DC 20005–2221.

PART 1304—PRODUCTION OR DISCLOSURE OF INFORMATION

Subpart A—Procedures for Requests for Disclosure of Records Under the Freedom of Information Act

Subpart B—[Reserved]

AUTHORITY: 5 U.S.C. 552, as amended.

SOURCE: 83 FR 35544, July 27, 2018, unless otherwise noted.

Subpart A—Procedures for Requests for Disclosure of Records Under the Freedom of Information Act

§ 1304.1 General provisions.

This part contains the rules that the Millennium Challenge Corporation ("MCC") follows in processing requests for records under the Freedom of Information Act ("FOIA") (5 U.S.C. 552). The rules in this part should be read in conjunction with the text of the FOIA and the Uniform Freedom of Information Act Fee Schedule and Guidelines published by the Office of Management and Budget ("OMB Fee Guidelines"). In addition, the MCC FOIA web page contains information about the specific procedures particular to MCC with respect to making FOIA requests. This resource is available at *www.mcc.gov/resources/foia*.

§ 1304.2 Definitions.

Administrative appeal. An independent review of the initial determination made in response to a FOIA request.

Agency. Any executive department, military department, government corporation, government controlled corporation, or other establishment in the executive branch of the Federal Government or any independent regulatory agency.

Business day or work day. A day of the week, excluding Saturday, Sunday, or legal public holidays.

Calendar days. Every day within a month, including Saturday, Sunday, and legal public holidays. Unless identified as a "business day" or "work day," all timeframes and days noted in this part shall be calculated in calendar days.

Chief FOIA Officer. A designated MCC employee who is a senior official, at the Assistant Secretary or equivalent level who, subject to the authority of the head of the agency, shall have agency wide responsibility for efficient and appropriate compliance with the FOIA. In addition, the Chief FOIA Officer shall monitor implementation of the FOIA throughout MCC and keep the head of the agency, the chief legal officer of the agency, and the Attorney General appropriately informed of the agency's performance in implementing the FOIA; recommend to the head of the agency such adjustments to MCC's practices, policies, personnel, and funding as may be necessary to improve its implementation of the FOIA; facilitate public understanding of the purposes of the statutory exemptions of the FOIA; offer training to MCC staff regarding their responsibilities under the FOIA, serve as the primary agency liaison with the Office of Government Information Services and the Office of Information policy; and designate one (1) or more FOIA Public Liaisons. The Chief FOIA Officer shall review, not less frequently than annually, all aspects of the administration of the FOIA by MCC to ensure compliance with the requirements of the FOIA, including—agency regulations; disclosure of records; assessment of fees and determination of eligibility for fee waivers; timely processing of requests for information; the use of exemptions; and dispute resolution services with the assistance of the Office of Government Information Services or the FOIA Public Liaison.

Commercial requester. Any person making a request for information for a use or purpose that furthers a commercial, trade, or profit interest, which can include furthering those interests through litigation.

Complex request. A FOIA request that MCC anticipates will involve a voluminous amount of material to review or will be time-consuming to process.

Confidential commercial information. Records provided to the government that contain material exempt from disclosure under Exemption 4 of the FOIA and disclosure of such records could reasonably be expected to cause substantial competitive harm.

Consultation. When MCC locates a record that contains information of interest to another agency, MCC shall ask the interested agency for their views on disclosing the records before any final determination is made.

Direct costs. Expenditures actually incurred by MCC for searching, duplicating, and in the case of commercial use requests, reviewing records in order to respond to a FOIA request.

Discretionary disclosure. The release of or portions of records to a FOIA requester that could be withheld by MCC under one or more of the FOIA exemptions.

Duplication. The process of making a copy of a record in order to respond to a FOIA request, including but not limited to paper copies, microfilm, audio-video materials, and computer diskettes or other electronic copies.

Duplication fees. The estimated direct costs of making a copy of a record in order to respond to a FOIA request.

Educational institution. Any school or institution that operates a program of scholarly research. A requester in this category must show that the request is made in connection with his or her role at the educational institution.

Educational requester. A student who makes a request in furtherance of their coursework or other school-sponsored activities and provides a copy of a course syllabus or other reasonable documentation to indicate the research purpose for the request, would qualify as part of this fee category.

Exemptions. Certain categories of information that are not required to be released in response to a FOIA request because release would be harmful to governmental or private interests.

Fee waiver. The waiver or reduction of processing fees if a requester can demonstrate that certain statutory standards are satisfied including that the information is in the public interest and is not requested for a commercial interest.

FOIA Appeals Officer. The MCC employee who is responsible for conducting an independent review of the initial determination of the FOIA request after the requester has requested an administrative appeal.

FOIA Public Liaison. The MCC employee who is responsible for assisting in the resolution of disputes in response to FOIA requests.

FOIA Program Officer. The MCC employee who receives and processes requests within the MCC FOIA Office.

Non-commercial scientific institution. An institution that does not operate on a commercial basis, but operates solely for the purpose of conducting scientific research and the results of the scientific research are not intended to promote any particular product or industry.

Record. Any item, collection, or grouping of information maintained by MCC in any form or format, including an electronic copy. A "record" can potentially constitute an entire document, a single page of a multipage document, an individual paragraph of a document, or an email within an email chain.

Referral. When an agency locates a record that originated with, or is of otherwise primary interest to another agency, it will forward that record to the other agency to process the record and to provide the final determination directly to the requester.

Representative of the news media. Any person or entity that gathers information of potential interest to a segment of the public, uses its editorial skills to turn the raw materials into a distinct work, and distributes that work to an audience. The term "news" means information that is about current events or that would be of current interest to the public. Examples of news media entities include television or radio stations that broadcast "news" to the public at large and publishers of periodicals that disseminate "news" and make their products available through a variety of means to the general public, including news organizations that disseminate solely on the internet. A request for records supporting the news-dissemination function of the requester will not be considered to be for a commercial use. "Freelance" journalists who demonstrate a solid basis for expecting publication through a news media entity will be considered as a representative of the news media. A publishing contract would provide the clearest evidence that publication is expected; however, agencies can also consider a requester's past publication record in making this determination.

Review. The process of examining a record to determine whether all or part of the record may be released or withheld, and includes redacting or otherwise processing the record for disclosure to a requester. The review process does not include time spent resolving legal or policy issues regarding the application of exemptions to a record. The review process also does not include time spent reviewing records at the administrative appeal level unless, MCC determines that the exemption under which it withheld records does not apply and the records are reviewed again to determine whether a different exemption may apply.

Requester category. One of the three categories that agencies place requesters in for the purpose of determining whether a requester will be charged fees for search, review and duplication, including commercial requesters; noncommercial scientific or educational institutions or news media requesters, and all other requesters.

Search. The time spent locating records that may be responsive to a request, manually or by electronic means, including page-by-page or line-by-line identification of responsive material within a record.

Search fees. Estimated direct costs of the time spent locating records by either manual or electronic means.

Submitter. Any person or entity who provides information directly or indirectly to MCC. The term includes, but is not limited to, corporations, state governments, and foreign governments.

§ 1304.3 Proactive disclosure of MCC records.

Records that are required by the FOIA to be made available for public inspection in an electronic format may be accessed through the MCC website. MCC is responsible for determining which of its records are required to be made publicly available, identifying additional records in the interest of the public that are appropriate for public disclosure, and posting such records. MCC shall ensure that its website of posted records is reviewed and updated on an ongoing basis. The FOIA Program Officer may assist individuals in locating records on the MCC website and FOIA reading room.

§ 1304.4 Requirements for making requests.

(a) Requests for access to, or copies of, MCC records other than those identified in § 1304.3, shall be in writing and addressed to the MCC Chief FOIA Officer at 1099 14th St. NW, Washington, DC 20005 or *FOIA@mcc.gov*. All requests for records shall be deemed to have been made pursuant to the FOIA, regardless of whether the request specifically mentions the Freedom of Information Act. To facilitate processing, the requester should place the phrase "FOIA REQUEST" in capital letters on the front of the envelope or subject line of the email.

(b) Each request shall include the following:

(1) A description of the record(s) that provides sufficient detail to enable MCC to locate the record(s) with a reasonable amount of effort; such as the date, title or name, author, recipient, subject matter of the record, case number, file designation, or reference number. Before submitting their requests, requesters may contact the MCC FOIA Program Officer to discuss the records the are seeking and receive assistance in describing the records;

(2) The preferred format of the records;

(3) The requestor's full name, mailing address or email address, and telephone number where the requester can be reached during business hours; and

(4) If applicable, the maximum amount the requester is willing to pay or dollar limit on the fees MCC may incur to respond to the request for records. When this information is specified, MCC shall not exceed such limit.

(c) If a request does not meet all of the requirements of paragraph (b) of this section, the FOIA Program Officer may advise the requester that additional information is needed. Requesters who are attempting to reformulate or modify a request may engage with the MCC Program Officer to clarify their request.

§ 1304.5 Responsibility for acknowledgment and initial determinations.

(a) Upon receipt of a request for records, the FOIA Program Officer will acknowledge receipt of the request in writing within ten (10) business days. In responding to a request for records, MCC shall make reasonable efforts to search for the records in electronic format, except when such efforts would significantly interfere with the operation of the agency's automated information system.

(b) The Chief FOIA Officer shall make an initial determination, within twenty (20) business days, to either grant or deny, in whole or in part, a request for records. If the Chief FOIA Officer shall notify the requester making such a request of the following information:

(1) The determination whether grant or deny the request and reasons for the determination;

(2) The right of the requester to seek assistance from the FOIA Public Liaison; and in the case of an adverse determination;

(3) The right of the requester to seek dispute resolution services via the Office of Government Information Services of the National Archives and Records Administration (OGIS); and

(4) The right to file an administrative appeal to the FOIA Appeals Officer within 90 calendar days after the date of the adverse determination.

§ 1304.6 Timing of responses to requests.

(a) *General information.* The twenty (20) business day period identified in § 1304.5(b) shall commence on the date that the request is first received by the MCC FOIA office and an acknowledgment of the request shall be sent no later than ten (10) business days after receipt of the request. The twenty (20) business day period shall not be tolled except that MCC may make one request to the requester for information and toll the twenty (20) business day period while it is awaiting receipt of the information, or the twenty (20) business day period may be tolled if it is necessary to clarify issues regarding fees with the requester.

(b) *Unusual circumstances.* If MCC cannot meet the statutory time limit for processing a request because of "unusual circumstances" as defined in the FOIA and MCC extends the time limit on that basis, MCC will, before expiration of the twenty (20) business day period, notify the requester in writing of the unusual circumstances involved and of the date by which MCC estimates processing of the request will be completed. Where the extension exceeds ten (10) business days, MCC will provide the requester with an opportunity to modify the request or arrange an alternative time period for processing the original or modified request. MCC must make its designated FOIA Program Officer or FOIA Public Liaison available for this purpose. To aid the requester, the MCC FOIA Public Liaison shall assist in the resolution of any disputes between the requester and MCC, and notify the requester of the right to seek dispute resolution services from the Office of Government Information Services.

(c) *Aggregating requests.* MCC may aggregate requests where it reasonably appears that multiple requests, submitted either by a requester or by a group of requesters acting in concert, constitute a single request that would otherwise involve unusual circumstances. Requests that involve unrelated matters shall not be aggregated.

(d) *Multitrack processing.* MCC may use multitrack processing in responding to requests. This process entails separating simple requests that require rather limited review from more lengthy and complex requests. Requests in each track are then processed in their respective track. The FOIA Program Officer may provide requesters in the slower track an opportunity to limit the scope of their requests in order to decrease the processing time required. The FOIA Program Officer may provide the opportunity to limit the scope of the request by contacting the requester by letter, email, or telephone.

(e) *Expedited processing of requests.* The FOIA Program Officer must determine whether to grant a request for expedited processing within ten (10) calendar days of its receipt. Requests will receive expedited processing if one of the following criteria are met:

(1) The requester can establish that failure to receive the records quickly could reasonably be expected to pose an imminent threat to the life or physical safety of an individual;

(2) The requester is primarily engaged in disseminating information and can demonstrate that an urgency to inform the public concerning actual

or alleged Federal Government activity exists; or

(3) As determined by the Chief FOIA Officer.

(f) *Written expedited requests.* A requester who seeks expedited processing must submit a written statement explaining in detail the basis for making the request for expedited processing. This statement must be certified to be true and correct. The MCC Chief FOIA Officer may waive the formal certification requirement.

§ 1304.7 Responses to requests.

(a) *General information.* MCC, to the extent practicable, will communicate with requesters who have access to the internet via email or web portal.

(b) *Acknowledgment of requests.* MCC shall acknowledge the request in writing and assign a tracking number for processing purposes.

(c) *Estimated dates of completion and interim responses.* Upon request, MCC shall provide an estimated response date. If a request involves a voluminous amount of material or searches in multiple locations, MCC shall provide interim responses by releasing the records on a rolling basis.

(d) *Granting requests.* MCC will notify the requestor in writing if it determines that it will grant a request in full or in part. MCC shall inform the requester of any fees charged and shall disclose the requested records to the requester promptly upon payment of any applicable fees.

(e) *Partial grant of requests.* MCC shall consider whether partial disclosure of information is possible whenever the agency determines that a full disclosure of a requested record is not possible. MCC shall take reasonable steps necessary to segregate and release nonexempt information.

(f) *Denial or adverse determination of requests.* Except as otherwise provided in this part, MCC shall withhold information only if—

(1) It reasonably foresees that disclosure would harm an interest protected by an exemption under the FOIA or disclosure is prohibited by law;

(2) The request does not reasonably describe the records sought;

(3) The information sought is not a record subject to the FOIA;

(4) The information sought does not exist, cannot be located, or has been destroyed; or

(5) The records are not in the readily producible form or format sought by the requester.

(g) *Markings on released documents.* Records disclosed in part shall be marked clearly to show the amount of information deleted and the exemption under which the deletion was made unless doing so would harm an interest protected by an applicable exemption.

§ 1304.8 Confidential commercial information.

(a) *Designation of confidential commercial information.* A submitter of confidential commercial information must use good faith efforts to designate by appropriate markings, either at the time of the submission or within a reasonable time thereafter, any portion of its submission that it considers to be protected from disclosure under Exemption 4 of the FOIA. These designations shall expire ten (10) years after the date of submission unless the submitter requests and provides justification for a longer designation period.

(b) *Required notice.* Written notice shall be provided to a submitter of confidential commercial information whenever records containing such information are requested under the FOIA if, after reviewing the request, the responsive records, and any appeal by the requester, it is determined that MCC may be required to disclose the records, provided:

(1) The requested information has been designated in good faith by the submitter as information considered protected from disclosure under Exemption 4 of the FOIA; or

(2) MCC has reason to believe that the requested information may be protected from disclosure under Exemption 4 of the FOIA, but has not yet determined whether the information is protected from disclosure under that exemption or any other applicable exemption.

(c) *Information.* The notices shall either describe the commercial information requested or include a copy of the requested records or portions of records containing information. In cases involving a voluminous number of submitters, notice may be made by posting or publishing the notice in a place or manner reasonably likely to accomplish it.

(d) *Exceptions to notice requirements.* The notices requirements of this section shall not apply if:

(1) The Chief FOIA Officer determines that the information is exempt under the FOIA;

(2) The information has been lawfully published or has officially been made available to the public;

(3) Disclosure of the information is required by a statute other than the FOIA or by a regulation issued in accordance with the requirements of Executive Order 12600 of June 23, 1987; or

(4) The designation made by the submitter under paragraph (b) of this section appears obviously frivolous, except that, in such a case, the component shall give the submitter written notice of any final decision to disclose the information and must provide that notice within a reasonable number of days prior to the disclosure date.

(e) *Opportunity to object to disclosure.* A submitter may provide the Chief FOIA Officer with a detailed written statement of any objection to disclosure within ten (10) days of notification. The statement shall specify all grounds for withholding any of the information under any exemption of the FOIA, and if Exemption 4 applies, shall demonstrate the reasons the submitter believes the information to be confidential commercial information that is exempt from disclosure. Whenever possible, the submitter's claim of confidentiality shall be supported by a statement or certification by an officer or authorized representative of the submitter. In the event a submitter fails to respond to the notice in the time specified, the submitter will be considered to have no objection to the disclosure of the information. Information provided by the submitter that is received after the disclosure decision has been made will not be considered. Information provided by a submitter pursuant to this paragraph may itself be subject to disclosure under the FOIA.

(f) *Notice of intent to disclose.* The Chief FOIA Officer shall consider a submitter's objections and specific grounds for nondisclosure prior to determining whether to disclose the information requested. Whenever the Chief FOIA Officer determines that disclosure is appropriate, the Chief FOIA Officer shall, within a reasonable number of days prior to disclosure, provide the submitter with written notice of the intent to disclose which shall include a statement of the reasons for which the submitter's objections were overruled, a description of the information to be disclosed, and a specific disclosure date. The Chief FOIA Officer shall also notify the requester that the requested records will be made available.

(g) *Notice of lawsuit.* If the requester files a lawsuit seeking to compel disclosure of confidential commercial information, MCC shall promptly notify the submitter of this action. If a submitter files a lawsuit seeking to prevent disclosure of confidential commercial information, MCC shall promptly notify the requester.

§ 1304.9 Administrative appeals.

(a) *Requirements for appealing an adverse determination.* A requester may appeal any adverse determination to MCC. The requester must submit a written notice of appeal and it must be postmarked or, in the case of electronic submissions, transmitted within ninety (90) calendar days after the date of the response. The appeal should clearly identify the determination that is being appealed and the assigned tracking number. To facilitate handling, the requester should mark both the appeal letter and envelope, or subject line of the electronic transmission, "Freedom of Information Act Appeal."

(b) *Appeals address.* Requesters can submit appeals by mail by addressing it to Millennium Challenge Corporation, Attn.: FOIA Appeals Officer, 1099 14th St. NW, Washington, DC 20005 or online at *FOIA@mcc.gov.*

(c) *Adjudication of appeals.* The MCC FOIA Appeals Officer will adjudicate the appeal within twenty (20) business days after the receipt of such appeal. An appeal ordinarily will not be adjudicated if the request becomes a matter of the subject of litigation. On receipt of any appeal involving classified information, the MCC FOIA Appeals Officer must take appropriate action to ensure compliance with applicable classification rules.

(d) *Final agency determinations.* The FOIA Appeals Officer shall issue a final written determination, stating the basis for the decision, within twenty (20) business days after receipt of a notice of appeal. Any decision that upholds MCC's determination in whole or in part must contain a statement that identifies the reason(s) for the decision, including any FOIA exemptions applied. The decision will provide the requester with notification of the statutory right to file a lawsuit and will inform the requester of the dispute resolution services offered by the OGIS of the National Archives and Records Administration as a non-exclusive alternative to litigation. If the Chief FOIA Officer's decision is remanded or modified on appeal, the FOIA Appeals Officer will notify the requester of the determination in writing. MCC will then further process the request in accordance with the appeal determination and will respond directly to the requester.

(e) *Engaging in dispute resolution services provided by OGIS.* Dispute resolution is a voluntary process. If MCC agrees to participate in the dispute resolution services provided by OGIS, MCC will actively engage as a partner to the process in an attempt to resolve the dispute.

(f) *When an appeal is required.* Before seeking review by a court of MCC's adverse determination, a requester generally must first submit a timely administrative appeal.

§ 1304.10 Preservation of records.

MCC shall preserve all correspondence pertaining to the requests that it receives under this part, as well as copies of all requested records, until disposition or destruction is authorized pursuant to Title 44 of the United States Code or the General Records Schedule 4.2 of the National Archives and Records Administration. MCC shall not dispose of or destroy records while they are the subject of a pending request, appeal, or lawsuit under the FOIA.

§ 1304.11 Fees.

(a) *General information.* (1) MCC's fee provisions are governed by the FOIA and by the Office of Management and Budget's Uniform FOIA Fee Schedule and Guidelines. For purposes of assessing fees, the FOIA establishes the following categories of requesters:

(i) Commercial use;

(ii) Non-commercial scientific or educational institutions;

(iii) Representative of the news media; and

(iv) All other requesters.

(2) Fees will be assessed pursuant to the category of requester and detailed in paragraph (b) of this section. Requesters may seek a fee waiver. To resolve any fee issues that arise under this section, MCC may contact a requester for additional information. MCC will ensure that searches, review, and duplication are conducted in the most efficient and the least expensive manner. MCC ordinarily will collect all applicable fees before sending copies of records to a requester. Requesters must pay fees to the Treasury of the United States. All fee information is available at *www.mcc.gov/resources/foia.*

(b) *Charging fees.* Because the fee amounts provided already account for the direct costs associated with the given fee type, MCC will not add any additional costs to charges calculated under this section. In responding to FOIA requests, MCC shall charge fees for the following unless a waiver or reduction of fees has been granted:

(1) *Search time fees.* Search time includes page-by-page or line-by-line identification of information within records and the reasonable efforts expended to locate and retrieve information from electronic records.

(i) Requests made by education institutions, non-commercial scientific institutions, or representatives of the news media are not subject to search time fees. Search time fees shall be charged for all other requesters, subject to the restrictions identified in this section. MCC may properly charge for time spent searching even if no responsive records are located if it is determined that the records are entirely exempt from disclosure.

(ii) Requesters shall be charged the direct costs associated with conducting any searches that require the creation of a new computer program to locate the requested records. Requesters shall be notified of the costs associated with creating such a program and must agree to pay the associated costs before the costs may be incurred.

(iii) For requests that require the retrieval of records stored by an agency at the Federal Records Centers operated by the National Archives and Records Administration (NARA), additional costs shall be charged in accordance with the Transactional Billing Range Schedule established by NARA.

(2) *Duplication fees.* Duplication fees shall be charged to all requesters, subject to the restrictions in this section. MCC shall honor a requester's preference for receiving a record in a particular form or format where it is readily reproducible by MCC in the form or format requested. Where photocopies are supplied, MCC shall provide one copy per request and charge fees calculated per page. For copies of records produced on tapes, disks, or other media, MCC shall charge the direct costs of producing the copy, including operator time. Where paper documents must be scanned in order to comply with a requester's preference to receive the records in an electronic format, the requester shall be charged direct costs associated with scanning those materials. For other forms of duplication, MCC shall charge the direct costs.

(3) *Review.* Review fees shall be charged to requesters who make commercial use requests. Review fees shall be assessed in connection with the initial review of the record. No charge will be made for review at the administrative appeal state of exemptions applied at the initial review stage. If a particular exemption is deemed to no longer apply, any costs associated with MCC's subsequent review following the administrative appeal of the records in order to consider the use of other exemptions may be assessed as review fees.

(c) *Restrictions on charging fees.* The following restrictions shall apply to MCC FOIA requests:

(1) If MCC fails to comply with the FOIA's time limits to respond to a request, MCC may not charge fees, except as described in paragraphs (c)(3) through (5) of this section;

(2) If MCC has determined that unusual circumstances as defined by the FOIA apply and the agency provided timely written notice to the requester in accordance with the FOIA, a failure to comply with the time limit shall be excused for an additional ten (10) calendar days;

(3) If MCC has determined that unusual circumstances as defined by the FOIA apply, and more than five-thousand (5,000) pages are necessary to respond to the request, MCC may charge search time fees or duplication fees where applicable, if MCC has provided timely written notice of the unusual circumstances to the requester in accordance with the FOIA and has discussed with the requester via written mail, email, or telephone (or made a minimum of three (3) good-faith attempts to do so) how the requester could effectively limit the scope of the request;

(4) If a court has determined that exceptional circumstances exist as defined by the FOIA, a failure to comply with the time limits shall be excused for the length of time provided by the court order; and

(5) No search time or review fees will be charged for a quarter-hour period unless more than half of that period is required for search or review.

(d) *Fee exceptions.* Except for requesters seeking records for commercial use, MCC shall provide without charge:

(1) The first one-hundred (100) pages of duplication (or the cost equivalent for other media); and

(2) The first two (2) hours of search time. When, after deducting the first one-hundred (100) free pages (or its cost equivalent) and the first two (2) hours of search time, a total fee calculated under this section is $25.00 or less for any request, no fee will be charged.

(e) *Notice of anticipated fees in excess of $25.00.* (1) When MCC determines that the fees to be assessed will exceed $25.00, the requester shall be notified of the actual or estimated amount of the fees, including the breakdown of the fees for search time, review or duplication, unless the requester has indicated a willingness to pay fees as high as those anticipated. If only a portion of the fee can be estimated readily, MCC shall advise the requester accordingly. If the requester is not a commercial use requester, the notice shall specify that the requester is entitled to the statutory requirements of one-hundred (100) pages of duplication at no charge and, if the requester is charged search time fees, two (2) hours of search time at no charge, and shall advise the requester whether those entitlements have been provided.

(2) In cases in which a requester has been notified that the actual or estimated fees are in excess of $25.00, the request shall not be considered received and further work will not be completed until the requester commits, in writing, to pay the actual or estimated total fee, or designates some amount of fees the requester is willing to pay, or in the case of a requester who is not a commercial use requester who has not yet been provided with the requester's statutory entitlements, designates that the requester seeks only that which can be provided by the statutory entitlements. The requester must provide the commitment or designation in writing, and must, when applicable designate an exact dollar amount the requester is willing to pay. MCC is not required to accept payments in installments.

(3) If the requester has indicated a willingness to pay some designated amount of fees, and MCC estimates that the total fee will exceed that amount, MCC shall toll the processing of the request when it notifies the requester of the estimated fees in excess of the amount the requester has indicated a willingness to pay. MCC shall inquire whether the requester wishes to revise the amount of fees the requester is willing to pay or modify the request. Once the requester responds, the time to respond will resume from where it was at the date of the notification.

(4) The FOIA Program Officer will assist any requester in reformulating a request to meet the requester's needs at a lower cost.

(f) *Waiver or reduction of fees*. Documents shall be furnished without charge or at a charge below that listed in this section based upon information provided by a requester or otherwise made known to the Chief FOIA Officer that disclosure of the requested information is in the public interest. Disclosure is in the public interest if it is likely to contribute significantly to public understanding of government operations and is not primarily for commercial purposes. Requests for a waiver or reduction of fees shall be considered on a case by case basis. Where only some of the records to be released satisfy the requirements for waiver of fees, a waiver shall be granted to those records. In order to determine whether the fee waiver requirement is met, the Chief FOIA Officer shall consider the following factors:

(1) The subject of the request. Whether the subject of the requested records concerns the operations or activities of the government;

(2) The informative value of the information to be disclosed; and

(3) The significance of the contribution to public understanding.

(g) *Fees pending a waiver request*. Requests for a waiver or reduction of fees should be made when the request is first submitted to the agency and should address the criteria referenced in this section. A requester may submit a fee waiver request at a later time so long as the underlying record request is pending or on administrative appeal. When a requester who has committed to pay fees subsequently asks for a waiver of those fees and that waiver is denied, the requester must pay any costs incurred up to the date the fee waiver request was received.

(h) *Types of requesters*. There are four categories of FOIA requesters: Commercial use requesters, educational and non-commercial scientific institutional requesters; representatives of the news media; and all other requesters. The following specific levels of fees are prescribed for each of these categories:

(1) Commercial requesters shall be charged the full direct costs of searching for, reviewing, and duplicating requested records;

(2) Educational and non-commercial scientific institution requesters shall be charged for document duplication only and the first one-hundred (100) pages of paper copies shall be provided without charge;

(3) Representative of the news media requesters shall be charged for document duplication costs only, except that the first one-hundred (100) pages of paper copies shall be provided without charge; and

(4) All other requesters who do not fall into any of the categories in paragraphs (h)(1) through (3) of this section shall be charged fees which recover the full reasonable direct costs incurred for searching for and reproducing records if that total costs exceeds $25.00, except that the first one-hundred (100) pages of duplication and the first two hours of manual search time shall not be charged.

(i) *Charges for unsuccessful searches.* If the requester has been notified of the estimated cost of the search time and has been advised specifically that the requested records may not exist or may be withheld as exempt, fees may be charged.

(j) *Charges for other services.* Although MCC is not required to provide special services, if it chooses to do so as a matter of administrative discretion, the direct costs of providing the service shall be charged. Examples of such services include certifying that records are true copies, providing multiple copies of the same document, or sending records by means other than first class mail.

(k) *Charging interest.* MCC may charge interest on any unpaid bill starting on the 31st day following the date of billing the requester. Interest charges shall be assessed at the rate provided in 31 U.S.C. 3717 and will accrue from the billing date until payment is received. MCC shall follow the provisions of the Debt Collection Act of 1982, as amended, and its administrative procedures, including the use consumer reporting agencies, collection agencies, and offset.

(l) *Aggregating requests.* The requester or a group of requesters may not submit multiple requests at the same time, each seeking portions of a document or documents solely in order to avoid payment of fees. When the FOIA Program Officer reasonably believes that a requester is attempting to divide a request into a series of requests to evade an assessment of fees, the FOIA Program Officer may aggregate such requests and charge accordingly. MCC may presume that multiple requests of this type made within a thirty (30) calendar day period have been made in order to avoid fees. For requests separated by a longer period, MCC will aggregate them only where there is a reasonable basis for determining that aggregation is warranted in view of all the circumstances involved. Multiple requests involving unrelated matters cannot be aggregated.

(m) *Advance payment of fees.* (1) MCC may require an advanced payment of fees if the requestor previously failed to pay fees or if the FOIA Program Officer determines the total fee will exceed $250.00. When payment is required in advance of the processing of a request, the time limits prescribed in §1304.5 shall not be deemed to begin until the requester has paid the assessed fees.

(2) In cases in which MCC requires advance payment, the request will not be considered received and further work will not be completed until the required payment is received. If the requester does not pay the advance payment within thirty (30) calendar days after the date of the fee determination, the request will be closed. Where it is anticipated that the cost of providing the requested record will exceed $25.00 but falls below $250.00 after the free duplication and search time has been calculated, MCC may, in its discretion may require either an advance deposit of the entire estimated charges or written confirmation of the requester's willingness to pay such charges.

(3) Where the requester has previously failed to pay a properly charged FOIA fee within thirty (30) calendar days of the billing date, MCC may require the requester to pay the full amount due plus any applicable interest on that prior request, and/or require that the requester make an advance payment of the full amount of the anticipated fee before MCC begins a new request or continues to process a pending request or any pending appeal. If MCC has a reasonable basis to believe that a requester has misrepresented the requester's identity in order to avoid paying outstanding fees, MCC may require that the requester provide proof of identity.

§ 1304.12 Other rights and services.

Nothing in this part shall be construed to entitle any person a right to any service or to the disclosure of any record to which such person is not entitled under the FOIA.

Subpart B—[Reserved]

PART 1305—RELEASE OF OFFICIAL INFORMATION AND TESTIMONY BY MCC PERSONNEL AS WITNESSES

AUTHORITY: 5 U.S.C. 301.

SOURCE: 79 FR 44278, July 31, 2014, unless otherwise noted.

§ 1305.1 Purpose and scope.

Pursuant to 5 U.S.C. 301, the head of an executive department or military department may prescribe regulations for the government of his/her department, the conduct of its employees, the distribution and performance of its business, and the custody, use, and preservation of its records, papers, and property. Section 301 does not authorize withholding information from the public or limiting the availability of records to the public. This part contains the regulations of the Millennium Challenge Corporation (MCC) concerning procedures to be followed when a request, subpoena, order or other demand (hereinafter in this part referred to as a "demand") of a court or other authorities in any state or federal proceeding is issued for the production or disclosure of:

(a) Any material contained in the files of MCC;

(b) Any information relating to materials contained in the files of MCC; or

(c) Any information or material acquired by an employee of MCC during the performance of the employee's official duties or because of the employee's official status.

§ 1305.2 Definitions.

For purposes of this part:

(a) *Demand* means a request, order, or subpoena for testimony or documents related to or for possible use in a legal proceeding.

(b) *Document* means any record or other property, no matter what media and including copies thereof, held by MCC, including without limitation, official letters, telegrams, memoranda, reports, studies, calendar and diary entries, maps, graphs, pamphlets, notes, charts, tabulations, analyses, statistical or informational accumulations, any kind of summaries of meetings and conversations, film impressions, magnetic tapes and sound or mechanical reproductions.

(c) *Employee* means all employees and officers of MCC, including contractors who have been appointed by, or are subject to the supervision, jurisdiction or control of MCC. The procedures established within this part also apply to former employees and contractors of MCC.

(d) *General Counsel* means the General Counsel or MCC employee to whom the General Counsel has delegated authority to act under this subpart.

§ 1305.3 Production prohibited unless approved.

No employee or former employee shall, in response to a demand of a court or other authority, disclose any information relating to materials contained in the files of MCC, or disclose any information or produce any material acquired as part of the performance of the person's official duties, or because of the person's official status, without the prior, written approval of the General Counsel.

§ 1305.4 Factors to be considered by the General Counsel.

(a) In deciding whether to authorize the release of official information or the testimony of employees concerning official information, the General Counsel shall consider the following factors:

(1) Whether the demand is unduly burdensome;

(2) MCC's ability to maintain impartiality in conducting its business;

(3) Whether the time and money of the United States would be used for private purposes;

(4) The extent to which the time of employees for conducting official business would be compromised;

(5) Whether the public might misconstrue variances between personal opinions of employees and MCC policy;

(6) Whether the demand demonstrates that the information requested is relevant and material to the action pending, genuinely necessary to the proceeding, unavailable from other sources, and reasonable in its scope;

(7) Whether the number of similar demands would have a cumulative effect on the expenditure of agency resources;

(8) Whether disclosure otherwise would be inappropriate under the circumstances; and

(9) Any other factor that is appropriate.

(b) Among those demands in response to which compliance will not ordinarily be authorized are those with respect to which any of the following factors exists:

(1) The disclosure would violate a statute, Executive order, or regulation;

(2) The integrity of the administrative and deliberative processes of MCC would be compromised;

(3) The disclosure would not be appropriate under the rules of procedure governing the case or matter in which the demand arose;

(4) The disclosure, including release in camera, is not appropriate or necessary under the relevant substantive law concerning privilege;

(5) The disclosure, except when in camera and necessary to assert a claim of privilege, would reveal information properly classified or other matters exempt from unrestricted disclosure; or

(6) The disclosure would interfere with ongoing enforcement proceedings, compromise constitutional rights, reveal the identity of an intelligence source or confidential informant, or disclose trade secrets or similarly confidential commercial or financial information.

§ 1305.5 Service of demands.

Demands for official documents, information or testimony must be in writing, and served on the General Counsel, Millennium Challenge Corporation, 875 Fifteenth Street NW., Washington, DC 20005–2221.

§ 1305.6 Processing demands.

(a) After service of a demand to produce or disclose official documents and information, the General Counsel will review the demand and, in accordance with the provisions of this subpart, determine whether, or under what conditions, to authorize the employee to testify on matters relating to official information and/or produce official documents.

(b) If information or material is sought by a demand in any case or matter in which MCC is not a party, an affidavit or, if that is not feasible, a statement by the party seeking the information or material, or by his/her attorney setting forth a summary of the information or material sought and its relevance to the proceeding, must be submitted before a decision is made as to whether materials will be produced or permission to testify or otherwise provide information will be granted. Any authorization for testimony by a present or former employee of MCC shall be limited to the scope of the demand.

(c) When necessary, the General Counsel will coordinate with the Department of Justice to file appropriate motions, including motions to remove the matter to Federal court, to quash, or to obtain a protective order.

(d) If a demand fails to follow the requirements of these regulations, MCC will not allow the testimony or produce the documents.

(e) MCC will process demands in the order in which they are received. Absent unusual circumstances, MCC will respond within 45 days of the date that the demand was received. The time for response will depend upon the scope of the demand.

(f) The General Counsel may grant a waiver of any procedure described by this subpart where a waiver is considered necessary to promote a significant interest of MCC or the United States or for other good cause.

§ 1305.7 Final determination.

The General Counsel makes the final determination on demands to employees for production of official documents and information or testimony. All final determinations are within the sole discretion of the General Counsel. The General Counsel will notify the requester and the Court or other authority of the final determination, the reasons for the grant or denial of the demand, and any conditions that the General Counsel may impose on the release of documents, or on the testimony of an employee. When in doubt about the propriety of granting or denying a demand for testimony or documents, the General Counsel should consult with the Department of Justice.

§ 1305.8 Restrictions that apply to testimony.

(a) The General Counsel may impose conditions or restrictions on the testimony of MCC employees including, for example, limiting the areas of testimony or requiring the requester and other parties to the legal proceeding to agree that the transcript of the testimony will be kept under seal or will only be used or made available in the particular legal proceeding for which testimony was requested. The General Counsel may also require a copy of the transcript of testimony at the requester's expense.

(b) MCC may offer the employee's declaration in lieu of testimony, in whatever form the court finds acceptable.

(c) If authorized to testify pursuant to this part, an employee may testify to relevant unclassified materials or information within his or her personal knowledge, but, unless specifically authorized to do so by the General Counsel, the employee shall not:

(1) Disclose confidential or privileged information; or

(2) For a current MCC employee, testify as an expert or opinion witness with regard to any matter arising out of the employee's official duties or the functions of MCC, unless testimony is being given on behalf of the United States.

§ 1305.9 Restrictions that apply to released documents.

(a) The General Counsel may impose conditions or restrictions on the release of official documents and information, including the requirement that parties to the proceeding obtain a protective order or execute a confidentiality agreement to limit access and any further disclosure. The terms of the protective order or of the confidentiality agreement must be acceptable to the General Counsel. In cases where protective orders or confidentiality agreements have already been executed, MCC may condition the release of official documents and information on an amendment to the existing protective order or confidentiality agreement.

(b) If the General Counsel so determines, original MCC documents may be presented in response to a demand, but they are not to be presented as evidence or otherwise used in a manner by which they could lose their identity as official MCC documents nor are they to be marked or altered. In lieu of original records, certified copies will be presented for evidentiary purposes. (See 28 U.S.C. 1733).

§ 1305.10 Procedure when a decision is not made prior to the time a response is required.

If a response to a demand is required before the General Counsel can make the determination referred to above, the General Counsel, when necessary, will provide the court or other competent authority with a copy of this part, inform the court or other competent authority that the demand is being reviewed, and respectfully seek a stay of the demand pending a final determination.

§ 1305.11 Procedure in the event of an adverse ruling.

If the court or other competent authority declines to stay the demand in response to a request made in accordance with § 1305.10, or if the court or other competent authority rules that the demand must be complied with irrespective of the instructions from the General Counsel not to produce the material or disclose the information sought, the employee or former employee upon whom the demand has been made shall respectfully decline to comply with the demand (*United States ex rel. Touhy* v. *Ragen*, 340 U.S. 462 (1951)).

§ 1305.12 No private right of action.

This part is intended only to provide guidance for the internal operations of MCC, and is not intended to, and does not, and may not be relied upon, to create a right or benefit, substantive or procedural, enforceable at law by a party against the United States.

PART 1306—DEBT COLLECTION

Subpart A—General Provisions

AUTHORITY: 31 U.S.C. 3701–3719; 5 U.S.C. 5514; 31 CFR part 285; 31 CFR parts 900–904; 5 CFR part 550 subpart K.

SOURCE: 81 FR 59441, Aug. 30, 2016, unless otherwise noted.

Subpart A—General Provisions

§ 1306.1 Purpose.

The regulations in this part prescribe the procedures to be used by the Millennium Challenge Corporation (MCC) in the collection and/or disposal of non-tax debts owed to MCC and to the United States.

§ 1306.2 Scope.

(a) *Applicability of Federal Claims Collection Standards (FCCS).* MCC hereby adopts the provisions of the Federal Claims Collections Standards (31 CFR parts 900–904) and, except as set forth in this part or otherwise provided by law, MCC will conduct administrative actions to collect claims (including offset, compromise, suspension, termination, disclosure and referral) in accordance with the FCCS.

(b) This part is not applicable to any debt or claim for which collection is explicitly provided for or prohibited under other statutory authorities. This includes, but is not limited to:

(1) MCC claims against another Federal agency, any foreign country or any political subdivision thereof, or any public international organization.

(2) Debts arising out of acquisitions subject to the Federal Acquisition Regulation (FAR) which shall be determined, collected, compromised, terminated, or settled in accordance with the regulations published at 48 CFR part 32.

(3) Debts arising from the audit of transportation accounts pursuant to 31 U.S.C. 3726 which shall be determined, collected, compromised, terminated, or settled in accordance with the regulations published at 41 CFR parts 102–118.

(4) Debts based in whole or in part on conduct in violation of the antitrust laws, or in regard to which there is an indication of fraud, presentation of a false claim, or misrepresentation on the part of the debtor or any other party having an interest in the claim,

which shall be referred to the Department of Justice for compromise, suspension, or termination of collection action.

(5) Tax debts.

§ 1306.3 Definitions.

For purposes of this part:

(a) *Administrative offset* means withholding funds payable by the United States to, or held by the United States for, a person to satisfy a debt owed by the person to the United States.

(b) *Administrative wage garnishment* means the process by which a Federal agency orders a non-Federal employer to withhold amounts from a debtor's wages to satisfy a debt owed to the United States.

(c) *Compromise* means that the creditor agency accepts less than the full amount of an outstanding debt in full satisfaction of the entire amount of the debt.

(d) *Creditor agency* means the Federal agency to which a debt is owed including a debt collection center when acting in behalf of a creditor agency in matters pertaining to the collection of a debt (as provided in 5 CFR 550.1110).

(e) *Debt* or *claim* means an amount of money which has been determined to be owed to the United States from any person. A debtor's liability arising from a particular contract or transaction shall be considered a single claim for purposes of the monetary ceilings of the FCCS.

(f) *Debtor* means a person who owes the Federal government money.

(g) *Delinquent debt* means a debt that has not been paid by the date specified in MCC's written notification or applicable contractual agreement, unless other satisfactory arrangements have been made by that date, or that has not been paid in accordance with a payment agreement with MCC.

(h) *Discharge* means the release of a debtor from personal liability for a debt. Further collection action is prohibited.

(i) *Disposable pay* means the amount that remains from an employee's current basic pay, special pay, incentive pay, retired pay, retainer pay, or in the case of an employee not entitled to basic pay, other authorized pay remaining after required deductions for Federal, State and local income taxes; Social Security taxes, including Medicare taxes; Federal retirement programs; normal premiums for life and health insurance benefits and such other deductions that are required by law to be withheld, excluding garnishments.

(j) *FCCS* means the Federal Claims Collection Standards published jointly by the Departments of the Treasury and Justice and codified at 31 CFR parts 900–904.

(k) *Person* means an individual, corporation, partnership, association, organization, State or local government, or any other type of entity other than a Federal agency, Foreign Government, or public international organization.

(l) *Salary offset* means an administrative offset to collect a debt under 5 U.S.C. 5514 by deduction(s) at one or more officially established pay intervals from the current pay account of a Federal employee without his or her consent to satisfy a debt owed by that employee to the United States.

(m) *Suspension* means the temporary cessation of active debt collection pending the occurrence of an anticipated event.

(n) *Termination* means the cessation of all active debt collection action for the foreseeable future.

(o) *Waiver* means the cancellation, remission, forgiveness, or non-recovery of a debt allegedly owed by an employee to an agency as permitted or required by 5 U.S.C. 5522, 5 U.S.C. 5584, 5 U.S.C. 5922, 5 U.S.C. 8346(b), or any other law.

§ 1306.4 Other procedures or actions.

(a) Nothing contained in this part is intended to require MCC to duplicate administrative proceedings required by contract or other laws or regulations.

(b) Nothing in this part is intended to preclude utilization of informal administrative actions or remedies which may be available.

(c) Nothing contained in this part is intended to deter MCC from demanding the return of specific property or from demanding the return of the property or the payment of its value.

(d) The failure of MCC to comply with any provision in this part shall not serve as defense to the debt.

§ 1306.5 Interest, penalties, and administrative costs.

Except as otherwise provided by statute, contract or excluded in accordance with the FCCS, MCC will assess:

(a) Interest on delinquent debts in accordance with 31 CFR 901.9.

(b) Penalties at the rate of 6 percent a year or such other rate as authorized by law on any portion of a debt that is delinquent for more than 90 days.

(c) Administrative costs to cover the costs of processing and calculating delinquent debts.

(d) Late payment charges under paragraphs (a) and (b) of this section shall be computed from the date of delinquency.

(e) When a debt is paid in partial or installment payments, amounts received shall be applied first to outstanding penalty and administrative cost charges, second to accrued interest, and then to outstanding principal.

(f) MCC shall consider waiver of interest, penalties and/or administrative costs in accordance with the FCCS, 31 CFR 901.9(g).

§ 1306.6 Collection in installments.

(a) Whenever feasible, and except as required otherwise by law, debts owed to the United States, together with interest, penalties, and administrative costs as required by this part, should be collected in one lump sum. This is true whether the debt is being collected under administrative offset, including salary offset, or by another method, including voluntary payment. However, if the debtor is financially unable to pay the indebtedness in one lump sum or the amount of debt exceeds 15 percent of disposable pay for an officially established pay interval collection must be made in regular installments. If possible, the installment payments should be sufficient in size and frequency to liquidate the Government's claim within three years, and in the case of a current MCC employee, installment repayment plans must be made over a period not greater than the anticipated period of employment, except as provided in paragraph (b) in this section. However, the amount deducted for any period under this section and § 1306.16 may not exceed 15 percent of the disposable pay from which the deduction is made, unless the employee has agreed in writing to the deduction of a greater amount or a higher deduction has been ordered by a court.

(b) If the employee retires or resigns or if his or her employment ends before collection of the debt is completed, MCC may collect the debt from subsequent payments of any nature (e.g., final salary payment, lump-sum leave, etc.) due the employee from the paying agency as of the date of separation to the extent necessary to liquidate the debt. Following the employee's separation, MCC may collect any later payments of any kind that are due to the former employee from the United States to the extent necessary to liquidate the debt.

§ 1306.7 Designation.

The Chief Financial Officer is delegated authority and designated to perform all the duties for which head of the agency is responsible under the forgoing statutes and joint regulations. The authority delegated hereunder may be further delegated by the Chief Financial Officer subject to applicable laws, regulations and MCC policies.

§ 1306.8 Application.

(a) MCC shall aggressively collect claims and debts in accordance with this part and applicable law.

(b) In accordance with the FCCS:

(1) MCC will transfer to the Department of the Treasury, Financial Management Service (FMS) any past due, legally enforceable non-tax debt that has been delinquent for 180 days or more so that FMS may take appropriate action to collect the debt or take other appropriate action in accordance with applicable law and regulation; and

(2) MCC may transfer any past due, legally enforceable debt that has been delinquent for fewer than 180 days to FMS for collection in accordance with applicable law and regulation. (See 31 CFR part 285).

§ 1306.9 Administrative wage garnishment.

MCC hereby adopts the administrative wage garnishment rules issued by the Department of the Treasury at 31 CFR 285.11.

§ 1306.10 Scope.

(a) This subpart sets forth MCC's procedures for the collection of a Federal employee's current pay by salary offset to satisfy certain debts owed to the United States.

(b) This subpart applies to:

(1) Current employees of MCC and other agencies who owe debts to MCC;

(2) Current employees of MCC who owe debts to other agencies.

(c) This subpart does not apply to:

(1) Debts or claims arising under the Internal Revenue Code of 1954 (26 U.S.C. 1 *et seq.*); the Social Security Act (42 U.S.C. 301 *et seq.*); the tariff laws of the United States.

(2) Any case where collection of a debt by salary offset is explicitly provided for or prohibited by another statute (e.g., travel advances in 5 U.S.C. 5705 and employee training expenses in 5 U.S.C. 4108); or

(3) Any other debts excluded by the Federal Claims Collections Standards (31 CFR parts 900–904) or 31 CFR part 285.

(d) This part does not preclude an employee from requesting waiver of the debt, if waiver is available under subpart C of this part or by other regulation or statute.

(e) Nothing in this part precludes the compromise, suspension or termination of collection actions where appropriate under § 1306.18 or other regulations or statutes.

§ 1306.11 Coordinating offset with another Federal agency.

(a) When MCC is owed a debt by an employee of another agency, MCC shall provide the agency with a written certification that the debtor owes MCC a debt (including the amount and basis of the debt and the due date of payment) and that MCC has complied with this part.

(b) When another agency is owed the debt, MCC may use salary offset against one of its employees who is indebted to another agency, if requested to do so by that agency. Such request must be accompanied by a certification that the person owes the debt (including the amount and basis of the debt and the due date of payment) and that the agency has complied with its regulations as required by 5 U.S.C. 5514 and 5 CFR part 550, subpart K.

§ 1306.12 Notice requirements before offset.

(a) Deductions under the authority of 5 U.S.C. 5514 shall not be made unless the creditor agency first provides the employee with written notice that he/she owes a debt to the Federal Government at least 30 calendar days before salary offset is to be initiated. When MCC is the creditor agency this notice of intent to offset an employee's salary shall be hand-delivered or sent by certified mail to the most current address that is available. The written notice will state:

(1) That MCC has reviewed the records relating to the claim and has determined that a debt is owed, its origin and nature, and the amount of the debt;

(2) The intention of MCC to collect the debt by means of deduction from the employee's current disposable pay account until the debt, all accumulated interest, penalties and administrative costs are paid in full;

(3) The amount, frequency, approximate beginning date, and duration of the intended deductions;

(4) An explanation of MCC's policy concerning interest, penalties and administrative costs, including a statement that such assessments must be made unless excused in accordance with the FCCS;

(5) The employee's right to inspect and copy all records of MCC pertaining to the debt claimed or to receive copies of such records if personal inspection is impractical;

(6) If not previously provided, the opportunity (under terms agreeable to MCC) to establish a schedule for the voluntary repayment of the debt or to enter into a written agreement to establish a schedule for repayment of the debt in lieu of offset. The agreement must be in writing, signed by both the employee and MCC, and documented in MCC's files;

(7) The employee's right to a hearing conducted by a hearing official (an administrative law judge, or alternatively, an individual not under the

supervision or control of MCC, but in each case arranged by MCC) with respect to the existence and amount of the debt claimed, or the repayment schedule, so long as a petition is filed by the employee in accordance with this part;

(8) The name, address and telephone number of an official to whom questions and correspondence regarding this notice may be directed;

(9) The method and time period for requesting a hearing;

(10) That the timely filing of a petition for a hearing as prescribed by this part will stay the commencement of collection proceedings;

(11) The name and address of the office to which the petition for hearing should be sent;

(12) That MCC will initiate certification procedures to implement a salary offset, as appropriate, (which may not exceed 15 percent of the employee's disposable pay) not less than 30 calendar days from the date of delivery of the notice of debt, unless the employee files a timely petition for a hearing;

(13) That a final decision on the hearing (if one is requested) will be issued at the earliest practical date, but not later than 60 calendar days after the filing of the petition requesting the hearing, unless the employee requests and the hearing official grants a delay in the proceedings;

(14) That any knowingly false or frivolous statements, representation, or evidence may subject the employee to disciplinary procedures (5 U.S.C. Chapter 75, 5 CFR part 752 or other applicable statutes or regulations); penalties (31 U.S.C. 3729–3731 or other applicable statutes or regulations); or criminal penalties (18 U.S.C. 286, 287, 1001, and 1002 or other applicable statutes or regulations);

(15) Any other rights and remedies available to the employee under statutes or regulations governing the program for which the collection is being made;

(16) That unless there are applicable contractual or statutory provisions to the contrary, amounts paid on or deducted for the debt which are later waived or found not owed to the United States will be promptly refunded to the employee; and

(17) That proceedings with respect to such debt are governed by 5 U.S.C. 5514.

(b) MCC is not required to provide prior notice to an employee when the following adjustments are made by MCC to an MCC employee's pay:

(1) Any adjustment to pay arising out of an employee's election of coverage or a change in coverage under a Federal benefits program requiring periodic deductions from pay if the amount to be recovered was accumulated over four pay periods or less;

(2) A routine adjustment of pay that is made to correct an overpayment of pay attributable to clerical or administrative errors or delays in processing pay documents, if the overpayment occurred within the four pay periods preceding the adjustment, and, at the time of such adjustment, or as soon thereafter as practical, the individual is provided written notice of the nature and the amount of the adjustment and a point of contact for contesting the adjustment; or

(3) Any adjustment to collect a debt of $50 or less, if, at the time of such adjustment, or as soon thereafter as practical, the individual is provided written notice of the nature of the amount of the adjustment and a point of contact for contesting the adjustment.

§ 1306.13 Employee response.

(a) *Voluntary repayment agreement.* An employee may submit a request to enter into a written repayment agreement of the debt in lieu of offset. The request must be made within 7 days of receipt of notice under § 1306.12 to the official identified in § 1306.12(a)(8). The agreement must be in writing signed by both the employee and the appropriate official within MCC. Acceptance of such an agreement is discretionary with the Agency. An employee who enters into such an agreement may, nevertheless, seek a waiver under § 1306.18.

(b) *Reconsideration.* (1) An employee may seek a reconsideration of MCC's determination regarding the existence and/or amount of the debt. The request must be made within 7 days of receipt of notice under § 1306.12 to the official identified in 1306.12(a)(8). Within 20 days of receipt of this notice, the employee must submit a detailed statement of reasons for reconsideration that must be accompanied by supporting documentation.

(2) An employee may seek a reconsideration of MCC's proposed offset schedule. The request must be made within 7 days of receipt of notice under § 1306.12 to the official identified in § 1306.12(a)(8). Within 20 days of receipt of this notice, the employee must submit an alternative repayment schedule accompanied by a detailed statement, supported by documentation, evidencing financial hardship resulting from MCC's proposed schedule. Acceptance of the request is at MCC's discretion. MCC will notify the employee in writing of its decision concerning the request to reduce the rate of an involuntary deduction.

§ 1306.14 Request for a hearing for certain debts.

(a) Except as provided in paragraphs (d) and (e) of this section, an employee must file a request that is received by the official identified in the notice provided pursuant to § 1306.12(a)(11) not later than 15 calendar days from the date of MCC's notice if an employee wants a hearing concerning:

(1) The existence or amount of the debt; or

(2) MCC's proposed offset schedule.

(b) The request must be signed by the employee and should identify and explain with reasonable specificity and brevity the facts, evidence and witnesses, if any, which the employee believes support his or her position. If the employee objects to the percentage of disposable pay to be deducted from each check, the request should state the objection and the reasons for it.

(c) The employee must also specify whether an oral or paper hearing is requested. If an oral hearing is desired, the request should explain why the matter cannot be resolved by review of the documentary evidence alone.

(d) If the employee files a request for a hearing later than the required 15 calendar days as described in paragraph (a) of this section, MCC may accept the request if the employee can show that the delay was because of circumstances beyond his or her control or because of failure to receive notice of the filing deadline (unless the employee otherwise has actual notice of the filing deadline).

(e) If the employee files a timely request for reconsideration pursuant to § 1306.13(b), the employee must file a request for a hearing by the official identified in the notice provided pursuant to § 1306.12(a)(11) not later than 15 calendar days from the date of MCC's written decision concerning the reconsideration request.

(f) An employee waives the right to a hearing and will have his or her pay offset if the employee fails to file a petition for a hearing in accordance with this section.

§ 1306.15 Hearings.

(a) If an employee timely files a request for a hearing under § 1306.14, pursuant to 5 U.S.C. 5514(a)(2), the hearing official shall select the time, date, and location of the hearing.

(b) Hearings shall be conducted by a hearing official not under the supervision or control of MCC or an administrative law judge.

(c) *Procedure.* (1) After the employee requests a hearing, the hearing official shall notify the employee of the form of the hearing to be provided. If the hearing will be oral, notice shall set forth the date, time and location of the hearing. If the hearing will be paper, the employee shall be notified that he or she should submit arguments in writing to the hearing official by a specified date after which the record shall be closed. This date shall give the employee reasonable time to submit documentation.

(2) *Oral hearing.* An employee who requests an oral hearing shall be provided an oral hearing if the hearing official determines that the matter cannot be resolved by review of documentary evidence alone (e.g., when an issue of credibility or veracity is involved). The hearing is not an adversarial adjudication, and need not take the form of an evidentiary hearing.

(3) *Paper hearing.* If the hearing official determines that an oral hearing is not necessary, he or she will make a decision based upon a review of the available written record.

(4) *Record.* The hearing official must maintain a summary record of any

hearing provided by this subpart. Witnesses who provide testimony will do so under oath or affirmation.

(5) *Content of decision.* The written decision shall include:

(i) A statement of the facts presented to support the origin, nature, and amount of the debt;

(ii) The hearing official's findings, analysis, and conclusions; and

(iii) The terms of any repayment schedules, or the date salary offset will commence, if applicable.

(6) Failure to appear. In the absence of good cause shown (e.g., excused illness), an employee who fails to appear at an oral hearing shall be deemed, for the purpose of this part, to admit the existence and amount of the debt as described in the notice of intent. The hearing official shall schedule a new hearing date upon the request of MCC's representative when good cause is shown.

(d) A hearing official's decision is considered to be an official certification regarding the existence and amount of the debt for purposes of executing salary offset under 5 U.S.C. 5514 only.

§ 1306.16 Procedures for salary offset.

Unless otherwise provided by statute, regulation, or contract, the following procedures apply to salary offset:

(a) *Method.* Salary offset will be made by deduction at one or more officially established pay intervals from the current pay account of the employee without his or her consent.

(b) *Source.* The source of salary offset is current disposable pay.

(c) *Types of collection.* (1) *Lump sum payment.* Ordinarily debts will be collected by salary offset in one lump sum if possible. However, if the amount of the debt exceeds 15 percent of disposable pay for an officially established pay interval, the collection by salary offset must be made in installment deductions, except as provided by other laws or regulations or unless the employee has agreed in writing to a greater amount.

(2) *Installment deductions.* (i) The size of installment deductions must bear a reasonable relation to the size of the debt and the employee's ability to pay. If possible, the size of the deduction will be that necessary to liquidate the debt in no more than 1 year. However, the amount deducted for any period must not exceed 15 percent of the disposable pay from which the deduction is made, except as provided by other laws or regulations or unless the employee has agreed in writing to a greater amount.

(ii) Installment payments of less than $50 per pay period will be accepted only in unusual circumstances such as when that amount exceeds 15% of disposable pay.

(iii) Installment deductions should be sufficient in size and frequency to liquidate the Government's claim within three years and must be made over a period not greater than the anticipated period of employment.

§ 1306.17 Non-waiver of rights by payments.

So long as there are no statutory or contractual provisions to the contrary, no employee payment (of all or a portion of a debt) collected under this part will be interpreted as a waiver of any rights that the employee may have under 5 U.S.C. 5514.

§ 1306.18 Waiver of indebtedness.

(a) An employee may request a waiver of indebtedness. When an employee makes a request under a statutory right, further collection may be stayed pending an administrative determination on the request. During the period of any suspension, interest, penalties and administrative charges may be held in abeyance. MCC will not duplicate, for purposes of salary offset, any of the notices/procedures already provided the debtor prior to a request for waiver.

(b) Waiver of indebtedness is an equitable remedy and as such must be based on an assessment of the facts involved in the individual case under consideration. The burden is on the employee to demonstrate that the applicable waiver standard has been met in accordance with MCC's Policy on Waivers of Indebtedness.

(c) A debtor requesting a waiver shall do so in writing to the official identified in § 1306.12(a)(8) and within the timeframe stated within the initial notice sent under § 1306.12. The debtor's written response shall state the basis for the dispute and include any relevant documentation in support.

(d) While a waiver request is pending, MCC may suspend collection, including the accrual of interest and penalties, on the debt if MCC determines that suspension is in the agency's best interest or would serve equity and good conscience.

§ 1306.19 Compromise.

MCC may attempt to effect a compromise with respect to the debt in accordance with the process and standards set forth in the FCCS, 31 CFR part 902.

§ 1306.20 Suspension.

Any suspension of collection action shall be made in accordance with the standards set forth in the FCCS, 31 CFR 903.1–903.2.

§ 1306.21 Termination.

Any termination of a collection action shall be made in accordance with the standards set forth in the FCCS, 31 CFR 903.1 and 903.3–903.4.

§ 1306.22 Discharge.

Once a debt has been closed out for accounting purposes and collection has been terminated, the debt is discharged. MCC must report discharged debt as income to the debtor to the Internal Revenue Service per 26 U.S.C. 6050P and 26 CFR 1.6050P–1.

§ 1306.23 Bankruptcy.

A debtor should notify MCC at the contact office provided in the original notice of the debt, if the debtor has filed for bankruptcy. MCC will require documentation from the applicable court indicating the date of filing and type of bankruptcy. Pursuant to the laws of bankruptcy, MCC will suspend debt collection upon such filing unless the automatic stay is no longer in effect or has been lifted. In general, collection of a debt discharged in bankruptcy shall be terminated unless otherwise provided for by bankruptcy law.

§ 1306.24 Refunds.

(a) MCC will refund promptly to the appropriate individual amounts offset under this part when:

(1) A debt is waived or otherwise found not owing the United States (unless expressly prohibited by statute or regulation); or

(2) MCC is directed by an administrative or judicial order to make a refund.

(b) Refunds do not bear interest unless required or permitted by law or contract.

PARTS 1307–1399 [RESERVED]

CHAPTER XIV—FOREIGN SERVICE LABOR RELATIONS BOARD; FEDERAL LABOR RELATIONS AUTHORITY; GENERAL COUNSEL OF THE FEDERAL LABOR RELATIONS AUTHORITY; AND THE FOREIGN SERVICE IMPASSE DISPUTES PANEL

SUBCHAPTER A [RESERVED]

SUBCHAPTER B—GENERAL PROVISIONS

SUBCHAPTER C—FOREIGN SERVICE LABOR RELATIONS BOARD AND GENERAL COUNSEL OF THE FEDERAL LABOR RELATIONS AUTHORITY

SUBCHAPTER D—FOREIGN SERVICE IMPASSE DISPUTES PANEL

SUBCHAPTER A [RESERVED]
SUBCHAPTER B—GENERAL PROVISIONS

PARTS 1400–1410 [RESERVED]

PART 1411—AVAILABILITY OF OFFICIAL INFORMATION

AUTHORITY: 5 U.S.C. 552.

SOURCE: 46 FR 45854, Sept. 15, 1981, unless otherwise noted.

§ 1411.1 Purpose and scope.

This part contains the regulations of the Foreign Service Labor Relations Board (the Board), the General Counsel of the Federal Labor Relations Authority (the General Counsel) and the Foreign Service Impasse Disputes Panel (the Panel) providing for public access to information from the Board, the General Counsel or the Panel. These regulations implement the Freedom of Information Act, as amended, 5 U.S.C. 552, and the policy of the Board, the General Counsel and the Panel to disseminate information on matters of interest to the public and to disclose to members of the public on request such information contained in records insofar as is compatible with the discharge of their responsibilities, consistent with applicable law.

§ 1411.2 Delegation of authority.

(a) *Foreign Service Labor Relations Board/General Counsel of the Federal Labor Relations Authority.* Regional Directors of the Federal Labor Relations Authority, the Freedom of Information Officer of the Office of the General Counsel, Washington, DC, and the Solicitor of the Federal Labor Relations Authority are delegated the exclusive authority to act upon all requests for information, documents and records which are received from any person or organization under § 1411.4(a).

(b) *Foreign Service Impasse Disputes Panel.* The Executive Director of the Federal Service Impasses Panel is delegated the exclusive authority to act upon all requests for information, documents and records which are received from any person or organization under § 1411.4(b).

§ 1411.3 Information policy.

(a) *Foreign Service Labor Relations Board/General Counsel of the Federal Labor Relations Authority.* (1) It is the policy of the Foreign Service Labor Relations Board and the General Counsel of the Federal Labor Relations Authority to make available for public inspection and copying: (i) Final decisions and orders of the Board and administrative rulings of the General Counsel; (ii) statements of policy and interpretations which have been adopted by the Board or by the General Counsel and are not published in the FEDERAL REGISTER; and (iii) administrative staff manuals and instructions to staff that affect a member of the public (except those establishing internal operating rules, guidelines, and procedures for the investigation, trial, and settlement of cases). Any person may examine and copy items in paragraphs (a)(1) (i) through (iii) of this section at each regional office of the Authority and at the offices of the Authority and the General Counsel, respectively, in Washington, DC, under conditions prescribed by the Board and the General Counsel, respectively, and at reasonable times during normal working hours so long as it does not interfere with the efficient operations of the Authority, the Board and the General Counsel. To the extent required to prevent a clearly unwarranted invasion of personal privacy, identifying details may be deleted and, in each case, the justification for the deletion shall be fully explained in writing.

(2) It is the policy of the Board and the General Counsel to make promptly available for public inspection and copying, upon request by any person, other records where the request reasonably describes such records and otherwise conforms with the rules provided herein.

(b) *Foreign Service Impasse Disputes Panel.* (1) It is the policy of the Foreign Service Impasse Disputes Panel to make available for public inspection and copying: (i) Procedural determinations of the Panel; (ii) factfinding and arbitration reports; (iii) final decisions and orders of the Panel; (iv) statements of policy and interpretations which have been adopted by the Panel and are not published in the FEDERAL REGISTER; and (v) administrative staff manuals and instructions to staff that affect a member of the public. Any person may examine and copy items in paragraphs (b)(1)(i) through (v) of this section at the offices of the Federal Service Impasses Panel in Washington, DC, under conditions prescribed by the Panel, and at reasonable times during normal working hours so long as it does not interfere with the efficient operations of the Federal Service Impasses Panel and the Panel. To the extent required to prevent a clearly unwarranted invasion of personal privacy, identifying details may be deleted and, in each case, the justification for the deletion shall be fully explained in writing.

(2) It is the policy of the Panel to make promptly available for public inspection and copying, upon request by any person, other records where the request reasonably describes such records and otherwise conforms with the rules provided herein.

(c) The Board, the General Counsel and the Panel shall maintain and make available for public inspection and copying the current indexes and supplements thereto which are required by 5 U.S.C. 552(a)(2) and, as appropriate, a record of the final votes of each member of the Board and of the Panel in every agency proceeding. Any person may examine and copy such document or record of the Board, the General Counsel or the Panel at the offices of the Authority, the General Counsel, or the Federal Service Impasses Panel, as appropriate, in Washington, DC, under conditions prescribed by the Board, the General Counsel or the Panel at reasonable times during normal working hours so long as it does not interfere with the efficient operations of the Authority, the Board, the General Counsel, the Federal Service Impasses Panel, or the Panel.

(d) The Board, the General Counsel or the Panel may decline to disclose any matters exempted from the disclosure requirements in 5 U.S.C. 552(b), particularly those that are:

(1)(i) Specifically authorized under criteria established by an executive order to be kept secret in the interest of national defense or foreign policy and (ii) are in fact properly classified pursuant to such executive order;

(2) Related solely to internal personnel rules and practices of the Authority, the General Counsel or the Federal Service Impasses Panel;

(3) Specifically exempted from disclosure by statute (other than 5 U.S.C. 552(b)): *Provided,* That such statute:

(i) Requires that the matters be withheld from the public in such a manner as to leave no discretion on the issue; or

(ii) Establishes particular criteria for withholding or refers to particular types of matters to be withheld;

(4) Trade secrets and commercial or financial information obtained from a person and privileged or confidential;

(5) Interagency or intra-agency memoranda or letters which would not be available by law to a party other than an agency in litigation with the agency;

(6) Personnel and medical files and similar files the disclosure of which would constitute a clearly unwarranted invasion of personal privacy; or

(7) Investigatory records compiled for law enforcement purposes, but only to the extent that the production of such records would:

(i) Interfere with an enforcement proceeding;

(ii) Deprive a person of a right to a fair trial or an impartial adjudication;

(iii) Constitute an unwarranted invasion of personal privacy;

(iv) Disclose the identity of a confidential source and, in the case of a record compiled by a criminal law enforcement authority in the course of a criminal investigation, or by an agency conducting a lawful national security intelligence investigation, confidential information furnished only by the confidential source;

(v) Disclose investigative techniques and procedures; or

(vi) Endanger the life or physical safety of law enforcement personnel.

(e)(1) The formal documents constituting the record in a case or proceeding are matters of official record and, until destroyed pursuant to applicable statutory authority, are available to the public for inspection and copying at the appropriate regional office of the Authority, or the offices of the Authority, the General Counsel or the Federal Service Impasses Panel in Washington, DC, as appropriate, under conditions prescribed by the Authority, the General Counsel or the Federal Service Impasses Panel at reasonable times during normal working hours so long as it does not interfere with the efficient operations of the Authority, the General Counsel or the Federal Service Impasses Panel.

(2) The Board, the General Counsel or the Panel, as appropriate, shall certify copies of the formal documents upon request made a reasonable time in advance of need and payment of lawfully prescribed costs.

(f)(1) Copies of forms prescribed by the Board for the filing of charges and petitions may be obtained without charge from any regional office of the Authority.

(2) Copies of forms prescribed by the Panel for the filing of requests may be obtained without charge from the offices of the Federal Service Impasses Panel in Washington, DC.

§ 1411.4 Procedure for obtaining information.

(a) *Foreign Service Labor Relations Board/General Counsel of the Federal Labor Relations Authority.* Any person who desires to inspect or copy any records, documents or other information of the Board or the General Counsel, covered by this part, other than those specified in paragraphs (a) (1) and (c) of § 1411.3, shall submit a written request to that effect as follows:

(1) If the request is for records, documents or other information in a regional office of the Authority, it should be made to the appropriate Regional Director;

(2) If the request is for records, documents or other information in the Office of the General Counsel and located in Washington, DC, it should be made to the Freedom of Information Officer, Office of the General Counsel, Washington, DC; and

(3) If the request is for records, documents or other information in the offices of the Authority in Washington, DC, it should be made to the Solicitor of the Authority, Washington, DC.

(b) *Foreign Service Impasse Disputes Panel.* Any person who desires to inspect or copy any records, documents or other information of the Panel covered by this part, other than those specified in paragraphs (b) (1) and (c) of § 1411.3, shall submit a written request to that effect to the Executive Director, Federal Service Impasses Panel, Washington, DC.

(c) All requests under this part should be clearly and prominently identified as a request for information under the Freedom of Information Act and, if submitted by mail or otherwise submitted in an envelope or other cover, should be clearly identified as such on the envelope or other cover. If a request does not comply with the provisions of this paragraph, it shall not be deemed received by the appropriate Regional Director, the Freedom of Information Officer of the Office of the General Counsel, the Solicitor of the Authority, or the Executive Director of the Federal Service Impasses Panel, as appropriate, until the time it is actually received by such person.

§ 1411.5 Identification of information requested.

(a) Each request under this part should reasonbaly describe the records being sought in a way that they can be identified and located. A request should include all pertinent details that will help identify the records sought.

(b) If the description is insufficient, the officer processing the request will so notify the person making the request and indicate the additional information needed. Every reasonable effort shall be made to assist in the identification and location of the record sought.

(c) Upon receipt of a request for records, the appropriate Regional Director, the Freedom of Information Officer of the Office of the General Counsel, the Solicitor of the Authority, or the Executive Director of the Federal Service Impasses Panel, as appropriate, shall enter it in a public log. The log shall state the date and time received, the name and address of the person making the request, the nature of the records requested, the action taken on the request, the date of the determination letter sent pursuant to paragraphs (b) and (c) of §1411.6, the date(s) any records are subsequently furnished, the number of staff-hours and grade levels of persons who spent time responding to the request, and the payment requested and received.

§1411.6 Time limits for processing requests.

(a) All time limits established pursuant to this section shall begin as of the time at which a request for records is logged in by the appropriate Regional Director, the Freedom of Information Officer of the Office of the General Counsel, the Solicitor of the Authority, or the Executive Director of the Federal Service Impasses Panel, as appropriate, processing the request pursuant to paragraph (c) of §1411.5. An oral request for records shall not begin any time requirement. A written request for records sent to other than the appropriate officer will be forwarded to that officer by the receiving officer, but in that event the applicable time limit for response set forth in paragraph (b) of this section shall begin upon the request being logged in as required by paragraph (c) of §1411.5.

(b) Except as provided in §1411.8, the appropriate Regional Director, the Freedom of Information Officer of the Office of the General Council, the Solicitor of the Authority, or the Executive Director of the Federal Service Impasses Panel, as appropriate, shall, within ten (10) working days following receipt of the request, respond in writing to the requester, determining whether, or the extent to which, the request shall be complied with.

(1) If all the records requested have been located and a final determination has been made with respect to disclosure of all of the records requested, the response shall so state.

(2) If all of the records have not been located or a final determination has not been made with respect to disclosure of all the records requested, the response shall state the extent to which the records involved shall be disclosed pursuant to the rules established in this part.

(3) If the request is expected to involve an assessed fee in excess of $25.00, the response shall specify or estimate the fee involved and shall require prepayment of any charges in accordance with the provisions of paragraph (a) of §1411.10 before the records are made available.

(4) Whenever possible, the response relating to a request for records that involves a fee of less than $25.00 shall be accompanied by the requested records. Where this is not possible, the records shall be forwarded as soon as possible thereafter, consistent with other obligations of the Board, the General Counsel or the Panel.

(c) If any request for records is denied in whole or in part, the response required by paragraph (b) of this section shall notify the requester of the denial. Such denial shall specify the reason therefor, set forth the name and title or position of the person responsible for the denial, and notify the person making the request of the right to appeal the denial under the provisions of §1411.7.

§1411.7 Appeal from denial of request.

(a) *Foreign Service Labor Relations Board/General Counsel of the Federal Labor Relations Authority.* (1) Whenever any request for records is denied, a written appeal may be filed within thirty (30) days after the requester receives notification that the request has been denied or after the requester receives any records being made available, in the event of partial denial. If the denial was made by a Regional Director or by the Freedom of Information Officer of the Office of the General

Counsel, the appeal shall be filed with the General Counsel in Washington, DC. If the denial was made by the Solicitor of the Authority, the appeal shall be filed with the Chairperson of the Board in Washington, DC.

(2) The Chairperson of the Board or the General Counsel, as appropriate, shall, within twenty (20) working days from the time of receipt of the appeal, except as provided in § 1411.8, make a determination on the appeal and respond in writing to the requester, determining whether, or the extent to which, the request shall be complied with.

(i) If the determination is to comply with the request and the request is expected to involve an assessed fee in excess of $25.00, the determination shall specify or estimate the fee involved and shall require prepayment of any charges due in accordance with the provisions of paragraph (a) of § 1411.10 before the records are made available.

(ii) Whenever possible, the determination relating to a request for records that involves a fee of less than $25.00 shall be accompanied by the requested records. Where this is not possible, the records shall be forwarded as soon as possible thereafter, consistent with other obligations of the Board or the General Counsel.

(b) *Foreign Service Impasse Disputes Panel.* (1) Whenever any request for records is denied by the Executive Director of the Federal Service Impasses Panel, a written appeal may be filed with the Chairperson of the Panel within thirty (30) days after the requester receives notification that the request has been denied or after the requester receives any records being made available, in the event of partial denial.

(2) The Chairperson of the Panel, within twenty (20) working days from the time of receipt of the appeal, except as provided in § 1411.8, shall make a determination on the appeal and respond in writing to the requester, determining whether, or the extent to which, the request shall be complied with.

(i) If the determination is to comply with the request and the request is expected to involve an assessed fee in excess of $25.00, the determination shall specify or estimate the fee involved and shall require prepayment of any charges due in accordance with the provisions of paragraph (a) of § 1411.10 before the records are made available.

(ii) Whenever possible, the determination relating to a request for records that involves a fee of less than $25.00 shall be accompanied by the requested records. Where this is not possible, the records shall be forwarded as soon as possible thereafter, consistent with other obligations of the Panel.

(c) If on appeal the denial of the request for records is upheld in whole or in part by the Chairperson of the Board, the General Counsel, or the Chairperson of the Panel, as appropriate, the person making the request shall be notified of the reasons for the determination, the name and title or position of the person responsible for the denial, and the provisions for judicial review of that determination under 5 U.S.C. 552(a)(4). Even though no appeal is filed from a denial in whole or in part of a request for records by the person making the request, the Chairperson of the Board, the General Counsel or the Chairperson of the Panel, as appropriate, may, without regard to the time limit for filing of an appeal, sua sponte initiate consideration of a denial under this appeal procedure by written notification to the person making the request. In such event, the time limit for making the determination shall commence with the issuance of such notification.

§ 1411.8 Extension of time limits.

In unusual circumstances as specified in this section, the time limits prescribed with respect to initial determinations or determinations on appeal may be extended by written notice from the officer handling the request (either initial or on appeal) to the person making such request setting forth the reasons for such extension and the date on which a determination is expected to be dispatched. No such notice shall specify a date that would result in a total extension of more than ten (10) working days. As used in this section, "unusual circumstances" means, but only to the extent reasonably necessary to the proper processing of the particular request:

(a) The need to search for and collect the requested records from field facilities or other establishments that are separate from the office processing the request;

(b) The need to search for, collect and appropriately examine a voluminous amount of separate and distinct records which are demanded in a single request; or

(c) The need for consultation, which shall be conducted with all practicable speed, with another agency having a substantial interest in the determination of the request or among two or more components of the agency having substantial subject matter interest therein.

§ 1411.9 Effect of failure to meet time limits.

Failure by the Board, the General Counsel or the Federal Service Impasses Panel either to deny or grant any request under this part within the time limits prescribed by the Freedom of Information Act, as amended, 5 U.S.C. 552, and these regulations shall be deemed to be an exhaustion of the administrative remedies available to the person making this request.

§ 1411.10 Fees.

Persons requesting records from the Board, the General Counsel or the Panel shall be subject to a charge of fees for the direct cost of document search and duplication in accordance with the following schedules, procedures and conditions:

(a) The following fees shall be charged for disclosure of any record pursuant to this part:

(1) *Copying of records.* Ten cents per copy of each page.

(2) *Clerical searches.* $1.25 for each one-quarter hour spent by clerical personnel searching for and producing a requested record, including time spent copying any record.

(3) *Nonclerical searches.* $2.50 for each one-quarter hour spent by professional or managerial personnel searching for and producing a requested record, including time spent copying any record.

(4) *Forwarding material to destination.* Postage, insurance and special fees will be charged on an actual cost basis.

(b) All charges may be waived or reduced whenever it is in the public interest to do so.

(c) Requests for copies of transcripts of hearings should be made to the official hearing reporter. However, a person may request a copy of a transcript of a hearing from the Board, the Panel or the General Counsel, as appropriate. In such instance, the Board, the Panel or the General Counsel, as appropriate, may, by agreement with the person making the request, make arrangements with commercial firms for required services to be charged directly to the requester.

(d) No charge shall be made for the time spent in resolving legal or policy issues or in examining records for the purpose of deleting nondisclosable portions thereof.

(e) Payment of fees shall be made by check or money order payable to the U.S. Treasury.

§ 1411.11 Compliance with subpoenas.

No member of the Board or the Panel, or the General Counsel, or employee of the Authority, the Federal Service Impasses Panel, or the General Counsel shall produce or present any files, documents, reports, memoranda, or records of the Board, the Panel or the General Counsel, or testify in behalf of any party to any cause pending in any arbitration or in any court or before the Board or the Panel, or any other board, commission, or administrative agency of the United States, territory, or the District of Columbia with respect to any information, facts, or other matter to their knowledge in their official capacity or with respect to the contents of any files, documents, reports, memoranda, or records of the Board, the Panel or the General Counsel, whether in answer to a subpoena, subpoena duces tecum, or otherwise, without the written consent of the Board, the Panel or the General Counsel, as appropriate. Whenever any subpoena, the purpose for which is to adduce testimony or require the production of records as described in this section, shall have been served on any member of the Board or of the Panel or employee of the Authority, the Federal Service Impasses Panel or the General

Counsel, such person will, unless otherwise expressly directed by the Board, the Panel or the General Counsel, as appropriate, and as provided by law, move pursuant to the applicable procedure to have such subpoena invalidated on the ground that the evidence sought is privileged against disclosure by this rule.

§ 1411.12 Annual report.

On or before March 1 of each calendar year, the Executive Director of the Authority shall submit a report of the activities of the Board, the General Counsel and the Panel with regard to public information requests during the preceding calendar year to the Speaker of the House of Representatives and the President of the Senate for referral to the appropriate committees of the Congress. The report shall include for such calendar year all information required by 5 U.S.C. 552(d) and such other information as indicates the efforts of the Board, the General Counsel and the Panel to administer fully the provisions of the Freedom of Information Act, as amended.

PART 1413—OPEN MEETINGS

Sec.

AUTHORITY: 5 U.S.C. 552b.

SOURCE: 46 FR 45858, Sept. 15, 1981, unless otherwise noted.

§ 1413.1 Purpose and scope.

This part contains the regulations of the Foreign Service Labor Relations Board implementing the Government in the Sunshine Act, 5 U.S.C. 552b.

§ 1413.2 Public observation of meetings.

Every portion of every meeting of the Board shall be open to public observation, except as provided in § 1413.4, and Board members shall not jointly conduct or dispose of agency business other than in accordance with the provisions of this part.

§ 1413.3 Definition of meeting.

For purposes of this part, *meeting* shall mean the deliberations of at least two (2) members of the Board where such deliberations determine or result in the joint conduct or disposition of official agency business, but does not include deliberations to determine whether a meeting should be closed to public observation in accordance with the provisions of this part.

§ 1413.4 Closing of meetings; reasons therefor.

(a) Except where the Board determines that the public interest requires otherwise, meetings, or portions thereof, shall not be open to public observation where the deliberations concern the issuance of a subpoena, the Board participation in a civil action or proceeding or an arbitration, or the initiation, conduct or disposition by the Board of particular cases of formal agency adjudication pursuant to the procedures in 5 U.S.C. 554 or otherwise involving a determination on the record after opportunity for a hearing, or any court proceedings collateral or ancillary thereto.

(b) Meetings, or portions thereof, may also be closed by the Board, except where it determines that the public interest requires otherwise, when the deliberations concern matters or information falling within the reasons for closing meetings specified in 5 U.S.C. 552b(c)(1) (secret matters concerning national defense or foreign policy); (c)(2) (internal personnel rules and practices); (c)(3) (matters specifically exempted from disclosure by statute); (c)(4) (privileged or confidential trade secrets and commercial or financial information); (c)(5) (matters of alleged criminal conduct or formal censure); (c)(6) (personal information where disclosure would cause a clearly unwarranted invasion of personal privacy); (c)(7) (certain materials or information from investigatory files compiled for law enforcement purposes); or (c)(9)(B) (disclosure would significantly frustrate implementation of a proposed agency action).

§ 1413.5 Action necessary to close meeting; record of votes.

A meeting shall be closed to public observation under § 1413.4, only when a majority of the members of the Board who will participate in the meeting vote to take such action.

(a) When the meeting deliberations concern matters specified in § 1413.4(a), the Board members shall vote at the beginning of the meeting, or portion thereof, on whether to close such meeting, or portion thereof, to public observation and on whether the public interest requires that a meeting which may properly be closed should nevertheless be open to public observation. A record of such vote, reflecting the vote of each member of the Board, shall be kept and made available to the public at the earliest practicable time.

(b) When the meeting deliberations concern matters specified in § 1413.4(b), the Board shall vote on whether to close such meeting, or portion thereof, to public observation, and on whether there is a public interest which requires that a meeting which may properly be closed should nevertheless be open to public observation. The vote shall be taken at a time sufficient to permit inclusion of information concerning the open or closed status of the meeting in the public announcement thereof. A single vote may be taken with respect to a series of meetings at which the deliberations will concern the same particular matters where such subsequent meetings are scheduled to be held within thirty (30) days after the initial meeting. A record of such vote, reflecting the vote of each member of the Board, shall be kept and made available for the public within one (1) day after the vote is taken.

(c) Whenever any person whose interests may be directly affected by deliberations during a meeting, or a portion thereof, requests that the Board close that meeting, or portion thereof, to public observation for any of the reasons specified in 5 U.S.C. 552b(c)(5) (matters of alleged criminal conduct or formal censure), (c)(6) (personal information where disclosure would cause a clearly unwarranted invasion of personal privacy), or (c)(7) (certain materials or information from investigatory files compiled for law enforcement purposes), the Board members participating in the meeting, upon request of any one of its members, shall vote on whether to close such meeting, or a portion thereof, for that reason. A record of such vote, reflecting the vote of each member of the Board participating in the meeting, shall be kept and made available to the public within one (1) day after the vote is taken.

(d) After public announcement of a meeting as provided in § 1413.6, a meeting, or portion thereof, announced as closed may be opened, or a meeting, or portion thereof, announced as open may be closed only if a majority of the members of the Board who will participate in the meeting determine by a recorded vote that Board business so requires and that an earlier announcement of the change was not possible. The change made and the vote of each member on the change shall be announced publicly at the earliest practicable time.

(e) Before a meeting may be closed pursuant to § 1413.4, the Solicitor of the Authority shall certify that in the Solicitor's opinion the meeting may properly be closed to public observation. The certification shall set forth each applicable exemptive provision for such closing. Such certification shall be retained by the agency and made publicly available as soon as practicable.

§ 1413.6 Notice of meetings; public announcement and publication.

(a) A public announcement setting forth the time, place and subject matter of meetings, or portions thereof, closed to public observation pursuant to the provisions of § 1413.4(a), shall be made at the earliest practicable time.

(b) Except for meetings closed to public observation pursuant to the provisions of § 1413.4(a), the agency shall make public announcement of each meeting to be held at least seven (7) days before the scheduled date of the meeting. The announcement shall specify the time, place and subject matter of the meeting, whether it is to be open to public observation or closed, and the name, address, and phone number of an agency official designated to respond to requests for information about the meeting. The seven (7) day period for advance notice may be shortened only upon a determination by a majority of the members of the Board who will participate in the meeting that agency business requires that such meeting be called at an earlier date, in which event the public announcements shall be made at the earliest practicable time. A record of the vote to schedule a meeting at an earlier date shall be kept and made available to the public.

(c) Within one (1) day after a vote to close a meeting, or any portion thereof, pursuant to the provisions of § 1413.4(b), the agency shall make publicly available a full written explanation of its action closing the meeting, or portion thereof, together with a list of all persons expected to attend the meeting and their affiliation.

(d) If after public announcement required by paragraph (b) of this section has been made, the time and place of the meeting are changed, a public announcement shall be made at the earliest practicable time. The subject matter of the meeting may be changed after the public announcement only if a majority of the members of the Board who will participate in the meeting determine that agency business so requires and that no earlier announcement of the change was possible. When such a change in subject matter is approved, a public announcement of the change shall be made at the earliest practicable time. A record of the vote to change the subject matter of the meeting shall be kept and made available to the public.

(e) All announcements or changes thereto issued pursuant to the provisions of paragraphs (b) and (d) of this section or pursuant to the provisions of § 1413.5(d) shall be submitted for publication in the FEDERAL REGISTER immediately following their release to the public.

(f) Announcements of meetings made pursuant to the provisions of this section shall be made publicly available by the Executive Director of the Authority.

§ 1413.7 Transcripts, recordings or minutes of closed meeting; public availability; retention.

(a) For every meeting, or portion thereof, closed under the provisions of § 1413.4, the presiding officer shall prepare a statement setting forth the time and place of the meeting and the persons present, which statement shall be retained by the agency. For each such meeting, or portion thereof, there shall also be maintained a complete transcript or electronic recording of the proceedings, except that for meetings closed pursuant to § 1413.4(a), the Board may, in lieu of a transcript or electronic recording, maintain a set of minutes fully and accurately summarizing any action taken, the reasons therefor and views thereon, documents considered and the members' vote on each roll-call vote.

(b) The agency shall make promptly available to the public copies of transcripts, recordings or minutes maintained as provided in accordance with paragraph (a) of this section, except to the extent the items therein contain information which the agency determines may be withheld pursuant to the provisions of 5 U.S.C. 552b(c). Copies of transcripts or minutes, or transcriptions of electronic recordings including the indentification of speakers, shall to the extent determined to be publicly available, be furnished to any person, subject to the payment of duplication costs in accordance with the schedule of fees set forth in § 1411.10 of this subchapter and the actual cost of transcription.

(c) The agency shall maintain a complete verbatim copy of the transcript, a complete copy of the minutes, or a complete electronic recording of each meeting, or portion of a meeting, closed to the public, for a period of at least two (2) years after such meeting or until one (1) year after the conclusion of any agency proceeding with respect to which the meeting or portion was held whichever occurs later.

PART 1414—EX PARTE COMMUNICATIONS

Sec.

AUTHORITY: 22 U.S.C. 4107(c).

SOURCE: 46 FR 45859, Sept. 15, 1981, unless otherwise noted.

§ 1414.1 Purpose and scope.

This part contains the regulations of the Foreign Service Labor Relations Board relating to ex parte communications.

§ 1414.2 Unauthorized communications.

(a) No interested person outside this agency shall, in any Board proceeding subject to 5 U.S.C. 557(a), make or knowingly cause to be made any prohibited ex parte communication to any Board member or Authority employee who is or may reasonably be expected to be involved in the decisional process of the proceeding.

(b) No Board member or Authority employee who is or may reasonably be expected to be involved in the decisional process of the proceeding relevant to the merits of the proceeding shall: (1) Request any prohibited ex parte communications; or (2) make or knowingly cause to be made any prohibited ex parte communications about the proceeding to any interested person outside this agency relevant to the merits of the proceeding.

§ 1414.3 Definitions.

When used in this part:

(a) The term *person outside this agency*, to whom the prohibitions apply, shall include any individual outside the Board or the Authority, labor organization, agency, or other entity, or an agent thereof, and the General Counsel or his representative when prosecuting an unfair labor practice proceeding before the Board pursuant to 22 U.S.C. 4116.

(b) The term *ex parte communication* means an oral or written communication not on the public record with respect to which reasonable prior notice to all parties is not given, subject however, to the provisions of §§ 1414.5 and 1414.6.

§ 1414.4 Duration of prohibition.

Unless otherwise provided by specific order of the Board entered in the proceeding, the prohibition of § 1414.2 shall be applicable in any Board proceeding subject to 5 U.S.C. 557(a) beginning at the time of which the proceeding is noticed for hearing, unless the person responsible for the communication has knowledge that it will be noticed, in which case the prohibitions shall apply beginning at the time of such person's acquisition of such knowledge.

§ 1414.5 Communications prohibited.

Except as provided in § 1414.6, ex parte communications prohibited by § 1414.2 shall include:

(a) Such communications, when written, if copies thereof are not contemporaneously served by the communicator on all parties to the proceeding in accordance with the provisions of part 1429 of this chapter; and

(b) Such communications, when oral, unless advance notice thereof is given by the communicator to all parties in the proceeding and adequate opportunity afforded to them to be present.

§ 1414.6 Communications not prohibited.

Ex parte communications prohibited by § 1414.2 shall not include:

(a) Oral or written communications which relate solely to matters which the Hearing Officer, Regional Director, Administrative Law Judge, General Counsel or member of the Board is authorized by law or Board rules to entertain or dispose of on an ex parte basis;

(b) Oral or written requests for information solely with respect to the status of a proceeding;

(c) Oral or written communications which all the parties to the proceeding agree, or which the responsible official formally rules, may be made on an ex parte basis;

(d) Oral or written communications proposing settlement or an agreement for disposition of any or all issues in the proceeding;

(e) Oral or written communications which concern matters of general significance to the field of labor-management relations or administrative practice and which are not specifically related to any agency proceeding subject to 5 U.S.C. 557(a); or

(f) Oral or written communications from the General Counsel to the Board when the General Counsel is acting on behalf of the Board under 22 U.S.C. 4109(d).

§ 1414.7 Solicitation of prohibited communications.

No person shall knowingly and willfully solicit the making of an unauthorized ex parte communication by any other person.

§ 1414.8 Reporting of prohibited communications; penalties.

Any Board member or Authority employee who is or may reasonably be expected to be involved in the decisional process of the proceeding relevant to the merits of the proceeding to whom a prohibited oral ex parte communication is attempted to be made, shall refuse to listen to the communication, inform the communicator of this rule, and advise such person that if the person has anything to say it should be said in writing with copies to all parties. Any such Board member or Authority employee who is or may reasonably be expected to be involved in the decisional process of the proceeding relevant to the merits of the proceeding who receives, or who makes or knowingly causes to be made, an unauthorized ex parte communication, shall place or cause to be placed on the public record of the proceeding: (a) The communication, if it was written; (b) a memorandum stating the substance of the communication, if it was oral; (c) all written responses to the prohibited communication; and (d) memoranda stating the substance of all oral responses to the prohibited communication. The Executive Director of the Authority, if the proceeding is then pending before the Board, the Administrative Law Judge, if the proceeding is then pending before any such judge, or the Regional Director, if the proceeding is then pending before a Hearing Officer or the Regional Director, shall serve copies of all such materials placed on the public record of the proceeding on all other parties to the proceeding and on the attorneys of record for the parties. Within ten (10) days after the mailing of such copies, any party may file with the Executive Director of the Authority, Administrative Law Judge, or Regional Director serving the communication, as appropriate, and serve on all other parties, a statement setting forth facts or contentions to rebut those contained in the prohibited communication. All such responses shall be placed in the public record of the proceeding, and provision may be made for any further action, including reopening of the record, which may be required under the circumstances. No action taken pursuant to this provision shall constitute a waiver of the power of the Board to impose an appropriate penalty under § 1414.9

§ 1414.9 Penalties and enforcement.

(a) Where the nature and circumstances of a prohibited communication made by or caused to be made by a party to the proceeding are such that the interests of justice and statutory policy may require remedial action, the Board, Administrative Law Judge, or Regional Director, as appropriate, may issue to the party making the communication a notice to show cause, returnable before the Board, Administrative Law Judge, or Regional Director, within a stated period not less than seven (7) days from the date thereof, why the Board, Administrative Law Judge, or Regional Director should not determine that the interests of justice and statutory policy require that the claim or interest in the proceeding of a party who knowingly makes a prohibited communication or knowingly causes a prohibited communication to be made, should be dismissed, denied, disregarded or otherwise adversely affected on account of such violation.

(b) Upon notice and hearing, the Board may censure, suspend or revoke the privilege of practice before the agency of any person who knowingly and willfully makes or solicits the making of a prohibited ex parte communication. However, before the Board institutes formal proceedings under this section, it shall first advise the person or persons concerned in writing that it proposes to take such action and that they may show cause, within a period to be stated in such written advice, but not less than seven (7) days from the date thereof, why it should not take such action.

(c) The Board may censure, or, to the extent permitted by law, suspend, dismiss, or institute proceedings for the dismissal of, any Board agent who knowingly and willfully violates the prohibitions and requirements of this rule.

SUBCHAPTER C—FOREIGN SERVICE LABOR RELATIONS BOARD AND GENERAL COUNSEL OF THE FEDERAL LABOR RELATIONS AUTHORITY

PART 1420—PURPOSE AND SCOPE

§ 1420.1 Purpose and scope.

The regulations contained in this subchapter are designed to implement the provisions of the Foreign Service Labor-Management Relations Statute. They prescribe the procedures and basic principles or criteria under which the Foreign Service Labor Relations Board or the General Counsel of the Federal Labor Relations Authority, as applicable, will:

(a) Supervise or conduct elections and determine whether a labor organization has been selected as an exclusive representative by a majority of the employees who cast valid ballots and otherwise administer the provisions of the Statute relating to the according of exclusive recognition to a labor organization;

(b) Resolve complaints of alleged unfair labor practices;

(c) Resolve issues relating to the obligation to bargain in good faith;

(d) Resolve disputes concerning the effects, the interpretation, or a claim of breach of collective bargaining agreement, in accord with 22 U.S.C. 4114; and

(e) Take any action considered necessary to administer effectively the provisions of the Foreign Service Labor-Management Relations Statute.

(Authority: 22 U.S.C. 4107(c))

[46 FR 45861, Sept. 15, 1981]

PART 1421—MEANING OF TERMS AS USED IN THIS SUBCHAPTER

Sec.

AUTHORITY: 22 U.S.C. 4107(c).

SOURCE: 46 FR 45861, Sept. 15, 1981, unless otherwise noted.

§ 1421.1 Foreign Service Labor-Management Relations Statute.

The term *Foreign Service Labor-Management Relations Statute* means chapter 10 of title 1 of the Foreign Service Act of 1980, codified as chapter 41 of title 22 of United States Code.

§ 1421.2 Terms defined in section 1002 of the Foreign Service Act of 1980 (22 U.S.C. 4102).

(a) The terms *Authority*, *Board*, *collective bargaining*, *collective bargaining agreement conditions of employment*, *confidential employee*, *dues*, *exclusive representative*, *General Counsel*, *labor organization*, *management official*, *Panel*, and *person*, as used herein shall have the meaning set forth in 22 U.S.C. 4102.

(b) The term *Assistant Secretary* means the Assistant Secretary of Labor for Labor-Management Relations.

§ 1421.3 Exclusive recognition; Unfair labor practices.

(a) *Exclusive Recognition* has the meaning as set forth in 22 U.S.C. 4111; and

(b) *Unfair labor practices* has the meaning as set forth in 22 U.S.C. 4115.

§ 1421.4 Department.

Department means the Department of State, except that with reference to the exercise of functions under this Act with respect to another agency authorized by law to utilize the Foreign Service personnel system, such term means that other agency.

§ 1421.5 Regional Director.

Regional Director means the Director of a region of the Authority with geographical boundaries as fixed by the Authority.

§ 1421.6 Executive Director.

Executive Director means the Executive Director of the Authority.

§ 1421.7 Hearing Officer.

Hearing Officer means the individual designated to conduct a hearing involving a question concerning the appropriateness of a unit or such other matters as may be assigned.

§ 1421.8 Administrative law judge.

Administrative law judge means the Chief Administrative Law Judge or any administrative law judge designated by the Chief Administrative Law Judge to conduct a hearing in cases under 22 U.S.C. 4115, and such other matters as may be assigned.

§ 1421.9 Chief Administrative Law Judge.

Chief Administrative Law Judge means the Chief Administrative Law Judge of the Authority.

§ 1421.10 Secretary.

Secretary means the Secretary of State, except that (subject to 22 U.S.C. 3921) with reference to the exercise of functions under the Foreign Service Act of 1980 with respect to any agency authorized by law to utilize the Foreign Service personnel system, such term means the head of that agency.

§ 1421.11 Party.

Party means (a) any person: (1) Filing a charge, petition, or request; (2) named in a charge, complaint, petition, or request; (3) whose intervention in a proceeding has been permitted or directed by the Board; (4) who participated as a party (i) in a matter that was decided by an agency head under 22 U.S.C. 4105 or (ii) in a matter where action by the Grievance Board was taken; and (b) the General Counsel, or the General Counsel's designated representative, in appropriate proceedings.

§ 1421.12 Intervenor.

Intervenor means a party in a proceeding whose intervention has been permitted or directed by the Authority, its agents or representatives.

§ 1421.13 Certification.

Certification means the determination by the Board, its agents or representatives, of the results of an election.

§ 1421.14 Bargaining unit.

Bargaining unit has the meaning as set forth in 22 U.S.C. 4112 for the purpose of exclusive recognition under 22 U.S.C. 4111, and for purposes of allotments to representatives under 22 U.S.C. 4118.

§ 1421.15 Secret ballot.

Secret ballot means the expression by ballot, voting machine or otherwise, but in no event by proxy, of a choice with respect to any election or vote taken upon any matter, which is cast in such a manner that the person expressing such choice cannot be identified with the choice expressed, except in that instance in which any determinative challenged ballot is opened.

§ 1421.16 Showing of interest.

Showing of interest means evidence of membership in a labor organization; employees' signed and dated authorization cards or petitions authorizing a labor organization to represent them for purposes of exclusive recognition; allotment of dues forms executed by an employee and the labor organization's authorized official; current dues records; and existing or recently expired agreement; current exclusive recognition or certification; employees' signed and dated petitions or cards indicating that they no longer desire to be represented for the purposes of exclusive recognition by the currently recognized or certified labor organization; or other evidence approved by the Authority.

§ 1421.17 Grievance Board.

Grievance Board means the Foreign Service Grievance Board established under 22 U.S.C. 4135.

§ 1421.18 Regular and substantially equivalent employment.

Regular and substantially equivalent employment means employment that entails substantially the same amount of work, rate of pay, hours, working conditions, location of work, and seniority rights if any, of an employee prior to the cessation of employment in a Department because of any unfair labor practice under 22 U.S.C. 4115.

PART 1422—REPRESENTATION PROCEEDINGS

Sec.

AUTHORITY: 22 U.S.C. 4107.

SOURCE: 46 FR 45862, Sept. 15, 1981, unless otherwise noted.

§ 1422.1 Who may file petitions.

(a) A petition for exclusive recognition may be filed by a labor organization requesting an election to determine whether it should be recognized as the exclusive representative of employees of the Department in the unit described in 22 U.S.C. 4112 or should replace another labor organization as the exclusive representative of employees in such unit.

(b) A petition for any election to determine if a labor organization should cease to be the exclusive representative because it does not represent a majority of employees in the unit described in 22 U.S.C. 4112 may be filed by an employee or employees or an individual acting on behalf of any employee(s).

(c) A petition seeking to clarify a matter relating to representation may be filed by the Department where the Department has a good faith doubt, based on objective considerations, that the currently recognized or certified labor organization represents a majority of the employees in the unit described in 22 U.S.C. 4112.

(d) A petition for clarification of the unit described in 22 U.S.C. 4112 or for amendment of recognition or certification may be filed by the Department or by a labor organization which is currently recognized by the Department as the exclusive representative.

(e) A petition for determination of eligibility for dues allotment may be filed by a labor organization in accordance with 22 U.S.C. 4118(c).

§ 1422.2 Contents of petition; filing and service of petition; challenges to petition.

(a) *Petition for exclusive recognition.* A petition by a labor organization for exclusive recognition shall be submitted on a form prescribed by the Board and shall contain the following:

(1) The name of the Department, its address, telephone number, and the persons to contact and their titles, if known;

(2) A description of the unit described in 22 U.S.C. 4112. Such description shall indicate the classifications of employees sought to be included and those sought to be excluded and the approximate number of employees in the unit;

(3) Name, address, and telephone number of the recognized or certified representative, if any, and the date of such recognition or certification and the expiration date of any applicable agreement, if known to the peititioner;

(4) Names, addresses, and telephone numbers of any other interested labor organizations, if known to the petitioner;

(5) Name and affiliation, if any, of the petitioner and its address and telephone number;

(6) A statement that the petitioner has submitted to the Department and to the Assistant Secretary a roster of its officers and representatives, a copy of its constitution and bylaws, and a statement of its objectives;

(7) A declaration by such person signing the petition, under the penalties of the Criminal Code (18 U.S.C. 1001), that its contents are true and correct to the best of such person's knowledge and belief;

(8) The signature of the petitioner's representative, including such person's title and telephone number; and

(9) The petition shall be accompanied by a showing of interest of not less than thirty percent (30%) of the employees in the unit described in 22 U.S.C. 4112 and an alphabetical list of names constituting such showing.

(b) *Department petition seeking clarification of a matter relating to representation; employee petition for an election to determine whether a labor organization should cease to be an exclusive representative.* (1) A petition by the Department shall be submitted on a form prescribed by the Board and shall contain the information set forth in paragraph (a) of this section, except paragraphs (a) (6), and (9), and a statement that the Department has a good faith doubt, based on objective considerations, that the currently recognized or certified labor organization represents a majority of the employees in the unit described in 22 U.S.C. 4112. Attached to the petition shall be a detailed explanation of the reasons supporting the good faith doubt.

(2) A petition by any employee or employees or an individual acting on behalf of any employee(s) shall contain the information set forth in paragraph (a) of this section, except paragraphs (a) (6) and (9), and it shall be accompanied by a showing of interest of not less than thirty percent (30%) of the employees in the unit indicating that the employees no longer desire to be represented for the purposes of exclusive recognition by the currently recognized or certified labor organization and an alphabetical list of names constituting such showing.

(c) *Petition for clarification of unit or for amendment of recognition or certification.* A petition for clarification of unit or for amendment of recognition or certification shall be submitted on a form prescribed by the Board and shall contain the information required by paragraph (a) of this section, except paragraphs (a) (2), (6) and (9), and shall set forth:

(1) A description of the unit and the date of recognition or certification;

(2) The proposed clarification or amendment of the recognition or certification; and

(3) A statement of reasons why the proposed clarification or amendment is requested.

(d) *Petition for determination of eligibility for dues allotment.* A petition for determination of eligibility for dues allotment in the unit may be filed if there is no exclusive representative. The petition shall be submitted on a form prescribed by the Board and shall contain the information required in paragraphs (a) (1), (4), (5), (6), (7), and (8) of this section, and shall set forth:

(1) A description of the unit described in 22 U.S.C. 4112. Such description shall indicate the classifications of employees sought to be included and those sought to be excluded and the approximate number of employees in the unit; and

(2) The petition shall be accompanied by a showing of membership in the petitioner of not less than ten percent (10%) of the employees in the unit and an alphabetical list of names constituting such showing.

(e) *Filing and service of petition and copies.* (1) A petition for exclusive recognition, for an election to determine if a labor organization should cease to be the exclusive representative, for clarification of unit, for amendment of recognition or certification, or for determination of eligibility for dues allotment, filed pursuant to paragraphs (a), (b), (c), or (d) of this section respectively, shall be filed with the Regional Director for the region in which the unit exists, or, if the claimed unit exists in two or more regions, the petition shall be filed with the Regional Director for the region in which the affected employees are located.

(2) An original and four (4) copies of a petition shall be filed, together with a statement of any other relevant facts and of all correspondence relating to the question concerning representation.

(3) Copies of the petition together with any attachments shall be served by the petitioner on all known interested parties, and a written statement of such service shall be filed with the Regional Director: *Provided, however,* That the showing of interest or the showing of membership submitted with a petition filed pursuant to paragraphs (a), (b)(2), (d), or (h) of this section shall not furnished to any other person.

(f) *Adequacy and validity of showing of interest or showing of membership.* (1) The Regional Director shall determine the adequacy of the showing of interest or the showing of membership administratively, and such determination shall not be subject to collateral attack at a unit or representation hearing. If the petition is dismissed or the intervention sought pursuant to § 1422.5 is denied, a request for review of such dismissal or denial may be filed with the Board in accordance with the procedures set forth in § 1422.6(d).

(2) Any party challenging the validity of any showing of interest or showing of membership of a petitioner, or a cross-petitioner filing pursuant to § 1422.5(b), or of a labor organization seeking to intervene pursuant to § 1422.5, must file its challenge with the Regional Director, with respect to the petitioner or a cross-petitioner, within twenty (20) days after the initial date of posting of the notice of petition as provided in § 1422.4(a), and with respect to any labor organization seeking to intervene, within twenty (20) days of service of a copy of the request for intervention on the challenging party. The challenge shall be supported with evidence including signed statements of employees and any other written evidence. The Regional Director shall investigate the challenge and thereafter shall take such action as the Regional Director deems appropriate which shall be final and not subject to review by the Board, unless the petition is dismissed or the intervention is denied on the basis of the challenge. Such request for review shall be filed with the Board in accordance with the procedures set forth in § 1422.6(d).

(g) *Challenge to status of a labor organization.* Any party challenging the status of a labor organization under chapter 41 of title 22 of the United States Code must file its challenge with the Regional Director and support the challenge with evidence. With respect to the petitioner or a cross-petitioner filing pursuant to § 1422.5(b), such a challenge must be filed within twenty (20) days after the initial date of posting of the notice of petition as provided in § 1422.4(a), and with respect to a labor organization seeking to intervene pursuant to § 1422.5, within twenty (20) days after service of a copy of the request for intervention on the challenging party. The Regional Director shall investigate the challenge and thereafter shall take such action as the Regional Director deems appropriate, which shall be subject to review by the Board. Such request for review shall be filed with the Board in accordance with the procedures set forth in § 1422.6(d).

§ 1422.3 Timeliness of petition.

(a) When there is no certified exclusive representative of the employees, a petition will be considered timely filed provided a valid election has not been held within the preceding twelve (12) month period in the unit described in 22 U.S.C. 4112.

(b) When there is a certified exclusive representative of the employees, a petition will not be considered timely if filed within twenty-four (24) months after the certification as the exclusive representative of employees in unit described in 22 U.S.C. 4112, unless a signed and dated collective bargaining agreement covering the unit has been entered into in which case paragraphs

(c) and (d) of this section shall be applicable.

(c) When a collective bargaining agreement covering the unit described in 22 U.S.C. 4112 has been signed and dated by the Department and the incumbent exclusive representative, a petition for exclusive recognition or other election petition will not be considered timely if filed during the period of review by the Secretary as set forth in 22 U.S.C. 4113(f), absent unusual circumstances.

(d) A petition for exclusive recognition or other election petition will be considered timely when filed as follows:

(1) Not more than one hundred and five (105) days and not less than (60) days prior to the expiration date of a collective bargaining agreement having a term of three (3) years or less from the date it became effective.

(2) Not more than one hundred and five (105) days and not less than sixty (60) days prior to the expiration of the initial three (3) year period of a collective bargaining agreement having a term of more than three (3) years from the date it became effective, and any time after the expiration of the initial three (3) year period of such a collective bargaining agreement; and

(3) Any time when unusual circumstances exist which substantially affect the unit or the majority representation.

(e) When a collective bargaining agreement having a term of three (3) years or less is in effect between the Department and the incumbent exclusive representative, and a petition has been filed challenging the representation status of the incumbent exclusive representative and the petition is subsequently withdrawn or dismissed less than sixty (60) days prior to the expiration date of that collective bargaining agreement, or any time thereafter, the Department and incumbent exclusive representative shall be afforded a ninety (90) day period from the date the withdrawal is approved or the petition is dismissed free from rival claim within which to consummate a collective bargaining agreement: *Provided, however*, That the provisions of this paragraph shall not be applicable when any other petition is pending which has been filed pursuant to paragraph (d)(1) of this section.

(f) When an extension of a collective bargaining agreement having a term of three (3) years or less has been signed more than sixty (60) days before its expiration date, such extension shall not serve as a basis for the denial of a petition submitted in accordance with the time limitations provided herein.

(g) Collective bargaining agreements which go into effect automatically pursuant to 22 U.S.C. 4113(f) and which do not contain the date on which the agreement became effective shall not constitute a bar to an election petition.

(h) A petitioner who withdraws a petition after the issuance of a notice of hearing or after the approval of an agreement for an election, shall be barred from filing another petition for the unit described in 22 U.S.C. 4112 for six (6) months, unless a withdrawal request has been received by the Regional Director not later than three (3) days before the date of the hearing.

(i) The time limits set forth in this section shall not apply to a petition for clarification of unit or for amendment of recognition or certification, or to a petition for dues allotment.

§ 1422.4 Investigation of petition and posting of notice of petition; action by Regional Director.

(a) Upon the request of the Regional Director, after the filing of a petition, the Department shall post copies of a notice to all employees in places where notices are normally posted affecting the employees in the unit described in 22 U.S.C. 4112.

(b) Such notice shall set forth:

(1) The name of the petitioner;

(2) The description of the unit;

(3) If appropriate, the proposed clarification of unit or the proposed amendment of recognition or certification; and

(4) A statement that all interested parties are to advise the Regional Director in writing of their interest and position within twenty (20) days after the date of posting of such notice: *Provided, however*, That the notice in a petition for determination of eligibility

for dues allotment shall contain the information required in paragraphs (a) (1), (2), and (4) of this section.

(c) The notice shall remain posted for a period of twenty (20) days. The notice shall be posted conspicuously and shall not be covered by other material, altered or defaced.

(d) The Department shall furnish the Regional Director and all known interested parties with the following:

(1) Names, addresses and telephone numbers of all labor organizations known to represent any of the employees in the unit described in 22 U.S.C. 4112;

(2) A copy of all relevant correspondence;

(3) A copy of existing or recently expired agreement(s) covering any of the employees described in the petition;

(4) A current alphabetized list of employees included in the unit, together with their job classifications; and

(5) A current alphabetized list of employees described in the petition as excluded from the unit, together with their job classifications.

(e) The parties are expected to meet as soon as possible after the expiration of the twenty (20) day posting period of the notice of petition as provided in paragraph (a) of this section and use their best efforts to secure agreement on the unit.

(f) The Regional Director shall make such investigation as the Regional Director deems necessary and thereafter shall take action which may consist of the following, as appropriate:

(1) Approve an agreement for consent election in the unit as provided under § 1422.7;

(2) Approve a withdrawal request;

(3) Dismiss the petition; or

(4) Issue a notice of hearing.

(g) In processing a petition for clarification of unit or for amendment of recognition or certification, or dues allotment, where appropriate, the Regional Director shall prepare and serve a report and findings upon all parties to the proceedings and shall state therein, among other pertinent matters, the Regional Director's conclusions and the action contemplated. A party may file with the Board a request for review of such action of the Regional Director in accordance with the procedures set forth in § 1422.6(d). If no request for review is filed, or if one is filed and denied, the Regional Director shall take such action as may be appropriate, which may include issuing a clarification of unit or an amendment of recognition or certification, or determination of eligibility for dues allotment.

(h) A determination by the Regional Director to issue a notice of hearing shall not be subject to review by the Board.

§ 1422.5 Intervention.

(a) No labor organization will be permitted to intervene in any proceeding involving a petition filed pursuant to § 1422.2 (a) or (b) unless it has submitted to the Regional Director a showing of interest of ten percent (10%) or more of the employees in the unit described in 22 U.S.C. 4112 together with an alphabetical list of names constituting such showing, or has submitted a current or recently expired agreement with the Department covering any of the employees involved, or has submitted evidence that it is currently recognized or certified exclusive representative of any of the employees involved: *Provided, however*, That an incumbent exclusive representative shall be deemed to be an intervenor in the proceeding unless it serves on the Regional Director a written disclaimer of any representation interest for the employees involved: *Provided, further*, That any such incumbent exclusive representative that declines to sign an agreement for consent election because of a disagreement on the matters contained in § 1422.7(c) as decided by the Regional Director, or fails to appear at a hearing held pursuant to § 1422.9, shall be denied its status as an intervenor.

(b) No labor organization may participate to any extent in any representation proceeding unless it has notified the Regional Director in writing, accompanied by its showing of interest as specified in paragraph (a) of this section, of its desire to intervene within twenty (20) days after the initial date of posting of the notice of petition as provided in § 1422.4(a), unless good cause is shown for extending the period. A copy of the request for intervention filed with the Regional Director, excluding the showing of interest, shall be served on all known interested parties, and a written statement of such service should be filed with the Regional Director: *Provided, however*, That an incumbent exclusive representative shall be deemed to be an intervenor in the proceeding in accordance with paragraph (a) of this section.

(c) Any labor organization seeking to intervene in a proceeding involving a petition for determination of eligibility for dues allotment filed pursuant to §1422.2(d) may intervene solely on the basis it claims to be the exclusive representative of some or all the employees specified in the petition and shall submit to the Regional Director a current or recently expired agreement with the Department covering any of the employees involved, or evidence that it is the currently recognized or certified exclusive representative of any of the employees involved.

(d) Any labor organization seeking to intervene must submit to the Regional Director a statement that it has submitted to the Department and to the Assistant Secretary a roster of its officers and representatives, a copy of its constitution and bylaws, and a statement of its objectives.

(e) The Regional Director may grant intervention to a labor organization in a proceeding involving a petition for clarification of unit or a petition for amendment of recognition or certification filed pursuant to §1422.2(c), or a petition for determination of eligibility for dues allotment filed pursuant to §1422.2(d), based on a showing that the proposed clarification, amendment or dues allotment affects that labor organizations's existing exclusively recognized unit(s) in that it would cover one or more employees who are included in such unit(s).

§1422.6 Withdrawal, dismissal or deferral of petitions; consolidation of cases; denial of intervention; review of action by Regional Director.

(a) If the Regional Director determines, after such investigation as the Regional Director deems necessary, that the petition has not been timely filed, the unit is not as described in 22 U.S.C. 4114, the petitioner has not made a sufficient showing of interest, the petition is not otherwise actionable, or an intervention is not appropriate, the Regional Director may request the petitioner or intervenor to withdraw the petition or the request for intervention. In the absence of such withdrawal within a reasonable period of time, the Regional Director may dismiss the petition or deny the request for intervention.

(b) If the Regional Director determines, after investigation, that a valid issue has been raised by a challenge under §1422.2 (f) or (g), the Regional Director may take action which may consist of the following, as appropriate:

(1) Request the petitioner or intervenor to withdraw the petition or the request for intervention;

(2) Dismiss the petition and/or deny the request for intervention if a withdrawal request is not submitted within a reasonable period of time;

(3) Defer action on the petition or request for intervention until such time as issues raised by the challenges have been resolved pursuant to this part; or

(4) Consolidate such issues with the representation matter for resolution of all issues.

(c) If the Regional Director dismisses the petition and/or denies the request for intervention, the Regional Director shall serve on the petitioner or the party requesting intervention a written statement of the grounds for the dismissal or the denial, and serve a copy of such statement on the Department, and on the petitioner and any intervenors, as appropriate.

(d) The petitioner or party requesting intervention may obtain a review of such dismissal and/or denial by filing a request for review with the Board within twenty-five (25) days after service of the notice of such action. Copies of the request for review shall be served on the Regional Director and the other parties, and a statement of service shall be filed with the request for review. Requests for extensions of time shall be in writing and received by the Board not later than five (5) days before the date the request for review is due. The request for review shall contain a complete statement setting forth facts and reasons upon which the request is based. Any party may file an opposition to a request for review with the Board within ten (10) days after service of the request for review. Copies of the opposition to the request for review shall be served on the Regional Director and the other parties, and a statement of service shall be filed with the opposition to the request for review. The Board may issue a decision or ruling affirming or reversing the Regional Director in whole or in part or making any other disposition of the matter as it deems appropriate.

§ 1422.7 Agreement for consent election.

(a) All parties desiring to participate in an election being conducted pursuant to this section or § 1422.16, including intervenors who have met the requirements of § 1422.5, must sign an agreement providing for such an election on a form prescribed by the Board. An original and one (1) copy of the agreement shall be filed with the Regional Director.

(b) The Department, a petitioner, and any intervenors who have complied with the requirements set forth in § 1422.5 may agree that a secret ballot election shall be conducted among the employees in the unit to determine whether the employees desire to be represented for purposes of exclusive recognition by any or none of the labor organizations involved.

(c) The parties shall agree on the eligibility period for participation in the election, the date(s), hour(s), and place(s) of the election, the designations on the ballot and other related election procedures.

(d) In the event that the parties cannot agree on the matters contained in paragraph (c) of this section, the Regional Director, acting on behalf of the Board, shall decide these matters without prejudice to the right of a party to file objections to the procedural conduct of the election under § 1422.20(b).

(e) If the Regional Director approves the agreement, the election shall be conducted by the Department, as appropriate, under the supervision of the Regional Director, in accordance with § 1422.17.

(f) Any qualified intervenor who refuses to sign an agreement for an election may express its objections to the agreement in writing to the Regional Director. The Regional Director, after careful consideration of such objections, may approve the agreement or take such other action as the Regional Director deems appropriate.

§ 1422.8 Notice of hearing; contents; attachments; procedures.

(a) The Regional Director may cause a notice of hearing to be issued involving any matters related to the petition.

(b) The notice of hearing shall be served on all interested parties and shall include:

(1) The name of the Department, petitioner, and intervenors, if any;

(2) A statement of the time and place of the hearing, which shall be not less than twenty (20) days after service of the notice of hearing, except in extraordinary circumstances;

(3) A statement of the nature of the hearing; and

(4) A statement of the authority and jurisdiction under which the hearing is to be held.

(c) A copy of the petition shall be attached to the notice of hearing.

(d) Hearings on matters related to the petition pursuant to paragraph (a) of this section shall be conducted by a Hearing Officer in accordance with §§ 1422.9 through 1422.15.

§ 1422.9 Conduct of hearing.

(a) Hearings shall be conducted by a Hearing Officer and shall be open to the public unless otherwise ordered by the Hearing Officer. At any time another Hearing Officer may be substituted for the Hearing Officer previously presiding. It shall be the duty of the Hearing Officer to inquire fully into all matters in issue and the Hearing Officer shall obtain a full and complete record upon which the Board can make an appropriate decision. An official reporter shall make the only official transcript of such proceedings. Copies of the official transcript may be examined in the appropriate regional office during normal working hours. Requests by parties for copies of transcripts should be made to the official hearing reporter.

(b) Hearings under this section are considered investigatory and not adversary. Their purpose is to develop a full and complete factual record. The rules of relevancy and materiality are paramount; there are no burdens of proof and the technical rules of evidence do not apply.

§ 1422.10 Motions.

(a) *General.* (1) A motion shall state briefly the order or relief sought and the grounds for the motion: *Provided, however,* That a motion to intervene will not be entertained by the Hearing Officer. Intervention will be permitted only to those who have met the requirements of § 1422.5.

(2) A motion prior to, and after a hearing and any response thereto, shall be made in writing. A response shall be filed within five (5) days after service of the motion. An original and two (2) copies of such motion and any response thereto shall be filed and copies shall be served on the parties and the Regional Director. A statement of such service shall be filed with the original.

(3) During a hearing a motion may be made and responded to orally on the record.

(4) The right to make motions, or to make objections to rulings on motions, shall not be deemed waived by participation in the proceeding.

(5) All motions, rulings, and orders shall become part of the record.

(b) *Filing of motions.* (1) Motions and responses thereto prior to a hearing shall be filed with the Regional Director. During the hearing motions shall be made to the Hearing Officer.

(2) After the transfer of the case to the Board, except as otherwise provided, motions and responses thereto shall be filed with the Board: *Provided,* That following the close of a hearing, motions to correct the transcript should be filed with the Hearing Officer within ten (10) days after the transcript is received in the regional office.

(c) *Rulings on motions.* (1) Regional Directors may rule on all motions filed with them, or they may refer them to the Hearing Officer. A ruling by a Regional Director granting a motion to dismiss a petition may be reviewed by the Board upon the filing by the petitioner of a request for review pursuant to § 1422.6(d).

(2) Hearing Officers shall rule, either orally on the record or in writing, on all motions made at the hearing or referred to them, except that a motion to dismiss a petition shall be referred for appropriate action at such time as the record is considered by the Regional Director or the Board. Rulings by a Hearing Officer reduced to writing shall be served on the parties.

(3) The Board shall consider the rulings by the Regional Director and the Hearing Officer when the case is transferred to it for decision.

§ 1422.11 Rights of the parties.

(a) A party shall have the right to appear at any hearing in person, by counsel, or by other representative, and to examine and cross-examine witnesses, and to introduce into the record documentary or other relevant evidence. Two (2) copies of documentary evidence shall be submitted and a copy furnished to each of the other parties. Stipulations of fact may be introduced in evidence with respect to any issue.

(b) A party shall be entitled, upon request, to a reasonable period at the close of the hearing for oral argument, which shall be included in the stenographic report of the hearing. Such oral argument shall not preclude a party from filing a brief under § 1422.14.

§ 1422.12 Duties and powers of the Hearing Officer.

It shall be the duty of Hearing Officers to inquire fully into the facts as they relate to the matters before them. With respect to cases assigned to them between the time they are designated and the transfer of the case to the Board, Hearing Officers shall have the authority to:

(a) Grant requests for subpenas pursuant to § 1429.7 of this subchapter;

(b) Rule upon offers of proof and receive relevant evidence and stipulations of fact;

(c) Take or cause depositions or interrogatories to be taken whenever the ends of justice would be served thereby;

(d) Limit lines of questioning or testimony which are immaterial, irrelevant or unduly repetitious;

(e) Regulate the course of the hearing and, if appropriate, exclude from the hearing persons who engage in misconduct;

(f) Strike all related testimony of witnesses refusing to answer any questions ruled to be proper;

(g) Hold conferences for the settlement or simplification of the issues by consent of the parties or upon the Hearing Officer's own motion;

(h) Dispose of procedural requests, motions, or similar matters, which shall be made part of the record of the proceedings, including motions referred to the Hearing Officer by the Regional Director and motions to amend petitions;

(i) Call and examine and cross-examine witnesses and introduce into the record documentary or other evidence;

(j) Request the parties at any time during the hearing to state their respective positions concerning any issue in the case or theory in support thereof;

(k) Continue the hearing from day-to-day, or adjourn it to a later date or to a different place, by announcement thereof at the hearing or by other appropriate notice;

(l) Rule on motions to correct the transcript which are received within ten (10) days after the transcript is received in the regional office; and

(m) Take any other action necessary under this section and not prohibited by the regulations in this subchapter.

§ 1422.13 Objections to conduct of hearing.

Any objection to the introduction of evidence may be stated orally or in writing and shall be accompanied by a short statement of the grounds of such objection, and be included in the record. No such objection shall be deemed waived by further participation in the hearing. Automatic exceptions will be allowed to all adverse rulings.

§ 1422.14 Filing of briefs.

A party desiring to file a brief with the Board shall file the original and three (3) copies within thirty (30) days from the close of the hearing. Copies thereof shall be served on all other parties to the proceeding. Requests for additional time in which to file a brief under authority of this section shall be made to the Regional Director, in writing, and copies thereof shall be served on the other parties and a statement of such service shall be filed with the Regional Director. Requests for extension of time shall be in writing and received not later than five (5) days before the date such briefs are due. No reply brief may be filed in any proceeding except by special permission of the Board.

§ 1422.15 Transfer of case to the Board; contents of record.

Upon the close of the hearing the case is transferred automatically to the Board. The record of the proceeding shall include the petition, notice of hearing, service sheet, motions, rulings, orders, official transcript of the hearing with any corrections thereto, stipulations, objections, depositions, interrogatories, exhibits, documentary evidence, and any briefs or other documents submitted by the parties.

§ 1422.16 Decision.

The Board will issue a decision directing an election or dismissing the petition, or making other disposition of the matters before it.

§ 1422.17 Election procedure; request for authorized representation election observers.

This section governs all elections conducted under the supervision of the Regional Director pursuant to § 1422.7 or § 1422.16. The Regional Director may conduct elections in unusual circumstances in accordance with terms and conditions set forth in the notice of election.

(a) Appropriate notices of election shall be posted by the Department. Such notices shall set forth the details and procedures for the election, the unit described in 22 U.S.C. 4112, the eligibility period, the date(s), hour(s) and place(s) of the election and shall contain a sample ballot.

(b) The reproduction of any document purporting to be a copy of the official ballot, other than one completely unaltered in form and content and clearly marked "sample" on its face, which suggests either directly or indirectly to employees that the Board endorses a particular choice, may constitute grounds for setting aside an election upon objections properly filed.

(c) All elections shall be by secret ballot. An exclusive representative shall be chosen by a majority of the valid ballots cast.

(d) Whenever two or more labor organizations are included as choices in an election, any intervening labor organization may request the Regional Director to remove its name from the ballot. The request must be in writing and received not later than seven (7) days before the date of the election. Such request shall be subject to the approval of the Regional Director whose decision shall be final.

(e) In a proceeding involving an election to determine if a labor organization should cease to be the exclusive representative filed by the Department or any employee or employees or an individual acting on behalf of any employee(s) under § 1422.2(b), an organization currently recognized or certified may not have its name removed from the ballot without having served the written request submitted pursuant to paragraph (d) of this section on all parties. Such request shall contain an express disclaimer of any representation interest among the employees in the unit.

(f) Any party may be represented at the polling place(s) by observers of its own selection, subject to such limitations as the Regional Director may prescribe.

(g) A party's request to the Regional Director for named observers shall be in writing and filed with the Regional Director not less than fifteen (15) days prior to an election to be supervised or conducted pursuant to this part. The request shall name and identify the authorized representation election observers sought, and state the reasons therefor. Copies thereof shall be served on the other parties and a written statement of such service shall be filed with the Regional Director. Within five (5) days after service of a copy of the request, a party may file objections to the request with the Regional Director and state the reasons therefor. Copies thereof shall be served on the other parties and a written statement of such service shall be filed with the Regional Director. The Regional Director shall rule upon the request not later than five (5) days prior to the date of the election. However, for good cause shown by a party, or on the Regional Director's own motion, the Regional Director may vary the time limits prescribed in this paragraph.

§ 1422.18 Challenged ballots.

Any party or the representative of the Board may challenge, for good cause, the eligibility of any person to participate in the election. The ballots of such challenged persons shall be impounded.

§ 1422.19 Tally of ballots.

Upon the conclusion of the election, the Regional Director shall cause to be furnished to the parties a tally of ballots.

§ 1422.20 Certification; objections to election; determination on objections and challenged ballots.

(a) The Regional Director shall issue to the parties a certification of results of the election or a certification of representative, where appropriate: *Provided, however,* That no objections are filed within the time limit set forth below; the challenged ballots are insufficient in number to affect the results of the election; and no rerun election is to be held.

(b) Within twenty (20) days after the tally of ballots has been furnished, a party may file objections to the procedural conduct of the election, or to conduct which may have improperly affected the results of the election, setting forth a clear and concise statement of the reasons therefor. The objecting party shall bear the burden of proof at all stages of the proceeding regarding all matters raised in its objections. An original and two (2) copies of the objections shall be filed with the Regional Director and copies shall be served on the parties. A statement of such service shall be filed with the Regional Director. Such filing must be timely whether or not the challenged ballots are sufficient in number to affect the results of the election. Within ten (10) days after the filing of the objections, unless an extension of time has been granted by the Regional Director, the objecting party shall file with the Regional Director evidence, including signed statements, documents and other material supporting the objections.

(c) If objections are filed or challenged ballots are sufficient in number to affect the results of the election, the Regional Director shall investigate the objections or challenged ballots, or both.

(d) When the Regional Director determines that no relevant question of fact exists, the Regional Director (1) shall find whether improper conduct occurred of such a nature as to warrant the setting aside of the election and, if so, indicate an intention to set aside the election, or (2) shall rule on determinative challenged ballots, if any, or both. The Regional Director shall issue a report and findings on objections and/or challenged ballots which shall be served upon all parties to the proceeding. Such report and findings shall state therein any additional pertinent matters such as an intent to rerun the election or count ballots at a specified date, time, and place, and if appropriate, that the Regional Director will cause to be issued a revised tally of ballots.

(e) When the Regional Director determines that no relevant question of fact exists, but that a substantial question of interpretation or policy exists, the Regional Director shall notify the parties in the report and findings and transfer the case to the Board in accordance with of this subchapter.

(f) Any party aggrieved by the findings of a Regional Director with respect to objections to an election or challenged ballots may obtain a review of such action by the Board by following the procedure set forth in § 1422.6(d) of this subchapter: *Provided, however*, That a determination by the Regional Director to issue a notice of hearing shall not be subject to review by the Board.

(g) Where it appears to the Regional Director that the objections or challenged ballots raise any relevant question of fact which may have affected the results of the election, the Regional Director shall cause to be issued a notice of hearing. Hearings shall be conducted and decisions issued by Administrative Law Judges and exceptions and related submissions filed with the Board in accordance with §§ 1423.14 through 1423.28 of this subchapter excluding § 1423.18 and § 1423.19(j), with the following exceptions:

(1) The Administrative Law Judge may not recommend remedial action to be taken or notices to be posted, as provided under § 1423.26(a); and

(2) Reference to "charge, complaint" in § 1423.26(b) shall be read as "report and findings of the Regional Director."

(h) At a hearing conducted pursuant to paragraph (g) of this section the party filing the objections shall have the burden of proving all matters alleged in its objections by a preponderance of the evidence. With respect to challenged ballots, no burden of proof is imposed on any party.

(i) The Board shall take action which may consist of the following, as appropriate:

(1) Issue a decision adopting, modifying, or rejecting the Administrative Law Judge's decision;

(2) Issue a decision in any case involving a substantial question of interpretation or policy transferred pursuant to paragraph (e) of this section; or

(3) Issue a ruling with respect to a request for review filed pursuant to paragraph (f) of this section affirming or reversing, in whole or in part, the Regional Director's findings, or make such other disposition as may be appropriate.

§ 1422.21 Preferential voting.

In any election in which more than two choices are on the ballot and no choice receives a majority of first preferences the Board shall distribute to the two choices having the most first preferences the preferences as between those two of the other valid ballots cast. The choice receiving a majority of preferences shall be declared the winner. A labor organization which is declared the winner of the election shall be certified by the Board as the exclusive representative.

§ 1422.22 Inconclusive elections.

(a) An inconclusive election is one in which none of the choices on the ballot is declared the winner. If there are no challenged ballots that would affect the results of the election, the Regional Director may declare the election a nullity and may order another election providing for a selection from among the choices afforded in the previous ballot.

(b) Only one further election pursuant to this section may be held.

PART 1423—UNFAIR LABOR PRACTICE PROCEEDINGS

Sec.

AUTHORITY: 22 U.S.C. 4107.

SOURCE: 46 FR 45868, Sept. 15, 1981, unless otherwise noted.

§ 1423.1 Applicability of this part.

This part is applicable to any charge of alleged unfair labor practices filed with the Board on or after February 15, 1981.

§ 1423.2 Informal proceedings.

(a) The purposes and policies of the Foreign Service Labor-Management Relations Statute can best be achieved by the cooperative efforts of all persons covered by the program. To this end, it shall be the policy of the Board and the General Counsel to encourage all persons alleging unfair labor practices and persons against whom such allegations are made to meet and, in good faith, attempt to resolve such matters prior to the filing of unfair labor practice charges with the Board.

(b) In furtherance of the policy referred to in paragraph (a) of this section, and noting the six (6) month period of limitation set forth in 22 U.S.C. 4116(d), it shall be the policy of the Board and the General Counsel to encourage the informal resolution of unfair labor practice allegations subsequent to the filing of a charge and prior to the issuance of a complaint by the Regional Director.

§ 1423.3 Who may file charges.

The Department or labor organization may be charged by any person with having engaged in or engaging in any unfair labor practice prohibited under 22 U.S.C. 4115.

§ 1423.4 Contents of the charge; supporting evidence and documents.

(a) A charge alleging a violation of 22 U.S.C. 4115 shall be submitted on forms prescribed by the Board and shall contain the following:

(1) The name, address and telephone number of the person(s) making the charge;

(2) The name, address and telephone number of the Department or labor organization against whom the charge is made;

(3) A clear and concise statement of the facts constituting the alleged unfair labor practice, a statement of the

section(s) and subsection(s) of chapter 41 of title 22 of the United States Code alleged to have been violated, and the date and place of occurrence of the particular acts; and

(4) A statement of any other procedure invoked involving the subject matter of the charge and the results, if any, including whether the subject matter raised in the charge (i) has been raised previously in a grievance procedure; (ii) has been referred to the Foreign Service Impasse Disputes Panel or the Foreign Service Grievance Board for consideration or action; or (iii) involves a negotiability issue raised by the charging party in a petition pending before the Board pursuant to part 1424 of this subchapter.

(b) Such charge shall be in writing and signed and shall contain a declaration by the person signing the charge, under the penalties of the Criminal Code (18 U.S.C. 1001), that its contents are true and correct to the best of that person's knowledge and belief.

(c) When filing a charge, the charging party shall submit to the Regional Director any supporting evidence and documents.

§ 1423.5 Selection of the unfair labor practice procedure or the negotiability procedure.

(a) Where a labor organization files an unfair labor practice charge pursuant to this part which involves a negotiability issue, and the labor organization also files pursuant to part 1424 of this subchapter a petition for review of the same negotiability issue, the Board and the General Counsel ordinarily will not process the unfair labor practice charge and the petition for review simultaneously.

(b) Under such circumstances, the labor organization must select under which procedure to proceed. Upon selection of one procedure, further action under the other procedure will ordinarily be suspended. Such selection must be made regardless of whether the unfair labor practice charge or the petition for review of a negotiability issue is filed first. Notification of this selection must be made in writing at the time that both procedures have been invoked, and must be served on the Board, the appropriate Regional Director and all parties to both the unfair labor practice case and the negotiability case.

(c) Cases which solely involve an agency's allegation that the duty to bargain in good faith does not extend to the matter proposed to be bargained and which do not involve actual or contemplated changes in conditions of employment may only be filed under part 1424 of this subchapter.

§ 1423.6 Filing and service of copies.

(a) An original and four (4) copies of the charge together with one copy for each additional charged party named shall be filed with the Regional Director for the region in which the alleged unfair labor practice has occurred or is occurring. A charge alleging that an unfair labor practice has occurred or is occurring in two or more regions may be filed with the Regional Director for any such region.

(b) Upon the filing of a charge, the charging party shall be responsible for the service of a copy of the charge (without the supporting evidence and documents) upon the person(s) against whom the charge is made, and for filing a written statement of such service with the Regional Director. The Regional Director will, as a matter of course, cause a copy of such charge to be served on the person(s) against whom the charge is made, but shall not be deemed to assume responsibility for such service.

§ 1423.7 Investigation of charges.

(a) The Regional Director, on behalf of the General Counsel, shall conduct such investigation of the charge as the Regional Director deems necessary.

(b) During the course of the investigation all parties involved will have an opportunity to present their evidence and views to the Regional Director.

(c) In connection with the investigation of charges, all persons are expected to cooperate fully with the Regional Director.

(d) The purposes and policies of the Foreign Service Labor-Management Relations Statute can best be achieved by the full cooperation of all parties involved and the voluntary submission of all potentially relevant information from all potential sources during the course of the investigation. To this end, it shall be the policy of the Board and the General Counsel to protect the identity of individuals and the substance of the statements and information they submit or which is obtained during the investigation as a means of assuring the Board's and the General Counsel's continuing ability to obtain all relevant information.

§ 1423.8 Amendment of charges.

Prior to the issuance of a complaint, the charging party may amend the charge in accordance with the requirements set forth in § 1423.6.

§ 1423.9 Action by the Regional Director.

(a) The Regional Director shall take action which may consist of the following, as appropriate:

(1) Approve a request to withdraw a charge;

(2) Refuse to issue a complaint;

(3) Approve a written settlement agreement in accordance with the provisions of § 1423.11;

(4) Issue a complaint;

(5) Upon agreement of all parties, transfer to the Board for decision, after issuance of a complaint, a stipulation of facts in accordance with the provisions of § 1429.1(a) this subchapter; or

(6) Withdraw a complaint.

(b) Parties may request the General Counsel to seek appropriate temporary relief (including a restraining order) under 22 U.S.C. 4109(d). The General Counsel will initiate and prosecute injunctive proceedings under 22 U.S.C. 4109(d) only upon approval of the Board. A determination by the General Counsel not to seek approval of the Board for such temporary relief is final and may not be applied to the Board.

(c) Upon a determination to issue a complaint, whenever it is deemed advisable by the Board to seek appropriate temporary relief (including a restraining order) under 22 U.S.C. 4109(d), the Regional Attorney or other designated agent of the Board to whom the matter has been referred will make application for appropriate temporary relief (including a restraining order) in the United States District Court for the District of Columbia. Such temporary relief will not be sought unless the record establishes probable cause that an unfair labor practice is being committed, or if such temporary relief will interfere with the ability of the Department to carry out its essential functions.

(d) Whenever temporary relief has been obtained pursuant to 22 U.S.C. 4109(d) and thereafter the Administrative Law Judge hearing the complaint, upon which the determination to seek such temporary relief was predicated, recommends dismissal of such complaint, in whole or in part, the Regional Attorney or other designated agent of the Board handling the case for the Board shall inform the United States District Court for the District of Columbia of the possible change in circumstances arising out of the decision of the Administrative Law Judge.

§ 1423.10 Determination not to issue complaint; review of action by the Regional Director.

(a) If the Regional Director determines that the charge has not been timely filed, that the charge fails to state an unfair labor practice, or for other appropriate reasons, the Regional Director may request the charging party to withdraw the charge, and in the absence of such withdrawal within a reasonable time, decline to issue a complaint.

(b) If the Regional Director determines not to issue a complaint on a charge which is not withdrawn, the Regional Director shall provide the parties with a written statement of the reasons for not issuing a complaint.

(c) The charging party may obtain a review of the Regional Director's decision not to issue a complaint by filing an appeal with the General Counsel within twenty-five (25) days after service of the Regional Director's decision. The appeal shall contain a complete statement setting forth the facts and reasons upon which it is based. A copy of the appeal shall also be filed with the Regional Director. In addition, the charging party should notify all other parties of the fact that an appeal has been taken, but any failure to give such notice shall not affect the validity of the appeal.

(d) A request for extension of time to file an appeal shall be in writing and received by the General Counsel not later than five (5) days before the date the appeal is due. The charging party should notify the Regional Director and all other parties that it has requested an extension of time in which to file an appeal, but any failure to give such notice shall not affect the validity of its request for an extension of time to file an appeal.

(e) The General Counsel may sustain the Regional Director's refusal to issue or re-issue a complaint, stating the grounds of affirmance, or may direct the Regional Director to take further action. The General Counsel's decision shall be served on all the parties. The decision of the General Counsel shall be final.

§ 1423.11 Settlement or adjustment of issues.

GENERAL SETTLEMENT POLICY

(a) At any stage of a proceeding prior to hearing, where time, the nature of the proceeding, and the public interest permit, all interested parties shall have the opportunity to submit to the Regional Director with whom the charge was filed, for consideration, all facts and arguments concerning offers of settlement, or proposals of adjustment.

PRECOMPLAINT INFORMAL SETTLEMENTS

(b)(1) Prior to the issuance of any complaint or the taking of other formal action, the Regional Director will afford the charging party and the respondent a reasonable period of time in which to enter into an informal settlement agreement to be approved by the Regional Director. Upon approval by the Regional Director and compliance with the terms of the informal settlement agreement, no further action shall be taken in the case. If the respondent fails to perform its obligations under the informal settlement agreement, the Regional Director may determine to institute further proceedings.

(2) In the event that the charging party fails or refuses to become a party to an informal settlement agreement offered by the respondent, if the Regional Director concludes that the offered settlement will effectuate the policies of the Foreign Service Labor-Management Relations Statute, the agreement shall be between the respondent and the Regional Director and the latter shall decline to issue a complaint. The charging party may obtain a review of the Regional Director's action by filing an appeal with the General Counsel in accordance with § 1423.10(c). The General Counsel shall take action on such appeal as set forth in § 1423.10(e).

POST COMPLAINT SETTLEMENT POLICY

(c) Consistent with the policy reflected in paragraph (a) of this section, even after the issuance of a complaint, the Board favors the settlement of issues. Such settlements may be either informal or formal. Informal settlement agreements shall be accomplished as provided in paragraph (b) of this section. Formal settlement agreements are subject to the approval of the Board. In such formal settlement agreements, the parties shall agree to waive their right to a hearing and agree further that the Board may issue an order requiring the respondent to take action appropriate to the terms of the settlement. Ordinarily the formal settlement agreement also contains the respondent's consent to the Board application for the entry of a decree by the United States Court of Appeals for the District of Columbia enforcing the Board's order.

POST COMPLAINT—PREHEARING FORMAL SETTLEMENTS

(d)(1) If, after issuance of a complaint but before opening of the hearing, the charging party and the respondent enter into a formal settlement agreement, and such agreement is accepted by the Regional Director, the formal settlement agreement shall be submitted to the Board for approval.

(2) If, after issuance of a complaint but before opening of the hearing, the charging party fails or refuses to become a party to a formal settlement agreement offered by the respondent, and the Regional Director concludes

that the offered settlement will effectuate the policies of the Foreign Service Labor-Management Relations Statute, the agreement shall be between the respondent and the Regional Director. The charging party will be so informed and provided a brief written statement by the Regional Director of the reasons therefor. The formal settlement agreement together with the charging party's objections, if any, and the Regional Director's written statements, shall be submitted to the Board for approval. The Board may approve or disapprove any formal settlement agreement or return the case to the Regional Director for other appropriate action.

POST COMPLAINT—PREHEARING INFORMAL SETTLEMENTS

(3) After the issuance of a complaint but before opening of the hearing, if the Regional Director concludes that it will effectuate the policies of the Foreign Service Labor-Management Relations Statute, the Regional Director may withdraw the complaint and approve an informal settlement agreement pursuant to paragraph (b) of this section.

INFORMAL SETTLEMENTS AFTER THE OPENING OF THE HEARING

(e)(1) After issuance of a complaint and after opening of the hearing, if the Regional Director concludes that it will effectuate the policies of the Foreign Service Labor-Management Relations Statute, the Regional Director may request the Administrative Law Judge for permission to withdraw the complaint and, having been granted such permission to withdraw the complaint, may approve an informal settlement pursuant to paragraph (b) of this section.

FORMAL SETTLEMENTS AFTER THE OPENING OF THE HEARING

(2) If, after issuance of a complaint and after opening of the hearing, the parties enter into a formal settlement agreement, the Regional Director may request the Administrative Law Judge to approve such formal settlement agreement, and upon such approval, to transmit the agreement to the Board for approval.

(3) If the charging party fails or refuses to become a party to a formal settlement agreement offered by the respondent, and the Regional Director concludes that the offered settlement will effectuate the policies of the Foreign Service Labor-Management Relations Statute, the agreement shall be between the respondent and the Regional Director. After the charging party is given an opportunity to state on the record or in writing the reasons for opposing the formal settlement, the Regional Director may request the Administrative Law Judge to approve such formal settlement agreement, and upon such approval, to transmit the agreement to the Board for approval. The Board may approve or disapprove any formal settlement agreement or return the case to the Administrative Law Judge for another appropriate action.

§ 1423.12 Issuance and contents of the complaint.

(a) After a charge is filed, if it appears to the Regional Director that formal proceedings in respect thereto should be instituted, the Regional Director shall issue and cause to be served on all other parties a formal complaint: *Provided, however,* That a determination by a Regional Director to issue a complaint shall not be subject to review.

(b) The complaint shall include:

(1) Notice of the charge;

(2) Notice that a hearing will be held before an Adminsitrative Law Judge;

(3) Notice of the time and place fixed for the hearing which shall not be earlier than five (5) days after service of the complaint;

(4) A statement of the nature of the hearing;

(5) A clear and concise statement of the facts upon which assertion of jurisdiction by the Board is predicated;

(6) A reference to the particular sections of chapter 41 of title 22 of the United States Code and the rules and regulations involved; and

(7) A clear and concise description of the acts which are claimed to constitute unfair labor practices, including, where known, the approximate

dates and places of such acts and the names of respondent's agents or other representatives by whom committed.

(c) The Chief Administrative Law Judge may, upon such judge's own motion or upon proper cause shown by any other party, extend the date of the hearing or may change the place at which it is to be held.

(d) A complaint may be amended, upon such terms as may be deemed just, prior to the hearing, by the Regional Director issuing the complaint; at the hearing and until the case has been transmitted to the Board pursuant to § 1423.26, upon motion by the Administrative Law Judge designated to conduct the hearing; and after the case has been transmitted to the Board pursuant to § 1423.26, upon motion by the Board at any time prior to the issuance of an order based thereon by the Board.

(e) Any such complaint may be withdrawn before the hearing by the Regional Director.

§ 1423.13 Answer to the complaint; extension of time for filing; amendment.

(a) Except in extraordinary circumstances as determined by the Regional Director, within twenty (20) days after the complaint is served upon the respondent, the respondent shall file the original and four (4) copies of the answer thereto, signed by the respondent or its representative, with the Regional Director who issued the complaint. The respondent shall serve a copy of the answer on the Chief Administrative Law Judge and on all other parties.

(b) The answer: (1) Shall specifically admit, deny, or explain each of the allegations of the complaint unless the respondent is without knowledge, in which case the answer shall so state; or (2) Shall state that the respondent admits all of the allegations in the complaint. Failure to file an answer or to plead specifically to or explain any allegation shall constitute an admission of such allegation and shall be so found by the Board, unless good cause to the contrary is shown.

(c) Upon the Regional Director's own motion or upon proper cause shown by any other party, the Regional Director issuing the complaint may by written order extend the time within which the answer shall be filed.

(d) The answer may be amended by the respondent at any time prior to the hearing. During the hearing or subsequent thereto, the answer may be amended in any case where the complaint has been amended, within such period as may be fixed by the Administrative Law Judge or the Board. Whether or not the complaint has been amended, the answer may, in the discretion of the Administrative Law Judge or the Board, upon motion, be amended upon such terms and within such periods as may be fixed by the Administrative Law Judge or the Board.

§ 1423.14 Conduct of hearing.

(a) Hearings shall be conducted not earlier than five (5) days after the date on which the complaint is served. The hearing shall be open to the public unless otherwise ordered by the Administrative Law Judge. A substitute Administrative Law Judge may be designated at any time to take the place of the Administrative Law Judge previously designated to conduct the hearing. Such hearing shall, to the extent practicable, be conducted in accordance with the provisions of subchapter II of chapter 5 of title 5 of the United States Code, except that the parties shall not be bound by the rules of evidence, whether statutory, common law, or adopted by a court.

(b) An official reporter shall make the only official transcript of such proceedings. Copies of the official transcript may be examined in the appropriate regional office during normal working hours. Requests by parties for copies of transcripts should be made to the official hearing reporter.

§ 1423.15 Intervention.

Any person involved and desiring to intervene in any proceeding pursuant to this part shall file a motion in accordance with the procedures set forth in § 1423.22. The motion shall state the grounds upon which such person claims involvement.

§ 1423.16 Rights of parties.

A party shall have the right to appear at any hearing in person, by counsel, or by other representative, and to examine and cross-examine witnesses, and to introduce into the record documentary or other relevant evidence, and to submit rebuttal evidence, except that the participation of any party shall be limited to the extent prescribed by the Administrative Law Judge. Two (2) copies of documentary evidence shall be submitted and a copy furnished to each of the other parties. Stipulations of fact may be introduced in evidence with respect to any issue.

§ 1423.17 Rules of evidence.

The parties shall not be bound by the rules of evidence, whether statutory, common law, or adopted by court. Any evidence may be received, except that an Administrative Law Judge may exclude any evidence which is immaterial, irrelevant, unduly repetitious or customarily privileged.

§ 1423.18 Burden of proof before the Administrative Law Judge.

The General Counsel shall have the responsibility of presenting the evidence in support of the complaint and shall have the burden of proving the allegations of the complaint by a preponderance of the evidence.

§ 1423.19 Duties and powers of the Administrative Law Judge.

It shall be the duty of the Administrative Law Judge to inquire fully into the facts as they relate to the matter before such judge. Subject to the rules and regulations of the Board and the General Counsel, an Administrative Law Judge presiding at a hearing may:

(a) Grant requests for subpoenas pursuant to § 1429.7 of this subchapter;

(b) Rule upon petitions to revoke subpoenas pursuant to § 1429.7 of this subchapter;

(c) Administer oaths and affirmations;

(d) Take or order the taking of a deposition whenever the ends of justice would be served thereby;

(e) Order responses to written interrogatories whenever the ends of justice would be served thereby unless it would interfere with the Board's and the General Counsel's policy of protecting the personal privacy and confidentiality of sources of information as set forth in § 1423.7(d);

(f) Call, examine and cross-examine witnesses and introduce into the record documentary or other evidence;

(g) Rule upon offers of proof and receive relevant evidence and stipulations of fact with respect to any issue;

(h) Limit lines of questioning or testimony which are immaterial, irrelevant, unduly repetitious, or customarily privileged;

(i) Regulate the course of the hearing and, if appropriate, exclude from the hearing persons who engage in contemptuous conduct and strike all related testimony of witnesses refusing to answer any questions ruled to be proper;

(j) Hold conferences for the settlement or simplification of the issues by consent of the parties or upon the judge's own motion;

(k) Dispose of procedural requests, motions, or similar matters, including motions referred to the Administrative Law Judge by the Regional Director and motions for summary judgment or to amend pleadings; dismiss complaints or portions thereof; order hearings reopened; and, upon motion, order proceedings consolidated or severed prior to issuance of the Administrative Law Judge's decision;

(l) Request the parties at any time during the hearing to state their respective positions concerning any issue in the case or theory in support thereof;

(m) Continue the hearing from day-to-day or adjourn it to a later date or to a different place, by announcement thereof at the hearing or by other appropriate notice;

(n) Prepare, serve and transmit the decision pursuant to § 1423.26;

(o) Take official notice of any material fact not appearing in evidence in the record, which is among the traditional matters of judicial notice: *Provided, however*, That the parties shall be given adequate notice, at the hearing or by reference in the Administrative Law Judge's decision of the matters so noticed, and shall be given adequate opportunity to show the contrary;

(p) Approve requests for withdrawal of complaints based on informal settlements occurring after the opening of the hearing pursuant to § 1423.11(e)(1), and transmit formal settlement agreements to the Board for approval pursuant to § 1423.11(e) (2) and (3);

(q) Grant or deny requests made at the hearing to intervene and to present testimony;

(r) Correct or approve proposed corrections of the official transcript when deemed necessary;

(s) Sequester witnesses where appropriate; and

(t) Take any other action deemed necessary under the foregoing and not prohibited by the regulations in this subchapter.

§ 1423.20 Unavailability of Administrative Law Judges.

In the event the Administrative Law Judge designated to conduct the hearing becomes unavailable, the Chief Administrative Law Judge shall designate another Administrative Law Judge for the purpose of further hearing or issuance of a decision on the record as made, or both.

§ 1423.21 Objection to conduct of hearing.

(a) Any objection with respect to the conduct of the hearing, including any objection to the introduction of evidence, may be stated orally or in writing accompanied by a short statement of the grounds for such objection, and included in the record. No such objection shall be deemed waived by further participation in the hearing. Such objection shall not stay the conduct of the hearing.

(b) Formal exceptions to adverse rulings are unnecessary. Automatic exceptions will be allowed to all adverse rulings. Except by special permission of the Board, and in view of § 1429.11 of this subchapter, rulings by the Administrative Law Judge shall not be appealed prior to the transmittal of the case to the Board, but shall be considered by the Board only upon the filing of exceptions to the Administrative Law Judge's decision in accordance with § 1423.27. In the discretion of the Administrative Law Judge, the hearing may be continued or adjourned pending any such request for special permission to appeal.

§ 1423.22 Motions.

(a) *Filing of Motions.* (1) Motions made prior to a hearing and any response thereto shall be made in writing and filed with the Regional Director: *Provided, however,* That after the issuance of a complaint by the Regional Director any motion to postpone the hearing should be filed with the Chief Administrative Law Judge at least five (5) days prior to the opening of the scheduled hearing. Motions made after the hearing opens and prior to the transmittal of the case to the Board shall be made in writing to the Administrative Law Judge or orally on the record. After the transmittal of the case to the Board, motions and any response thereto shall be filed in writing with the Board: *Provided, however,* That a motion to correct the transcript shall be filed with the Administrative Law Judge.

(2) A response to a motion shall be filed within five (5) days after service of the motion, unless otherwise directed.

(3) An original and two (2) copies of the motions and responses shall be filed, and copies shall be served on the parties. A statement of such service shall accompany the original.

(b) *Rulings on motions.* (1) Regional Directors may rule on all motions filed with them before the hearing, or they may refer them to the Chief Administrative Law Judge.

(2) Except by special permission of the Board, and in view of § 1429.11 of this subchapter, rulings by the Regional Director shall not be appealed prior to the transmittal of the case to the Board, but shall be considered by the Board when the case is transmitted to it for decision.

(3) Administrative Law Judges may rule on motions referred to them prior to the hearing and on motions filed after the beginning of the hearing and before the transmittal of the case to the Board. Such motions may be ruled upon by the Chief Administrative Law Judge in the absence of an Administrative Law Judge.

(4) Except by special permission of the Board, and in view of § 1429.11 of this subchapter, rulings by Administrative Law Judges shall not be appealed prior to the transmittal of the case to

the Board, but shall be considered by the Board when the case is transmitted to it for decision. In the discretion of the Administrative Law Judge, the hearing may be continued or adjourned pending any such request for special permission to appeal.

§ 1423.23 Waiver of objections.

Any objection not made before an Administrative Law Judge shall be deemed waived.

§ 1423.24 Oral argument at the hearing.

Any party shall be entitled, upon request, to a reasonable period prior to the close of the hearing for oral argument, which shall be included in the official transcript of the hearing.

§ 1423.25 Filing of brief.

Any party desiring to submit a brief to the Administrative Law Judge shall file the original and two (2) copies within a reasonable time fixed by the Administrative Law Judge, but not in excess of thirty (30) days from the close of the hearing. Copies of any brief shall be served on all other parties to the proceeding and a statement of such service shall be filed with the Administrative Law Judge. Requests for additional time to file a brief shall be made to the Chief Administrative Law Judge, in writing, and copies thereof shall be served on the other parties. A statement of such service shall be furnished. Requests for extension of time shall be received not later than five (5) days before the date such briefs are due. No reply brief may be filed except by special permission of the Administrative Law Judge.

§ 1423.26 Transmittal of the Administrative Law Judge's decision to the Board; exceptions.

(a) After the close of the hearing, and the receipt of brief, if any, the Administrative Law Judge shall prepare the decision expeditiously. The Administrative Law Judge shall prepare a decision even when the parties enter into a stipulation of fact at the hearing. The decision shall contain findings of fact, conclusions, and the reasons or basis therefor including credibility determinations, and conclusions as to the disposition of the case including, where appropriate, the remedial action to be taken and notices to be posted.

(b) The Administrative Law Judge shall cause the decision to be served promptly on all parties to the proceeding. Thereafter, the Administrative Law Judge shall transmit the case to the Board including the judge's decision and the record. The record shall include the charge, complaint, service sheet, answer, motions, rulings, orders, official transcript of the hearing, stipulations, objections, depositions, interrogatories, exhibits, documentary evidence and any briefs or other documents submitted by the parties.

(c) An original and three (3) copies of any exception to the Administrative Law Judge's decision and briefs in support of exceptions may be filed by any party with the Board within twenty-five (25) days after service of the decision: *Provided, however*, That the Board may for good cause shown extend the time for filing such exceptions. Requests for additional time in which to file exceptions shall be in writing, and copies thereof shall be served on the other parties. Requests for extension of time must be received no later than five (5) days before the date the exceptions are due. Copies of such exceptions and any supporting briefs shall be served on all other parties, and a statement of such service shall be furnished to the Board.

§ 1423.27 Contents of exceptions to the Administrative Law Judge's decision.

(a) Exceptions to an Administrative Law Judge's decision shall:

(1) Set forth specifically the questions upon which exceptions are taken;

(2) Identify that part of the Administrative Law Judge's decision to which objection is made; and

(3) Designate by precise citation of page the portions of the record relied on, state the grounds for the exceptions, and include the citation of authorities unless set forth in a supporting brief.

(b) Any exception to a ruling, finding or conclusion which is not specifically urged shall be deemed to have been waived. Any exception which fails to comply with the foregoing requirements may be disregarded.

§ 1423.28 Briefs in support of exceptions; oppositions to exceptions; cross-exceptions.

(a) Any brief in support of exceptions shall contain only matters included within the scope of the exceptions and shall contain, in the order indicated, the following:

(1) A concise statement of the case containing all that is material to the consideration of the questions presented;

(2) A specification of the questions involved and to be argued; and

(3) The argument, presenting clearly the points of fact and law relied on in support of the position taken on each question, with specific page reference to the transcript and the legal or other material relied on.

(b) Any party may file an opposition to exceptions and cross-exceptions and a supporting brief with the Board within ten (10) days after service of any exceptions to an Administrative Law Judge's decision. Copies of the opposition to exceptions and the cross-exceptions and any supporting briefs shall be served on all other parties, and a statement of service shall be filed with the opposition to exceptions and cross-exceptions and any supporting briefs.

§ 1423.29 Action by the Board.

(a) After considering the Administrative Law Judge's decision, the record, and any exceptions and related submissions filed, the Board shall issue its decision affirming or reversing the Administrative Law Judge, in whole, or in part, or making such other disposition of the matter as it deems appropriate: *Provided, however*, That unless exceptions are filed which are timely and in accordance with § 1423.27, the Board may, at its discretion, adopt without discussion the decision of the Administrative Law Judge, in which event the findings and conclusions of the Administrative Law Judge, as contained in such decision shall, upon appropriate notice to the parties, automatically become the decision of the Board.

(b) Upon finding a violation, the Board shall issue an order:

(1) To cease and desist from any such unfair labor practice in which the Department or labor organization is engaged;

(2) Requiring the parties to renegotiate a collective bargaining agreement in accordance with the order of the Board and requiring that the agreement, as amended, be given retroactive effect;

(3) Requiring reinstatement of an employee with backpay in accordance with 5 U.S.C. 5596; or

(4) Including any combination of the actions described in paragraphs (b) (1) through (3) of this section or such other action as will carry out the purpose of the Foreign Service Labor-Management Relations Statute.

(c) Upon finding no violation, the Board shall dismiss the complaint.

§ 1423.30 Compliance with decisions and orders of the Board.

When remedial action is ordered, the respondent shall report to the appropriate Regional Director within a specified period that the required remedial action has been effected. When the General Counsel finds that the required remedial action has not been effected, the General Counsel shall take such action as may be appropriate, including referral to the Board for enforcement.

§ 1423.31 Backpay proceedings.

After the entry of a Board order directing payment of backpay, or the entry of a court decree enforcing such order, if it appears to the Regional Director that a controversy exists between the Board and a respondent which cannot be resolved without a formal proceeding, the Regional Director may issue and serve on all parties a backpay specification accompanied by a notice of hearing or a notice of hearing without a specification. The respondent shall, within twenty (20) days after the service of a backpay specification accompanied by a notice of hearing, file an answer thereto in accordance with § 1423.13 with the Regional Director issuing such specification. No answer need be filed by the respondent to a notice of hearing issued without a specification. After the issuance of a notice of hearing, with or without a backpay specification, the procedures provided in §§1423.14 to 1423.29, inclusive, shall be followed insofar as applicable.

PART 1424—EXPEDITED REVIEW OF NEGOTIABILITY ISSUES

AUTHORITY: 22 U.S.C. 4107(c).

SOURCE: 46 FR 45873, Sept. 15, 1981, unless otherwise noted.

§1424.1 Conditions governing review.

Pursuant to the authority contained in 22 U.S.C. 4107 (a)(3) and (c)(1) the Board will consider a direct appeal concerning whether a matter proposed to be bargained is within the obligation to bargain under the Foreign Service Act of 1980 as follows: If the Department is involved in collective bargaining with an exclusive representative and alleges that the duty to bargain in good faith does not extend to any matter proposed to be bargained because, as proposed, the matter is inconsistent with applicable law, rule or regulation the exclusive representative may appeal the allegation to the Board when it disagrees with Department's allegation that the matter as proposed to be bargained is inconsistent with applicable law, rule or regulation.

§1424.2 Who may file a petition.

A petition for review of a negotiability issue may be filed by the exclusive representative which is a party to the negotiations.

§1424.3 Time limits for filing.

(a) The time limit for filing an appeal under this part is fifteen (15) days from the Department's allegation, which was requested in writing by the exclusive representative, is served on the exclusive representative. The Department shall make the allegation in writing and serve a copy on the exclusive representative: *Provided, however,* That review of a negotiability issue may be requested by the exclusive representative under this part without a prior written allegation by the Department if a written allegation has not been served upon the exclusive representative within ten (10) days after the date of receipt by any Department bargaining representative at the negotiations of a written request for such allegation.

§1424.4 Content of petition; service.

(a) A petition for review shall be dated and shall contain the following:

(1) A statement setting forth the matter proposed to be bargained as submitted to the Department;

(2) A copy of all pertinent material, including the Department's allegation in writing that the matter, as proposed, is not within the duty to bargain in good faith, and other relevant documentary material; and

(3) Notification by the petitioning labor organization whether the negotiability issue is also involved in an unfair labor parctice charge filed by such labor organization under part 1423 of this subchapter and pending before the General Counsel.

(b) A copy of the petition including all attachments thereto shall be served on the Secretary and on the principal Department bargaining representative at the negotiations.

§1424.5 Selection of the unfair labor practice procedure or the negotiability procedure.

Where a labor organization files an unfair labor practice charge pursuant to part 1423 of this subchapter which involves a negotiability issue, and the labor organization also files pursuant to this part a petition for review of the same negotiability issue, the Board and the General Counsel ordinarily will not process the unfair labor practice charge and the petition for review simultaneously. Under such circumstances, the labor organization must select under which procedure to proceed. Upon selection of one procedure, further action under the other procedure will ordinarily be suspended. Such selection must be made regardless of whether the unfair labor practice charge or the petition for review of a negotiability issue is filed first. Notification of this selection must be made in writing at the time that both procedures have been invoked, and must be served on the Board, the appropriate Regional Director and all parties to both the unfair labor practice case and the negotiability case. Cases which solely involve the Department's allegation that the duty bargain in good faith does not extend to the matter proposed to be bargained and which do not involve actual or contemplated changes in conditions of employment may only be filed under this part.

§ 1424.6 Position of the Department; time limits for filing; service.

(a) Within thirty (30) days after the date of receipt by the Secretary of a copy of the petition for review of a negotiability issue the Department shall file a statement—

(1) Withdrawing the allegation that the duty to bargain in good faith does not extend to the matter proposed to be bargained; or

(2) Setting forth in full its position on any matters relevant to the petition which it wishes the Board to consider in reaching its decision, including a full and detailed statement of its reasons supporting the allegation. The statement shall cite the section of any law, rule or regulation relied upon as a basis for the allegation.

(b) A copy of the Department's statement of position including all attachments thereto shall be served on the exclusive representative.

§ 1424.7 Response of the exclusive representative; time limits for filing; service.

(a) Within fifteen (15) days after the date of receipt by an exclusive representative of a copy of the Department's statement of position the exclusive representative shall file a full and detailed response stating its position and reasons for disagreeing with the Department's allegation that the matter, as proposed to be bargained, is inconsistent with applicable law or rule or regulation.

(b) A copy of the response of the exclusive representative including all attachments thereto shall be served on the Secretary and on the Department's representative of record in the proceedings before the Board.

§ 1424.8 Additional submissions to the Board.

The Board will not consider any submission filed by any party, whether supplemental or responsive in nature, other than those authorized under §§ 1424.2 through 1424.7 unless such submission is requested by the Board; or unless, upon written request by any party, a copy of which is served on all other parties, the Board in its discretion grants permission to file such submission.

§ 1424.9 Hearing.

A hearing may be held, in the discretion of the Board, before a determination is made under 22 U.S.C. 4107(a)(3). If a hearing is held, it shall be expedited to the extent practicable and shall not include the General Counsel as a party.

§ 1424.10 Board decision and order; compliance.

(a) Subject to the requirements of this part the Board shall expedite proceedings under this part to the extent practicable and shall issue to the exclusive representative and to the Department a written decision on the allegation and specific reasons therefor at the earliest practicable date.

(b) If the Board finds that the duty to bargain extends to the matter proposed to be bargained, the decision of the Board shall include an order that the Department shall upon request (or as otherwise agreed to by the parties) bargain concerning such matter. If the Board finds that the duty to bargain does not extend to the matter proposed to be bargained, the Board shall so state and issue an order dismissing the petition for review of the negotiability issue. If the Board finds that the duty to bargain extends to the matter proposed to be bargained only at the election of the Department, the Board shall so state and issue an order dismissing the petition for review of the negotiability issue.

(c) When an order is issued as provided in paragraph (b) of this section, the Department or exclusive representative shall report to the appropriate Regional Director within a specified period failure to comply with an order that the Department shall upon request (or as otherwise agreed to by the parties) bargain concerning the disputed matter. If the Board finds such a failure to comply with its order, the Board shall take whatever action it deems necessary, including enforcement under 22 U.S.C. 4109(b).

PART 1425—REVIEW OF IMPLEMENTATION DISPUTE ACTIONS

Sec.

AUTHORITY: 22 U.S.C. 4107(c).

SOURCE: 46 FR 45875, Sept. 15, 1981, unless otherwise noted.

§ 1425.1 Who may file an exception; time limits for filing; opposition; service.

(a) Either party to an appeal to the Foreign Service Grievance Board under the provisions of 22 U.S.C. 4114 may file an exception to the action of the Foreign Service Grievance Board taken pursuant to the appeal.

(b) The time limit for filing an exception to a Foreign Service Grievance Board action is thirty (30) days after such action is communicated to the parties.

(c) An opposition to the exception may be filed by a party within thirty (30) days after the date of service of the exception.

(d) A copy of the exception and any opposition shall be served on the other party.

§ 1425.2 Content of exception.

An exception must be a dated, self-contained document which sets forth in full:

(a) A statement of the grounds on which review is requested;

(b) Evidence or rulings bearing on the issues before the Board;

(c) Arguments in support of the stated grounds, together with specific reference to the pertinent documents and citations of authorities; and

(d) A legible copy of the decision or other document representing the action taken by the Foreign Service Grievance Board, together with legible copies of other pertinent documents pertaining to the action.

§ 1425.3 Grounds for review.

The Board will review an action of the Foreign Service Grievance Board to which an exception has been filed to determine if it is deficient—

(a) Because it is contrary to any law, rule, or regulation; or

(b) On other grounds similar to those applied by Federal courts in private sector labor-management relations.

§ 1425.4 Board decision.

The Board shall issue its decision taking such action and making such recommendations concerning the Foreign Service Grievance Board action as it considers necessary, consistent with applicable laws, rules, and regulations.

PART 1427—GENERAL STATEMENTS OF POLICY OR GUIDANCE

Sec.

AUTHORITY: 22 U.S.C. 4107(c).

SOURCE: 46 FR 45875, Sept. 15, 1981, unless otherwise noted.

§ 1427.1 Scope.

This part sets forth procedures under which requests may be submitted to the Board seeking the issuance of general statements of policy or guidance under 22 U.S.C. 4107(c)(2)(F).

§ 1427.2 Requests for general statements of policy or guidance.

(a) The head of the Department (or designee), the national president of a labor organization (or designee), or the president of a labor organization not affiliated with a national organization (or designee) may separately or jointly ask the Board for a general statement of policy or guidance. The head of any lawful association not qualified as a labor organization may also ask the Board for such a statement provided the request is not in conflict with the provisions of the Foreign Service Labor-Management Relations Statute.

(b) The Board ordinarily will not consider a request related to any matter pending before the Board, General Counsel, Panel or Assistant Secretary.

§ 1427.3 Content of request.

(a) A request for a general statement of policy or guidance shall be in writing and must contain:

(1) A concise statement of the question with respect to which a general statement of policy or guidance is requested together with background information necessary to an understanding of the question;

(2) A statement of the standards under § 1427.5 upon which the request is based;

(3) A full and detailed statement of the position or positions of the requesting party or parties

(4) Identification of any cases or other proceedings known to bear on the question which are pending under the Foreign Service Labor-Management Statute.

(5) Identification of other known interested parties.

(b) A copy of each document also shall be served on all known interested parties, including the General Counsel, the Panel, and the Assistant Secretary, where appropriate.

§ 1427.4 Submissions from interested parties.

Prior to issuance of a general statement of policy or guidance the Board, as it deems appropriate, will afford an opportunity to interested parties to express their views orally or in writing.

§ 1427.5 Standards governing issuance of general statements of policy or guidance.

In deciding whether to issue a general statement of policy or guidance, the Board shall consider:

(a) Whether the question presented can more appropriately be resolved by other means;

(b) Where other means are available, whether a Board statement would prevent the proliferation of cases involving the same or similar question;

(c) Whether the resolution of the question presented would have general applicability under the Foreign Service Labor-Management Relations Statute.

(d) Whether the question currently confronts parties in the context of a labor-management relationship;

(e) Whether the question is presented jointly by the parties involved; and

(f) Whether the issuance by the Board of a general statement of policy or guidance on the question would promote constructive and cooperative labor-management relationships in the Foreign Service and would otherwise promote the purposes of the Foreign Service Labor-Management Relations Statute.

PART 1428—ENFORCEMENT OF ASSISTANT SECRETARY STANDARDS OF CONDUCT DECISIONS AND ORDERS

AUTHORITY: 22 U.S.C. 4107(c).

SOURCE: 46 FR 45875, Sept. 15, 1981, unless otherwise noted.

§ 1428.1 Scope.

This part sets forth procedures under which the Board, pursuant to 22 U.S.C. 4107(a)(5) enforce decisions and orders of the Assistant Secretary in standards of conduct matters arising under 5 U.S.C. 7120.

§ 1428.2 Petitions for enforcement.

(a) The Assistant Secretary may petition the Board to enforce any Assistant Secretary decision and order in a standards of conduct case arising under 22 U.S.C. 4117. The Assistant Secretary shall transfer to the Board the record in the case, including a copy of the transcript if any, exhibits, briefs, and other documents filed with the Assistant Secretary. A copy of the petition for enforcement shall be served on the labor organization against which such order applies.

(b) An opposition to Board enforcement of any such Assistant Secretary decision and order may be filed by the labor organization against which such order applies twenty (20) days from the date of service of the petition, unless the Board, upon good cause shown by the Assistant Secretary, sets a shorter time for filing such position. A copy of the opposition to enforcement shall be served on the Assistant Secretary.

§ 1428.3 Board decision.

(a) A decision and order of the Assistant Secretary shall be enforced unless it is arbitrary and capricious or based upon manifest disregard of the law.

(b) The Board shall issue its decision on the case enforcing, enforcing as modified, refusing to enforce, or remanding the decision and order of the Assistant Secretary.

PART 1429—MISCELLANEOUS AND GENERAL REQUIREMENTS

Subpart A—Miscellaneous

Sec.

Subpart B—General Requirements

AUTHORITY: 22 U.S.C. 4107(c).

SOURCE: 46 FR 45876, Sept. 15, 1981, unless otherwise noted.

Subpart A—Miscellaneous

§ 1429.1 Transfer of cases to the Board.

(a) In any representation case under part 1422 of this subchapter in which the Regional Director determines, based upon a stipulation by the parties, that no material issue of fact exists, the Regional Director may transfer the case to the Board; and the Board may decide the case on the basis of the papers alone after having allowed twenty-five (25) days for the filing of briefs. In any unfair labor practice case under part 1423 of this subchapter in which, after the issuance of a complaint, the Regional Director determines, based upon a stipulation by the parties, that no material issue of fact exists, the Regional Director may upon agreement of all parties transfer the case to the Board; and the Board shall decide the case on the basis of the case papers alone after having allowed twenty-five (25) days for the filing of briefs. The Board may remand any such case to the Regional Director if it determines that a material question of fact does exist. Orders of transfer and remand shall be served on all parties.

(b) In any case under parts 1422 and 1423 of this subchapter in which it appears to the Regional Director that the proceedings raise questions which should be decided by the Board, the Regional Director may, at any time, issue an order transferring the case to the Board for decision or other appropriate action. Such an order shall be served on the parties.

§ 1429.2 Transfer and consolidation of cases.

In any matter arising pursuant to parts 1422 and 1423 of this subchapter, whenever it appears necessary in order to effectuate the purposes of the Foreign Service Labor-Management Relations Statute or to avoid unnecessary costs or delay, Regional Directors may consolidate cases within their own region or may transfer such cases to any other region, for the purpose of investigation or consolidation with any proceedings which may have been instituted in, or transferred to, such region.

§ 1429.3 Transfer of record.

In any case under part 1425 of this subchapter, upon request by the Board, the parties jointly shall transfer the record in the case, including a copy of the transcript, if any, exhibits, briefs and other documents filed with the Grievance Board, to the Board.

§ 1429.4 Referral of policy questions to the Board.

Notwithstanding the procedures set forth in this subchapter, the General Counsel, the Assistant Secretary, or the Panel may refer for review and decision or general ruling by the Board any case involving a major policy issue that arises in a proceeding before any of them. Any such referral shall be in writing and a copy of such referral shall be served on all parties to the proceeding. Before decision or general ruling, the Board shall obtain the views of the parties and other interested persons, orally or in writing, as it deems necessary and appropriate.

§ 1429.5 Matters not previously presented; official notice.

The Board will not consider evidence offered by a party, or any issue, which was not presented in the proceedings before the Regional Director, Hearing Officer, Administrative Law Judge, or Grievance Board. The Board may, however, take official notice of such matters as would be proper.

§ 1429.6 Oral argument.

The Board or the General Counsel, in their discretion, may request or permit oral argument in any matter arising under this subchapter under such circumstances and conditions as they deem appropriate.

§ 1429.7 Subpoenas.

(a) Any member of the Board, the General Counsel, any Administrative Law Judge appointed by the Board under 5 U.S.C. 3105, and any Regional Director, Hearing Officer, or other employee of the Board designated by the Board may issue subpoenas requiring the attendance and testimony of witnesses and the production of documentary or other evidence. However, no subpoena shall be issued under this section which requires the disclosure of intramanagement guidance, advice, counsel, or training within an agency or between an agency and the Office of Personnel Management.

(b) Where the parties are in agreement that the appearance of witnesses or the production of documents is necessary, and such witnesses agree to appear, no such subpoena need be sought.

(c) A request for a subpoena by any person, as defined in 22 U.S.C. 4102 shall be in writing and filed with the Regional Director, in proceedings arising under parts 1422 and 1423 of this subchapter, or filed with the Board, in proceedings arising under parts 1424 and 1425 of this subchapter, not less than fifteen (15) days prior to the opening of a hearing, or with the appropriate presiding official(s) during the hearing.

(d) All requests shall name and identify the witnesses or documents sought, and state the reasons therefor. The Board, General Counsel, Administrative Law Judge, Regional Director, Hearing Officer, or any other employee of the Board designated by the Board, as appropriate, shall grant the request upon the determination that the testimony or documents appear to be necessary to the matters under investigation and the request describes with sufficient particularity the documents sought. Service of an approved subpoena is the responsibility of the party on whose behalf the subpoena was issued. The subpoena shall show on its face the name and address of the party on whose behalf the subpoena was issued.

(e) Any person served with a subpoena who does not intend to comply, shall, within five (5) days after the date of service of the subpoena upon such person, petition in writing to revoke the subpoena. A copy of any petition to revoke a subpoena shall be served on the party on whose behalf the subpoena was issued. Such petition to revoke, if made prior to the hearing, and a written statement of service, shall be filed with the Regional Director, who may refer the petition to the Board, General Counsel, Administrative Law Judge, Hearing Officer, or any other employee of the Board designated by the Board, as appropriate, for ruling. A petition to revoke a subpoena filed during the hearing, and a written statement of service, shall be filed with the appropriate presiding official(s). The Regional Director, or the appropriate presiding official(s) will, as a matter of course, cause a copy of the petition to revoke to be served on the party on whose behalf the subpoena was issued, but shall not be deemed to assume responsibility for such service. The Board, General Counsel, Administrative Law Judge, Regional Director, Hearing Officer, or any other employee of the Board designated by the Board, as appropriate, shall revoke the subpoena if the evidence the production of which is required does not relate to any matter under investigation or in question in the proceedings, or the subpoena does not describe with sufficient particularity the evidence the production of which is required, or if for any other reason sufficient in law the subpoena is invalid. The Board, General Counsel, Administrative Law Judge, Regional Director, Hearing Officer, or any other employee of the Board designated by the Board, as appropriate, shall make a simple statement of procedural or other ground for the ruling on the petition to revoke. The petition to revoke, any answer thereto, and any ruling thereon shall not become part of the official record except upon the request of the party aggrieved by the ruling.

(f) Upon the failure of any person to comply with a subpoena issued, upon the request of the party on whose behalf the subpoena was issued, the General Counsel shall, on behalf of such party, institute proceedings in the appropriate district court for the enforcement thereof, unless, in the judgment of the General Counsel, the enforcement of such subpoena would be inconsistent with law and the policies of the Foreign Service Labor-Management Relations Statute. The General Counsel shall not be deemed thereby to have assumed responsibility for the effective prosecution of the same before the court thereafter.

§ 1429.8 Stay of action taken by Grievance Board; requests.

(a) A request for a stay shall be entertained only in conjunction with and as a part of an exception to an action taken by the Grievance Board under part 1425 of this subchapter. The filing of an exception shall not itself operate as a stay of the action involved in the proceedings.

(b) A timely request for a stay of an action taken by the Grievance Board to which an exception has been filed shall operate as a temporary stay of the award. Such temporary stay shall be deemed effective from the date of the action and shall remain in effect until the Board issues its decision and order on the exception, or the Board or its designee otherwise acts with respect to the request for the stay.

(c) A request for a stay of an action taken by the Grievance Board will be granted only where it appears, based upon the facts and circumstances presented, that:

(1) There is a strong likelihood of success on the merits of the appeal; and

(2) A careful balancing of all the equities, including the public interest, warrants issuance of a stay.

§ 1429.9 Amicus curiae.

Upon petition of an interested person, a copy of which petition shall be served on the parties, and as the Board deems appropriate, the Board may grant permission for the presentation of written and/or oral argument at any stage of the proceedings by an amicus curiae and the parties shall be notified of such action by the Board.

§ 1429.10 Advisory opinions.

The Board and the General Counsel will not issue advisory opinions.

§ 1429.11 Interlocutory appeals.

The Board and the General Counsel ordinarily will not consider interlocutory appeals.

§ 1429.12 Service of process and papers by the Board.

(a) *Methods of service.* Notices of hearings, reports and findings, decisions of

Administrative Law Judges, complaints, written rulings on motions, decisions and orders, and all other papers required by this subchapter to be issued by the Board, the General Counsel, Regional Directors, Hearing Officers and Administrative Law Judges, shall be served personally or by certified mail or by telegraph.

(b) *Upon whom served.* All papers required to be served under paragraph (a) of this section shall be served upon all counsel of record or other designated representative(s) of parties, and upon parties not so represented. Service upon such counsel or representative shall constitute service upon the party, but a copy also shall be transmitted to the party.

(c) *Proof of service.* Proof of service shall be the verified return by the individual serving the papers setting forth the manner of such service, the return post office receipt, or the return telegraph receipt. When service is by mail, the date of service shall be the day when the matter served is deposited in the United States mail. When service is to be made to an addressee outside the United States, the date of service shall be the date received, as evidenced by official receipt.

§ 1429.13 Official time.

If the participation of any employee in any phase of any proceeding before the Board, including the investigation of unfair labor practice charges and representation petitions and the participation in hearings and representation elections, is deemed necessary by the Board, the General Counsel, any Administrative Law Judge, Regional Director, Hearing Officer, or other agent of the Board designated by the Board, such employee shall be granted official time for such participation, including necessary travel time, as occurs during the employee's regular work hours and when the employee would otherwise be in a work or paid leave status. In addition, necessary transportation and per diem expenses shall be paid by the Department.

§ 1429.14 Witness Fees.

(a) Witnesses (whether appearing voluntarily, or under a subpoena) shall be paid the fee and mileage allowances which are paid subpoenaed witnesses in the courts of the United States: *Provided,* That any witness who is employed by the Federal Government shall not be entitled to receive witness fees in addition to compensation received pursuant to § 1429.13.

(b) Witness fees and mileage allowances shall be paid by the party at whose instance the witnesses appear, except when the witness receives compensation pursuant to (the preceding section).

§ 1429.15 Board requests for advisory opinions.

(a) Whenever the Board, pursuant to section 1007(c)(2)(f) of the Foreign Service Act of 1980 (22 U.S.C. 4107) requests an advisory opinion from the Director of the Office of Personnel Management concerning the proper interpretation of rules, regulations, or policy directives issued by that Office in connection with any matter before the Board, a copy of such request, and any response thereto, shall be served upon the parties in the matter.

(b) The parties shall have fifteen (15) days from the date of service a copy of the response of the Office of Personnel Management to file with the Board comments on that response which the parties wish the Board to consider before reaching a decision in the matter. Such comments shall be in writing and copies shall be served upon the parties in the manner and upon the Office of Personnel Management.

§ 1429.16 General remedial authority.

The Board shall take any actions which are necessary and appropriate to administer effectively the provisions of chapter 41 of title 22 of the United States Code.

Subpart B—General Requirements

§ 1429.21 Computation of time for filing papers.

In computing any period of time prescribed by or allowed by this subchapter, except in agreement bar situations described in § 1422.3(c) of this subchapter, the day of the act, event, or default from or after which the designated period of time begins to run, shall not be included. The last day of the period so computed is to be included unless it is a Saturday, Sunday, or a Federal legal holiday in which event the period shall run until the end of the next day which is neither a Saturday, Sunday, or a Federal legal holiday: *Provided, however*, In agreement bar situations described in § 1422.3 (c) and (d), if the sixtieth (60th) day prior to the expiration date of an agreement falls on Saturday, Sunday or a Federal legal holiday, a petition, to be timely, must be received by the close of business of the last official workday preceding the sixtieth (60th) day. When the period of time prescribed or allowed is seven (7) days or less, intermediate Saturdays, Sundays, and Federal legal holidays shall be excluded from the computations. When this subchapter requires the filing of any paper, such document must be received by the Board or the officer or agent designated to receive such matter before the close of business on the last day of the time limit, if any, for such filing or extension of time that may have been granted.

§ 1429.22 Additional time after service by mail.

Whenever a party has the right or is required to do some act pursuant to this subchapter within a prescribed period after service of a notice or other paper upon such party, and the notice or paper is served on such party by mail, five (5) days shall be added to the prescribed period.

§ 1429.23 Extension; waiver.

(a) Except as provided in paragraph (d) of this section, the Board or General Counsel, or their designated representatives, as appropriate, may extend any time limit provided in this subchapter for good cause shown, and shall notify the parties of any such extension. Requests for extensions of time shall be filed in writing no later than five (5) days before the established time limit for filing, shall state the position of the other parties on the request for extension, and shall be served on the other parties.

(b) Except as provided in paragraph (d) of this section, the Board or General Counsel, or their designated representatives, as appropriate, may waive any expired time limit in this subchapter in extraordinary circumstances. Request for a waiver of time limits shall state the position of the other parties and shall be served on the other parties.

(c) The time limits established in this subchapter may not be extended or waived in any manner other than that described in this subchapter.

(d) The time limits prescribed by 22 U.S.C. 4114(c) may not be waived.

§ 1429.24 Place and method of filing; acknowledgement.

(a) A document submitted to the Board pursuant to this subchapter shall be filed with the Board at the address set forth in appendix A to this chapter XIV.

(b) A document submitted to the General Counsel pursuant to this subchapter shall be filed with the General Counsel at the address set forth in appendix A.

(c) A document submitted to a Regional Director pursuant to this subchapter shall be filed with the appropriate regional office, as set forth in appendix A.

(d) A document submitted to an Administrative Law Judge pursuant to this subchapter shall be filed with the appropriate Administrative Law Judge, as set forth in appendix A.

(e) All documents filed pursuant to paragraphs (a), (b), (c) and (d) of this section shall be filed by certified mail or in person, or if the filing party is outside the United States, by the most appropriate available means.

(f) All matters filed under paragraphs (a), (b), (c) and (d) of this section shall be printed, typed, or otherwise legibly duplicated: Carbon copies of typewritten matter will be accepted if they are clearly legible.

(g) Documents in any proceedings under this subchapter, including correspondence, shall show the title of the proceeding and the case number, if any.

(h) The original of each document required to be filed under this subchapter shall be signed by the party or by an attorney or representative of record for the party, or by an officer of the party, and shall contain the address and telephone number of the person signing it.

(i) A return postal receipt may serve as acknowledgement of receipt by the Board, General Counsel, Administrative Law Judge, Regional Director, or Hearing Officer, as appropriate. The receiving officer will otherwise acknowledge receipt of documents filed only when the filing party so requests and includes an extra copy of the document or its transmittal letter which the receiving office will date stamp upon receipt and return. If return is to be made by mail, the filing party shall include a self-addressed, stamped envelope for the purpose.

§ 1429.25 Number of copies.

Unless otherwise provided by the Board or the General Counsel, or their designated representatives, as appropriate, or under this subchapter, any document or paper filed with the Board, General Counsel, Administrative Law Judge, Regional Director, or Hearing Officer, as appropriate, under this subchapter, together with any enclosure filed therewith, shall be submitted in an original and four (4) copies. A clean copy capable of being used as an original for purposes such as further reproduction may be substituted for the original.

§ 1429.26 Other documents.

(a) The Board or the General Counsel, or their designated representatives, as appropriate, may in their discretion grant leave to file other documents as they deem appropriate.

(b) A copy of such other documents shall be served on the other parties.

§ 1429.27 Service; statement of service.

(a) Except as provided in § 1423.10 (c) and (d), any party filing a document as provided in this subchapter is responsible for serving a copy upon all counsel of record or other designated representative(s) of parties, upon parties not so represented, and upon any interested person who has been granted permission by the Board pursuant to § 1429.9 to present written and/or oral argument as amicus curiae. Service upon such counsel or representative shall constitute service upon the party, but a copy also shall be transmitted to the party.

(b) Service of any document or paper under this subchapter, by any party, including documents and papers served by one party on another, shall be made by certified mail or in person. A return post office receipt or other written receipt executed by the party or person served shall be proof of service.

(c) A signed and dated statement of service shall be submitted at the time of filing. The statement of service shall include the names of the parties and persons served, their addresses, the date of service, the nature of the document served, and the manner in which service was made.

(d) The date of service or date served shall be in the day when the matter served is deposited in the U.S. mail or is delivered in person. When service is to be made to an addressee outside the United States, the date of service shall be the date received, as evidenced by official receipt.

§ 1429.28 Petitions for amendment of regulations.

Any interested person may petition the Board or General Counsel in writing for amendments to any portion of these regulations. Such petition shall identify the portion of the regulations involved and provide the specific language of the proposed amendment together with a statement of grounds in support of such petition.

SUBCHAPTER D—FOREIGN SERVICE IMPASSE DISPUTES PANEL

PART 1470—GENERAL

Subpart A—Purpose

Subpart B—Definitions

AUTHORITY: 22 U.S.C. 4107(c), 4110.

SOURCE: 46 FR 45879, Sept. 15, 1981, unless otherwise noted.

Subpart A—Purpose

§ 1470.1 Purpose.

The regulations contained in this subchapter are intended to implement the provisions of section 4110 of title 22 of the United States Code. They prescribed procedures and methods which the Foreign Service Impasse Disputes Panel may utilize in the resolution of negotiation impasses.

Subpart B—Definitions

§ 1470.2 Definitions.

(a) The term *Department* as used herein shall have the meaning set forth in 22 U.S.C. 3902 and 4103, and § 1421.4 of subchapter C of these regulations.

(b) The terms *labor organization*, and *conditions of employment* as used herein shall have the meanings set forth in 22 U.S.C. 4102.

(c) The term *Executive Director* means the Executive Director of the Federal Service Impasse Panel as defined in 5 U.S.C. 7119(c).

(d) The terms *designated representative* or *designee* of the Panel means a Panel member, a staff member, or other individual designated by the Panel to act on its behalf pursuant to 22 U.S.C. 4110(c)(1).

(e) The term *hearing* means a fact-finding hearing, arbitration hearing, or any other hearing procedure deemed necessary to accomplish the purposes of 22 U.S.C. 4110.

(f) The term *impasse* means that point in the negotiation of a collective bargaining agreement at which the parties are deadlocked, notwithstanding their efforts to reach agreement by direct negotiations and other voluntary arrangements, if any.

(g) The term *Panel* means the Foreign Service Impasse Disputes Panel described in 22 U.S.C. 4110(a) or a quorum thereof.

(h) The term *party* means the Department or the labor organization participating in the negotiation of a collective bargaining agreement.

(i) The term *quorum* means three (3) or more members of the Panel.

(j) The term *voluntary arrangements* means any appropriate technique, not inconsistent with the provisions of 22 U.S.C. 4110, used by the parties to assist in the negotiation of a collective bargaining agreement.

PART 1471—PROCEDURES OF THE PANEL

AUTHORITY: 22 U.S.C. 4107(c), 4110.

SOURCE: 46 FR 45879, Sept. 15, 1981, unless otherwise noted.

§ 1471.1 Request for Panel consideration.

If direct negotiations and other voluntary arrangements for settlement, if any, fail to resolve a negotiation impasse:

(a) Either party, or the parties jointly, may request the Panel to consider the matter by filing a request as hereinafter provided; or

(b) The Panel may, pursuant to 22 U.S.C. 4110(a), undertake consideration of the matter upon request of the Executive Director.

§ 1471.2 Content of request.

A request from a party or parties to the Panel for consideration of an impasse must be in writing and include the following information:

(a) Identification of the parties and individuals authorized to act on their behalf;

(b) Statement of issues at impasse and the summary of positions of the initiating party or parties with respect to those issues; and

(c) Number, length, and dates of negotiation sessions held, including the nature and extent of all other voluntary arrangements utilized.

§ 1471.3 Where to file.

Requests to the Panel provided for in this part, and inquiries or correspondence on the status of impasses or other related matters, should be directed to the Executive Director, Federal Service Impasses Panel, Suite 209, 1730 K Street NW., Washington, D.C. 20006.

§ 1471.4 Copies and service.

Any party submitting a request for Panel consideration of an impasse and any party submitting a response to such requests shall file an original and one copy with the Panel, shall serve a copy promptly on the other party to the dispute, and shall file a statement of such service with the Executive Director. When the Panel acts on a request from the Executive Director, it will notify the parties to the dispute.

§ 1471.5 Investigation of request; Panel recommendation and assistance.

Upon receipt of a request for consideration of an impasse, the Panel or its designee will promptly conduct an investigation. After due consideration, the Panel shall either:

(a) Decline to assert jurisdiction in the event that it finds that no impasse exists or that there is other good cause for not asserting jurisdiction, in whole or in part, and so advise the parties in writing, stating its reasons; or

(b) Recommend to the parties procedures, including but not limited to arbitration, for the resolution of the impasse and/or assist them in resolving the impasse through whatever methods and procedures the Panel considers appropriate.

§ 1471.6 Preliminary hearing procedures.

When the Panel determines that a hearing is necessary under § 1471.5 it will:

(a) Appoint one or more of its designees to conduct such hearing; and

(b) Issue and serve upon each of the parties a notice of hearing and a notice of prehearing conference, if any. The notice will state (1) the names of the parties to the dispute; (2) the date, time, place, type, and purpose of the hearing; (3) the date, time, place, and purpose of the prehearing conference, if any; (4) the name of the designated representative appointed by the Panel; and (5) the issues to be resolved.

§ 1471.7 Conduct of hearing and prehearing conference.

(a) A designated representative of the Panel, when so appointed to conduct a hearing, shall have the authority on behalf of the Panel to:

(1) Administer oaths, take the testimony or deposition of any person under oath, receive other evidence, and issue subpoenas;

(2) Conduct the hearing in open or in closed session at the discretion of the designated representative for good cause shown;

(3) Rule on motions and requests for appearance of witnesses and the production of records;

(4) Designate the date on which posthearing briefs, if any, shall be submitted (an original and one (1) copy of each brief, accompanied by a statement of service, shall be submitted to the designated representative of the Panel with a copy to the other party); and

(5) Determine all procedural matters concerning the hearing, including the length of sessions, conduct of persons

in attendance, recesses, continuances, and adjournments; and take any other appropriated procedural action which, in the judgment of the designated representative, will promote the purpose and objectives of the hearing.

(b) A prehearing conference may be conducted by the designated representative of the Panel in order to:

(1) Inform the parties of the purpose of the hearing and the procedures under which it will take place;

(2) Explore the possibilities of obtaining stipulations of fact;

(3) Clarify the positions of the parties with respect to the issues to be heard; and

(4) Discuss any other relevant matters which will assist the parties in the resolution of the dispute.

(c) An official reporter shall make the only official transcript of a hearing. Copies of the official transcript may be examined and copied at the Office of the Executive Director in accordance with part 1411 of this chapter.

§ 1471.8 Report and recommendations.

(a) When a report is issued after a hearing conducted pursuant to §§ 1471.6 and 1471.7, it normally shall be in writing and, when authorized by the Panel, shall contain recommendations.

(b) A report of the designated representative containing recommendations shall be submitted to the parties, with two (2) copies to the Executive Director, within a period normally not to exceed thirty (30) calendar days after receipt of the transcript or briefs, if any.

(c) A report of the designated representative not containing recommendations shall be submitted to the Panel with a copy to each party within a period normally not to exceed thirty (30) calendar days after receipt of the transcript or briefs, if any. The Panel shall then take whatever action it may consider appropriate or necessary to resolve the impasse.

§ 1471.9 Duties of each party following receipt of recommendations.

(a) Within thirty (30) days after receipt of a report containing recommendations of the Panel or its designated representative, each party shall, after conferring with the other, either:

(1) Accept the recommendations and so notify the Executive Director; or

(2) Reach a settlement of all unresolved issues and submit a written settlement statement to the Executive Director; or

(3) Submit a written statement to the Executive Director setting forth the reasons for not accepting the recommendations and for not reaching a settlement of all unresolved issues.

(b) A reasonable extension of time may be authorized by the Executive Director for good cause shown when requested in writing by either party prior to the expiration of the time limits.

(c) All papers submitted to the Executive Director under this section shall be filed in duplicate, along with a statement of service showing that a copy has been served on the other party to the dispute.

§ 1471.10 Final action by the Panel.

(a) If the parties do not arrive at a settlement as a result of or during action taken under §§ 1471.5(a)(2), 1471.6, 1471.7, 1471.8, and 1471.9, the Panel may take whatever action is necessary and not inconsistent with 22 U.S.C. 4110 to resolve the impasse, including but not limited to methods and procedures which the Panel considers appropriate, such as directing the parties to accept a factfinder's recommendations, ordering binding arbitration conducted according to whatever procedure the Panel deems suitable, and rendering a binding decision.

(b) In preparation for taking such final action, the Panel may hold hearings, administer oaths, take the testimony or deposition of any person under oath, and issue subpoenas as provided in 22 U.S.C. 4110(c)(2), or it may appoint or designate one or more individuals pursuant to 22 U.S.C. 4110(c)(1) to exercise such authority on its behalf.

(c) When the exercise of authority under this section requires the holding of a hearing, the procedure contained in § 1471.7 shall apply.

(d) Notice of any final action of the Panel shall be promptly served upon the parties, and the action shall be binding on such parties during the term of the agreement, unless they agree otherwise.

(e) All papers submitted to the Executive Director under this section shall be filed in duplicate, along with a statement of service showing that a copy has been served on the other party to the dispute.

PARTS 1472–1499 [RESERVED]

APPENDIX A TO CHAPTER XIV—CURRENT ADDRESSES AND GEOGRAPHIC JURISDICTIONS

(a) The Office address of the Board is as follows:

1900 E Street, NW., Room 7469, Washington, DC 20424. Telephone: Office of Executive Director, FTS—254-9595; Commercial—(202) 254-9595. Office of Operations, FTS—254-7362; Commercial—(202) 254-7362

(b) The Office address of the General Counsel is as follows:

1900 E Street, NW., Room 7469, Washington, DC 20424. Telephone: FTS—632-6264; Commercial—(202) 632-6264

(c) The Office address of the Chief Administrative Law Judge is as follows:

1111 20th Street, NW., Room 416, Washington, DC 20036. Telephone: FTS—653-7375; Commercial—(202) 653-7375

(d) The Office addresses of Regional Directors of the Authority are as follows:

(1) *Boston Regional Office,* 441 Stuart Street, 9th Floor, Boston, MA 02116. Telephone: FTS—223-0920; Commercial—(617) 223-0920

(2) *New York Regional Office,* 26 Federal Plaza, Room 241, New York, NY 10278. Telephone: FTS—264-4934; Commercial—(212) 264-4934

(i) *Philadelphia Sub-Regional Office,* 325 Chestnut Street, Mall Building, Room 5000, Philadelphia, PA 19106. Telephone: FTS—597-1527; Commercial—(215) 597-1527

(3) *Washington Regional Office,* 1133 15th Street, NW., Suite 300, Washington, DC 20005. Telephone: FTS—653-8452; Commercial—(202) 653-8452

(4) *Atlanta Regional Office,* 1776 Peachtree Street, NW., Suite 501, North Wing, Atlanta, GA 30309. Telephone: FTS—257-2324; Commercial—(404) 881-2324 or 881-2325

(5) *Chicago Regional Office,* 175 W. Jackson Blvd., Suite 1359-A, Chicago, IL 60604. Telephone: FTS—886-3468 or 886-3469; Commercial—(312) 353-6306

(i) *Cleveland Sub-Regional Office,* 1301 Superior Avenue, Suite 230, Cleveland, OH 44114. Telephone: FTS—293-2114; Commercial—(216) 522-2114

(6) *Dallas Regional Office,* Downtown Post Office Station, Bryan and Ervay Streets, P.O. Box 2640, Dallas, TX 75221. Telephone: FTS—729-4996; Commercial—(214) 767-4996

(7) *Kansas City Regional Office,* City Center Square, 1100 Main Street, Suite 680, Kansas City, MO 64105. Telephone: FTS—758-2199; Commercial—(816) 374-2199

(i) *Denver Sub-Regional Office,* 1531 Stout Street, Suite 301, Denver, CO 80202. Telephone: FTS—327-5224; Commercial—(303) 837-5224

(8) *Los Angeles Regional Office,* 350 So. Figueroa Street, 10th Floor, World Trade Center, Los Angeles, CA 90071. Telephone: FTS—798-3805; Commercial—(213) 688-3805

(i) *Honolulu Sub-Regional Office,* Room 3206, 300 Alamoana Blvd., Honolulu, Hawaii 96850. Telephone: FTS—556-0220 through San Francisco FTS Operator; Commercial—(808) 546-8355

(9) *San Francisco Regional Office,* 530 Bush Street, Room 542, San Francisco, CA 94108. Telephone: FTS—556-8105; Commercial—(415) 556-8105

(e) The Office address of the Panel is as follows:

1730 K Street, NW., Suite 209, Washington, DC 20006. Telephone: FTS—653-7078; Commercial—(202) 653-7078

(f) The geographic jurisdictions of the Regional Directors of the Authority, are as follows:

State or other locality	Regional office
Alabama	Atlanta
Alaska	San Francisco
Arizona	Los Angeles
Arkansas	Dallas
California	Los Angeles/San Francisco[1]
Colorado	Kansas City
Connecticut	Boston
Delaware	New York
District of Columbia	Washington, DC
Florida	Atlanta
Georgia	Atlanta
Hawaii and all land and water areas west of the continents of North and South America (except coastal islands) to long. 90¼E	Los Angeles
Idaho	San Francisco
Illinois	Chicago
Indiana	Chicago
Iowa	Kansas City
Kansas	Kansas City
Kentucky	Atlanta
Louisiana	Dallas

State or other locality	Regional office
Maine	Boston
Maryland	Washington, DC
Massachusetts	Boston
Michigan	Chicago
Minnesota	Chicago
Mississippi	Atlanta
Missouri	Kansas City
Montana	Kansas City
Nebraska	Kansas City
Nevada	San Francisco
New Hampshire	Boston
New Jersey	New York
New Mexico	Dallas
New York	Boston/New York [2]
North Carolina	Atlanta
North Dakota	Kansas City
Ohio	Chicago
Oklahoma	Dallas
Oregon	San Francisco
Pennsylvania	New York
Puerto Rico	New York
Rhode Island	Boston
South Carolina	Atlanta
South Dakota	Kansas City
Tennessee	Atlanta
Texas	Dallas
Utah	Kansas City
Vermont	Boston
Virginia	Washington, DC/ Atlanta [3]
Washington	San Francisco
West Virginia	Washington, DC
Wisconsin	Chicago
Wyoming	Kansas City
Virgin Islands	New York
Panama/Limited FLRA jurisdiction	Dallas
All land and water areas east of the continents of North and South America to long. 90¼E, except the Virgin Islands, Panama (limited FLRA jurisdiction), Puerto Rico and coastal islands	Washington

[1] San Francisco includes the following California counties: Monterey, Kings, Tulare, Inyo, and all counties north thereof. All counties in California south thereof are within the Los Angeles jurisdiction.

[2] New York includes the following counties: Ulster, Sullivan, Greene, Columbia and all counties south thereof. All counties in New York state north thereof are in the jurisdiction of Boston.

[3] Washington, DC includes the following counties in Virginia: Alexandria, Fairfax, Fauquier, Loudoun and Prince William. All other counties within Virginia are in the jurisdiction of Atlanta.

[46 FR 45881, Sept. 15, 1981]

APPENDIX B TO CHAPTER XIV—MEMORANDUM DESCRIBING THE AUTHORITY AND ASSIGNED RESPONSIBILITIES OF THE GENERAL COUNSEL OF THE FEDERAL LABOR RELATIONS AUTHORITY UNDER THE FOREIGN SERVICE LABOR-MANAGEMENT RELATIONS STATUTE

The statutory authority and responsibility of the General Counsel of the Federal Labor Relations Board are stated in section 4108 subsections (1), (2) and (3), of the Foreign Service Labor-Management Relations Statute as follows:

SECTION 4108 FUNCTIONS OF THE GENERAL COUNSEL

The General Counsel may—

(A) investigate alleged unfair labor practices under this chapter,

(B) file and prosecute complaints under this chapter, and

(C) exercise such other powers of the Board as the Board may prescribe.

This memorandum is intended to describe the statutory authority and set forth the prescribed duties and authority of the General Counsel of the Federal Labor Relations Authority under the Foreign Service Statute, effective February 15, 1981.

I. *Case handling*— A. *Unfair labor practice cases*. The General Counsel has full and final authority and responsibility, on behalf of the Board, to accept and investigate charges filed, to enter into and approve the informal settlement of charges, to approve withdrawal requests, to dismiss charges, to determine matters concerning the consolidation and severance of cases before complaint issues, to issue complaints and notices of hearing, to appear before Administrative Law Judges in hearings on complaints and prosecute as provided in the Board's and the General Counsel's rules and regulations, and to initiate and prosecute injunction proceedings as provided for in section 4109(d) of the Foreign Service Statute. After issuance of the Administrative Law Judge's decision, the General Counsel may file exceptions and briefs and appear before the Board in oral argument, subject to the Board's and the General Counsel's rules and regulations.

B. *Compliance actions (injunction proceedings)*. The General Counsel is authorized and responsible, on behalf of the Board, to seek and effect compliance with the Board's orders and make such compliance reports to the Board as it may from time to time require.

On behalf of the Board, the General Counsel will, in full accordance with the directions of the Board, initiate and prosecute injunction proceedings as provided in section 4109(d) of the Foreign Service Statute: *Provided however*, That the General Counsel will initiate and conduct injunction proceedings under section 4109(d) of the Foreign Service Statute only upon approval of the Board.

C. *Representation cases.* The General Counsel is authorized and has responsibility, on behalf of the Board, to receive and process, in accordance with the decisions of the Board and with such instructions and rules and regulations as may be issued by the Board from time to time, all petitions filed pursuant to sections 4111 and 4118(c) of the Foreign Service Statute. The General Counsel is also authorized and has responsibility to supervise or conduct elections pursuant to section 4111 of the Foreign Service Statute and to enter into consent election agreements in accordance with section 4111(g) of the Foreign Service Statute.

The authority and responsibility of the General Counsel in representation cases shall extend, in accordance with the rules and regulations of the Board and the General Counsel, to all phases of the investigation through the conclusion of the hearing (if a hearing should be necessary to resolve disputed issues), but all matters involving decisional action after such hearings are reserved by the Board to itself. In the event a direction of election should issue by the Board, the authority and responsibility of the General Counsel, as herein prescribed, shall attach to the conduct of the ordered election, the initial determination of the validity of challenges and objections to the conduct of the election and other similar matters, except that if appeals shall be taken from the General Counsel's action on the validity of challenges and objections, such appeals will be directed to and decided by the Board in accordance with its procedural requirements. If challenged ballots would not affect the election results and if no objections are filed within five days after the conduct of the Board-directed election under the provisions of section 4111 of the Foreign Service Statute, the General Counsel is authorized and has responsibility, on behalf of the Board, to certify to the parties the results of the election in accordance with regulations prescribed by the Board and the General Counsel.

Appeals from the refusal of the General Counsel to issue a notice of hearing, from the conclusions contained in a report and findings issued by the General Counsel, or from the dismissal by the General Counsel of any petition, will be directed to and decided by the Board, in accordance with its procedural requirements.

In processing election petitions filed pursuant to section 4111 of the Foreign Service Statute and petitions filed pursuant to section 4118(c) of the Foreign Service Statute, the General Counsel is authorized to conduct an appropriate investigation as to the authenticity of the prescribed showing of interest and, upon making a determination to proceed, where appropriate, to supervise or conduct a secret ballot election or certify the validity of a petition for determination of eligibility for dues allotment. After an election, if there are no challenges or objections which require a hearing by the Board, the General Counsel shall certify the results thereof, with appropriate copies lodged in the Washington, DC, files of the Board.

II. *Liaison with other governmental agencies.* The General Counsel is authorized and has responsibility, on behalf of the Board, to maintain appropriate and adequate liaison and arrangements with the Office of the Assistant Secretary of Labor for Labor-Management Relations with reference to the financial and other reports required to be filed with the Assistant Secretary pursuant to section 4117 of the Foreign Service Statute and the availability to the Board and the General Counsel of the contents thereof. The General Counsel is authorized and has responsibility, on behalf of the Board, to maintain appropriate and adequate liaison with the Foreign Service Grievance Board with respect to functions which may be performed by the Foreign Service Grievance Board.

III. To the extent that the above-described duties, powers and authority rest by statute with the Board, the foregoing statement constitutes a prescription and assignment of such duties, powers and authority, whether or not so specified.

[46 FR 45882, Sept. 15, 1981]

CHAPTER XV—AFRICAN DEVELOPMENT FOUNDATION

PART 1500—SUNSHINE REGULATIONS

AUTHORITY: 5 U.S.C. 552b.

SOURCE: 48 FR 55842, Dec. 16, 1983, unless otherwise noted.

§1500.1 Purpose and scope.

The purpose of this part is to effectuate the provisions of the Government in the Sunshine Act. These procedures apply to meetings of the Board of Directors of the African Development Foundation.

§1500.2 Policy.

It is the policy of the African Development Foundation to provide the public with the fullest practical information regarding its decision-making process, while protecting the rights of individuals and the ability of the Foundation to carry out its responsibilities.

§1500.3 Definitions.

As used in this part:

Board or Board of Directors means the collegial body that conducts the business of the African Development Foundation as specified in title V, section 507 of the International Security and Development Cooperation Act of 1980, Pub. L. 96–533 (22 U.S.C. 290 h–5).

Meeting means the deliberations of a quorum of the Directors of the Foundation required to take action on behalf of the Foundation where such deliberations determine or result in the joint conduct or disposition of official Foundation business, but does not apply to deliberations to take action to open or close a meeting. (See §1500.5.)

Member means an individual who belongs to the ADF Board of Directors.

Public Observation means attendance at any meeting but does not include participation, or attempted participation, in such meeting in any manner.

§1500.4 Open meetings.

(a) Members shall not jointly conduct or dispose of Foundation business other than in accordance with these procedures. Every portion of every meeting of the Board of Directors shall be open to public observation, subject to the exceptions provided in §1500.5.

(b) The Secretary of the Foundation shall be responsible for assuring that ample space, sufficient visibility, and adequate acoustics are provided for public observation of meetings of the Board of Directors.

§1500.5 Grounds on which meetings may be closed.

(a) The Foundation shall open every portion of every meeting of the Foundation for public observation, except where the Foundation determines that such portion or portions of its meeting or the disclosure of such information is likely to:

(1) Disclose matters that are:

(i) Specifically authorized under criteria established by an executive order to be kept secret in the interests of national defense on foreign policy, and

(ii) In fact properly classified pursuant to such executive order;

(2) Relate solely to the internal personnel rules and practice of the Foundation;

(3) Disclose matters specifically exempted from disclosure by statute, provided that such statute:

(i) Requires that the matters be withheld from the public in such manner as to leave no discretion on the issue, or

(ii) Has established practical criteria for withholding or refers to particular types of matters to be withheld;

(4) Disclose trade secrets and commercial or financial information which has been obtained from a person and is privileged or confidential;

(5) Involve accusing any person of a crime, or formally censuring any person;

(6) Disclose information of a personal nature where disclosure would constitute a clearly unwarrented invasion of personal privacy;

(7) Disclose investigatory records compiled for law enforcement purposes,

or information which if written would be contained in such records, but only to the extent that the production of such records or information would:

(i) Interfere with enforcement proceedings,

(ii) Deprive a person of a right to fair trial or an impartial adjudication,

(iii) Constitute an unwarranted invasion of personal privacy,

(iv) Disclose the identity of a confidential source and, in the case of a record compiled by a criminal law enforcement authority in the course of a criminal investigation or by an agency conducting a lawful national security intelligence investigation, confidential information furnished only by the confidential source,

(v) Disclose investigative techniques and procedures, or

(vi) Endanger the life or physical safety of law enforcement personnel;

(8) Disclose information the premature disclosure of which would be likely to significantly frustrate implementation of a proposed agency action. This shall not apply in any instance where the Foundation has already disclosed to the public the content or nature of its proposed action or where the Foundation is required by law to make such disclosure on its own initiative prior to taking final Foundation action on such proposal;

(9) Specifically concern the Foundation's issuance of a subpoena; the Foundation's participation in a civil action or proceeding, or an arbitration; or an action in a foreign court or international tribunal; or the initiation, conduct, or disposition by the Foundation of a particular case of formal agency adjudication pursuant to the procedures in section 554 of title 5 of the United States Code, or otherwise involving a determination on the record after an opportunity for a hearing.

(b) Meetings of the Board of Directors shall not be closed pursuant to paragraph (a) of this section when the Foundation finds that the public interest requires that they be open.

§ 1500.6 Procedure for announcing meetings.

(a) In the case of each meeting of the Board of Directors, the Foundation shall make public, at least one week before the meeting, the following information:

(1) Time of the meeting;

(2) Place of the meeting;

(3) Subject matter of the meeting;

(4) Whether the meeting or parts thereof are to be open or closed to the public; and

(5) The name and telephone number of the person designated by the Board to respond to requests for information about the meeting.

(b) The period of one week for the public announcement required by paragraph (a) of this section may be reduced if a majority of the Board of Directors of the Foundation determines by a recorded vote that the Foundation requires that such a meeting be called at an earlier date, in which case the Foundation shall make public announcement of the time, place, and subject matter of such meeting, and whether open or closed to the public, at the earliest practicable time.

(c) Immediately following the public announcement, the Foundation shall publish the announcement in the FEDERAL REGISTER.

(d) The *earliest practicable time,* as used in this subsection, means as soon as possible, which should not be later than the commencement of the meeting or portion in question.

(e) The Secretary of the Foundation shall use reasonable means to assure that the public is fully informed by the public announcements required by this section. Such public announcements may be made by posting notices in the public areas of the Foundation's headquarters and mailing notices to the persons on a list maintained for those who want to receive such announcements.

§ 1500.7 Procedure for closing meetings.

(a) Action to close a meeting or a portion thereof, pursuant to the exemptions set forth in § 1500.5, shall be taken only when:

(1) A majority of the membership of the Foundation's Board of Directors votes to take such action. That vote shall determine whether or not any portion or portions of a meeting or portions of a series of meetings may be

closed to public, obervation for any of the reasons provided in §1500.5 and whether or not the public interest nevertheless requires that portion of the meeting or meetings remain open. A single vote may be taken with respect to a series of meetings, a portion or portions of which are proposed to be closed to the public, or with respect to any information concerning such series of meetings, so long as each meeting in such series involves the same particular matters and is scheduled to be held no more than thirty days after the initial meeting in such series. The vote of each Board member participating in such vote shall be recorded, and no proxies shall be allowed.

(2) Whenever any person whose interests may be directly affected by a portion of a meeting requests that the Foundation close such portion to the public for any of the reasons referred to in §1500.5 (a) (5), (6), or (7), the Foundation, upon request of any one of its Board members, shall take a recorded vote whether to close such portion of the meeting.

(b) Within one day of any vote taken, the Foundation shall make publicly available a written copy of such vote, reflecting the vote of each member on the question, and a full written explanation of the action to close a portion of or the entire meeting, together with a list of persons expected to attend the meeting and their affiliations.

(c) For every closed meeting, the General Counsel of the Foundation shall publicly certify prior to a Board of Directors' vote on closing the meeting that, in his or her opinion, the meeting may be closed to the public, and shall state each relevant exemptive provision. A copy of such certification, together with a statement from the presiding officer of the meeting setting forth the time and place of the meeting and the persons present, shall be retained by the Foundation.

§1500.8 Changing the time and place of, and reconsideration of opening or closing a meeting.

The time or place of a Board meeting may be changed following the public announcement only if the Foundation publicly announces such change at the earliest practicable time. The subject matter of a meeting, or the determination of the Foundation to open or close a meeting, or portion of a meeting, to the public, may be changed following the public announcement only if a majority of the Board of Directors determines by a recorded vote that Foundation business so requires and that no earlier announcement of the change was possible, and the Foundation publicly announces such change and the vote of each member upon change at the earliest practicable time.

§1500.9 Transcripts, recording of closed meetings.

(a) The Foundation shall maintain a complete transcript or electronic recording adequate to record fully the proceedings of each meeting, or portion of a meeting, closed to the public.

(b) The Foundation, after review by the General Counsel, shall make promptly available to the public in a place easily accessible to the public the transcript or electronic recording of the discussion of any item on the agenda, or any item of the testimony of any witness received at the Board meeting, except for such item or items of discussion or testimony as the Foundation determines to contain information which may be withheld under §1500.5. Copies of such transcript, or a transcription of such recording, disclosing the identify of each speaker, shall be furnished to any person at the actual cost of duplication or transcription. The Foundation shall maintain a complete verbatim copy of the transcript or a complete electronic recording of each meeting, or portion of a meeting, closed to the public, for a period of at least two years after such meeting, or until one year after the conclusion of any Foundation proceeding with respect to which the meeting or portion was held, whichever occurs later.

PART 1501—ORGANIZATION

SUBSTANTIVE RULE OF GENERAL APPLICABILITY

Sec.

AUTHORITY: 22 U.S.C. 290h; 5 U.S.C. 552.

SOURCE: 50 FR 18861, May 3, 1985, unless otherwise noted.

SUBSTANTIVE RULE OF GENERAL APPLICABILITY

§ 1501.1 Introduction.

The regulations of this part are issued pursuant to the provisions of the Freedom of Information Act, 5 U.S,C. 552.

§ 1501.2 Background.

(a) The African Development Foundation ("ADF") is a wholly-owned corporation of the United States Government, created by the African Development Foundation Act (title V, Pub. L. 96–533, 94 Stat. 3151 (22 U.S.C. 290h)). It is a non-profit, non-stock issuing, tax-exempt corporation, and is subject to title I of the Government Corporation Control Act (31 U.S.C. 9101 *et seq.*).

(b) The primary function of ADF is to extend financial assistance in the form of grants, loans and loan guarantees to African private and public entities to support self-help activities at the local level in African countries, and to fund development research by Africans. Priority shall be given to projects which community groups undertake to foster their own development and which involve maximum feasible participation of the poor. The maximum assistance which may be extended for a single project is $250,000.

§ 1501.3 Description of central organization and location of offices.

(a) The management of ADF is vested in a Board of Directors (hereinafter referred to as the "Board") consisting of a Chairperson, a Vice Chairperson and five other members appointed by the President, by and with the advice and consent of the Senate. Five of the members are appointed from private life and two from among the officers and employees of agencies of the United States concerned with African affairs. The Board establishes policy for the Foundation and is responsible for its management.

(b) The Board is required to appoint a President of the Foundation upon such terms as it may determine. The President has responsibility for directing the day to day activities of the Foundation. He is assisted by a Vice President, a Congressional liaison officer, a Public Affairs officer, a General Counsel, and the following staff units:

(1) *Office of Administration and Finance.* This office is responsible for the management of the administrative, budgeting, financial and personnel activities of the Foundation.

(2) *Office of Research and Evaluation.* This office is responsible for evaluating, or assisting grantees to evaluate, ADF funded projects; for monitoring evaluations and analyses of grassroots projects conducted by other funding or research organizations; and for identifying and providing assistance to indigenous researchers in Africa working in development projects at the local level.

(3) *Office of Program and Field Operations.* This office is responsible for identifying, reviewing and monitoring projects funded by the Foundation.

(c) The Board is also required to establish an Advisory Council made up of individuals knowledgeable about development activities in Africa, and to consult with the Council at least once each year. The Council shall have not more than 25 members appointed for a period of two years with an option to be reappointed for an additional year.

(d) The Board of Directors and the aforementioned officers, together with the other employees of the Foundation, constitute the central organization of ADF, and are located and function at ADF headquarters, 1724 Massachusetts Avenue NW., Suite 200, Washington, DC 20036. It is anticipated that in the future a field organization will be established with offices in selected cities in Africa, but this has not yet occurred.

§ 1501.4 Availability of information pertaining to Foundation operations.

Rules of procedure and forms used for the funding of ADF projects may be obtained upon application to the Office of Program and Field Operations at ADF headquarters, 1724 Massachusetts Avenue NW., Suite 200, Washington, DC 20036.

§ 1501.5 Substantive rules of general applicability.

ADF's regulations published under the provisions of the Administrative Procedure Act are found in chapter XV of title 22 of the Code of Federal Regulations and the FEDERAL REGISTER. These regulations are supplemented from time to time by amendments appearing initially in the FEDERAL REGISTER.

PART 1502—AVAILABILITY OF RECORDS

AUTHORITY: Title V of the International Security and Development Cooperation Act of 1980, 22 U.S.C. 290h; 5 U.S.C. 552; FOIA Improvement Act of 2016, Public Law 114–185.

SOURCE: 82 FR 9130, Feb. 3, 2017, unless otherwise noted.

§ 1502.1 Introduction.

(a) The United States African Development Foundation makes information about its operations, procedures, and records freely available to the public in accordance with the provisions of the Freedom of Information Act (FOIA).

(b) The Foundation will make the fullest possible disclosure of its information and identifiable records consistent with the provisions of the Act and the regulations in this part.

(c) The Chief FOIA Officer shall be responsible for the Foundation's compliance with the processing requirements of the Freedom of Information Act.

§ 1502.2 Definitions.

As used in this part, the following words have the meanings set forth below:

(a) *Act* means the Act of June 5, 1967, sometimes referred to as the "Freedom of Information Act" or the Public Information Section of the Administrative Procedure Act, as amended, Public Law 90–23, 81 Stat. 54, codified at 5 U.S.C. 552.

(b) *Foundation* means the United States African Development Foundation.

(c) *President* means the President of the Foundation.

(d) *Record(s)* includes all books, papers, or other documentary materials made or received by the Foundation in connection with the transaction of its business which have been preserved or are appropriate for preservation by the Foundation as evidence of its organization, functions, policies, decisions, procedures, operations, or other activities, or because of the informational value of the data contained therein. Library or other material acquired and preserved solely for reference or exhibition purposes, and stocks of publications and other documents provided by the Foundation to the public in the normal course of doing business are not included within the definition of the word "records." The latter will continue to be made available to the public without charge.

§ 1502.3 Access to Foundation records.

Any person desiring to have access to Foundation records may call or apply in person between the hours of 10 a.m. and 4 p.m. on weekdays (holidays excluded) at the Foundation offices or mail a request to the Foundation at 1400 I Street NW., Suite 1000, Washington, DC 20005, or submit a request by email to *info@usadf.gov* on the Foundation's Web site, *www.usadf.gov*. Requests for access under the Freedom of Information Act should be made to the Chief FOIA Officer at the Foundation offices. If a request is made for copies of any record, the Chief FOIA Officer will assist the person making such request in seeing that such copies are provided according to the rules in this part.

§ 1502.4 Written requests.

In order to facilitate the processing of written requests, every petitioner should:

(a) Address his or her request to: Chief FOIA Officer, United States African Development Foundation, 1400 I Street NW., Suite 1000, Washington, DC 20005.

Both the envelope and the request itself, or the email, should be clearly marked: "Freedom of Information Act Request."

(b) Identify the desired record by name, title, author, a brief description, or number, and date, as applicable. The identification should be specific enough so that a record can be identified and found without unreasonably burdening or disrupting the operations of the Foundation. If the Foundation determines that a request does not reasonably describe the records sought, the requestor shall be advised what additional information is needed or informed why the request is insufficient.

(c) Include a check or money order to the order of the "United States African Development Foundation" covering the appropriate search and copying fees, or a request for determination of the fee, or a specified amount that the requestor is willing to pay in connection with the FOIA request.

§ 1502.5 Records available at the Foundation.

Records that the FOIA requires be made available for public inspection in an electronic format may be accessed through the Foundation's Web site.

§ 1502.6 Records of other departments and agencies.

Responsive records located by the Foundation which have been originated by, or are primarily the concerns of, another U.S. department or agency will be forwarded to the particular department or agency involved, and the requestor so notified. In response to requests for records or publications published by the Government Printing Office or other government printing activity, the Foundation will refer the petitioner to the appropriate sales office and refund any fee payments which accompanied the request.

§ 1502.7 Fees.

(a) *Authority.* USADF charges for processing FOIA requests in accordance with the Uniform Freedom of Information Act Fee Schedule and Guidelines of the Office of Management and Budget, 52 FR 10012–10020 (March 17, 1987).

(b) *When charged.* Fees shall be charged in accordance with the schedules contained in paragraph (c) of this section for services rendered in responding to requests for Foundation records under this subpart. Requestors may seek a waiver of fees by submitting a written application demonstrating how disclosure of the requested information is in the public interest because it is likely to contribute significantly to public understanding of the operations or activities of the government and is not primarily in the commercial interest of the requestor. Fees shall also not be charged where they would amount, in the aggregate, for a request or series of related requests, to $25 or less.

(c) *Services charged for and amount charged.* For the services listed below expended in locating or making available records or copies thereof, the following charges shall be assessed:

(1) *Copies.* For copies, $.10 per copy of each page.

(2) *Clerical searches.* For each one quarter hour spent by clerical personnel in excess of the first quarter hour in searching for and producing requested records, $4.75.

(3) *Non-routine, non-clerical searches.* Where the task of determining which records fall within a request and collecting them requires the time of professional or managerial personnel, and where the time required is substantial, for each one quarter hour spent in excess of the first quarter hour, $10.00. No charge shall be made for the time spent in resolving legal or policy issues affecting access to records of known contents.

(4) *Other charges.* When a response to a request requires services or materials other than those described in paragraphs (c)(1) through (3) of this section, the direct cost of such services to the Foundation may be charged, providing the requestor has been given an estimate of such cost before it is incurred.

§ 1502.8 Exemptions.

The categories of records maintained by the Foundation which may be exempted from disclosure are described in 5 U.S.C. 552(b).

§ 1502.9 Processing of requests.

(a) *Processing.* A person who has made a written request for records which meets the requirements of § 1502.4 shall be informed by the Chief FOIA Officer within 20 working days after receipt of the request of the Foundation's decision whether to deny or grant access to the records and the right of the requestor to seek assistance from the Foundation's Chief Public Liaison.

(b) *Denials.* If the Chief FOIA Officer, with the concurrence of the General Counsel, denies a request for records, the requestor will be informed of the name and title of the official responsible for the denial, the reasons for it, and the right to appeal the decision to the President of the Foundation within 90 calendar days of receipt of the denial. The President shall determine any appeal within 20 days of receipt and notify the requestor within the time period of the decision. If the decision is to uphold the denial, the requestor will be informed of the reasons for the decision, of the right to a judicial review of the decision in the federal courts, and of the dispute resolution services offered by the FOIA Public Liaison of the Foundation or the Office of Government Information Services of the National Archives and Records Administration as a non-exclusive alternative to litigation.

(c) *Extension of time.* In unusual circumstances, as defined by the FOIA, to the extent reasonably necessary to the proper processing of requests, the time required to respond to a FOIA request or an appeal may be extended for an additional 10 working days upon written notification to the requestor providing the reasons for the extension. If the extension goes beyond 10 working days, USADF will notify the requestor of services provided by the FOIA Public Liaison and the Office of Government Information Services.

(d) *Expedited processing.* USADF shall process requests and appeals on an expedited basis where the requestor demonstrates a compelling need for the records, as defined in 5 U.S.C. 552(a)(6)(E)(v). USADF shall make a determination of whether to provide expedited processing, and shall notify the requestor of the determination, within 10 calendar days after the receipt of the request. USADF shall provide expeditious consideration of administrative appeals of determinations of whether to provide expedited processing.

(e) *Confidential commercial information.* Whenever records containing confidential commercial information are requested under the FOIA and USADF determines that it may be required to disclose the records, USADF shall promptly provide written notice to the submitter of the confidential commercial information, in conformity with the procedures set forth in Executive Order 12600, Predisclosure Notification Procedures for Confidential Commercial Information, 3 CFR, 1987 Comp., p. 235.

§ 1502.10 Judicial review.

On complaint, the district court of the United States in the district in which the complainant resides, or has his/her principal place of business, or in which the agency records are situated, or in the District of Columbia, has jurisdiction to enjoin the Foundation from withholding Foundation records, and to order the production of any agency records improperly withheld from the complainant (5 U.S.C. 552(a)(4)(B)).

PART 1503—OFFICIAL SEAL

AUTHORITY: Pub. L. 95–533, 94 Stat. 3131 (22 U.S.C. 290h 4(2)(3)).

SOURCE: 50 FR 18634, May 2, 1985, unless otherwise noted.

§ 1503.1 Authority.

Pursuant to section 506(a)(3) of Pub. L. 96–533, the African Development Foundation official seal and design thereof, which accompanies and is made part of this document, is hereby adopted, approved, and judicially noticed.

§ 1503.2 Description.

The official seal of the African Development Foundation is described as follows:

(a) Forming an outer circle is a ring of type in dark blue capital letters spelling the words "AFRICAN DEVELOPMENT FOUNDATION—UNITED STATES OF AMERICA;"

(b) Within that circle is an inner circle with the stylized letters ADF in dark blue superimposed on a light grey background.

(c) The official seal of the African Development Foundation when reproduced in black and white and when embossed, is as it appears below.

§ 1503.3 Custody and authorization to affix.

(a) The seal is the official emblem of the African Development Foundation and its use is therefore permitted only as provided in this part.

(b) The seal shall be kept in the custody of the General Counsel, or any other person he authorizes, and should be affixed by him, the Chairman of the Board of Directors, or the President of the African Development Foundation to authenticate records of the Foundation and for other official purposes. The General Counsel may redelegate and authorize redelegation of this authority.

(c) The President of the African Development Foundation shall designate and prescribe by internal written delegation and policies the use of the seal for other publication and display purposes and those Foundation officials authorized to affix the seal for these purposes.

(d) Use by any person or organization outside of the Foundation may be made only with the Foundation's prior written approval. Such request must be made in writing to the General Counsel.

PART 1504—EMPLOYEE RESPONSIBILITIES AND CONDUCT

AUTHORITY: 5 U.S.C. 7301.

SOURCE: 61 FR 6507, Feb. 21, 1996, unless otherwise noted.

§ 1504.1 Cross-references to employee ethical conduct standards and financial disclosure regulations.

Directors and other employees of the African Development Foundation are subject to the Standards of Ethical Conduct for Employees of the Executive Branch at 5 CFR part 2635, and the executive branch financial disclosure regulations at 5 CFR part 2634.

PART 1506—COLLECTION OF CLAIMS

Subpart A—General Provisions

Sec.

Subpart B—Collection

Subpart C—Salary Offset

Subpart D—Compromise of Debts

Subpart E—Suspension or Termination of Collection Action

AUTHORITY: Title V of the International Security and Development Cooperation Act of 1980, 22 U.S.C. 290h; 31 U.S.C. 3701–3719; 5 U.S.C. 5514; 31 CFR part 285; 31 CFR 900–904; 5 CFR 550, subpart K; 31 U.S.C. 3720A.

SOURCE: 81 FR 95028, Dec. 27, 2016, unless otherwise noted.

Subpart A—General Provisions

§ 1506.1 What is the purpose of this part?

This part prescribes the standards and procedures to be used by the United States African Development Foundation (USADF) in the collection and disposal of non-tax debts owed to USADF and the United States. It covers USADF's collection, compromise, suspension, termination, and referral of claims to the Department of Justice.

§ 1506.2 What types of claims do these standards and procedures cover?

These standards and procedures are applicable to all claims and debts for which a statute, regulation or contract does not prescribe different standards or procedures.

§ 1506.3 Do these regulations adopt the Federal Claims Collection Standards (FCCS)?

This part adopts and incorporates all provisions of the FCCS. Except as otherwise provided by law, USADF will conduct administrative actions to collect claims (including offset, compromise, suspension termination, disclosure, and referral) in accordance with the FCCS.

§ 1506.4 What definitions apply to the regulations in this part?

Administrative offset means the withholding of funds payable by the United States to, or held by the United States for, a person to satisfy a debt the person owes to the Government.

Administrative wage garnishment means the process by which federal agencies require a private sector employer to withhold up to 15% of an employee's disposable pay to satisfy a delinquent debt owed to the Federal government. A court order is not required.

Agency means the United States African Development Foundation (USADF).

CFO means the Chief Financial Officer of USADF or the USADF official designated to act as the CFO.

Claim or debt means an amount of money, funds, or property that has been determined by an agency official to be due the United States from any person, organization, or entity, except another Federal agency.

Compromise means the creditor agency's acceptance of an amount less than the full amount of an outstanding debt in full satisfaction of the entire amount of the debt.

Creditor agency means the Federal agency to which the debt is owed, including a debt collection center when acting on behalf of a creditor agency in matters pertaining to the collection of a debt.

Debtor means an individual, organization, association, corporation, or a State or local government indebted to the United States or a person or entity with legal responsibility for assuming the debtor's obligation.

Delinquent claim or debt means any claim or debt that has not been paid by the date specified in the agency's Bill for Collection or demand letter for payment or which has not been satisfied in accordance with a repayment agreement.

Discharge means the release of a debtor from personal liability for the debt. Further collection action is prohibited.

Disposable pay means that part of current basic pay, special pay, incentive pay, retired pay, retainer pay, or in the case of the employee not entitled to basic pay, other authorized pay remaining after the deduction of any amount required by law to be withheld (other than deductions to execute garnishment orders) in accordance with 5 CFR parts 581 and 582. Among the legally required deductions that must be applied first to determine disposable pay are levies pursuant to the Internal Revenue Code (Title 26, United States Code) and deductions described in 5 CFR 581.105(b) through (f). These deductions include, but are not limited to: Social Security withholdings; Federal, State, and local tax withholdings; health insurance premiums; retirement contributions; and life insurance premiums.

Employee means a current employee of the Federal Government including a current member of the Armed Forces or a Reserve of the Armed Forces.

Employee salary offset means the administrative collection of a debt by deductions at one or more officially established pay intervals from the current pay account of an employee without the employee's consent.

Person means an individual, firm, partnership, corporation, association, organization, State or local government, or any other type of entity other than a Federal agency, foreign government, or public international organization.

Suspension means the temporary cessation of an active debt collection pending the occurrence of an anticipated event.

Termination means the cessation of all active debt collection action for the foreseeable future.

Waiver means the cancellation, remission, forgiveness or non-recovery of a debt or debt-related charge as permitted or required by law.

Withholding order means any order for withholding or garnishment of pay issued by USADF or a judicial or administrative body. For the purposes of this Part, wage garnishment order and garnishment order have the same meaning as withholding order.

§ 1506.5 Does the application of remedies prescribed in this part preclude USADF from imposing other sanctions or remedies?

(a) The remedies and sanctions available to USADF under this part for collecting debts are not intended to be exhaustive. USADF may impose, where authorized, other appropriate formal and informal sanctions upon a debtor for inexcusable, prolonged or repeated failure to pay a debt.

(b) Nothing in this part is intended to deter USADF from demanding the return of specific property or the payment of its value.

(c) This part does not supersede or require omission or duplication of administrative proceedings required by contract, statute, regulation or other USADF procedures, *e.g.*, resolution of audit findings under grants or contracts, informal grant appeals, formal grant appeals, or review under a procurement contract.

§ 1506.6 Will USADF subdivide a claim in excess of $100,000?

USADF will not subdivide a claim to avoid the $100,000 limit on the Agency's authority to compromise, suspend, or terminate a debt. A debtor's liability arising from a particular transaction or contract is a single claim.

§ 1506.7 How does USADF process claims involving fraud?

(a) The CFO will refer claims involving fraud, the presentation of a false claim, or misrepresentation on the part of the debtor or any party having an interest in the claim to the United States Agency for International Development (USAID) Office of Inspector General (OIG), which has statutory jurisdiction over USADF. The OIG has the responsibility for investigating or referring the matter, where appropriate, to the Department of Justice (DOJ), and/or returning it to USADF for further action.

(b) The CFO will not administratively compromise, terminate, suspend or otherwise dispose of debts involving fraud, the presentation of a false claim or misrepresentation on the part of the debtor or any party having an interest in the claim without the approval of DOJ.

§ 1506.8 Will an omission by the Agency in complying with this part serve as a debtor's defense against payment?

Failure by USADF to comply with any provision of this Part is not available to a debtor as a defense against payment of a debt.

Subpart B—Collection

§ 1506.9 What does a collection action entail?

(a) The Agency will undertake prompt action to collect all debts owed to the United States arising out of USADF activities and to reduce debt delinquencies. A collection action may include sending a written notice in the form of a Bill for Collection or demand letter to the debtor's last known address. When necessary to protect the Government's interest (for example, to prevent the running of a statute of limitations), a written demand may be preceded by other appropriate actions under the Federal Claims Collection Standards, including the immediate referral to DOJ for litigation or collection by salary offset. The CFO may contact the debtor by telephone, in person and/or in writing to demand prompt payment, to discuss the debtor's position regarding the existence, amount or repayment of the debt, to inform the debtor of its rights (*e.g.*, to apply for a waiver of indebtedness or to request an administrative review) and of the basis for the debt and the consequences of nonpayment or delay in payment.

(b) The CFO will maintain an administrative file for each claim. The administrative file will document the basis for the debt, all administrative collection actions regarding the debt (including communications to and from the debtor) and the final disposition of the debt. Information on an individual debtor may be disclosed only for purposes consistent with this Part, the Privacy Act of 1974, and other applicable law.

§ 1506.10 What information is included in a written demand for payment?

(a) The Bill for Collection or demand letter shall inform the debtor of:

(1) The amount, nature and basis of the debt;

(2) The right of the debtor to inspect and copy records related to the debt;

(3) The right of the debtor to discuss and propose a repayment agreement;

(4) Any rights available to the debtor to dispute the validity of the debt or to have recovery of the debt waived (citing the available review or waiver authority, the conditions for review or waiver, and the effects of the review or waiver request on the collection of the debt);

(5) The applicable standards for imposition of interest charges and penalty charges and administrative costs that may be assessed against a delinquent debt;

(6) The date by which payment should be made to avoid late charges (*i.e.* interest, penalties, and administrative costs), which may be not more than 30 days from the date that the demand letter is mailed or hand-delivered;

(7) The name, address, and telephone number of a person or office within USADF available to discuss the debt;

(8) The intention of USADF to enforce collection if the debtor fails to pay or otherwise resolve the debt, by taking one or more of the following actions:

(i) Offset from Federal payments otherwise due to the debtor, including income tax refunds, salary, certain benefit payments, retirement, vendor payments, travel reimbursement and advances, and other Federal payments;

(ii) Referral to a private collection agency;

(iii) Report to credit bureaus;

(iv) Administrative wage garnishment;

(v) Referral to the Department of Justice for litigation action if the debt cannot be collected administratively;

(vi) Transfer of any debt delinquent for more than 180 days to the Department of Treasury for collection; and

(vii) Other actions authorized by the FCCS and applicable law.

(9) Any rights available to the debtor to dispute the validity of the debt or to have recovery of the debt waived (citing the available review or waiver authority, the conditions for review or waiver, and the effects of the review or

waiver request on the collection of the debt);

(10) The instructions for making electronic payment; and

(11) Requirement that the debtor advise USADF of any bankruptcy proceeding.

(b) USADF may omit from the written demand for payment one or more of the provisions contained in paragraphs (a)(8) through (11) of this section if USADF determines that any provision is not legally required given the collection remedies to be applied to a particular debt, or which have already been provided by prior notice, applicable agreement, or contract.

(c) USADF will respond promptly to communications from the debtor. Responses will generally be made within 30 days of the receipt of the communication from the debtor.

§ 1506.11 May I request a review of the existence or amount of a claim?

(a) USADF shall provide the debtor with a reasonable opportunity for an internal review of the existence or amount of the debt. For offset of current Federal salary under 5 U.S.C. 5514, a debtor may also request a hearing. (See subpart C of this part).

(b) A request for a review must be submitted in writing to the appropriate contact office by the payment due date indicated in the Bill for Collection or demand letter. The request must state the basis for the debtor's dispute of the claim and include any relevant documentation in support.

(1) USADF will provide for an internal review of the debt by an appropriate official. The review may include examination of documents, internal discussions with relevant officials and discussions with the debtor, at USADF's discretion.

(2) An oral hearing is not required when USADF determines that the matter can be decided on the documentary record. When an oral hearing is not required, USADF shall accord the debtor a "paper hearing," that is, a determination of the request for reconsideration based upon a review of the written record.

(3) Unless otherwise required by law, an oral hearing under this section is not required to be a formal evidentiary hearing, although USADF will carefully document all significant matters discussed at the hearing.

§ 1506.12 What happens if my debt becomes past due?

USADF will transfer to the Department of Treasury's Bureau of Fiscal Services (BFS) any past due, legally enforceable non-tax debt that has been delinquent for 120 days or more for administrative offset, and delinquent for 180 days or more for other collections. BFS may take appropriate action to collect the debt in accordance with applicable law and regulation. USADF may transfer any past due, legally enforceable debt that has been delinquent for fewer than 120 days to BFS for collection in accordance with applicable law and regulation.

§ 1506.13 How are interest, penalty, and administrative costs determined?

(a) *Interest.* USADF will assess interest on all delinquent debts, unless prohibited by statute, regulation, or contract.

(1) Interest begins to accrue on all debts from the payment due date established in the initial notice to the debtor, or as otherwise provided by law. USADF shall charge an annual rate of interest that is equal to the rate established annually by the Secretary of the Treasury in accordance with 31 U.S.C. 3717 unless a different rate is necessary to protect the rights of the United States. USADF will notify the debtor of the basis for its finding that a different rate is necessary to protect the interest of the Government.

(2) The rate of interest, as initially assessed, shall remain fixed for the duration of the indebtedness. If a debtor defaults on a repayment agreement, interest may be set at the Treasury rate in effect on the date a new agreement is executed.

(3) Interest will not be assessed on interest charges, administrative costs or late payment penalties. However, where a debtor defaults on a previous repayment agreement and interest, administrative costs and penalty charges that had been waived under the defaulted agreement may be reinstated and added to the debt principal under

any new agreement and interest may be charged on the entire amount of the debt.

(b) *Administrative costs of collecting overdue debts.* The costs of USADF's administrative processing of overdue debts, including charges assessed by the Department of Treasury in cross-servicing the debts based on either actual or average cost incurred, will be charged on all debts. These costs include both direct and indirect costs.

(c) *Penalties.* Penalty charges will be assessed at 6 percent a year on any portion of a claim that is delinquent for more than 90 days.

(d) *Allocation of payments.* A partial payment by a debtor will be applied first towards outstanding administrative costs, penalty assessments, accrued interest and then towards the outstanding debt principal.

(e) *Waivers.* (1) USADF will waive the collection of interest and administrative charges on any portion of the debt that is paid within 30 days after the date on which late payment charges begin to accrue. This 30 day period may be extended on a case-by-case basis where the Agency determines that such action is in the best interest of the Government.

(2) USADF may (without regard to the amount of the debt) waive collection of all or part of accrued interest, penalty or administrative costs, where it determines that:

(i) Waiver is justified under the criteria of subpart D; or

(ii) Collection of these charges would be against equity and good conscience or not in the best interest of the United States.

(3) A decision to waive interest, penalty charges or administrative costs may be made at any time.

§ 1506.14 Does interest accrue during the period pending waiver or review?

During the period pending waiver or review, USADF may suspend accrual of interest, penalty charges, and administrative costs on any disputed portion of the debt if it is determined that suspension is in the Agency's best interest or would serve equity and good conscience. Interest, penalty, and administrative costs will not be assessed where a statute or regulation specifically prohibits collection of the debt during the period of the administrative appeal or the Agency review.

§ 1506.15 Does USADF contract with other agencies for collection services?

(a) USADF has entered into a cross-servicing agreement with the Bureau of Fiscal Services (BFS) of the Department of Treasury. BFS will take appropriate action to collect and/or compromise transferred debts in accordance with applicable statutory and regulatory requirements. BFS may take any of the following collection actions on behalf of USADF:

(1) Send demand letters on U.S. Treasury letterhead and telephone debtors;

(2) Refer accounts to credit bureaus;

(3) Purchase credit reports to assist in the collection effort;

(4) Refer accounts for offset, including tax refund, Federal employee salary, administrative wage garnishment, and general administrative offset under the Treasury Offset Program;

(5) Refer accounts to private collection agencies;

(6) Refer accounts to the Department of Justice for litigation;

(7) Report written off or discharged debt to the Internal Revenue Service (IRS) on the appropriate Form 1099;

(8) Take any additional steps necessary to enforce recovery; and

(9) Terminate collection action, as appropriate.

(b) BFS will maintain records on debt transferred to it, assure that accounts are updated as necessary, and modify its delinquent debt and debtor records with information obtained from its skip tracking and asset-location services as appropriate. In the event that a referred debtor disputes the validity of a debt or any terms and conditions related to any debt not reduced by judgment, BFS may return the disputed debt to USADF for its determination of debt validity.

§ 1506.16 Does USADF report delinquent debts to consumer reporting agencies?

USADF may report delinquent debts to appropriate credit reporting bureaus and other automated databases through the cross-servicing agreement with BFS. Any such disclosure will be done in accordance with 31 U.S.C. 3711(e) and the Federal Claims Collection Standards, 31 CFR 901.4, and in compliance with the Bankruptcy Code and Privacy Act 5 U.S.C. 552a.

§ 1506.17 For what purposes may USADF use my mailing address?

When attempting to locate a debtor in order to collect or compromise a debt, USADF may obtain the debtor's mailing address from the Internal Revenue Service. Addresses obtained from the Internal Revenue Service will be used by USADF, its officers, employees, agents or contractors and other Federal agencies only to collect or dispose of debts, and may be disclosed to other agencies and to collection agencies only for collection purposes.

§ 1506.18 Will USADF suspend or revoke my financial assistance or other privileges if I fail to pay my debt?

Unless waived by the Head of the Agency, USADF will not extend financial assistance in the form of a grant, loan, or loan guarantee to any person delinquent on a non-tax debt owed to a Federal agency. The authority to waive the application of this section may be delegated to the Chief Financial Officer and re-delegated. USADF may also suspend or revoke other privileges for any inexcusable, prolonged or repeated failure of a debtor to pay a claim. Additionally, the Agency may suspend or disqualify any contractor, lender, broker, borrower, grantee or other debtor from doing business with USADF or engaging in programs USADF sponsors or funds if a debtor fails to pay its debts to the Government within a reasonable time. Debtors will be notified before such action is taken and applicable debarment procedures will be used.

§ 1506.19 May I pay my debt in installments?

(a) Whenever feasible, USADF shall collect the total amount of a debt (including interest, penalty, and administrative cost) in one lump sum. If the debtor is financially unable to pay the debt in one lump sum, USADF may accept payment in regular installments. USADF will obtain financial statements from debtors who represent that they are unable to pay on one lump sum and independently verify such representations whenever possible. In addition, USADF will obtain a legally enforceable written agreement from the debtor that specifies all of the terms of the arrangement and contains a provision accelerating the debt in the event of a default.

(b) The size and frequency of the installment payments will bear a reasonable relation to the size of the debt and the debtor's ability to pay. To the extent possible, the installment payments will be sufficient in size and frequency to liquidate the debt in three years or less.

(c) In appropriate cases, the Agency will obtain security for deferred payments. However, USADF may accept installment payments notwithstanding the refusal of the debtor to execute a written agreement or to give security.

Subpart C—Administrative Offset

§ 1506.20 When and how will USADF collect past due debt through administrative offset?

(a) Payments otherwise due the debtor from the United States shall be offset from the debt in accordance with 31 CFR 901.3. These may be funds under the control of USADF or other Federal agencies. Collection may be through centralized offset by the Bureau of Fiscal Service (BFS) of the Department of the Treasury.

(b) Such payments include but are not limited to vendor payments, salary, retirement, lump sum payments due upon Federal employment separation, travel reimbursements, tax refunds, loans or other assistance. Offset of Federal salary payments will be in accordance with 5 U.S.C. 5514.

(c) Before administrative offset is instituted by another Federal agency or the BFS, USADF shall certify in writing to that entity that the debt is past due and legally enforceable and that USADF has complied with all applicable due process and other requirements as described in this part and other Federal law and regulations.

§ 1506.21 I am a USADF employee; when will the Agency offset my salary to satisfy a debt against me?

Any amount advanced to an employee for allowable travel expenses but not used for such purposes is recoverable from the employee, in accordance with 5 U.S.C. 5705, by salary offset without regard to the due process provisions in § 1506.22. This section does not apply to debts where collection by salary offset is explicitly prohibited by another statute. Collection of debt by salary offset will be in accordance with 5 U.S.C. 5514.

§ 1506.22 Am I entitled to notice and hearing prior to salary offset?

(a) *Due process requirements—Notice, hearing, written response and decision.* (1) Prior to initiating collection action through salary offset, the Agency will provide all employees that owe a debt to the Government an opportunity to repay in full the amount owed, unless such opportunity will compromise the Government's ultimate ability to collect the debt.

(2) Except as provided otherwise, each employee from whom the Agency proposes to collect a debt by salary offset will receive a written notice 30 days prior to any deductions from pay. The notification will include the Agency's determination that a debt is owed, the amount of the debt, the Agency's intention to collect the debt by means of deductions from the employee's pay account, and the employee's right to request a hearing on the claim.

(3) An employee facing collection of debt by salary offset is entitled to request a hearing on the claim. The request must be filed in writing and signed by the employee. It must be received by the Agency within 15 days of the employee's receipt of the notification of proposed deduction. Late request for a hearing may be accepted if the employee can show that the delay in filing the request was due to circumstances beyond the employee's control.

(4) The Agency will make hearing arrangements that are consistent with law and regulations. Where a hearing is held, the employee is entitled to a written decision on the following:

(i) A determination of the Agency concerning the existence and amount of the debt; and

(ii) A repayment schedule.

(b) *Exceptions to the due process requirements—pay and allowances.* The procedural requirements of paragraph (a) of this section are not applicable to overpayments of salary or allowances in the following situations:

(1) Adjustments of pay arising out of an employee's election of coverage or a change in coverage under a Federal benefits program requiring periodic deduction from payment, if the amount to be recovered accumulated over four pay periods or less;

(2) Routine intra-agency adjustments in pay or allowances that are made to correct overpayments of pay attributable to clerical or administrative errors or delays in processing pay documents, if the overpayments accrued over four pay periods or less; and

(3) Any adjustment to collect a debt amounting to $50 or less.

(c) *Form of hearing, written response and final decision.* (1) The hearing official will make a decision based upon a review of the claim and any additional material submitted by the debtor. Where the hearing official determines that the validity of the debt turns on an issue of veracity or credibility which cannot be resolved through a review of documentary evidence, the hearing official at his discretion may afford the debtor an opportunity for an oral hearing. An oral hearing will consist of an informal conference before a hearing official in which the employee and the Agency may present evidence, witnesses and arguments. The employee may be represented by an individual of his/her choosing. The Agency shall maintain a summary record of all oral hearings provided under the procedures of this section.

(2) Written decisions rendered pursuant to a hearing will include the hearing official's analysis, findings and conclusions. The decision will be final and binding on the parties.

(d) *Request for waiver.* In certain circumstances, an employee may have a statutory right to request a waiver of overpayment of pay or allowances, *e.g.*, 5 U.S.C. 5584 or 5 U.S.C. 5724(i). When an employee requests a waiver consideration under a right authorized by statue, further collection on the debt will be suspended until a final administrative decision is made on the waiver request.

(e) *Non-waiver of right by payment.* An employee's payment of all or any portion of a debt does not waive any rights that the employee may have under either the procedures in this section or any other provision of law.

§ 1506.23 Will the debt be collected in a lump sum or by installment deductions from my pay account?

A debt will be collected in a lump sum or by installment deductions at established pay intervals from an employee's current pay account. If the employee is financially unable to pay a debt in a lump sum or the amount of debt exceeds 15 percent of disposable pay, collection will be made in installments, unless the employee and the Agency agree to alternative arrangements for payment. Alternative payment schedules must be in writing, signed by both the employee and the CFO and will be documented in the Agency's files.

§ 1506.24 Are there any limitations on the amount of salary deduction?

Installment deduction will be made over the period of active duty or employment. The size and frequency of the installment deductions generally will bear a reasonable relation to the size of the debt and the employee's ability to pay. However, an amount deducted for any period may not exceed 15 percent of the disposable pay from which the deduction is made, unless the employee has agreed in writing to the deduction of a greater amount. If possible, the installment payments should be in amounts sufficient to liquidate the debt within a period of three years or less. Installment payments of less than $50 will be accepted only in the most unusual circumstances.

§ 1506.25 When will deduction from my pay account begin?

(a) Deductions to liquidate an employee's debt will begin on the date stated in the Agency's Bill for Collection or demand letter notice of intention to collect from the employee's current pay, unless the debt has been repaid in full or the employee has filed a timely request for hearing.

(b) If an employee files a timely request for hearing, deductions will begin after the hearing official has provided the employee with a final written decision indicating the amount owed to the Government. Following the decision by the hearing official, the employee will be given 30 days to repay the amount owed prior to collection through salary offset, unless otherwise provided by the hearing official.

§ 1506.26 What happens if my employment with USADF ends prior to repaying the full amount of my debt?

If the employee retires, resigns, or the period of employment ends before collection of the debt is completed, the remainder of the debt will be offset from subsequent payments of any nature due the employee (*e.g.* final salary payment, lump-sum leave, etc.).

§ 1506.27 How are interest, penalty, and administrative costs assessed?

USADF will assess interest, penalties and administrative costs on debts collected under the procedures in this section. Interest, penalty and administrative costs will continue to accrue during the period that the debtor is seeking formal or informal review of the debt or requesting a waiver. The following guidelines apply to the assessment of these costs on debts collected by salary offset:

(a) Interest will be assessed on all debts not collected by the payment due date specified in the Bill for Collection or demand letter. USADF will waive the interest and administrative charges on the portion of the debt that is paid within 30 days after the date on which interest begins to accrue.

(b) Administrative costs will be assessed if the debt is referred to Treasury for cross-servicing.

(c) Deductions by administrative offset normally begin prior to the time for assessment of a penalty. Therefore, a penalty charge will not be assessed unless deductions occur more than 90 days from the due date in the Bill for Collection or demand letter.

§ 1506.28 Will I receive a refund if the claim against me is found to be without merit?

USADF will promptly refund to the employee any amounts paid or deducted pursuant to this section that are subsequently waived or found not owing to the United States Government. Refunds do not bear interest unless specifically authorized by law.

§ 1506.29 Is there a time limit for initiating collection by salary offset?

USADF will not initiate salary offset to collect a debt more than 1 year after the Government's right to collect the debt first accrued, unless facts material to the right to collect the debt were not known and could not have been known through the exercise of reasonable care by the Government official responsible for discovering and collecting such debt.

§ 1506.30 Can USADF use salary offset means to collect a claim against me if USADF is not the creditor agency?

(a) USADF will use salary offset means of collecting debt against one of its employees that is indebted to another agency if requested to do so by that agency. The requesting agency must certify that the USADF employee owes a debt and that the procedural requirements of 5 U.S.C. 5514 and 5 CFR part 550, subpart K, have been met. The creditor agency must also advise USADF of the amount of debt, and the number and amount of the installments to be collected.

(b) Request for salary offset must be submitted to the CFO of USADF.

(c) Processing of the claim by USADF—

(1) *Incomplete claims.* A creditor agency will be required to supply USADF with all the required information prior to any salary offset from the employee's current pay account.

(2) *Complete claims.* If the claim procedures in paragraph (a) of this section have been properly completed, deduction will begin on the next established pay period. USADF will not review the merits of the creditor agency's determinations with respect to the amount or validity of the debt as stated in the debt claim form. USADF will not assess a handling or any other related charge to cover the cost of its processing the claim.

(d) Employees separating from USADF before a debt to another agency is collected—

(1) *Employees separating from Government service.* If an employee begins separation action before USADF collects the total debt due the creditor agency, the following actions will be taken:

(i) To the extent possible, the balance owed the creditor agency will be liquidated from subsequent payments of any nature due the employee from USADF;

(ii) If the total amount of the debt cannot be recovered, USADF will certify to the creditor agency and the employee the total amount of USADF's collection; and

(iii) If USADF is aware that the employee is entitled to payments from the Civil Service Retirement and Disability Fund, or other similar payments, it will provide such information to the creditor agency so that it can file a certified claim against the payments.

(2) *Employees who transfer to another Federal agency.* If an USADF employee transfers to another Federal agency before USADF collects the total amount due the creditor agency, USADF will certify the total amount of the collection made on the debt. It is the responsibility of the creditor agency to ensure that the collection is resumed by the new employing agency.

Subpart D—Compromise of Debts

§ 1506.31 May USADF reduce or negotiate a claim amount?

USADF may compromise claims for money or property where the principal balance of a claim, excluding interest, penalty and administrative costs, does not exceed $100,000. Where the claim exceeds $100,000, the authority to accept the compromise rests solely with DOJ. The CFO may reject an offer of compromise in any amount. Where the claim exceeds $100,000, USADF may refer the claim to DOJ for approval with a recommendation to accept an offer of compromise. The referral will be in the form of a Claims Collection

Litigation Report (CCLR) and will outline the basis for USADF's recommendation.

§ 1506.32 If I am jointly and severally liable on a claim, will USADF delay collection action against me until the other debtors pay their proportional share?

When two or more debtors are jointly and severally liable, collection action will not be withheld against one debtor until the other or others pay their proportionate share. The amount of a compromise with one debtor is not precedent in determining compromises from other debtors who have been determined to be jointly and severally liable on the claim.

§ 1506.33 Under what circumstances will USADF compromise a claim?

(a) USADF may compromise a claim pursuant to this section if the debtor does not have the financial ability to pay the full amount of the debt within a reasonable time, or the debtor refuses to pay the claim in full and the Government does not have the ability to enforce collection in full within a reasonable time by collection proceedings. In evaluating the acceptability of a compromise offer, the CFO may consider, among other factors, the following:

(1) Age and health of the debtor;

(2) Present and potential income;

(3) Inheritance prospects;

(4) The possibility that assets have been concealed or improperly transferred by the debtor;

(5) The availability of assets or income which may be realized by enforced collection proceedings; or

(6) The applicable exemptions available to the debtor under State and Federal law in determining the Government's ability to enforce collection.

(b) USADF may compromise a claim, or recommend acceptance of a compromise offer to DOJ, if:

(1) There is significant doubt concerning the Government's ability to prove its case in court for the full amount of the claim, either because of the legal issues involved or a bona fide dispute as to the facts; or

(2) The cost of collection does not justify the enforced collection of the full amount of the debt.

The amount accepted in compromise in such cases will reflect the costs of collection, the probability of prevailing on the legal issues involved, and the likely amount of court costs and attorney's fees in litigation.

(c) To assess the merits of a compromise offer, USADF generally will require a current financial statement from the debtor, executed under penalty of perjury, showing the debtor's assets, liabilities, income and expenses.

(d) Statutory penalties, forfeitures or debt established as an aid to enforcement and compel compliance may be compromised where the CFO determines that the Agency's enforcement policy, in terms of deterrence and securing compliance (both present and future), will be adequately served by accepting the offer.

§ 1506.34 Can I pay a compromised claim in installments?

The debtor may not pay a compromised claim in installments unless the CFO determines that payment in installments is necessary to effect collection.

§ 1506.35 Will USADF execute a release after full payment of a compromised amount?

Upon receipt of a payment in full or a compromised amount of a claim, USADF will prepare and execute a release.

Subpart E—Suspension or Termination of Collection Action

§ 1506.36 Under what circumstances may USADF suspend collection actions?

USADF may suspend or terminate the Agency's collection actions on a debt where the outstanding debt principal does not exceed $100,000. Unless otherwise provided by DOJ regulations, USADF must refer all requests for suspension of debt exceeding $100,000 to the Commercial Litigation Branch, Civil Division, Department of Justice, for approval. If prior to referral to DOJ, USADF determines that a debt is plainly erroneous or clearly without legal merit, the Agency may terminate collection activity regardless of the amount involved without obtaining

DOJ concurrence. USADF may waive the assessment of interest, penalty charges and administrative costs during the period of the suspension. Suspension will be for an estimated time period and generally will be reviewed at least every six months to ensure the continued propriety of the suspension.

§ 1506.37 What are the criteria for suspension?

(a) USADF may suspend collection action on a debt when:

(1) The debtor cannot be located;

(2) The debtor's financial condition is expected to improve; or

(3) The debtor has requested a waiver or review of the debt.

(b) Based on the current financial condition of the debtor, USADF may suspend collection activity on a debt when the debtor's future prospects justify retention of the claim for periodic review, and:

(1) The applicable statute of limitations has not expired; or

(2) Future collection can be effected by offset; or

(3) The debtor agrees to pay interest on the debt and suspension is likely to enhance the debtor's ability to fully pay the principal amount of the debt with interest at a later date.

(c) USADF will suspend collection activity during the time required for waiver consideration or administrative review prior to agency collection of a debt if the statute under which the request is sought prohibits the Agency from collecting the debt during that time. USADF will ordinarily suspend collection action during the pendency of its consideration of a waiver request or administrative review where statute and regulation preclude refund of amounts collected by the Agency should the debtor prevail.

(d) USADF may suspend collection activities on debts of $100,000 or less during the pendency of a permissive waiver or administrative review when there is no statutory requirement and where it determines that:

(1) There is a reasonable possibility that waiver will be granted and the debtor may be found not owing the debt (in whole or in part);

(2) The Government's interest is protected, if suspension is granted, by the reasonable assurance that the debt can be recovered if the debtor does not prevail; or

(3) Collection of the debt will cause undue hardship to the debtor.

(e) USADF will decline to suspend collection where it determines that the request for waiver or administrative review is frivolous or was made primarily to delay collection.

§ 1506.38 Under what circumstances may USADF terminate collection actions?

USADF may terminate collection actions including accrued interest, penalty and administrative costs, where the debt principal does not exceed $100,000. If the debt exceeds $100,000, USADF must obtain the approval from DOJ to terminate further collection actions. Unless otherwise provided for by DOJ regulations, requests to terminate collection on debts in excess of $100,000 are referred to the Commercial Litigation Branch, Civil Division, Department of Justice, for approval.

§ 1506.39 What are the criteria for termination?

A debt may be terminated where USADF determines that:

(a) The Government cannot collect or enforce collection of any significant sum from the debtor, having due regard for available judicial remedies, the debtor's ability to pay, and the exemptions available to the debtor under State and Federal law;

(b) The debtor cannot be located, there is no security remaining to be liquidated, and the prospects of collecting by offset are too remote to justify retention of the claim;

(c) The cost of further collection action is likely to exceed the amount recoverable;

(d) The claim is determined to be legally without merit or enforcement of the debt is barred by any applicable statute of limitations;

(e) The evidence necessary to prove the claim cannot be produced or the necessary witnesses are unavailable and efforts to induce voluntary payment have failed; or

(f) The debt against the debtor has been discharged in bankruptcy.

§ 1506.40 What actions by the Agency are permitted after termination of collection activity?

Termination ceases active collection of a debt. However, termination does not preclude the Agency from retaining a record of the account for purposes of:

(a) Selling the debt if the CFO determines that such sale is in the best interests of USADF;

(b) Pursuing collection at a subsequent date in the event there is a change in the debtor's status or a new collection tool becomes available;

(c) Offsetting against future income or assets not available at the time of termination of collection activity; or

(d) Screening future applicants for prior indebtedness.

§ 1506.41 Can the Agency collect against a debt that has been discharged in bankruptcy?

USADF will generally terminate collection activity on a debt that has been discharged in bankruptcy regardless of the amount. However, USADF may continue collection activity subject to the provisions of the Bankruptcy Code for any payments provided under a plan of reorganization. The CFO will seek legal advice from the General Counsel's office if s/he believes that any claims or offsets may have survived the discharge of a debtor.

Subpart F—Discharge of Indebtedness and Reporting Requirements

§ 1506.42 Under what circumstances will USADF discharge a delinquent debt?

Before discharging a delinquent debt, USADF will make a determination that collection action is no longer warranted and request that litigation counsel release any liens of record securing the debt. Discharge of indebtedness is distinct from termination or suspension of collection activity and is governed by the Internal Revenue Code. When collection action on a debt is suspended or terminated, the debt remains delinquent and further collection action may be pursued at a later date in accordance with the standards set forth in this part. When a debt is discharged in full or in part, further collection action is prohibited and USADF must terminate all debt collection activities.

§ 1506.43 Will USADF report a discharge of debt to the IRS?

Upon discharge of a debt, USADF will report the discharge to the IRS in accordance with the requirements of 26 U.S.C. 6050P and 26 CFR 1.6050P-1. USADF may request the Bureau of Fiscal Services of the Department of Treasury to file such a discharge report to the IRS on the agency's behalf.

Subpart G—Referrals to the Department of Justice

§ 1506.44 When will USADF refer claims to the Department of Justice for litigation?

Unless otherwise provided by DOJ regulations or procedures, USADF will refer for litigation debts of more than $2,500 but less than $1,000,000 to the Department of Justice's Nationwide Central Intake Facility as required by the Claims Collection Litigation Report (CCLR) instructions. Debts of over $1,000,000 shall be referred to the Civil Division at the Department of Justice. Any debt involving fraud, false claim, and misrepresentation will be referred to the Department of Justice.

Subpart H—Mandatory Transfer of Delinquent Debt to the Bureau of Fiscal Services (BFS) of the Department of Treasury

§ 1506.45 When is it mandatory for USADF to transfer debts to BFS?

(a) USADF will transfer legally enforceable debt to BFS 90 days after the Bill for Collection or demand letter is issued. A debt is legally enforceable if there has been a final agency determination that the debt is due and there are no legal bars to collection action. A debt is not legally enforceable for purposes of mandatory transfer to BFS if it is the subject of a pending administrative review process required by statute or regulation and collection action during the review process is prohibited.

(b) Except as set forth in paragraph (a) of this section, USADF will transfer any debt covered by this part that is more than 180 days delinquent to BFS for debt collection services. A debt is 180 days delinquent for purposes of this section if it is 180 days past due and is legally enforceable.

§ 1506.46 When is USADF not required to transfer a debt to BFS?

USADF is not required to transfer a debt to BFS pursuant to § 1506.37(b) during the period of time that the debt:

(a) Is in litigation or foreclosure;

(b) Is scheduled for sale;

(c) Is at a private collection contractor;

(d) Is at a debt collection center if the debt has been referred to a Treasury-designated debt collection center;

(e) Is being collected by internal offset; or

(f) Is covered by an exemption granted by Treasury.

PART 1507—RULES SAFEGUARDING PERSONAL INFORMATION

Sec.

AUTHORITY: 5 U.S.C. 522a.

SOURCE: 53 FR 40411, Oct. 17, 1988, unless otherwise noted.

§ 1507.1 Purpose.

The purpose of this part is to set forth the basic policies of the African Development Foundation ("the Foundation" or "ADF") governing the maintenance of systems of records containing personal information as defined in the Privacy Act of 1974 (5 U.S.C. 552a).

§ 1507.2 General policies.

It is the policy of the Foundation to safeguard the right of privacy of any individual as to whom the Foundation maintains personal information in any records system, and to provide such individuals with appropriate and complete access to such records, including adequate opportunity to correct any errors in said records. It is further the policy of the Foundation to maintain its records in such a fashion that the information contained therein is, and remains, material and relevant to the purposes for which it is collected. Information in such records will be collected, maintained, used or disseminated in a manner that assures that such action is for a necessary and lawful purpose, and that adequate safeguards are provided to prevent misuse of such information. Exemptions from records requirements provided in 5 U.S.C. 552a will be permitted only where an important public policy need for such exemptions has been determined pursuant to specific statutory authority.

§ 1507.3 Definitions.

(a) *Record* means any document, collection, or grouping of information about an individual maintained by the Foundation, including but not limited to information regarding education, financial transactions, medical history, criminal or employment history, or any other personal information which contains the name or personal identification number, symbol, photograph, or other identifying particular assigned to such individual, such as a finger or voiceprint.

(b) *System of Records* means a group of any records under the control of the Foundation from which information is retrieved by use of the name of an individual or by some identifying particular assigned to the individual.

(c) *Routine Use* means, with respect to the disclosure of a record, the use of such record for a purpose which is compatible with the purpose for which it was collected.

(d) The term *Foundation* means the African Development Foundation or any component thereof.

(e) The term *individual* means any citizen of the United States or an alien lawfully admitted to permanent residence.

(f) The term *maintain* includes the maintenance, collection, use or dissemination of any record.

(g) The term *Act* means the Privacy Act of 1974 (5 U.S.C. 552a) as amended from time to time.

§ 1507.4 Conditions of disclosure.

The Foundation will not disclose any record contained in a system of records by any means of communication to any person or any other agency except by written request or prior written consent of the individual to whom the record pertains or his or her agent or attorney, unless such disclosure is:

(a) To those officers and employees of the Foundation who have a need for the records in the official performance of their duties;

(b) Required under the Freedom of Information Act (5 U.S.C. 552);

(c) For a routine use of the record compatible with the purpose for which it was collected;

(d) To the Bureau of the Census for purpose of planning or carrying out a census or survey or related activity pursuant to title 13, United States Code;

(e) To a recipient who has provided the Foundation with advance adequate written assurance that the record will be used solely as a statistical research or reporting record, and the record is to be transferred to a form that is not individually identifiable;

(f) To the National Archives of the United States as a record which has sufficient historical or other value to warrant its continued preservation by the U.S. Government, or for evaluation by the Administrator of General Services, or designee, to determine whether the record has such value;

(g) To another agency or to an instrumentality of any governmental jurisdiction within or under the control of the United States for a civil or criminal law enforcement activity if the activity is authorized by law, and if the head of the agency or instrumentality has made a written request to the Foundation specifying the particular portion desired and the law enforcement activity for which the record is sought;

(h) To a person, pursuant to a showing of compelling circumstances affecting the health or safety of an individual, if, promptly following such disclosure, notification is transmitted to the last known address of the individual to whom the record pertains;

(i) To either House of Congress, or, to the extent of matters within its jurisdiction, any committee or subcommittee thereof, any joint committee of Congress or subcommittee of any such joint committee;

(j) To the Comptroller General, or any authorized representative, in the course of the performance of the duties of the General Accounting Office; or

(k) Pursuant to the order of a court of competent jurisdiction. If any record disclosed under compulsory legal process is subsequently made public by the court which issued it, the Foundation must make a reasonable effort to notify the individual to whom the record pertains of such disclosure.

(l) To consumer reporting agencies as defined in 31 U.S.C. 370(a)(3) in accordance with 31 U.S.C. 3711, and under contracts for collection services as authorized in 31 U.S.C. 3718.

§ 1507.5 Accounting for disclosure of records.

(a) With respect to each system of records under ADF control, the Foundation will keep an accurate accounting of routine disclosures, except those made to employees of the Foundation in the normal course of duties or pursuant to the provisions of the Freedom of Information Act. Such accounting shall contain the following:

(1) The date, nature and purpose of each disclosure, and the name and address of the person or agency to whom the disclosure is made:

(2) Sufficient information to permit the construction of a listing of all disclosures at appropriate periodic intervals; and

(3) The justification or basis upon which any release was made including any written documentation required.

(b) The Foundation will retain the accounting made under this section for at least 5 years or the life of the record, whichever is longer, after the disclosure for which the accounting is made.

(c) Except for disclosure made under paragraph (g) of § 1503.3, the Foundation will make the accounting under paragraph (a) of this section available to the individual named in the record at his or her request.

(d) The Foundation will inform any person or other agency about any correction or notation of dispute made by the agency of any record that has been disclosed to the person or agency if an accounting of the disclosure was made.

§ 1507.6 Access to records.

(a) Except as otherwise provided by law or regulation, any individual, upon request made either in writing or in person during regular business hours, shall be provided access to his or her record or to any information pertaining to him or her which is contained in a system of records maintained by the Foundation. The individual will be permitted to review the record and have a copy made of all or any portion thereof in a form comprehensible to him or her. Nothing in 5 U.S.C. 552a, however, allows an individual access to any information compiled in reasonable anticipation of a civil action or proceeding.

(b) An individual will be notified, upon request, if any Foundation system of records contains a record pertaining to him or her. Such request may be made in person during regular business hours, or in writing over the signature of the person making the request. Individuals requesting the information will be required to identify themselves by providing their names, addresses, and a signature. If they are requesting disclosure in person, they are also required to show an identification card, such as a drivers license, containing a photo and a sample signature. If the request is received through the mail, the Foundation may request such information as may be necessary to assure that the requesting individual is properly identified. This may include a requirement that the request be notarized with a notation that the notary received an acknowledgement of identity from the requester.

(c) A record may be disclosed to a representative of the person to whom a record relates when the representative is authorized in writing by such person to have access.

(d) Requests for access to or copies of records should contain, at a minimum, identifying information needed to locate any given record, and a brief description of the item or items of information required. If the individual wishes access to specific documents, the request should identify or describe, as nearly as possible, such documents. The request should be made to the Director, Administration and Finance, African Development Foundation, 1625 Massachusetts Avenue NW., Suite 600, Washington, DC 20036. Personal contacts should normally be made during the regular duty hours of the officer concerned, which are 8:30 a.m. to 5:00 p.m. Monday through Friday.

(e) A request made in person will be promptly complied with if the records sought are in the immediate custody of the Foundation. Mail or personal requests for documents which are not in the immediate custody of ADF or which are otherwise not immediately available, will be acknowledged within ten working days of receipt, and the records will be provided as promptly thereafter as possible.

(f) Special procedures may be established by the President of the Foundation governing the disclosure to an individual of his or her medical records, including psychological records.

(g) Any individual may request the Director, Administration and Finance, to amend any Foundation record pertaining to him or her. Not later than 10 working days after the date of receipt of such request, the Director, Administration and Finance, or his/her designee, will acknowledge such receipt in writing. Promptly after acknowledging receipt of a request, the Director, Administration and Finance or his/her designee will:

(1) Correct any portion of the record which the individual believes is not accurate, relevant, timely, or complete; or

(2) Inform the individual of the Foundation's refusal to amend the record in accordance with the request, the reason for the refusal, the procedures by which the individual may request a review of that refusal by the President of the Foundation, or his/her designee, and the name and address of such official; or

(3) Refer the request to the agency that has control of and maintains the record when the record requested is not

the property of the Foundation, but of the controlling agency.

(h) Any individual who disagrees with the refusal of the Director, Administration and Finance to amend his or her record may request a review of that refusal. Such request for review must be made within 30 days after receipt by the requester of the initial refusal to amend. The President of the Foundation, or designee, will complete such review not later than 30 working days from the date on which the individual requests such review, and make a final determination, unless for good cause shown, the President or designee extends such 30-day period and notifies the requester in writing that additional time is required to complete the review. If, after review, the President or designee refuses to amend the record in accordance with the request, the individual will be advised of the right to file with the Foundation a concise statement setting forth the reasons for his or her disagreement with the refusal, and also advised of the provisions in the Act for judicial review of the President's determination.

(i) In any disclosure containing information about which the individual has filed a statement under paragraph (g) of this section, the Foundation will clearly note any part of the record which is disputed and provide copies of the statement and, if the Foundation deems it appropriate, copies of a concise statement of the Foundation's reasons for not making the amendment requested, to persons or other agencies to whom the disputed record has been disclosed.

§ 1507.7 Contents of records systems.

(a) The Foundation will maintain in its records only such information about an individual as is accurate, relevant, and necessary to accomplish the purpose for which it was acquired as authorized by statute or Executive Order.

(b) The Foundation will collect information, to the greatest extent practicable, directly from the individual to whom the record pertains when the information may result in adverse determinations about the individual's rights, benefits and privileges under Federal programs.

(c) The Foundation will inform each individual whom it asks to supply information on any form which it uses to collect the information, or on a separate form that can be retained by the individual, of:

(1) The authority which authorizes the solicitation of the information and whether provision of such information is mandatory or voluntary;

(2) The purpose or purposes for which the information is intended to be used;

(3) The routine uses which may be made of the information, as published pursuant to paragraph (d) of this section; and

(4) The effects on the individual, if any, of not providing all or any part of the requested information.

(d) Subject to the provisions of paragraph (k) of this section, the Foundation will publish in the FEDERAL REGISTER, at least a notice of the existence and character of its sytem(s) of records upon establishment or revision. This notice will include:

(1) The name and location of the system or systems;

(2) The categories of individuals on whom records are maintained in the system or systems;

(3) The categories of records maintained in the system or sytems;

(4) Each routine use of the records contained in the system or systems, including the categories of users, and the purpose of such use;

(5) The policies and practices of the Foundation regarding storage, retrievability, access controls, retention, and disposal of the record;

(6) The title and business address of the Foundation official or officials responsible for the system or systems of records;

(7) The Foundation's procedures whereby an individual can be notified at his or her request if the system or systems of records contains a record pertaining to him or her;

(8) The Foundation's procedures whereby an individual can be notified at him or her request how he or she can gain access to any record pertaining to him or her contained in the system or systems of records, and how he or she can contest its content; and

(9) The categories of sources of records in the system or systems.

(e) All records used by the Foundation in making any determination about any individual will be maintained with such accuracy, relevance, timeliness, and completeness as is reasonably necessary to assure fairness to the individual in the determination.

(f) Before disseminating any record about an individual to any person other than an agency or pursuant to 5 U.S.C. 552, the Foundation will make reasonable efforts to assure that such records are accurate, complete, timely, and relevant for Foundation purposes.

(g) The Foundation will maintain no record describing how any individual exercises rights guaranteed by the First Amendment of the Constitution of the United States unless expressly authorized by statute or by the individual about whom the record is maintained, or unless pertinent to, and within the scope of, an authorized law enforcement activity.

(h) The Foundation will establish rules of conduct for persons involved in the design, development, operation, or maintenance of any system of records, or in maintaining any record. Each such person will be instructed regarding such rules and the requirements of 5 U.S.C. 552a. The instruction will include any other rules and procedures adopted pursuant to 5 U.S.C. 552a, and the penalties provided for noncompliance.

(i) The Foundation will establish appropriate administrative, technical, and physical safeguards to insure the security and confidentiality of records and to protect against any anticipated threats or hazards to their security or integrity which could result in substantial harm, embarrassment, inconvenience, or unfairness to any individual on whom information is maintained.

(j) At least 30 days prior to the publication of the notice in the FEDERAL REGISTER regarding the routine use of the records contained in the Foundation's system or systems of records, including the categories of users and the purpose of such use pursuant to paragraph (d) of this section, the Foundation will also:

(1) Publish a notice in the FEDERAL REGISTER of any new or revised use of the information in the system or systems maintained by the Foundation; and

(2) Provide an opportunity for interested persons to submit written data, views, or arguments to the Foundation.

§ 1507.8 Fees.

Fees to be charged, if any, to any individual for making copies of his or her record will be as follows:

(a) Photocopy reproductions from all types of copying processes, each reproduction image, $0.10 per page.

(b) Where the Foundation undertakes to perform for an individual making a request, or for any other person, services which are very clearly not required to be performed under section 552a, title 5, United States Code, either voluntarily or because such services are required by some other law (e.g., the formal certification of records as true copies, attestation under the seal of the Foundation, etc.), the question of charging fees for such services will be determined by the Director of Administration and Finance, in light of the Federal user charge statute (31 U.S.C. 483a), and any other applicable law.

(c) No fees shall be charged for search time expended by the Foundation to produce a record.

§ 1507.9 Judicial review.

Any person may file a complaint against the Foundation in the appropriate U.S. district court, as provided in 5 U.S.C. 552a(g), whenever the Foundation:

(a) Makes a determination not to amend an individual's record in accordance with his or her request, or fails to make such review in conformity with that section; or

(b) Refuses to comply with an individual's request; or

(c) Fails to maintain any record concerning an individual with such accuracy, relevance, timeliness, and completeness as is necessary to assure fairness in any determination relating to the qualifications, character, rights or opportunities of, or benefits to the individual that may be made on the basis of such record, and consequently a determination is made which is adverse to the individual; or

(d) Fails to comply with any other provision of 5 U.S.C. 552a, or any Foundation regulation promulgated thereunder, in any such a way as to have an adverse effect on an individual.

§ 1507.10 Exemptions.

No Foundation system or systems of records, as such, are exempted from the provisions of 5 U.S.C. 552a, as permitted under certain conditions by 5 U.S.C. 552a (j) and (k).

§ 1507.11 Mailing list.

An individual's name and address may not be sold or rented by the Foundation unless such action is specifically authorized by law. This section does not require the withholding of names and addresses otherwise permitted to be made public.

§ 1507.12 Criminal penalties.

Section 552a(e), title 5, United States Code, provides that:

(a) Any officer or employee of the Foundation, who, by virtue of his or her employment or official position, has possession of, or access to, Foundation records which contain individually identifiable information, the disclosure of which is prohibited by 5 U.S.C. 552a, and who knowing that disclosure of the specific material is so prohibited, willfully discloses the material in any manner to any person or agency not entitled to receive it, shall be guilty of a misdemeanor and fined not more than $5,000.

(b) Any officer or employee of the Foundation who willfully maintains a system of records without meeting the notice requirements of 5 U.S.C. 552a(e)(4) shall be guilty of a misdemeanor and fined not more than $5,000.

(c) Any person who knowingly and willfully requests or obtains any record concerning an individual from the Foundation under false pretenses shall be guilty of a misdemeanor and fined not more than $5,000.

§ 1507.13 Reports.

(a) The Foundation shall provide to Congress and the Office of Management and Budget advance notice of any proposal to establish or alter any system or records as defined herein. This report will be submitted in accordance with guidelines provided by the Office of Management and Budget.

(b) If at any time Foundation system or systems of records is determined to be exempt from the application of 5 U.S.C. 552a in accordance with the provisions of 5 U.S.C. 552a (j) and (k), the records contained in such system or systems will be separately listed and reported to the Office of Management and Budget in accordance with the then prevailing guidelines and instructions of that office.

PART 1508—GOVERNMENTWIDE DEBARMENT AND SUSPENSION (NONPROCUREMENT)

Sec.

Subpart A—General

Subpart B—Covered Transactions

Subpart C—Responsibilities of Participants Regarding Transactions

DOING BUSINESS WITH OTHER PERSONS

DISCLOSING INFORMATION—PRIMARY TIER PARTICIPANTS

DISCLOSING INFORMATION—LOWER TIER PARTICIPANTS

Subpart D—Responsibilities of ADF Officials Regarding Transactions

Subpart E—Excluded Parties List System

Subpart F—General Principles Relating to Suspension and Debarment Actions

Subpart G—Suspension

Subpart H—Debarment

Subpart I—Definitions

Subpart J [Reserved]

AUTHORITY: Sec. 2455, Pub.L. 103–355, 108 Stat. 3327; E.O. 12549, 3CFR, 1986 Comp., p.89; E.O. 12689, 3CFR, 1989 Comp., p. 235.

SOURCE: 68 FR 66590, 66592, Nov. 26, 2003, unless otherwise noted.

§ 1508.25 How is this part organized?

(a) This part is subdivided into ten subparts. Each subpart contains information related to a broad topic or specific audience with special responsibilities, as shown in the following table:

In subpart . . .	You will find provisions related to . . .
A	general information about this rule.
B	the types of ADF transactions that are covered by the Governmentwide nonprocurement suspension and debarment system.
C	the responsibilities of persons who participate in covered transactions.
D	the responsibilities of ADF officials who are authorized to enter into covered transactions.
E	the responsibilities of Federal agencies for the *Excluded Parties List System* (Disseminated by the General Services Administration).
F	the general principles governing suspension, debarment, voluntary exclusion and settlement.
G	suspension actions.
H	debarment actions.
I	definitions of terms used in this part.
J	[Reserved]

(b) The following table shows which subparts may be of special interest to you, depending on who you are:

If you are . . .	See subpart(s) . . .
(1) a participant or principal in a nonprocurement transaction.	A, B, C, and I.
(2) a respondent in a suspension action	A, B, F, G and I.
(3) a respondent in a debarment action	A, B, F, H and I.
(4) a suspending official	A, B, D, E, F, G and I.
(5) a debarring official	A, B, D, E, F, H and I.
(6) a (n) ADF official authorized to enter into a covered transaction.	A, B, D, E and I.
(7) Reserved	J.

§ 1508.50 How is this part written?

(a) This part uses a "plain language" format to make it easier for the general public and business community to use. The section headings and text, often in the form of questions and answers, must be read together.

(b) Pronouns used within this part, such as "I" and "you," change from subpart to subpart depending on the audience being addressed. The pronoun "we" always is the African Development Foundation.

(c) The "Covered Transactions" diagram in the appendix to this part shows the levels or "tiers" at which the African Development Foundation enforces an exclusion under this part.

§ 1508.75 Do terms in this part have special meanings?

This part uses terms throughout the text that have special meaning. Those terms are defined in Subpart I of this part. For example, three important terms are—

(a) *Exclusion or excluded*, which refers only to discretionary actions taken by a suspending or debarring official under this part or the Federal Acquisition Regulation (48 CFR part 9, subpart 9.4);

(b) *Disqualification or disqualified*, which refers to prohibitions under specific statutes, executive orders (other than Executive Order 12549 and Executive Order 12689), or other authorities. Disqualifications frequently are not subject to the discretion of an agency official, may have a different scope than exclusions, or have special conditions that apply to the disqualification; and

(c) *Ineligibility or ineligible*, which generally refers to a person who is either excluded or disqualified.

Subpart A—General

§ 1508.100 What does this part do?

This part adopts a governmentwide system of debarment and suspension for ADF nonprocurement activities. It also provides for reciprocal exclusion of persons who have been excluded under the Federal Acquisition Regulation, and provides for the consolidated listing of all persons who are excluded, or disqualified by statute, executive order, or other legal authority. This part satisfies the requirements in section 3 of Executive Order 12549, "Debarment and Suspension" (3 CFR 1986 Comp., p. 189), Executive Order 12689, "Debarment and Suspension" (3 CFR 1989 Comp., p. 235) and 31 U.S.C. 6101 note (Section 2455, Public Law 103–355, 108 Stat. 3327).

§ 1508.105 Does this part apply to me?

Portions of this part (see table at §1508.25(b)) apply to you if you are a(n)—

(a) Person who has been, is, or may reasonably be expected to be, a participant or principal in a covered transaction;

(b) Respondent (a person against whom the African Development Foundation has initiated a debarment or suspension action);

(c) ADF debarring or suspending official; or

(d) ADF official who is authorized to enter into covered transactions with non-Federal parties.

§ 1508.110 What is the purpose of the nonprocurement debarment and suspension system?

(a) To protect the public interest, the Federal Government ensures the integrity of Federal programs by conducting business only with responsible persons.

(b) A Federal agency uses the nonprocurement debarment and suspension system to exclude from Federal programs persons who are not presently responsible.

(c) An exclusion is a serious action that a Federal agency may take only to protect the public interest. A Federal agency may not exclude a person or commodity for the purposes of punishment.

§ 1508.115 How does an exclusion restrict a person's involvement in covered transactions?

With the exceptions stated in §§ 1508.120, 1508.315, and 1508.420, a person who is excluded by the African Development Foundation or any other Federal agency may not:

(a) Be a participant in a(n) ADF transaction that is a covered transaction under subpart B of this part;

(b) Be a participant in a transaction of any other Federal agency that is a covered transaction under that agency's regulation for debarment and suspension; or

(c) Act as a principal of a person participating in one of those covered transactions.

§ 1508.120 May we grant an exception to let an excluded person participate in a covered transaction?

(a) The ADF President may grant an exception permitting an excluded person to participate in a particular covered transaction. If the ADF President grants an exception, the exception must be in writing and state the reason(s) for deviating from the governmentwide policy in Executive Order 12549.

(b) An exception granted by one agency for an excluded person does not extend to the covered transactions of another agency.

§ 1508.125 Does an exclusion under the nonprocurement system affect a person's eligibility for Federal procurement contracts?

If any Federal agency excludes a person under its nonprocurement common rule on or after August 25, 1995, the excluded person is also ineligible to participate in Federal procurement transactions under the FAR. Therefore, an exclusion under this part has reciprocal effect in Federal procurement transactions.

§ 1508.130 Does exclusion under the Federal procurement system affect a person's eligibility to participate in nonprocurement transactions?

If any Federal agency excludes a person under the FAR on or after August 25, 1995, the excluded person is also ineligible to participate in nonprocurement covered transactions under this part. Therefore, an exclusion under the FAR has reciprocal effect in Federal nonprocurement transactions.

§ 1508.135 May the African Development Foundation exclude a person who is not currently participating in a nonprocurement transaction?

Given a cause that justifies an exclusion under this part, we may exclude any person who has been involved, is currently involved, or may reasonably be expected to be involved in a covered transaction.

§ 1508.140 How do I know if a person is excluded?

Check the *Excluded Parties List System (EPLS)* to determine whether a person is excluded. The General Services Administration (GSA) maintains the *EPLS* and makes it available, as detailed in subpart E of this part. When a Federal agency takes an action to exclude a person under the nonprocurement or procurement debarment and suspension system, the agency enters the information about the excluded person into the *EPLS*.

§ 1508.145 Does this part address persons who are disqualified, as well as those who are excluded from nonprocurement transactions?

Except if provided for in Subpart J of this part, this part—

(a) Addresses disqualified persons only to—

(1) Provide for their inclusion in the *EPLS;* and

(2) State responsibilities of Federal agencies and participants to check for disqualified persons before entering into covered transactions.

(b) Does not specify the—

(1) ADF transactions for which a disqualified person is ineligible. Those transactions vary on a case-by-case basis, because they depend on the language of the specific statute, Executive order, or regulation that caused the disqualification;

(2) Entities to which the disqualification applies; or

(3) Process that the agency uses to disqualify a person. Unlike exclusion, disqualification is frequently not a discretionary action that a Federal agency takes.

Subpart B—Covered Transactions

§ 1508.200 What is a covered transaction?

A covered transaction is a nonprocurement or procurement transaction that is subject to the prohibitions of this part. It may be a transaction at—

(a) The primary tier, between a Federal agency and a person (see appendix to this part); or

(b) A lower tier, between a participant in a covered transaction and another person.

§ 1508.205 Why is it important if a particular transaction is a covered transaction?

The importance of a covered transaction depends upon who you are.

(a) As a participant in the transaction, you have the responsibilities laid out in Subpart C of this part. Those include responsibilities to the person or Federal agency at the next higher tier from whom you received the transaction, if any. They also include responsibilities if you subsequently enter into other covered transactions with persons at the next lower tier.

(b) As a Federal official who enters into a primary tier transaction, you have the responsibilities laid out in subpart D of this part.

(c) As an excluded person, you may not be a participant or principal in the transaction unless—

(1) The person who entered into the transaction with you allows you to continue your involvement in a transaction that predates your exclusion, as permitted under § 1508.310 or § 1508.415; or

(2) A(n) ADF official obtains an exception from the ADF President to allow you to be involved in the transaction, as permitted under § 1508.120.

§ 1508.210 Which nonprocurement transactions are covered transactions?

All nonprocurement transactions, as defined in § 1508.970, are covered transactions unless listed in § 1508.215. (See appendix to this part.)

§ 1508.215 Which nonprocurement transactions are not covered transactions?

The following types of nonprocurement transactions are not covered transactions:

(a) A direct award to—

(1) A foreign government or foreign governmental entity;

(2) A public international organization;

(3) An entity owned (in whole or in part) or controlled by a foreign government; or

(4) Any other entity consisting wholly or partially of one or more foreign governments or foreign governmental entities.

(b) A benefit to an individual as a personal entitlement without regard to the individual's present responsibility (but benefits received in an individual's business capacity are not excepted). For example, if a person receives social security benefits under the Supplemental Security Income provisions of the Social Security Act, 42 U.S.C. 1301 *et seq.*, those benefits are not covered transactions and, therefore, are not affected if the person is excluded.

(c) Federal employment.

(d) A transaction that the African Development Foundation needs to respond to a national or agency-recognized emergency or disaster.

(e) A permit, license, certificate, or similar instrument issued as a means to regulate public health, safety, or the environment, unless the African Development Foundation specifically designates it to be a covered transaction.

(f) An incidental benefit that results from ordinary governmental operations.

(g) Any other transaction if the application of an exclusion to the transaction is prohibited by law.

§ 1508.220 Are any procurement contracts included as covered transactions?

(a) Covered transactions under this part—

(1) Do not include any procurement contracts awarded directly by a Federal agency; but

(2) Do include some procurement contracts awarded by non-Federal participants in nonprocurement covered transactions (see appendix to this part).

(b) Specifically, a contract for goods or services is a covered transaction if any of the following applies:

(1) The contract is awarded by a participant in a nonprocurement transaction that is covered under § 1508.210, and the amount of the contract is expected to equal or exceed $25,000.

(2) The contract requires the consent of a(n) ADF official. In that case, the contract, regardless of the amount, always is a covered transaction, and it does not matter who awarded it. For example, it could be a subcontract awarded by a contractor at a tier below a nonprocurement transaction, as shown in the appendix to this part.

(3) The contract is for federally-required audit services.

§ 1508.225 How do I know if a transaction in which I may participate is a covered transaction?

As a participant in a transaction, you will know that it is a covered transaction because the agency regulations governing the transaction, the appropriate agency official, or participant at the next higher tier who enters into the transaction with you, will tell you that you must comply with applicable portions of this part.

Subpart C—Responsibilities of Participants Regarding Transactions

DOING BUSINESS WITH OTHER PERSONS

§ 1508.300 What must I do before I enter into a covered transaction with another person at the next lower tier?

When you enter into a covered transaction with another person at the next lower tier, you must verify that the person with whom you intend to do business is not excluded or disqualified. You do this by:

(a) Checking the *EPLS;* or

(b) Collecting a certification from that person if allowed by this rule; or

(c) Adding a clause or condition to the covered transaction with that person.

§ 1508.305 May I enter into a covered transaction with an excluded or disqualified person?

(a) You as a participant may not enter into a covered transaction with an excluded person, unless the African Development Foundation grants an exception under § 1508.120.

(b) You may not enter into any transaction with a person who is disqualified from that transaction, unless you have obtained an exception under the disqualifying statute, Executive order, or regulation.

§ 1508.310 What must I do if a Federal agency excludes a person with whom I am already doing business in a covered transaction?

(a) You as a participant may continue covered transactions with an excluded person if the transactions were in existence when the agency excluded the person. However, you are not required to continue the transactions, and you may consider termination. You should make a decision about whether to terminate and the type of termination action, if any, only after a thorough review to ensure that the action is proper and appropriate.

(b) You may not renew or extend covered transactions (other than no-cost time extensions) with any excluded person, unless the African Development Foundation grants an exception under § 1508.120.

§ 1508.315 May I use the services of an excluded person as a principal under a covered transaction?

(a) You as a participant may continue to use the services of an excluded person as a principal under a covered transaction if you were using the services of that person in the transaction before the person was excluded. However, you are not required to continue using that person's services as a principal. You should make a decision about whether to discontinue that person's services only after a thorough review to ensure that the action is proper and appropriate.

(b) You may not begin to use the services of an excluded person as a principal under a covered transaction unless the African Development Foundation grants an exception under § 1508.120.

§ 1508.320 Must I verify that principals of my covered transactions are eligible to participate?

Yes, you as a participant are responsible for determining whether any of your principals of your covered transactions is excluded or disqualified from participating in the transaction. You may decide the method and frequency by which you do so. You may, but you are not required to, check the *EPLS*.

§ 1508.325 What happens if I do business with an excluded person in a covered transaction?

If as a participant you knowingly do business with an excluded person, we may disallow costs, annul or terminate the transaction, issue a stop work order, debar or suspend you, or take other remedies as appropriate.

§ 1508.330 What requirements must I pass down to persons at lower tiers with whom I intend to do business?

Before entering into a covered transaction with a participant at the next lower tier, you must require that participant to—

(a) Comply with this subpart as a condition of participation in the transaction. You may do so using any method(s), unless § 1508.440 requires you to use specific methods.

(b) Pass the requirement to comply with this subpart to each person with whom the participant enters into a covered transaction at the next lower tier.

DISCLOSING INFORMATION—PRIMARY TIER PARTICIPANTS

§ 1508.335 What information must I provide before entering into a covered transaction with the African Development Foundation?

Before you enter into a covered transaction at the primary tier, you as the participant must notify the ADF office that is entering into the transaction with you, if you know that you or any of the principals for that covered transaction:

(a) Are presently excluded or disqualified;

(b) Have been convicted within the preceding three years of any of the offenses listed in § 1508.800(a) or had a civil judgment rendered against you for one of those offenses within that time period;

(c) Are presently indicted for or otherwise criminally or civilly charged by a governmental entity (Federal, State or local) with commission of any of the offenses listed in § 1508.800(a); or

(d) Have had one or more public transactions (Federal, State, or local) terminated within the preceding three years for cause or default.

§ 1508.340 If I disclose unfavorable information required under § 1508.335, will I be prevented from participating in the transaction?

As a primary tier participant, your disclosure of unfavorable information about yourself or a principal under § 1508.335 will not necessarily cause us to deny your participation in the covered transaction. We will consider the information when we determine whether to enter into the covered transaction. We also will consider any additional information or explanation that you elect to submit with the disclosed information.

§ 1508.345 What happens if I fail to disclose information required under § 1508.335?

If we later determine that you failed to disclose information under § 1508.335 that you knew at the time you entered into the covered transaction, we may—

(a) Terminate the transaction for material failure to comply with the terms and conditions of the transaction; or

(b) Pursue any other available remedies, including suspension and debarment.

§ 1508.350 What must I do if I learn of information required under § 1508.335 after entering into a covered transaction with the African Development Foundation?

At any time after you enter into a covered transaction, you must give immediate written notice to the ADF office with which you entered into the transaction if you learn either that—

(a) You failed to disclose information earlier, as required by § 1508.335; or

(b) Due to changed circumstances, you or any of the principals for the transaction now meet any of the criteria in § 1508.335.

DISCLOSING INFORMATION—LOWER TIER PARTICIPANTS

§ 1508.355 What information must I provide to a higher tier participant before entering into a covered transaction with that participant?

Before you enter into a covered transaction with a person at the next higher tier, you as a lower tier participant must notify that person if you know that you or any of the principals are presently excluded or disqualified.

§ 1508.360 What happens if I fail to disclose the information required under § 1508.355?

If we later determine that you failed to tell the person at the higher tier that you were excluded or disqualified at the time you entered into the covered transaction with that person, we may pursue any available remedies, including suspension and debarment.

§ 1508.365 What must I do if I learn of information required under § 1508.355 after entering into a covered transaction with a higher tier participant?

At any time after you enter into a lower tier covered transaction with a person at a higher tier, you must provide immediate written notice to that person if you learn either that—

(a) You failed to disclose information earlier, as required by § 1508.355; or

(b) Due to changed circumstances, you or any of the principals for the transaction now meet any of the criteria in § 1508.355.

Subpart D—Responsibilities of ADF Officials Regarding Transactions

§ 1508.400 May I enter into a transaction with an excluded or disqualified person?

(a) You as an agency official may not enter into a covered transaction with an excluded person unless you obtain an exception under § 1508.120.

(b) You may not enter into any transaction with a person who is disqualified from that transaction, unless you obtain a waiver or exception under the statute, Executive order, or regulation that is the basis for the person's disqualification.

§ 1508.405 May I enter into a covered transaction with a participant if a principal of the transaction is excluded?

As an agency official, you may not enter into a covered transaction with a participant if you know that a principal of the transaction is excluded, unless you obtain an exception under § 1508.120.

§ 1508.410 May I approve a participant's use of the services of an excluded person?

After entering into a covered transaction with a participant, you as an agency official may not approve a participant's use of an excluded person as a principal under that transaction, unless you obtain an exception under § 1508.120.

§ 1508.415 What must I do if a Federal agency excludes the participant or a principal after I enter into a covered transaction?

(a) You as an agency official may continue covered transactions with an excluded person, or under which an excluded person is a principal, if the transactions were in existence when the person was excluded. You are not required to continue the transactions, however, and you may consider termination. You should make a decision about whether to terminate and the type of termination action, if any, only after a thorough review to ensure that the action is proper.

(b) You may not renew or extend covered transactions (other than no-cost time extensions) with any excluded person, or under which an excluded person is a principal, unless you obtain an exception under § 1508.120.

§ 1508.420 May I approve a transaction with an excluded or disqualified person at a lower tier?

If a transaction at a lower tier is subject to your approval, you as an agency official may not approve—

(a) A covered transaction with a person who is currently excluded, unless you obtain an exception under § 1508.120; or

(b) A transaction with a person who is disqualified from that transaction, unless you obtain a waiver or exception under the statute, Executive order, or regulation that is the basis for the person's disqualification.

§ 1508.425 When do I check to see if a person is excluded or disqualified?

As an agency official, you must check to see if a person is excluded or disqualified before you—

(a) Enter into a primary tier covered transaction;

(b) Approve a principal in a primary tier covered transaction;

(c) Approve a lower tier participant if agency approval of the lower tier participant is required; or

(d) Approve a principal in connection with a lower tier transaction if agency approval of the principal is required.

§ 1508.430 How do I check to see if a person is excluded or disqualified?

You check to see if a person is excluded or disqualified in two ways:

(a) You as an agency official must check the *EPLS* when you take any action listed in § 1508.425.

(b) You must review information that a participant gives you, as required by § 1508.335, about its status or the status of the principals of a transaction.

§ 1508.435 What must I require of a primary tier participant?

You as an agency official must require each participant in a primary tier covered transaction to—

(a) Comply with subpart C of this part as a condition of participation in the transaction; and

(b) Communicate the requirement to comply with Subpart C of this part to persons at the next lower tier with whom the primary tier participant enters into covered transactions.

§ 1508.440 What method do I use to communicate those requirements to participants?

To communicate the requirements to participants, you must include a term or condition in the transaction requiring the participant's compliance with subpart C of this part, and requiring them to include a similar term or condition in lower tier covered transactions.

§ 1508.445 What action may I take if a primary tier participant knowingly does business with an excluded or disqualified person?

If a participant knowingly does business with an excluded or disqualified person, you as an agency official may refer the matter for suspension and debarment consideration. You may also disallow costs, annul or terminate the transaction, issue a stop work order, or take any other appropriate remedy.

§ 1508.450 What action may I take if a primary tier participant fails to disclose the information required under § 1508.335?

If you as an agency official determine that a participant failed to disclose information, as required by § 1508.335, at the time it entered into a covered transaction with you, you may—

(a) Terminate the transaction for material failure to comply with the terms and conditions of the transaction; or

(b) Pursue any other available remedies, including suspension and debarment.

§ 1508.455 What may I do if a lower tier participant fails to disclose the information required under § 1508.355 to the next higher tier?

If you as an agency official determine that a lower tier participant failed to disclose information, as required by § 1508.355, at the time it entered into a covered transaction with a participant at the next higher tier, you may pursue any remedies available to you, including the initiation of a suspension or debarment action.

Subpart E—Excluded Parties List System

§ 1508.500 What is the purpose of the Excluded Parties List System (EPLS)?

The *EPLS* is a widely available source of the most current information about persons who are excluded or disqualified from covered transactions.

§ 1508.505 Who uses the EPLS?

(a) Federal agency officials use the *EPLS* to determine whether to enter into a transaction with a person, as required under § 1508.430.

(b) Participants also may, but are not required to, use the *EPLS* to determine if—

(1) Principals of their transactions are excluded or disqualified, as required under § 1508.320; or

(2) Persons with whom they are entering into covered transactions at the next lower tier are excluded or disqualified.

(c) The *EPLS* is available to the general public.

§ 1508.510 Who maintains the EPLS?

In accordance with the OMB guidelines, the General Services Administration (GSA) maintains the *EPLS*. When a Federal agency takes an action to exclude a person under the nonprocurement or procurement debarment and suspension system, the agency enters the information about the excluded person into the *EPLS*.

§ 1508.515 What specific information is in the EPLS?

(a) At a minimum, the *EPLS* indicates—

(1) The full name (where available) and address of each excluded or disqualified person, in alphabetical order, with cross references if more than one name is involved in a single action;

(2) The type of action;

(3) The cause for the action;

(4) The scope of the action;

(5) Any termination date for the action;

(6) The agency and name and telephone number of the agency point of contact for the action; and

(7) The Dun and Bradstreet Number (DUNS), or other similar code approved by the GSA, of the excluded or disqualified person, if available.

(b)(1) The database for the *EPLS* includes a field for the Taxpayer Identification Number (TIN) (the social security number (SSN) for an individual) of an excluded or disqualified person.

(2) Agencies disclose the SSN of an individual to verify the identity of an individual, only if permitted under the Privacy Act of 1974 and, if appropriate, the Computer Matching and Privacy Protection Act of 1988, as codified in 5 U.S.C. 552(a).

§ 1508.520 Who places the information into the EPLS?

Federal officials who take actions to exclude persons under this part or officials who are responsible for identifying disqualified persons must enter the following information about those persons into the *EPLS*:

(a) Information required by § 1508.515(a);

(b) The Taxpayer Identification Number (TIN) of the excluded or disqualified person, including the social security number (SSN) for an individual, if the number is available and may be disclosed under law;

(c) Information about an excluded or disqualified person, generally within five working days, after—

(1) Taking an exclusion action;

(2) Modifying or rescinding an exclusion action;

(3) Finding that a person is disqualified; or

(4) Finding that there has been a change in the status of a person who is listed as disqualified.

§ 1508.525 Whom do I ask if I have questions about a person in the EPLS?

If you have questions about a person in the *EPLS*, ask the point of contact for the Federal agency that placed the person's name into the *EPLS*. You may find the agency point of contact from the *EPLS*.

§ 1508.530 Where can I find the EPLS?

(a) You may access the *EPLS* through the Internet, currently at *http://epls.arnet.gov*.

(b) As of November 26, 2003, you may also subscribe to a printed version. However, we anticipate discontinuing the printed version. Until it is discontinued, you may obtain the printed version by purchasing a yearly subscription from the Superintendent of Documents, U.S. Government Printing Office, Washington, DC 20402, or by calling the Government Printing Office Inquiry and Order Desk at (202) 783–3238.

Subpart F—General Principles Relating to Suspension and Debarment Actions

§ 1508.600 How do suspension and debarment actions start?

When we receive information from any source concerning a cause for suspension or debarment, we will promptly report and investigate it. We refer the question of whether to suspend or debar you to our suspending or debarring official for consideration, if appropriate.

§ 1508.605 How does suspension differ from debarment?

Suspension differs from debarment in that—

A suspending official . . .	A debarring official . . .
(a) Imposes suspension as a temporary status of ineligibility for procurement and nonprocurement transactions, pending completion of an investigation or legal proceedings.	Imposes debarment for a specified period as a final determination that a person is not presently responsible.
(b) Must— (1) Have *adequate evidence* that there may be a cause for debarment of a person; and. (2) Conclude that *immediate action* is necessary to protect the Federal interest.	Must conclude, based on a *preponderance of the evidence,* that the person has engaged in conduct that warrants debarment.
(c) Usually imposes the suspension *first,* and then promptly notifies the suspended person, giving the person an opportunity to contest the suspension and have it lifted.	Imposes debarment *after* giving the respondent notice of the action and an opportunity to contest the proposed debarment.

§ 1508.610 What procedures does the African Development Foundation use in suspension and debarment actions?

In deciding whether to suspend or debar you, we handle the actions as informally as practicable, consistent with principles of fundamental fairness.

(a) For suspension actions, we use the procedures in this subpart and subpart G of this part.

(b) For debarment actions, we use the procedures in this subpart and subpart H of this part.

§ 1508.615 How does the African Development Foundation notify a person of a suspension or debarment action?

(a) The suspending or debarring official sends a written notice to the last known street address, facsimile number, or e-mail address of—

(1) You or your identified counsel; or

(2) Your agent for service of process, or any of your partners, officers, directors, owners, or joint venturers.

(b) The notice is effective if sent to any of these persons.

§ 1508.620 Do Federal agencies coordinate suspension and debarment actions?

Yes, when more than one Federal agency has an interest in a suspension or debarment, the agencies may consider designating one agency as the lead agency for making the decision. Agencies are encouraged to establish methods and procedures for coordinating their suspension and debarment actions.

§ 1508.625 What is the scope of a suspension or debarment?

If you are suspended or debarred, the suspension or debarment is effective as follows:

(a) Your suspension or debarment constitutes suspension or debarment of all of your divisions and other organizational elements from all covered transactions, unless the suspension or debarment decision is limited—

(1) By its terms to one or more specifically identified individuals, divisions, or other organizational elements; or

(2) To specific types of transactions.

(b) Any affiliate of a participant may be included in a suspension or debarment action if the suspending or debarring official—

(1) Officially names the affiliate in the notice; and

(2) Gives the affiliate an opportunity to contest the action.

§ 1508.630 May the African Development Foundation impute conduct of one person to another?

For purposes of actions taken under this rule, we may impute conduct as follows:

(a) *Conduct imputed from an individual to an organization.* We may impute the fraudulent, criminal, or other improper conduct of any officer, director, shareholder, partner, employee, or other individual associated with an organization, to that organization when the improper conduct occurred in connection with the individual's performance of duties for or on behalf of that organization, or with the organization's knowledge, approval or acquiescence. The organization's acceptance of the benefits derived from the conduct is evidence of knowledge, approval or acquiescence.

(b) *Conduct imputed from an organization to an individual, or between individuals.* We may impute the fraudulent, criminal, or other improper conduct of any organization to an individual, or from one individual to another individual, if the individual to whom the improper conduct is imputed either participated in, had knowledge of, or reason to know of the improper conduct.

(c) *Conduct imputed from one organization to another organization.* We may impute the fraudulent, criminal, or other improper conduct of one organization to another organization when the improper conduct occurred in connection with a partnership, joint venture, joint application, association or similar arrangement, or when the organization to whom the improper conduct is imputed has the power to direct, manage, control or influence the activities of the organization responsible for the improper conduct. Acceptance of the benefits derived from the conduct is evidence of knowledge, approval or acquiescence.

§ 1508.635 May the African Development Foundation settle a debarment or suspension action?

Yes, we may settle a debarment or suspension action at any time if it is in the best interest of the Federal Government.

§ 1508.640 May a settlement include a voluntary exclusion?

Yes, if we enter into a settlement with you in which you agree to be excluded, it is called a voluntary exclusion and has governmentwide effect.

§ 1508.645 Do other Federal agencies know if the African Development Foundation agrees to a voluntary exclusion?

(a) Yes, we enter information regarding a voluntary exclusion into the *EPLS*.

(b) Also, any agency or person may contact us to find out the details of a voluntary exclusion.

Subpart G—Suspension

§ 1508.700 When may the suspending official issue a suspension?

Suspension is a serious action. Using the procedures of this subpart and subpart F of this part, the suspending official may impose suspension only when that official determines that—

(a) There exists an indictment for, or other adequate evidence to suspect, an offense listed under § 1508.800(a), or

(b) There exists adequate evidence to suspect any other cause for debarment listed under § 1508.800(b) through (d); and

(c) Immediate action is necessary to protect the public interest.

§ 1508.705 What does the suspending official consider in issuing a suspension?

(a) In determining the adequacy of the evidence to support the suspension, the suspending official considers how much information is available, how credible it is given the circumstances, whether or not important allegations are corroborated, and what inferences can reasonably be drawn as a result. During this assessment, the suspending official may examine the basic documents, including grants, cooperative agreements, loan authorizations, contracts, and other relevant documents.

(b) An indictment, conviction, civil judgment, or other official findings by Federal, State, or local bodies that determine factual and/or legal matters, constitutes adequate evidence for purposes of suspension actions.

(c) In deciding whether immediate action is needed to protect the public interest, the suspending official has wide discretion. For example, the suspending official may infer the necessity for immediate action to protect the public interest either from the nature of the circumstances giving rise to a cause for suspension or from potential business relationships or involvement with a program of the Federal Government.

§ 1508.710 When does a suspension take effect?

A suspension is effective when the suspending official signs the decision to suspend.

§ 1508.715 What notice does the suspending official give me if I am suspended?

After deciding to suspend you, the suspending official promptly sends you a Notice of Suspension advising you—

(a) That you have been suspended;

(b) That your suspension is based on—

(1) An indictment;

(2) A conviction;

(3) Other adequate evidence that you have committed irregularities which seriously reflect on the propriety of further Federal Government dealings with you; or

(4) Conduct of another person that has been imputed to you, or your affiliation with a suspended or debarred person;

(c) Of any other irregularities in terms sufficient to put you on notice without disclosing the Federal Government's evidence;

(d) Of the cause(s) upon which we relied under § 1508.700 for imposing suspension;

(e) That your suspension is for a temporary period pending the completion of an investigation or resulting legal or debarment proceedings;

(f) Of the applicable provisions of this subpart, Subpart F of this part, and any other ADF procedures governing suspension decision making; and

(g) Of the governmentwide effect of your suspension from procurement and nonprocurement programs and activities.

§ 1508.720 How may I contest a suspension?

If you as a respondent wish to contest a suspension, you or your representative must provide the suspending official with information in opposition to the suspension. You may do this orally or in writing, but any information provided orally that you consider important must also be submitted in writing for the official record.

§ 1508.725 How much time do I have to contest a suspension?

(a) As a respondent you or your representative must either send, or make rrangements to appear and present, the information and argument to the suspending official within 30 days after you receive the Notice of Suspension.

(b) We consider the notice to be received by you—

(1) When delivered, if we mail the notice to the last known street address, or five days after we send it if the letter is undeliverable;

(2) When sent, if we send the notice by facsimile or five days after we send it if the facsimile is undeliverable; or

(3) When delivered, if we send the notice by e-mail or five days after we send it if the e-mail is undeliverable.

§ 1508.730 What information must I provide to the suspending official if I contest a suspension?

(a) In addition to any information and argument in opposition, as a respondent your submission to the suspending official must identify—

(1) Specific facts that contradict the statements contained in the Notice of Suspension. A general denial is insufficient to raise a genuine dispute over facts material to the suspension;

(2) All existing, proposed, or prior exclusions under regulations implementing E.O. 12549 and all similar actions taken by Federal, state, or local agencies, including administrative agreements that affect only those agencies;

(3) All criminal and civil proceedings not included in the Notice of Suspension that grew out of facts relevant to the cause(s) stated in the notice; and

(4) All of your affiliates.

(b) If you fail to disclose this information, or provide false information, the African Development Foundation may seek further criminal, civil or administrative action against you, as appropriate.

§ 1508.735 Under what conditions do I get an additional opportunity to challenge the facts on which the suspension is based?

(a) You as a respondent will not have an additional opportunity to challenge the facts if the suspending official determines that—

(1) Your suspension is based upon an indictment, conviction, civil judgment, or other finding by a Federal, State, or local body for which an opportunity to contest the facts was provided;

(2) Your presentation in opposition contains only general denials to information contained in the Notice of Suspension;

(3) The issues raised in your presentation in opposition to the suspension are not factual in nature, or are not material to the suspending official's initial decision to suspend, or the official's decision whether to continue the suspension; or

(4) On the basis of advice from the Department of Justice, an office of the United States Attorney, a State attorney general's office, or a State or local prosecutor's office, that substantial interests of the government in pending or contemplated legal proceedings based on the same facts as the suspension would be prejudiced by conducting fact-finding.

(b) You will have an opportunity to challenge the facts if the suspending official determines that—

(1) The conditions in paragraph (a) of this section do not exist; and

(2) Your presentation in opposition raises a genuine dispute over facts material to the suspension.

(c) If you have an opportunity to challenge disputed material facts under this section, the suspending official or designee must conduct additional proceedings to resolve those facts.

§ 1508.740 Are suspension proceedings formal?

(a) Suspension proceedings are conducted in a fair and informal manner. The suspending official may use flexible procedures to allow you to present matters in opposition. In so doing, the suspending official is not required to follow formal rules of evidence or procedure in creating an official record upon which the official will base a final suspension decision.

(b) You as a respondent or your representative must submit any documentary evidence you want the suspending official to consider.

§ 1508.745 How is fact-finding conducted?

(a) If fact-finding is conducted—

(1) You may present witnesses and other evidence, and confront any witness presented; and

(2) The fact-finder must prepare written findings of fact for the record.

(b) A transcribed record of fact-finding proceedings must be made, unless you as a respondent and the African Development Foundation agree to waive it in advance. If you want a copy of the transcribed record, you may purchase it.

§ 1508.750 What does the suspending official consider in deciding whether to continue or terminate my suspension?

(a) The suspending official bases the decision on all information contained in the official record. The record includes—

(1) All information in support of the suspending official's initial decision to suspend you;

(2) Any further information and argument presented in support of, or opposition to, the suspension; and

(3) Any transcribed record of fact-finding proceedings.

(b) The suspending official may refer disputed material facts to another official for findings of fact. The suspending official may reject any resulting findings, in whole or in part, only after specifically determining them to be arbitrary, capricious, or clearly erroneous.

§ 1508.755 When will I know whether the suspension is continued or terminated?

The suspending official must make a written decision whether to continue, modify, or terminate your suspension within 45 days of closing the official record. The official record closes upon the suspending official's receipt of final submissions, information and findings of fact, if any. The suspending official may extend that period for good cause.

§ 1508.760 How long may my suspension last?

(a) If legal or debarment proceedings are initiated at the time of, or during your suspension, the suspension may continue until the conclusion of those proceedings. However, if proceedings are not initiated, a suspension may not exceed 12 months.

(b) The suspending official may extend the 12 month limit under paragraph (a) of this section for an additional 6 months if an office of a U.S. Assistant Attorney General, U.S. Attorney, or other responsible prosecuting official requests an extension in writing. In no event may a suspension exceed 18 months without initiating proceedings under paragraph (a) of this section.

(c) The suspending official must notify the appropriate officials under paragraph (b) of this section of an impending termination of a suspension at least 30 days before the 12 month period expires to allow the officials an opportunity to request an extension.

Subpart H—Debarment

§ 1508.800 What are the causes for debarment?

We may debar a person for—

(a) Conviction of or civil judgment for—

(1) Commission of fraud or a criminal offense in connection with obtaining, attempting to obtain, or performing a public or private agreement or transaction;

(2) Violation of Federal or State antitrust statutes, including those proscribing price fixing between competitors, allocation of customers between competitors, and bid rigging;

(3) Commission of embezzlement, theft, forgery, bribery, falsification or destruction of records, making false statements, tax evasion, receiving stolen property, making false claims, or obstruction of justice; or

(4) Commission of any other offense indicating a lack of business integrity or business honesty that seriously and directly affects your present responsibility;

(b) Violation of the terms of a public agreement or transaction so serious as to affect the integrity of an agency program, such as—

(1) A willful failure to perform in accordance with the terms of one or more public agreements or transactions;

(2) A history of failure to perform or of unsatisfactory performance of one or more public agreements or transactions; or

(3) A willful violation of a statutory or regulatory provision or requirement applicable to a public agreement or transaction;

(c) Any of the following causes:

(1) A nonprocurement debarment by any Federal agency taken before October 1, 1988, or a procurement debarment by any Federal agency taken pursuant to 48 CFR part 9, subpart 9.4, before August 25, 1995;

(2) Knowingly doing business with an ineligible person, except as permitted under § 1508.120;

(3) Failure to pay a single substantial debt, or a number of outstanding debts (including disallowed costs and overpayments, but not including sums owed the Federal Government under the Internal Revenue Code) owed to any Federal agency or instrumentality, provided the debt is uncontested by the debtor or, if contested, provided that the debtor's legal and administrative remedies have been exhausted;

(4) Violation of a material provision of a voluntary exclusion agreement entered into under § 1508.640 or of any settlement of a debarment or suspension action; or

(5) Violation of the provisions of the Drug-Free Workplace Act of 1988 (41 U.S.C. 701); or

(d) Any other cause of so serious or compelling a nature that it affects your present responsibility.

§ 1508.805 What notice does the debarring official give me if I am proposed for debarment?

After consideration of the causes in § 1508.800 of this subpart, if the debarring official proposes to debar you, the official sends you a Notice of Proposed Debarment, pursuant to § 1508.615, advising you—

(a) That the debarring official is considering debarring you;

(b) Of the reasons for proposing to debar you in terms sufficient to put you on notice of the conduct or transactions upon which the proposed debarment is based;

(c) Of the cause(s) under § 1508.800 upon which the debarring official relied for proposing your debarment;

(d) Of the applicable provisions of this subpart, Subpart F of this part, and any other ADF procedures governing debarment; and

(e) Of the governmentwide effect of a debarment from procurement and nonprocurement programs and activities.

§ 1508.810 When does a debarment take effect?

A debarment is not effective until the debarring official issues a decision. The debarring official does not issue a decision until the respondent has had an opportunity to contest the proposed debarment.

§ 1508.815 How may I contest a proposed debarment?

If you as a respondent wish to contest a proposed debarment, you or your representative must provide the debarring official with information in opposition to the proposed debarment. You may do this orally or in writing, but any information provided orally that you consider important must also be submitted in writing for the official record.

§ 1508.820 How much time do I have to contest a proposed debarment?

(a) As a respondent you or your representative must either send, or make arrangements to appear and present, the information and argument to the debarring official within 30 days after you receive the Notice of Proposed Debarment.

(b) We consider the Notice of Proposed Debarment to be received by you—

(1) When delivered, if we mail the notice to the last known street address, or five days after we send it if the letter is undeliverable;

(2) When sent, if we send the notice by facsimile or five days after we send it if the facsimile is undeliverable; or

(3) When delivered, if we send the notice by e-mail or five days after we send it if the e-mail is undeliverable.

§ 1508.825 What information must I provide to the debarring official if I contest a proposed debarment?

(a) In addition to any information and argument in opposition, as a respondent your submission to the debarring official must identify—

(1) Specific facts that contradict the statements contained in the Notice of Proposed Debarment. Include any information about any of the factors listed in § 1508.860. A general denial is insufficient to raise a genuine dispute over facts material to the debarment;

(2) All existing, proposed, or prior exclusions under regulations implementing E.O. 12549 and all similar actions taken by Federal, State, or local agencies, including administrative agreements that affect only those agencies;

(3) All criminal and civil proceedings not included in the Notice of Proposed Debarment that grew out of facts relevant to the cause(s) stated in the notice; and

(4) All of your affiliates.

(b) If you fail to disclose this information, or provide false information, the African Development Foundation may seek further criminal, civil or administrative action against you, as appropriate.

§ 1508.830 Under what conditions do I get an additional opportunity to challenge the facts on which a proposed debarment is based?

(a) You as a respondent will not have an additional opportunity to challenge the facts if the debarring official determines that—

(1) Your debarment is based upon a conviction or civil judgment;

(2) Your presentation in opposition contains only general denials to information contained in the Notice of Proposed Debarment; or

(3) The issues raised in your presentation in opposition to the proposed debarment are not factual in nature, or are not material to the debarring official's decision whether to debar.

(b) You will have an additional opportunity to challenge the facts if the debarring official determines that—

(1) The conditions in paragraph (a) of this section do not exist; and

(2) Your presentation in opposition raises a genuine dispute over facts material to the proposed debarment.

(c) If you have an opportunity to challenge disputed material facts under this section, the debarring official or designee must conduct additional proceedings to resolve those facts.

§ 1508.835 Are debarment proceedings formal?

(a) Debarment proceedings are conducted in a fair and informal manner. The debarring official may use flexible procedures to allow you as a respondent to present matters in opposition. In so doing, the debarring official is not required to follow formal rules of evidence or procedure in creating an official record upon which the official will base the decision whether to debar.

(b) You or your representative must submit any documentary evidence you want the debarring official to consider.

§ 1508.840 How is fact-finding conducted?

(a) If fact-finding is conducted—

(1) You may present witnesses and other evidence, and confront any witness presented; and

(2) The fact-finder must prepare written findings of fact for the record.

(b) A transcribed record of fact-finding proceedings must be made, unless you as a respondent and the African Development Foundation agree to waive it in advance. If you want a copy of the transcribed record, you may purchase it.

§ 1508.845 What does the debarring official consider in deciding whether to debar me?

(a) The debarring official may debar you for any of the causes in § 1508.800. However, the official need not debar you even if a cause for debarment exists. The official may consider the seriousness of your acts or omissions and the mitigating or aggravating factors set forth at § 1508.860.

(b) The debarring official bases the decision on all information contained in the official record. The record includes—

(1) All information in support of the debarring official's proposed debarment;

(2) Any further information and argument presented in support of, or in opposition to, the proposed debarment; and

(3) Any transcribed record of fact-finding proceedings.

(c) The debarring official may refer disputed material facts to another official for findings of fact. The debarring official may reject any resultant findings, in whole or in part, only after specifically determining them to be arbitrary, capricious, or clearly erroneous.

§ 1508.850 What is the standard of proof in a debarment action?

(a) In any debarment action, we must establish the cause for debarment by a preponderance of the evidence.

(b) If the proposed debarment is based upon a conviction or civil judgment, the standard of proof is met.

§ 1508.855 Who has the burden of proof in a debarment action?

(a) We have the burden to prove that a cause for debarment exists.

(b) Once a cause for debarment is established, you as a respondent have the burden of demonstrating to the satisfaction of the debarring official that you are presently responsible and that debarment is not necessary.

§ 1508.860 What factors may influence the debarring official's decision?

This section lists the mitigating and aggravating factors that the debarring official may consider in determining whether to debar you and the length of your debarment period. The debarring official may consider other factors if appropriate in light of the circumstances of a particular case. The existence or nonexistence of any factor, such as one of those set forth in this section, is not necessarily determinative of your present responsibility. In making a debarment decision, the debarring official may consider the following factors:

(a) The actual or potential harm or impact that results or may result from the wrongdoing.

(b) The frequency of incidents and/or duration of the wrongdoing.

(c) Whether there is a pattern or prior history of wrongdoing. For example, if you have been found by another Federal agency or a State agency to have engaged in wrongdoing similar to that found in the debarment action, the existence of this fact may be used by the debarring official in determining that you have a pattern or prior history of wrongdoing.

(d) Whether you are or have been excluded or disqualified by an agency of the Federal Government or have not been allowed to participate in State or local contracts or assistance agreements on a basis of conduct similar to one or more of the causes for debarment specified in this part.

(e) Whether you have entered into an administrative agreement with a Federal agency or a State or local government that is not governmentwide but is based on conduct similar to one or more of the causes for debarment specified in this part.

(f) Whether and to what extent you planned, initiated, or carried out the wrongdoing.

(g) Whether you have accepted responsibility for the wrongdoing and recognize the seriousness of the misconduct that led to the cause for debarment.

(h) Whether you have paid or agreed to pay all criminal, civil and administrative liabilities for the improper activity, including any investigative or administrative costs incurred by the government, and have made or agreed to make full restitution.

(i) Whether you have cooperated fully with the government agencies during the investigation and any court or administrative action. In determining the extent of cooperation, the debarring official may consider when the cooperation began and whether you disclosed all pertinent information known to you.

(j) Whether the wrongdoing was pervasive within your organization.

(k) The kind of positions held by the individuals involved in the wrongdoing.

(l) Whether your organization took appropriate corrective action or remedial measures, such as establishing ethics training and implementing programs to prevent recurrence.

(m) Whether your principals tolerated the offense.

(n) Whether you brought the activity cited as a basis for the debarment to the attention of the appropriate government agency in a timely manner.

(o) Whether you have fully investigated the circumstances surrounding the cause for debarment and, if so, made the result of the investigation available to the debarring official.

(p) Whether you had effective standards of conduct and internal control systems in place at the time the questioned conduct occurred.

(q) Whether you have taken appropriate disciplinary action against the individuals responsible for the activity which constitutes the cause for debarment.

(r) Whether you have had adequate time to eliminate the circumstances within your organization that led to the cause for the debarment.

(s) Other factors that are appropriate to the circumstances of a particular case.

§ 1508.865 How long may my debarment last?

(a) If the debarring official decides to debar you, your period of debarment will be based on the seriousness of the cause(s) upon which your debarment is based. Generally, debarment should not exceed three years. However, if circumstances warrant, the debarring official may impose a longer period of debarment.

(b) In determining the period of debarment, the debarring official may consider the factors in § 1508.860. If a suspension has preceded your debarment, the debarring official must consider the time you were suspended.

(c) If the debarment is for a violation of the provisions of the Drug-Free Workplace Act of 1988, your period of debarment may not exceed five years.

§ 1508.870 When do I know if the debarring official debars me?

(a) The debarring official must make a written decision whether to debar within 45 days of closing the official record. The official record closes upon the debarring official's receipt of final submissions, information and findings of fact, if any. The debarring official may extend that period for good cause.

(b) The debarring official sends you written notice, pursuant to § 1508.615 that the official decided, either—

(1) Not to debar you; or

(2) To debar you. In this event, the notice:

(i) Refers to the Notice of Proposed Debarment;

(ii) Specifies the reasons for your debarment;

(iii) States the period of your debarment, including the effective dates; and

(iv) Advises you that your debarment is effective for covered transactions and contracts that are subject to the Federal Acquisition Regulation (48 CFR chapter 1), throughout the executive branch of the Federal Government unless an agency head or an authorized designee grants an exception.

§ 1508.875 May I ask the debarring official to reconsider a decision to debar me?

Yes, as a debarred person you may ask the debarring official to reconsider the debarment decision or to reduce the time period or scope of the debarment. However, you must put your request in writing and support it with documentation.

§ 1508.880 What factors may influence the debarring official during reconsideration?

The debarring official may reduce or terminate your debarment based on—

(a) Newly discovered material evidence;

(b) A reversal of the conviction or civil judgment upon which your debarment was based;

(c) A bona fide change in ownership or management;

(d) Elimination of other causes for which the debarment was imposed; or

(e) Other reasons the debarring official finds appropriate.

§ 1508.885 May the debarring official extend a debarment?

(a) Yes, the debarring official may extend a debarment for an additional period, if that official determines that an extension is necessary to protect the public interest.

(b) However, the debarring official may not extend a debarment solely on the basis of the facts and circumstances upon which the initial debarment action was based.

(c) If the debarring official decides that a debarment for an additional period is necessary, the debarring official must follow the applicable procedures in this subpart, and subpart F of this part, to extend the debarment.

Subpart I—Definitions

§ 1508.900 Adequate evidence.

Adequate evidence means information sufficient to support the reasonable belief that a particular act or omission has occurred.

§ 1508.905 Affiliate.

Persons are *affiliates* of each other if, directly or indirectly, either one controls or has the power to control the other or a third person controls or has the power to control both. The ways we use to determine control include, but are not limited to—

(a) Interlocking management or ownership;

(b) Identity of interests among family members;

(c) Shared facilities and equipment;

(d) Common use of employees; or

(e) A business entity which has been organized following the exclusion of a person which has the same or similar management, ownership, or principal employees as the excluded person.

§ 1508.910 Agency.

Agency means any United States executive department, military department, defense agency, or any other agency of the executive branch. Other agencies of the Federal government are not considered "agencies" for the purposes of this part unless they issue regulations adopting the governmentwide Debarment and Suspension system under Executive orders 12549 and 12689.

§ 1508.915 Agent or representative.

Agent or representative means any person who acts on behalf of, or who is authorized to commit, a participant in a covered transaction.

§ 1508.920 Civil judgment.

Civil judgment means the disposition of a civil action by any court of competent jurisdiction, whether by verdict, decision, settlement, stipulation, other disposition which creates a civil liability for the complained of wrongful acts, or a final determination of liability under the Program Fraud Civil Remedies Act of 1988 (31 U.S.C. 3801–3812).

§ 1508.925 Conviction.

Conviction means—

(a) A judgment or any other determination of guilt of a criminal offense by any court of competent jurisdiction, whether entered upon a verdict or plea, including a plea of nolo contendere; or

(b) Any other resolution that is the functional equivalent of a judgment, including probation before judgment and deferred prosecution. A disposition without the participation of the court is the functional equivalent of a judgment only if it includes an admission of guilt.

§ 1508.930 Debarment.

Debarment means an action taken by a debarring official under subpart H of this part to exclude a person from participating in covered transactions and transactions covered under the Federal Acquisition Regulation (48 CFR chapter 1). A person so excluded is debarred.

§ 1508.935 Debarring official.

(a) *Debarring official* means an agency official who is authorized to impose debarment. A debarring official is either—

(1) The agency head; or

(2) An official designated by the agency head.

(b) [Reserved]

§ 1508.940 Disqualified.

Disqualified means that a person is prohibited from participating in specified Federal procurement or nonprocurement transactions as required under a statute, Executive order (other than Executive Orders 12549 and 12689) or other authority. Examples of disqualifications include persons prohibited under—

(a) The Davis-Bacon Act (40 U.S.C. 276(a));

(b) The equal employment opportunity acts and Executive orders; or

(c) The Clean Air Act (42 U.S.C. 7606), Clean Water Act (33 U.S.C. 1368) and Executive Order 11738 (3 CFR, 1973 Comp., p. 799).

§ 1508.945 Excluded or exclusion.

Excluded or exclusion means—

(a) That a person or commodity is prohibited from being a participant in covered transactions, whether the person has been suspended; debarred; proposed for debarment under 48 CFR part 9, subpart 9.4; voluntarily excluded; or

(b) The act of excluding a person.

§ 1508.950 Excluded Parties List System

Excluded Parties List System (EPLS) means the list maintained and disseminated by the General Services Administration (GSA) containing the names and other information about persons who are ineligible. The *EPLS* system includes the printed version entitled, "List of Parties Excluded or Disqualified from Federal Procurement and Nonprocurement Programs," so long as published.

§ 1508.955 Indictment.

Indictment means an indictment for a criminal offense. A presentment, information, or other filing by a competent authority charging a criminal offense shall be given the same effect as an indictment.

§ 1508.960 Ineligible or ineligibility.

Ineligible or ineligibility means that a person or commodity is prohibited from covered transactions because of an exclusion or disqualification.

§ 1508.965 Legal proceedings.

Legal proceedings means any criminal proceeding or any civil judicial proceeding, including a proceeding under the Program Fraud Civil Remedies Act (31 U.S.C. 3801–3812), to which the Federal Government or a State or local government or quasi-governmental authority is a party. The term also includes appeals from those proceedings.

§ 1508.970 Nonprocurement transaction.

(a) *Nonprocurement transaction* means any transaction, regardless of type (except procurement contracts), including, but not limited to the following:

(1) Grants.

(2) Cooperative agreements.

(3) Scholarships.

(4) Fellowships.

(5) Contracts of assistance.

(6) Loans.

(7) Loan guarantees.

(8) Subsidies.

(9) Insurances.

(10) Payments for specified uses.

(11) Donation agreements.

(b) A nonprocurement transaction at any tier does not require the transfer of Federal funds.

§ 1508.975 Notice.

Notice means a written communication served in person, sent by certified mail or its equivalent, or sent electronically by e-mail or facsimile. (See § 1508.615.)

§ 1508.980 Participant.

Participant means any person who submits a proposal for or who enters into a covered transaction, including an agent or representative of a participant.

§ 1508.985 Person.

Person means any individual, corporation, partnership, association, unit of government, or legal entity, however organized.

§ 1508.990 Preponderance of the evidence.

Preponderance of the evidence means proof by information that, compared with information opposing it, leads to the conclusion that the fact at issue is more probably true than not.

§ 1508.995 Principal.

Principal means—

(a) An officer, director, owner, partner, principal investigator, or other person within a participant with management or supervisory responsibilities related to a covered transaction; or

(b) A consultant or other person, whether or not employed by the participant or paid with Federal funds, who—

(1) Is in a position to handle Federal funds;

(2) Is in a position to influence or control the use of those funds; or,

(3) Occupies a technical or professional position capable of substantially influencing the development or outcome of an activity required to perform the covered transaction.

§ 1508.1000 Respondent.

Respondent means a person against whom an agency has initiated a debarment or suspension action.

§ 1508.1005 State.

(a) *State* means—

(1) Any of the states of the United States;

(2) The District of Columbia;

(3) The Commonwealth of Puerto Rico;

(4) Any territory or possession of the United States; or

(5) Any agency or instrumentality of a state.

(b) For purposes of this part, *State* does not include institutions of higher education, hospitals, or units of local government.

§ 1508.1010 Suspending official.

(a) *Suspending official* means an agency official who is authorized to impose suspension. The suspending official is either:

(1) The agency head; or

(2) An official designated by the agency head.

(b) [Reserved]

§ 1508.1015 Suspension.

Suspension is an action taken by a suspending official under subpart G of this part that immediately prohibits a person from participating in covered transactions and transactions covered under the Federal Acquisition Regulation (48 CFR chapter 1) for a temporary period, pending completion of an agency investigation and any judicial or administrative proceedings that may ensue. A person so excluded is suspended.

§ 1508.1020 Voluntary exclusion or voluntarily excluded.

(a) *Voluntary exclusion* means a person's agreement to be excluded under the terms of a settlement between the person and one or more agencies. Voluntary exclusion must have governmentwide effect.

(b) *Voluntarily excluded* means the status of a person who has agreed to a voluntary exclusion.

Subpart J [Reserved]

APPENDIX TO PART 1508—COVERED TRANSACTIONS

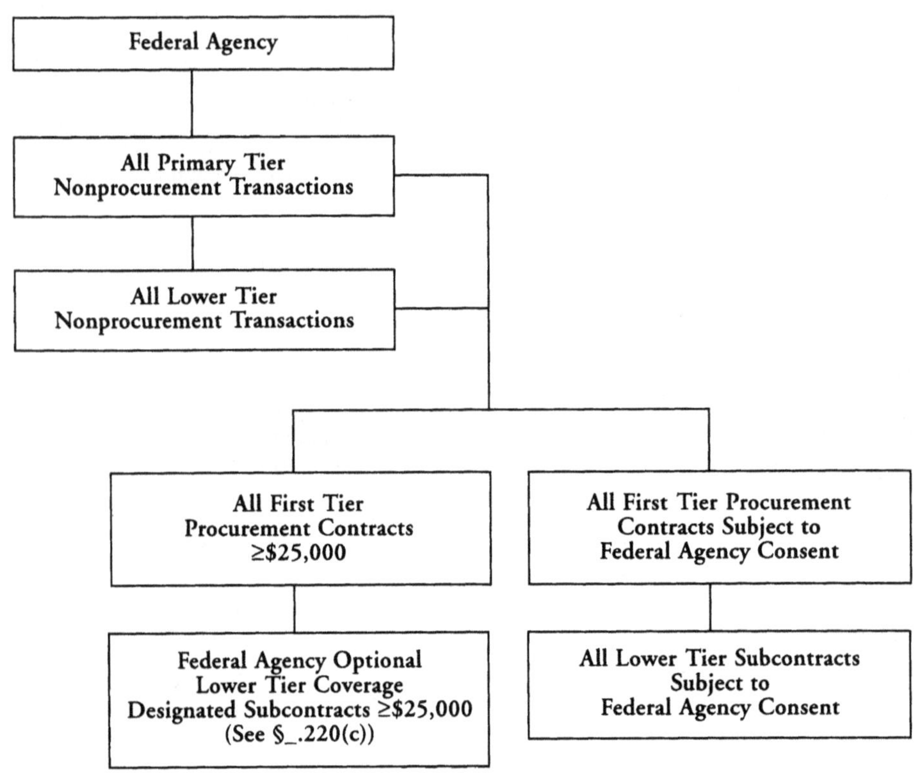

PART 1509—GOVERNMENTWIDE REQUIREMENTS FOR DRUG-FREE WORKPLACE (FINANCIAL ASSISTANCE)

Subpart A—Purpose and Coverage

Sec.

Subpart B—Requirements for Recipients Other Than Individuals

Subpart C—Requirements for Recipients Who Are Individuals

AUTHORITY: 41 U.S.C. 701 *et seq.*

SOURCE: 68 FR 66592, Nov. 26, 2003, unless otherwise noted.

Subpart A—Purpose and Coverage

§ 1509.100 What does this part do?

This part carries out the portion of the Drug-Free Workplace Act of 1988 (41 U.S.C. 701 *et seq.*, as amended) that applies to grants. It also applies the provisions of the Act to cooperative agreements and other financial assistance awards, as a matter of Federal Government policy.

§ 1509.105 Does this part apply to me?

(a) Portions of this part apply to you if you are either—

(1) A recipient of an assistance award from the African Development Foundation; or

(2) A(n) ADF awarding official. (See definitions of award and recipient in §§ 1509.605 and 1509.660, respectively.)

(b) The following table shows the subparts that apply to you:

If you are . . .	see subparts . . .
(1) A recipient who is not an individual	A, B and E.
(2) A recipient who is an individual	A, C and E.
(3) A(n) ADF awarding official	A, D and E.

§ 1509.110 Are any of my Federal assistance awards exempt from this part?

This part does not apply to any award that the ADF President determines that the application of this part would be inconsistent with the international obligations of the United States or the laws or regulations of a foreign government.

§ 1509.115 Does this part affect the Federal contracts that I receive?

It will affect future contract awards indirectly if you are debarred or suspended for a violation of the requirements of this part, as described in § 1509.510(c). However, this part does not apply directly to procurement contracts. The portion of the Drug-Free Workplace Act of 1988 that applies to Federal procurement contracts is carried out through the Federal Acquisition Regulation in chapter 1 of Title 48 of the Code of Federal Regulations (the drug-free workplace coverage currently is in 48 CFR part 23, subpart 23.5).

Subpart B—Requirements for Recipients Other Than Individuals

§ 1509.200 What must I do to comply with this part?

There are two general requirements if you are a recipient other than an individual.

(a) First, you must make a good faith effort, on a continuing basis, to maintain a drug-free workplace. You must agree to do so as a condition for receiving any award covered by this part. The specific measures that you must take in this regard are described in more detail in subsequent sections of this subpart. Briefly, those measures are to—

(1) Publish a drug-free workplace statement and establish a drug-free awareness program for your employees (see §§1509.205 through 1509.220); and

(2) Take actions concerning employees who are convicted of violating drug statutes in the workplace (see §1509.225).

(b) Second, you must identify all known workplaces under your Federal awards (see §1509.230).

§1509.205 What must I include in my drug-free workplace statement?

You must publish a statement that—

(a) Tells your employees that the unlawful manufacture, distribution, dispensing, possession, or use of a controlled substance is prohibited in your workplace;

(b) Specifies the actions that you will take against employees for violating that prohibition; and

(c) Lets each employee know that, as a condition of employment under any award, he or she:

(1) Will abide by the terms of the statement; and

(2) Must notify you in writing if he or she is convicted for a violation of a criminal drug statute occurring in the workplace and must do so no more than five calendar days after the conviction.

§1509.210 To whom must I distribute my drug-free workplace statement?

You must require that a copy of the statement described in §1509.205 be given to each employee who will be engaged in the performance of any Federal award.

§1509.215 What must I include in my drug-free awareness program?

You must establish an ongoing drug-free awareness program to inform employees about—

(a) The dangers of drug abuse in the workplace;

(b) Your policy of maintaining a drug-free workplace;

(c) Any available drug counseling, rehabilitation, and employee assistance programs; and

(d) The penalties that you may impose upon them for drug abuse violations occurring in the workplace.

§1509.220 By when must I publish my drug-free workplace statement and establish my drug-free awareness program?

If you are a new recipient that does not already have a policy statement as described in §1509.205 and an ongoing awareness program as described in §1509.215, you must publish the statement and establish the program by the time given in the following table:

If . . .	then you . . .
(a) The performance period of the award is less than 30 days	must have the policy statement and program in place as soon as possible, but before the date on which performance is expected to be completed.
(b) The performance period of the award is 30 days or more ...	must have the policy statement and program in place within 30 days after award.
(c) You believe there are extraordinary circumstances that will require more than 30 days for you to publish the policy statement and establish the awareness program.	may ask the ADF awarding official to give you more time to do so. The amount of additional time, if any, to be given is at the discretion of the awarding official.

§1509.225 What actions must I take concerning employees who are convicted of drug violations in the workplace?

There are two actions you must take if an employee is convicted of a drug violation in the workplace:

(a) First, you must notify Federal agencies if an employee who is engaged in the performance of an award informs you about a conviction, as required by §1509.205(c)(2), or you otherwise learn of the conviction. Your notification to the Federal agencies must—

(1) Be in writing;

(2) Include the employee's position title;

(3) Include the identification number(s) of each affected award;

(4) Be sent within ten calendar days after you learn of the conviction; and

(5) Be sent to every Federal agency on whose award the convicted employee was working. It must be sent to every awarding official or his or her official designee, unless the Federal agency has specified a central point for the receipt of the notices.

(b) Second, within 30 calendar days of learning about an employee's conviction, you must either_

(1) Take appropriate personnel action against the employee, up to and including termination, consistent with the requirements of the Rehabilitation Act of 1973 (29 U.S.C. 794), as amended; or

(2) Require the employee to participate satisfactorily in a drug abuse assistance or rehabilitation program approved for these purposes by a Federal, State or local health, law enforcement, or other appropriate agency.

§ 1509.230 How and when must I identify workplaces?

(a) You must identify all known workplaces under each ADF award. A failure to do so is a violation of your drug-free workplace requirements. You may identify the workplaces_

(1) To the ADF official that is making the award, either at the time of application or upon award; or

(2) In documents that you keep on file in your offices during the performance of the award, in which case you must make the information available for inspection upon request by ADF officials or their designated representatives.

(b) Your workplace identification for an award must include the actual address of buildings (or parts of buildings) or other sites where work under the award takes place. Categorical descriptions may be used (*e.g.*, all vehicles of a mass transit authority or State highway department while in operation, State employees in each local unemployment office, performers in concert halls or radio studios).

(c) If you identified workplaces to the ADF awarding official at the time of application or award, as described in paragraph (a)(1) of this section, and any workplace that you identified changes during the performance of the award, you must inform the ADF awarding official.

Subpart C—Requirements for Recipients Who Are Individuals

§ 1509.300 What must I do to comply with this part if I am an individual recipient?

As a condition of receiving a(n) ADF award, if you are an individual recipient, you must agree that—

(a) You will not engage in the unlawful manufacture, distribution, dispensing, possession, or use of a controlled substance in conducting any activity related to the award; and

(b) If you are convicted of a criminal drug offense resulting from a violation occurring during the conduct of any award activity, you will report the conviction:

(1) In writing.

(2) Within 10 calendar days of the conviction.

(3) To the ADF awarding official or other designee for each award that you currently have, unless § 1509.301 or the award document designates a central point for the receipt of the notices. When notice is made to a central point, it must include the identification number(s) of each affected award.

§ 1509.301 [Reserved]

Subpart D—Responsibilities of ADF Awarding Officials

§ 1509.400 What are my responsibilities as a(n) ADF awarding official?

As a(n) ADF awarding official, you must obtain each recipient's agreement, as a condition of the award, to comply with the requirements in—

(a) Subpart B of this part, if the recipient is not an individual; or

(b) Subpart C of this part, if the recipient is an individual.

Subpart E—Violations of this Part and Consequences

§ 1509.500 How are violations of this part determined for recipients other than individuals?

A recipient other than an individual is in violation of the requirements of this part if the ADF President determines, in writing, that—

(a) The recipient has violated the requirements of subpart B of this part; or

(b) The number of convictions of the recipient's employees for violating criminal drug statutes in the workplace is large enough to indicate that the recipient has failed to make a good faith effort to provide a drug-free workplace.

§ 1509.505 How are violations of this part determined for recipients who are individuals?

An individual recipient is in violation of the requirements of this part if the ADF President determines, in writing, that—

(a) The recipient has violated the requirements of subpart C of this part; or

(b) The recipient is convicted of a criminal drug offense resulting from a violation occurring during the conduct of any award activity.

§ 1509.510 What actions will the Federal Government take against a recipient determined to have violated this part?

If a recipient is determined to have violated this part, as described in § 1509.500 or § 1509.505, the African Development Foundation may take one or more of the following actions—

(a) Suspension of payments under the award;

(b) Suspension or termination of the award; and

(c) Suspension or debarment of the recipient under 22 CFR part 1508, for a period not to exceed five years.

§ 1509.515 Are there any exceptions to those actions?

The ADF President may waive with respect to a particular award, in writing, a suspension of payments under an award, suspension or termination of an award, or suspension or debarment of a recipient if the ADF President determines that such a waiver would be in the public interest. This exception authority cannot be delegated to any other official.

Subpart F—Definitions

§ 1509.605 Award.

Award means an award of financial assistance by the African Development Foundation or other Federal agency directly to a recipient.

(a) The term award includes:

(1) A Federal grant or cooperative agreement, in the form of money or property in lieu of money.

(2) A block grant or a grant in an entitlement program, whether or not the grant is exempted from coverage under the Governmentwide rule [Agency-specific CFR citation] that implements OMB Circular A–102 (for availability, see 5 CFR 1310.3) and specifies uniform administrative requirements.

(b) The term award does not include:

(1) Technical assistance that provides services instead of money.

(2) Loans.

(3) Loan guarantees.

(4) Interest subsidies.

(5) Insurance.

(6) Direct appropriations.

(7) Veterans' benefits to individuals (*i.e.*, any benefit to veterans, their families, or survivors by virtue of the service of a veteran in the Armed Forces of the United States).

(c) Notwithstanding paragraph (a)(2) of this section, this paragraph is not applicable for ADF.

§ 1509.610 Controlled substance.

Controlled substance means a controlled substance in schedules I through V of the Controlled Substances Act (21 U.S.C. 812), and as further defined by regulation at 21 CFR 1308.11 through 1308.15.

§ 1509.615 Conviction.

Conviction means a finding of guilt (including a plea of nolo contendere) or imposition of sentence, or both, by any judicial body charged with the responsibility to determine violations of the Federal or State criminal drug statutes.

§ 1509.620 Cooperative agreement.

Cooperative agreement means an award of financial assistance that, consistent with 31 U.S.C. 6305, is used to enter into the same kind of relationship as a grant (see definition of grant in

§ 1509.650), except that substantial involvement is expected between the Federal agency and the recipient when carrying out the activity contemplated by the award. The term does not include cooperative research and development agreements as defined in 15 U.S.C. 3710a.

§ 1509.625 Criminal drug statute.

Criminal drug statute means a Federal or non-Federal criminal statute involving the manufacture, distribution, dispensing, use, or possession of any controlled substance.

§ 1509.630 Debarment.

Debarment means an action taken by a Federal agency to prohibit a recipient from participating in Federal Government procurement contracts and covered nonprocurement transactions. A recipient so prohibited is debarred, in accordance with the Federal Acquisition Regulation for procurement contracts (48 CFR part 9, subpart 9.4) and the common rule, Government-wide Debarment and Suspension (Nonprocurement), that implements Executive Order 12549 and Executive Order 12689.

§ 1509.635 Drug-free workplace.

Drug-free workplace means a site for the performance of work done in connection with a specific award at which employees of the recipient are prohibited from engaging in the unlawful manufacture, distribution, dispensing, possession, or use of a controlled substance.

§ 1509.640 Employee.

(a) *Employee* means the employee of a recipient directly engaged in the performance of work under the award, including—

(1) All direct charge employees;

(2) All indirect charge employees, unless their impact or involvement in the performance of work under the award is insignificant to the performance of the award; and

(3) Temporary personnel and consultants who are directly engaged in the performance of work under the award and who are on the recipient's payroll.

(b) This definition does not include workers not on the payroll of the recipient (*e.g.*, volunteers, even if used to meet a matching requirement; consultants or independent contractors not on the payroll; or employees of subrecipients or subcontractors in covered workplaces).

§ 1509.645 Federal agency or agency.

Federal agency or agency means any United States executive department, military department, government corporation, government controlled corporation, any other establishment in the executive branch (including the Executive Office of the President), or any independent regulatory agency.

§ 1509.650 Grant.

Grant means an award of financial assistance that, consistent with 31 U.S.C. 6304, is used to enter into a relationship—

(a) The principal purpose of which is to transfer a thing of value to the recipient to carry out a public purpose of support or stimulation authorized by a law of the United States, rather than to acquire property or services for the Federal Government's direct benefit or use; and

(b) In which substantial involvement is not expected between the Federal agency and the recipient when carrying out the activity contemplated by the award.

§ 1509.655 Individual.

Individual means a natural person.

§ 1509.660 Recipient.

Recipient means any individual, corporation, partnership, association, unit of government (except a Federal agency) or legal entity, however organized, that receives an award directly from a Federal agency.

§ 1509.665 State.

State means any of the States of the United States, the District of Columbia, the Commonwealth of Puerto Rico, or any territory or possession of the United States.

§ 1509.670 Suspension.

Suspension means an action taken by a Federal agency that immediately prohibits a recipient from participating in Federal Government procurement contracts and covered nonprocurement transactions for a temporary period, pending completion of an investigation and any judicial or administrative proceedings that may ensue. A recipient so prohibited is suspended, in accordance with the Federal Acquisition Regulation for procurement contracts (48 CFR part 9, subpart 9.4) and the common rule, Governmentwide Debarment and Suspension (Nonprocurement), that implements Executive Order 12549 and Executive Order 12689. Suspension of a recipient is a distinct and separate action from suspension of an award or suspension of payments under an award.

PART 1510—ENFORCEMENT OF NONDISCRIMINATION ON THE BASIS OF HANDICAP IN PROGRAMS OR ACTIVITIES CONDUCTED BY THE AFRICAN DEVELOPMENT FOUNDATION

Sec.

AUTHORITY: 29 U.S.C. 794.

SOURCE: 53 FR 25883, 25885, July 8, 1988, unless otherwise noted.

§ 1510.101 Purpose.

The purpose of this regulation is to effectuate section 119 of the Rehabilitation, Comprehensive Services, and Developmental Disabilities Amendments of 1978, which amended section 504 of the Rehabilitation Act of 1973 to prohibit discrimination on the basis of handicap in programs or activities conducted by Executive agencies or the United States Postal Service.

§ 1510.102 Application.

This regulation (§§ 1510.101–1510.170) applies to all programs or activities conducted by the agency, except for programs or activities conducted outside the United States that do not involve individuals with handicaps in the United States.

§ 1510.103 Definitions.

For purposes of this regulation, the term—

Assistant Attorney General means the Assistant Attorney General, Civil Rights Division, United States Department of Justice.

Auxiliary aids means services or devices that enable persons with impaired sensory, manual, or speaking skills to have an equal opportunity to participate in, and enjoy the benefits of, programs or activities conducted by the agency. For example, auxiliary aids useful for persons with impaired vision include readers, Brailled materials, audio recordings, and other similar services and devices. Auxiliary aids useful for persons with impaired hearing include telephone handset amplifiers, telephones compatible with hearing aids, telecommunication devices for deaf persons (TDD's), interpreters, notetakers, written materials, and other similar services and devices.

Complete complaint means a written statement that contains the complainant's name and address and describes the agency's alleged discriminatory action in sufficient detail to inform the agency of the nature and date of the alleged violation of section 504. It shall be signed by the complainant or by someone authorized to do so on his or her behalf. Complaints filed on behalf of classes or third parties shall describe or identify (by name, if possible) the alleged victims of discrimination.

Facility means all or any portion of buildings, structures, equipment, roads, walks, parking lots, rolling stock or other conveyances, or other real or personal property.

Historic preservation programs means programs conducted by the agency that have preservation of historic properties as a primary purpose.

Historic properties means those properties that are listed or eligible for listing in the National Register of Historic Places or properties designated as historic under a statute of the appropriate State or local government body.

Individual with handicaps means any person who has a physical or mental impairment that substantially limits one or more major life activities, has a record of such an impairment, or is regarded as having such an impairment.

As used in this definition, the phrase:

(1) *Physical or mental impairment* includes—

(i) Any physiological disorder or condition, cosmetic disfigurement, or anatomical loss affecting one or more of the following body systems: Neurological; musculoskeletal; special sense organs; respiratory, including speech organs; cardiovascular; reproductive; digestive; genitourinary; hemic and lymphatic; skin; and endocrine; or

(ii) Any mental or psychological disorder, such as mental retardation, organic brain syndrome, emotional or mental illness, and specific learning disabilities. The term *physical or mental impairment* includes, but is not limited to, such diseases and conditions as orthopedic, visual, speech, and hearing impairments, cerebral palsy, epilepsy, muscular dystrophy, multiple sclerosis, cancer, heart disease, diabetes, mental retardation, emotional illness, and drug addiction and alcoholism.

(2) *Major life activities* includes functions such as caring for one's self, performing manual tasks, walking, seeing, hearing, speaking, breathing, learning, and working.

(3) *Has a record of such an impairment* means has a history of, or has been misclassified as having, a mental or physical impairment that substantially limits one or more major life activities.

(4) *Is regarded as having an impairment* means—

(i) Has a physical or mental impairment that does not substantially limit major life activities but is treated by the agency as constituting such a limitation;

(ii) Has a physical or mental impairment that substantially limits major life activities only as a result of the attitudes of others toward such impairment; or

(iii) Has none of the impairments defined in paragraph (1) of this definition but is treated by the agency as having such an impairment.

Qualified individual with handicaps means—

(1) With respect to preschool, elementary, or secondary education services provided by the agency, an individual with handicaps who is a member of a class of persons otherwise entitled by statute, regulation, or agency policy to receive education services from the agency;

(2) With respect to any other agency program or activity under which a person is required to perform services or to achieve a level of accomplishment, an individual with handicaps who meets the essential eligibility requirements and who can achieve the purpose of the program or activity without modifications in the program or activity that the agency can demonstrate would result in a fundamental alteration in its nature;

(3) With respect to any other program or activity, an individual with handicaps who meets the essential eligibility requirements for participation in, or receipt of benefits from, that program or activity; and

(4) *Qualified handicapped person* as that term is defined for purposes of employment in 29 CFR 1613.702(f), which is made applicable to this regulation by § 1510.140.

Section 504 means section 504 of the Rehabilitation Act of 1973 (Pub. L. 93–112, 87 Stat. 394 (29 U.S.C. 794)), as amended by the Rehabilitation Act Amendments of 1974 (Pub. L. 93–516, 88 Stat. 1617); the Rehabilitation, Comprehensive Services, and Developmental Disabilities Amendments of 1978 (Pub. L. 95–602, 92 Stat. 2955); and the Rehabilitation Act Amendments of 1986 (Pub. L. 99–506, 100 Stat. 1810). As used in this regulation, section 504 applies only to programs or activities conducted by Executive agencies and not to federally assisted programs.

Substantial impairment means a significant loss of the integrity of finished materials, design quality, or special character resulting from a permanent alteration.

§§ 1510.104–1510.109 [Reserved]

§ 1510.110 Self-evaluation.

(a) The agency shall, by September 6, 1989, evaluate its current policies and practices, and the effects thereof, that do not or may not meet the requirements of this regulation and, to the extent modification of any such policies and practices is required, the agency shall proceed to make the necessary modifications.

(b) The agency shall provide an opportunity to interested persons, including individuals with handicaps or organizations representing individuals with handicaps, to participate in the self-evaluation process by submitting comments (both oral and written).

(c) The agency shall, for at least three years following completion of the self-evaluation, maintain on file and make available for public inspection:

(1) A description of areas examined and any problems identified; and

(2) A description of any modifications made.

§ 1510.111 Notice.

The agency shall make available to employees, applicants, participants, beneficiaries, and other interested persons such information regarding the provisions of this regulation and its applicability to the programs or activities conducted by the agency, and make such information available to them in such manner as the head of the agency finds necessary to apprise such persons of the protections against discrimination assured them by section 504 and this regulation.

§§ 1510.112–1510.129 [Reserved]

§ 1510.130 General prohibitions against discrimination.

(a) No qualified individual with handicaps shall, on the basis of handicap, be excluded from participation in, be denied the benefits of, or otherwise be subjected to discrimination under any program or activity conducted by the agency.

(b)(1) The agency, in providing any aid, benefit, or service, may not, directly or through contractual, licensing, or other arrangements, on the basis of handicap—

(i) Deny a qualified individual with handicaps the opportunity to participate in or benefit from the aid, benefit, or service;

(ii) Afford a qualified individual with handicaps an opportunity to participate in or benefit from the aid, benefit, or service that is not equal to that afforded others;

(iii) Provide a qualified individual with handicaps with an aid, benefit, or service that is not as effective in affording equal opportunity to obtain the same result, to gain the same benefit, or to reach the same level of achievement as that provided to others;

(iv) Provide different or separate aid, benefits, or services to individuals with handicaps or to any class of individuals with handicaps than is provided to others unless such action is necessary to provide qualified individuals with handicaps with aid, benefits, or services that are as effective as those provided to others;

(v) Deny a qualified individual with handicaps the opportunity to participate as a member of planning or advisory boards;

(vi) Otherwise limit a qualified individual with handicaps in the enjoyment of any right, privilege, advantage, or opportunity enjoyed by others receiving the aid, benefit, or service.

(2) The agency may not deny a qualified individual with handicaps the opportunity to participate in programs or activities that are not separate or different, despite the existence of permissibly separate or different programs or activities.

(3) The agency may not, directly or through contractual or other arrangements, utilize criteria or methods of administration the purpose or effect of which would—

(i) Subject qualified individuals with handicaps to discrimination on the basis of handicap; or

(ii) Defeat or substantially impair accomplishment of the objectives of a program or activity with respect to individuals with handicaps.

(4) The agency may not, in determining the site or location of a facility, make selections the purpose or effect of which would—

(i) Exclude individuals with handicaps from, deny them the benefits of, or otherwise subject them to discrimination under any program or activity conducted by the agency; or

(ii) Defeat or substantially impair the accomplishment of the objectives of a program or activity with respect to individuals with handicaps.

(5) The agency, in the selection of procurement contractors, may not use criteria that subject qualified individuals with handicaps to discrimination on the basis of handicap.

(6) The agency may not administer a licensing or certification program in a manner that subjects qualified individuals with handicaps to discrimination on the basis of handicap, nor may the agency establish requirements for the programs or activities of licensees or certified entities that subject qualified individuals with handicaps to discrimination on the basis of handicap. However, the programs or activities of entities that are licensed or certified by the agency are not, themselves, covered by this regulation.

(c) The exclusion of nonhandicapped persons from the benefits of a program limited by Federal statute or Executive order to individuals with handicaps or the exclusion of a specific class of individuals with handicaps from a program limited by Federal statute or Executive order to a different class of individuals with handicaps is not prohibited by this regulation.

(d) The agency shall administer programs and activities in the most integrated setting appropriate to the needs of qualified individuals with handicaps.

§§ 1510.131–1510.139 [Reserved]

§ 1510.140 Employment.

No qualified individual with handicaps shall, on the basis of handicap, be subject to discrimination in employment under any program or activity conducted by the agency. The definitions, requirements, and procedures of section 501 of the Rehabilitation Act of 1973 (29 U.S.C. 791), as established by the Equal Employment Opportunity Commission in 29 CFR part 1613, shall apply to employment in federally conducted programs or activities.

§§ 1510.141–1510.148 [Reserved]

§ 1510.149 Program accessibility: Discrimination prohibited.

Except as otherwise provided in § 1510.150, no qualified individual with handicaps shall, because the agency's facilities are inaccessible to or unusable by individuals with handicaps, be denied the benefits of, be excluded from participation in, or otherwise be subjected to discrimination under any program or activity conducted by the agency.

§ 1510.150 Program accessibility: Existing facilities.

(a) *General.* The agency shall operate each program or activity so that the program or activity, when viewed in its entirety, is readily accessible to and usable by individuals with handicaps. This paragraph does not—

(1) Necessarily require the agency to make each of its existing facilities accessible to and usable by individuals with handicaps;

(2) In the case of historic preservation programs, require the agency to take any action that would result in a substantial impairment of significant historic features of an historic property; or

(3) Require the agency to take any action that it can demonstrate would result in a fundamental alteration in the nature of a program or activity or in undue financial and administrative burdens. In those circumstances where agency personnel believe that the proposed action would fundamentally alter the program or activity or would result in undue financial and administrative burdens, the agency has the burden of proving that compliance with § 1510.150(a) would result in such alteration or burdens. The decision that compliance would result in such alteration or burdens must be made by the agency head or his or her designee after considering all agency resources available for use in the funding and operation of the conducted program or activity, and must be accompanied by a written statement of the reasons for

reaching that conclusion. If an action would result in such an alteration or such burdens, the agency shall take any other action that would not result in such an alteration or such burdens but would nevertheless ensure that individuals with handicaps receive the benefits and services of the program or activity.

(b) *Methods*—(1) *General.* The agency may comply with the requirements of this section through such means as redesign of equipment, reassignment of services to accessible buildings, assignment of aides to beneficiaries, home visits, delivery of services at alternate accessible sites, alteration of existing facilities and construction of new facilities, use of accessible rolling stock, or any other methods that result in making its programs or activities readily accessible to and usable by individuals with handicaps. The agency is not required to make structural changes in existing facilities where other methods are effective in achieving compliance with this section. The agency, in making alterations to existing buildings, shall meet accessibility requirements to the extent compelled by the Architectural Barriers Act of 1968, as amended (42 U.S.C. 4151–4157), and any regulations implementing it. In choosing among available methods for meeting the requirements of this section, the agency shall give priority to those methods that offer programs and activities to qualified individuals with handicaps in the most integrated setting appropriate.

(2) *Historic preservation programs.* In meeting the requirements of §1510.150(a) in historic preservation programs, the agency shall give priority to methods that provide physical access to individuals with handicaps. In cases where a physical alteration to an historic property is not required because of §1510.150(a) (2) or (3), alternative methods of achieving program accessibility include—

(i) Using audio-visual materials and devices to depict those portions of an historic property that cannot otherwise be made accessible;

(ii) Assigning persons to guide individuals with handicaps into or through portions of historic properties that cannot otherwise be made accessible; or

(iii) Adopting other innovative methods.

(c) *Time period for compliance.* The agency shall comply with the obligations established under this section by November 7, 1988, except that where structural changes in facilities are undertaken, such changes shall be made by September 6, 1991, but in any event as expeditiously as possible.

(d) *Transition plan.* In the event that structural changes to facilities will be undertaken to achieve program accessibility, the agency shall develop, by March 6, 1989, a transition plan setting forth the steps necessary to complete such changes. The agency shall provide an opportunity to interested persons, including individuals with handicaps or organizations representing individuals with handicaps, to participate in the development of the transition plan by submitting comments (both oral and written). A copy of the transition plan shall be made available for public inspection. The plan shall, at a minimum—

(1) Identify physical obstacles in the agency's facilities that limit the accessibility of its programs or activities to individuals with handicaps;

(2) Describe in detail the methods that will be used to make the facilities accessible;

(3) Specify the schedule for taking the steps necessary to achieve compliance with this section and, if the time period of the transition plan is longer than one year, identify steps that will be taken during each year of the transition period; and

(4) Indicate the official responsible for implementation of the plan.

§ 1510.151 Program accessibility: New construction and alterations.

Each building or part of a building that is constructed or altered by, on behalf of, or for the use of the agency shall be designed, constructed, or altered so as to be readily accessible to and usable by individuals with handicaps. The definitions, requirements, and standards of the Architectural Barriers Act (42 U.S.C. 4151–4157), as established in 41 CFR 101–19.600 to 101–19.607, apply to buildings covered by this section.

§§ 1510.152–1510.159 [Reserved]

§ 1510.160 Communications.

(a) The agency shall take appropriate steps to ensure effective communication with applicants, participants, personnel of other Federal entities, and members of the public.

(1) The agency shall furnish appropriate auxiliary aids where necessary to afford an individual with handicaps an equal opportunity to participate in, and enjoy the benefits of, a program or activity conducted by the agency.

(i) In determining what type of auxiliary aid is necessary, the agency shall give primary consideration to the requests of the individual with handicaps.

(ii) The agency need not provide individually prescribed devices, readers for personal use or study, or other devices of a personal nature.

(2) Where the agency communicates with applicants and beneficiaries by telephone, telecommunication devices for deaf persons (TDD's) or equally effective telecommunication systems shall be used to communicate with persons with impaired hearing.

(b) The agency shall ensure that interested persons, including persons with impaired vision or hearing, can obtain information as to the existence and location of accessible services, activities, and facilities.

(c) The agency shall provide signage at a primary entrance to each of its inaccessible facilities, directing users to a location at which they can obtain information about accessible facilities. The international symbol for accessibility shall be used at each primary entrance of an accessible facility.

(d) This section does not require the agency to take any action that it can demonstrate would result in a fundamental alteration in the nature of a program or activity or in undue financial and administrative burdens. In those circumstances where agency personnel believe that the proposed action would fundamentally alter the program or activity or would result in undue financial and administrative burdens, the agency has the burden of proving that compliance with § 1510.160 would result in such alteration or burdens. The decision that compliance would result in such alteration or burdens must be made by the agency head or his or her designee after considering all agency resources available for use in the funding and operation of the conducted program or activity and must be accompanied by a written statement of the reasons for reaching that conclusion. If an action required to comply with this section would result in such an alteration or such burdens, the agency shall take any other action that would not result in such an alteration or such burdens but would nevertheless ensure that, to the maximum extent possible, individuals with handicaps receive the benefits and services of the program or activity.

§§ 1510.161–1510.169 [Reserved]

§ 1510.170 Compliance procedures.

(a) Except as provided in paragraph (b) of this section, this section applies to all allegations of discrimination on the basis of handicap in programs and activities conducted by the agency.

(b) The agency shall process complaints alleging violations of section 504 with respect to employment according to the procedures established by the Equal Employment Opportunity Commission in 29 CFR part 1613 pursuant to section 501 of the Rehabilitation Act of 1973 (29 U.S.C. 791).

(c) The Personnel Officer, Office of Administration and Finance, shall be responsible for coordinating implementation of this section. Complaints may be sent to Personnel Officer, Office of Administration and Finance, African Development Foundation, 1625 Massachusetts Avenue, NW., Suite 600, Washington, DC, 20036.

(d) The agency shall accept and investigate all complete complaints for which it has jurisdiction. All complete complaints must be filed within 180 days of the alleged act of discrimination. The agency may extend this time period for good cause.

(e) If the agency receives a complaint over which it does not have jurisdiction, it shall promptly notify the complainant and shall make reasonable efforts to refer the complaint to the appropriate Government entity.

(f) The agency shall notify the Architectural and Transportation Barriers Compliance Board upon receipt of any complaint alleging that a building or facility that is subject to the Architectural Barriers Act of 1968, as amended (42 U.S.C. 4151–4157), is not readily accessible to and usable by individuals with handicaps.

(g) Within 180 days of the receipt of a complete complaint for which it has jurisdiction, the agency shall notify the complainant of the results of the investigation in a letter containing—

(1) Findings of fact and conclusions of law;

(2) A description of a remedy for each violation found; and

(3) A notice of the right to appeal.

(h) Appeals of the findings of fact and conclusions of law or remedies must be filed by the complainant within 90 days of receipt from the agency of the letter required by §1510.170(g). The agency may extend this time for good cause.

(i) Timely appeals shall be accepted and processed by the head of the agency.

(j) The head of the agency shall notify the complainant of the results of the appeal within 60 days of the receipt of the request. If the head of the agency determines that additional information is needed from the complainant, he or she shall have 60 days from the date of receipt of the additional information to make his or her determination on the appeal.

(k) The time limits cited in paragraphs (g) and (j) of this section may be extended with the permission of the Assistant Attorney General.

(l) The agency may delegate its authority for conducting complaint investigations to other Federal agencies, except that the authority for making the final determination may not be delegated to another agency.

[53 FR 25883, 25885, July 8, 1988, as amended at 53 FR 25883, July 8, 1988]

§§ 1510.171–1510.999 [Reserved]

PARTS 1511–1599 [RESERVED]

CHAPTER XVI—JAPAN-UNITED STATES FRIENDSHIP COMMISSION

PART 1600—ENFORCEMENT OF NONDISCRIMINATION ON THE BASIS OF HANDICAP IN PROGRAMS OR ACTIVITIES CONDUCTED BY THE JAPAN-UNITED STATES FRIENDSHIP COMMISSION

AUTHORITY: 29 U.S.C. 794.

SOURCE: 51 FR 22891, 22896, June 23, 1986, unless otherwise noted.

§ 1600.101 Purpose.

This part effectuates section 119 of the Rehabilitation, Comprehensive Services, and Developmental Disabilities Amendments of 1978, which amended section 504 of the Rehabilitation Act of 1973 to prohibit discrimination on the basis of handicap in programs or activities conducted by Executive agencies or the United States Postal Service.

§ 1600.102 Application.

This part applies to all programs or activities conducted by the agency.

§ 1600.103 Definitions.

For purposes of this part, the term—

Assistant Attorney General means the Assistant Attorney General, Civil Rights Division, United States Department of Justice.

Auxiliary aids means services or devices that enable persons with impaired sensory, manual, or speaking skills to have an equal opportunity to participate in, and enjoy the benefits of, programs or activities conducted by the agency. For example, auxiliary aids useful for persons with impaired vision include readers, brailled materials, audio recordings, telecommunications devices and other similar services and devices. Auxiliary aids useful for persons with impaired hearing include telephone handset amplifiers, telephones compatible with hearing aids, telecommunication devices for deaf persons (TDD's), interpreters, notetakers, written materials, and other similar services and devices.

Complete complaint means a written statement that contains the complainant's name and address and describes the agency's alleged discriminatory action in sufficient detail to inform the agency of the nature and date of the alleged violation of section 504. It shall be signed by the complainant or by someone authorized to do so on his or her behalf. Complaints filed on behalf of classes or third parties shall describe or identify (by name, if possible) the alleged victims of discrimination.

Facility means all or any portion of buildings, structures, equipment, roads, walks, parking lots, rolling stock or other conveyances, or other real or personal property.

Handicapped person means any person who has a physical or mental impairment that substantially limits one or more major life activities, has a record of such an impairment, or is regarded as having such an impairment.

As used in this definition, the phrase:

(1) *Physical or mental impairment* includes—

(i) Any physiological disorder or condition, cosmetic disfigurement, or anatomical loss affecting one or more of the following body systems: Neurological; musculoskeletal; special sense organs; respiratory, including speech organs; cardiovascular; reproductive; digestive; genitourinary; hemic and lymphatic; skin; and endocrine; or

(ii) Any mental or psychological disorder, such as mental retardation, organic brain syndrome, emotional or mental illness, and specific learning disabilities. The term *physical or mental impairment* includes, but is not limited to, such diseases and conditions as orthopedic, visual, speech, and hearing impairments, cerebral palsy, epilepsy, muscular dystrophy, multiple sclerosis, cancer, heart disease, diabetes, mental retardation, emotional illness, and drug addiction and alocoholism.

(2) *Major life activities* includes functions such as caring for one's self, performing manual tasks, walking, seeing, hearing, speaking, breathing, learning, and working.

(3) *Has a record of such an impairment* means has a history of, or has been misclassified as having, a mental or physical impairment that substantially limits one or more major life activities.

(4) *Is regarded as having an impairment* means—

(i) Has a physical or mental impairment that does not substantially limit major life activities but is treated by the agency as constituting such a limitation;

(ii) Has a physical or mental impairment that substantially limits major life activities only as a result of the attitudes of others toward such impairment; or

(iii) Has none of the impairments defined in paragraph (1) of this definition but is treated by the agency as having such an impairment.

Historic preservation programs means programs conducted by the agency that have preservation of historic properties as a primary purpose.

Historic properties means those properties that are listed or eligible for listing in the National Register of Historic Places or properties designated as historic under a statute of the appropriate State or local government body.

Qualified handicapped person means—

(1) With respect to preschool, elementary, or secondary education services provided by the agency, a handicapped person who is a member of a class of persons otherwise entitled by statute, regulation, or agency policy to receive education services from the agency.

(2) With respect to any other agency program or activity under which a person is required to perform services or to achieve a level of accomplishment, a handicapped person who meets the essential eligibility requirements and who can acheive the purpose of the program or activity without modifications in the program or activity that the agency can demonstrate would result in a fundamental alteration in its nature;

(3) With respect to any other program or activity, a handicapped person who meets the essential eligibility requirements for participation in, or receipt of benefits from, that program or activity; and

(4) *Qualified handicapped person* is defined for purposes of employment in 29 CFR 1613.702(f), which is made applicable to this part by § 1600.140.

Section 504 means section 504 of the Rehabilitation Act of 1973 (Pub. L. 93–112, 87 Stat. 394 (29 U.S.C. 794)), as amended by the Rehabilitation Act Amendments of 1974 (Pub. L. 93–516, 88 Stat. 1617), and the Rehabilitation, Comprehensive Services, and Developmental Disabilities Amendments of 1978 (Pub. L. 95–602, 92 Stat. 2955). As used in this part, section 504 applies only to programs or activities conducted by Executive agencies and not to federally assisted programs.

Substantial impairment means a significant loss of the integrity of finished materials, design quality, or special character resulting from a permanent alteration.

§§ 1600.104–1600.109 [Reserved]

§ 1600.110 Self-evaluation.

(a) The agency shall, by August 24, 1987, evaluate its current policies and practices, and the effects thereof, that do not or may not meet the requirements of this part, and, to the extent modification of any such policies and practices is required, the agency shall proceed to make the necessary modifications.

(b) The agency shall provide an opportunity to interested persons, including handicapped persons or organizations representing handicapped persons, to participate in the self-evaluation process by submitting comments (both oral and written).

(c) The agency shall, until three years following the completion of the self-evaluation, maintain on file and make available for public inspection:

(1) A description of areas examined and any problems identified, and

(2) A description of any modifications made.

§ 1600.111 Notice.

The agency shall make available to employees, applicants, participants, beneficiaries, and other interested persons such information regarding the provisions of this part and its applicability to the programs or activities conducted by the agency, and make such information available to them in such manner as the head of the agency finds necessary to apprise such persons of the protections against discrimination assured them by section 504 and this regulation.

§§ 1600.112–1600.129 [Reserved]

§ 1600.130 General prohibitions against discrimination.

(a) No qualified handicapped person shall, on the basis of handicap, be excluded from participation in, be denied the benefits of, or otherwise be subjected to discrimination under any program or activity conducted by the agency.

(b)(1) The agency, in providing any aid, benefit, or service, may not, directly or through contractual, licensing, or other arrangements, on the basis of handicap—

(i) Deny a qualified handicapped person the opportunity to participate in or benefit from the aid, benefit, or service;

(ii) Afford a qualified handicapped person an opportunity to participate in or benefit from the aid, benefit, or service that is not equal to that afforded others;

(iii) Provide a qualified handicapped person with an aid, benefit, or service that is not as effective in affording equal opportunity to obtain the same result, to gain the same benefit, or to reach the same level of achievement as that provided to others;

(iv) Provide different or separate aid, benefits, or services to handicapped persons or to any class of handicapped persons than is provided to others unless such action is necessary to provide qualified handicapped persons with aid, benefits, or services that are as effective as those provided to others;

(v) Deny a qualified handicapped person the opportunity to participate as a member of planning or advisory boards; or

(vi) Otherwise limit a qualified handicapped person in the enjoyment of any right, privilege, advantage, or opportunity enjoyed by others receiving the aid, benefit, or service.

(2) The agency may not deny a qualified handicapped person the opportunity to participate in programs or activities that are not separate or different, despite the existence of permissibly separate or different programs or activities.

(3) The agency may not, directly or through contractual or other arrangments, utilize criteria or methods of administration the purpose or effect of which would—

(i) Subject qualified handicapped persons to discrimination on the basis of handicap; or

(ii) Defeat or substantially impair accomplishment of the objectives of a program or activity with respect to handicapped persons.

(4) The agency may not, in determining the site or location of a facility, make selections the purpose or effect of which would—

(i) Exclude handicapped persons from, deny them the benefits of, or otherwise subject them to discrimination under any program or activity conducted by the agency; or

(ii) Defeat or substantially impair the accomplishment of the objectives of a program or activity with respect to handicapped persons.

(5) The agency, in the selection of procurement contractors, may not use criteria that subject qualified handicapped persons to discrimination on the basis of handicap.

(6) The agency may not administer a licensing or certification program in a manner that subjects qualified handicapped persons to discrimination on the basis of handicap, nor may the agency establish requirements for the programs or activities of licensees or certified entities that subject qualified handicapped persons to discrimination on the basis of handicap. However, the programs or activities of entities that are licensed or certified by the agency

are not, themselves, covered by this part.

(c) The exclusion of nonhandicapped persons from the benefits of a program limited by Federal statute or Executive order to handicapped persons or the exclusion of a specific class of handicapped persons from a program limited by Federal statute or Executive order to a different class of handicapped persons is not prohibited by this part.

(d) The agency shall administer programs and activities in the most integrated setting appropriate to the needs of qualified handicapped persons.

§§ 1600.131–1600.139 [Reserved]

§ 1600.140 Employment.

No qualified handicapped person shall, on the basis of handicap, be subjected to discrimination in employment under any program or activity conducted by the agency. The definitions, requirements, and procedures of section 501 of the Rehabilitation Act of 1973 (29 U.S.C. 791), as established by the Equal Employment Opportunity Commission in 29 CFR part 1613, shall apply to employment in federally conducted programs or activities.

§§ 1600.141–1600.148 [Reserved]

§ 1600.149 Program accessibility: Discrimination prohibited.

Except as otherwise provided in § 1600.150, no qualified handicapped person shall, because the agency's facilities are inaccessible to or unusable by handicapped persons, be denied the benefits of, be excluded from participation in, or otherwise be subjected to discrimination under any program or activity conducted by the agency.

§ 1600.150 Program accessibility: Existing facilities.

(a) *General.* The agency shall operate each program or activity so that the program or activity, when viewed in its entirety, is readily accessible to and usable by handicapped persons. This paragraph does not—

(1) Necessarily require the agency to make each of its existing facilities accessible to and usable by handicapped persons;

(2) In the case of historic preservation programs, require the agency to take any action that would result in a substantial impairment of significant historic features of an historic property; or

(3) Require the agency to take any action that it can demonstrate would result in a fundamental alteration in the nature of a program or activity or in undue financial and administrative burdens. In those circumstances where agency personnel believe that the proposed action would fundamentally alter the program or activity or would result in undue financial and administrative burdens, the agency has the burden of proving that compliance with § 1600.150(a) would result in such alteration or burdens. The decision that compliance would result in such alteration or burdens must be made by the agency head or his or her designee after considering all agency resources available for use in the funding and operation of the conducted program or activity, and must be accompanied by a written statement of the reasons for reaching that conclusion. If an action would result in such an alteration or such burdens, the agency shall take any other action that would not result in such an alteration or such burdens but would nevertheless ensure that handicapped persons receive the benefits and services of the program or activity.

(b) *Methods*—(1) *General.* The agency may comply with the requirements of this section through such means as redesign of equipment, reassignment of services to accessible buildings, assignment of aides to beneficiaries, home visits, delivery of services at alternate accessible sites, alteration of existing facilities and construction of new facilities, use of accessible rolling stock, or any other methods that result in making its programs or activities readily accessible to and usable by handicapped persons. The agency is not required to make structural changes in existing facilities where other methods are effective in achieving compliance with this section. The agency, in making alterations to existing buildings, shall meet accessibility requirements to the extent compelled by the Architectural Barriers Act of 1968, as amended (42 U.S.C. 4151–4157), and any regulations implementing it. In choosing among available methods for meeting the requirements of this section, the agency shall give priority to those methods that offer programs and activities to qualified handicapped persons in the most integrated setting appropriate.

(2) *Historic preservation programs.* In meeting the requirements of § 1600.150(a) in historic preservation programs, the agency shall give priority to methods that provide physical access to handicapped persons. In cases where a physical alteration to an historic property is not required because of § 1600.150(a)(2) or (a)(3), alternative methods of achieving program accessibility include—

(i) Using audio-visual materials and devices to depict those portions of an historic property that cannot otherwise be made accessible;

(ii) Assigning persons to guide handicapped persons into or through portions of historic properties that cannot otherwise be made accessible; or

(iii) Adopting other innovative methods.

(c) *Time period for compliance.* The agency shall comply with the obligations established under this section by October 21, 1986, except that where structural changes in facilities are undertaken, such changes shall be made by August 22, 1989, but in any event as expeditiously as possible.

(d) *Transition plan.* In the event that structural changes to facilities will be undertaken to achieve program accessibility, the agency shall develop, by February 23, 1987, a transition plan setting forth the steps necessary to complete such changes. The agency shall provide an opportunity to interested persons, including handicapped persons or organizations representing handicapped persons, to participate in the development of the transition plan by submitting comments (both oral and written). A copy of the transition plan shall be made available for public inspection. The plan shall, at a minimum—

(1) Identify physical obstacles in the agency's facilities that limit the accessibility of its programs or activities to handicapped persons;

(2) Describe in detail the methods that will be used to make the facilities accessible;

(3) Specify the schedule for taking the steps necessary to achieve compliance with this section and, if the time period of the transition plan is longer than one year, identify steps that will be taken during each year of the transition period; and

(4) Indicate the official responsible for implementation of the plan.

§ 1600.151 Program accessibility: New construction and alterations.

Each building or part of a building that is constructed or altered by, on behalf of, or for the use of the agency shall be designed, constructed, or altered so as to be readily accessible to and usable by handicapped persons. The definitions, requirements, and standards of the Architectural Barriers Act (42 U.S.C. 4151–4157), as established in 41 CFR 101–19.600 to 101–19.607, apply to buildings covered by this section.

§§ 1600.152–1600.159 [Reserved]

§ 1600.160 Communications.

(a) The agency shall take appropriate steps to ensure effective communication with applicants, participants, personnel of other Federal entities, and members of the public.

(1) The agency shall furnish appropriate auxiliary aids where necessary to afford a handicapped person an equal opportunity to participate in, and enjoy the benefits of, a program or activity conducted by the agency.

(i) In determining what type of auxiliary aid is necessary, the agency shall give primary consideration to the requests of the handicapped person.

(ii) The agency need not provide individually prescribed devices, readers for personal use or study, or other devices of a personal nature.

(2) Where the agency communicates with applicants and beneficiaries by telephone, telecommunication devices for deaf person (TDD's) or equally effective telecommunication systems shall be used.

(b) The agency shall ensure that interested persons, including persons with impaired vision or hearing, can obtain information as to the existence and location of accessible services, activities, and facilities.

(c) The agency shall provide signage at a primary entrance to each of its inaccessible facilities, directing users to a location at which they can obtain information about accessible facilities. The international symbol for accessibility shall be used at each primary entrance of an accessible facility.

(d) This section does not require the agency to take any action that it can demonstrate would result in a fundamental alteration in the nature of a program or activity or in undue financial and adminstrative burdens. In those circumstances where agency personnel believe that the proposed action would fundamentally alter the program or activity or would result in undue financial and administrative burdens, the agency has the burden of proving that compliance with § 1600.160 would result in such alteration or burdens. The decision that compliance would result in such alteration or burdens must be made by the agency head or his or her designee after considering all agency resources available for use in the funding and operation of the conducted program or activity, and must be accompanied by a written statement of the reasons for reaching that conclusion. If an action required to comply with this section would result in such an alteration or such burdens, the agency shall take any other action that would not result in such an alteration or such burdens but would nevertheless ensure that, to the maximum extent possible, handicapped persons receive the benefits and services of the program or activity.

§§ 1600.161–1600.169 [Reserved]

§ 1600.170 Compliance procedures.

(a) Except as provided in paragraph (b) of this section, this section applies to all allegations of discrimination on the basis of handicap in programs or activities conducted by the agency.

(b) The agency shall process complaints alleging violations of section 504 with respect to employment according to the procedures established by the Equal Employment Opportunity Commission in 29 CFR part 1613 pursuant to section 501 of the Rehabilitation Act of 1973 (29 U.S.C. 791).

(c) The Executive Director, Japan-U.S. Friendship Commission, shall be responsible for coordinating implementation of this section. Complaints may be sent to Executive Director, Japan-U.S. Friendship Commission, 1200 Pennsylvania Avenue, NW., Washington, DC 20004.

(d) The agency shall accept and investigate all complete complaints for which it has jurisdiction. All complete complaints must be filed within 180 days of the alleged act of discrimination. The agency may extend this time period for good cause.

(e) If the agency receives a complaint over which it does not have jurisdiction, it shall promptly notify the complainant and shall make reasonable efforts to refer the complaint to the appropriate government entity.

(f) The agency shall notify the Architectural and Transportation Barriers Compliance Board upon receipt of any complaint alleging that a building or facility that is subject to the Architectural Barriers Act of 1968, as amended (42 U.S.C. 4151–4157), or section 502 of the Rehabilitation Act of 1973, as amended (29 U.S.C. 792), is not readily accessible to and usable by handicapped persons.

(g) Within 180 days of the receipt of a complete complaint for which it has jurisdiction, the agency shall notify the complainant of the results of the investigation in a letter containing—

(1) Findings of fact and conclusions of law;

(2) A description of a remedy for each violation found; and

(3) A notice of the right to appeal.

(h) Appeals of the findings of fact and conclusions of law or remedies must be filed by the complainant within 90 days of receipt from the agency of the letter required by § 1600.170(g). The agency may extend this time for good cause.

(i) Timely appeals shall be accepted and processed by the head of the agency.

(j) The head of the agency shall notify the complainant of the results of the appeal within 60 days of the receipt of the request. If the head of the agency determines that additional information is needed from the complainant, he or she shall have 60 days from the date of receipt of the additional information to make his or her determination on the appeal.

(k) The time limits cited in paragraphs (g) and (j) of this section may be extended with the permission of the Assistant Attorney General.

(l) The agency may delegate its authority for conducting complaint investigations to other Federal agencies, except that the authority for making the final determination may not be delegated to another agency.

[51 FR 22891, 22896, June 23, 1986, as amended at 51 FR 22891, June 23, 1986]

§§ 1600.171–1600.999 [Reserved]

PARTS 1601–1699 [RESERVED]

CHAPTER XVII—UNITED STATES INSTITUTE OF PEACE

PART 1700 [RESERVED]

PART 1701—ENFORCEMENT OF NONDISCRIMINATION ON THE BASIS OF HANDICAP IN PROGRAMS OR ACTIVITIES CONDUCTED BY THE UNITED STATES INSTITUTE OF PEACE

AUTHORITY: 29 U.S.C. 794.

SOURCE: 58 FR 57697, 57699, Oct. 26, 1993, unless otherwise noted.

§ 1701.101 Purpose.

The purpose of this part is to implement the spirit of section 119 of the Rehabilitation, Comprehensive Services and Developmental Disabilities Amendments of 1978, which amended section 504 of the Rehabilitation Act of 1973 to prohibit discrimination on the basis of handicap in programs or activities conducted by various Executive agencies. Although the USIP does not believe that Congress contemplated coverage of independent Federal institutions, such as the USIP, it has chosen to promulgate this part.

[58 FR 57697, Oct. 26, 1993]

§ 1701.102 Application.

This part (§§ 1701.101–1701.170) applies to all programs or activities conducted by the agency, except for programs or activities conducted outside the United States that do not involve individuals with handicaps in the United States.

§ 1701.103 Definitions.

For purposes of this part, the term—

Assistant Attorney General means the Assistant Attorney General, Civil Rights Division, United States Department of Justice.

Auxiliary aids means services or devices that enable persons with impaired sensory, manual, or speaking skills to have an equal opportunity to participate in, and enjoy the benefits of, programs or activities conducted by the agency. For example, auxiliary aids useful for persons with impaired vision include readers, Brailled materials, audio recordings, and other similar services and devices. Auxiliary aids useful for persons with impaired hearing include telephone handset amplifiers, telephones compatible with hearing aids, telecommunication devices for deaf persons (TTD's), interpreters, notetakers, written materials, and other similar services and devices.

Complete complaint means a written statement that contains the complainant's name and address and describes the agency's alleged discriminatory action in sufficient detail to inform the agency of the nature and date of the alleged violation of section 504. It shall be signed by the complainant or by someone authorized to do so on his or her behalf. Complaints filed on behalf of classes or third parties shall describe or identify (by name, if possible) the alleged victims of discrimination.

Facility means all or any portion of buildings, structures, equipment, roads, walks, parking lots, rolling stock or other conveyances, or other real or personal property.

Historic preservation programs means programs conducted by the agency that have preservation of historic properties as a primary purpose.

Historic properties means those properties that are listed or eligible for listing in the National Register of Historic Places or properties designated as historic under a statute of the appropriate State or local government body.

Individual with handicaps means any person who has a physical or mental impairment that substantially limits one or more major life activities, has a record of such an impairment, or is regarded as having such an impairment. As used in this definition, the phrase:

(1) *Physical or mental impairment* includes—

(i) Any physiological disorder or condition, cosmetic disfigurement, or anatomical loss affecting one or more of the following body systems: Neurological; musculoskeletal; special sense organs; respiratory, including speech organs; cardiovascular; reproductive; digestive; genitourinary; hemic and lymphatic; skin; and endocrine; or

(ii) Any mental or psychological disorder, such as mental retardation, organic brain syndrome, emotional or mental illness, and specific learning disabilities. The term "physical or mental impairment" includes, but is not limited to, such diseases and conditions as orthopedic, visual, speech, and hearing impairments, cerebral palsy, epilepsy, muscular dystrophy, multiple sclerosis, cancer, heart disease, diabetes, mental retardation, emotional illness, HIV disease (whether symptomatic or asymptomatic), and drug addiction and alcoholism.

(2) *Major life activities* include functions such as caring for one's self, performing manual tasks, walking, seeing, hearing, speaking, breathing, learning, and working.

(3) *Has a record of such an impairment* means has a history of, or has been misclassified as having, a mental or physical impairment that substantially limits one or more major life activities.

(4) *Is regarded as having an impairment* means—

(i) Has a physical or mental impairment that does not substantially limit major life activities but is treated by the agency as constituting such a limitation;

(ii) Has a physical or mental impairment that substantially limits major life activities only as a result of the attitudes of others toward such impairment; or

(iii) Has none of the impairments defined in paragraph (1) of this definition but is treated by the agency as having such an impairment.

Qualified individual with handicaps means—

(1) With respect to preschool, elementary, or secondary education services provided by the agency, an individual with handicaps who is a member of a class of persons otherwise entitled by statute, regulation, or agency policy to receive education services from the agency;

(2) With respect to any other agency program or activity under which a person is required to perform services or to achieve a level of accomplishment, an individual with handicaps who meets the essential eligibility requirements and who can achieve the purpose of the program or activity without modifications in the program or activity that the agency can demonstrate would result in a fundamental alteration in its nature;

(3) With respect to any other program or activity, an individual with handicaps who meets the essential eligibility requirements for participation in, or receipt of benefits from, that program or activity; and

(4) *Qualified handicapped person* as that term is defined for purposes of employment in 29 CFR 1614.203(a)(6), which is made applicable to this part by §1701.140.

Section 504 means section 504 of the Rehabilitation Act of 1973 (Pub. L. 93–112, 87 Stat. 394 (29 U.S.C. 794)), as amended. As used in this part, section 504 applies only to programs or activities conducted by Executive agencies and not to federally assisted programs.

Substantial impairment means a significant loss of the integrity of finished materials, design quality, or special character resulting from a permanent alteration.

§§ 1701.104–1701.109 [Reserved]

§ 1701.110 Self-evaluation.

(a) The agency shall, by November 28, 1994, evaluate its current policies and practices, and the effects thereof, that do not or may not meet the requirements of this part and, to the extent modification of any such policies and practices is required, the agency shall proceed to make the necessary modifications.

(b) The agency shall provide an opportunity to interested persons, including individuals with handicaps or organizations representing individuals with handicaps, to participate in the self-evaluation process by submitting comments (both oral and written).

(c) The agency shall, for at least three years following completion of the self-evaluation, maintain on file and make available for public inspection:

(1) A description of areas examined and any problems identified; and

(2) A description of any modifications made.

§ 1701.111 Notice.

The agency shall make available to employees, applicants, participants, beneficiaries, and other interested persons such information regarding the provisions of this part and its applicability to the programs or activities conducted by the agency, and make such information available to them in such manner as the head of the agency finds necessary to apprise such persons of the protections against discrimination assured them by section 504 and this part.

§§ 1701.112–1701.129 [Reserved]

§ 1701.130 General prohibitions against discrimination.

(a) No qualified individual with handicaps shall, on the basis of handicap, be excluded from participation in, be denied the benefits of, or otherwise be subjected to discrimination under any program or activity conducted by the agency.

(b)(1) The agency, in providing any aid, benefit, or service, may not, directly or through contractual, licensing, or other arrangements, on the basis of handicap—

(i) Deny a qualified individual with handicaps the opportunity to participate in or benefit from the aid, benefit, or service;

(ii) Afford a qualified individual with handicaps an opportunity to participate in or benefit from the aid, benefit, or service that is not equal to that afforded others;

(iii) Provide a qualified individual with handicaps with an aid, benefit, or service that is not as effective in according equal opportunity to obtain the same result, to gain the same benefit, or to reach the same level of achievement as that provided to others;

(iv) Provide different or separate aid, benefits, or services to individuals with handicaps or to any class of individuals with handicaps than is provided to others unless such action is necessary to provide qualified individuals with handicaps with aid, benefits, or services that are as effective as those provided to others;

(v) Deny a qualified individual with handicaps the opportunity to participate as a member of planning or advisory boards;

(vi) Otherwise limit a qualified individual with handicaps in the enjoyment of any right, privilege, advantage, or opportunity enjoyed by others receiving the aid, benefit, or service.

(2) The agency may not deny a qualified individual with handicaps the opportunity to participate in programs or activities that are no separate or different, despite the existence of permissibly separate or different programs or activities.

(3) The agency may not, directly or through contractual or other arrangements, utilize criteria or methods of administration the purpose or effect of which would—

(i) Subject qualified individuals with handicaps to discrimination on the basis of handicap; or

(ii) Defeat or substantially impair accomplishment of the objectives of a program or activity with respect to individuals with handicaps.

(4) The agency may not, in determining the site or location of a facility, make selections the purpose or effect of which would—

(i) Exclude individuals with handicaps from, deny them the benefits of, or otherwise subject them to discrimination under any program or activity conducted by the agency; or

(ii) Defeat or substantially impair the accomplishment of the objectives of a program or activity with respect to individuals with handicaps.

(5) The agency, in the selection of procurement contractors, may not use

criteria that subject qualified individuals with handicaps to discrimination on the basis of handicap.

(6) The agency may not administer a licensing or certification program in a manner that subjects qualified individuals with handicaps to discrimination on the basis of handicap, nor may the agency establish requirements for the programs or activities of licensees or certified entities that subject qualified individuals with handicaps to discrimination on the basis of handicap. However, the programs or activities of entities that are licensed or certified by the agency are not, themselves, covered by this part.

(c) The exclusion of nonhandicapped persons from the benefits of a program limited by Federal statute or Executive order to individuals with handicaps or the exclusion of a specific class of individuals with handicaps from a program limited by Federal statute or Executive order to a different class of individuals with handicaps is not prohibited by this part.

(d) The agency shall administer programs and activities in the most integrated setting appropriate to the needs of qualified individuals with handicaps.

§§ 1701.131–1701.139 [Reserved]

§ 1701.140 Employment.

No qualified individual with handicaps shall, on the basis of handicap, be subjected to discrimination in employment under any program or activity conducted by the agency. The definitions, requirements, and procedures of section 501 of the Rehabilitation Act of 1973 (29 U.S.C. 791), as established by the Equal Employment Opportunity Commission in 29 CFR part 1614, shall apply to employment in federally conducted programs or activities.

§§ 1701.141–1701.148 [Reserved]

§ 1701.149 Program accessibility: Discrimination prohibited.

Except as otherwise provided in § 1701.150, no qualified individual with handicaps shall, because the agency's facilities are inaccessible to or unusable by individuals with handicaps, be denied the benefits of, be excluded from participation in, or otherwise be subjected to discrimination under any program or activity conducted by the agency.

§ 1701.150 Program accessibility: Existing facilities.

(a) *General.* The agency shall operate each program or activity so that the program or activity, when viewed in its entirety, is readily accessible to and usable by individuals with handicaps. This paragraph does not—

(1) Necessarily require the agency to make each of its existing facilities accessible to and usable by individuals with handicaps;

(2) In the case of historic preservation programs, require the agency to take any action that would result in a substantial impairment of significant historic features of an historic property; or

(3) Require the agency to take any action that it can demonstrate would result in a fundamental alteration in the nature of a program or activity or in undue financial and administrative burdens. In those circumstances where agency personnel believe that the proposed action would fundamentally alter the program or activity or would result in undue financial and administrative burdens, the agency has the burden of proving that compliance with § 1701.150(a) would result in such alteration or burdens. The decision that compliance would result in such alteration or burdens must be made by the agency head or his or her designee after considering all agency resources available for use in the funding and operation of the conducted program or activity, and must be accompanied by a written statement of the reasons for reaching that conclusion. If an action would result in such an alteration or such burdens, the agency shall take any other action that result in such an alteration or such burdens but would nevertheless ensure that individuals with handicaps receive the benefits and services of the program or activity.

(b) *Methods*—(1) *General.* The agency may comply with the requirements of this section through such means as redesign of equipment, reassignment of services to accessible buildings, assignment of aides to beneficiaries, home visits, delivery of services at alternate accessible sites, alteration of existing facilities and construction of new facilities, use of accessible rolling stock, or any other methods that result in making its programs or activities readily accessible to and usable by individuals with handicaps. The agency is not required to make structural changes in existing facilities where other methods are effective in achieving compliance with this section. The agency, in making alterations to existing buildings, shall meet accessibility requirements to the extent compelled by the Architectural Barriers Act of 1968, as amended (42 U.S.C. 4151–4157), and any regulations implementing it. In choosing among available methods for meeting the requirements of this section, the agency shall give priority to those methods that offer programs and activities to qualified individuals with handicaps in the most integrated setting appropriate.

(2) *Historic preservation programs.* In meeting the requirements of § 1701.150(a) in historic preservation programs, the agency shall give priority to methods that provide physical access to individuals with handicaps. In cases where a physical alteration to an historic property is not required because of § 1701.150(a)(2) or (a)(3), alternative methods of achieving program accessibility include—

(i) Using audio-visual materials and devices to depict those portions of an historic property that cannot otherwise be made accessible;

(ii) Assigning persons to guide individuals with handicaps into or through portions of historic properties that cannot otherwise be made accessible; or

(iii) Adopting other innovative methods.

(c) *Time period for compliance.* The agency shall comply with the obligations established under this section by January 24, 1994, except that where structural changes in facilities are undertaken, such changes shall be made by November 26, 1996, but in any event as expeditiously as possible.

(d) *Transition plan.* In the event that structural changes to facilities will be undertaken to achieve program accessibility, the agency shall develop, by May 26, 1994, a transition plan setting forth the steps necessary to complete such changes. The agency shall provide an opportunity to interested persons, including individuals with handicaps or organizations representing individuals with handicaps, to participate in the development of the transition plan by submitting comments (both oral and written). A copy of the transition plan shall be made available for public inspection. The plan shall, at a minimum—

(1) Identify physical obstacles in the agency's facilities that limit the accessibility of its programs or activities to individuals with handicaps;

(2) Describe in detail the methods that will be used to make the facilities accessible;

(3) Specify the schedule for taking the steps necessary to achieve compliance with this section and, if the time period of the transition plan is longer than one year, identify steps that will be taken during each year of the transition period; and

(4) Indicate the official responsible for implementation of the plan.

§ 1701.151 Program accessibility: New construction and alterations.

Each building or part of a building that is constructed or altered by, on behalf of, or for the use of the agency shall be designed, constructed, or altered so as to be readily accessible to and usable by individuals with handicaps. The definitions, requirements, and standards of the Architectural Barriers Act (42 U.S.C. 4151–4157), as established in 41 CFR 101–19.600 to 101–19.607, apply to buildings covered by this section.

§§ 1701.152–1701.159 [Reserved]

§ 1701.160 Communications.

(a) The agency shall take appropriate steps to ensure effective communication with applicants, participants, personnel of other Federal entities, and members of the public.

(1) The agency shall furnish appropriate auxiliary aids where necessary to afford an individual with handicaps an equal opportunity to participate in, and enjoy the benefits of, a program or activity conducted by the agency.

(i) In determining what type of auxiliary aid is necessary, the agency shall give primary consideration to the requests of the individual with handicaps.

(ii) The agency need not provide individually prescribed devices, readers for personal use or study, or other devices of a personal nature.

(2) Where the agency communicates with applicants and beneficiaries by telephone, telecommunication devices for deaf persons (TDD's) or equally effective telecommunication systems shall be used to communicate with persons with impaired hearing.

(b) The agency shall ensure that interested persons, including persons with impaired vision or hearing, can obtain information as to the existence and location of accessible services, activities, and facilities.

(c) The agency shall provide signage at a primary entrance to each of its inaccessible facilities, directing users to a location at which they can obtain information about accessible facilities. The international symbol for accessibility shall be used at each primary entrance of an accessible facility.

(d) This section does not require the agency to take any action that it can demonstrate would result in a fundamental alteration in the nature of a program or activity or in undue financial and administrative burdens. In those circumstances where agency personnel believe that the proposed action would fundamentally alter the program or activity or would result in undue financial and administrative burdens, the agency has the burden of proving that compliance with § 1701.160 would result in such alteration or burdens. The decision that compliance would result in such alteration or burdens must be made by the agency head or his or her designee after considering all agency resources available for use in the funding and operation of the conducted program or activity and must be accompanied by a written statement of the reasons for reaching that conclusion. If an action required to comply with this section would result in such an alteration or such burdens, the agency shall take any other action that would not result in such an alteration or such burdens but would nevertheless ensure that, to the maximum extent possible, individuals with handicaps receive the benefits and services of the program or activity.

§§ 1701.161–1701.169 [Reserved]

§ 1701.170 Compliance procedures.

(a) Except as provided in paragraph (b) of this section, this section applies to all allegations of discrimination on the basis of handicap in programs and activities conducted by the agency.

(b) The agency shall process complaints alleging violations of section 504 with respect to employment according to the procedures established by the Equal Employment Opportunity Commission in 29 CFR part 1614 pursuant to section 501 of the Rehabilitation Act of 1973 (29 U.S.C. 791).

(c) The Director for Administration, United States Institute of Peace, shall be responsible for coordinating implementation of this section. Complaints may be sent to Director of Administration at the following address: 1550 M Street, NW., suite 700, Washington, DC 20005.

(d) The agency shall accept and investigate all complete complaints for which it has jurisdiction. All complete complaints must be filed within 180 days of the alleged act of discrimination. The agency may extend this time period for good cause.

(e) If the agency receives a complaint over which it does not have jurisdiction, it shall promptly notify the complainant and shall make reasonable efforts to refer the complaint to the appropriate Government entity.

(f) The agency shall notify the Architectural and Transportation Barriers Compliance Board upon receipt of any complaint alleging that a building or facility that is subject to the Architectural Barriers Act of 1968, as amended (42 U.S.C. 4151–4157), is not readily accessible to and usable by individuals with handicaps.

(g) Within 180 days of the receipt of a complete complaint for which it has jurisdiction, the agency shall notify the complainant of the results of the investigation in a letter containing—

(1) Findings of fact and conclusions of law;

(2) A description of a remedy for each violation found; and

(3) A notice of the right to appeal.

(h) Appeals of the findings of fact and conclusions of law or remedies must be filed by the complainant within 90 days of receipt from the agency of the letter required by § 1701.170(g). The agency may extend this time for good cause.

(i) Timely appeals shall be accepted and processed by the head of the agency.

(j) The head of the agency shall notify the complainant of the results of the appeal within 60 days of the receipt of the request. If the head of the agency determines that additional information is needed from the complainant, he or she shall have 60 days from the date of receipt of the additional information to make his or her determination on the appeal.

(k) The time limits cited in paragraphs (g) and (j) of this section may be extended with the permission of the Assistant Attorney General.

(l) The agency may delegate its authority for conducting complaint investigations to other Federal agencies, except that the authority for making the final determination may not be delegated to another agency.

[58 FR 57697, 57699, Oct. 26, 1993, as amended at 58 FR 57697, Oct. 26, 1993]

§§ 1701.171–1701.999 [Reserved]

PARTS 1702–1799 [RESERVED]

FINDING AIDS

A list of CFR titles, subtitles, chapters, subchapters and parts and an alphabetical list of agencies publishing in the CFR are included in the CFR Index and Finding Aids volume to the Code of Federal Regulations which is published separately and revised annually.

Table of CFR Titles and Chapters

(Revised as of April 1, 2019)

Title 1—General Provisions

I Administrative Committee of the Federal Register (Parts 1—49)
II Office of the Federal Register (Parts 50—299)
III Administrative Conference of the United States (Parts 300—399)
IV Miscellaneous Agencies (Parts 400—599)
VI National Capital Planning Commission (Parts 600—699)

Title 2—Grants and Agreements

SUBTITLE A—OFFICE OF MANAGEMENT AND BUDGET GUIDANCE FOR GRANTS AND AGREEMENTS

I Office of Management and Budget Governmentwide Guidance for Grants and Agreements (Parts 2—199)
II Office of Management and Budget Guidance (Parts 200—299)

SUBTITLE B—FEDERAL AGENCY REGULATIONS FOR GRANTS AND AGREEMENTS

III Department of Health and Human Services (Parts 300—399)
IV Department of Agriculture (Parts 400—499)
VI Department of State (Parts 600—699)
VII Agency for International Development (Parts 700—799)
VIII Department of Veterans Affairs (Parts 800—899)
IX Department of Energy (Parts 900—999)
X Department of the Treasury (Parts 1000—1099)
XI Department of Defense (Parts 1100—1199)
XII Department of Transportation (Parts 1200—1299)
XIII Department of Commerce (Parts 1300—1399)
XIV Department of the Interior (Parts 1400—1499)
XV Environmental Protection Agency (Parts 1500—1599)
XVIII National Aeronautics and Space Administration (Parts 1800—1899)
XX United States Nuclear Regulatory Commission (Parts 2000—2099)
XXII Corporation for National and Community Service (Parts 2200—2299)
XXIII Social Security Administration (Parts 2300—2399)
XXIV Department of Housing and Urban Development (Parts 2400—2499)
XXV National Science Foundation (Parts 2500—2599)
XXVI National Archives and Records Administration (Parts 2600—2699)

Title 2—Grants and Agreements—Continued

Chap.	
XXVII	Small Business Administration (Parts 2700—2799)
XXVIII	Department of Justice (Parts 2800—2899)
XXIX	Department of Labor (Parts 2900—2999)
XXX	Department of Homeland Security (Parts 3000—3099)
XXXI	Institute of Museum and Library Services (Parts 3100—3199)
XXXII	National Endowment for the Arts (Parts 3200—3299)
XXXIII	National Endowment for the Humanities (Parts 3300—3399)
XXXIV	Department of Education (Parts 3400—3499)
XXXV	Export-Import Bank of the United States (Parts 3500—3599)
XXXVI	Office of National Drug Control Policy, Executive Office of the President (Parts 3600—3699)
XXXVII	Peace Corps (Parts 3700—3799)
LVIII	Election Assistance Commission (Parts 5800—5899)
LIX	Gulf Coast Ecosystem Restoration Council (Parts 5900—5999)

Title 3—The President

I	Executive Office of the President (Parts 100—199)

Title 4—Accounts

I	Government Accountability Office (Parts 1—199)

Title 5—Administrative Personnel

I	Office of Personnel Management (Parts 1—1199)
II	Merit Systems Protection Board (Parts 1200—1299)
III	Office of Management and Budget (Parts 1300—1399)
IV	Office of Personnel Management and Office of the Director of National Intelligence (Parts 1400—1499)
V	The International Organizations Employees Loyalty Board (Parts 1500—1599)
VI	Federal Retirement Thrift Investment Board (Parts 1600—1699)
VIII	Office of Special Counsel (Parts 1800—1899)
IX	Appalachian Regional Commission (Parts 1900—1999)
XI	Armed Forces Retirement Home (Parts 2100—2199)
XIV	Federal Labor Relations Authority, General Counsel of the Federal Labor Relations Authority and Federal Service Impasses Panel (Parts 2400—2499)
XVI	Office of Government Ethics (Parts 2600—2699)
XXI	Department of the Treasury (Parts 3100—3199)
XXII	Federal Deposit Insurance Corporation (Parts 3200—3299)
XXIII	Department of Energy (Parts 3300—3399)
XXIV	Federal Energy Regulatory Commission (Parts 3400—3499)
XXV	Department of the Interior (Parts 3500—3599)
XXVI	Department of Defense (Parts 3600—3699)

Title 5—Administrative Personnel—Continued

Chap.	
LXXIV	Federal Mine Safety and Health Review Commission (Parts 8400—8499)
LXXVI	Federal Retirement Thrift Investment Board (Parts 8600—8699)
LXXVII	Office of Management and Budget (Parts 8700—8799)
LXXX	Federal Housing Finance Agency (Parts 9000—9099)
LXXXIII	Special Inspector General for Afghanistan Reconstruction (Parts 9300—9399)
LXXXIV	Bureau of Consumer Financial Protection (Parts 9400—9499)
LXXXVI	National Credit Union Administration (Parts 9600—9699)
XCVII	Department of Homeland Security Human Resources Management System (Department of Homeland Security—Office of Personnel Management) (Parts 9700—9799)
XCVIII	Council of the Inspectors General on Integrity and Efficiency (Parts 9800—9899)
XCIX	Military Compensation and Retirement Modernization Commission (Parts 9900—9999)
C	National Council on Disability (Parts 10000—10049)
CI	National Mediation Board (Part 10101)

Title 6—Domestic Security

I	Department of Homeland Security, Office of the Secretary (Parts 1—199)
X	Privacy and Civil Liberties Oversight Board (Parts 1000—1099)

Title 7—Agriculture

	SUBTITLE A—OFFICE OF THE SECRETARY OF AGRICULTURE (PARTS 0—26)
	SUBTITLE B—REGULATIONS OF THE DEPARTMENT OF AGRICULTURE
I	Agricultural Marketing Service (Standards, Inspections, Marketing Practices), Department of Agriculture (Parts 27—209)
II	Food and Nutrition Service, Department of Agriculture (Parts 210—299)
III	Animal and Plant Health Inspection Service, Department of Agriculture (Parts 300—399)
IV	Federal Crop Insurance Corporation, Department of Agriculture (Parts 400—499)
V	Agricultural Research Service, Department of Agriculture (Parts 500—599)
VI	Natural Resources Conservation Service, Department of Agriculture (Parts 600—699)
VII	Farm Service Agency, Department of Agriculture (Parts 700—799)
VIII	Grain Inspection, Packers and Stockyards Administration (Federal Grain Inspection Service), Department of Agriculture (Parts 800—899)

Chap.	
IX	Agricultural Marketing Service (Marketing Agreements and Orders; Fruits, Vegetables, Nuts), Department of Agriculture (Parts 900—999)
X	Agricultural Marketing Service (Marketing Agreements and Orders; Milk), Department of Agriculture (Parts 1000—1199)
XI	Agricultural Marketing Service (Marketing Agreements and Orders; Miscellaneous Commodities), Department of Agriculture (Parts 1200—1299)
XIV	Commodity Credit Corporation, Department of Agriculture (Parts 1400—1499)
XV	Foreign Agricultural Service, Department of Agriculture (Parts 1500—1599)
XVI	Rural Telephone Bank, Department of Agriculture (Parts 1600—1699)
XVII	Rural Utilities Service, Department of Agriculture (Parts 1700—1799)
XVIII	Rural Housing Service, Rural Business-Cooperative Service, Rural Utilities Service, and Farm Service Agency, Department of Agriculture (Parts 1800—2099)
XX	Local Television Loan Guarantee Board (Parts 2200—2299)
XXV	Office of Advocacy and Outreach, Department of Agriculture (Parts 2500—2599)
XXVI	Office of Inspector General, Department of Agriculture (Parts 2600—2699)
XXVII	Office of Information Resources Management, Department of Agriculture (Parts 2700—2799)
XXVIII	Office of Operations, Department of Agriculture (Parts 2800—2899)
XXIX	Office of Energy Policy and New Uses, Department of Agriculture (Parts 2900—2999)
XXX	Office of the Chief Financial Officer, Department of Agriculture (Parts 3000—3099)
XXXI	Office of Environmental Quality, Department of Agriculture (Parts 3100—3199)
XXXII	Office of Procurement and Property Management, Department of Agriculture (Parts 3200—3299)
XXXIII	Office of Transportation, Department of Agriculture (Parts 3300—3399)
XXXIV	National Institute of Food and Agriculture (Parts 3400—3499)
XXXV	Rural Housing Service, Department of Agriculture (Parts 3500—3599)
XXXVI	National Agricultural Statistics Service, Department of Agriculture (Parts 3600—3699)
XXXVII	Economic Research Service, Department of Agriculture (Parts 3700—3799)
XXXVIII	World Agricultural Outlook Board, Department of Agriculture (Parts 3800—3899)
XLI	[Reserved]
XLII	Rural Business-Cooperative Service and Rural Utilities Service, Department of Agriculture (Parts 4200—4299)

Title 8—Aliens and Nationality

Chap.

I Department of Homeland Security (Immigration and Naturalization) (Parts 1—499)

V Executive Office for Immigration Review, Department of Justice (Parts 1000—1399)

Title 9—Animals and Animal Products

I Animal and Plant Health Inspection Service, Department of Agriculture (Parts 1—199)

II Grain Inspection, Packers and Stockyards Administration (Packers and Stockyards Programs), Department of Agriculture (Parts 200—299)

III Food Safety and Inspection Service, Department of Agriculture (Parts 300—599)

Title 10—Energy

I Nuclear Regulatory Commission (Parts 0—199)

II Department of Energy (Parts 200—699)

III Department of Energy (Parts 700—999)

X Department of Energy (General Provisions) (Parts 1000—1099)

XIII Nuclear Waste Technical Review Board (Parts 1300—1399)

XVII Defense Nuclear Facilities Safety Board (Parts 1700—1799)

XVIII Northeast Interstate Low-Level Radioactive Waste Commission (Parts 1800—1899)

Title 11—Federal Elections

I Federal Election Commission (Parts 1—9099)

II Election Assistance Commission (Parts 9400—9499)

Title 12—Banks and Banking

I Comptroller of the Currency, Department of the Treasury (Parts 1—199)

II Federal Reserve System (Parts 200—299)

III Federal Deposit Insurance Corporation (Parts 300—399)

IV Export-Import Bank of the United States (Parts 400—499)

V (Parts 500—599) [Reserved]

VI Farm Credit Administration (Parts 600—699)

VII National Credit Union Administration (Parts 700—799)

VIII Federal Financing Bank (Parts 800—899)

IX Federal Housing Finance Board (Parts 900—999)

X Bureau of Consumer Financial Protection (Parts 1000—1099)

XI Federal Financial Institutions Examination Council (Parts 1100—1199)

XII Federal Housing Finance Agency (Parts 1200—1299)

XIII Financial Stability Oversight Council (Parts 1300—1399)

Title 12—Banks and Banking—Continued

Chap.	
XIV	Farm Credit System Insurance Corporation (Parts 1400—1499)
XV	Department of the Treasury (Parts 1500—1599)
XVI	Office of Financial Research (Parts 1600—1699)
XVII	Office of Federal Housing Enterprise Oversight, Department of Housing and Urban Development (Parts 1700—1799)
XVIII	Community Development Financial Institutions Fund, Department of the Treasury (Parts 1800—1899)

Title 13—Business Credit and Assistance

I	Small Business Administration (Parts 1—199)
III	Economic Development Administration, Department of Commerce (Parts 300—399)
IV	Emergency Steel Guarantee Loan Board (Parts 400—499)
V	Emergency Oil and Gas Guaranteed Loan Board (Parts 500—599)

Title 14—Aeronautics and Space

I	Federal Aviation Administration, Department of Transportation (Parts 1—199)
II	Office of the Secretary, Department of Transportation (Aviation Proceedings) (Parts 200—399)
III	Commercial Space Transportation, Federal Aviation Administration, Department of Transportation (Parts 400—1199)
V	National Aeronautics and Space Administration (Parts 1200—1299)
VI	Air Transportation System Stabilization (Parts 1300—1399)

Title 15—Commerce and Foreign Trade

	SUBTITLE A—OFFICE OF THE SECRETARY OF COMMERCE (PARTS 0—29)
	SUBTITLE B—REGULATIONS RELATING TO COMMERCE AND FOREIGN TRADE
I	Bureau of the Census, Department of Commerce (Parts 30—199)
II	National Institute of Standards and Technology, Department of Commerce (Parts 200—299)
III	International Trade Administration, Department of Commerce (Parts 300—399)
IV	Foreign-Trade Zones Board, Department of Commerce (Parts 400—499)
VII	Bureau of Industry and Security, Department of Commerce (Parts 700—799)
VIII	Bureau of Economic Analysis, Department of Commerce (Parts 800—899)
IX	National Oceanic and Atmospheric Administration, Department of Commerce (Parts 900—999)
XI	National Technical Information Service, Department of Commerce (Parts 1100—1199)

Chap.

XIII East-West Foreign Trade Board (Parts 1300—1399)

XIV Minority Business Development Agency (Parts 1400—1499)

SUBTITLE C—REGULATIONS RELATING TO FOREIGN TRADE AGREEMENTS

XX Office of the United States Trade Representative (Parts 2000—2099)

SUBTITLE D—REGULATIONS RELATING TO TELECOMMUNICATIONS AND INFORMATION

XXIII National Telecommunications and Information Administration, Department of Commerce (Parts 2300—2399) [Reserved]

Title 16—Commercial Practices

I Federal Trade Commission (Parts 0—999)

II Consumer Product Safety Commission (Parts 1000—1799)

Title 17—Commodity and Securities Exchanges

I Commodity Futures Trading Commission (Parts 1—199)

II Securities and Exchange Commission (Parts 200—399)

IV Department of the Treasury (Parts 400—499)

Title 18—Conservation of Power and Water Resources

I Federal Energy Regulatory Commission, Department of Energy (Parts 1—399)

III Delaware River Basin Commission (Parts 400—499)

VI Water Resources Council (Parts 700—799)

VIII Susquehanna River Basin Commission (Parts 800—899)

XIII Tennessee Valley Authority (Parts 1300—1399)

Title 19—Customs Duties

I U.S. Customs and Border Protection, Department of Homeland Security; Department of the Treasury (Parts 0—199)

II United States International Trade Commission (Parts 200—299)

III International Trade Administration, Department of Commerce (Parts 300—399)

IV U.S. Immigration and Customs Enforcement, Department of Homeland Security (Parts 400—599) [Reserved]

Title 20—Employees' Benefits

I Office of Workers' Compensation Programs, Department of Labor (Parts 1—199)

II Railroad Retirement Board (Parts 200—399)

III Social Security Administration (Parts 400—499)

Title 20—Employees' Benefits—Continued

Chap.

IV	Employees' Compensation Appeals Board, Department of Labor (Parts 500—599)
V	Employment and Training Administration, Department of Labor (Parts 600—699)
VI	Office of Workers' Compensation Programs, Department of Labor (Parts 700—799)
VII	Benefits Review Board, Department of Labor (Parts 800—899)
VIII	Joint Board for the Enrollment of Actuaries (Parts 900—999)
IX	Office of the Assistant Secretary for Veterans' Employment and Training Service, Department of Labor (Parts 1000—1099)

Title 21—Food and Drugs

I	Food and Drug Administration, Department of Health and Human Services (Parts 1—1299)
II	Drug Enforcement Administration, Department of Justice (Parts 1300—1399)
III	Office of National Drug Control Policy (Parts 1400—1499)

Title 22—Foreign Relations

I	Department of State (Parts 1—199)
II	Agency for International Development (Parts 200—299)
III	Peace Corps (Parts 300—399)
IV	International Joint Commission, United States and Canada (Parts 400—499)
V	Broadcasting Board of Governors (Parts 500—599)
VII	Overseas Private Investment Corporation (Parts 700—799)
IX	Foreign Service Grievance Board (Parts 900—999)
X	Inter-American Foundation (Parts 1000—1099)
XI	International Boundary and Water Commission, United States and Mexico, United States Section (Parts 1100—1199)
XII	United States International Development Cooperation Agency (Parts 1200—1299)
XIII	Millennium Challenge Corporation (Parts 1300—1399)
XIV	Foreign Service Labor Relations Board; Federal Labor Relations Authority; General Counsel of the Federal Labor Relations Authority; and the Foreign Service Impasse Disputes Panel (Parts 1400—1499)
XV	African Development Foundation (Parts 1500—1599)
XVI	Japan-United States Friendship Commission (Parts 1600—1699)
XVII	United States Institute of Peace (Parts 1700—1799)

Title 23—Highways

I	Federal Highway Administration, Department of Transportation (Parts 1—999)

Title 23—Highways—Continued

Chap.

II National Highway Traffic Safety Administration and Federal Highway Administration, Department of Transportation (Parts 1200—1299)

III National Highway Traffic Safety Administration, Department of Transportation (Parts 1300—1399)

Title 24—Housing and Urban Development

SUBTITLE A—OFFICE OF THE SECRETARY, DEPARTMENT OF HOUSING AND URBAN DEVELOPMENT (PARTS 0—99)

SUBTITLE B—REGULATIONS RELATING TO HOUSING AND URBAN DEVELOPMENT

I Office of Assistant Secretary for Equal Opportunity, Department of Housing and Urban Development (Parts 100—199)

II Office of Assistant Secretary for Housing-Federal Housing Commissioner, Department of Housing and Urban Development (Parts 200—299)

III Government National Mortgage Association, Department of Housing and Urban Development (Parts 300—399)

IV Office of Housing and Office of Multifamily Housing Assistance Restructuring, Department of Housing and Urban Development (Parts 400—499)

V Office of Assistant Secretary for Community Planning and Development, Department of Housing and Urban Development (Parts 500—599)

VI Office of Assistant Secretary for Community Planning and Development, Department of Housing and Urban Development (Parts 600—699) [Reserved]

VII Office of the Secretary, Department of Housing and Urban Development (Housing Assistance Programs and Public and Indian Housing Programs) (Parts 700—799)

VIII Office of the Assistant Secretary for Housing—Federal Housing Commissioner, Department of Housing and Urban Development (Section 8 Housing Assistance Programs, Section 202 Direct Loan Program, Section 202 Supportive Housing for the Elderly Program and Section 811 Supportive Housing for Persons With Disabilities Program) (Parts 800—899)

IX Office of Assistant Secretary for Public and Indian Housing, Department of Housing and Urban Development (Parts 900—1699)

XII Office of Inspector General, Department of Housing and Urban Development (Parts 2000—2099)

XV Emergency Mortgage Insurance and Loan Programs, Department of Housing and Urban Development (Parts 2700—2799) [Reserved]

XX Office of Assistant Secretary for Housing—Federal Housing Commissioner, Department of Housing and Urban Development (Parts 3200—3899)

XXIV Board of Directors of the HOPE for Homeowners Program (Parts 4000—4099) [Reserved]

XXV Neighborhood Reinvestment Corporation (Parts 4100—4199)

Title 25—Indians

Chap.

I Bureau of Indian Affairs, Department of the Interior (Parts 1—299)

II Indian Arts and Crafts Board, Department of the Interior (Parts 300—399)

III National Indian Gaming Commission, Department of the Interior (Parts 500—599)

IV Office of Navajo and Hopi Indian Relocation (Parts 700—899)

V Bureau of Indian Affairs, Department of the Interior, and Indian Health Service, Department of Health and Human Services (Part 900—999)

VI Office of the Assistant Secretary, Indian Affairs, Department of the Interior (Parts 1000—1199)

VII Office of the Special Trustee for American Indians, Department of the Interior (Parts 1200—1299)

Title 26—Internal Revenue

I Internal Revenue Service, Department of the Treasury (Parts 1—End)

Title 27—Alcohol, Tobacco Products and Firearms

I Alcohol and Tobacco Tax and Trade Bureau, Department of the Treasury (Parts 1—399)

II Bureau of Alcohol, Tobacco, Firearms, and Explosives, Department of Justice (Parts 400—699)

Title 28—Judicial Administration

I Department of Justice (Parts 0—299)

III Federal Prison Industries, Inc., Department of Justice (Parts 300—399)

V Bureau of Prisons, Department of Justice (Parts 500—599)

VI Offices of Independent Counsel, Department of Justice (Parts 600—699)

VII Office of Independent Counsel (Parts 700—799)

VIII Court Services and Offender Supervision Agency for the District of Columbia (Parts 800—899)

IX National Crime Prevention and Privacy Compact Council (Parts 900—999)

XI Department of Justice and Department of State (Parts 1100—1199)

Title 29—Labor

SUBTITLE A—OFFICE OF THE SECRETARY OF LABOR (PARTS 0—99)

SUBTITLE B—REGULATIONS RELATING TO LABOR

I National Labor Relations Board (Parts 100—199)

Title 29—Labor—Continued

Chap.	
II	Office of Labor-Management Standards, Department of Labor (Parts 200—299)
III	National Railroad Adjustment Board (Parts 300—399)
IV	Office of Labor-Management Standards, Department of Labor (Parts 400—499)
V	Wage and Hour Division, Department of Labor (Parts 500—899)
IX	Construction Industry Collective Bargaining Commission (Parts 900—999)
X	National Mediation Board (Parts 1200—1299)
XII	Federal Mediation and Conciliation Service (Parts 1400—1499)
XIV	Equal Employment Opportunity Commission (Parts 1600—1699)
XVII	Occupational Safety and Health Administration, Department of Labor (Parts 1900—1999)
XX	Occupational Safety and Health Review Commission (Parts 2200—2499)
XXV	Employee Benefits Security Administration, Department of Labor (Parts 2500—2599)
XXVII	Federal Mine Safety and Health Review Commission (Parts 2700—2799)
XL	Pension Benefit Guaranty Corporation (Parts 4000—4999)

Title 30—Mineral Resources

I	Mine Safety and Health Administration, Department of Labor (Parts 1—199)
II	Bureau of Safety and Environmental Enforcement, Department of the Interior (Parts 200—299)
IV	Geological Survey, Department of the Interior (Parts 400—499)
V	Bureau of Ocean Energy Management, Department of the Interior (Parts 500—599)
VII	Office of Surface Mining Reclamation and Enforcement, Department of the Interior (Parts 700—999)
XII	Office of Natural Resources Revenue, Department of the Interior (Parts 1200—1299)

Title 31—Money and Finance: Treasury

	Subtitle A—Office of the Secretary of the Treasury (Parts 0—50)
	Subtitle B—Regulations Relating to Money and Finance
I	Monetary Offices, Department of the Treasury (Parts 51—199)
II	Fiscal Service, Department of the Treasury (Parts 200—399)
IV	Secret Service, Department of the Treasury (Parts 400—499)
V	Office of Foreign Assets Control, Department of the Treasury (Parts 500—599)
VI	Bureau of Engraving and Printing, Department of the Treasury (Parts 600—699)
VII	Federal Law Enforcement Training Center, Department of the Treasury (Parts 700—799)

Title 31—Money and Finance: Treasury—Continued

Chap.

VIII Office of Investment Security, Department of the Treasury (Parts 800—899)

IX Federal Claims Collection Standards (Department of the Treasury—Department of Justice) (Parts 900—999)

X Financial Crimes Enforcement Network, Department of the Treasury (Parts 1000—1099)

Title 32—National Defense

SUBTITLE A—DEPARTMENT OF DEFENSE

I Office of the Secretary of Defense (Parts 1—399)

V Department of the Army (Parts 400—699)

VI Department of the Navy (Parts 700—799)

VII Department of the Air Force (Parts 800—1099)

SUBTITLE B—OTHER REGULATIONS RELATING TO NATIONAL DEFENSE

XII Defense Logistics Agency (Parts 1200—1299)

XVI Selective Service System (Parts 1600—1699)

XVII Office of the Director of National Intelligence (Parts 1700—1799)

XVIII National Counterintelligence Center (Parts 1800—1899)

XIX Central Intelligence Agency (Parts 1900—1999)

XX Information Security Oversight Office, National Archives and Records Administration (Parts 2000—2099)

XXI National Security Council (Parts 2100—2199)

XXIV Office of Science and Technology Policy (Parts 2400—2499)

XXVII Office for Micronesian Status Negotiations (Parts 2700—2799)

XXVIII Office of the Vice President of the United States (Parts 2800—2899)

Title 33—Navigation and Navigable Waters

I Coast Guard, Department of Homeland Security (Parts 1—199)

II Corps of Engineers, Department of the Army, Department of Defense (Parts 200—399)

IV Saint Lawrence Seaway Development Corporation, Department of Transportation (Parts 400—499)

Title 34—Education

SUBTITLE A—OFFICE OF THE SECRETARY, DEPARTMENT OF EDUCATION (PARTS 1—99)

SUBTITLE B—REGULATIONS OF THE OFFICES OF THE DEPARTMENT OF EDUCATION

I Office for Civil Rights, Department of Education (Parts 100—199)

II Office of Elementary and Secondary Education, Department of Education (Parts 200—299)

III Office of Special Education and Rehabilitative Services, Department of Education (Parts 300—399)

Title 34—Education—Continued

Chap.

IV Office of Career, Technical and Adult Education, Department of Education (Parts 400—499)

V Office of Bilingual Education and Minority Languages Affairs, Department of Education (Parts 500—599) [Reserved]

VI Office of Postsecondary Education, Department of Education (Parts 600—699)

VII Office of Educational Research and Improvement, Department of Education (Parts 700—799) [Reserved]

SUBTITLE C—REGULATIONS RELATING TO EDUCATION

XI (Parts 1100—1199) [Reserved]

XII National Council on Disability (Parts 1200—1299)

Title 35 [Reserved]

Title 36—Parks, Forests, and Public Property

I National Park Service, Department of the Interior (Parts 1—199)

II Forest Service, Department of Agriculture (Parts 200—299)

III Corps of Engineers, Department of the Army (Parts 300—399)

IV American Battle Monuments Commission (Parts 400—499)

V Smithsonian Institution (Parts 500—599)

VI [Reserved]

VII Library of Congress (Parts 700—799)

VIII Advisory Council on Historic Preservation (Parts 800—899)

IX Pennsylvania Avenue Development Corporation (Parts 900—999)

X Presidio Trust (Parts 1000—1099)

XI Architectural and Transportation Barriers Compliance Board (Parts 1100—1199)

XII National Archives and Records Administration (Parts 1200—1299)

XV Oklahoma City National Memorial Trust (Parts 1500—1599)

XVI Morris K. Udall Scholarship and Excellence in National Environmental Policy Foundation (Parts 1600—1699)

Title 37—Patents, Trademarks, and Copyrights

I United States Patent and Trademark Office, Department of Commerce (Parts 1—199)

II U.S. Copyright Office, Library of Congress (Parts 200—299)

III Copyright Royalty Board, Library of Congress (Parts 300—399)

IV National Institute of Standards and Technology, Department of Commerce (Parts 400—599)

Title 38—Pensions, Bonuses, and Veterans' Relief

I Department of Veterans Affairs (Parts 0—199)

II Armed Forces Retirement Home (Parts 200—299)

Title 39—Postal Service

Chap.

I United States Postal Service (Parts 1—999)

III Postal Regulatory Commission (Parts 3000—3099)

Title 40—Protection of Environment

I Environmental Protection Agency (Parts 1—1099)

IV Environmental Protection Agency and Department of Justice (Parts 1400—1499)

V Council on Environmental Quality (Parts 1500—1599)

VI Chemical Safety and Hazard Investigation Board (Parts 1600—1699)

VII Environmental Protection Agency and Department of Defense; Uniform National Discharge Standards for Vessels of the Armed Forces (Parts 1700—1799)

VIII Gulf Coast Ecosystem Restoration Council (Parts 1800—1899)

Title 41—Public Contracts and Property Management

SUBTITLE A—FEDERAL PROCUREMENT REGULATIONS SYSTEM [NOTE]

SUBTITLE B—OTHER PROVISIONS RELATING TO PUBLIC CONTRACTS

50 Public Contracts, Department of Labor (Parts 50–1—50–999)

51 Committee for Purchase From People Who Are Blind or Severely Disabled (Parts 51–1—51–99)

60 Office of Federal Contract Compliance Programs, Equal Employment Opportunity, Department of Labor (Parts 60–1—60–999)

61 Office of the Assistant Secretary for Veterans' Employment and Training Service, Department of Labor (Parts 61–1—61–999)

62—100 [Reserved]

SUBTITLE C—FEDERAL PROPERTY MANAGEMENT REGULATIONS SYSTEM

101 Federal Property Management Regulations (Parts 101–1—101–99)

102 Federal Management Regulation (Parts 102–1—102–299)

103—104 [Reserved]

105 General Services Administration (Parts 105–1—105–999)

109 Department of Energy Property Management Regulations (Parts 109–1—109–99)

114 Department of the Interior (Parts 114–1—114–99)

115 Environmental Protection Agency (Parts 115–1—115–99)

128 Department of Justice (Parts 128–1—128–99)

129—200 [Reserved]

SUBTITLE D—OTHER PROVISIONS RELATING TO PROPERTY MANAGEMENT [RESERVED]

SUBTITLE E—FEDERAL INFORMATION RESOURCES MANAGEMENT REGULATIONS SYSTEM [RESERVED]

SUBTITLE F—FEDERAL TRAVEL REGULATION SYSTEM

300 General (Parts 300–1—300–99)

301 Temporary Duty (TDY) Travel Allowances (Parts 301–1—301–99)

Title 41—Public Contracts and Property Management—Continued

Title 42—Public Health

Title 43—Public Lands: Interior

Title 44—Emergency Management and Assistance

Title 45—Public Welfare

Title 45—Public Welfare—Continued

Chap.

V Foreign Claims Settlement Commission of the United States, Department of Justice (Parts 500—599)

VI National Science Foundation (Parts 600—699)

VII Commission on Civil Rights (Parts 700—799)

VIII Office of Personnel Management (Parts 800—899)

IX Denali Commission (Parts 900—999)

X Office of Community Services, Administration for Children and Families, Department of Health and Human Services (Parts 1000—1099)

XI National Foundation on the Arts and the Humanities (Parts 1100—1199)

XII Corporation for National and Community Service (Parts 1200—1299)

XIII Administration for Children and Families, Department of Health and Human Services (Parts 1300—1399)

XVI Legal Services Corporation (Parts 1600—1699)

XVII National Commission on Libraries and Information Science (Parts 1700—1799)

XVIII Harry S. Truman Scholarship Foundation (Parts 1800—1899)

XXI Commission of Fine Arts (Parts 2100—2199)

XXIII Arctic Research Commission (Parts 2300—2399)

XXIV James Madison Memorial Fellowship Foundation (Parts 2400—2499)

XXV Corporation for National and Community Service (Parts 2500—2599)

Title 46—Shipping

I Coast Guard, Department of Homeland Security (Parts 1—199)

II Maritime Administration, Department of Transportation (Parts 200—399)

III Coast Guard (Great Lakes Pilotage), Department of Homeland Security (Parts 400—499)

IV Federal Maritime Commission (Parts 500—599)

Title 47—Telecommunication

I Federal Communications Commission (Parts 0—199)

II Office of Science and Technology Policy and National Security Council (Parts 200—299)

III National Telecommunications and Information Administration, Department of Commerce (Parts 300—399)

IV National Telecommunications and Information Administration, Department of Commerce, and National Highway Traffic Safety Administration, Department of Transportation (Parts 400—499)

V The First Responder Network Authority (Parts 500—599)

Title 48—Federal Acquisition Regulations System

Title 49—Transportation

Chap.

SUBTITLE A—OFFICE OF THE SECRETARY OF TRANSPORTATION (PARTS 1—99)

SUBTITLE B—OTHER REGULATIONS RELATING TO TRANSPORTATION

I Pipeline and Hazardous Materials Safety Administration, Department of Transportation (Parts 100—199)

II Federal Railroad Administration, Department of Transportation (Parts 200—299)

III Federal Motor Carrier Safety Administration, Department of Transportation (Parts 300—399)

IV Coast Guard, Department of Homeland Security (Parts 400—499)

V National Highway Traffic Safety Administration, Department of Transportation (Parts 500—599)

VI Federal Transit Administration, Department of Transportation (Parts 600—699)

VII National Railroad Passenger Corporation (AMTRAK) (Parts 700—799)

VIII National Transportation Safety Board (Parts 800—999)

X Surface Transportation Board (Parts 1000—1399)

XI Research and Innovative Technology Administration, Department of Transportation (Parts 1400—1499) [Reserved]

XII Transportation Security Administration, Department of Homeland Security (Parts 1500—1699)

Title 50—Wildlife and Fisheries

I United States Fish and Wildlife Service, Department of the Interior (Parts 1—199)

II National Marine Fisheries Service, National Oceanic and Atmospheric Administration, Department of Commerce (Parts 200—299)

III International Fishing and Related Activities (Parts 300—399)

IV Joint Regulations (United States Fish and Wildlife Service, Department of the Interior and National Marine Fisheries Service, National Oceanic and Atmospheric Administration, Department of Commerce); Endangered Species Committee Regulations (Parts 400—499)

V Marine Mammal Commission (Parts 500—599)

VI Fishery Conservation and Management, National Oceanic and Atmospheric Administration, Department of Commerce (Parts 600—699)

Alphabetical List of Agencies Appearing in the CFR

(Revised as of April 1, 2019)

Agency	CFR Title, Subtitle or Chapter
Administrative Conference of the United States	1, III
Advisory Council on Historic Preservation	36, VIII
Advocacy and Outreach, Office of	7, XXV
Afghanistan Reconstruction, Special Inspector General for	5, LXXXIII
African Development Foundation	22, XV
Federal Acquisition Regulation	48, 57
Agency for International Development	2, VII; 22, II
Federal Acquisition Regulation	48, 7
Agricultural Marketing Service	7, I, IX, X, XI
Agricultural Research Service	7, V
Agriculture, Department of	2, IV; 5, LXXIII
Advocacy and Outreach, Office of	7, XXV
Agricultural Marketing Service	7, I, IX, X, XI
Agricultural Research Service	7, V
Animal and Plant Health Inspection Service	7, III; 9, I
Chief Financial Officer, Office of	7, XXX
Commodity Credit Corporation	7, XIV
Economic Research Service	7, XXXVII
Energy Policy and New Uses, Office of	2, IX; 7, XXIX
Environmental Quality, Office of	7, XXXI
Farm Service Agency	7, VII, XVIII
Federal Acquisition Regulation	48, 4
Federal Crop Insurance Corporation	7, IV
Food and Nutrition Service	7, II
Food Safety and Inspection Service	9, III
Foreign Agricultural Service	7, XV
Forest Service	36, II
Grain Inspection, Packers and Stockyards Administration	7, VIII; 9, II
Information Resources Management, Office of	7, XXVII
Inspector General, Office of	7, XXVI
National Agricultural Library	7, XLI
National Agricultural Statistics Service	7, XXXVI
National Institute of Food and Agriculture	7, XXXIV
Natural Resources Conservation Service	7, VI
Operations, Office of	7, XXVIII
Procurement and Property Management, Office of	7, XXXII
Rural Business-Cooperative Service	7, XVIII, XLII
Rural Development Administration	7, XLII
Rural Housing Service	7, XVIII, XXXV
Rural Telephone Bank	7, XVI
Rural Utilities Service	7, XVII, XVIII, XLII
Secretary of Agriculture, Office of	7, Subtitle A
Transportation, Office of	7, XXXIII
World Agricultural Outlook Board	7, XXXVIII
Air Force, Department of	32, VII
Federal Acquisition Regulation Supplement	48, 53
Air Transportation Stabilization Board	14, VI
Alcohol and Tobacco Tax and Trade Bureau	27, I
Alcohol, Tobacco, Firearms, and Explosives, Bureau of	27, II
AMTRAK	49, VII
American Battle Monuments Commission	36, IV
American Indians, Office of the Special Trustee	25, VII
Animal and Plant Health Inspection Service	7, III; 9, I

Agency	CFR Title, Subtitle or Chapter
Appalachian Regional Commission	5, IX
Architectural and Transportation Barriers Compliance Board	36, XI
Arctic Research Commission	45, XXIII
Armed Forces Retirement Home	5, XI
Army, Department of	32, V
Engineers, Corps of	33, II; 36, III
Federal Acquisition Regulation	48, 51
Bilingual Education and Minority Languages Affairs, Office of	34, V
Blind or Severely Disabled, Committee for Purchase from People Who Are	41, 51
Broadcasting Board of Governors	22, V
Federal Acquisition Regulation	48, 19
Career, Technical, and Adult Education, Office of	34, IV
Census Bureau	15, I
Centers for Medicare & Medicaid Services	42, IV
Central Intelligence Agency	32, XIX
Chemical Safety and Hazardous Investigation Board	40, VI
Chief Financial Officer, Office of	7, XXX
Child Support Enforcement, Office of	45, III
Children and Families, Administration for	45, II, III, IV, X, XIII
Civil Rights, Commission on	5, LXVIII; 45, VII
Civil Rights, Office for	34, I
Council of the Inspectors General on Integrity and Efficiency	5, XCVIII
Court Services and Offender Supervision Agency for the District of Columbia	5, LXX
Coast Guard	33, I; 46, I; 49, IV
Coast Guard (Great Lakes Pilotage)	46, III
Commerce, Department of	2, XIII; 44, IV; 50, VI
Census Bureau	15, I
Economic Analysis, Bureau of	15, VIII
Economic Development Administration	13, III
Emergency Management and Assistance	44, IV
Federal Acquisition Regulation	48, 13
Foreign-Trade Zones Board	15, IV
Industry and Security, Bureau of	15, VII
International Trade Administration	15, III; 19, III
National Institute of Standards and Technology	15, II; 37, IV
National Marine Fisheries Service	50, II, IV
National Oceanic and Atmospheric Administration	15, IX; 50, II, III, IV, VI
National Technical Information Service	15, XI
National Telecommunications and Information Administration	15, XXIII; 47, III, IV
National Weather Service	15, IX
Patent and Trademark Office, United States	37, I
Secretary of Commerce, Office of	15, Subtitle A
Commercial Space Transportation	14, III
Commodity Credit Corporation	7, XIV
Commodity Futures Trading Commission	5, XLI; 17, I
Community Planning and Development, Office of Assistant Secretary for	24, V, VI
Community Services, Office of	45, X
Comptroller of the Currency	12, I
Construction Industry Collective Bargaining Commission	29, IX
Consumer Financial Protection Bureau	5, LXXXIV; 12, X
Consumer Product Safety Commission	5, LXXI; 16, II
Copyright Royalty Board	37, III
Corporation for National and Community Service	2, XXII; 45, XII, XXV
Cost Accounting Standards Board	48, 99
Council on Environmental Quality	40, V
Court Services and Offender Supervision Agency for the District of Columbia	5, LXX; 28, VIII
Customs and Border Protection	19, I
Defense Contract Audit Agency	32, I
Defense, Department of	2, XI; 5, XXVI; 32, Subtitle A; 40, VII
Advanced Research Projects Agency	32, I
Air Force Department	32, VII

Agency	CFR Title, Subtitle or Chapter
Army Department	32, V; 33, II; 36, III; 48, 51
Defense Acquisition Regulations System	48, 2
Defense Intelligence Agency	32, I
Defense Logistics Agency	32, I, XII; 48, 54
Engineers, Corps of	33, II; 36, III
National Imagery and Mapping Agency	32, I
Navy Department	32, VI; 48, 52
Secretary of Defense, Office of	2, XI; 32, I
Defense Contract Audit Agency	32, I
Defense Intelligence Agency	32, I
Defense Logistics Agency	32, XII; 48, 54
Defense Nuclear Facilities Safety Board	10, XVII
Delaware River Basin Commission	18, III
Denali Commission	45, IX
Disability, National Council on	5, C; 34, XII
District of Columbia, Court Services and Offender Supervision Agency for the	5, LXX; 28, VIII
Drug Enforcement Administration	21, II
East-West Foreign Trade Board	15, XIII
Economic Analysis, Bureau of	15, VIII
Economic Development Administration	13, III
Economic Research Service	7, XXXVII
Education, Department of	2, XXXIV; 5, LIII
Bilingual Education and Minority Languages Affairs, Office of	34, V
Career, Technical, and Adult Education, Office of	34, IV
Civil Rights, Office for	34, I
Educational Research and Improvement, Office of	34, VII
Elementary and Secondary Education, Office of	34, II
Federal Acquisition Regulation	48, 34
Postsecondary Education, Office of	34, VI
Secretary of Education, Office of	34, Subtitle A
Special Education and Rehabilitative Services, Office of	34, III
Educational Research and Improvement, Office of	34, VII
Election Assistance Commission	2, LVIII; 11, II
Elementary and Secondary Education, Office of	34, II
Emergency Oil and Gas Guaranteed Loan Board	13, V
Emergency Steel Guarantee Loan Board	13, IV
Employee Benefits Security Administration	29, XXV
Employees' Compensation Appeals Board	20, IV
Employees Loyalty Board	5, V
Employment and Training Administration	20, V
Employment Policy, National Commission for	1, IV
Employment Standards Administration	20, VI
Endangered Species Committee	50, IV
Energy, Department of	2, IX; 5, XXIII; 10, II, III, X
Federal Acquisition Regulation	48, 9
Federal Energy Regulatory Commission	5, XXIV; 18, I
Property Management Regulations	41, 109
Energy, Office of	7, XXIX
Engineers, Corps of	33, II; 36, III
Engraving and Printing, Bureau of	31, VI
Environmental Protection Agency	2, XV; 5, LIV; 40, I, IV, VII
Federal Acquisition Regulation	48, 15
Property Management Regulations	41, 115
Environmental Quality, Office of	7, XXXI
Equal Employment Opportunity Commission	5, LXII; 29, XIV
Equal Opportunity, Office of Assistant Secretary for	24, I
Executive Office of the President	3, I
Environmental Quality, Council on	40, V
Management and Budget, Office of	2, Subtitle A; 5, III, LXXVII; 14, VI; 48, 99
National Drug Control Policy, Office of	2, XXXVI; 21, III
National Security Council	32, XXI; 47, 2

Agency	CFR Title, Subtitle or Chapter
Presidential Documents	3
Science and Technology Policy, Office of	32, XXIV; 47, II
Trade Representative, Office of the United States	15, XX
Export-Import Bank of the United States	2, XXXV; 5, LII; 12, IV
Family Assistance, Office of	45, II
Farm Credit Administration	5, XXXI; 12, VI
Farm Credit System Insurance Corporation	5, XXX; 12, XIV
Farm Service Agency	7, VII, XVIII
Federal Acquisition Regulation	48, 1
Federal Aviation Administration	14, I
Commercial Space Transportation	14, III
Federal Claims Collection Standards	31, IX
Federal Communications Commission	5, XXIX; 47, I
Federal Contract Compliance Programs, Office of	41, 60
Federal Crop Insurance Corporation	7, IV
Federal Deposit Insurance Corporation	5, XXII; 12, III
Federal Election Commission	5, XXXVII; 11, I
Federal Emergency Management Agency	44, I
Federal Employees Group Life Insurance Federal Acquisition Regulation	48, 21
Federal Employees Health Benefits Acquisition Regulation	48, 16
Federal Energy Regulatory Commission	5, XXIV; 18, I
Federal Financial Institutions Examination Council	12, XI
Federal Financing Bank	12, VIII
Federal Highway Administration	23, I, II
Federal Home Loan Mortgage Corporation	1, IV
Federal Housing Enterprise Oversight Office	12, XVII
Federal Housing Finance Agency	5, LXXX; 12, XII
Federal Housing Finance Board	12, IX
Federal Labor Relations Authority	5, XIV, XLIX; 22, XIV
Federal Law Enforcement Training Center	31, VII
Federal Management Regulation	41, 102
Federal Maritime Commission	46, IV
Federal Mediation and Conciliation Service	29, XII
Federal Mine Safety and Health Review Commission	5, LXXIV; 29, XXVII
Federal Motor Carrier Safety Administration	49, III
Federal Prison Industries, Inc.	28, III
Federal Procurement Policy Office	48, 99
Federal Property Management Regulations	41, 101
Federal Railroad Administration	49, II
Federal Register, Administrative Committee of	1, I
Federal Register, Office of	1, II
Federal Reserve System	12, II
Board of Governors	5, LVIII
Federal Retirement Thrift Investment Board	5, VI, LXXVI
Federal Service Impasses Panel	5, XIV
Federal Trade Commission	5, XLVII; 16, I
Federal Transit Administration	49, VI
Federal Travel Regulation System	41, Subtitle F
Financial Crimes Enforcement Network	31, X
Financial Research Office	12, XVI
Financial Stability Oversight Council	12, XIII
Fine Arts, Commission of	45, XXI
Fiscal Service	31, II
Fish and Wildlife Service, United States	50, I, IV
Food and Drug Administration	21, I
Food and Nutrition Service	7, II
Food Safety and Inspection Service	9, III
Foreign Agricultural Service	7, XV
Foreign Assets Control, Office of	31, V
Foreign Claims Settlement Commission of the United States	45, V
Foreign Service Grievance Board	22, IX
Foreign Service Impasse Disputes Panel	22, XIV
Foreign Service Labor Relations Board	22, XIV
Foreign-Trade Zones Board	15, IV
Forest Service	36, II
General Services Administration	5, LVII; 41, 105

Agency	CFR Title, Subtitle or Chapter
Contract Appeals, Board of	48, 61
Federal Acquisition Regulation	48, 5
Federal Management Regulation	41, 102
Federal Property Management Regulations	41, 101
Federal Travel Regulation System	41, Subtitle F
General	41, 300
Payment From a Non-Federal Source for Travel Expenses	41, 304
Payment of Expenses Connected With the Death of Certain Employees	41, 303
Relocation Allowances	41, 302
Temporary Duty (TDY) Travel Allowances	41, 301
Geological Survey	30, IV
Government Accountability Office	4, I
Government Ethics, Office of	5, XVI
Government National Mortgage Association	24, III
Grain Inspection, Packers and Stockyards Administration	7, VIII; 9, II
Gulf Coast Ecosystem Restoration Council	2, LIX; 40, VIII
Harry S. Truman Scholarship Foundation	45, XVIII
Health and Human Services, Department of	2, III; 5, XLV; 45, Subtitle A
Centers for Medicare & Medicaid Services	42, IV
Child Support Enforcement, Office of	45, III
Children and Families, Administration for	45, II, III, IV, X, XIII
Community Services, Office of	45, X
Family Assistance, Office of	45, II
Federal Acquisition Regulation	48, 3
Food and Drug Administration	21, I
Indian Health Service	25, V
Inspector General (Health Care), Office of	42, V
Public Health Service	42, I
Refugee Resettlement, Office of	45, IV
Homeland Security, Department of	2, XXX; 5, XXXVI; 6, I; 8, I
Coast Guard	33, I; 46, I; 49, IV
Coast Guard (Great Lakes Pilotage)	46, III
Customs and Border Protection	19, I
Federal Emergency Management Agency	44, I
Human Resources Management and Labor Relations Systems	5, XCVII
Immigration and Customs Enforcement Bureau	19, IV
Transportation Security Administration	49, XII
HOPE for Homeowners Program, Board of Directors of	24, XXIV
Housing and Urban Development, Department of	2, XXIV; 5, LXV; 24, Subtitle B
Community Planning and Development, Office of Assistant Secretary for	24, V, VI
Equal Opportunity, Office of Assistant Secretary for	24, I
Federal Acquisition Regulation	48, 24
Federal Housing Enterprise Oversight, Office of	12, XVII
Government National Mortgage Association	24, III
Housing—Federal Housing Commissioner, Office of Assistant Secretary for	24, II, VIII, X, XX
Housing, Office of, and Multifamily Housing Assistance Restructuring, Office of	24, IV
Inspector General, Office of	24, XII
Public and Indian Housing, Office of Assistant Secretary for	24, IX
Secretary, Office of	24, Subtitle A, VII
Housing—Federal Housing Commissioner, Office of Assistant Secretary for	24, II, VIII, X, XX
Housing, Office of, and Multifamily Housing Assistance Restructuring, Office of	24, IV
Immigration and Customs Enforcement Bureau	19, IV
Immigration Review, Executive Office for	8, V
Independent Counsel, Office of	28, VII
Independent Counsel, Offices of	28, VI
Indian Affairs, Bureau of	25, I, V
Indian Affairs, Office of the Assistant Secretary	25, VI

Agency	CFR Title, Subtitle or Chapter
Indian Arts and Crafts Board	25, II
Indian Health Service	25, V
Industry and Security, Bureau of	15, VII
Information Resources Management, Office of	7, XXVII
Information Security Oversight Office, National Archives and Records Administration	32, XX
Inspector General	
Agriculture Department	7, XXVI
Health and Human Services Department	42, V
Housing and Urban Development Department	24, XII, XV
Institute of Peace, United States	22, XVII
Inter-American Foundation	5, LXIII; 22, X
Interior, Department of	2, XIV
American Indians, Office of the Special Trustee	25, VII
Endangered Species Committee	50, IV
Federal Acquisition Regulation	48, 14
Federal Property Management Regulations System	41, 114
Fish and Wildlife Service, United States	50, I, IV
Geological Survey	30, IV
Indian Affairs, Bureau of	25, I, V
Indian Affairs, Office of the Assistant Secretary	25, VI
Indian Arts and Crafts Board	25, II
Land Management, Bureau of	43, II
National Indian Gaming Commission	25, III
National Park Service	36, I
Natural Resource Revenue, Office of	30, XII
Ocean Energy Management, Bureau of	30, V
Reclamation, Bureau of	43, I
Safety and Enforcement Bureau, Bureau of	30, II
Secretary of the Interior, Office of	2, XIV; 43, Subtitle A
Surface Mining Reclamation and Enforcement, Office of	30, VII
Internal Revenue Service	26, I
International Boundary and Water Commission, United States and Mexico, United States Section	22, XI
International Development, United States Agency for	22, II
Federal Acquisition Regulation	48, 7
International Development Cooperation Agency, United States	22, XII
International Joint Commission, United States and Canada	22, IV
International Organizations Employees Loyalty Board	5, V
International Trade Administration	15, III; 19, III
International Trade Commission, United States	19, II
Interstate Commerce Commission	5, XL
Investment Security, Office of	31, VIII
James Madison Memorial Fellowship Foundation	45, XXIV
Japan–United States Friendship Commission	22, XVI
Joint Board for the Enrollment of Actuaries	20, VIII
Justice, Department of	2, XXVIII; 5, XXVIII; 28, I, XI; 40, IV
Alcohol, Tobacco, Firearms, and Explosives, Bureau of	27, II
Drug Enforcement Administration	21, II
Federal Acquisition Regulation	48, 28
Federal Claims Collection Standards	31, IX
Federal Prison Industries, Inc.	28, III
Foreign Claims Settlement Commission of the United States	45, V
Immigration Review, Executive Office for	8, V
Independent Counsel, Offices of	28, VI
Prisons, Bureau of	28, V
Property Management Regulations	41, 128
Labor, Department of	2, XXIX; 5, XLII
Employee Benefits Security Administration	29, XXV
Employees' Compensation Appeals Board	20, IV
Employment and Training Administration	20, V
Employment Standards Administration	20, VI
Federal Acquisition Regulation	48, 29
Federal Contract Compliance Programs, Office of	41, 60

Agency	CFR Title, Subtitle or Chapter
Federal Procurement Regulations System	41, 50
Labor-Management Standards, Office of	29, II, IV
Mine Safety and Health Administration	30, I
Occupational Safety and Health Administration	29, XVII
Public Contracts	41, 50
Secretary of Labor, Office of	29, Subtitle A
Veterans' Employment and Training Service, Office of the Assistant Secretary for	41, 61; 20, IX
Wage and Hour Division	29, V
Workers' Compensation Programs, Office of	20, I, VII
Labor-Management Standards, Office of	29, II, IV
Land Management, Bureau of	43, II
Legal Services Corporation	45, XVI
Libraries and Information Science, National Commission on	45, XVII
Library of Congress	36, VII
Copyright Royalty Board	37, III
U.S. Copyright Office	37, II
Local Television Loan Guarantee Board	7, XX
Management and Budget, Office of	5, III, LXXVII; 14, VI; 48, 99
Marine Mammal Commission	50, V
Maritime Administration	46, II
Merit Systems Protection Board	5, II, LXIV
Micronesian Status Negotiations, Office for	32, XXVII
Military Compensation and Retirement Modernization Commission	5, XCIX
Millennium Challenge Corporation	22, XIII
Mine Safety and Health Administration	30, I
Minority Business Development Agency	15, XIV
Miscellaneous Agencies	1, IV
Monetary Offices	31, I
Morris K. Udall Scholarship and Excellence in National Environmental Policy Foundation	36, XVI
Museum and Library Services, Institute of	2, XXXI
National Aeronautics and Space Administration	2, XVIII; 5, LIX; 14, V
Federal Acquisition Regulation	48, 18
National Agricultural Library	7, XLI
National Agricultural Statistics Service	7, XXXVI
National and Community Service, Corporation for	2, XXII; 45, XII, XXV
National Archives and Records Administration	2, XXVI; 5, LXVI; 36, XII
Information Security Oversight Office	32, XX
National Capital Planning Commission	1, IV, VI
National Counterintelligence Center	32, XVIII
National Credit Union Administration	5, LXXXVI; 12, VII
National Crime Prevention and Privacy Compact Council	28, IX
National Drug Control Policy, Office of	2, XXXVI; 21, III
National Endowment for the Arts	2, XXXII
National Endowment for the Humanities	2, XXXIII
National Foundation on the Arts and the Humanities	45, XI
National Geospatial-Intelligence Agency	32, I
National Highway Traffic Safety Administration	23, II, III; 47, VI; 49, V
National Imagery and Mapping Agency	32, I
National Indian Gaming Commission	25, III
National Institute of Food and Agriculture	7, XXXIV
National Institute of Standards and Technology	15, II; 37, IV
National Intelligence, Office of Director of	5, IV; 32, XVII
National Labor Relations Board	5, LXI; 29, I
National Marine Fisheries Service	50, II, IV
National Mediation Board	5, CI; 29, X
National Oceanic and Atmospheric Administration	15, IX; 50, II, III, IV, VI
National Park Service	36, I
National Railroad Adjustment Board	29, III
National Railroad Passenger Corporation (AMTRAK)	49, VII
National Science Foundation	2, XXV; 5, XLIII; 45, VI
Federal Acquisition Regulation	48, 25
National Security Council	32, XXI

Agency	CFR Title, Subtitle or Chapter
National Security Council and Office of Science and Technology Policy	47, II
National Technical Information Service	15, XI
National Telecommunications and Information Administration	15, XXIII; 47, III, IV, V
National Transportation Safety Board	49, VIII
Natural Resources Conservation Service	7, VI
Natural Resource Revenue, Office of	30, XII
Navajo and Hopi Indian Relocation, Office of	25, IV
Navy, Department of	32, VI
Federal Acquisition Regulation	48, 52
Neighborhood Reinvestment Corporation	24, XXV
Northeast Interstate Low-Level Radioactive Waste Commission	10, XVIII
Nuclear Regulatory Commission	2, XX; 5, XLVIII; 10, I
Federal Acquisition Regulation	48, 20
Occupational Safety and Health Administration	29, XVII
Occupational Safety and Health Review Commission	29, XX
Ocean Energy Management, Bureau of	30, V
Oklahoma City National Memorial Trust	36, XV
Operations Office	7, XXVIII
Overseas Private Investment Corporation	5, XXXIII; 22, VII
Patent and Trademark Office, United States	37, I
Payment From a Non-Federal Source for Travel Expenses	41, 304
Payment of Expenses Connected With the Death of Certain Employees	41, 303
Peace Corps	2, XXXVII; 22, III
Pennsylvania Avenue Development Corporation	36, IX
Pension Benefit Guaranty Corporation	29, XL
Personnel Management, Office of	5, I, XXXV; 5, IV; 45, VIII
Human Resources Management and Labor Relations Systems, Department of Homeland Security	5, XCVII
Federal Acquisition Regulation	48, 17
Federal Employees Group Life Insurance Federal Acquisition Regulation	48, 21
Federal Employees Health Benefits Acquisition Regulation	48, 16
Pipeline and Hazardous Materials Safety Administration	49, I
Postal Regulatory Commission	5, XLVI; 39, III
Postal Service, United States	5, LX; 39, I
Postsecondary Education, Office of	34, VI
President's Commission on White House Fellowships	1, IV
Presidential Documents	3
Presidio Trust	36, X
Prisons, Bureau of	28, V
Privacy and Civil Liberties Oversight Board	6, X
Procurement and Property Management, Office of	7, XXXII
Public Contracts, Department of Labor	41, 50
Public and Indian Housing, Office of Assistant Secretary for	24, IX
Public Health Service	42, I
Railroad Retirement Board	20, II
Reclamation, Bureau of	43, I
Refugee Resettlement, Office of	45, IV
Relocation Allowances	41, 302
Research and Innovative Technology Administration	49, XI
Rural Business-Cooperative Service	7, XVIII, XLII
Rural Development Administration	7, XLII
Rural Housing Service	7, XVIII, XXXV
Rural Telephone Bank	7, XVI
Rural Utilities Service	7, XVII, XVIII, XLII
Safety and Environmental Enforcement, Bureau of	30, II
Saint Lawrence Seaway Development Corporation	33, IV
Science and Technology Policy, Office of	32, XXIV
Science and Technology Policy, Office of, and National Security Council	47, II
Secret Service	31, IV
Securities and Exchange Commission	5, XXXIV; 17, II

Agency	CFR Title, Subtitle or Chapter
Selective Service System	32, XVI
Small Business Administration	2, XXVII; 13, I
Smithsonian Institution	36, V
Social Security Administration	2, XXIII; 20, III; 48, 23
Soldiers' and Airmen's Home, United States	5, XI
Special Counsel, Office of	5, VIII
Special Education and Rehabilitative Services, Office of	34, III
State, Department of	2, VI; 22, I; 28, XI
Federal Acquisition Regulation	48, 6
Surface Mining Reclamation and Enforcement, Office of	30, VII
Surface Transportation Board	49, X
Susquehanna River Basin Commission	18, VIII
Tennessee Valley Authority	5, LXIX; 18, XIII
Trade Representative, United States, Office of	15, XX
Transportation, Department of	2, XII; 5, L
Commercial Space Transportation	14, III
Emergency Management and Assistance	44, IV
Federal Acquisition Regulation	48, 12
Federal Aviation Administration	14, I
Federal Highway Administration	23, I, II
Federal Motor Carrier Safety Administration	49, III
Federal Railroad Administration	49, II
Federal Transit Administration	49, VI
Maritime Administration	46, II
National Highway Traffic Safety Administration	23, II, III; 47, IV; 49, V
Pipeline and Hazardous Materials Safety Administration	49, I
Saint Lawrence Seaway Development Corporation	33, IV
Secretary of Transportation, Office of	14, II; 49, Subtitle A
Transportation Statistics Bureau	49, XI
Transportation, Office of	7, XXXIII
Transportation Security Administration	49, XII
Transportation Statistics Bureau	49, XI
Travel Allowances, Temporary Duty (TDY)	41, 301
Treasury, Department of the	2, X;5, XXI; 12, XV; 17, IV; 31, IX
Alcohol and Tobacco Tax and Trade Bureau	27, I
Community Development Financial Institutions Fund	12, XVIII
Comptroller of the Currency	12, I
Customs and Border Protection	19, I
Engraving and Printing, Bureau of	31, VI
Federal Acquisition Regulation	48, 10
Federal Claims Collection Standards	31, IX
Federal Law Enforcement Training Center	31, VII
Financial Crimes Enforcement Network	31, X
Fiscal Service	31, II
Foreign Assets Control, Office of	31, V
Internal Revenue Service	26, I
Investment Security, Office of	31, VIII
Monetary Offices	31, I
Secret Service	31, IV
Secretary of the Treasury, Office of	31, Subtitle A
Truman, Harry S. Scholarship Foundation	45, XVIII
United States and Canada, International Joint Commission	22, IV
United States and Mexico, International Boundary and Water Commission, United States Section	22, XI
U.S. Copyright Office	37, II
Utah Reclamation Mitigation and Conservation Commission	43, III
Veterans Affairs, Department of	2, VIII; 38, I
Federal Acquisition Regulation	48, 8
Veterans' Employment and Training Service, Office of the Assistant Secretary for	41, 61; 20, IX
Vice President of the United States, Office of	32, XXVIII
Wage and Hour Division	29, V
Water Resources Council	18, VI
Workers' Compensation Programs, Office of	20, I, VII
World Agricultural Outlook Board	7, XXXVIII

List of CFR Sections Affected

All changes in this volume of the Code of Federal Regulations (CFR) that were made by documents published in the FEDERAL REGISTER since January 1, 2014 are enumerated in the following list. Entries indicate the nature of the changes effected. Page numbers refer to FEDERAL REGISTER pages. The user should consult the entries for chapters, parts and subparts as well as sections for revisions.

For changes to this volume of the CFR prior to this listing, consult the annual edition of the monthly List of CFR Sections Affected (LSA). The LSA is available at *www.govinfo.gov*. For changes to this volume of the CFR prior to 2001, see the "List of CFR Sections Affected, 1949–1963, 1964–1972, 1973–1985, and 1986–2000" published in 11 separate volumes. The "List of CFR Sections Affected 1986–2000" is available at *www.govinfo.gov*.

2014

22 CFR

79 FR Page

Chapter III

303.2 (d) through (i) redesignated as (g) through (j), (l) and (m); new (d), (e), (f), (k) and (n) added; new (h) revised 19818
303.3 Revised 19818
303.5 (a), (b) introductory text and (d) revised; (e) removed 19818
303.6 Revised 19818
303.8 (a), (b), (c), (h)(1) and (l)(1)(iv) revised 19818
303.9 (a)(8) and (9) added; (b) revised.......................................19819
303.10 (a), (c)(1)(i), (ii), (2)(ii) and (3) revised 19819
303.12 (a) revised; (b) redesignated as (c); new (b) added 19819
303.13 (b) revised 19820
303.14 (a)(5)(i) and (ii) revised 19820

Chapter VII

706 Revised 8608
707 Revised 8614
713.2 Revised 8619
713.3 Revised 8619
713.5 Revised 8619
713.10 Heading revised 8619

22 CFR—Continued

79 FR Page

Chapter XIII

1305 Added 44278

2015

(No regulations published]

2016

22 CFR

81 FR Page

Chapter XIII

1306 Added 59441

Chapter XV

1506 Revised 95028

2017

22 CFR

82 FR Page

Chapter III

305 Revised 1188

Chapter VII

706 Revised...................................20434

Chapter XIII

1502 Revised; eff. 4-4-17 9130

2018

22 CFR

83 FR Page

Chapter XIII

1304 Revised 35544

2019

(No regulations published from January 1, 2019, through April 1, 2019)

○

www.ingramcontent.com/pod-product-compliance
Lightning Source LLC
Chambersburg PA
CBHW060419220326
41598CB00021BA/2219

* 9 7 8 1 6 4 0 2 4 5 6 3 1 *